LATIN *FOR THE* NEW MILLENNIUM

STUDENT TEXT

LEVEL 2

LATIN FOR THE NEW MILLENNIUM
Series Information

LEVEL ONE

Student Text (2008)

Student Workbook (2008)

Teacher's Manual (2008)

Teacher's Manual for Student Workbook (2008)

ANCILLARIES

From Romulus to Romulus Augustulus:
Roman History for the New Millennium (2008)

The Original Dysfunctional Family:
Basic Classical Mythology for the New Millennium (2008)

LEVEL TWO

Student Text (2009)

Student Workbook (2009)

Teacher's Manual (2009)

Teacher's Manual for Student Workbook (2009)

ANCILLARIES

From Rome to Reformation:
Early European History for the New Millennium (2009)

The Clay-footed SuperHeroes:
Mythology Tales for the New Millennium (2009)

ELECTRONIC RESOURCES

(See page 570 for detailed description)

www.lnm.bolchazy.com

Quia Question Bank

Latin-only Villa in Teen Second Life™

Carpe Praedam

LATIN *FOR THE* NEW MILLENNIUM

STUDENT TEXT

LEVEL 2

Milena Minkova and Terence Tunberg

Bolchazy-Carducci Publishers, Inc.
Mundelein, Illinois USA

Series Editor: LeaAnn A. Osburn

Volume Editors: LeaAnn A. Osburn, Donald E. Sprague

Contributing Editors: Judith P. Hallett, Laurie Haight Keenan, Andrew Reinhard, Karen Lee Singh, Vicki A. Wine

Historical Timeline: Rose Williams

Cover Design & Typography: Adam Phillip Velez

Cover Illustration: Colosseum ©Bettmann/CORBIS

Other Illustrations: Photo Credits appear on pp. 551–554

Cartography: Mapping Specialists

Indexing: Michael Hendry

Proofreading: Gary Varney

Latin for the New Millennium
Student Text, Level 2

Milena Minkova and Terence Tunberg

©2009 Bolchazy-Carducci Publishers, Inc.

Bolchazy-Carducci Publishers, Inc.
1570 Baskin Road
Mundelein, Illinois 60060
www.bolchazy.com

Printed in Canada
2010
by Friesens

ISBN 978-0-86516-563-2

Library of Congress Cataloging-in-Publication Data

Minkova, Milena.
  Latin for the new millennium : student text, level 1 / Milena Minkova and
Terence Tunberg.
      p. cm.
  Includes bibliographical references.
  ISBN 978-0-86516-560-1 (v. 1 : hardbound : alk. paper) 1. Latin language--
Grammar. I. Tunberg, Terence. II. Title.

  PA2087.5.M562 2008
  478.2'421--dc22

                                                            2008014705

CONTENTS

Reading: Bede, "About Britain"

Language Facts: First Conjugation Verbs: Present Active and Passive
    Subjunctive; The Subjunctive Mood; Volitive and Optative Subjunctive;
    Present Subjunctive of *Sum* and *Possum*

Talking About a Reading: The Origin of My Family

Classical Latin: The Life of Cicero's Best Friend—The Family of Atticus

Reading: Einhard, "About Charlemagne"

Language Facts: Second, Third, Fourth Conjugations and –*iō* Verbs of Third
    Conjugation: Present Active and Passive Subjunctive; Place Where, Place
    to Which, and Place From Which with the Names of Towns

Talking About a Reading: A European Trip

Classical Latin: The Life of Cicero's Best Friend—Atticus Excels in School

Reading: Heloise to Abelard

Language Facts: Imperfect Active and Passive Subjunctive of All
    Conjugations; Purpose Clauses; Sequence of Tenses

Talking About a Reading: About Love

Classical Latin: The Life of Cicero's Best Friend—Atticus Goes to Athens

---

LIST OF MAPS

# FOREWORD

Latin for the New Millennium, Level 2, is just as *mīrābile vīsū* and *mīrābile doctū* as Level 1. All the strengths of LNM1 continue with LNM2. Every aspect of this book truly does take the study of Latin into the new millennium. This textbook series is not only student friendly but also teacher friendly.

The literary sections demonstrate the influence of the Latin language throughout the ages up to the current time (see p. xxvi for more on this important topic) and focus on real people facing real challenges. Students will find the stories interesting because of the diversity of the authors, time periods, and subject matter. Students will be able to relate the literary selections to their own lives (e.g., parental interference in the story of Heloise and Abelard), and to other subject areas (e.g., world history in the reading selections about Charlemagne and Christopher Columbus) and to current world events such as the crisis in the Mideast (e.g., in the Latin reading and English information about the Crusades). Essays by current practicing scholars in each review section further explore subjects that are relevant to life today, such as the development of the sciences from its ancient roots to its modern manifestation and Cicero's influence through the ages.

What an inspired choice to include the unadapted *Life of Atticus* by Cornelius Nepos! Students will certainly empathize with a friend torn between two other friends as Atticus was torn between Cicero and Antony. Likewise the emotions concerning an arranged marriage are sure to elicit strong student response.

The quote, labeled *memorābile dictū* at the beginning of each chapter, reinforces the diversity of the Latin language and the influence which Latin has exerted throughout the centuries up to the modern age. In this section, students will become familiar with authors such as Thomas More (Chapter 11) whom they will encounter in their history and English literature classes. This also allows the student and the teacher to connect Latin with other subject areas and to engage in cross-curricula discussions.

The grammar is explained at a good pace with a reasonable amount covered in each chapter. The explanations are clear and concise. They promote student success by building on the similarities with what the students have already learned. Study tips aid students in remembering the grammar and syntax. Then what makes the concept difficult to understand is pointed out in the "By the Way" section thus limiting student frustration by alerting them to what is difficult.

The exercises in each chapter are of varying levels of difficulty. Thus drills are available for students of different ability levels and each student's needs are met. In addition to exercises that test a student's mastery of forms, sentences and reading passages allow students to improve their reading comprehension. This same methodology characterizes the workbook which features similar kinds of exercises as well as additional Latin readings.

Every textbook raises student questions and inquiring minds need to know. The Teacher's Manual teaching tips enable teachers to add depth to their instruction with suggestions that encourage higher level thinking skills. Teaching tips also lessen frustration for teachers and students by pointing out how to build on previously learned materials and the exceptions to the current lesson. In addition, excellent explanations address questions that students ask about Latin such as "How did Latin survive after the Roman Empire?" This enables the teacher to use class time wisely when answering and allows beginning as well as veteran teachers to enhance instruction. In addition, many teaching tips suggest techniques such as TPR (Total Physical Response) that have proven successful in many language classrooms. This allows students to develop language skills that they can apply to learning any world language.

The general vocabulary words, which are used over and over again, are starred in each chapter alerting students to which words are needed for mastery. English derivatives from the Latin vocabulary words are used in English sentences in *Latin for the New Millennium*. The students have to analyze the context of the sentence while finding the English words derived from the Latin vocabulary words, thereby encouraging higher level thinking skills. Having students write the Latin word as well as the derivative enables the students to store the words in their long term memory and better prepares them for the vocabulary encountered on standardized tests as well as academic competitions. A special feature called "Take Note" provides unique background about certain words, sometimes about their technical use and other times—as with *pecus* and *virtus*—about the evolution of the word's meaning. These notes, like the Latin reading passages, promote cross-curricular discussion.

One of the distinctive characteristics of *Latin for the New Millennium* is the emphasis on conversational Latin. The conversational Latin dialogues reinforce the chapters' grammar forms and vocabulary, thus improving the student's comprehension. By providing oral and aural language learning training, the text prepares students to learn modern languages while improving their mastery of the Latin language.

Teachers today not only have to teach, they have to document that they have adhered to the national standards in teaching their subject. By including national standards correlations to all the aspects of this series, *Latin for the New Millennium* easily allows teachers to teach and to fulfill all the demands made on them in writing and implementing standards-based lesson plans and providing individualized student instruction. Students benefit when teachers' energies focus on maximizing classroom instruction and interaction with students.

The series also encourages the incorporation of technology on a daily basis in the classroom, another demand of the new millennium. The resources at the *Latin for the New Millennium* website provide a constant stream of teaching and learning ideas for classroom activities and student assessments. They also provide teachers with a means to publish student work online in the Student Project Gallery. Students and teachers are encouraged to join eClassics, to play *Carpe Praedam,* and to listen to MP3 recordings of the Latin readings. A dedicated Quia test bank provides teachers and students with quiz, test, and review options with instant feedback. Electronic flash cards allow students to learn their vocabulary with their iPods while traveling to school.

As with Level 1, a review section follows every three chapters. A set of review exercises reinforces mastery. The mythology essays introduce the major classical heroes and their stories while a background essay discusses a major topic of the post-ancient world such as the medieval university. Throughout the text, vibrant full color illustrations with captions that instruct enrich the lessons and show the ongoing influence of the Romans and their descendants. Essays by current scholars reveal how practices, customs, thoughts, and words from previous eras have taken root in modern society. This multidisciplinary approach is a boon to understanding Latin's place at the center of the history of ideas in the western world.

Latin for the New Millennium, Level 2, pulls together the genius and creativity of the authors along with other classical scholars and teachers throughout our great country to provide materials that will carry the importance of learning Latin well into the next century. They all deserve our greatest thanks.

Dawn LaFon
White Station High School
Memphis, Tennessee

PREFACE

Learning Latin helps you learn English and other languages better, and, perhaps even more importantly, it offers you the linguistic key to the thoughts that shaped European (and therefore American) culture from the Romans to the age of the scientific revolution in early modern times. Latin was the language the leading minds of the West used to express themselves and to record their ideas in permanent, classical form for a long time after the disappearance of the ancient Western Roman Empire (see p. xxvi for more on this important topic). In this book you will learn each step of the language by using it. Doing is learning!

CHAPTER COMPONENTS

READING PASSAGES

Each chapter begins with a reading passage well supplied with notes that help you understand all elements you have not seen previously. You meet these new elements by reading them first and by seeing them in context. Often you do not need an explanation to understand how they function, because they are surrounded by everything you already know and they naturally fit into the context. The reading notes feature an alphabetical listing of the vocabulary words you have not yet learned and those words that you will need to learn later in the chapter are marked with an asterisk.

These reading passages are adapted from real works of Latin literature, and they are placed in chronological order. So, as you complete each chapter, you follow the story of Latin as a literary language and the people who used it during the Middle Ages, Renaissance, and early modern period. In the process you learn about the culture and the periods of time in which the featured reading of each chapter was produced.

LANGUAGE FACTS AND EXERCISES

In the body of each chapter you will find simple explanations of the language facts used in the chapter reading, along with many exercises that allow you to apply all the elements you are learning. By doing all the exercises in each chapter and in the student workbook, you will not only be reading and writing Latin, you'll be speaking it too! Many of these exercises involve oral exchange with the instructor and with other students. A person who gains an active facility in any language, in addition to a reading ability, is more likely to progress quickly to a deep understanding of the language and the works written in it. If you can speak and write in a language, you will probably not need to be reminded about forms and grammatical rules as often as a learner who lacks active practice. In this book you will build on this active oral facility begun in Level 1 as a basic part of learning the language.

CONVERSATIONAL LATIN AND NEPOS' *LIFE OF ATTICUS*

Near the end of each chapter you will find a Latin dialogue in which the modern students you met in Level 1 discuss in Latin situations encountered in modern life. By the end of each dialogue these characters introduce you to reading an unadapted piece of Latin from the *Life of Atticus* (Cicero's best friend) by Cornelius Nepos, who knew both Atticus and Cicero in person. These passages are completely unadapted, and they are equipped with both vocabulary words that you have not been required to learn and with notes that help you understand all new features. The vocabulary words and reading notes are in two columns by line number.

ADDITIONAL FEATURES

In each chapter you will also find many other things that will help you learn and enjoy Latin.

- *Memorābile Dictū* A famous saying labeled with this Latin phrase begins each chapter. The Latin saying is often so well known that it has become a proverb in many languages. Learning each famous saying will increase your understanding not just of Latin, but also of the thoughts and ideas which were important in the Middle Ages and the Renaissance and which have continued to play a role in modern life.

- **Study Tips** Each chapter contains rhymes, mnemonic devices, and tips that will help you master Latin.

- **By the Way** In each chapter this phrase appears to alert you to some additional information that is being presented or to an additional explanation of something that is difficult.

- **Illustrations** The text is richly illustrated with images that both complement and enhance the text. Illustrations of archaeological and historical sites, of the writers and places associated with their lives, and of artworks connected to the stories stimulate visual learning. The captions for these illustrations provide additional information about the writers and their cultural context.

- **Take Note** In the chapter reading vocabulary, words marked with a double dagger are explained with additional details (linguistic, cultural, or historical) in a Take Note section that immediately follows.

REVIEW COMPONENTS

At the end of each set of three chapters a review contains various components.

VOCABULARY TO KNOW

The Vocabulary to Learn from each of the three preceding chapters is put together to form a complete list of these words. This list is called Vocabulary to Know and is an excellent way to study the cumulative vocabulary for each set of chapters.

EXERCISES

Here you will see many new exercises that will help you review the material in each unit. Often an additional reading passage in Latin will be found among the exercises and this passage will offer more information about the time period being studied and will help you understand Latin literature and its heritage today.

CLASSICAL MYTHOLOGY

This section is titled Considering the Classical Heroes. It includes in English some of the principal stories about the Greek and Roman heroes and is followed by a passage in Latin that supplies some additional information on the same topic. These stories provide some of the main themes for literature and art from classical to modern times.

ASPECTS OF MEDIEVAL, RENAISSANCE, AND EARLY MODERN LIFE

In this section, entitled Connecting with the Post-Ancient World, you will read in English about some important aspect of the history of western European culture in which Latin played a vital role.

EXPLORING THE INFLUENCE OF LATIN ON MODERN LIFE

Here you will find an essay in English on how Latin has influenced modern times. Each of these essays has been written by a university scholar with special expertise in this field of study.

MĪRĀBILE AUDĪTŪ

The final component in each review section is a list of Latin quotations, mottoes, phrases, or abbreviations used in English. These sayings relate to one of the unit topics.

COMPONENTS IN ADDITIONAL READINGS FROM NEPOS' *LIFE OF ATTICUS*

UNADAPTED READINGS

Following Chapter Fifteen, you will find ten sections which are entirely devoted to segments from the *Life of Atticus* by Cornelius Nepos. On the page facing each Latin section, there are copious notes, both vocabulary notes and reading notes. The two types of notes are arranged in a two-column format which will allow you to read across both pages and often see in one horizontal line the vocabulary words with their definition, the information presented in the reading note, and the line of Latin text. This format has been specially designed to aid students in making the transition from their Latin I and II textbooks to the reading of continuous, unadapted Latin text.

VOCABULARY TO LEARN AND EXERCISES

Each segment of Latin is followed by vocabulary to learn and exercises that give you valuable practice in some fundamental grammatical constructions and also help you to understand the readings more thoroughly by actually using Latin.

Each author of this book has written different sections of the textbook but both authors have benefited, throughout the composition of the textbook, from continuous mutual advice and support.

M.M. and T.T.
2009

Visit www.lnm.bolchazy.com to see the electronic resources
that accompany *Latin for the New Millennium.*

AUTHORS

MILENA MINKOVA

MA and PhD, Christian and Classical Philology, Pontifical Salesian University, Rome, Italy; MA and PhD, Classics, University of Sofia, Bulgaria

Associate Professor of Classics, University of Kentucky, Lexington, Kentucky

Milena Minkova has studied, conducted research, and taught in Bulgaria, Switzerland, Germany, Italy, the Vatican City, and the USA. Minkova has authored three book monographs: *The Personal Names of the Latin Inscriptions from Bulgaria* (Peter Lang, 2000); *The Protean Ratio* (Peter Lang, 2001); and *Introduction to Latin Prose Composition* (Bolchazy-Carducci, 2007, reprint; Wimbledon, 2001). She has also published numerous articles on Latin medieval philosophy, Latin literature, Latin composition, and Latin pedagogy.

TERENCE TUNBERG

BA and MA, Classics, University of Southern California; Postgraduate researcher, and doctoral student, Medieval Studies, University of London, England; PhD, Classical Philology, University of Toronto, Canada

Professor of Classics, University of Kentucky, Lexington, Kentucky

Terence Tunberg has taught in Belgium and Canada, as well as in the USA. He is a specialist in Latin composition, and an expert in the history of the approaches to writing Latin prose from antiquity to early modern times. His works include an edition of collection of Medieval Latin speeches, commentaries on Latin works, and numerous studies of the history of imitation in Latin writing. In addition, for more than a decade he has offered summer seminars designed to introduce people to the use of spoken Latin.

JOINT PUBLICATIONS BY THE AUTHORS

Minkova and Tunberg have coauthored the following books: *Readings and Exercises in Latin Prose Composition* (Focus, 2004); *Reading Livy's Rome. Selections from Livy, Books I–VI* (Bolchazy-Carducci, 2005); *Mater Anserina. Poems in Latin for Children* (Focus, 2006); and *Latin for the New Millennium*, Level 1. They are the directors of the Institute for Latin Studies at the University of Kentucky, in which students study the history of Latin from ancient to modern times, and they conduct seminars in which Latin is the working language of all activities. Both Minkova and Tunberg are elected fellows of the Rome-based *Academia Latinitati Fovendae*, the primary learned society devoted to the preservation and promotion of the use of Latin.

EDITORS, CONSULTANTS, AND PILOT TEACHER

VOLUME EDITORS

LeaAnn A. Osburn
Editor, Bolchazy-Carducci Publishers
Barrington High School, Emerita
Barrington, Illinois

Donald E. Sprague
Editor, Bolchazy-Carducci Publishers
Professor of Humanities
Kennedy-King College
City Colleges of Chicago, Illinois

BOARD OF CONSULTANTS

Ronnie Ancona
Professor of Classics
Hunter College
New York, New York

Virginia Anderson
Latin Teacher
Illinois Virtual High School
Barrington Middle School, Emerita
Barrington, Illinois

Jill M. Crooker
Latin Teacher
Pittsford-Mendon High School, Emerita
Pittsford, New York

Judith Peller Hallett
Professor of Classics
University of Maryland
College Park, Maryland

Sherwin D. Little
1–12 Foreign Language Program Leader
Indian Hill High School
Cincinnati, Ohio

Sherrilyn Martin
Chair, Department of Foreign Languages
Keith Country Day School
Rockford, Illinois

Mary Pendergraft
Professor of Classical Languages
Wake Forest University
Winston-Salem, North Carolina

John Traupman
Professor of Classics
St. Joseph's University, Emeritus
Philadelphia, Pennsylvania

Jeremy M. Walker
Latin Teacher
Crown Point High School
Crown Point, Indiana

Lanetta Warrenburg
Latin Teacher
Elgin High School
Elgin, Illinois

Cynthia White
Associate Professor of Classics
University of Arizona
Tucson, Arizona

Rose Williams
McMurry College, Emerita
Abilene High School, Emerita
Abilene, Texas

Donna Wright
Latin Teacher
Lawrence North and Lawrence Central High
  Schools
Indianapolis, Indiana

PILOT TEACHER

Craig Bebergal
Latin Teacher
Florida State University School
Tallahassee, Florida

VOLUME EDITORS

LEAANN A. OSBURN

BA Monmouth College, Illinois; MA Loyola University Chicago

While teaching Latin for many years at Barrington High School in Barrington, Illinois, LeaAnn Osburn served as both vice-president and president of the Illinois Classical Conference. She has authored several Latin workbooks and teacher resources. Osburn received the Illinois Latin Teacher of the Year award in 1989, the Illinois Lt. Governor's Award in 1990, the Classical Association of the Middle, West, and South Good Teacher Award in 1996, and the Illinois Classical Conference Lifetime Achievement Award in 2008.

DONALD E. SPRAGUE

BA Williams College, Massachusetts; MPS Loyola University Chicago

Donald Sprague also studied at the Intercollegiate Center for Classical Studies in Rome. He taught Latin and Greek, founded the Honors Program, established a summer study tour of Italy and Greece, and served as an administrator for many years at Loyola Academy in Wilmette, Illinois. He regularly develops and leads adult education tours of Roman sites. He served as treasurer of the Illinois Classical Conference for fourteen years and two terms as president of the Chicago Classical Club. In 1990, Sprague received the Illinois Latin Teacher of the Year award and the Illinois Lt. Governor's Award.

BOARD OF CONSULTANTS

RONNIE ANCONA

BA, MA University of Washington, PhD The Ohio State University

Ronnie Ancona is Professor of Classics at Hunter College and The Graduate Center of the City University of New York. For many years she directed Hunter's MA in the teaching of Latin program. Ancona has authored or coauthored several Latin textbooks. She recently served on the American Philological Association/American Classical League Joint Task Force on Teacher Training. She taught Latin at the secondary school level for five years.

VIRGINIA ANDERSON

BA Loyola University Chicago; MAT St. Xavier University

Virginia Anderson taught Latin for thirty years in private and public high schools and middle schools in the Chicago area. In 1999 she was awarded the Lt. Governor's Award for Enhancement of the Teaching Profession and in 2003 was named Illinois Latin Teacher of the Year.

JILL M. CROOKER

BA University of Illinois; MSEd Nazareth College of Rochester, New York

Jill Crooker taught Latin for many years at Pittsford-Mendon High School in Pittsford, New York. She has served as the College Board Advisor to the AP Latin Test Development Committee and in 1996 received the Morton E. Spillenger Award for Distinguished Leadership to the Classical Association of the Empire State. In 2003 she received the ACL Merita Award and in 2006 an Ovatio from the Classical Association of the Atlantic States.

JUDITH PELLER HALLETT

BA Wellesley, Massachusetts; MA, PhD Harvard University

In addition to studying at the American Academy in Rome, the Institute of Classical Studies in London, and the University of Maastricht in Holland, Judith Hallett is a former president of the Classical Association of the Atlantic States and Vice-President for Outreach of the American Philological Association. She was named a Distinguished Scholar-Teacher in 1992 by the University of Maryland.

SHERWIN LITTLE

BA University of Cincinnati, Ohio; MA University of Colorado

Sherwin Little has taught Latin from sixth grade through Latin AP at Indian Hill Exempted Village School District since 1983. Sherwin has received an Ovatio and the Good Teacher Award from Classical Association of the Middle, West, and South and the Hildesheim Vase Award from the Ohio Classical Conference in 1986 and 2007. Little holds National Board Certification in World Languages Other than English and has been both Vice President and President of the American Classical League.

SHERRILYN MARTIN

BA Wilson College; MA, PhD University of Cincinnati

Sherrilyn Martin was named Illinois Latin Teacher of the Year in 1993, was a recipient of the Lt. Governor's Award for Foreign Language Teaching in 2001, and was named a Claes Nobel Teacher of Distinction in 2007. She is a past president of the Illinois Classical Conference and is active in the Rockford Society of the Archaeological Institute of America. Martin spent a year in independent study at the University of Thessaloniki, Greece.

MARY PENDERGRAFT

AB, PhD University of North Carolina, Chapel Hill

After teaching at UNC-Greensboro and Duke University, Mary Pendergraft began teaching classics full-time at Wake Forest. Pendergraft is a former President of the North Carolina Classical Association and participated in the focus group that wrote the North Carolina Standard Course of Study for Latin.

JOHN TRAUPMAN

BA Moravian College, Pennsylvania; MA, PhD Princeton University

John Traupman is professor emeritus from St. Joseph's University in Philadelphia where he taught for thirty-eight years. Among his many awards, Traupman received the Distinguished Teaching Award from St. Joseph's University in 1982, a certificate of appreciation from the Pennsylvania Department of Education in 1990, and the Special Award from the Classical Association of the Atlantic States in 1996. Traupman is especially well-known as the author of *Conversational Latin* and *The New College Latin and English Dictionary*.

JEREMY M. WALKER

AB Wabash College, Indiana; MA Indiana University

Jeremy Walker has taught Latin at Crown Point High School in Crown Point, Indiana since 1995. He has served as the Co-Chair of the Indiana Junior Classical League and Membership and Public Relations Chair of the National Junior Classical League. In addition to studying in Italy at the Intercollegiate Center for Classical Studies and in Greece at the American School for Classical Studies, he was president of the Indiana Classical Conference. In 2003, Walker was recognized as the Latin Teacher of the Year in Indiana, and in 2004 was recognized by the Indiana State Teachers Association as a Torch of Knowledge Recipient.

LANETTA WARRENBURG

BA Indiana University; MAT Indiana University-Purdue University, Indianapolis

Lanetta Warrenburg taught high school English and Latin for thirty-three years at schools in Indiana and Illinois. Her last twenty-four years of teaching Latin were at Elgin High School in Elgin, Illinois. While teaching Latin there, she served as the Illinois Classical Conference chairperson for Chicago Classics Day, as co-chair for the Illinois Certamen League since 1993, and as state chair for the Illinois Junior Classical League from 1999–2001. Warrenburg was honored as the Illinois Latin Teacher of the Year in 2001, was president of the Chicago Classical Club from 2005–2007, and received the Illinois Classical Conference Lifetime Achievement Award in 2008.

CYNTHIA WHITE

BA Chestnut Hill College, Pennsylvania; MA Villanova University; PhD Catholic University of America

Cynthia White is the Director of the Undergraduate Latin Program and supervises teacher training and K–12 Latin Teacher Certification at the University of Arizona. She regularly teaches at the *Istituto Internazionale di Studi Classici di Orvieto*, the Classics Department's Study Abroad Program in Orvieto, Italy and has studied in Rome with the Papal Latinist Reginald Foster, O.D.C.

ROSE WILLIAMS

BA Baylor University, Texas; MA University of North Carolina, Chapel Hill

In addition to postgraduate work in Latin and Humanities at the University of Dallas and the University of Texas at Arlington, on a Rockefeller Grant Rose Williams did research at the Bodleian Library, Oxford University in England and at the University of Pisa. She taught Latin for over thirty years at both high school and university levels in Texas and is now the author of more than ten books about the Classics.

DONNA WRIGHT

BA, MA Ball State University, Indiana

After teaching Latin at Carmel High School, Donna Wright currently teaches at both Lawrence North and Lawrence Central High Schools in Indianapolis, Indiana. She has been an active member of the Indiana Classical Conference, being named Creative Latin Teacher of the Year in 1976. She has also been active in the American Classical League, sponsoring a JCL chapter, and leading Italy trips for nearly twenty years. Wright also served as an officer, speaker, and board member of Pompeiiana, Inc.

PILOT TEACHER

CRAIG BEBERGAL

BA Florida State University; MEd Florida Atlantic University

Craig Bebergal has taught Latin for seven years, three of which have been at his current position at the Florida State University School where he teaches Latin I–AP to eighth through twelfth graders. He has also taught as an adjunct professor for Florida Atlantic University's College of Education. Bebergal is currently serving as co-chair of the Florida JCL speech and costume committee while working on a PhD in Humanities with a concentration in Latin Literature.

INTRODUCTION

To say that Latin literature did not end with the Romans would be an understatement. In fact the Roman contribution to Latin, however fundamental, is a mere beginning. The amount of surviving Latin literature written in Europe since the collapse of the Western Roman Empire in the late fifth century CE is almost inconceivably larger than the surviving corpus of literature left by the Romans themselves.

This heritage of post-Roman Latin literature was anything but a sterile idiom reserved for a few reclusive monks. The very pulse of western European civilization, as it developed through the Middle Ages and the Renaissance, moved primarily to the rhythms of Latin prose and poetry.

The language of Caesar and Cicero performed new functions and came to be used in ways unimagined by the ancient Romans. Latin became the vehicle for sciences as refined as ballistics and hydrodynamics. Latin exclusively provided the academic and philosophical vocabulary for the expression of Europe's most sophisticated thoughts. Latin was the language in which fundamental concepts, such as gravity and the heliocentric solar system, received their first coherent expression. Latin, along with some revived terms from ancient Greek, supplied the language of botany and zoology. Latin was the international language of cartography, geography, history, and ethnography, the sciences through which the discoveries of Renaissance explorers gradually became part of the consciousness of European civilization. Latin, and not any of the nascent national tongues, was the primary linguistic vehicle for all of this before about 1750 CE.

But medieval and Renaissance Latin was not merely the language of scholars, scientists, and philosophers; it also produced poetry, letters, satire, fiction, and many other genres—including works widely recognized as monuments and masterpieces of world literature, ranging from the stories of the Venerable Bede and the *Carmina Burāna* to Thomas More's *Ūtopia* and Erasmus' *Praise of Folly*. Even as the language of creative literature, Latin still rivaled the vernacular tongues in the Renaissance.

This international and multicultural role of Latin was in some ways already anticipated in the literature of the Roman Empire, when the peoples of the Roman provinces, especially in the West, began using Latin and not their native tongues as their means of literary expression. Thus Petronius and Seneca, who were from Spain, wrote in Latin just as the African Apuleius also produced his literary work in Latin. This multicultural role for Latin was even more pronounced in the Middle Ages and Renaissance, when Latin served as an international language and a vehicle for a literary tradition which eventually extended even to the New World. Moreover, in the Middle Ages and Renaissance Latin was no longer anyone's native tongue, and this long-lasting phenomenon of the Latin language, based on stable written sources rather than fluid popular usage, supporting such a vast, varied, and dynamic literature from about 450 CE to about 1750 CE is arguably more distinctive and significant than any literature produced by people who wrote in their native tongue.

The existence of Latin curricula in the secondary schools is often defended because Latin offers access to the origins of western civilization. The literary heritage of the Romans is certainly fundamental. But the Latin literature produced after the time of the ancient Romans is no less central to our culture, language, and institutions than the literature of the ancient Romans. If "cultural literacy" is one of the goals of our education, teachers of Latin should think seriously about broadening their perspective and consistently exploiting post-antique as well as Roman Latin.

Latin helps students build vocabulary and verbal skills in English and modern languages. Students who have taken Latin in secondary school typically earn higher verbal scores in college entrance exams than their peers who never studied Latin. However, Latin could offer even more linguistic resources and verbal power if more attention were paid to post-antique Latin in secondary school curricula. Medieval Latin lies at the basis of nearly the whole spectrum of the vocabulary for modern universities, degrees, and academic institutions (and this includes basic English words, such as "faculty," "dean," "chancellor," "graduate," etc.). Medieval and Renaissance Latin is the source for our terminology for telling time (the Romans had no mechanical clocks). The list of our word debts to post-Roman Latin would embrace physics, astronomy, botany, and many other sciences, not to mention such disciplines as philosophy and law.

Yet Latin is typically taught, and Latin teachers are typically prepared, in a way that assumes that Latin is only about the ancient Romans—and not even the entire Roman tradition (since most of Roman literature produced after about 120 CE has little place in canonical curricula). What other literary and linguistic discipline focuses so exclusively on its origins alone? It is time for a change. Both teachers and students of Latin should make the most of what the Latin tradition actually has to offer. In the long run, the place of Latin in our educational system will be more secure, if such a broadening of perspective can be achieved. Some idea of the immense contributions to our culture made by Latin after the time of the Romans, and selected readings of some of the astoundingly rich post-Roman Latin literature, should be a basic part of the teaching of Latin today at all levels. In *Latin for the New Millennium*, Level 2, we have endeavored to provide teachers and students, who are still learning the fundamentals of the Latin language, with the readings and cultural information that will help to add this wider and richer perspective to the Latin classroom.

This wider perspective added by Level 2 is in no way inconsistent with standard placement tests and activities commonly employed by Latin teachers today. In LNM Level 2 the Vocabulary to Learn is composed of a selection of words most commonly employed in such authors as Cicero and Virgil. These words remain common throughout the entire Latin tradition, and our reading selections consistently highlight this vocabulary. LNM Level 1 is filled to the brim with information on Roman authors, Roman culture, and Roman history. More information on things Roman is offered in LNM Level 2, both in the notes to each chapter, and in the concluding part of each chapter, where the reader will find unadapted readings from the *Life of Atticus* by Cornelius Nepos, a contemporary of Cicero.

Latin teaching in the new millennium should take full account of the fact that Latin literature is a phenomenon spanning the millennia.

POST-ANCIENT EUROPE

ŌCEANUS
ĀTLANTICUS

NORVEGIA
Berga
Upsala
SUECIA
DĀNIA
Lunda Gothōrum
Hafnia
Sarmaticus Ōceanus
Frombork
Torunur
BORUSIA
Berolīnum
POLŌNIA
HIBERNIA
ANGLIA
BRITANNIA
BATĀVIA
Delfta
Roterodamum
Bruxellae
Lovānium
BELGICA
Aquīsgrānum
GERMĀNIA
Praga
Cracōvia
TZECHIA
EURŌPA
Argentolium
Lutetia
Parīsiōrum
GALLIA
Stutgardia
Tubinga
BADENIA-
VIRTEMBERGA
Basilēa
HELVĒTIA
AUSTRIA
PANNONI
Gradecium
Claromōns
ALPĒS MONTĒS
CROĀTIA
Patavium
Ferrāra
Mutina
Bonōnia
Pīsae
Flōrentia
DALMATIA
ILLYRICU
Mare Hādriāticum
PRŌVINCIA
ĪTALIA
Massilia
PĪRĒNAEĪ MONTĒS
HISPĀNIA
Matrītum
Barcinō
Nōmentum
Rōma
Alba Longa
Neāpolis
▲ *Vesuvius Mōns*
LŪSITĀNIA
Olisīpō
Tolētum
Hispalis
Corduba
Grānāta
Gāditānum
Fretum
SICILIA
Syrācūsae
Carthāgō
Mare

AFRICA

SCYTHIA

CAUCASUS

COLCHIS

Pontus Euxīnus

ASIA

Constantīnopolis

MACEDONIA

ASIA MINOR

Olympus Mōns ▲   Trôia

SYRIA

Mare Aegaeum

ΞPĪRUS

ITHACA

Thēbae

SAMOS

Castellum equitum

GRAECIA

Athēnae

Olympia

Sparta

PHOENĪCIA

CRĒTA

Tyrus

Hierosolyma

Internum

Cȳrēnē

Alexandrēa

AEGYPTUS

© 2009 Bolchazy–Carducci Publishers

First Conjugation Verbs: Present Active and Passive Subjunctive; The Subjunctive Mood; Volitive and Optative Subjunctive; Present Subjunctive of *Sum* and *Possum*

Englishman John White based his depiction of a female Pict on his encounter with Native Americans while serving as illustrator for Sir Walter Raleigh's expeditions in Virginia.

MEMORĀBILE DICTŪ

Nēmō mē impūne lacessit.

"Nobody provokes me with impunity."

A Royal Scottish motto which is inscribed on Scottish pound coins. According to an ancient legend, an enemy soldier attacking Scottish territory stepped on a thistle and shouted in pain.

READING

Even after the Roman Empire disappeared in Western Europe, Latin remained the language of educated people throughout the continent. Yet the language spoken by those lacking education during the Roman Empire evolved into other tongues, direct ancestors of what would eventually become the national languages in various western European countries: they are known as "vernacular" languages, from the Latin word for homeborn slaves.

In Britain Anglo-Saxons were among the very earliest non-Romans to begin writing texts in their native tongue, in this case Old English. However, as was the case elsewhere, the educated classes in Anglo-Saxon Britain who were either clerics or monks wrote in Latin. It was their use of Latin which ensured that the British Isles would remain culturally a part of Western Europe, where Latin played a major role.

By far the most famous Latin author of Anglo-Saxon England is Bede, known as "the venerable" because of the great veneration he received from later medieval writers. Bede (ca. 673–735) was a lover of learning, and avidly studied all of the earlier Latin texts he could find. He is best known today for his contributions to the fields of biography and history and for his *Historia ecclēsiastica gentis Anglōrum* (*Ecclesiastical History of the People of the Angles*). This work serves not only as a remarkable historical source for early medieval Britain, but is also noteworthy for its colorful narratives and vivid character sketches. It begins in 55 BCE, when Julius Caesar first set foot on British soil. Bede's simple and clear Latin follows established rules of grammar from classical times.

DĒ BRITANNIĀ

1   Īnsula Britannia ab Eurōpā marī sēpārātur; ā merīdiē Galliam Belgicam
     habet, ā tergō ōceanum īnfīnītum. Arborum, pōmōrum, animālium
     est plēna. Piscibus abundat: capiuntur etiam ibi delphīnēs et bālaenae.
     Inveniuntur quoque ostreae, in quibus sunt pulchrae margarītae. Terra
5   multa metalla gignit: aes, ferrum, plumbum, argentum. Īnsula in parte
     septentriōnālī mundī iacet et aestāte noctēs lūcidās habet. Ita mediō
     noctis tempore hominēs prō certō nōn habent esse noctem.
          Incolae Britanniae erant Britonēs, ā quibus nōmen īnsulae est datum.
     Posteā Pictōrum gēns ex Scythiā per ōceanum nāvibus vēnit
10   ad īnsulam Hiberniam, quae prope Britanniam est sita. Pictī in illā
     īnsulā habitāre dēcrēvērunt, sed Scottī, quī eō tempore in Hiberniā
     habitābant, eīs dīxērunt: "Haec īnsula est parva: et nōs et vōs tenēre
     nōn poterit. Cōnsilium tamen bonum vōbīs dabimus. Scīmus ad ortum

sōlis nōn procul ā nostrā aliam īnsulam esse, cūius lītora diēbus
15 lūcidīs aspicere solēmus. Ad eam īnsulam nāvigētis et eam occupētis!"
Itaque Pictī partēs Britanniae septentriōnālēs occupāvērunt. Nam ad
merīdiem Britonēs habitābant. Pictī, quī uxōrēs nōn habēbant, fēminās
ā Scottīs petīvērunt. Scottī hoc respondērunt: "Uxōrēs vōbīs dabuntur,
sed prōmittere dēbētis vōs nōn rēgēs, sed rēgīnās esse habitūrōs." Hic
20 mōs etiam hodiē apud eōs manet.

READING VOCABULARY

aes, aeris, n. – bronze

aestās, aestātis, f. – summer (*aestāte* "in the summer")

argentum, ī, n. – silver

*aspiciō, ere, aspexī, aspectum – to look at, catch a glimpse of

bālaena, ae, f. – whale

Britannia, ae, f. – Britain

Britō, Britonis, m. – Briton

*cōnsilium, ī, n. – advice‡

delphīn, delphīnis, m. – dolphin

*et . . . et . . . – both . . . and . . .

Eurōpa, ae, f. – Europe

ferrum, ī, n. – iron

Gallia Belgica, ae, f. – Belgium

*gēns, gentis, f. – tribe, population

*gignō, ere, genuī, genitum – to produce, give birth

Hibernia, ae, f. – Ireland

*hodiē (adv.) – today

*incola, ae, m. – inhabitant

īnfīnītus, a, um – infinite, immense

*īnsula, ae, f. – island

*inveniō, īre, invēnī, inventum – to come upon, find

lūcidus, a, um – bright, clear

medius, a, um – middle

margarīta, ae, f. – pearl

*merīdiēs, merīdiēī, m. – south, midday

metallum, ī, n. – metal

*mōs, mōris, m. – custom, habit, pl. morals

*mundus, ī, m. – world

nāvigētis (present active subjunctive) – you (pl.) should sail

occupētis (present active subjunctive) – you (pl.) should occupy

*occupō, āre, āvī, ātum – to occupy

ōceanus, ī, m. – ocean

*ortus, ortūs, m. – raising, beginning, origin
ortus sōlis – east

ostrea, ae, f. – oyster

Pictus, ī, m. – Pict‡

*piscis, piscis, m. – fish

plumbum, ī, n. – lead

*procul (adv.) – far, far away

*prōmittō, ere, prōmīsī, prōmissum – to promise

Scottus, ī, m. – Scot

Scythia, ae, f. – Scythia‡

*septentriōnālis, septentriōnāle – northern

*situs, a, um – situated, located

*sōl, sōlis, m. – sun

tergum, ī, n. – back

*Words marked with an asterisk will need to be memorized later in the chapter.

‡Additional information about the words marked with the double dagger will be in the **Take Note** section that follows the Reading Vocabulary.

TAKE NOTE

cōnsilium, ī In this context, *cōnsilium* means "advice;" in other contexts you have already learned that this word means "plan."

Pictus, ī The Picts' name literally means "a painted one," because of the custom of painting faces.

Scythia Today this is a territory in southern Russia.

COMPREHENSION QUESTIONS

1. Where did the Britons and the Scots live?

2. What is the route of the Picts described in the passage above? Where did they finally settle and why?

3. What was the agreement finally made between the Scots and the Picts?

LANGUAGE FACT I

FIRST CONJUGATION VERBS: PRESENT ACTIVE AND PASSIVE SUBJUNCTIVE

In the chapter reading passage you notice two new forms which belong to verbs you already know. When the Scots want to send the Picts away from Ireland to Britain on account of the small size of their island, they give them this advice:

> *Ad eam īnsulam nāvigētis et eam occupētis!*
> "You should sail to that island and you should occupy it!"

The forms *nāvigētis* and *occupētis* are clearly second person plural (as you can guess from the ending *–tis*), but they are different from the well-known present active indicative forms *nāvigātis* and *occupātis*.

Nāvigētis and *occupētis* are present active subjunctive.

The present subjunctive of the first conjugation (to which both *nāvigō* and *occupō* belong) is formed by subtracting the stem vowel *–a–,* substituting in its place the vowel *–e–,* and attaching the verb endings.

First Conjugation: Present Active Subjunctive		
	Singular	**Plural**
First person	parem	parēmus
Second person	parēs	parētis
Third person	paret	parent

First Conjugation: Present Passive Subjunctive		
	Singular	**Plural**
First person	parer	parēmur
Second person	parēris	parēminī
Third person	parētur	parentur

There are many different ways to translate the subjunctive and you will learn about some of them in the next section.

▶ EXERCISE 1

Change the indicative verbs into the subjunctive keeping the same person, number, tense, and voice.

Example: nāvigō   nāvigem

1. aestimātur
2. cōgitant
3. dēvastantur
4. exspectāris
5. firmāmur
6. līberantur
7. occultās
8. pugnat
9. sānāmus
10. servātis
11. temptor

VOCABULARY TO LEARN

NOUNS

cōnsilium, ī, n. – advice
gēns, gentis, f. – tribe, population
incola, ae, m. – inhabitant
īnsula, ae, f. – island
merīdiēs, merīdiēī, m. – south, midday
mōs, mōris, m. – custom, habit, pl. morals
mundus, ī, m. – world
ortus, ortūs, m. – rising, beginning, origin
ortus sōlis – east
piscis, piscis, m. – fish
sōl, sōlis, m. – sun

ADJECTIVES

septentriōnālis, septentriōnāle – northern
situs, a, um – situated, located

VERBS

aspiciō, ere, aspexī, aspectum – to look at, catch a glimpse of
gignō, ere, genuī, genitum – to produce, give birth
inveniō, īre, invēnī, inventum – to come upon, find
occupō, āre, āvī, ātum – to occupy
prōmittō, ere, prōmīsī, prōmissum – to promise

ADVERBS

hodiē – today
nē – negative particle with the subjunctive
procul – far, far away
utinam – I wish that, if only (a particle of wishing)

CONJUNCTIONS

et . . . et . . . – both . . . and . . .

Bede describes the island of Britain making references to the directions indicated on the points of a compass. Cite the specific Latin words from the Vocabulary to Learn which relate to the compass.

▶ EXERCISE 2

Find the English derivatives based on the Vocabulary to Learn in the following sentences. Write the corresponding Latin word. Some of the sentences may contain more than one derivative.

1. There were no occupants in the building.
2. It is time to seek counsel.
3. Our home is totally heated by solar power.
4. Let us consider the moral aspect of this story.
5. I think that the telephone is one of the greatest inventions of our time.
6. Every day we must deal with the mundane affairs of ordinary life.
7. During the trip, we visited some archaeological sites.
8. The new findings of genetics are very promising for humanity.
9. He is a real gentleman.
10. The Office of Insular Affairs manages the United States Virgin Islands, Guam, and some other islands.

BY THE WAY

In some of its forms, the present subjunctive of the first conjugation resembles the present indicative of the second conjugation and the future indicative of the third conjugation. So be careful when you see a verb whose ending includes the vowel –*e*–, which may be a

> present active subjunctive like *parēs* – "you should prepare"
> present active indicative like *tenēs* – "you hold"
> future active indicative like *colēs* – "you will worship"

Knowing your principal parts is critical for making these distinctions.

THE BRITISH ISLES

BRITANNIA

CALĒDONIA

Lindisfarna

Vallum Hadriānum

Dunelmum

Ouedra/Adron

Eborācum

HIBERNIA

ANGLIA

Cantabrigia

Oxonium

Londīnium

Thamesis

Aquae Sūlis

Dubrī

Cornūbia

Fretum Gallicum

Septentriōnēs

Occāsus sōlis — Ortus sōlis

Merīdiēs

▶ **EXERCISE 3**

Identify each of the following forms as present subjunctive (first conjugation), present indicative (second conjugation), or future indicative (third conjugation).

Example: ambulet, ardet, aget

ambulet	present subjunctive
ardet	present indicative
aget	future indicative

1. dēlēmus, dēlectem, dīcēmus

2. dētis, dolētis, discēdētis

3. movēmur, mūtēmur, mittēmur

4. petēs, possidēs, putēs

5. rogent, respondent, relinquent

6. temptētur, timētur, tangētur

7. vincentur, vulnerentur, videntur

LANGUAGE FACT II

THE SUBJUNCTIVE MOOD

Until now, you have learned two verb moods: indicative and imperative. The mood shows how the action of the verb is related to reality. The indicative shows the action as real, the imperative as ordered.

> *Legō librum.* "I read a book." (indicative)
>
> *Lege librum.* "Read the book!" (imperative)

The subjunctive in a main clause usually shows the action as desirable or possible. In addition the subjunctive has several specific meanings in a main clause and especially in subordinate clauses that you will learn later in this book.

Look at the following examples.

> *Nāvigātis.* "You (pl.) sail." Indicative: a real action.
>
> *Nāvigāte.* "You (pl.) sail!" Imperative: an order.
>
> *Nāvigētis.* "You (pl.) should sail." or "You (pl.) may sail." Subjunctive: desirable or possible action.

The church nave at Lindisfarne Priory which was made famous by Cuthbert and became one of the most significant centers of early Christianity in Anglo-Saxon England. Also important were the monasteries at Jarrow and Wearmouth where Bede served. One of Bede's major works was to rewrite the *Life of St. Cuthbert*.

LANGUAGE FACT III
THE VOLITIVE AND OPTATIVE SUBJUNCTIVE

You just learned that the subjunctive in the main clause may indicate a desirable action.

Such a "desirable" subjunctive may be volitive or optative.

A **volitive** subjunctive is similar to an imperative. The only difference between the volitive subjunctive and the imperative is that the volitive subjunctive indicates a somewhat milder command than the imperative. The volitive subjunctive is translated with an imperative or with the words "you should . . . /you may. . . ."

> *Rēs parēs!*
> "Prepare the things!" *or* "You should/may prepare the things!"

When this subjunctive is in the first or in the third person, it is often translated with the words "let me/her/him/us/them . . ."

> *Ad īnsulam nāvigēmus!*
> "Let us sail to the island!"

The **optative** subjunctive indicates a wish. It is often, but not always, accompanied by the word **utinam**. The optative subjunctive is usually translated with the word "may" and **utinam** means "if only."

> *Utinam dī nōs ament!*
> "May the gods love us!" *or* "If only the gods may love us!"

The optative subjunctive and the volitive subjunctive in the **first** and **third** person is negative when **nē** is added. In the case of the negative optative, we sometimes see **utinam nē.**

> *Utinam nē pauper sim!*
> "May I not be poor" *or* "If only I may not be poor!"

> *Nē ad īnsulam nāvigent!*
> "Let them not sail to the island!"

> *Nē malae rēs nōs exspectent!*
> "Let bad things not await us!"

BY THE WAY

The negative of the volitive subjunctive in the **second** person is formed in the same way as the negative imperative: ***nōlī, nōlīte* + infinitive**.

> *Nōlīte ad īnsulam nāvigāre!*
> Do not sail to the island!

Beautifully situated overlooking the Wear River, the Cathedral of Durham was begun in 1093 CE and retains most of its Norman craftsmanship and original design. It was built to house the shrine of St. Cuthbert, Bede's beloved spiritual mentor, and Bede's own remains were transferred to Durham there. A shrine houses them in the cathedral's Galilee Chapel.

LANGUAGE FACT IV
PRESENT SUBJUNCTIVE OF *SUM* AND *POSSUM*

Present Subjunctive of *sum*

	Singular	Plural
First person	sim	sīmus
Second person	sīs	sītis
Third person	sit	sint

Present Subjunctive of *possum*

	Singular	Plural
First person	possim	possīmus
Second person	possīs	possītis
Third person	possit	possint

STUDY TIP

Remember the vowel –*i*– in the present subjunctive of *sum* and *possum*! That makes it **sim**ple to remember!

▶ EXERCISE 4

Translate into English.

Example: Nē diū exspectēmus!
Let us not wait for a long time!

1. Fābulam illam omnibus gentibus celeriter nārrēs!

2. Nōlī procul occultārī!

3. Nē septentriōnālēs gentēs terram occupent!

4. Omnibus cum incolīs pugnēmus!

5. Utinam adulēscēns, quem amō, hodiē mē amet!

6. Nē sīmus pauperēs!

7. Utinam possīmus hodiē multōs piscēs invenīre!

8. Fābulam mihi nārrēs!

9. Nē hostēs terram nostram occupent!

10. Omnibus vīribus pugnēmus!

11. Utinam fēmina, quam amō, mē amet!

12. Nē sīmus miserī!

▶ EXERCISE 5

Translate into Latin using the various types of subjunctives you have just learned.

1. You (pl.) should think about these customs!
2. Let not/may not the world be bad!
3. You should walk far away today!
4. You (pl.) should be strong!
5. May we learn new customs on this island!
6. Let the inhabitants build new homes not far away!
7. May you be able to find what you are seeking!
8. You should prepare all the things you promised!

▶ EXERCISE 6

Give the negative of the following sentences. Translate the negative sentences.

Example: Nunc ambulētis!
Nōlīte nunc ambulāre!
Do not walk now!   You should not/may not walk now!

1. Apud nōs habitent!
2. Hostem accūsā!
3. Fābulās nārrēmus!
4. Utinam sīmus prīmī!

▶ EXERCISE 7

Read the following conversation held between the Picts and the Scots after the Picts' arrival in Ireland. Translate the English parts into Latin and the Latin parts into English.

Picts: Tandem ad terram nāvigāvimus. Cum gaudiō exclāmēmus! Utinam hāc in īnsulā manēre possīmus!

Scots: Who are you? What are you seeking in our land?

Picts: Sumus Pictī et novam patriam diū quaesīvimus. Utinam haec patria multa bona nōbīs det!

Scots: You cannot remain on this island. For it is very small and there is no space for everybody. You should sail to another island! You should prepare your ships!

Picts: Sītis amīcī! Auxilium nōbīs dētis!

Scots: Be brave! From this island you can catch a glimpse of another island. May you be able to find for yourselves a place on that island!

Picts: Utinam bona fortūna in aliā īnsulā nōs exspectet! Dē aliā quoque rē vōs rogāre cupimus.

Scots: You should ask now.

Picts: Dētis nōbīs mulierēs! Nam nōs uxōribus egēmus: nōn enim sunt nōbīs mulierēs.

Scots: Mulierēs vōbīs dabimus, sed hoc prōmittere dēbētis: tantum mulierēs erunt rēgīnae, virī nōn erunt rēgēs.

Picts: May your advice be good!

Scots: Prōmittitisne?

Picts: We promise, we promise. Give the women now!

This stone monument sculpted by the Picts during the seventh to ninth centuries CE stands with two others in Aberlemno, Scotland, not far from Dundee. The north face depicted here contains a Celtic-style cross flanked by angels holding books. Similar sculpted stones throughout Scotland attest to the presence of the Picts.

TALKING ABOUT A READING

ABOUT THE ORIGIN OF MY FAMILY AND UNADAPTED LATIN: THE FAMILY OF ATTICUS

In Chapter 8 of Level 1 you read an adaptation of the life of Themistocles by Cornelius Nepos. Cornelius Nepos (100–25 BCE) wrote a book of short biographies about famous Greeks, and some Romans, entitled *Dē virīs illūstribus* (*About Famous Men*). Here, together with our friends from the first volume, Mary, Christy, Helen, and Mark, you will read the unadapted version of Cornelius Nepos' biography of Cicero's best friend Atticus.

The friends gather and first make some remarks about Bede's text that they have just read. Then they read part of Nepos' life of Atticus and later conclude their conversation.

DĒ FAMILIAE MEAE ORTŪ

Marīa: Salvēte, amīcī!

Mārcus, Helena et Christīna: Salva (*in good health*) sīs, Marīa!

Marīa: Bonum erat legere dē familiae meae ortū. Nam familiae meae patria est Calēdonia (*Scotland*). Nōn sciēbam Pictōs ex Scythiā vēnisse.

Mārcus: Et familiae meae patria est Hibernia. Ego autem nōn sciēbam Scottōs prīmum (*first*) in Hiberniā habitāvisse, deinde Calēdoniam petīvisse. Mea familia familiae tuae fēminās dedisse vidētur. Nam Pictī mulierēs nōn habēbant. Rēgīnae igitur, quae in Calēdoniā fuērunt, omnēs ex Hiberniā vēnerant.

Marīa: Hoc nōn est prorsus (*completely*) vērum. Prīmae tantum mulierēs ex Hiberniā vēnērunt. Posteā novae mulierēs nātae sunt (*were born*) in Calēdoniā, nōn in Hiberniā.

Helena: Audiātis! Mea autem familia patriam habet Britanniam. Diū in Britanniā meī vīxērunt, tandem Americam petīvērunt.

Christīna: Cūr dīcitis vōs esse Pictōs, Scottōs, Britonēs? Nōs omnēs nunc sumus Americānī!

Marīa: Bene dīcis, Christīna. Patriam, quam nunc habēmus, amāre dēbēmus, sed etiam dē familiae ortū bonum est scīre. Hoc nōn significat (*does not mean*) nōs patriam nostram minus (*less*) amāre . . . Sed quid aliud hodiē legēmus?

Mārcus: Vītam Atticī quam scrīpsit (*wrote*) Cornēlius Nepos.

Helena: Nē sit valdē difficilis! Timeō.

Mārcus: Nē cōgitēmus librum esse difficilem! Timōre līberēmur! Iam multa scīmus.

Christīna: Utinam nunc incipere (*begin*) possīmus! Nam dē Cicerōnis amīcō scīre cupiō.

THE FAMILY OF ATTICUS

CORNĒLIĪ NEPŌTIS ATTICUS, 1.1–2

Atticus came from an old family, but not one of the highest nobility. His father was well-to-do, and was deeply interested in literature, an interest which was transmitted to Atticus.

1   1. Titus Pompōnius Atticus, ab orīgine ultimā stirpis Rōmānae
     generātus, perpetuō ā māiōribus acceptam equestrem obtinuit
     dignitātem. 2. Patre ūsus est dīligente et, ut tum erant tempora, dītī in
     prīmīsque studiōsō litterārum. Hic, prout ipse amābat litterās, omnibus
5   doctrīnīs, quibus puerīlis aetās impertīrī dēbet, fīlium ērudīvit.

VOCABULARY

1   orīgō, orīginis, f. – origin
     ultimus, a, um – farthest, most remote
     stirps, stirpis, f. – stock, descent, race
2   generō, āre, āvī, ātum – to give birth, procreate; *pass.* to descend from
     perpetuō (adv.) – without interruption
     māiōrēs, māiōrum, m. pl. – ancestors
     equestris, equestre – equestrian, related to the social class of knights
     obtineō, ēre, obtinuī, obtentum – to hold
3   dignitās, dignitātis, f. – dignity, social position
     pater, patris, m. – father
     ūsus est + ablative – he enjoyed
     dīligēns, dīligentis – diligent
     ut – as, when, according to
     dītī = dīvite
3–4 in prīmīs – especially, first of all
4   studiōsus, a, um + gen. – interested in
     prout (conj.) – as
     ipse – himself
5   doctrīna, ae, f. – learning, erudition
     puerīlis, puerīle – related to *puer*; puerīlis aetās – boyhood
     aetās, aetātis, f. – age
     impertiō, īre, impertīvī, impertītum – to share, provide (to give a *pars*)
     ērudiō, īre, ērudīvī, ērudītum – to educate, instruct

READING NOTES

1–2 *ab orīgine ultimā stirpis Rōmānae generātus* Understand *generātus* with *ab*. Atticus was "descended from the remotest/most ancient origin of Roman stock."

2   *acceptam* Perfect passive participle of *accipiō* – to accept, receive.

2–3 *equestrem . . . dignitātem* This phrase means "the social position of an equestrian/knight."

3   *ūsus est* This passive looking verb has the active meaning "he enjoyed" and it governs the ablative phrase *patre dīligente*.

     ut tum erant tempora With an indicative verb *ut* means "when/as." This phrase means "as the times/standards then were." In other words, Atticus' father was rich by the standards of an earlier age.

3–4 *dītī in prīmīsque studiōsō litterārum* "Rich and especially interested in literature."

4–5 *omnibus doctrīnīs, quibus puerīlis aetās impertīrī dēbet, fīlium ērudīvit* The pronoun *quibus* referring to *doctrīnīs* is an ablative of means with the verb *impertīrī*; *omnibus doctrīnīs* is an ablative of means to be taken with *ērudīvit*. The phrase *quibus puerīlis aetās impertīrī dēbet* means "with which boyhood ought to be provided."

QUESTIONS ABOUT THE TEXT
Answer in complete Latin sentences.

1. Eratne familia Atticī vetusta?

2. Quam dignitātem habēbat Atticus?

3. Habēbantne māiōrēs Atticī dignitātem equestrem?

4. Quālis (*what sort of*) erat pater Atticī?

5. Fuitne valdē dīves?

6. Cūius reī pater Atticī erat in prīmīs studiōsus?

7. Cupīvitne pater Atticī fīlium litterīs ērudīrī?

8. Cūr hoc cupīvit?

DĒ FAMILIAE MEAE ORTŪ CONTINUED

Mārcus: Meus pater quoque litterās valdē amat. Cupīvit igitur mē litterīs Latīnīs ērudīrī.

Marīa: Putābam patrem tuum esse astronautam (*astronaut*).

Mārcus: Hoc est vērum. Tantum hominēs doctī possunt esse astronautae. Sīmus dīligentēs!

Second, Third, Fourth, Conjugations and *-iō* Verbs of Third Conjugation: Present Active and Passive Subjunctive; Place Where, Place to Which, and Place from Which with the Names of Towns

Without a portrait as model, Albrecht Dürer (1471–1528), the most famous of German Renaissance artists, used his imagination to create this oil image of the Charlemagne. With sword in his right hand and in his left an orb surmounted by a cross, Dürer portrays Carolus Magnus as Holy Roman Emperor. This role is reinforced by the cross atop the elaborate crown.

MEMORĀBILE DICTŪ

Sacrum Rōmānum imperium.

"Holy Roman Empire."

The Holy Roman Empire continued the empire founded in 800 CE by Charlemagne, who revived the title of Roman Empire in Western Europe. Charlemagne's successors, the Carolingians, considered the Roman Empire suspended, rather than ended, by the abdication in 476 CE by Romulus Augustus. As a phrase, "Holy Roman Empire" designated a political entity that originated with the coronation of the German king Otto I as emperor and survived until Francis II renounced the imperial title in 1806.

READING

In the eighth century much of Western Europe once again became part of a substantial empire—this time that of the Franks, a German tribe who, after invading the Roman Empire centuries earlier, were recovering from many years of division and strife. This recovery had resulted from the unifying leadership of a new dynasty called the "Carolingians," which derived its name from Carolus, the Latin name of its greatest ruler Charles the Great or, as he is called in French, Charlemagne. Leo III, who was Pope from 795–816 CE, a highly astute leader from relatively humble beginnings who had risen through the ranks of the Roman church, regarded Charles as a great ally and protector. In a ceremony held on Christmas Day 800 CE in St. Peter's Basilica, Leo actually crowned Charles Roman Emperor of the West. In a sense, then, Charlemagne's coronation revived the Western Roman Empire. Once again, after an interval of three centuries, an emperor in the west seemed to be the counterpart of the eastern emperor in Constantinople: we must not forget that the eastern Roman Empire never fell, but continued to exist without interruption from the fourth century CE onwards.

Charlemagne's rule was of particular cultural importance because he made Latin the official language of his empire. As he needed an educated class of administrators capable of expressing themselves in Latin, at his court in Aachen, known in French as Aix-la-Chapelle, Charlemagne patronized a group of the greatest Latin writers, scholars, and teachers of his day.

The biography of Charlemagne by Einhard (775–840), of the German region known as Franconia, furnishes much information about the reign of the emperor. In certain respects the biography resembles the lives of ancient Roman emperors written by the biographer Suetonius in the second century CE.

DĒ CAROLŌ MĀGNŌ

1 Carolus erat altus, ēius corpus māgnum et forte, cervīx brevis, venter prōiectus, capillī cānī, vultus gravis, oculī vegetī, vōx clāra. Bene valēbat, sed ultimīs annīs ante mortem febrī corripiēbātur. Medicōs tamen odiō habēbat, quī eum nōn sinēbant carnēs assās comedere, sed

5 tantum ēlixās. Itaque eōrum cōnsilia numquam petēbat. Carolus erat eques assiduus, ut omnēs Francī, atque vēnātor. Valdē dēlectābātur vapōribus aquārum nātūrāliter calentium, in quibus cum gaudiō natābat. Rēgiam Aquīsgrānī aedificāverat et ibi ad fīnem vītae habitāvit. Nōn sōlum fīliōs, sed etiam amīcōs et corporis custōdēs invītābat:

10 "Veniātis omnēs et mēcum natētis." Interdum centum hominēs cum eō ūnā natābant. Vestis ēius erat simplex, ut Francī gerēbant. Gladiō semper accingēbātur, cūius capulus erat ex aurō vel ex argentō factus. Vīnum nōn amābat nec hominēs ēbriōs tolerābat. Dum comedēbat,

librī legēbantur: valdē dēlectābātur historicīs et librīs Augustīnī.

15　Post merīdiem dormīre solēbat; noctū somnus saepe interpellābātur.
Māne, cum vestīmenta induēbat, hominēs accipere solēbat: nōn sōlum
amīcōs, sed etiam sī erant lītēs, dē quibus dēcernere dēbēbat.

READING VOCABULARY

accingō, ere, accīnxī, accīnctum – to gird on, arm

aliquot (indeclinable indefinite pronoun/adjective) –
　some, a few

*altus, a, um – tall, deep

*annus, ī, m. – year

Aquīsgrānī – at Aachen

Aquīsgrānum, ī, n. – Aachen‡

*argentum, ī, n. – silver

assiduus, a, um – diligent, dedicated

assus, a, um – roasted

Augustīnus, ī, m. – Augustine‡

*aurum, ī, n. – gold

*brevis, breve – short

calēns, calentis – hot;
　aquae nātūrāliter calentēs – hot water springs

cānus, a, um – grey (for hair)

capillus, ī, m. – hair

capulus, ī, m. – handle, hilt

Carolus, ī, m. – Charles

centum (numeral) – one hundred

cervīx, cervīcis, f. – neck

*clārus, a, um – clear, distinguished

*custōs, custōdis, m. – guard

ēbrius, a, um – drunk

ēlixus, a, um – boiled

*eques, equitis, m. – horseman

febris, febris, f. – fever

*fīnis, fīnis, m. – end

Francus, ī, m. – Frank

*gerō, ere, gessī, gestum – to wear, carry

*gravis, grave – heavy, serious

historicus, ī, m. – historian

induō, ere, induī, indūtum – to put on (a piece of
　clothing)

*interdum (adv.) – sometimes

interpellō, āre, āvī, ātum – to interrupt

invītō, āre, āvī, ātum – to invite

*līs, lītis, f. – dispute, quarrel

*māne (adv.) – in the morning

medicus, ī, m. – doctor

natō, āre, āvī, ātum – to swim

nātūrāliter (adv.) – naturally

*odium, ī, n. – hatred;
　odiō habeō + accusative – I hate somebody

prōiciō, ere, prōiēcī, prōiectum – to send forth; (in
　passive participle) protruding

rēgia, ae, f. – royal palace

simplex, simplicis – simple

*sinō, ere, sīvī, situm + accusative + infinitive – to al-
　low somebody to do something

tolerō, āre, āvī, ātum – to tolerate, bear

ultimus, a, um – last

*ut (conj.) – as

*valeō, ēre, valuī, — – to be in good health

vapor, vapōris, m. – steam, vapor

vegetus, a, um – lively, vigorous

*vel (conj.) – or

vēnātor, vēnātōris, m. – hunter

veniātis – present active subjunctive of *veniō*

venter, ventris, m. – stomach, belly

*vestis, vestis, f. – clothes, attire

vīnum, ī, n. – wine

*vōx, vōcis, f. – voice

*vultus, vultūs, m. – face

*Words marked with an asterisk will need to be
　memorized later in the chapter.

‡Additional information about the words marked with
　the double dagger will be in the **Take Note** section
　that follows the Reading Vocabulary.

TAKE NOTE

Aquīsgrānum Called Aachen in German or Aix-la-Chapelle in French, this town is in western Germany and was a seat of the Holy Roman Empire. The town was known for its mineral waters as the root *"aqu"* in the name indicates.

Augustīnus You learned about Augustine in Chapter 20 of Level 1.

COMPREHENSION QUESTIONS

1. Why did Charlemagne dislike doctors?

2. What were Charlemagne's favorite pastimes?

3. Of which customs did Charlemagne approve during mealtime and of which did he disapprove?

Charlemagne spent several months traveling through Italy with his son Pippin in 800. In November he arrived in Rome resolved to strengthen his position and his alliance with Pope Leo III. Charlemagne was crowned in the basilica built by Constantine, which, unlike the Renaissance St. Peter's (pictured here on the right with its impressive dome), would have blended into its surroundings.

The flags of Belgium and the European Union hang on the façade of City Hall, Mechelen, Belgium. The European flag flies above a statue of Charlemagne who ruled a united Holy Roman Empire which included today's modern state of Belgium. Founded in 1992, the European Union is headquartered in nearby Brussels, Belgium. It is conceived as a reincarnation of a united Europe including a broader swath of Europe than that of the historical Holy Roman Empire.

LANGUAGE FACT 1

SECOND, THIRD, FOURTH, CONJUGATIONS AND *-IŌ* VERBS OF THE THIRD CONJUGATION: PRESENT ACTIVE AND PASSIVE SUBJUNCTIVE

In the text above, you encountered the form *veniātis*, "May you all come!" which is a present subjunctive of the verb *veniō*.

Verbs of the second, third and fourth conjugation form the present subjunctive by adding the vowel *–a–* to their verbal stem, and then the same endings as the verbs of the first conjugation. Third conjugation *–iō* verbs resemble verbs of the fourth conjugation in their present subjunctive.

tene-a-m	tene-a-r
pet-a-m	pet-a-r
audi-a-m	audi-a-r
cap-ia-m	cap-ia-r

STUDY TIP

You can easily remember what vowels are used in the present subjunctive with this mnemonic:

H**e** F**ea**rs **a** G**ia**nt L**ia**r

Second Conjugation: Present Active Subjunctive

	Singular	Plural
First person	teneam	teneāmus
Second person	teneās	teneātis
Third person	teneat	teneant

Second Conjugation: Present Passive Subjunctive

	Singular	Plural
First person	tenear	teneāmur
Second person	teneāris	teneāminī
Third person	teneātur	teneantur

Third Conjugation: Present Active Subjunctive

	Singular	Plural
First person	petam	petāmus
Second person	petās	petātis
Third person	petat	petant

Third Conjugation: Present Passive Subjunctive

	Singular	Plural
First person	petar	petāmur
Second person	petāris	petāminī
Third person	petātur	petantur

Fourth Conjugation: Present Active Subjunctive

	Singular	Plural
First person	audiam	audiāmus
Second person	audiās	audiātis
Third person	audiat	audiant

Fourth Conjugation: Present Passive Subjunctive

	Singular	Plural
First person	audiar	audiāmur
Second person	audiāris	audiāminī
Third person	audiātur	audiantur

-iō Verbs of Third Conjugation: Present Active Subjunctive

	Singular	Plural
First person	capiam	capiāmus
Second person	capiās	capiātis
Third person	capiat	capiant

-iō Verbs of Third Conjugation: Present Passive Subjunctive

	Singular	Plural
First person	capiar	capiāmur
Second person	capiāris	capiāminī
Third person	capiātur	capiantur

BY THE WAY

Since there are several ways of translating the subjunctive, depending on whether it is in a main or in a subordinate clause, and depending on its meaning, no translation is given with the conjugation of these subjunctive verbs.

STUDY TIP

The present subjunctive of fourth conjugation verbs and the *–iō* verbs of the third conjugation look the same: *audiam – capiam*.

BY THE WAY

All forms of the present subjunctive of third conjugation verbs (except in the first person) resemble the present indicative of first conjugation verbs. Compare: *amās – petās*; *amāris – petāris*.

▶ EXERCISE 1

Change the indicative verbs into the subjunctive keeping the same person, number, tense, and voice. Give the basic meaning of the verb.

Example: valētis   valeātis   to be well, be strong

1. sinuntur
2. geris
3. prōmittitur
4. gignō
5. aspiciminī
6. invenīmur
7. occupātur
8. gignimus
9. doceor
10. invenit
11. movēris

VOCABULARY TO LEARN

NOUNS

annus, ī, m. – year

argentum, ī, n. – silver

aurum, ī, n. – gold

custōs, custōdis, m. – guard

eques, equitis, m. – horseman

fīnis, fīnis, m. – end

līs, lītis, f. – dispute, quarrel

odium, ī, n. – hatred

vestis, vestis, f. – clothes, attire

vōx, vōcis, f. – voice

vultus, vultūs, m. – face

ADJECTIVES

altus, a, um – tall, deep

brevis, breve – short

clārus, a, um – clear, distinguished

gravis, grave – heavy, serious

VERBS

gerō, ere, gessī, gestum – to wear (you already know the meaning "carry")

sinō, ere, sīvī, situm + accusative + infinitive – to allow somebody to do something

valeō, ēre, valuī, — – to be in good health

ADVERBS

interdum – sometimes

māne – in the morning

CONJUNCTIONS

ut – as

vel – or

PHRASE

odiō habeō + accusative – I hate somebody

▶ EXERCISE 2

Write the Latin word from the Vocabulary to Learn on which each derivative is based.

final	litigator	gesture	gravity	clarity	brevity
altitude	equestrian	custody	infinity	annual	vocal
valor	odious	valedictorian	vocative	litigation	

▶ EXERCISE 3

Give the first and second principal part and the conjugation of the verb from which each form comes and identify whether the form is present indicative, present subjunctive, or future indicative. Give the basic meaning of the verb.

Example: accūset   accūsō, āre   first conjugation   present subjunctive   to accuse

1. gignet
2. occupet
3. prōmittet
4. aspiciat
5. accipiet
6. valet
7. exspectat
8. sinat
9. faciat
10. fugiat
11. occupat
12. gerat
13. gerit
14. valeat
15. inveniet
16. invideat
17. prōmittat
18. intret
19. mittat
20. moveat
21. occultet
22. sinet

▶ EXERCISE 4

Read the following dialogue between Charlemagne and his doctor. Find all the imperatives and subjunctives and identify each by type. The Reading Vocabulary may be consulted.

Example:

Medicus: Salvus (*healthy*) sīs (*salvus sīs = salvē*; a greeting), rēx praeclāre!

sīs – optative subjunctive

> **Carolus Māgnus:** Salvē, medice!
>
> **Medicus:** Utinam possīs per multōs annōs bene valēre et rēx Francōrum esse!
>
> **Carolus Māgnus:** Prō certō erō. Cūr hoc dīcis?
>
> **Medicus:** Corpus tuum nōn iam est forte et febribus corripitur. Cōnsilia bona tibi dabō. Ita corpus curāre poteris. Audiās!
>
> **Carolus Māgnus:** Audiāmus (*kings sometimes talk in the plural to enhance their majesty*)! Dīcās ea quae dīcere cupis.
>
> **Medicus:** Iam carnēs assās comedere nōn dēbēs, sed tantum carnēs ēlixās.
>
> **Carolus Māgnus:** Verba tua odiō habeō. Nōlī mē docēre! Ego enim sum rēx Francōrum. Fugiās nunc! Nam īra mea est terribilis.

Imposing statues of Charlemagne and of Louis IX King of France (not pictured) flank the entrance to the Église Saint-Louis des In-valides. Charles Antoine Coysevox (1640–1720) had previously com-pleted several sculpture commis-sions for the Palace at Versailles. Louis XIV, the Sun King, founded Les Invalides as an old soldiers' home in 1670. He had intended the chapel to be the royal family's burial place. While that wish did not come to pass, French Emperor Napoleon I is buried beneath the chapel's dome.

▶ EXERCISE 5

The following dialogues are held in Charlemagne's dressing room and at his table. Translate the following Latin sentences into English, and the English sentences into Latin. The Reading Vocabulary may be consulted.

Custōs: Licetne intrāre, rēx? Sunt enim duō (*two*) virī, inter quōs est līs.

Carolus Māgnus: Let them enter!

Custōs: Intrētis et rem vestram rēgī nārrētis!

Vir prīmus: This man takes fruit from my tree. Punish him, just king!

Vir secundus (second): Mihi crēdās, rēx! Arbor est mea, nōn ēius.

Carolus Māgnus: Quō locō est arbor?

Virī ambō (both): Invenītur in fīne agrī meī.

Carolus Māgnus: Et tibi et tibi ex illā arbore pōma capere licēbit. Nunc mē relinquātis! Nam vestīmenta induere dēbeō.

Carolus Māgnus: Comedāmus! Nē exspectēmus! Venter meus vocat.

Servus (servant): Everything is prepared.

Carolus Māgnus: Carnēs in mensam (*table*) pōnās, sed nōlī pōnere vīnum! Nōn enim amō hominēs ēbriōs.

Servus: Say, king! Which book do you want to hear today? One of Cicero's (Cicero, Cicerōnis, m.)?

Carolus Māgnus: Nē nōmen Cicerōnis audiātur! Augustīnum legāmus!

Amīcī: May we be pleased by the book of Augustine! For sure we will be pleased by the meats, but we will not be pleased by the water.

LANGUAGE FACT II

PLACE WHERE, PLACE TO WHICH, AND PLACE FROM WHICH WITH NAMES OF TOWNS

In the text above, you read that Charlemagne had built a royal palace *Aquīsgrānī* (in Aachen). The form *Aquīsgrānī* is not a genitive of *Aquīsgrānum*, as it may seem. It is a locative. The **locative** is a case which had died out in very early Latin, but a few forms remained in use.

You have learned that Latin uses *in* with the ablative to express **place where**.

> *Vīvō in pulchrā terrā.*
> "I live in a nice land."

However, "place where" with the names of **cities**, **towns**, and **small islands** is expressed with a special case form called the **locative**. The ending of the locative singular for the first declension is *–ae* and for the second declension is *–ī*. The locative looks exactly like the ablative in 3ʳᵈ declension singular and in 1ˢᵗ, 2ⁿᵈ, and 3ʳᵈ declension plurals. (There are no such nouns belonging to the fourth and the fifth declensions.)

> *Vīvō Rōmae.* – "I live in Rome."

> *Carolus vīvit Aquīsgrānī.* – "Charles lives in Aachen."

> *Vīvō Athēnīs.* – "I live in Athens." (Athēnae, ārum, f. pl. – Athens)

> *Hannibal vīvēbat Carthāgine.* – "Hannibal lived in Carthage." (Carthāgō, Carthāginis, f. – Carthage)

Note these special forms with the noun *rūs, rūris*, n., which means "countryside."

> *rūrī* (locative) – in the country

> *rūre* (place from which) – from the country

> *rūs* (place to which) – to the country

The domed octagon caps the Palatine Chapel around which the larger Cathedral of Aachen was built. Charlemagne constructed the chapel ca. 796–805 CE as part of his palace. Inspired by early Christian and Byzantine churches, many see it as a direct echo of the Emperor Justinian's San Vitale in Ravenna.

BY THE WAY

In Level 1 you learned that *domī* could mean "at home." This is actually the locative singular form of *domus*.

You have learned that Latin uses *in* or *ad* with the accusative to express **place to which**.

However, "place to which" with the names of **cities, towns**, and **small islands** is expressed with a simple accusative without a Latin preposition.

> *Mīlitēs Rōmam, Aquīsgrānum, Athēnās, Carthāginem dūcō.*
> "I lead soldiers to Rome, Aachen, Athens, Carthage."

You have learned that Latin uses *ab, dē,* or *ex* with the ablative to express **place from which.**

However, "place from which" with the names of **cities, towns**, and **small islands** is expressed with a simple ablative without a Latin preposition.

> *Rōmā, Aquīsgrānō, Athēnīs, Carthāgine veniō.*
> "I am coming from Rome, Aachen, Athens, Carthage."

Place Constructions	Without a Preposition	With a Preposition
Ablative – Place Where	Carthāgine - in Carthage	in Graeciā – in Greece
Locative – Place Where	Rōmae – in/at Rome	————
Accusative – Place to Which	Athēnās – to Athens	ad Eurōpam – to Europe
Ablative – Place from Which	Carthāgine – from Carthage	ā Siciliā – from Sicily

▶ EXERCISE 6

For each of the cities listed, compose three sentences that will start with:

Cupiō vīvere . . . (place where)
Amīcōs dūcere cupiō . . . (place to which)
Veniō . . . (place from which)

Example: Novum Eborācum
Cupiō vīvere Novī Eborācī (*New York*).
Amīcōs dūcere cupiō Novum Eborācum.
Veniō Novō Eborācō.

1. Vasintōnia, ae, f. – Washington

2. Sicāgum, ī, n. – Chicago

3. Angelopolis, Angelopolis, f. – Los Angeles (Nom. Angelopolis, Gen. Angelopolis, Dat. Angelopolī, Acc. Angelopolim, Abl. Angelopolī)

4. Bostōnia, ae, f. – Boston

5. Cincinnātī, ōrum, m. pl. – Cincinnati

6. Dallasia, ae, f. – Dallas

TALKING ABOUT A READING

ABOUT A EUROPEAN TRIP AND UNADAPTED LATIN: ATTICUS EXCELS IN SCHOOL

DĒ ITINERE IN EURŌPAM FACTŌ

Mārcus: Audiātis mē! Nunc meminī (*remember*). Ego et parentēs fuimus Aquīsgrānī. Est urbs in Germāniā occidentālī (*western Germany*) sita. Fuerāmus Berolīnī (*Berolīnum, ī, n. – Berlin*), deinde iter (*trip, journey*) fēcimus in Galliam (*Gallia, ae, f. – France*). Nam parentēs cupiēbant petere Lutetiam (*Lutetia, ae, f. – Paris*). In itinere constitimus (*stopped*) Aquīsgrānī. Ibi est māgna ecclēsia cathedrālis (*cathedral church*). Urbs erat valdē pulchra.

Marīa: Utinam mihi liceat Lutetiam petere, turrim Eiffeliānam (*Eiffel Tower*) vidēre, Lutetiae ambulāre atque dēlectārī! Dūcēsne mē, Mārce, Lutetiam?

While Mary is speaking, Helen goes away. Mark runs after her.

Mārcus: Ego, Helena, cupiō ūnā tēcum esse Lutetiae. Sī ūnā erimus Lutetiae, quāsdam rēs (*some things*) ibi tibi dīcam.

Helena: Ego cupiō quoque Rōmam, imperiī (*empire*) Rōmānī caput, vidēre.

Mārcus: Poterimus etiam Aquīsgrānum petere, quod erat imperiī Rōmānī caput novum. Tēcum omnī locō erō fēlīx!

Helena: Redeāmus (*let us return*) ad aliōs!

Helen and Mark return to the others.

Mārcus: Satis superque (*more than enough*) dē itineribus dīximus. Nunc librum dē Atticō Cicerōnis amīcō scrīptum legāmus.

Marīa: Erant tamen in illō librō multa verba difficilia. Relinquātur ille liber!

Helena: Nōlī, Marīa, hoc dīcere! Et ego timēbam, sed nōn iam. Audiās nunc!

Utinam mihi liceat Lutetiam petere, turrim Eiffeliānam vidēre, Lutetiae ambulāre atque dēlectārī! Dūcēsne mē, Mārce, Lutetiam?

ATTICUS EXCELS IN SCHOOL

CORNĒLIĪ NEPŌTIS ATTICUS, 1.3–4

Atticus did better in school than many boys of more noble origin. In doing so, he gave incentives to his classmates to strive even harder in their studies. During this period of childhood and early youth, he made a number of friendships that would be lifelong, including his friendship with Cicero.

1   3. Erat autem in puerō praeter docilitātem ingeniī summa suāvitās
     ōris atque vōcis, ut nōn sōlum celeriter acciperet, quae trādēbantur,
     sed etiam excellenter prōnūntiāret. Quā ex rē in pueritiā nōbilis inter
     aequālēs ferēbātur clāriusque exsplendēscēbat, quam generōsī
5   condiscipulī animō aequō ferre possent. 4. Itaque incitābat omnēs
     studiō suō. Quō in numerō fuērunt L. Torquātus, C. Marius fīlius,
     M. Cicero; quōs cōnsuētūdine suā sīc dēvīnxit, ut nēmō hīs umquam
     fuerit cārior.

VOCABULARY

1   praeter + accusative – besides, in addition to

     docilitās, docilitātis, f. – aptness for being taught, docility

     summus, a, um – supreme

     suāvitās, suāvitātis, f. – sweetness

2   trādō, ere, trādidī, trāditum – to give, teach

3   excellenter (adv.) – in an excellent way

     prōnūntiō, āre, āvī, ātum – to pronounce

     pueritia, ae, f. – childhood

     nōbilis, nōbile – noble, distinguished

4   ferēbātur – was told, was regarded, was said

     clārius . . . quam . . . possent . . . – more brilliantly . . . than . . . they were able . . .

     explendēscō, ere, exsplenduī, — — to shine forth, be famous

     generōsus, a, um – of noble birth

5   condiscipulus, ī, m. – classmate

     ferō, ferre – to carry, bear

     incitō, āre, āvī, ātum – to stimulate, instigate

6   studium, ī, n. – zeal, eagerness

     L. = Lūcius, Roman first name

     C. = Gāius, Roman first name

     numerus, ī, m. – number

7   quō in numerō = et in eō numerō

     sīc (adv.) – in such a way

     M. = Mārcus, Roman first name

     cōnsuētūdō, cōnsuētūdinis, f. – custom, companionship

     dēvinciō, īre, dēvīnxī, dēvīnctum – to tie up, oblige, attach

READING NOTES

1   *praeter docilitātem ingeniī* "in addition to an aptitude of (i.e., for) being taught" or "in addition to an ability to learn quickly."

1–2   *summa suāvitās ōris atque vōcis* "the utmost sweetness of mouth and voice." I.e., Atticus modulated his words with care, the pitch of his voice was pleasing, and his delivery was good.

2–3   *ut nōn sōlum . . . acciperet, sed etiam . . . prōnūntiāret* "so that he would not only receive . . . but also pronounce"

3   *Quā ex rē =et eā ex rē;* "On account of this fact." This refers back to what has been said so far about Atticus' qualities.

4   *ferēbātur* "he was said to be" or "he was regarded as."

4–5   *clāriusque exsplendēscēbat, quam . . . condiscipulī . . . ferre possent.* Here the clause with its verb in the subjunctive (*possent*) means: "he shone forth more brilliantly than his classmates were able to bear."

6   *Quō* The relative pronoun at the beginning of a sentence often translates as the demonstrative "this" or "that," as is the case here.

7–8   *cōnsuētūdine suā sīc dēvīnxit, ut nēmō hīs . . . fuerit cārior* Here *ut* introduces a clause with a verb in the subjunctive (*fuerit*) that expresses the result of an action or state. (See Chapter 14). The whole phrase, including the *ut* clause, means "<whom> he attached <to himself> through his companionship in such a way that nobody was ever dearer to them . . . "

QUESTIONS ABOUT THE TEXT

Answer in complete Latin sentences.

1. Quōmodō docēbātur Atticus?

2. Quid Atticus in scholā bene faciēbat?

3. Eratne Atticus generōsus?

4. Eratne Atticus melior quam (*better than*) condiscipulī generōsī?

5. Quid condiscipulī generōsī dē Atticō sentiēbant?

6. Quī erant inter amīcōs Atticī?

7. Quamdiū illī Atticī amīcī fuērunt?

DĒ ITINERE IN EURŌPAM FACTŌ CONTINUED

Christīna: Nōs quoque maneāmus semper amīcī!

Mārcus: Ita, maneāmus!

Helena: Bene dīcitis.

Imperfect Subjunctive Active and Passive Subjunctive of All Conjugations; Purpose Clauses; Sequence of Tenses

The fourteenth century illuminated manuscript containing the poems of Charles, Duke of Orléans, includes this image of the ill-starred lovers Heloise and Abelard.

MEMORĀBILE DICTŪ

Nec sine tē nec tēcum vīvere possum.

"I can live neither without you nor with you." (Ovid, *Love Affairs*, 3.11b.7)

A witty description of the emotional difficulties that love brings. Ovid dramatizes the eternal and irreconcilable conflicts typical of human love affairs. It emphasizes that physical beauty makes the beloved desirable not only to the lover, but to others as well; the beloved's appearance, therefore, may also be a cause of anxiety. What is more, even if the behavior of the beloved causes resentment in the lover, it may also lead to greater desire, to the point where the lover feels subjected to the beloved, in a form of painful but welcome servitude. The reading in this chapter deals with one of the most celebrated and tragic love stories of all time.

READING

Peter Abelard was an eminent philosopher and theologian of the twelfth century who had acquired the reputation of a free thinker. He is remembered not only for his rigorous application of logical analysis in his studies, but also for his tragic personal life. When the uncle of a learned young woman named Heloise sought out a tutor for her, Abelard—who had been eager to meet her—applied for the position. The text below narrates what happened as a result.

This reading is an adaptation of a letter to Abelard from Heloise, in which she reacts to his *Historia calamitātum meārum* (*A Story of My Sufferings*), an autobiography presented in the form of a letter.

HELOĪSA AD ABAELARDUM

1   Abaelardō dominō (immō patrī), coniugī (immō frātrī) Heloīsa ancilla
      (immō fīlia), uxor (immō soror) salūtem dīcit.

      Lēgī epistulam quam ad amīcum scrīpserās ut dē calamitātibus tuīs
      nārrārēs. Propter verba tua māgnō dolōre sum capta. Discipula

5   eram et tū magister mē docēre dēbēbās. At ex tē nōn sōlum dē litterīs
      discēbam, sed etiam dē amōre. Nam amor fortis inter nōs ārsit.
      Avunculus meus putābat nōs librōs legere, sed nōs manūs tenēbāmus.
      Mē tamen uxōrem diū nōn dūcēbās, nē fāmam perderēs. Tunc fīlium[†]
      peperī et clam mātrimōniō sumus iūnctī. Avunculus īrā est correptus

10   et hominēs improbōs mīsit ut tē vulnerārent. Tandem sumus sēparātī:
      uterque monasterium intrāvit. Nunc tū in monasteriō tuō, ego in meō
      vīvimus. Soror tua fīlium meum cūrat; ego et fīliō et marītō misera
      egeō. Animus autem meus mēcum nōn est, sed tēcum. Sī tēcum nōn
      est, nusquam est; nam sine tē esse nōn potest. At tū dē mē cōgitāre nōn

15   vidēris. Ad mē, cum ūnā manēbāmus, carmina longa saepe scrībēbās.
      Nunc, cum sēparāmur, vōcem tuam nōn audiō. Scrībās ad mē!
      Epistulam mittās ut sciam tē bene valēre! Amōrem nostrum colāmus!
      Nōlī mē relinquere! Valē, ūnice!

[†]The parents gave their offspring the unorthodox name Astralabe which is the name of an instrument for measuring the stars. Astralabe, son of Abelard, seems to have followed a career in the church but not much is known about the details of his life or death.

READING VOCABULARY

Abaelardus, ī, m. – Abelard

ancilla, ae, f. – female servant

*at (conj.) – but

avunculus, ī, m. – (maternal) uncle

calamitās, calamitātis, f. – calamity, disaster

carmen, carminis, n. – poem, song

clam (adv.) – secretly

*coniūnx, coniugis, m./f. – spouse

*discipula, ae, f. – student (female)

*discō, ere, didicī, — – to learn

*dominus, ī, m. – master, lord

et . . . et – both . . . and

*fāma, ae, f. – fame, name, reputation

*frāter, frātris, m. – brother

Heloīsa, ae, f. – Heloise

immō (conj.) – on the contrary, nay rather

*improbus, a, um – bad, wicked

*iungō, ere, iūnxī, iūnctum – to join

*magister, magistrī, m. – teacher (male)

*mātrimōnium, ī, n. – marriage

monasterium, ī, n. – monastery

nārrārēs – imperfect subjunctive of *nārrō*

*nē (conj. + subjunctive) – in order not to, lest

*nusquam (adv.) – nowhere

*pariō, ere, peperī, partum – to give birth to

pater, patris, m. – father

perderēs – imperfect subjunctive of *perdō*

*perdō, ere, perdidī, perditum – to lose, waste

*salūs, salūtis, f. – health, welfare

salūtem dīcō + dative – I greet (a customary way to begin a letter)

*scrībō, ere, scrīpsī, scrīptum – to write

ūnicus, a, um – only one

*ut (conj. + subjunctive) – in order to, so that

uterque – each (of two)

*uxōrem dūcō – to marry (a woman), take as a wife

vulnerārent – imperfect subjunctive of *vulnerō*

*Words marked with an asterisk will need to be memorized later in the chapter.

COMPREHENSION QUESTIONS

1. What has prompted Heloise to write to Abelard?

2. Why did Heloise's uncle arrange for Abelard to be attacked?

3. Where are Abelard, Heloise, and their son during the time Heloise is writing the letter?

The astrolabe is a two-dimensional model of the celestial sphere elaborately inscribed on a brass disc. Its portability and usefulness made it the most used, multipurpose astronomical instrument until the seventeenth century. Conceived by the ancient Greeks, perfected by the Muslims, the astrolabe was introduced to Europe from Islamic Spain in the twelfth century.

LANGUAGE FACT I

IMPERFECT ACTIVE AND PASSIVE SUBJUNCTIVE OF ALL CONJUGATIONS

In Heloise's letter you encounter two new forms of verbs you already know: the forms *nārrārēs* and *vulnerārent* from the verbs *nārrō* and *vulnerō*. These forms belong to the imperfect subjunctive.

Find one more imperfect subjunctive in the Latin reading passage at the beginning of the chapter.

The imperfect subjunctive is easily formed by adding the endings of the present subjunctive to the present infinitive. You can recognize in the forms above the present infinitive: *nārrāre, vulnerāre*.

First Conjugation: Imperfect Active Subjunctive

	Singular	Plural
First person	parārem	parārēmus
Second person	parārēs	parārētis
Third person	parāret	parārent

First Conjugation: Imperfect Passive Subjunctive

	Singular	Plural
First person	parārer	parārēmur
Second person	parārēris	parārēminī
Third person	parārētur	parārentur

Second Conjugation: Imperfect Active Subjunctive

	Singular	Plural
First person	tenērem	tenērēmus
Second person	tenērēs	tenērētis
Third person	tenēret	tenērent

Second Conjugation: Imperfect Passive Subjunctive

	Singular	Plural
First person	tenērer	tenērēmur
Second person	tenērēris	tenērēminī
Third person	tenērētur	tenērentur

Third Conjugation: Imperfect Active Subjunctive

	Singular	Plural
First person	peterem	peterēmus
Second person	peterēs	peterētis
Third person	peteret	peterent

Third Conjugation: Imperfect Passive Subjunctive

	Singular	Plural
First person	peterer	peterēmur
Second person	peterēris	peterēminī
Third person	peterētur	peterentur

Fourth Conjugation: Imperfect Active Subjunctive

	Singular	Plural
First person	audīrem	audīrēmus
Second person	audīrēs	audīrētis
Third person	audīret	audīrent

Fourth Conjugation: Imperfect Passive Subjunctive

	Singular	Plural
First person	audīrer	audīrēmur
Second person	audīrēris	audīrēminī
Third person	audīrētur	audīrentur

-iō Verbs of Third Conjugation: Imperfect Active Subjunctive

	Singular	Plural
First person	caperem	caperēmus
Second person	caperēs	caperētis
Third person	caperet	caperent

-iō Verbs of Third Conjugation: Imperfect Passive Subjunctive

	Singular	Plural
First person	caperer	caperēmur
Second person	caperēris	caperēminī
Third person	caperētur	caperentur

BY THE WAY

The imperfect subjunctive of the third conjugation verbs and of the *–iō* verbs of the third conjugation look the same:

peterem – caperem.

STUDY TIP

Remember that *–re–* before the endings is often a clue for the imperfect subjunctive! Similarly, if you see an infinitive with a verb (personal) ending, you know you're looking at the imperfect subjunctive!

The irregular verbs *sum* and *possum* form the imperfect subjunctive in the same manner as the other verbs.

Imperfect Subjunctive of sum

	Singular	Plural
First person	essem	essēmus
Second person	essēs	essētis
Third person	esset	essent

Imperfect Subjunctive of possum

	Singular	Plural
First person	possem	possēmus
Second person	possēs	possētis
Third person	posset	possent

▶ EXERCISE 1

Change the present or imperfect indicative verb forms into the present or imperfect subjunctive, keeping the same tense, person, number, and voice. Give the basic meaning of the verb.

Example: discit – discat   to learn

1. iungēbātur
2. perduntur
3. discis
4. aspiciēbam
5. prōmittitis
6. inveniēbant
7. occupāminī
8. gignuntur
9. valeō
10. sinimus
11. gignimus

VOCABULARY TO LEARN

NOUNS

coniūnx, coniugis, m./f. – spouse

discipula, ae, f. – student (female)

dominus, ī, m. – master, lord

fāma, ae, f. – fame, name, reputation

frāter, frātris, m. – brother

magister, magistrī, m. – teacher (male)

mātrimōnium, ī, n. – marriage

salūs, salūtis, f. – health, welfare

ADJECTIVES

improbus, a, um – bad, wicked

VERBS

discō, ere, didicī, — – to learn

iungō, ere, iūnxī, iūnctum – to join

pariō, ere, peperī, partum – to give birth to

perdō, ere, perdidī, perditum – to lose, waste

scrībō, ere, scrīpsī, scrīptum – to write

ADVERBS

nusquam – nowhere

CONJUNCTIONS

at – but

nē + subjunctive – in order not to, lest . . . should

ut + subjunctive – in order to, so that

PHRASE

salūtem dīcō + dative – I greet (a customary way to begin a letter)

uxōrem dūcō – to marry (a woman), take as a wife

▶ EXERCISE 2

Find the English derivatives based on the Vocabulary to Learn in the following sentences. Write the corresponding Latin word. Some of the sentences may contain more than one derivative.

1. After the delivery of a child, a postpartum depression may occur.

2. There has been conjugal discord between this husband and wife recently.

3. Matrimonial happiness depends on the husband and wife's tolerance of each other's habits.

4. You need to salute when you meet a superior officer.

5. In my college years, I belonged to a fraternity.

6. He is an expert in his discipline.

7. Drive one mile to the junction and then turn right.

8. When I grow up, I will become famous.

9. After the conquests of Alexander the Great, his dominion stretched from the Mediterranean Sea all the way to India.

10. You will readily recognize the master among his disciples.

▶ EXERCISE 3

Change the present subjunctive forms into the imperfect subjunctive, keeping the same person and number.

Example: sint   essent

1. possim
2. sīs
3. possītis
4. sīmus
5. possit
6. possint
7. sītis
8. sim
9. sit
10. possīs
11. possīmus

LANGUAGE FACT II

PURPOSE CLAUSES; SEQUENCE OF TENSES

In her letter, Heloise says to Abelard:

> *Lēgī epistulam quam ad amīcum scrīpserās **ut** dē calamitātibus tuīs **nārrārēs**.*
> "I read the letter which you had written to your friend in order to tell about your calamities."

The clause ***ut** dē calamitātibus tuīs **nārrārēs*** is a purpose clause, which explains the purpose of Abelard's writing a letter.

In Latin, purpose is very often expressed with a clause introduced by the conjunction *ut* with the subjunctive.

Ut in a purpose clause is usually translated "in order to" (or its shortened form "to") or "so that."

An engraving depicts Heloise in the garb of a nun at her desk in the convent. Having read a page of a letter from her beloved Abelard, she has dropped it from her hands. Note the skull on the desk, a reminder of mortality. The Roman home often had such a *mementō morī* as well.

BY THE WAY

You have seen *ut* with the indicative meaning "as." However, the *ut* that introduces purpose clauses always requires the subjunctive.

The subjunctive used in a purpose clause is either present or imperfect. The **present** subjunctive is used after a primary tense main verb. The present, the future, and the future perfect are primary tenses. The **imperfect** subjunctive is used after a secondary tense main verb. The imperfect, the perfect, and the pluperfect are secondary tenses. This relation between the tense of the main verb and the tense of the subjunctive verb depending on it is called the **sequence of tenses.**

Heloise asks Abelard to write a few lines:

> *Epistulam mittās* **ut sciam** *tē bene valēre!*
> "Send a letter so that I know that you are well!"

Heloise wants to know that Abelard is well. *Sciam* is a present subjunctive because the verb *mittās* is present tense.

Negative purpose is expressed with the conjunction *nē* and the subjunctive.

Heloise remembers:

> *Mē tamen uxōrem diū nōn dūcēbās, nē fāmam tuam perderēs.*
> "However, for a long time you were not taking me as a wife, lest you should lose your reputation."

Nē in the negative purpose clause is translated "in order not to" or "lest."

Sequence of Tenses – Shortened Version	
Independent (Main) Clause (Verb)	**Subordinate (Purpose) Clause**
Primary Tense Verb/Primary Sequence Present, Future, Future Perfect Indicative	Present Subjunctive
Secondary Tense Verb/Secondary Sequence Imperfect, Perfect, Pluperfect Indicative	Imperfect Subjunctive

Find one more purpose clause in the Latin reading passage at the beginning of the chapter. Explain whether it is positive or negative, and whether a present or an imperfect subjunctive is used in it.

Heloise and Abelard's letters would have looked similar to this script. The most popular ink, brown made from iron and oak leaves, would be applied to sheets of vellum or parchment made from the skins of animals. Today's calligraphers are masters of the various medieval fonts.

▶ EXERCISE 4

Fill in the first blank with either *ut* or *nē* according to the sense of the sentence. Fill in the second blank with the correct form of the verb in parentheses. Translate each sentence. The Reading Vocabulary may be consulted.

Example: Heloīsa ad Abaelardum scrībit _____ dē dolōre suō eī _____. (nārrō)
Heloīsa ad Abaelardum scrībit **ut** dē dolōre suō eī **nārret.**
Heloise writes to Abelard in order to tell him about her pain.

1. Heloīsa ad Abaelardum scrībēbat _____ dē gravī dolōre suō eī _____. (nārrō)

2. Māne Abaelardus magister ad domum Heloīsae discipulae venit _____ eam _____. (doceō)

3. Māne Abaelardus magister ad domum Heloīsae discipulae vēnit _____ eam _____. (doceō)

4. Hodiē Abaelardus et Heloīsa in monasteria mittuntur _____ ūnā _____. (sum)

5. Abaelardus et Heloīsa in monasteria sunt missī _____ ūnā _____. (sum)

6. Fīlius Heloīsae cum sorōre Abaelardī per multōs annōs manet _____ ab illā _____. (cūrō)

7. Fīlius Heloīsae cum sorōre Abaelardī manēbat per multōs annōs _____ ab illā _____. (cūrō)

The arched windows and the barrel vaulted ceiling of the monastery dormitory bear witness to their Roman roots and give this style the name Romanesque. Founded in 1146, Thoronet Abbey in southern France is contemporaneous with Heloise and Abelard's time in the convent and the monastery.

▶ EXERCISE 5

Construct from each pair of sentences a complex sentence that contains a purpose clause. Translate the new sentences. The Reading Vocabulary may be consulted.

Example: Librōs legō. Rēs discō.
Librōs legō ut rēs discam.
I read books in order to learn things.

1. Abaelardus ad amīcum scrībit. Dē rēbus suīs nārrat.

2. Abaelardus et Heloīsa occultābantur. Avunculus dē amōre nōn discēbat.

3. Abaelardus et Heloīsa sunt tandem sēpārātī. Ūnā nōn erant.

4. Abaelardus ad Heloīsam nōn scrībit. Ēius animus est in pāce.

▶ EXERCISE 6

Find all the subjunctives and imperatives, both positive and negative, in the Latin reading passage at the beginning of the chapter. Identify what type of subjunctive or imperative each is.

A Gothic-revival tomb with two full-length figures of a monk and a nun atop a sarcophagus protects the remains of Heloise and Abelard. The French honored their story through the ages and in 1804, Napoleon and Joséphine Bonaparte brought the lovers' remains to Paris for final resting at Père-Lachaise cemetery in 1817.

TALKING ABOUT A READING
ABOUT LOVE AND UNADAPTED LATIN: ATTICUS GOES TO ATHENS

DĒ AMŌRE

Helen and Mark are alone.

Mārcus: Dum epistulam Heloīsae legēbāmus, dē tē, Helena, cōgitābam.

Helena: Cūr? Putāsne mē esse tam doctam quam (*as*) Heloīsam?

Mārcus: Nōn sōlum putō tē esse tam doctam et pulchram quam Heloīsam, sed quoque intellegō Abaelardī amōrem.

Helena: Tūne Marīam amās? Saepe enim cum eā verba facere solēs et gaudium hāc ex rē capere vidēris.

Mārcus: Audiās mē, Helena! Marīa est bona amīca. At est alia puella, quam uxōrem dūcere cupiō.

Helena: Quam?

Mārcus: Nōnne (*don't you*) intellegis?

Helena: Nōn intellegō. Nōmen ēius audīre dēbeō.

Mārcus: Idem (*the same*) nōmen habet quod mulier quae fuit bellī Trōiānī causa.

Helena (blushing): Dēbeō tamen aliōs nunc vocāre. . . . Veniātis, amīcī!

Marīa: Cūr venīre dēbēmus?

Helena: Venīre dēbētis ut dē Atticō ūnā legāmus.

Marīa: Legās tū, Helena!

Athens had long served as an intellectual capital in the ancient world. Romans went there to study with scholars in much the same way as modern students go away to university. Intellectual debates regularly took place in the agora (depicted above), the central gathering place of Athens. The temple of Hephaestus overlooks the agora.

ATTICUS GOES TO ATHENS

CORNĒLIĪ NEPŌTIS ATTICUS, 2.1–2

Atticus grew up in a period of civil strife in which Marius was the leader on one side and Sulla on the other. Not wishing to take sides and make enemies of people in the opposing party, Atticus decided to move to Athens, which was in any case an appropriate place for him to complete his studies.

1. 1. Pater matūrē dēcessit. Ipse adulēscentulus propter affīnitātem
P. Sulpiciī, quī tribūnus plēbī interfectus est, nōn expers fuit illīus
perīculī. Namque Anicia, Pomponiī consōbrīna, nūpserat Serviō, frātrī
Sulpiciī. 2. Itaque interfectō Sulpiciō, posteāquam vīdit Cinnānō
5. tumultū cīvitātem esse perturbātam neque sibi darī facultātem prō
dignitāte vīvendī, quīn alterutram partem offenderet, dissociātīs animīs
cīvium, cum aliī Sullānīs, aliī Cinnānīs favērent partibus, idōneum
tempus ratus studiīs obsequendī suīs, Athēnās sē contulit. Neque eō
sētius adulēscentem Marium hostem iūdicātum iūvit opibus suīs, cūius
10. fugam pecūniā sublevāvit.

VOCABULARY

1   matūrē (adv.) – early

      dēcēdō, ere, dēcessī, dēcessum – to die

      ipse – himself

      adulēscentulus, ī, m. – very young man

      affīnitās, affīnitātis, f. – relationship by marriage

2   P. = Pūblius

      tribūnus, ī, m. plēbī – tribune of the plebs

      interficiō, ere, interfēcī, interfectum – to kill

      expers, expertis + genitive – devoid of, free from

      illīus (gen.) – of that

3   namque = nam

      consōbrīna, ae, f. – cousin

      nūbō, ere, nūpsī, nūptum + dat. – to marry (a man)

4   posteāquam = postquam

      Cinnānus, a, um – related to Cinna, ae, m.

5   cīvitās, cīvitātis, f. – city, community of citizens, state

      perturbō, āre, āvī, ātum – to throw into confusion

6   quīn . . . offenderet – without offending

      alteruter, alterutra, alterutrum – either of two

7   aliī . . . aliī . . . – some . . . others . . .

      Sullānus, a, um – related to Sulla, ae, m

      faveō, ēre, fāvī, fautum + dative – to favor

8   Athēnae, ārum, f. pl. – Athens

      sē contulit – went

      neque = nec

8–9 neque eō sētius – nevertheless

9   Marius, ī, m. – civil war leader against Sulla

      iūvō, āre, iūvī, iūtum – to help

      opēs, opium, f. pl. – resources, money

10 fuga, ae, f. – flight

      pecūnia, ae, f. – money

      sublevō, āre, āvī, ātum – to support, help

READING NOTES

1–2 *propter affīnitātem P. Sulpiciī* "because of his relationship with Publius Sulpicius." Latin uses the genitive with *affīnitās* whereas an English speaker would use the preposition "with."

2   *quī tribūnus plēbī* "who as a tribune of the plebs." A tribune of the plebs was a magistrate elected to defend the rights of the lower class.

4   *Itaque interfectō Sulpiciō* This ablative absolute, a construction you will learn later in this book, means the same as *postquam Sulpicius est interfectus* or "after Sulpicius was killed."

4–5 *posteāquam vīdit Cinnānō tumultū cīvitātem esse perturbātam* "after he saw that the state had been thrown into confusion because of the uproar by Cinna." Cinna, a leader in the Roman civil wars, was on Marius' side.

5–6 *facultās (facultātis, f.) prō dignitāte vīvendī* This phrase means "a possibility of living according to one's dignity."

6   *quīn alterutram partem offenderet* "without offending either of the two sides."

6–7 *dissociātīs animīs cīvium* "<with> the minds of the citizens having been put at odds."

7   *Sullānīs* Sulla was a major leader in the Roman civil wars and later a celebrated Roman dictator.

      partibus This noun which ordinarily means "part," here means "party."

7–8 *idōneum tempus ratus studiīs obsequendī suīs* "having deemed the time appropriate for attending to his studies."

9   *adulēscentem Marium hostem iūdicātum* "the young man Marius having been judged (who had been judged) an enemy."

QUESTIONS ABOUT THE TEXT

Answer in complete Latin sentences.

1. Vīxitne diū pater Atticī?

2. Eratne Atticus in perīculō?

3. Cūr Atticus erat in perīculō?

4. Quid tunc Atticus fēcit?

5. Cūr Atticus Athēnās sē contulit? (answer with a purpose clause containing the verb *discō*)

6. Eratne eō tempore Rōmae pāx?

7. Inter quōs erat bellum?

8. Cūr timēbat Atticus?

9. Quem tamen iūvit Atticus?

10. Cūr Atticus Marium iūvit?

DĒ AMŌRE CONTINUED

Marīa: Cūr patriam relīquit Atticus? Hoc est malum.

Helena: Atticus hoc fēcit ut sē servāret. Nam ēius vīta in perīculō erat. At poterat Athēnīs litterīs studēre.

Christīna: Ego cupiō Rōmae esse ut litterīs Latīnīs studeam.

VOCABULARY TO KNOW

NOUNS

annus, ī, m. – year

argentum, ī, n. – silver

aurum, ī, n. – gold

coniūnx, coniugis, m./f. – spouse

cōnsilium, ī, n. – advice (you already know the meaning "plan")

custōs, custōdis, m. – guard

discipula, ae, f. – student (female)

dominus, ī, m. – master, lord

eques, equitis, m. – horseman

fāma, ae, f. – fame, name, reputation

fīnis, fīnis, m. – end

frāter, frātris, m. – brother

gēns, gentis, f. – tribe, population

incola, ae, m. – inhabitant

īnsula, ae, f. – island

līs, lītis, f. – dispute, quarrel

magister, magistrī, m. – teacher (male)

mātrimōnium, ī, n. – marriage

merīdiēs, merīdiēī, m. – south (you already know the meaning "midday")

mōs, mōris, m. – custom, habit, pl. morals

mundus, ī, m. – world

odium, ī, n. – hatred

ortus, ortūs, m. – rising, beginning, origin; ortus sōlis – east

piscis, piscis, m. – fish

salūs, salūtis, f. – health, welfare

sōl, sōlis, m. – sun

vestis, vestis, f. – clothes, attire

vōx, vōcis, f. – voice

vultus, vultūs, m. – face

ADJECTIVES

altus, a, um – tall, deep

brevis, breve – short

clārus, a, um – clear, distinguished

gravis, grave – heavy, serious

improbus, a, um – bad, wicked

septentriōnālis, septentriōnāle – northern

situs, a, um – situated, located

VERBS

aspiciō, ere, aspexī, aspectum – to look at, catch a glimpse of

discō, ere, didicī, —— – to learn

gerō, ere, gessī, gestum – to wear (you already know the meaning "carry")

gignō, ere, genuī, genitum – to produce, give birth

inveniō, īre, invēnī, inventum – to come upon, find

iungō, ere, iūnxī, iūnctum – to join

occupō, āre, āvī, ātum – to occupy

pariō, ere, peperī, partum – to give birth to

perdō, ere, perdidī, perditum – to lose, waste

prōmittō, ere, prōmīsī, prōmissum – to promise

scrībō, ere, scrīpsī, scrīptum – to write

sinō, ere, sīvī, situm + accusative + infinitive – to allow somebody to do something

valeō, ēre, valuī, —— – to be in good health

ADVERBS

hodiē – today

interdum – sometimes

māne – in the morning

nē – negative particle with the subjunctive

nusquam – nowhere

procul – far away

utinam – I wish that, if only (a particle of wishing)

CONJUNCTIONS

at – but

et ... et ... – both ... and ...

nē + subjunctive – in order not to, lest should

ut + indicative – as

ut + subjunctive – in order to, so that

vel – or

PHRASES

odiō habeō + accusative – I hate somebody

salūtem dīcō + dative – I greet (a customary way to begin a letter)

uxōrem dūcō – to marry (a woman), take as a wife

▶ EXERCISE 1

Conjugate the following verbs in the present and imperfect subjunctive, both active and passive.

1. *occupō, occupāre, occupāvī, occupātum*

2. *prōmittō, prōmittere, prōmisī, prōmissum*

▶ EXERCISE 2

Change the indicative verbs into the subjunctive, keeping the same person, number, tense, and voice. Give the basic meaning of each verb.

Example: parās parēs to prepare

1. iungēbantur
2. aspicitur
3. poterās
4. inveniunt
5. valēmus
6. occupāris

7. pariēbam
8. gereris
9. gignēbāminī
10. discō
11. perdit
12. sinēbāmus

▶ EXERCISE 3

Translate into Latin.

1. In Paris Heloise was a student and Abelard her teacher.

2. Charlemagne was an emperor not in Rome but in Aachen.

3. Caesar sailed to Dover in order to occupy Britain.

4. After Abelard and Heloise were separated, Heloise went to Argenteuil. For a long time Heloise was not able to leave Argenteuil. She had to live at Argenteuil.

Aachen – Aquisgrānum, ī, n.
Abelard – Abaelardus, ī, m.
Argenteuil – Argentiōlum, ī, n.
Britain – Britannia, ae, f.
Caesar – Caesar, Caesaris, m.

Charlemagne – Carolus, ī, m. Māgnus
Dover – Dubrī, ōrum, m. pl.
Heloise – Heloīsa, ae, f.
Paris – Lutetia, ae, f.

The White Cliffs of Dover, a chalk formation, face continental Europe at the narrowest point of the English Channel.
The armed Britons standing on the cliffs forced Caesar to beach down the coast. The Norman forces in 1066
also landed down the coast at Pevensey where the Romans had built a fort.

▶ EXERCISE 4

Identify the subjunctive in each sentence as a volitive, an optative, or a negative imperative used as a negative volitive. Translate the sentences.

Example: Magistrum audiās!
audiās   volitive subjunctive   You should listen to the teacher!

1. Dēs mihi argentum et aurum!

2. Nōlīte magistrōs odiō habēre!

3. Scrībāmus epistulam ad patrem, ad mātrem, ad frātrem et ad improbum coniugem!

4. Utinam māgnam fāmam in mundō habeam!

5. Utinam nē sint lītēs in hāc gente!

6. Bonī mōrēs colantur!

▶ EXERCISE 5

Fill in the blanks with the correct form of the verb in parentheses. Translate the sentences.

Example: Comedō ut _____ (vīvō).
Comedō ut vīvam.   I eat in order to live.

1. Pictī ad īnsulam nāvigāvērunt ut domum _____. (inveniō)
     Pictī, ōrum, m. pl. – Picts

2. Hibernī nōn sinēbant Pictōs ibi manēre nē multī incolae in illā īnsulā _____. (sum)
     Hibernī, ōrum, m. pl. – Irishmen

3. Tandem Pictī discessērunt ut aliam īnsulam _____. (quaerō)

4. Carolus Māgnus cōnsilia aliōrum nōn petēbat nē mala cōnsilia _____. (accipiō)
     Carolus, ī, m. Māgnus – Charlemagne

5. Dum comedēbat, Carolus Māgnus cupiēbat librōs legī ut eōs _____. (audiō)

6. Abaelardus et Heloīsa ūnā manēbant ut amōrem _____. (colō)
     Abaelardus, ī, m. – Abelard   Heloīsa, ae, f. – Heloise

▶ EXERCISE 6

Fill in the blank with the correct form of the verb keeping the same person, number, and voice. Translate the changed sentence.

Example: Comedō ut vīvam.
Comēdēbam ut <u>vīverem</u>.   I ate in order to live.

1. Omnia parant ut mātrimōniō iungantur.

    Omnia parābant ut mātrimōniō _____.

2. Aurum et argentum cupiō ut dīvitiās habeam.

    Aurum et argentum cupiēbam ut dīvitiās _____.

3. Ambulant ad merīdiem ut novam patriam inveniant.

    Ambulābant ad merīdiem ut novam patriam _____.

4. Piscēs comedimus ut bene valeāmus.

    Piscēs comedēbāmus ut bene _____.

CONSIDERING THE HEROES OF CLASSICAL MYTHOLOGY

Our ancient sources on Greek mythological heroes portray them as extraordinary individuals. For one thing, they are said to have been born in unusual circumstances, often to mortal mothers and divine fathers. For another, these sources report that upon reaching manhood all of these heroes were compelled to leave their familiar surroundings, to undertake a quest that required the performance of difficult deeds, and through these experiences to learn more not only about the wider world but also about themselves.

PERSEUS

Perseus, for example, was the son of a mortal princess named Danaë and the god Zeus. Because an oracle told her father Acrisius that his grandson would kill him, Acrisius locked Danaë up in a bronze tower. Nevertheless, after Zeus managed to visit her there by disguising himself as a shower of golden rain, Danaë gave birth to Perseus. Enraged, Acrisius set both his daughter and grandson adrift in a boat, hoping Perseus would die, but the two were saved. When Perseus grew up, he was forced to go on a quest to kill the Gorgon Medusa.

The three Gorgons of Greek mythology were the daughters of Phorcys and Ceto. Hideous creatures covered with scales, they had hair writhing with snakes and hands made out of brass. They were said to reside in the far west of the ancient Mediterranean world, near the ocean, and to guard the entrance to the underworld. Of the three sisters, Medusa was the only mortal.

A triumphant Perseus holds the head of the Gorgon Medusa. The Renaissance produced many artworks inspired by classical mythology. Benvenuto Cellini (1500–1571) signed his 18-foot bronze statue along the strap over Perseus' torso.

The Gorgon Medusa was a frightening female monster with snakes for hair and a boar-like snout. Those who looked at her turned to stone. Since the goddess Athena had equipped Perseus with a shield, he was able to kill Medusa by looking at her reflection on the shield and in this way avoid being turned to stone. While returning from his heroic venture, Perseus was also able to free the princess Andromeda, who had been bound to a rock and was under attack by a sea monster.

Andromeda was an Ethiopian princess. Her mother Cassiopeia had dared to compare her own beauty to that of the sea nymphs known as Nereids. Cassiopeia's behavior so enraged both the Nereids and the sea god Poseidon that he sent the sea monster to ravage her country.

Many men had sought to marry Andromeda, but they had done nothing to help when the sea monster threatened her life. Once Perseus rescued her, however, they claimed the right to her hand in marriage. Perseus proceeded to turn all of these suitors into stone by using Medusa's head, and to wed Andromeda himself. After Perseus and Andromeda were married, he accidentally killed his grandfather Acrisius, who happened to be among the spectators on an occasion when Perseus was playing with a discus. Thus Acrisius met the fate prophesied by the oracle, even though he tried to escape it.

HERACLES

Heracles is the greatest of the ancient Greek heroes, since he alone among them achieved immortality. His father, the god Zeus, had visited his mother, a mortal woman named Alcmene, disguised as her husband Amphitryon. Once Alcmene gave birth to Heracles, Zeus' wife Hera, ever jealous, sent a pair of snakes to attack the baby in his cradle. Heracles strangled them with his bare hands. According to one Greek legend, Zeus then put the baby to Hera's own breast while she was sleeping, so that his son might drink the milk of immortality. Hera, however, woke up suddenly and threw Heracles out of heaven: the milk that then flowed out of her breast was said to have poured into the sky as the Milky Way.

Hercules' character is full of contradictions. He is described as having enormous, indeed divine, physical strength, but in combination with mortal flesh. Consequently, he is portrayed as frequently

Temples to Hercules from the Greco-Roman world abound from Rome's seaport Ostia to Egypt. The temple on the citadel in Amman, Jordan, larger than any temple in Rome itself, was built from 162–166 CE. During the 2008 presidential campaign, Barack Obama held his first press conference in a foreign nation at this site.

violent, unbalanced, and unable to control both his body and his emotions. He is best known for the twelve labors that he performed, and for traveling to the outer limits of the ancient Mediterranean world in order to perform them. Here are two of Hercules' labors. The first involved a journey to the underworld to retrieve Cerberus, a three-headed dog who guards its gates. The second was the killing of the Nemean lion, again with his bare hands, after he realized that the lion's skin was impervious to all weapons.

Heracles' violent disposition led him to kill his first wife and children in a fit of rage. His own death resulted from a cruel misunderstanding by his second wife Deianira. She dipped Heracles' cloak in a liquid that she thought was a love potion, but turned out to be poison, and burned her husband's body badly. He was so tortured by physical pain that he set fire to himself on his own funeral pyre. Unable to endure the prospect of having his favorite son dwell in the underworld, Zeus arranged for Heracles to be transported to the abode of the gods on Mount Olympus, and granted him immortality.

A Roman mosaic depicts Heracles destroying the Stymphalian birds, winged creatures whose bronze beaks and claws readily destroyed humans. A large mosaic in Volubilis, Morocco illustrating all twelve of Heracles' labors includes the scene excerpted here.

THESEUS

Theseus is celebrated in ancient Greek legends for his exploits that protected the city of Athens, particularly the slaying of the Cretan Minotaur, half-human and half-bull. When Theseus was a young man, the Athenians were forced to pay a terrible tribute to King Minos of Crete: each year seven young men and seven young women were sent there to be devoured by the Minotaur, who dwelled in a maze under Minos' palace known as the labyrinth. Having resolved to slay the monster, Theseus sailed to Crete with the fourteen prospective victims; the princess Ariadne, Minos' daughter, promptly fell in love with him and aided him by providing him with a sword and a ball of thread. Theseus unrolled the thread as he entered the labyrinth so that he could find the exit

Through the ages the figure of the Minotaur has fascinated artists from the Greek vase painters to Picasso. Theseus killing the Minotaur sculpted by Étienne-Jules Ramey (1796–1852) stands in the Tuileries Gardens in Paris, France.

when the time came to leave. In gratitude, he took Ariadne away with him, promising to marry her. While they were traveling back to Athens, however, he abandoned her on the island of Naxos while she was fast asleep. Upon awakening, she cursed Theseus in anger and despair, and the gods punished him in the following manner.

Theseus had sailed to and from Crete in a ship with black sails. He had promised his father upon his departure from Athens that if he were to be successful in slaying the Minotaur, he would change these black sails to white sails as he approached Athens. If the Minotaur were to have slain him, however, his ship would continue to have black sails. As a result of Ariadne's curse, Theseus forgot to change the sails from black to white, leading his father Aegeus to believe that his son was dead. Aegeus is said to have then jumped into the sea out of grief and despair, giving his own name to what was thereafter called the Aegean Sea.

Excavations of King Minos' palace at Knossos provide some of the factual evidence that gave rise to the Minotaur myth. With its multiple stories, staircases, lightwells, and 600–700 rooms, the palace was labyrinthine. A fresco showing young men leaping over a bull suggests an alternative view of the annual tribute.

JASON

Jason was the least physically impressive of the Greek mythic heroes, perhaps because he was the son of two mortals. His quest involved retrieving the Golden Fleece from the eastern shore of the Black Sea. After sailing there on a ship called the "Argo" with a crew of sailors called the "Argonauts," he benefited from the help of Medea, daughter of the king who possessed the Golden Fleece, and a skillful sorceress. She went so far as to kill her own brother and scatter his body parts in the sea in order to delay her father, who was pursuing her and Jason. For Medea knew that her father would abandon his pursuit in order to retrieve his son's remains and give them a proper burial.

Medea and Jason fled to Greece, and lived there as exiles with their two sons. But eventually Jason decided to abandon her for a younger Greek princess, whose father was king of Corinth. The despairing Medea took revenge by killing her rival, and her own two children as well. Greek myths claim that Jason met his own death while sleeping under the Argo, after the rotten prow of the ship fell and crushed him.

The Argonauts find the Golden Fleece which the Colchians had placed in a spring to collect alluvial gold dust. The woodcut was published in Georgius Agricola's 1556 treatise on mining *Dē rē metallicā*. Note that the author chose to Latinize his name, George Bauer. His treatise remained the authoritative text in geology for 250 years.

READ THE FOLLOWING PASSAGE

Ariadna aspexit nāvem, quā Thēseus discēdēbat, et exclāmāvit: "Cūr mē, improbe, relinquis? Crētam, in patriam meam, vēnistī ut cum Mīnōtaurō pugnārēs. Auxilium tibi dedī ut eum vincere possēs. Prōmīsistī tē mē uxōrem ductūrum. Mēcum Crētā nāve discessistī. Deinde hanc parvam īnsulam petīvimus. Et hīc, dum dormiēbam, Athēnās sine mē nāvigāvistī. Audiās verba mea et mēcum maneās! Mē uxōrem dūcās! Nōlī mē relinquere! . . . At nōn audīre vidēris. Utinam deī tē familiamque tuam pūniant! Utinam omnia tibi sint fūnesta!"

Ariadna, ae, f. – Ariadne
Athēnae, ārum, f. pl. – Athens
Crēta, ae, f. – Crete

hīc (adv.) – here
Mīnōtaurus, ī, m. – Minotaur
Thēseus, ī, m. – Theseus

CONNECTING WITH THE POST-ANCIENT WORLD

A scene from the Bayeux Tapestry shows the Anglo-Saxon defenders confronting William's Norman invaders. The tapestry provides a visual account of events leading up to the Battle of Hastings as well as scenes of the conflict itself. Notations in Latin identify individuals in the 230 foot cloth panel. Halley's Comet of 1066 is depicted on the tapestry.

THE ORDERS OF MEDIEVAL SOCIETY

Three different classes comprised medieval western European society from the Frankish era until the mid-eleventh century CE. The rulers in theory were the warrior class, who also constituted the nobility. Next were the clerics, who held various positions in the ecclesiastical hierarchy of the Roman church throughout all of Western Europe. To appreciate the importance of this particular group, we must realize that clerics made up a far larger percentage of the population than they do today. The clerics included not only those who performed strictly religious functions but also doctors, educators, record-keepers for the nobility, and lawyers. Last, but by no means least, were the peasants and agricultural workers, without whose labors Western Europe could not have sustained itself. The origins of these social distinctions are not altogether clear, but they appear to have emerged from hierarchies already present in Germanic societies as well as from relations of protection and dependence typical of late imperial Roman society. The social organization formed by the nobility and the peasants, an entity that also included the church in some regions and some periods, is referred to as "feudalism." This word did not actually exist in the Middle Ages as a

King Harold II is killed by a Norman arrow in the Battle of Hastings in 1066. The victorious William henceforth known as William the Conqueror relied on his cavalry to defeat the Anglo-Saxons. The Norman Conquest brought to England a French-speaking court whose legacy is found in so many Latin-based words in the English language.

description of this specific form of social organization, but was devised by legal scholars in the seventeenth and eighteenth centuries to describe the system of lords and their dependents in earlier, medieval times. We still employ this word today for social and economic systems involving human dependence. Yet it is worth noting that medieval feudalism adopted different forms in different circumstances. Feudalism spread from France to England with the conquest of the Anglo-Saxons by the Normans in 1066, and then to Germany, but never took strong root in Italy.

The feudal system centered on land-holding. A knight, or *eques* in Latin, often served as the "vassal," or dependent of a more powerful lord, who was called by the Latin word for leader, *dux* (from which English derives the title "duke"), or the Latin word for companion, *comes* (from which comes the English title "count"). The use of these terms to denote nobles of high status seems to have its origins in Diocletian's reorganization of the Roman provinces at the end of the third century CE; these words were at that time applied to Roman magistrates.

The word *eques* of course had already existed in the Roman republic, but in ancient Roman society it referred to the class of well-to-do Romans excluded at first from senatorial status because of their connections with commerce and trade. Originally, however, Roman *equitēs* had supplied the cavalry for Rome's fighting forces; this association with horses is what they shared with *equitēs* in the medieval period.

The knight astride his horse was a formidable sight. The armor, which weighed as much as fifty pounds, protected the knight from an array of weapons. Carefully made to fit, the armor was a status symbol. This modern Renaissance Faire knight's equipment is a collection of items based on fifteenth and sixteenth century models.

In medieval society, vassals were given a parcel of land, or "fief" (sometimes referred to as *feudum* in medieval Latin) to use. Attached to it were tenant farmers or peasants, who would live from the produce of the land. In return, the vassal would recognize the higher lord as his superior, and pay him in the form of military service, for approximately forty days each year, as a member of the overlord's

Carisbrooke Castle on England's Isle of Wight stands on a former Roman site. Earthworks were constructed in 1070 CE and construction continued to include massive towers in the fourteenth and fifteenth centuries.

comitātus, or "retinue." If either the overlord or the vassal were to die, the feudal contract would be renewed between the successor of either party in a ceremony called "homage" (at times called *homāgium* in medieval Latin). In this way the fief would remain in the same family for generations. This system was able to function without the exchange of any money; by the mid-eleventh century CE, however, the rise of towns—in which economics based on money, trade, craftsmen, and banking flourished—caused a gradual erosion of feudal society.

Kings and the highest-ranking nobles tended to favor dealing with towns: not only could they cash in on their economic profits, but they could then use this money to hire soldiers for standing armies that would be more than a match for any feudal *comitātus*. Monarchs were, in fact, eager to weaken the power of the feudal nobility in their territories. In certain European regions, especially what is now Belgium, northern Germany, and Italy, individual towns and even city states grew very powerful indeed. In them developed a new aristocracy which owed its influence to money, banking, and trade, rather than to hereditary noble rank and the possession of feudal domains.

The stained glass windows of the Gothic cathedrals and churches provide a glimpse into the everyday life of the medieval period. Here the noble seated on his throne with sword in hand receives two gentlemen.

The hilltop town of Carcassonne in southern France is considered a superb example of a medieval walled town. The inner wall was built by the Romans and the Visigoths while the outer wall with its towers was built by Louis IX in 1240 CE. The Trencavel family ruled the area from their fortified palace.

The official language of the clerical class throughout the Middle Ages was Latin, although we should not suppose that every individual cleric was as proficient in Latin as he was expected to be. Communications among the feudal nobility and agricultural peasantry were in the vernacular languages that would develop into the national languages we know today, such as French, English, German and others. This communication was chiefly oral in nature; in fact, it was unusual for documents and texts to be written in these languages before 1200 CE, with the partial exception of those written in pre-Norman England under Saxon rulers. Latin tended to be the language employed for administration and record-keeping, and was virtually the exclusive language of the academic world, the sciences, and the church. Nevertheless, with the development of towns, and especially after the start of what we call the "Renaissance" in Italy around 1400 CE, non-clerical nobility started to become literate, learning and actively using Latin. A Latin education became a status symbol for the non-clerical nobility, especially after the late fifteenth century CE.

EXPLORING TRAGIC LOVE STORIES THROUGH THE AGES

LOVE AND LONGING

Love stories such as that of Heloise and Abelard have moved us for centuries, particularly when we find the story to be "tragic" in some way. But what makes any story tragic? To answer this question, we must reach back to the ancient world, where our notions of tragedy (in western culture), and our ideas about "true love" or even "soul mates" first take shape.

Performances of tragic plays occurred in Athens annually for the better part of two centuries, and such performances were an important aspect of the life of the city. It was the Greek philosopher Aristotle who made a formal study of the genre of tragedy in an attempt to analyze what tragedy is and why human beings react to it so profoundly. In Aristotle's view, we derive a certain emotional benefit called "catharsis"—an emotional release—through watching a tragic performance, which should inspire reactions consisting of both "pity and fear" in its audience. We feel pity for the poor characters experiencing whatever disaster is part of the play's action, and we feel fear that something like that could happen to us. According to Aristotle, the best tragic performances elicited these fundamental emotions.

But tragedy was a complex genre, and there are other features that should be part of a good tragic performance. First, the characters must be good—otherwise, we could not relate to them or care about what happens to them. Second, there was often a reversal of circumstances, in which a character's life shifts from a position of prosperity to one of suffering. Third, there was often a sense of irony regarding that shift—and most often, the character him- or herself was in some way, often unwittingly, personally responsible for that change or suffering.

When the Greek philosopher Plato wrote about love in the *Symposium*, he presented early human beings in a light that was both comical and tragic. He described their bodies as spherical, with two faces (looking in opposite directions), four arms and four legs, traveling about by doing cartwheels. While this image is comical, the important point of this depiction was to portray humans as reaching beyond their means and ending up in a tragic state; for, as Plato tells the story, these early humans decided to challenge the Olympian gods

A spectacular sand sculpture reconstructs the ancient Greek bust of Plato that is on display in the Capitoline Museum in Rome. Plato's theories have strongly influenced the thought of successive ages. The rediscovery of Plato's theories on love deeply affected the writers, artists, and thinkers of the Renaissance.

themselves, and were punished by Zeus—who split them in half. This aetiological myth (one which gives us an *aitia*, a cause or explanation for why things are the way they are) serves to explain why human beings seem to wander the earth searching for their "other half," and simultaneously presents the human condition in a manner that enhances our understanding of tragedy as part of our essence. In this view (even though, as stated above, Plato tells the story with comic overtones), humans are incomplete in themselves and remain incomplete until they find their "soul mate," so to speak, whom they embrace in an effort to grow together once again—which, of course, they cannot do. Therefore, even if we are fortunate enough to find our soul mate, we can never be as truly united as we long to be.

A full page from the illuminated manuscript containing the love poems of Charles (1391–1465), Duke of Orléans, depicts Heloise and Abelard. After his defeat at the Battle of Agincourt, Charles was taken as captive to England. During his twenty-five years in various prisons including the Tower of London, Charles composed hundreds of short poems in French.

It is this profound longing to be together that often characterizes any story of tragic love. The letter of Heloise to Abelard expresses this longing—due to the unjust separation of these lovers—in compelling terms, for Heloise describes her isolation as arising from the pain of living not only without Abelard but also without their child. Her sense of connection to Abelard on various levels—as she considers him her father, brother, husband, and teacher—demonstrates the extent to which she finds her entire world in him, and indeed, she states that her *animus* cannot exist without him. In this story of tragic love, as in others, our lovers are often individuals who seem "made for each other" in some respect, and they are often separated due to familial or social pressures of some kind.

This was certainly true of Dido and Aeneas. In many ways, they seemed like the perfect couple. She was a widow, he a widower; both had tragically lost their spouses to the turmoil of war or political unrest. Each of them had taken on the responsibility of leading a group of their compatriots to a new location where they would establish a new home. Both of them were thus good leaders, strong individuals capable of responding to difficult situations, willing to take on personal responsibility for others, and instrumental in moving their people toward the future. Both knew how to help others in need. As such, they seemed two halves of the same soul. In fact, although Dido was Carthaginian and not Roman, Vergil portrayed her as having the most important quality of a respectable Roman matron—she was a *ūnivira*—a "one man woman." This important attribute marked the behavior of women in ancient Rome even after their husbands had died, as many of them chose not to remarry since that could have been perceived as being unfaithful to their husbands, even though they were deceased. Dido expresses this sentiment for her deceased husband and hesitates to allow her feelings for Aeneas to grow, but she is persuaded to surrender to her love for Aeneas by her sister, Anna. This attitude is one that Heloise also expresses in her address to Abelard as *ūnice*, "my one and only"; it is perhaps first expressed in western literature by Andromache in Homer's *Iliad*, when she described her husband Hector as her father, mother and brothers, who had all been killed in the war.

Despite their intense connection, it was because of (perhaps ironically) his social responsibility to his compatriots that Aeneas had to leave Dido to found Rome. The profundity of her emotional response compelled her to take her own life—an event described by Vergil as occurring outside of what was expected, for "she died neither on account of destiny nor through a deserved death" (*Aeneid* 6.696, *nec fātō meritā nec morte perībat*). Thus, Dido experiences the reversal of fortune from prosperity to suffering (and sometimes death) that is the hallmark of so many tragic figures.

A story need not end in death for it to be tragic, but many such tales do. The ancient story of Pyramus and Thisbe, for example, told by the Roman author Ovid and the Greek writer Hyginus, depicts a pair of lovers whose families were opposed to their marriage. As they were neigh-

The high Renaissance painter Dosso Dossi (ca. 1490–1542) served as court artist to the humanist Dukes of Ferrara, Italy. Dossi was very familiar with the stories of the *Aeneid* and he had painted a series of friezes for the palace. Dossi's richly dressed Dido clings to Aeneas' helmet as she cries over his departure.

bors, they used to go into their yards and speak through a small opening in the stone wall. They planned to run off secretly one night to meet and embark on their life together, but a misunderstanding of circumstances led Pyramus to believe that Thisbe was dead, and he took his life. She then found him just as he was dying, and joined him in death, so profound was their desire to remain together. This ancient tale was the predecessor of William Shakespeare's *Romeo and Juliet* and both stories dramatize the tragic circumstances that can result when families attempt to keep lovers apart.

This kind of story has found many representations in literature and art throughout the centuries; one recent example is the story of Jack and Rose in the film *Titanic*. Once again, the lovers seem to be kindred spirits—Rose longs for the freedom in life that Jack has experienced and Jack's artistic talents inspire appreciation in Rose, who possesses a great love for art and its various representations of the human condition. Yet, Rose's social standing, her mother's influence, and her fiancé's meddling butler all conspire to separate Rose and Jack—until the horrifying demise of the Titanic allows the couple first a way to remain together, then the most tragic of separations. Rose, however, expresses the faithfulness of a *ūnivira* when she adopts the name of Dawson, Jack's last name, upon her rescue. Even though Rose goes on to live her life, her love for Jack and their kindred desires remain an integral part of who she is.

Shakespeare may well have been writing about any one of these tales when he penned, "the course of true love never did run smooth" (*A Midsummer Night's Dream*, Act I, Scene I, line 134). This line, like the tale from Plato's *Symposium*, occurs in a comic setting, as Lysander describes some of the mixed-up circumstances of the various couples in the play. However, whether comic or tragic, the tales of lovers who yearn to be together despite great odds, who seem meant for one another yet cannot bring togetherness to pass—like Dido and Aeneas, Heloise and Abelard, Pyramus and Thisbe, or Rose and Jack—continue to compel us to ponder our own desires to love and be loved and the difficulties we may experience along the way.

Friar Lawrence prays for Romeo who, thinking Juliet was dead, chose death rather than life without his beloved. When Juliet awakens to find Romeo dead she too takes her life. Finding Romeo's poison gone, she takes his sword to her breast. The French artists Achille Devéria (1800–1857) and Louis Boulanger (1806–1867) regularly collaborated.

The *Titanic* shipwreck is memorialized in Belfast, Ireland at whose shipyards the ocean liner was built. The people of Belfast raised the money to pay for the marble memorial by Thomas Brock (1847–1922). The 1920 neoclassical sculpture honors the victims of the disaster.

Perfect and Pluperfect Active Subjunctive of All Conjugations; Perfect and Pluperfect Subjunctive of *Sum* and *Possum*; Wishes for the Present and the Past; Indirect Question; Sequence of Tenses

An unknown Flemish artist records the crusaders' bloody capture of Jerusalem in 1099 CE.

MEMORĀBILE DICTŪ

Rādīx omnium malōrum est cupiditās.

"The root of all evil is greed." (I *Timothy* 6.10)

Paul made this famous statement in the first of his letters to Timothy. The text is quoted from the Latin translation of the scriptures, known as the Vulgate, which was mostly the work of Jerome, and completed in the fourth century CE.

READING

The origins of the Crusades are complex. When the Muslims occupied two former territories of the eastern Roman Empire, Syria and Palestine, they allowed Christian pilgrims to visit the holy sites there, particularly Jerusalem. But from the middle of the eleventh century CE onward, a new and militant group, the Turks, began to occupy these areas and made access to the holy regions unsafe for pilgrims. At the Council of Clermont in 1095, the Bishop of Rome, Pope Urban II reacted by pronouncing a holy war to liberate the "Holy Land." The pope's pronouncement elicited a huge response from the poor and noble classes alike. In 1099, after many setbacks, the forces of the Crusaders laid siege to Jerusalem, and captured the city. A terrible slaughter of its inhabitants ensued, and the unrestrained greed and brutality of this event foreshadows many others in the subsequent history of imperialism.

Many of the narratives about the first crusade, and the crusades that followed, are written in Latin, the main literary language of Western Europe. Perhaps the best narrative about the first phase of the crusades is *Historia rērum in partibus transmarīnīs gestārum* (*The Narrative of Deeds Done in Regions Across the Sea*), written by William of Tyre. The passage below, which tells about the capture of Jerusalem in 1099 CE, is adapted from chapters 18 and 19 of Book VIII in this lengthy work.

William himself, a grandson of an original European crusader, was born in the Latin kingdom of Jerusalem at some time in the 1130s. After entering the church, he traveled to France and Italy as a young man to complete his studies of the liberal arts and theology. He returned to Palestine to pursue a career in the Latin Church there, and eventually became Bishop of Tyre, a major eastern Mediterranean port.

HIEROSOLYMA CAPIUNTUR Ā FRANCĪS MĪLITIBUS

1   Ventus in vultūs hostium flābat. Godefrīdus igitur mīlitēs incendium
     māgnum prope mūrōs facere iussit. Hostēs, quī mūrōs dēfendere
     dēbēbant sed oculōs propter fūmum aperīre nōn valēbant, ē mūrīs
     fūgērunt. Nostrī, quī pontem ligneum aedificāverant ut mūrōs
5   scanderent, loca hostibus vacua iam occupāvērunt. Postquam nōn
     sōlum Godefrīdus, sed etiam Comes Flandrēnsium et Tancrēdus
     Normannus et aliī ducēs ūnā cum multīs mīlitibus intrāvērunt, dux
     paucōs mīlitēs ad urbis portam septentriōnālem, quae hodiē dīcitur
     Sānctī Stephanī, mīsit ut aliōs mīlitēs, quī extrā mūrōs exspectābant,
10   statim admitterent. Tunc ingēns agmen nostrōrum in urbem prōcessit.
     Hostēs, quī mīlitibus nostrīs restitērunt, celeriter sunt occīsī. Aliī
     fūgērunt. At nostrī īrā et dolōre incēnsī furēbant nec ūllīs pepercērunt
     incolīs, quōs cōnspexērunt. Aliud simul agmen mīlitum nostrōrum,

quod dūcēbat Comes Tolosānus, in partem urbis merīdiānam violenter
15 invāsit. Hī cum hostibus prope montem Siōn pugnāre coepērunt.
Tumultum autem in aliā urbis parte ēditum subitō audīvērunt. Prīmō
nec nostrī nec hostēs sciēbant quid hominēs in aliā urbis parte fēcissent.
Nōn enim sciēbant aliōs cum Godefrīdō urbem iam intrāvisse. Tunc
hostēs intellēxērunt quanta esset clādēs. Territī fūgērunt et sē in arcem
20 recēpērunt. At nostrī etiam in arcem intrāvērunt. Nē illī quidem, quī
in templum fūgērunt, tūtī erant. Etiam victōrēs sentīre possunt quam
terribilis fuerit haec clādēs.

READING VOCABULARY

admittō, ere, admīsī, admissum – to admit, let in

*agmen, agminis, n. – marching column

*aperiō, īre, aperuī, apertum – to open

arx, arcis, f. – citadel

*coepī, coepisse, coeptum + infinitive – to begin (NB: this verb has perfect forms only)

Comes Flandrēnsium – Robert II, Count of Flanders‡

Comes Tolosānus – Raymond IV, Count of Toulouse‡

*dēfendō, ere, dēfendī, dēfēnsum – to defend

*ēdō, ere, ēdidī, ēditum – to produce, give forth

*extrā + accusative – outside of

flō, āre, āvī, ātum – to blow

Francī, ōrum, m. pl. – the Franks‡

*furō, ere, furuī, — – to rage, be insane

Godefrīdus – Godfrey of Bouillon‡

Hierosolyma, ōrum, n. pl. – Jerusalem

incendō, ere, incendī, incēnsum – to set fire, irritate

*ingēns, ingentis – huge

*invādō, ere, invāsī, — – to burst in

*ligneus, a, um – made of wood

merīdiānus, a, um – southern

nē . . . quidem – not even

*nec . . . nec . . . – neither . . . nor . . .

nostrī, ōrum, m. pl. – our people, men

*parcō, ere, pepercī, — + dative – to spare (somebody or something)

*pōns, pontis, m. – bridge

*porta, ae, f. – gate

*prīmō (adv.) – at first

prōcēdō, ere, prōcessī, prōcessum – to advance, proceed

*quam (adv.) – how (in indirect questions and exclamations)

quam terribilis fuerit . . . clādēs – how terrible the disaster was

quanta esset clādēs – how great the disaster was

*quantus, a, um – how great, how much

quid hominēs . . . fēcissent – what men . . . had done

*resistō, ere, restitī, — + dative – to resist (somebody or something)

Sanctī Stephanī <porta> – the gate of St. Stephen‡

scandō, ere, —, — – to climb over, mount

*(mē, tē, sē . . .) recipiō, ere, recēpī, — – to retreat

*simul (adv.) – at the same time, simultaneously

Siōn, Siōnis, m./f. – a hill in Jerusalem

Tancrēdus Normannus – Tancred of Hauteville‡

territus, a, um – terrified

*tūtus, a, um – safe

*vacuus, a, um + ablative – empty of

*valeō, ēre, valuī, — + infinitive – to be able; to be in good health

*victor, victōris, m. – victor

violenter (adv.) – violently

*Words marked with an asterisk will need to be memorized.

‡Additional information about the words marked with the double dagger will be in the **Take Note** section that follows the Reading Vocabulary.

TAKE NOTE

Comes Flandrēnsium Robert II, the Count of Flanders (a region of Belgium today), was one of the principal generals in the First Crusade.

Comes Tolosānus Raymond IV, the Count of Toulouse (in southern France) was one of the leaders of the First Crusade.

The Place Royale in Brussels, Belgium celebrates Godfrey of Bouillon, one of the leaders of the First Crusade. The equestrian bronze was placed here in front of the Art Museum in 1843 when the new state of Belgium wanted to legitimize its historic roots and several statues celebrating famous Belgians were erected across the country.

Francī The Franks were, properly speaking, a Germanic group who had settled in parts of modern France (hence the name "France") and Germany in the later Roman empire. By the eleventh century CE, this word was often used loosely to describe all western Europeans.

Godefrīdus Godfrey of Bouillon was a noble from the area of modern Belgium, who became the principal leader of the First Crusade. He became an almost legendary figure in later medieval culture, when he was celebrated in song and literature as the model of the "chivalric knight."

nostrī Used as a substantive, this adjective literally means "our <people>." In the history of William of Tyre and in other crusade chronicles, this phrase always refers to the Frankish warriors from the Latin West.

Sanctī Stephanī <porta> The gate of St. Stephen led into the city of Jerusalem.

Tancrēdus Normannus Tancred of Hauteville and Bohemond of Taranto that is located in southern Italy led a powerful contingent of Normans in the First Crusade.

COMPREHENSION QUESTIONS

1. Why were the soldiers under Godfrey able to scale the walls of the city without opposition?

2. Where did the inhabitants flee before the victorious invaders?

3. What is the author's view of the behavior of the Franks in the capture of Jerusalem?

LANGUAGE FACT I
PERFECT ACTIVE SUBJUNCTIVE OF ALL CONJUGATIONS AND OF *SUM* AND *POSSUM*

In the very last sentence of the chapter reading passage, notice the form *fuerit*, which looks exactly like the third person singular of the future perfect indicative of the verb *sum, esse, fuī, —*. This is not, however, a form in the future perfect indicative, but in the **perfect subjunctive**.

So far you have learned the forms of the present and imperfect tenses of the subjunctive mood. In this chapter you meet the perfect active subjunctive of all conjugations. Forming the perfect active subjunctive is extremely easy, and is the same for **all** conjugations.

Find the perfect stem of the verb (in the third principal part), subtract the ending –*ī*, and replace it with the perfect subjunctive active endings which are: –*erim*, –*eris*, –*erit*, –*erimus*, –*eritis*, –*erint*. All four verb conjugations in the perfect active subjunctive are formed this same way.

"David's Tower" from fortifications dating from the second BCE stands on the remains of the Tower of Phasael, which Herod named for his brother. After the destruction of Jerusalem in 70 CE, the Romans garrisoned troops there. The Muslims withstood the Crusader assault here in their fortress and only surrendered with the promise of safe passage.

Perfect Active Subjunctive: parō

	Singular	Plural
First person	parāverim	parāverimus
Second person	parāveris	parāveritis
Third person	parāverit	parāverint

The irregular verbs *sum* and *possum* form the perfect subjunctive in exactly the same way as do other verbs. In the case of these verbs too, the perfect stem is the key.

Perfect Subjunctive: sum

	Singular	Plural
First person	fuerim	fuerimus
Second person	fueris	fueritis
Third person	fuerit	fuerint

Perfect Subjunctive: possum

	Singular	Plural
First person	potuerim	potuerimus
Second person	potueris	potueritis
Third person	potuerit	potuerint

STUDY TIP

Note that the forms of the perfect active subjunctive look exactly like those of the future perfect active indicative, with the exception of the first person singular: the first person singular ending for the perfect active subjunctive is *–erim*, while the first person singular ending of the future perfect active indicative is *–erō*. Remember that you will usually find the perfect subjunctive within a subordinate clause and that will help you distinguish it from the future perfect.

▶ EXERCISE 1

Change the indicative verbs into the subjunctive keeping the same person, number, tense, and voice.

Example: ēgimus   ēgerimus

1. aspexī
2. gessērunt
3. valuistī
4. sīvī
5. iūnxit
6. prōmīsistis
7. sēdistī
8. ārsērunt
9. neglēxistī
10. lēgimus

VOCABULARY TO LEARN

NOUNS

agmen, agminis, n. – marching column
pōns, pontis, m. – bridge
porta, -ae, f. – gate
victor, victōris, m. – victor

ADJECTIVES

ingēns, ingentis – huge
ligneus, a, um – made of wood
quantus, a, um – how much, how great
tūtus, a, um – safe
vacuus, a, um + ablative – empty of

VERBS

aperiō, īre, aperuī, apertum – to open
coepī, coepisse, coeptum + infinitive – to begin (NB: this verb has perfect forms only)
dēfendō, ere, dēfendī, dēfēnsum – to defend
ēdō, ere, ēdidī, ēditum – to produce, give forth
furō, ere, furuī, —— – to rage, be insane
invādō, ere, invāsī, —— – to burst in
parcō, ere, pepercī, —— + dative – to spare (somebody or something)
resistō, ere, restitī, —— + dative – to resist (somebody or something)
recipiō, ere, recēpī, receptum – to receive; mē recipiō – I retreat
valeō, ēre, valuī, —— + infinitive – to be able; to be in good health

ADVERBS

prīmō – at first

quam – how (in indirect questions and exclamations)

simul – at the same time, simultaneously

PREPOSITIONS

extrā + accusative – outside of

CONJUNCTIONS

nec . . . nec – neither . . . nor . . .

utinam – if only; (may precede a wish in the subjunctive). The negative is *utinam nē.*

▶ EXERCISE 2

Find the English derivatives based on the Vocabulary to Learn in the following sentences. Write the corresponding Latin word.

1. His parents died when he was still an infant, so he was raised under the tutelage of his aunt and uncle.

2. Your textbook is now available in a new edition.

3. The south portal of this cathedral was rebuilt at a later date.

4. Water is a resource of prime importance.

5. Vegetables kept on the shelf too long lose their taste and acquire a ligneous texture.

6. There is a large quantity of water in that reservoir, but its quality is not very high.

7. The final notes of the symphony and the enthusiastic applause were almost simultaneous.

8. A temporary bridge supported by pontoons was constructed by the soldiers.

9. The small apertures in the castle wall were designed so that defenders could shoot arrows through them at those besieging the castle.

10. The castle was so well fortified that no invader could ever capture it.

11. Fallacious arguments are not valid.

12. Whoever finishes this exercise without a single mistake will get extra credit.

13. The characters in that show seem to me to be completely vacuous.

14. In every contest she was victorious.

LANGUAGE FACT II

PLUPERFECT ACTIVE SUBJUNCTIVE OF ALL CONJUGATIONS AND OF *SUM* AND *POSSUM*; WISHES FOR THE PRESENT AND THE PAST

Look at another new verb form from the chapter reading passage. This is *fēcissent,* the third person plural pluperfect active subjunctive of the verb *faciō, ere, fēcī, factum.*

Forming the pluperfect active subjunctive of any verb is just as easy as forming the perfect active subjunctive. Like the perfect active subjunctive, you form the pluperfect active subjunctive in the same way for **all** the conjugations.

Find the perfect stem of the verb (in the third principal part), subtract the ending –*ī*, and re-place it with the pluperfect active subjunctive endings which are: –*issem*, –*issēs*, –*isset*, –*issēmus*, –*issētis*, –*issent*.

Pluperfect Active Subjunctive: parō

	Singular	Plural
First person	parāvissem	parāvissēmus
Second person	parāvissēs	parāvissētis
Third person	parāvisset	parāvissent

BY THE WAY

Since there are many different ways to translate the subjunctive in a main and in a subordinate clause, no specific translation is provided for the perfect and pluperfect active subjunctives.

The irregular verbs *sum* and *possum* form the pluperfect subjunctive in exactly the same way as do other verbs.

Pluperfect Subjunctive: sum

	Singular	Plural
First person	fuissem	fuissēmus
Second person	fuissēs	fuissētis
Third person	fuisset	fuissent

Pluperfect Subjunctive: possum

	Singular	Plural
First person	potuissem	potuissēmus
Second person	potuissēs	potuissētis
Third person	potuisset	potuissent

STUDY TIP

Another way to look at forming the pluperfect active subjunctive of any verb is to regard it as consisting of the perfect active infinitive form, plus the endings –*m*, –*s*, –*t*, –*mus*, –*tis*, –*nt*. If, however, you take this approach, you must be sure to learn that the vowel –*e* before these endings becomes **long** in the second person singular, the first person plural, and the second person plural. When recognizing the pluperfect active subjunctive, note that –**ISSE**– makes for an easy tipoff!

BY THE WAY

In chapter 1 you learned that the **optative** subjunctive, with or without the word *utinam,* indicates a wish, and that *nē* is added (also with or without *utinam*) for a negative wish. You saw only the present subjunctive in these wishes. The present subjunctive is used for a wish about the **future**, which could still come true. Now that you know the imperfect and pluperfect subjunctive, you know how to express wishes for the present or the past which cannot come true. In these cases the imperfect subjunctive is used for a wish about the present while the pluperfect subjunctive is used for one about the past. Look at the examples:

Wish for the future   Present Subjunctive
(Utinam) illam vōcem audiam!   "If only I may hear that voice!"
(Utinam) nē illam vōcem audiam!   "May I not hear that voice!"

Wish for the present   Imperfect Subjunctive
(Utinam) illam vōcem audīrem!   "If only I were hearing that voice!"
(Utinam) nē illam vōcem audīrem!   "If only I were not hearing that voice!"

Wish for the past   Pluperfect Subjunctive
(Utinam) illam vōcem audīvissem!   "If only I had heard that voice!"
(Utinam) nē illam vōcem audīvissem!   "If only I had not heard that voice!"

▶ EXERCISE 3

Change the perfect active indicative verbs into the pluperfect active subjunctive, keeping the same person and number. Give the basic meaning of the word.

Example: ēgimus ēgissēmus to do, drive

1. scrīpsī
2. valuimus
3. aperuistī
4. pepercērunt
5. invāsit
6. mūtāvit
7. ēdidistis

8. furuī
9. occupāvimus
10. invāsērunt
11. restitistī
12. recēpī
13. occupāvit
14. invēnit

▶ EXERCISE 4

Translate into Latin.

1. May these horsemen (knights) defend our huge city!

2. If only these horsemen (knights) were defending our wooden gate!

3. If only these horsemen had found the wooden bridge!

4. May you not find the wicked guard!

5. If only you were not afraid of the wicked guard!

6. If only you had not received the wicked guard!

LANGUAGE FACT III

INDIRECT QUESTIONS

Look again at these sentences from the chapter reading passage.

> *Prīmō nec nostrī nec hostēs sciēbant quid hominēs in aliā urbis parte fēcissent.*
> "At first, neither our men nor the enemy were aware of what people had done in the other part of the city."

> *Tunc hostēs intellēxērunt quanta esset clādēs.*
> "Then the enemy realized how great the disaster was."

> *Etiam victōrēs sentīre possunt quam terribilis fuerit haec clādēs.*
> "Even the victors can feel how terrible this disaster was."

All three sentences contain an indirect expression depending on a verb of thinking. But these subordinate thoughts are not indirect statements (which, as you have learned in Level 1, are constructed with the accusative and infinitive). These are **indirect questions**.

In classical Latin the verb in an indirect question is always in the subjunctive.

How are indirect questions different from indirect statements? If you ask yourself what the direct expression would have been, it will always appear as a question or an exclamatory statement beginning with an interrogative word. The following would be the direct expression of all the indirect questions above, i.e., if you take away the main verb of thinking.

> *Quid hominēs in aliā urbis parte fēcērunt?*
> "What did the people in the other part of the city do?"

> *Quanta est clādēs!*
> "How great is the disaster!"

> *Quam terribilis fuit haec clādēs!*
> "How terrible was this disaster!"

Indirect questions, like direct questions, begin with an interrogative word, such as the interrogative pronoun or adjective (which you have already learned), or other interrogatives such as *quam* ("how"), *quantus* ("how much")—as in the sentences above—or the suffix *–ne*.

A medieval manuscript records the Council at Jerusalem deciding to attack Damascus in the upper portion and the attack in the lower portion. The unsuccessful four-day siege of Damascus and losses incurred while retreating back to Christian territory marked the end of the Second Crusade. King Louis VII (1120–1180) of France and King Conrad III (1093–1152) of Germany served as leaders of the campaign.

BY THE WAY

The indirect questions on p. 78 illustrate the fact that in Latin, just as in English, the main verb introducing an indirect question does not have to be a verb of asking. The verbs that introduce indirect questions can be **any** verb of saying or thinking, **including** verbs of asking. So both the sentences "I know how many they are," and "I ask how many they are," are indirect questions. Both sentences are indirect questions because the **indirect** part is introduced by an interrogative word.

STUDY TIP

Verbs of cognition or, in other words, verbs that originate above the neck (seeing, saying, thinking, hearing, knowing, etc.) introduce indirect questions and indirect statements.

LANGUAGE FACT IV
SEQUENCE OF TENSES

Which tense of the subjunctive should be used in an indirect question? In the case of indirect questions, and a number of other types of subordinate expressions with a subjunctive verb, the tense of the subordinate subjunctive is **relative** to that of the main verb. Here are the rules for what is called the **sequence of tenses**:

1. If the main verb is in **a present or future tense**:

   - the **present subjunctive** is used in the subordinate clause if the action in the subjunctive is happening at the **same time as** (or just after) that of the main verb.

   - the **perfect subjunctive** is used in the subordinate clause if the action in the subjunctive happened **before** that of the main verb.

   The tense sequence with the main verb in the present or future tense is called **primary sequence**.

   Look again at this sentence:

   > *Etiam victōrēs sentīre possunt **quam** terribilis **fuerit** haec clādēs.*
   > "Even the victors can feel how terrible this disaster was."

   The subordinate verb is *fuerit* (perfect subjunctive) because the disaster happened in the past, while the main clause *sentīre possunt* refers to what the victors can feel in the present (at the time of the writer). If the indirect question were about a disaster in the present, the sentence would read as follows:

   > *Etiam victōrēs sentīre possunt **quam** terribilis **sit** haec clādēs.*
   > "Even the victors can feel how terrible this disaster is."

2. If the main verb is in **any past tense (imperfect, perfect, pluperfect):**

   - the **imperfect subjunctive** is used in the subordinate clause if the action in the subjunctive is happening at the **same time as** (or just after) that of the main verb.

   - the **pluperfect subjunctive** is used in the subordinate clause if the action in the subjunctive happened **before** that of the main verb.

   The tense sequence with the main verb in any past tense is called **secondary sequence**.

   Look again at these sentences:

   > *Tunc hostēs intellēxērunt **quanta** esset clādēs.*
   > "Then the enemy realized how great the disaster was."

   Here the subordinate verb is *esset* (imperfect subjunctive) because it refers to a disaster going on at the same time as the main verb *intellēxērunt* (perfect) "they realized."

   > *Prīmō nec nostrī nec hostēs sciēbant **quid** hominēs in aliā urbis parte **fēcissent**.*
   > "At first, neither our men nor the enemy were aware of what people had done in the other part of the city."

The white cross against a black garment readily identifies this group from a crusader reenactment as Knights Hospitaler. The Knights began as a group attending the poor in a Jerusalem hospital in 1080 CE and following the First Crusade became a religious/military order charged with the care and defense of the Holy Lands.

Here the subordinate verb is *fēcissent* (pluperfect subjunctive) because it refers to what people had done at a time earlier than the time expressed by the main verb *sciēbant* ("they were <not> aware") in the imperfect indicative.

Sequence of Tenses – Complete Version		
Independent (Main) Clause (Verb)	Subordinate Clause Same Time, Time After	Subordinate Clause Time Before
Primary Tense Verb/Primary Sequence Present, Future, Future Perfect Indicative	Present Subjunctive	Perfect Subjunctive
Secondary Sequence Imperfect, Perfect, Pluperfect Indicative	Imperfect Subjunctive	Pluperfect Subjunctive

▶ EXERCISE 5

Translate into Latin.

1. You were asking how beautiful that city was.

2. You were asking how beautiful that city had been.

3. You are asking how beautiful that city is.

4. You are asking how beautiful that city was.

5. You will ask how beautiful that city is.

6. We are learning which soldiers are coming to our city.

7. We are learning which soldiers came to our city.

8. We learned which soldiers were coming to our city.

9. We learned which soldiers had come to our city.

The Crusades consumed the energy and attention of rulers and soldiers for over two centuries and also seized the imagination of artists who filled manuscripts and canvases with images from these campaigns. The manuscript "Overseas Voyages" inspired by the maritime exploits following the Fall of Constantinople and illustrated by Sebastian Marmoret (ca. 1490) includes this image of fighting crusaders.

▶ EXERCISE 6

A modern tourist visiting Syria gazes at a huge crusader castle, many of which survive nearly intact in the Middle East, and questions the tour guide about the imposing structure. Translate this dialogue into English. The Reading Vocabulary may be consulted. Other words you have not yet learned are explained below.

Viātor: Quam ingēns est castellum!

Mystagōgus: Pauca castella sunt māiōra.

Viātor: Quandō hominēs hoc castellum aedificāvērunt?

Mystagōgus: Hierosolyma sunt ā mīlitibus Francīs capta. At victōrēs multīs in Palaestīnae Syriaeque partibus tūtī esse nōn poterant. Nam incolae in Francōs impetūs saepe faciēbant. Itaque Francī et hoc castellum et multa alia castella aedificāvērunt.

Viātor: Quamdiū Francī hoc castellum tenēbant?

Mystagōgus: Francī hoc castellum paene duo saecula tenēbant.

Viātor: Quot custōdēs castellum tenēbant?

Mystagōgus: Quam paucī mīlitēs castellum dēfendere poterant!

Viātor: Hoc discere cupiō.

Mystagōgus: Ducentī mīlitēs in hōc castellō manentēs ingentem exercitum facile dēpellere poterant.

Viātor: Quanta et quam alta sunt mūnimenta et prōpugnācula!

altus, a, um – high

castellum, ī, n. – castle

dēpellō, ere, dēpulī, dēpulsum – to repel

ducentī, ae, a – two hundred

duo saecula – for two centuries: note that the phrase is in the accusative neuter plural, since the accusative case is used to signify duration of time

exercitus, exercitūs, m. – army

impetus, impetūs, m. – attack

māiōra (n. pl.) – larger

manentēs (nom. pl.) – staying, remaining

mūnimenta, ōrum, n. pl. – fortifications

mystagōgus, ī, m. – guide (especially to sanctuaries)

Palaestīna, ae, f. – Palestine

prōpugnāculum, ī, n. – battlement, bulwark

quamdiū (adv.) – how long

quandō (adv.) – when

quot (indeclinable) – how many

Syria, ae, f. – Syria

viātor, viātōris, m. – tourist, traveler

▶ EXERCISE 7

Below is the dialogue you have just read in Exercise 6. Rewrite the dialogue using the verbs in parentheses to construct indirect questions or indirect statements as the sense requires. Note that *hic, haec, hoc* in direct speech become *ille, illa, illud* in indirect speech. Translate the rewritten dialogue. The Reading Vocabulary and the added vocabulary in Exercise 6 may be consulted.

Example:

Viātor: (rogāvit) Quī hominēs hoc castellum aedificāvērunt?
Mystagōgus: (dīxit) Francī hoc castellum aedificāvērunt.

Viātor rogāvit quī hominēs illud castellum aedificāvissent.
Mystagōgus dīxit Francōs illud castellum aedificāvisse.

Viātor: (exclāmāvit) Quam ingēns est castellum!

Mystagōgus: (dīxit) Pauca castella sunt māiōra.

Viātor: (rogāvit) Quandō hominēs hoc castellum aedificāvērunt?

Mystagōgus: (respondit) Hierosolyma sunt ā mīlitibus Francīs capta; at victōrēs multīs in Palaestīnae Syriaeque partibus tūtī esse nōn poterant; nam incolae in Francōs impetūs saepe faciēbant; itaque Francī et hoc castellum et multa alia castella aedificāvērunt.

Viātor: (rogāvit) Quamdiū Francī hoc castellum tenēbant?

Mystagōgus: (respondit) Francī hoc castellum paene duo saecula tenēbant.

Viātor: (rogāvit) Quot custōdēs castellum tenēbant?

Mystagōgus: (exclāmāvit) Quam paucī mīlitēs castellum dēfendere poterant!

Viātor: (dīxit) Hoc discere cupiō.

Mystagōgus: (dīxit) Ducentī mīlitēs in hōc castellō manentēs ingentem exercitum facile dēpellere poterant.

Viātor: (exclāmāvit) Quanta et quam alta sunt mūnimenta et prōpugnācula!

Krak de Chevaliers, the largest of the crusader fortresses, housed the Knights Hospitaler. Located in Syria near Tripoli, Lebanon, the fort was built in 1031 CE for the Muslim Emir of Aleppo, Syria. Raymond of Toulouse captured it in 1099 during the First Crusade and from 1150 to 1250 it received its present plan and was enlarged to house 2,000 troops.

This detail from a fresco in the Hall of Hannibal in the Capitoline Museum, Rome shows Hannibal's celebrated march with elephants from Spain over the Alps to Italy. This feat has fascinated people ever since.

TALKING ABOUT A READING
ABOUT TRIPS TO FARAWAY PLACES AND UNADAPTED LATIN: ATTICUS HELPS THE ATHENIANS

DĒ ITINERIBUS AD LOCA LONGINQUA

Marīa: Mīlitēs igitur Eurōpaeī longum iter fēcērunt ūsque ad (*up to*) Hierosolyma. Utinam ego tam longa itinera facere possem!

Mārcus: Quae loca, Marīa, vidēre cupis?

Marīa: Cupiō loca longinqua vidēre, montēs altōs petere. Cupiō iter facere in Alpēs (*Alps*) et vidēre quae loca Hannibal cum elephantīs (*elephants*) trānsīverit (*passed through*) ut Ītaliam peteret et cum Rōmānīs pugnāret. Illīs in locīs sunt māgnae nivēs (*snow*).

Christīna: Mē dēlectat lītus; nam mare ā mē amātur. Cupiō petere īnsulās Caribbicās (*Caribbean islands*) ut discam quae loca Christophorus Colōnus (*Christopher Columbus*) invēnerit. Bonum quoque erit illīs in aquīs limpidīs (*transparent*) natāre (*to swim*). At vōs, Helena et Mārce, quae loca petere cupitis?

Helena: Nōn sciō quae loca Mārcus vidēre cupiat, sed ego cupiō Ītaliam et Graeciam petere, Rōmae et Athēnīs esse.

Marīa: Dē Rōmā et dē Athēnīs iam multa ex librīs discimus. Hodiē Mārcus dē Atticō leget.

QUESTIONS ABOUT THE TEXT

Answer in complete Latin sentences.

1. Cūr Atticus in peregrīnātiōne rēs suās Athēnās (*to Athens*) trāiēcit?

2. Quantam partem fortūnārum suārum Athēnās trāiēcit Atticus?

3. Quid de Atticō sentiēbant ūniversī Athēniēnsēs?

4. Quanta in Atticō adulēscentulō grātia erat?

5. Quibus rēbus Atticus inopiam Athēniēnsium pūblicam levāvit?

6. Eratne Athēniēnsibus necesse versūram pūblicē facere?

7. Cum Athēniēnsēs versūram facere pūblicē dēbērent neque ēius condiciōnem aequam habērent, quis sē interposuit?

8. Umquamne Atticus ūsūram ab Athēniēnsibus accēpit?

9. Quā rē aliā Atticus ūniversōs Athēniēnsēs dōnāvit?

DĒ ITINERIBUS AD LOCA LONGINQUA CONTINUED

Mārcus: Bene. Lēgī. Quid didicistis?

Helena: Grātiam in Atticō fuisse didicī.

Christīna: Inopiam Athēniēnsium ab Atticō levātam esse didicī.

Marīa: Athēniēnsēs frūmentō ab Atticō esse dōnātōs didicī. Sed tē, Mārce, rogō quid didiceris.

Mārcus: Mē saepius (*more often*) legere dēbēre didicī.

CHAPTER 5

Perfect and Pluperfect Passive Subjunctive of All Conjugations; Indirect Command

The Collegium Maius of Cracow's Jagiellonian University has preserved
several medieval era rooms including the student dining area.

MEMORĀBILE DICTŪ

Eheu . . . fugācēs lābuntur annī!

"Alas . . . the fleeting years pass away." (Horace, *Odes* 2.14.1)

READING

The eleventh and twelfth centuries CE witnessed the production of Latin poetry on a grand scale. Some of this poetry followed the conventions established by ancient Roman poets. Several medieval epics, such as the twelfth century *Alexandreis*, which narrates the exploits of Alexander the Great, closely resemble ancient Roman epics. Extremely popular in the years after it was written, the *Alexandreis* was read in schools along with Vergil's *Aeneid*.

But the poets of the twelfth century also developed a new kind of rhythmical verse with many similarities to the popular songs of the day, particularly because it contained rhymes. This rhythmical poetry includes all kinds of themes: religious and secular, amatory and mournful. Probably the best-known collection of medieval poems in this vein is the *Carmina Burāna*. These poems are preoccupied with love, wine, jealousy, power, poverty, the changeable nature of fortune, and generally the problems of scholars who wandered in search of money from powerful patrons in order to write and study. The Latin poets of this period performed their verses orally—frequently singing and chanting to musical accompaniment—to audiences of those educated in Latin, in cathedral towns, and in the increasingly splendid courts of bishops and other important churchmen.

One of the poets whose works are included in the *Carmina Burāna* was the Archpoet, probably given this name ironically, since he was attached to the court of the German archbishop Rainald of Dassel (died 1167 CE). Here are excerpts from the *Cōnfessiō Goliae*, perhaps the most famous Latin poem. It is a parody of the confession ritual—which involves the acknowledgment of sin, either by a congregation in the course of worship, or, more typically, by individuals speaking privately to a priest. Parts of the text have been transformed into prose.

CŌNFESSIŌ GOLIAE

1   Aestuāns intrīnsecus īrā vehementī
      in amāritūdine loquor meae mentī.
      Factus dē māteriā levis elementī
      Foliō sum similis, dē quō lūdunt ventī.

5   Similis sum flūminī, quod numquam manet, sed semper fluit; similis sum nāvī sine nautā; similis sum avī.
      Nōn mē tenent vincula, nōn mē tenet clāvis,
      Quaerō meī similēs et adiungor prāvīs.
Dīves nōn sum, sed pauper, quī nihil possidet. Nam fūr esse nōlō nec

10   agrōs colere cupiō. Rēbus sevērīs nōn dēlector; rēbus dulcibus dēlector atque iocīs. Placet mihi dē pulchrīs puellīs cōgitāre atque amōrem colere.
      Viā lātā gradior mōre iuventūtis,
      implicō mē vitiīs immemor virtūtis.

Nōn mihi placet cibīs bonīs egēre. Sī bene nōn comedō, carmina
15 scrībere nōn possum. Sī tamen bene comēderō et sī multum vīnī
bīberō, tam pulchra carmina scrībere poterō quam scrīpsit Nāsō poēta.

> Meum est prōpositum in tabernā morī,
> Ut sint vīna proxima morientis ōrī.

Rogātis cūr tam multa ā mē contrā mē sint dicta. Vīta vetus mihi iam
20 nōn placet, sed mōrēs novōs habēre cupiō. Vitia iam nōn amō, sed
virtūtēs amō. Haēc omnia nārrāvī ut vītam meam mūtāre possem!
Ōrō ut mihi parcātis.

READING VOCABULARY

adiungō, ere, adiūnxī, adiūnctum + dative = iungō

aestuāns – being in violent commotion, burning (present active participle)

aestuō, āre, āvī, ātum – to be in violent commotion, burn

amāritūdō, amāritūdinis, f. – bitterness

avis, avis, f. – bird

*bibō, ere, bibī, — – to drink

*carmen, carminis, n. – poem

*cibus, ī, m. – food

clāvis, clāvis, f. – key

cōnfessiō, cōnfessiōnis, f. – confession

dē – from

*dulcis, dulce – sweet

elementum, ī, n. – element

*flūmen, flūminis, n. – river

folium, ī, n. – leaf

Golia, Goliae, m. – name of a wandering scholar

gradior – I walk‡

iam – any more

*immemor, immemoris + genitive – forgetful of

implicō, āre, āvī, ātum + dative – to involve into, implicate

intrīnsecus (adv.) – on the inside

*iocus, ī, m. – joke

*iuventūs, iuventūtis, f. – youth

lātus, a, um – broad, wide

*levis, leve – light

loquor – I speak‡

māteria, ae, f. – material

*mēns, mentis, f. – mind, spirit

morī – to die‡

multum + partitive genitive – a lot of

Nāsō, Nāsōnis, m. – Ovid

*ōrō, āre, āvī, ātum – to ask, entreat

*ōrō ut – I ask that

*placeō, ēre, placuī, placitum + dative – to please, be agreeable to somebody

prāvus, a, um – crooked, bad

prōpositum, ī, n. – plan

*proximus, a, um – nearest

sint dicta – are said

taberna, ae, f. – wine shop‡

*tam . . . quam . . . – so . . . as . . .

*vehemēns, vehementis – violent, vehement

*vetus, veteris – old

*vīnum, ī, n. – wine

*virtūs, virtūtis, f. – virtue, courage‡

*vitium, ī, n. – vice

*Words marked with an asterisk will need to be memorized later in the chapter.

‡Additional information about the words marked with the double dagger will be in the **Take Note** section that follows the Reading Vocabulary.

TAKE NOTE

gradior, loquor, morior These three verbs belong to a group of verbs called deponents, which have passive forms but active meanings. Deponent verbs will be introduced in a later chapter.

taberna The word *taberna* in both classical and medieval Latin means any kind of shop but in medieval Latin the specialized meaning "wine shop" becomes common. From this source comes the English "tavern."

virtūs The meaning of *virtūs* in the Christian writers of the later Roman period already had a specifically Christian meaning. In addition to the Roman sense of "manliness," "uprightness" and "courage," it also denotes "piety" and "sanctity." This meaning persists in medieval Latin.

COMPREHENSION QUESTIONS

1. Why is the poet comparing himself to a leaf?

2. What does the poet say about dying?

3. What are the poet's thoughts at the end of the passage?

Foliō sum similis, dē quō lūdunt ventī.

LANGUAGE FACT I

PERFECT AND PLUPERFECT PASSIVE SUBJUNCTIVE

In the chapter reading passage, the poet says the following to his readers:

> *Rogātis cūr tam multa ā mē contrā mē sint dicta.*
> "You (pl.) are asking me why so many things have been said by me against me <myself>."

You already know that the form *dicta* is a perfect passive participle, and that the form *sint* is a present subjunctive of *sum*. However, the perfect passive participle and the present subjunctive of *sum*, when taken together, provide the forms of the perfect passive subjunctive.

Perfect Passive Subjunctive: parō		
	Singular	**Plural**
First person	parātus, parāta, (parātum) sim	parātī, parātae, (parāta) sīmus
Second person	parātus, parāta, (parātum) sīs	parātī, parātae, (parāta) sītis
Third person	parātus, parāta, parātum sit	parātī, parātae, parāta sint

Once you know how the perfect passive subjunctive is formed, it is very easy to learn the formation of the pluperfect passive subjunctive. Use the perfect passive participle and the imperfect subjunctive form of *sum* to form the pluperfect passive subjunctive.

BY THE WAY

The imperfect subjunctive is one degree further in the past than the present subjunctive, much in the same way as the pluperfect tense is one degree further in the past than the perfect tense.

Pluperfect Passive Subjunctive: parō		
	Singular	**Plural**
First person	parātus, parāta, (parātum) essem	parātī, parātae, (parāta) essēmus
Second person	parātus, parāta, (parātum) essēs	parātī, parātae, (parāta) essētis
Third person	parātus, parāta, parātum esset	parātī, parātae, parāta essent

STUDY TIP

The perfect and the pluperfect passive subjunctives are formed in the same way for all the conjugations. Just remember to use the perfect passive participle (the fourth principal part of the verb) with the conjugation of *sim* and *essem*. You should readily master these two tenses!

BY THE WAY

Since there are many different ways to translate the subjunctive in main and in subordinate clauses, no specific translation is provided with the perfect and pluperfect passive subjunctives.

Perfect and pluperfect passive subjunctives are used in the same way that perfect and pluperfect active subjunctives are used in indirect questions. Both subjunctives indicate that the **action in the indirect question has happened before the action in the main clause**.

- The **perfect** subjunctive is used after a **primary** tense in the main clause (present, future, future perfect)
- The **pluperfect** subjunctive is used after a **secondary** tense in the main clause (imperfect, perfect, pluperfect).

The perfect and pluperfect subjunctive have other uses, which you will learn later.

STUDY TIP

The chart in Chapter 4 for the sequence of tenses works just as well for the passive tenses as for the active ones.

▶ EXERCISE 1

Change the following active verbs into the passive, keeping the same person, number, tense, and mood.

Example: amāverim   amātus, a, (um) sim

1. ōrāvisset
2. aspexerint
3. iūnxerim
4. audīvissēmus
5. tenueritis

6. coluissēs
7. cēpissem
8. prōmīseris
9. scrīpissent
10. dīxeris

VOCABULARY TO LEARN

NOUNS

carmen, carminis, n. – poem, song

cibus, ī, m. – food

flūmen, flūminis, n. – river

iocus, ī, m. – joke

iuventūs, iuventūtis, f. – youth

mēns, mentis, f. – mind, spirit

vīnum, ī, n. – wine

virtūs, virtūtis, f. – virtue, courage

vitium, ī, n. – vice

ADJECTIVES

dulcis, dulce – sweet

immemor, immemoris + genitive – forgetful of

levis, leve – light

proximus, a, um – nearest

vehemēns, vehementis – violent, vehement

vetus, veteris – old

VERBS

bibō, ere, bibī, — – to drink

ōrō, āre, āvī, ātum – to ask, entreat

placeō, ēre, placuī, placitum + dative – to please, be
  agreeable to somebody

CONJUNCTIONS

nē – that not, not to

ut – that, to

tam . . . quam . . . – so . . . as . . .

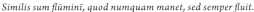

Similis sum flūminī, quod numquam manet, sed semper fluit.

▶ EXERCISE 2

Find the English derivatives based on the Vocabulary to Learn in the following sentences. Write the corresponding Latin word.

1. Don't take this seriously. I said it in a jocular manner.
2. There is no bank in the proximity of these shops.
3. Your levity and flippancy are becoming annoying.
4. The monument is dedicated to the memory of all those who defended our country.
5. It is illegal for people under eighteen to imbibe alcoholic beverages.
6. This case will be handled by the court of juvenile justice.
7. This dietary supplement will help mental alertness.
8. We went to a wine-tasting at the vineyard.
9. I am amazed by the complacency of people who are satisfied with everything as it now exists.
10. Everybody was persuaded by his splendid oratory.
11. Sometimes a placebo is used in tests instead of the real medicine.

▶ EXERCISE 3

Translate the following direct questions and then change them into Latin indirect questions using the verbs *rogō* and *rogāvī*. The Reading Vocabulary may be consulted.

Example: Quid dictum est?
What was said?
Rogō quid dictum sit.
Rogāvī quid dictum esset.

1. Quā dē māteriā es factus?
2. Cui es adiūnctus?
3. Esne vinculīs tentus?
4. Suntne bonī cibī ā tē amātī?
5. Suntne ā tē pulchra carmina scrīpta?

▶ EXERCISE 4

Change the following indirect questions into the passive voice and then translate the changed sentence.

Example: Rogō quis hanc domum aedificāverit.
Rogō ā quō sit haec domus aedificāta.
I ask by whom this house was built.

1. Rogō perdiderisne vīnum.

2. Rogāvī quis hanc portam prīmō aperuisset.

3. Rogō invēneritisne flūmina.

4. Rōgāvī quis ingentem pontem dēfendisset.

This modern statue of Alexander the Great, Alexander III of Macedon (356–323 BCE) astride his favorite horse, Bucephalus, with spear in hand, guards the main road along the harbor in Thessaloniki, Greece. Tutored by Aristotle, Alexander proved a brilliant general and diplomat, whose accomplishments by age 33 continue to impress. The medieval epic *Alexandreis* celebrates his achievement.

▶ EXERCISE 5

Change the main verb into the imperfect, change the tense of the verb in the indirect question as required, and translate the sentences.

Example: Rogō ā quō haec domus sit aedificāta.
Rogābam ā quō haec domus esset aedificāta.
I asked by whom this house had been built.

1. Nōn sciō ā quō sit hoc ōrātum.

2. Rogō ā quō māne sītis iūnctī.

3. Rogō cūr agrī sint occupātī.

4. Scītisne quā viā sint agmina ducta?

LANGUAGE FACT II

INDIRECT COMMAND

The poet in the chapter reading passage ends his confession with these words:

> Ōrō ut mihi parcātis.
> "I beg that you spare me (be lenient with me)."

You already know the use of *ut* as a conjunction which introduces a purpose clause.

However, *ut* in the sentence above does not introduce a purpose clause but instead introduces an indirect command.

The direct command of the example above would be:

> Mihi parcite!
> "Spare me!"

The indirect command is used after verbs that express a request or a command like *ōrō*, "to ask, entreat" or *rogō*, "to ask." It is introduced with the conjunction *ut*, or with the conjunction *nē*, if the command is negative. The indirect command uses the present subjunctive, if the tense in the main clause is primary, and the imperfect subjunctive, if the tense in the main clause is secondary.

	Positive	**Negative**
Primary Sequence:	Ōrō ut ad mē veniās.	Ōrō nē ad mē veniās.
	"I ask you to come to me."	"I ask you not to come to me."
Secondary Sequence:	Ōrāvī ut ad mē venīrēs.	Ōrāvī nē ad mē venīrēs.
	"I asked you to come to me."	"I asked you not to come to me."

BY THE WAY

The verb *iubeō*, "to order," takes the accusative and infinitive.

Example: *Iubeō tē ad mē venīre.* "I order you to come to me."

▶ EXERCISE 6

Change the following direct commands into indirect commands using the verb in parentheses. Use the sequence of tenses to determine the tense of the verb in the indirect question. Translate the sentences.

Example: Scrībe epistulam! (Ōrō tē . . .)
Ōrō tē ut epistulam scrībās.
I ask you to write a letter.

1. Nōn sōlum iuventūtem, sed etiam senectūtem amā! (Ōrō tē . . .)
2. Nōlī carmina scrībere! (Ōrō tē . . .)
3. Nōlī vīnum bibere! (Ōrāvī tē . . .)
4. Cole virtūtēs, nōn vitia! (Ōrāvī tē . . .)
5. Nōlīte tam multōs cibōs comedere! (Ōrō vōs . . .)
6. Nōlīte īrā vehementī capī! (Ōrāvī vōs . . .)
7. Cōgitā dē iocīs! (Ōrō tē . . .)
8. Placē omnibus! (Ōrāvī tē . . .)

STUDY TIP

Remember this about indirect questions, indirect commands, and indirect statements:

- the construction for an indirect statement is the accusative and infinitive.
- the indirect question is introduced by an interrogative pronoun, adjective, adverb, or particle and has a subjunctive verb.
- the indirect command is introduced by *ut* or *nē* and has its verb in the subjunctive.

Another way to tell the three constructions apart is to put the indirect part of the sentence into direct form: if the direct proposition is a statement, then the subordinate construction is an indirect statement; if the direct proposition is a question, then the subordinate construction is an indirect question; if the direct proposition is a command, then the subordinate construction is an indirect command.

Since the time of the Romans, wine has been a mainstay of the European diet. The Romans spread viticulture throughout the empire. Vineyards take great pride when able to point to their Roman roots. Traditionally, many monastic communities cultivated grapes for the production of altar wine as well as table wine.

Examples:

Indirect:	*Dīcō tē esse ducem.*	"I say that you are the leader."
Direct:	*Tū es dux.*	"You are the leader."

NB: The direct proposition is a statement; so the indirect proposition must be an indirect statement.

Indirect:	*Scīre volō quid fēcerit.*	"I want to know what s/he did."
Direct:	*Quid fēcit?*	"What did s/he do?"

NB: The direct proposition is a question; so the indirect proposition must be an indirect question.

Indirect:	*Rogō ut multōs librōs legās.*	"I ask you to read many books."
Direct:	*Multōs librōs lege!*	"Read many books!"

NB: The direct proposition is an imperative; so the indirect proposition must be an indirect command.

Medieval literature and art extol courtly love as illustrated in this fifteenth century tapestry detail. Set in a hunt scene, the gentleman, literally heart in hand, offers his love to the lady. The hunt as an allegory for love has its antecedents in classical literature—Aeneas and Dido's affair is cast in hunt imagery.

▶ EXERCISE 7

Translate into Latin.

1. I ask you not to be forgetful of the sweet things!

2. I do not know what plan has been made.

3. I know that this is the plan.

4. You (pl.) asked what plans had been made.

5. You (pl.) knew that these plans had been made.

6. They asked me to have all things in mind.

TALKING ABOUT A READING

ABOUT THE JOYS OF LIFE AND UNADAPTED LATIN: ATTICUS HONORED IN ATHENS

DĒ VĪTAE GAUDIĪS

Marīa: Ego quoque bonam vītam habēre cupiō, ut dīcit poēta, cūius verba lēgimus. Utinam māgnam pecūniam possideam, ut omnia emere (*buy*) possim quae amō. Nam in vīcō tabernārum (*mall*) ambulāre et novās rēs mihi emere amō.

Christīna: At novae rēs nōs nōn diū faciunt fēlīcēs. Mihi placet corpus exercēre (*to exercise*). Placet mihi natāre (*to swim*) in natātōriō (*swimming pool*).

Marīa: Mihi quoque placet corpus exercēre: birotā vehī (*ride a bicycle*), palaestram (*fitness center*) petere. At vespere (*in the evening*) mē dēlectat saltātōrium (*dance club*) petere, ubi hominēs modōs mūsicōs (*music*) audiunt et saltant (*dance*). Cupisne, Mārce, mox mēcum in saltātōrium venīre?

Mārcus (*looks at Helen*): Nōn sciō habeamne tempus vacuum. Quid tibi, Helena, placet?

Helena: Dulcia mihi placent. Theobrōma (*chocolate*) comedere amō.

Mārcus: Nōn sōlum theobrōma est dulce, sed aliae quoque rēs. Amor est dulcis . . .

Dulcia mihi placent. Theobrōma comedere amō.

Marīa: Poēta dīcit dulce esse vīnum bibere.

Christīna: At adulēscentibus nōn licet vīnum bibere nec aliās potiōnēs inebriantēs (*alcoholic beverages*). Mihi placet pelliculās (*films*) in televīsōriō (*television*) spectāre (*to watch*), in computātoriō (*computer*) lūdere vel bonōs librōs legere. Nunc autem scīre cupiō quid dē Atticō ā nōbīs legātur.

Helena: Atticus erat in Graeciā, Athēnīs (*Athēnae, ārum, f. pl.*), et Athēniēnsibus auxilium dabat.

Christīna: Ōrō ut pergāmus (*pergō, ere – continue*).

ATTICUS HONORED IN ATHENS

CORNĒLIĪ NEPŌTIS ATTICUS, 3

Atticus' kind and civil behavior towards all classes of Athenians won him great popularity. The Athenians gave him many honors and wanted to make him an Athenian citizen. Atticus refused this last mark of respect, fearing that Roman citizenship might be taken from him if he accepted citizenship of another state.

1   1. Hic autem sīc sē gerēbat, ut commūnis īnfimīs, pār prīncipibus vidērētur. Quō factum est, ut huic omnēs honōrēs, quōs possent, pūblicē habērent cīvemque facere studērent; quō beneficiō ille ūtī nōluit, quod nōnnūllī ita interpretantur, āmittī cīvitātem Rōmānam,

5   aliā ascītā. 2. Quamdiū adfuit, nē quae sibi statua pōnerētur, restitit; absēns prohibēre nōn potuit . . . 3. Igitur prīmum illud mūnus fortūnae, quod in eā potissimum urbe nātus est, in quā domicilium orbis terrārum esset imperiī, ut eandem et patriam habēret et domum; hoc specimen prūdentiae, quod, cum in eam sē cīvitātem cōntulisset, quae antīquitāte,

10   hūmānitāte doctrīnāque praestāret omnēs, ūnus eī fuerit cārissimus.

VOCABULARY

1   īnfimus, a, um – lowest
    pār, paris – equal
    prīnceps, prīncipis – distinguished, first

3   pūblicē (adv.) – publicly
    beneficium, ī, n. – benefit, favor, service
    ūtor, ūtī, ūsus sum + ablative – to use

4   nōluit – perfect of *nōlō*
    nōnnūllī, ae, a – some
    interpretantur – interpret
    cīvitās, cīvitātis, f. – city; citizenship

5   ascīscō, ere, ascīvī, ascītum – to receive, adopt
    quamdiū (conj.) – as long as
    adsum, adesse, adfuī, — – to be present
    resistō, ere, restitī, — – to resist, oppose

6   absēns, absentis – absent
    prohibeō, ēre, prohibuī, prohibitum – to prevent
    mūnus, mūneris, n. – gift

7   potissimum (adv.) – especially
    nātus, a, um – born
    domicilium, ī, n. – dwelling, abode
    orbis, orbis, m. – circle; orbis terrārum – world

8   imperium, ī, n. – dominion, command
    eandem – the same (acc. sg. f. of *īdem, eadem, idem*)
    specimen, speciminis, n. – mark, example, proof

9   prūdentia, ae, f. – prudence, foreseeing
    antīquitās, antīquitātis, f. – ancient tradition

10 hūmānitās, hūmānitātis, f. – humanity, refinement befitting a man
    doctrīna, ae, f. – learning, erudition
    praestō, āre, praestitī, — – to surpass, exceed
    cārissimus, a, um – dearest

READING NOTES

1   *sīc sē gerēbat, ut commūnis* "He behaved in such a way . . . that" *ut* starts a result clause (see Chapter 14). Here *commūnis* (common) means "ordinary person."

2   *Quō factum est, ut huic omnēs honōrēs, quōs possent* The pronoun *Quō* refers to the whole previous action. *Quō factum est* means "By this it was brought about that." The verb *possent* is subjunctive to express a restriction about the honors given to Atticus, i.e., "all honors, <all, at least> which they could <give>."

2–3   *ut . . . habērent* – that they held

4   *quod nōnnūllī ita interpretantur* The verb *interpretantur* (see Chapter 8) is deponent and this clause means "because some interpret <it> in this way (*ita*)."

    āmittī cīvitātem Rōmānam This indirect statement means "that Roman citizenship is lost."

5   *aliā ascītā* Like its implied antecedent *cīvitātem, aliā* is feminine. The ablative absolute (see Chapter 13) means "with another <citizenship> having been adopted."

    nē quae sibi statua pōnerētur, restitit Note that *nē* depends on *restitit.* The phrase means "he opposed any statue being set up to himself."

6–7   *Igitur prīmum illud mūnus fortūnae, quod in eā . . . urbe nātus est* Explaining *illud mūnus, quod* means "the fact that." "First therefore <there was> that gift of fortune; the fact that he was born . . . in that city."

7–8   *in quā domicilium orbis terrārum esset imperiī* "In which there was the abode of the dominion of the world."

8–9   *hoc specimen prūdentiae, quod* An example of the same use of *quod,* "the fact that."

9   *cum in eam sē cīvitatem contulisset* The clause starting with the conjunction *cum* that often takes a subjunctive verb means "when he had gone to that state/city." (*mē, tē, sē*) *cōnferō* means "I go."

9–10   *quae antīquitāte, hūmānitāte doctrīnāque praestāret omnēs* The verb *praestāret* is in the subjunctive after *quae* because it expresses a restriction.

QUESTIONS ABOUT THE TEXT

Answer in complete Latin sentences.

Athēnae, ārum, f. pl. – Athens   Athēniēnsis, Athēniēnsis, m./f. – Athenian

1. Eratne Atticus amīcus omnibus Athēniēnsibus, et pauperibus et dīvitibus?

2. Quōmodo sē gerēbat Atticus?

3. Quōmodo Athēniēnsēs ostendēbant sē esse Atticī amīcōs?

4. Cupīvitne Atticus cīvis Athēniēnsis esse? Cūr?

5. Estne statua Atticō Athēnīs posita annōn? Quōmodo hoc est factum?

6. Quod mūnus fortūna Atticō dedit?

7. Quod mūnus prūdentia Atticī Atticō dedit?

DĒ VĪTAE GAUDIĪS CONTINUED

Marīa: Bene fēcit Atticus. Cupīvit cīvis Rōmānus tantum manēre. Nōn est bonum aliam patriam petere.

Helena: Nōn sciō benene haec sint ā tē dicta. Nam Atticus et patriam suam amāvit, et honōrēs ā cīvibus Graecīs accēpit. Hoc est valdē bonum. Sumus enim cīvēs nōn sōlum patriae nostrae, sed etiam mundī. Quid vōs hāc dē rē putātis?

CHAPTER 6

Comparative and Superlative Adjectives; Comparative and Superlative
-*er* Adjectives; Comparative and Superlative Adverbs; Ways of Expressing
a Comparison

Emperor Theodosius the Great at the circus with his court holds a laurel wreath destined for the chariot race victor.

MEMORĀBILE DICTŪ

Obsequium amīcōs, vēritās odium parit.

"Indulgence produces friends, the truth hatred." (Terence, *The Woman of Andros*, 68)

The Roman playwright Terence expressed this bitter observation about human nature.

READING

Collections of stories, fables, anecdotes, and moral examples were popular in medieval Latin literature. The *Gesta Rōmānōrum*, probably compiled in the late thirteenth and early fourteen centuries CE, is such a collection and contains stories about the ancient Romans and other peoples.

The following fictitious tale purports to be about the emperor Theodosius and his daughters. Reliable historical sources report that the Roman emperor known as Theodosius the Great, who ruled from 379 to 395 CE, was the last to rule both the eastern and western halves of the Roman Empire. Theodosius II (408–450 CE) ruled only in the eastern half of the empire. But the *Gesta Rōmānōrum* does not even mention these facts; instead, it tells a story that may have provided the basis for Shakespeare's tragedy *King Lear*. The *Gesta Rōmānōrum* had a significant influence on later literature, and appears to have inspired tales related by Chaucer, Boccaccio, and Shakespeare.

DĒ THEODOSIŌ IMPERĀTŌRE

1 Theodosius imperātor Rōmānus clārissimus trēs fīliās pulcherrimās habuit. Quōdam diē fīliam nātū maximam rogāvit quantum patrem dīligeret. Tunc fīlia, "Tē," inquit, "vehementius dīligō quam mē." Haec verba imperātōrī vehementissimē placuērunt et fīliam rēgī omnium

5 praeclārissimō dedit, ut rēx eam in mātrimōnium dūceret.

Post haec imperātor ad fīliam secundam vēnit et eam rogāvit quantum patrem dīligeret. Tunc fīlia secunda, "Tantum," inquit, "tē dīligō quantum mē." Haec verba imperātōrī satis bene placuērunt, et fīliam secundam cuidam ducī dedit, ut dux eam in mātrimōnium dūceret.

10 Tandem imperātor ad fīliam nātū minimam vēnit et eam rogāvit quantum patrem dīligeret. Tunc fīlia tertia, "Tantum," inquit, "tē dīligō quantum merēris." Haec verba imperātōrī nōn valdē placuērunt, et fīliam tertiam cuidam equitī dedit, ut eques eam in mātrimōnium dūceret.

Paulō posteā Theodosius imperātor in bellō est victus, et imperātōrī

15 ē terrīs suīs fugere necesse erat. Itaque imperātor ad fīliam nātū maximam scrīpsit, ut auxilium ab eā peteret. Fīlia autem nātū maxima tantum quīnque mīlitēs ex exercitū marītī ad patrem mīsit. Imperātor valdē dolēbat et "Nēmō," inquit, "est miserior quam ego. Crēdēbam fīliam meam prīmam māgnum auxilium ad mē missūram esse."

20 Tunc imperātor ad fīliam secundam statim scrīpsit, quae respondit

patrem posse apud sē et marītum habitāre et cibum et vestīmenta habēre. Sed nihil aliud prōmīsit. Imperātor tunc erat valdē tristis et "Duābus," inquit, "fīliābus sum dēceptus."

Tunc imperātor ad fīliam tertiam statim scrīpsit, quae inopiam patris
25   intellēxit. Fīlia nātū minima auxilium marītī petīvit, et hī duo exercitum māgnum parāvērunt, quem contrā hostēs imperātōris dūxērunt. Postquam hostēs sunt victī, fīlia tertia et marītus imperātōrem in imperium restituērunt. Pater igitur fīliam tertiam vehementer laudāvit, quae fuerat fidēlior quam aliae fīliae. Haec fīlia hērēs
30   imperātōris facta est, et post patris mortem summam imperiī multōs annōs in pāce tenēbat.

READING VOCABULARY

clārissimus, a, um – most distinguished

cuidam (dative singular) – to a certain

*dēcipiō, ere, dēcēpī, dēceptum – to deceive

*dīligō, ere, dīlēxī, dīlēctum – to love, esteem highly

*duo, duae, duo – two

dux, ducis, m. – leader, duke‡

eques, equitis, m. – knight‡

*exercitus, exercitūs, m. – army

*fidēlior – more loyal

gesta, ōrum, n. pl. – deeds (from the perfect participle of gerō)

*hērēs, hērēdis, m./f. – heir

*imperium, ī, n. – rule, power, empire

*inopia, ae, f. – want, helplessness

maximus, a, um – greatest

*laudō, āre, āvī, ātum – to praise

merēris – you deserve‡

minimus, a, um – least

miserior – more wretched

multōs annōs – for many years

nātū maxima/minima – oldest/youngest

*necesse est + dative + infinitive – it is necessary for someone to do something

*nēmō, m. – no one‡

*pater, patris, m. – father

*paulō (adv.) – a little bit, to a small extent

praeclārissimus, a, um omnium – most excellent, renowned of all

pulcherrimus, a, um – most beautiful, very beautiful

*quam (adv.) – than (with comparative words)

*quantum (adv.) – how much, to what extent

quīnque (indeclinable) – five

quōdam diē – on a certain day

*restituō, ere, restituī, restitūtum – to restore

*satis (adv.) – enough, sufficiently

*secundus, a, um – second

summa, ae, f. – high point, sum total
    summa imperiī – pinnacle of power

tantum . . . quantum . . . – as much . . . as . . .

*tertius, a, um – third

Theodosius, ī, m. – Theodosius

*trēs, tria – three

*tristis, triste – sad

*vehementer (adv.) – vehemently, strongly

vehementissimē – most/very vehemently, most/very strongly

vehementius – more vehemently, more strongly

*Words marked with an asterisk will need to be memorized later in the chapter.

‡Additional information about the words marked with the double dagger will be in the **Take Note** section that follows the Reading Vocabulary.

TAKE NOTE

dux In medieval Latin *dux* typically means "duke."

duo The forms of the declension of *duo, duae, duo* can be seen on p. 113.

eques Ancient Roman authors used *eques* with the same sense of meaning, "knight," as did the medieval writers. In the Roman world, however, the knight held a much higher position.

merēris This verb form comes from *mereor* which belongs to a class of verbs called deponents, which have passive forms but active meanings. Deponent verbs will be introduced in a later chapter.

nēmō The forms of *nēmō* are *nullīus* in the genitive, *nēminī* in the dative, *nēminem* in the accusative, and *nūllō* in the ablative.

trēs The forms of the declension of *trēs, tria* can be seen on p. 113.

COMPREHENSION QUESTIONS

1. By what standard did the emperor in this tale decide on the rank of his daughters' husbands?

2. Which daughters let the emperor down, and why?

3. What was the reward for the third daughter who helped her father in need?

Fīlia nātū minima auxilium marītī petīvit, et hī duo exercitum māgnum parāvērunt, quem contrā hostēs imperātōris dūxērunt. NB: This modern reenactment participant wears an amalgam of armor styled from the late thirteenth century onward.

LANGUAGE FACT I

COMPARATIVE AND SUPERLATIVE ADJECTIVES

In the chapter reading passage, notice some new forms of adjectives:

>*clārissimus* "most illustrious/very illustrious"
>
>*pulcherrimās* "most beautiful/very beautiful"
>
>*praeclārissimō* "most distinguished/very distinguished"
>
>*miserior* "more wretched"

The first three words are called **superlatives;** and the last one is called a **comparative**.

Adjectives have three degrees:

- **Positive degree** – the basic form of any adjective you have learned up to this point and the form that appears in all vocabularies. For example, the adjective *dulcis*, *dulce*, which means "sweet," is in the positive degree. In the simple statement "sweet fruit," the noun ("fruit") modified by the adjective is described, but nothing is said about the level or degree of sweetness.

- **Comparative degree** – this is formed in English by adding the suffix *–er* or sometimes by adding the adverb "more." If we say the fruit is "sweeter," this adjective rates the degree of sweetness in the noun by relation to some other standard—in this case, probably another fruit. The comparative degree indicates a level above the positive degree.

- **Superlative degree** – this is formed in English by adding the suffix *–est* or sometimes by adding the adverb "most" or "very." If we say the fruit is "sweetest," this adjective indicates the noun surpasses all others in respect to the quality indicated by the adjective. The "sweetest" fruit is not merely higher in sweetness than some other or others, but surpasses all others. The superlative degree indicates the highest level, and a level that nothing else in the same class reaches.

The **comparative** degree of most Latin adjectives can be formed by subtracting the genitive singular ending of the positive form, and adding to the base of the adjective the endings *–ior* for the masculine and feminine nominative singular, and *–ius* for the neuter nominative singular.

Comparatives are third declension adjectives of the type with two nominative forms (e.g., *fortis, forte* or *omnis, omne*), but with the following differences:

- The ablative singular ends in *–e* instead of *–ī*.

- The genitive plural ends in *–um* instead of *–ium*.

- The neuter nominative and accusative plural end in *–a* instead of *–ia*.

Comparative Adjectives

Singular

	Masculine and Feminine	Neuter
Nominative	fortior	fortius
Genitive	fortiōris	fortiōris
Dative	fortiōrī	fortiōrī
Accusative	fortiōrem	fortius
Ablative	fortiōre	fortiōre
Vocative	fortior	fortius

Plural

	Masculine and Feminine	Neuter
Nominative	fortiōrēs	fortiōra
Genitive	fortiōrum	fortiōrum
Dative	fortiōribus	fortiōribus
Accusative	fortiōrēs	fortiōra
Ablative	fortiōribus	fortiōribus
Vocative	fortiōrēs	fortiōra

STUDY TIP

Another way to remember the declension endings of the comparative forms of adjectives is to consider them third declension adjectives of the type with two nominative forms but with endings that look like **nouns** of the third declension that are **not i–stems**, e.g., *passer, passeris, m.* or *corpus, corporis, n.*

The **superlative** degree of most Latin adjectives can be formed by adding *-issimus, a, um* to the base of the positive adjective.

Superlative forms are adjectives of the first and second declensions.

Superlative Adjectives

Singular

	Masculine	Feminine	Neuter
Nominative	fortissimus	fortissima	fortissimum
Genitive	fortissimī	fortissimae	fortissimī
Dative	fortissimō	fortissimae	fortissimō
Accusative	fortissimum	fortissimam	fortissimum
Ablative	fortissimō	fortissimā	fortissimō
Vocative	fortissime	fortissima	fortissimum

Plural

	Masculine	Feminine	Neuter
Nominative	fortissimī	fortissimae	fortissima
Genitive	fortissimōrum	fortissimārum	fortissimōrum
Dative	fortissimīs	fortissimīs	fortissimīs
Accusative	fortissimōs	fortissimās	fortissima
Ablative	fortissimīs	fortissimīs	fortissimīs
Vocative	fortissimī	fortissimae	fortissima

BY THE WAY

The comparatives of adjectives belong to the third declension, regardless of the declension of the positive form, and the superlatives belong to the first and second declensions, regardless of the declension of the positive form. For example, consider the third declension adjective *fortis*, whose superlative form, as indicated above, is *fortissimus, a, um*—an adjective of the first and second declensions. Likewise, the first and second declension adjective *altus, a, um* in the comparative is *altior, altius*—a third declension form.

Declensions and Degrees			
Positive-Declension I + II	Positive-Declension III	Comparative-Declension III	Superlative-Declension I + II
altus, a, um		altior, altius	altissimus, a, um
	fortis, forte	fortior, fortius	fortissimus, a, um
	fēlix, fēlīcis	fēlīcior, fēlīcius	fēlīcissimus, a, um

BY THE WAY

The comparative degree not only means "more" of a certain quality, it can also mean "rather" or even "too," depending on the context. So the word *doctior* can mean not only "more learned," but also "rather learned" or even "too learned." Similarly the superlative degree does not only mean "most" of a certain quality, it can also mean "very" or even "extremely." So *doctissimus* can mean not only "most learned," but also "very learned."

▶ EXERCISE 1

Write the nominative singular forms of the comparative and the superlative of the following adjectives.

Example: fortis, forte – fortior, fortius (comparative); fortissimus, a, um (superlative)

1. fūnestus, a, um
2. plēnus, a, um
3. ferōx, ferōcis
4. gravis, grave
5. iūstus, a, um
6. dulcis, dulce
7. doctus, a, um
8. fēlīx, fēlīcis
9. clārus, a, um
10. longus, a, um
11. altus, a, um
12. crūdēlis, crūdēle
13. vehemēns, vehementis
14. aequus, a, um

VOCABULARY TO LEARN

NOUNS

exercitus, exercitūs, m. – army
hērēs, hērēdis, m./f. – heir
imperium, ī, n. – rule, power, empire
inopia, ae, f. – want, helplessness
nēmō (genitive *nūllīus*, dative *nēminī*, accusative *nēminem*, ablative *nūllō*), m. – no one

ADJECTIVES

fidēlis, fidēle – faithful, loyal
secundus, a, um – second
tertius, a, um – third
tristis, triste – sad

NUMERALS

duo, duae, duo– two
trēs, tria – three

VERBS

dēcipiō, ere, dēcēpī, dēceptum – to deceive
dīligō, ere, dīlēxī, dīlēctum – to esteem highly, love
laudō, āre, āvī, ātum – to praise
restituō, ere, restituī, restitūtum – to restore

IMPERSONAL PHRASE

necesse est + dative + infinitive – it is necessary for someone to do something

ADVERBS

paulō – a little bit, to a small extent
quam – than (with comparative words)
quantum – how much, to what extent
satis – enough, sufficiently
vehementer – vehemently, strongly

BY THE WAY

The Latin cardinal numbers for "one," "two," and "three" decline and, like all other adjectives, agree with the noun that they modify in case, number, and gender. The other cardinal numbers from "four" to "ten" do not decline. A chart of the cardinal numbers from one to ten can be found in the appendix to this book. The declension forms for one, two, and three are as follows.

	Ūnus			Duo			Trēs	
Nominative	ūnus	ūna	ūnum	duo	duae	duo	trēs	tria
Genitive	ūnīus	ūnīus	ūnīus	duōrum	duārum	duōrum	trium	trium
Dative	ūnī	ūnī	ūnī	duōbus	duābus	duōbus	tribus	tribus
Accusative	ūnum	ūnam	ūnum	duōs	duās	duo	trēs	tria
Ablative	ūnō	ūnā	ūnō	duōbus	duābus	duōbus	tribus	tribus

▶ EXERCISE 2

Find the English derivatives based on the Vocabulary to Learn in the following sentences. Write the corresponding Latin word.

1. The vehemence of his speech surprised all of us.

2. Liberty, fraternity, and equality are the triad of values that lie at the basis of the republic of France.

3. Ulysses, who devised the Trojan horse, by which trickery Troy was captured when force had failed, is the most skilled in deception of all the Greek heroes.

4. Several ancient religions, such as Zoroastrianism, conceived of a universe governed by a duality: a supreme good force opposed to a supreme evil power.

5. Fidelity, the bond of steadfast loyalty shown by dependents to their social superiors, was supposed to be fundamental in both the ancient Roman client system and the feudal order of the Middle Ages.

6. Some illnesses are said to be transmitted by heredity from one generation to the next in the same family.

7. The development of the microchip constituted a quantum leap in communications technology.

8. The Roman empire was officially divided into an eastern and a western half after the reign of Diocletian in the late third century CE.

9. That recipe is so delicious that I cannot restrain myself from asking for a second helping.

10. After the Romans had expelled the kings, they never wanted a restitution of monarchy or kingship.

11. I have heard only praise and laudatory words about her.

LANGUAGE FACT II

COMPARATIVE AND SUPERLATIVE –ER ADJECTIVES

If the nominative masculine singular of an adjective in the positive degree ends in –er, the superlative of these adjectives is formed by adding the ending –rimus, –rima, –rimum directly to the ending of the masculine nominative singular.

The comparative degree of adjectives that end in *–er*, end in *–ior* just as other comparative adjectives. But remember that the base of an adjective that ends in *–er* may keep the *–e–* as in *miser, misera, miserum* or may lose the *–e–* as in *pulcher, pulchra, pulchrum*. If the base keeps its *–e–*, the comparative will also keep the *–e–* also, as in *miserior*. If the base loses its *–e–*, the comparative will similarly lose the *–e–* likewise, as in *acrior*.

Examples

Positive degree: *pulcher, pulchra, pulchrum* – beautiful

Comparative degree: *pulchrior, pulchrius* – more beautiful

Superlative degree: *pulcherrimus, pulcherrima, pulcherrimum* – most beautiful

You have already met the superlative form of *pulcher* in this sentence at the beginning of the chapter reading passage.

Theodosius imperātor Rōmānus clārissimus trēs fīliās **pulcherrimās** *habuit.*
"Theodosius, a most illustrious Roman emperor, had three very beautiful daughters."

The Romans brought obelisks from Egypt to both capitals, Rome and Constantinople, and often placed them along the *spīna* of the circus. Theodosius placed this obelisk with his image on the base in the hippodrome at Constantinople in 390 CE. It had previously stood outside the Karnak Temple at Thebes, Egypt to commemorate Pharaoh Thutmose III's conquest of Syria.

▶ EXERCISE 3

Write the comparative and superlative forms of the adjectives listed below keeping the same case, number, and gender. For some, more than one answer is possible. Give the basic meaning of the adjective.

Example pulchrā   pulchriōre, pulcherrimā   beautiful, nice

1. tūtae
2. ācrēs
3. celebrium
4. tūtās
5. tristī

6. vehementem
7. ferōcibus
8. clāra
9. paucōrum

LANGUAGE FACT III

COMPARATIVE AND SUPERLATIVE ADVERBS

In the chapter reading passage, notice the comparative and superlative adverbs:

> *vehementius* "more strongly/vehemently"
>
> *vehementissimē* "most strongly/vehemently"

The **comparative** adverb is the same form as the **neuter accusative singular** of the comparative adjective. For example, the comparative adverb from the adjective *brevis, breve* would be *brevius*.

The **superlative** adverb is formed by dropping the *–us* of the masculine nominative singular of the superlative adjective and adding *–ē* to this base. For example, the superlative adverb from the adjective *brevis, breve* would be *brevissimē*.

▶ EXERCISE 4

Write the comparative and the superlative adverbs of the following adjectives. Translate each adverb.

Example: fortis
fortius (comparative) – more/too/rather bravely
fortissimē (superlative) – most/very bravely

1. tūtus
2. tristis
3. vehemēns
4. pulcher

5. levis
6. dulcis
7. ācer

▶ EXERCISE 5

The "Pirate's Daughter" is yet another tale included in the *Gesta Rōmānōrum*. The version below has been very freely adapted from the original. Carefully read the text and change all the positive or comparative adjectives and adverbs into the superlative forms. Finally, translate the changed passage. The Reading Vocabulary may be consulted.

DĒ PĪRĀTAE FĪLIĀ

Iuvenis ā pīrātīs est captus, quī eum in carcere tenēbant. Rēx pīrātārum erat crūdēlis. Nōlēbat iuvenem līberāre.

"Numquam," inquit, "tē līberābō, sī pecūniae cōpiam amplam mihi nōn dederis."

Iuvenis erat miser; pecūniam enim nōn habuit. Itaque ad patrem tandem scrīpsit, ut pater pecūniam mitteret. Respondit autem pater sē paucās rēs habēre: filium igitur in carcere manēre dēbēre. Nihil mīsit pater improbus ut fīlius līberārētur. Fīlia autem rēgis pīrātārum, quae misericordiā et amōre vehementer movēbātur, ad iuvenem tristem saepius veniēbat.

Puella quōdam diē, "Līberāre tē," inquit, "temptābō, sī mē in mātrimōnium posteā dūxeris."

Iuvenis propter haec verba laetus, "Libenter," inquit, "hanc condiciōnem accipiō!"

Noctū puella clāvēs ē rēge, quī dormiēbat, cautē surripuit, quibus iuvenem ā vinculīs līberāvit. Tunc puella ūnā cum iuvene ad patriam iuvenis fūgit. Cum autem pater iuvenis audīvisset fīlium illam puellam in mātrimōnium ductūrum esse, īrā vehementī mōtus est.

"Fēminam nōbilem in mātrimōnium dūcere dēbēbis," inquit pater, "nōn illam pauperem! Sī eam dūxeris, nōn iam eris hērēs meus!"

Acerbē respondit iuvenis. "Vītam," inquit, "huic puellae dēbeō, quae mē carcere et perīculō līberāvit: nihil tibi dēbeō, quī mē līberāre nōluistī. Dīxistī tunc tē paucās rēs habēre. Itaque cūr hērēs tuus esse cupiam?"

"Haec puella patrem suum," inquit pater, "dēcēpit, ut tē līberāret. Putāsne eam futūram esse tibi fidēlem? Puella cupīdine suā tē marītum habēre voluit."

Iuvenis ā pīrātīs est captus, quī eum in carcere tenēbant.

Haec verba audīvit puella. "Dicta tua sunt inīqua," inquit. "Hominēs, quī cupīdine moventur, aut pulchritūdinem, aut dīvitiās, aut auxilium petunt. Hārum rērum nihil habuit fīlius tuus. Pulchritūdinem in carcere perdidit mācerātus; nūllam pecūniam habuit, nūllum auxilium mihi dare potuit. Pietāte et amōre mōta eum marītum petīvī."

Pater iuvenis respondēre nōn potuit. Itaque iuvenis puellam in mātrimōnium dūxit, et coniugēs vītam honestē et piē ēgērunt.

acerbē – bitterly; adverb from *acerbus, a, um* – bitter, harsh

amplus, a, um – ample, large

(cum) audīvisset – when he had heard

carcer, carceris, m. – prison

cautē – adverb from *cautus, a, um* – cautious

clāvis, clāvis, f. – key

condiciō, condiciōnis, f. – condition, terms

cōpia, ae, f. – amount

cupiam – should I want?

cupīdō, cupīdinis, f. – greed, desire; cupīdine suā – because of her own desire

dicta, ōrum, n. pl. – things said, words

honestē – adverb from *honestus, a, um* – moral, upright

inīquus, a, um – unjust

iuvenis, is, m./f. – youth

laetus, a, um – happy

libenter (adv.) – willingly

mācerātus, a, um – (a participle) emaciated, weakened

misericordia, ae, f. – pity, compassion

nōbilis, nōbile – noble

nōlēbat – he did not want

nōluistī – you did not want

nūllus, a, um – none (obviously, there is no comparative or superlative of this adjective)

pecūnia, ae, f. – money

piē – adverb from *pius, a, um* – dutiful, good

pietās, pietātis, f. – dutifulness

pīrāta, ae, m. – pirate

pulchritūdō, pulchritūdinis, f. – beauty, handsomeness

quōdam diē – on a certain day

saepius – more frequently, more often; comparative adverb from *saepe*

surripiō, ere, surripuī, surreptum – to snatch away by stealth

voluit – she wanted

LANGUAGE FACT IV

WAYS OF EXPRESSING A COMPARISON

When two or more things are compared with a comparative adjective or adverb, the word for "than" is the adverb **quam**. You have already seen this in the following sentence from the chapter reading passage:

*Nēmō ... est miserior **quam ego** ...*   "No one is more wretched than I ..."

Another way of saying "than" in Latin is to put the second member of the comparison in the **ablative case** with no preposition. So the same sentence could read:

*Nēmō est ... miserior **mē** ...*   "No one is more wretched than I ..."

BY THE WAY

Be cautious with the ablative of comparison! It is not used unless the first of the two things being compared is in the nominative or accusative, and it is usually avoided when the second member of the comparison has a modifier.

Sometimes comparatives, but especially superlatives, express a part of a whole. The whole then is expressed by a **genitive**. You have already seen this in the chapter reading.

> *Fīliam rēgī **omnium** praeclārissimō dedit.*
> "He gave his daughter to the most distinguished king of all."

Sometimes this "part of the whole" or "partitive" relationship can be expressed with the prepositions *ex* or *inter* instead of the genitive. So the "most distinguished king of all" might also be called *ex omnibus praeclārissimus.*

▶ EXERCISE 6

Each of the following sentences contains a comparative statement with *quam.* Change each sentence replacing *quam* with the ablative of comparison. Translate each sentence.

Example: Cōnsulēs sevēriōrēs quam rēgēs videntur esse.
Cōnsulēs sevēriōrēs rēgibus videntur esse.
The consuls seem to be more severe than the kings.

1. Mīlitēs nostrōs ācriōrēs quam hostēs esse crēdō.

2. Cōnsilia tua clāriōra sunt quam lūx (*lūx, lūcis, f.* light).

3. Nēminem pulchriōrem quam hanc puellam vīdistis.

4. Paucī hominēs sunt fēlīciōrēs quam ego.

5. Pauperēs crēduntur esse miseriōrēs quam dīvitēs.

King Lear Act IV, Scene 7 finds the ailing King Lear in bed surrounded by his daughters. The youngest daughter, Cordelia, whom he had disowned because she did not flatter him asks, "Sir, do you know me?" Lear expects his daughter to hate him but she forgives him. Scholars believe the *Gesta Rōmānōrum* may have inspired Shakespeare.

▶ EXERCISE 7

Translate into Latin. The Reading Vocabulary may be consulted.

1. This daughter seems to be more just than the other ones.
2. I believe that this one is the most learned of all your daughters.
3. Nothing is more serious than this oracle of the gods.
4. The emperor's soldiers were fighting very keenly against most ferocious enemies.
5. We seem to be happier now than we were earlier.
6. Afterwards I will be obliged to bear (*tolerō, tolerāre*) bad fortune with more indifference.
7. We do not believe that the Greeks were more learned than the Romans.
8. We are most vehemently afraid of this very deadly war.
9. The most famous of all the Roman poets was Vergil (*Vergilius*).

Sulla (138 BCE–78 BCE) stands in the pose of an orator clutching his rolled speech in his left hand. This first-century sculpture shows Sulla dressed as a public official in his toga. It is a valued part of the classical collection at the Louvre Museum in Paris, France.

TALKING ABOUT A READING

ABOUT MODERN STORIES AND UNADAPTED LATIN: THE SCHOLAR AND THE WARLORD

DĒ FĀBULĪS HODIERNĪS

Magistra: Placuēruntne vōbīs fābulae quās lēgimus?

Christīna: Mihi placuērunt, sed magis mihi placent fābulae hodiernae (*modern/of this time*). Mē valdē dēlectant librī dē Henrīcō Figulō (*Harry Potter*) scrīptī.

Magistra: Cūr Henrīcum Figulum tam amās?

Christīna: Rēs magicās (*magic*) valdē amō, et Henrīcus Figulus rēbus magicīs semper studet. Et tū, Helena?

Helena: Ego autem amō fābulās dē Virō Arāneō (*Spiderman*). Ille vir pugnat prō rēbus iūstīs et contrā inīquitātem.

Marīa: Inter omnēs fābulās hodiernās maximē (*most*) amō Bella stellāria (*Star Wars*). Cōgitāte dē Dīrō Patre Tenebrārum (*Darth Vader*)! "Nōlī Vim contemnere! (*Don't underestimate the Force!*)," ut dīcit ille.

Mārcus: Hae pelliculae (*movies*) quibus nārrantur bella ingentia animum meum quoque movent. Quam terribilis est Dīrus Pater Tenebrārum!

Christīna: Satis hīs dē rēbus . . . Quondam (*once*) didicī Atticum et Sullam fuisse amīcōs. Mīror! (*I marvel/am surprised!*). Nam dīcunt omnium ducum Rōmānōrum Sullam fuisse crūdēlissimum.

Helena: Ita. Sed nēmō erat doctior quam Atticus. Etiam hominēs ferōcissimī, sīcut Sulla, doctrīnā (*learning*) interdum capiuntur (i.e., *are captivated, won over*)

Christīna: Quōmodo (*how*) hoc sit factum audīre cupiō.

THE SCHOLAR AND THE WARLORD

CORNĒLIĪ NEPŌTIS ATTICUS, 4.1–2

When the fierce Roman general Sulla came to Athens, even he was won over by Atticus' urbane good manners, his cultured polish, and his fluency in Greek. Sulla, as it happened, had a liking for Greek and Latin poetry, which Atticus could recite with consummate skill. Sulla wanted to take Atticus with him back to Italy. But Atticus had no wish to be drawn into the civil strife (of which Sulla was one of the leaders) ravaging the Roman state.

1   1. Hūc ex Asiā Sulla dēcēdēns cum vēnisset, quamdiū ibi fuit, sēcum habuit Pompōnium, captus adulēscentis et hūmānitāte et doctrīnā. Sīc enim Graecē loquēbātur, ut Athēnīs nātus vidērētur; tanta autem suāvitās erat sermōnis Latīnī, ut appārēret in eō nātīvum quendam
5   lepōrem esse, nōn ascītum. Item poēmata prōnūntiābat et Graecē et Latīnē sīc, ut suprā nihil posset addī. 2. Quibus rēbus factum est ut Sulla nusquam eum ā sē dīmitteret cuperetque sēcum dēdūcere. Quī cum persuādēre temptāret, "Nōlī, ōrō tē," inquit Pompōnius, "adversum eōs mē velle dūcere, cum quibus nē contrā tē arma ferrem, Ītaliam
10   relīquī." At Sulla adulēscentis officiō collaudātō omnia mūnera eī, quae Athēnīs accēperat, proficīscēns iussit darī.

VOCABULARY

1 hūc (adv.) – to this place, hither
   quamdiū (adv.) – as long as
   sēcum = cum sē

2 Pompōnius, ī, m. – the first name of Atticus
   hūmānitās, hūmānitātis, f. – culture
   doctrīna, ae, f. – learning

3 sīc (adv.) – so, in such a way
   Graecē (adv.) – in Greek
   loquēbātur – he used to speak
   nātus, a, um – born

4 suāvitās, suāvitātis, f. – sweetness, pleasantness
   sermō, sermōnis, m. – conversation, speech
   appāret, ēre – it is clear, obvious
   nātīvus, a, um – inborn, native

5 lepor, lepōris, m. – charm, agreeableness
   ascīscō, ere, ascīvī, ascītum – to summon from
      elsewhere
   item (adv.) – likewise
   poēma, poēmatis, n. – poem
   prōnūntiō, āre, āvī, ātum – to recite, to deliver (of
      a speech)

6 Latīnē (adv.) – in Latin
   suprā (adv.) – beyond, in addition
   addō, ere, addidī, additum – to add

7 dīmittō, ere, dīmīsī, dīmissum – to send away
   dēdūcō, ere, dēdūxī, dēductum – to lead away

7–8 quī cum = et cum ille

8 persuādeō, ēre, persuāsī, persuāsum – to per-
      suade
   adversum + accusative – against

9 velle – infinitive of volō, "to wish"

10 officium, ī, n. – duty, sense of duty
    collaudō, āre, āvī, ātum – to praise warmly
    mūnus, mūneris, n. – gift

READING NOTES

1 *Hūc ex Asiā Sulla dēcēdēns cum vēnisset* The present active participle *dēcēdēns* (see Chapter 11)
   modifies Sulla (Lūcius Cornēlius Sulla) and
   means "leaving." The temporal conjunction
   cum means "when" and takes a subjunctive verb
   in its clause.

3 *ut Athēnīs nātus vidērētur* The result clause (see
   Chapter 14) *ut . . . vidērētur* means "so that he
   seemed."

3–4 *tanta autem suāvitās erat sermōnis Latīnī, ut
   appārēret* This result clause means: "there was
   such great sweetness in his Latin conversation,
   that it was obvious." The impersonal verb
   appārēret is used with an accusative and infinitive.

6 *ut suprā nihil posset addī* The result clause *ut . . .
   nihil posset addī* means "in such a way that nothing in addition could be added."

6–7 *Quibus rēbus factum est ut Sulla nusquam eum ā
   sē dīmitteret* "Because of these factors it came
   about that Sulla nowhere sent him (Atticus)
   away from him (Sulla)."

7–8 *Quī cum persuādēre temptāret* The conjunction
   cum means "when." The connecting relative
   Quī refers back to Sulla. Connecting relative
   pronouns link a sentence to something in the
   previous sentence and translate as a demonstrative or personal pronoun. "When he tried to
   persuade <Atticus>."

9 *nē . . . ferrem* "lest I bear." The first person singular
   ferrem is imperfect subjunctive from *ferō*, an irregular verb meaning "to bear."

10 *officiō collaudātō* The ablative absolute (see Chap-
    ter 13) means "<with> the young man's sense of
    duty having been warmly praised."
    eī "to him (i.e., Atticus)"

11 *proficīscēns* This present participle agrees with
    Sulla and means "setting out."

QUESTIONS ABOUT THE TEXT

Answer in complete Latin sentences.

1. In quam urbem ex Asiā Sulla dēcēdēns vēnit?

2. Quem sēcum Sulla Athēnīs habuit?

3. Cūr Sulla Atticum dīligēbat?

4. Quōmodo Atticus Graecē loquēbātur?

5. Quanta erat Atticō sermōnis Latīnī suāvitās?

6. Quōmodo Atticus poēmata Graecē et Latīnē prōnūntiābat?

7. Cupiēbatne Sulla Atticum Athēnīs relinquere?

8. Cum Sulla Athēnās relīquisset, quid Atticō darī iussit?

DĒ FĀBULĪS HODIERNĪS CONTINUED

Mārcus: Bene fēcit Atticus. Multō (*by much*) fēlīcior erat, quam multī aliī, quī ā Sullā sunt occīsī.

Marīa: Ego cupiō Latīnē loquī (*infinitive "to speak/converse"*), sīcut Atticus Graecē loquēbātur!

VOCABULARY TO KNOW

NOUNS

agmen, agminis, n. – marching column

carmen, carminis, n. – poem, song

cibus, ī, m. – food

exercitus, exercitūs, m. – army

flūmen, flūminis, n. – river

hērēs, hērēdis, m./f. – heir

imperium, ī, n. – rule, power, empire

inopia, ae, f. – want, helplessness

iocus, ī, m. – joke

iuventūs, iuventūtis, f. – youth

mēns, mentis, f. – mind, spirit

nēmō (genitive *nūllīus*, dative *nēminī*, accusative *nēminem*, ablative *nūllō*), m. – no one

pōns, pontis, m. – bridge

porta, ae, f. – gate

victor, victōris, m. – victor

vīnum, ī, n. – wine

virtūs, virtūtis, f. – virtue, courage

vitium, ī, n. – vice

ADJECTIVES

dulcis, dulce – sweet

fidēlis, fidēle – faithful, loyal

immemor, immemoris + genitive – forgetful of

ingēns, ingentis – huge

levis, leve – light

ligneus, a, um – made of wood

proximus, a, um – nearest

quantus, a, um – how much, how great

secundus, a, um – second

tertius, a, um – third

tristis, triste – sad

tūtus, a, um – safe

vacuus, a, um + ablative – empty of

vehemēns, vehementis – violent, vehement

vetus, veteris – old

NUMERALS

duo, duae, duo – two

trēs, tria – three

VERBS

aperiō, īre, aperuī, apertum – to open

bibō, ere, bibī, — – to drink

coepī, coepisse, coeptum + infinitive – to begin (this verb has perfect forms only)

dēcipiō, ere, dēcēpī, dēceptum – to deceive

dēfendō, ere, dēfendī, dēfēnsum – to defend

dīligō, ere, dīlēxī, dīlēctum – to esteem highly, love

ēdō, ere, ēdidī, ēditum – to produce, give forth

furō, ere, furuī, — – to rage, be insane

invādō, ere, invāsī, — – to burst in

laudō, āre, āvī, ātum – to praise

ōrō, āre, āvī, ātum – to ask, entreat

parcō, ere, pepercī, — + dative – to spare (somebody or something)

placeō, ēre, placuī, placitum + dative – to please, be agreeable to somebody

recipiō, ere, recēpī, receptum – to receive

resistō, ere, restitī, — + dative – to resist (somebody or something)

restituō, ere, restituī, restitūtum – to restore

valeō, ēre, valuī, — + infinitive – to be in good health; to be able

ADVERBS

paulō – a little bit, to a small extent

prīmō – at first

quam – how (in indirect questions and exclamations)

quam – than (with comparative words)

quantum – how much, to what extent

satis – enough, sufficiently

simul – at the same time, simultaneously

vehementer – vehemently, strongly

PREPOSITIONS

extrā + accusative – outside of

CONJUNCTIONS

nē – that not, not to

nec . . . nec – neither . . . nor . . .

tam . . . quam . . . – so . . . as . . .

ut – that, to

utinam – if only; (may precede a wish in the subjunctive); the negative is *utinam nē.*

PHRASES

mē recipiō – I retreat

necesse est + dative + infinitive – it is necessary for someone to do something

▶ EXERCISE 1

Conjugate the following verbs in the perfect and pluperfect subjunctive, both active and passive.

1. *laudō, laudāre, laudāvī, laudātum*

2. *dēcipiō, dēcipere, dēcēpī, dēceptum*

▶ EXERCISE 2

Change the indicative verbs to the subjunctive keeping the same person, number, tense and voice. Give the basic meaning of each verb.

Example: amāvī   amāverim   love

1. fueram
2. apertum erat
3. dīlēxerāmus
4. bibit
5. potuērunt
6. fuī
7. pepercistis
8. ēditus es
9. restitūtī erant
10. furuit
11. valuistī

▶ EXERCISE 3

Decline the following adjectives in the comparative and superlative degrees.

1. *dulcis, dulce* – sweet

2. *miser, misera, miserum* – wretched

▶ EXERCISE 4

Give the comparative and the superlative degree of the following adjectives keeping the same number, gender, and case. Often more than one answer is possible.

Example: longae   longiōris, longiōrī, longiōrēs   longissimae

1. fidēlī
2. levia
3. tūtā
4. tristium

5. vehemēns
6. fortibus
7. fēlīcēs
8. aequō

▶ EXERCISE 5

Translate the English sentences into Latin and the Latin sentences into English.

1. Incolae urbis rogābant cūius esset exercitus, quem ex mūrīs cōnspicere poterant.

2. Immemor omnium nōn sciō quae gaudia mihi hāc in vītā maneant.

3. Rēx fīliās rogābat ut patrem vehementissimē dīligerent.

4. If only life were longer and more full of jokes and lighter things!

5. If only huge marching columns of armed people had not burst into the city!

6. The father who had to wage war asked his daughters to give help, but only the third daughter was extremely loyal.

▶ EXERCISE 6

Fill in the blanks with the correct form of the word in parentheses. Sometimes a preposition may need to be added. Translate the sentences.

1. Hic pōns erat tūtissimus _____ quī umquam sunt aedificātī. (omnis)

2. Porta nostra est perdita. Utinam eam _____! (dēfendō)

3. Pater _____ prīmam propter ēius verba dulcia vehementissimē amāverat. (trēs fīliae; do not use the ablative of comparison)

4. "Tertia fīlia," rēx tandem dīxit, "mē vehementius amat quam _____ et _____." (prīma, secunda)

5. Ōrō ut cibus et vīnum mihi statim _____. (inveniō)

6. Nōn sciēbam quās virtūtēs laudāre _____. (dēbeō)

CONSIDERING THE HEROES OF CLASSICAL MYTHOLOGY

THE TROJAN WAR

Ancient writers trace the motivations behind the Trojan War to the wedding of the mortal Peleus and the sea nymph Thetis. All of the gods were invited to the celebration except Eris, the goddess of discord. Even so, she appeared at the event, and tossed into the crowd of celebrants a golden apple, on which were inscribed the following words: "To the Most Beautiful." After three different goddesses—Juno, Minerva, and Venus—claimed the title, much disagreement ensued. Annoyed at the quarreling, Zeus then tossed

To avenge being snubbed by the other gods, Eris disrupted Peleus and Thetis' wedding feast with the golden apple, "*mālum aureum*," inscribed "*Pulcherrimae*." True to her nature, the goddess stirred up discord. Her Greek name means "strife" and yields the English derivative "eristic" meaning "characterized by disputatious and often subtle and specious reasoning."

the apple onto the earth. It landed at Troy, where the Trojan prince Paris immediately found it. He was then summoned to judge which of the three goddesses was the most beautiful and each offered him substantial rewards if he chose her. Juno promised him a great kingdom; Minerva military power; Venus the love of the most beautiful woman in the world, who was Helen of Sparta, wife of King Menelaus. Paris selected Venus and proceeded to claim his prize, by visiting Sparta as Menelaus' guest and abducting Helen from Sparta to Troy. Helen was part divine herself, the daughter of a mortal woman, Leda, and Zeus.

This statue of Achilles Triumphant stands in the gardens of the Achillion Palace on the Greek island of Corfu. The palace of the Empress Elisabeth of Austria was named Achillion in honor of Achilles whom the empress, widely known as Sissi, admired. In 1909, German Kaiser Wilhelm II, who then owned the palace, commissioned Johannes Goetz to sculpt a reproduction of this statue of Achilles.

Helen's beauty had attracted many suitors. Before finally giving her to Menelaus, Tyndareus, Leda's mortal husband, asked all of them to swear a solemn oath that they would come to her aid if any difficulties should befall her. Thus, when Paris abducted Helen to Troy, all of her former suitors were summoned to wage war against the Trojans to recover her. Thus the Trojan War began. Agamemnon, brother of Menelaus, was commander-in-chief of the Greek forces. Among the other important Greek figures who fought in the Trojan War are Achilles, the greatest and strongest Greek hero after Heracles, Achilles' close friend Patroclus, and Odysseus.

The Greeks traveled to Troy, which is located in northwestern Asia Minor (Turkey today), and besieged the city for ten years without managing to capture it. Homer's epic poem the *Iliad* begins in the tenth year of the war.

At the opening of the *Iliad*, Agamemnon has been living with Chryseis, a woman he has captured and enslaved in war, whose father is a Trojan priest of the god Apollo. But Apollo has punished the Greeks, forcing Agamemnon to return Chryseis; the arrogant Agamemnon then demands Achilles' captive slave woman Briseis as a replacement. Angered, Achilles withdraws from the fighting against the Trojans, so alienated from all of his Greek comrades that he even wishes for a Trojan victory, hoping that in this way the other Greeks may see how indispensable he is to their endeavors. He descends into the depths of his own hatred and isolation, a psychological equivalent of the underworld that other Greek heroes in crisis must visit. After the Greeks start losing badly, however, Achilles' dear friend Patroclus goes into battle wearing Achilles' armor, in an effort to raise the spirits of the Greek soliders. But Patroclus dies at the hands of the valiant Trojan prince Hector, brother of Paris, who seizes Achilles' armor as a trophy. Grief-stricken, Achilles turns for help to his mother, the sea goddess Thetis; she then asks the god Hephaestus to forge new armor for him, and he returns to the battle, eventually defeating Hector in single combat.

After Achilles kills Hector, he desecrates Hector's corpse by dragging it behind his chariot for several days. But this act of vengeance does not make him feel better. One night Hector's aged father, King Priam, sneaks into the Greek camp to beg for his son's body. He and Achilles speak to one another with sympathy and dignity, each voicing his own heartbreak, and Achilles agrees to return Hector's body. The *Iliad* ends with the scene of Hector's funeral.

A Greek vase shows Achilles tending Patroclus' wounds. Through the centuries the stories of the Trojan War provided substantial subject matter for Greek writers and artists. Scenes like this attest to the significance of the war, which pitted the civilized Greeks against a barbarian foe, according to the Greeks.

But Hector's burial did not end the Trojan War. Achilles, who was half mortal and half immortal, had the choice of a long and quiet life without glory, or an early death and eternal renown. Because he sought immortality, he chose the latter option. His mother Thetis had tried to make him immortal as an infant by dropping him in the waters of the river Styx in the underworld. Yet she left one part of his body unprotected: his heel, by which she held him. Paris thus managed to kill Achilles by shooting an arrow into his heel. Today we refer to an individual's greatest weakness as his or her "Achilles' heel."

Troy was eventually captured, not by the brawn of Achilles but the brains of Odysseus, who devised the stratagem of the Trojan horse. A large wooden structure, its hollow belly hid a force of armed Greek soldiers. After the rest of the Greek army sailed away to a nearby island, pretending to abandon Troy and the fighting, they left the horse at the gates of the city. They convinced the Trojans that the horse was a gift they

King Priam of Troy mourns over the body of his son Hector. Priam's appearance in the Greek camp to ransom his son's body results in a reconciliation for Achilles who gives the body to the grieving father. This scene in a sixteenth century manuscript dresses the Trojans in contemporary garb.

were dedicating to the gods. Although some of the Trojans were skeptical, warning about their fear of "Greeks bearing gifts," most welcomed the horse and urged that it be brought into the city. Once the horse was inside the city walls, Troy could no longer protect itself. During the night the soldiers concealed in the horse came out; they opened the city gates to admit the rest of the Greek army, which had secretly returned. The Greeks burned down the entire city. The Romans claimed that Aeneas, the major Trojan leader who survived, was their nation's forefather, a remote ancestor of Julius and Augustus Caesar.

READ THE FOLLOWING PASSAGE

The passage narrates how the participants of the so-called Oath of Tyndareus were called to war after the abduction of Helen by Paris.

Māter Achillis fīlium occultāverat, nē ad bellum dūcerētur. Nam dē fīliī vītā timēbat. Itaque vestīmenta fēminīna Achilles gerēbat nec hominēs quī vēnerant ut Achillem ad bellum vocārent sciēbant quis ille esset. Inter eōs hominēs tamen erat Ulixes quī mente callidā erat celeberrimus. Ulixes Achillem agnōvit et eum dēcipere dēcrēvit. Sciēbat enim eum esse armōrum valdē studiōsum. Itaque multa arma ante oculōs Achillis posuit, quī statim dīxit sē esse Achillem et arma cēpit.

Ulixes ipse tamen nōn cupiēbat ad bellum dūcī. Itaque fīnxit sē esse insānum. Coepit harēnam arāre. Cupiēbat enim aliīs insānus vidērī et in pāce relinquī. Ducēs tamen intellēxērunt Ulixem fingere. Ēius fīlium ante arātrum posuērunt. Tunc Ulixes arātrum relīquit, fīlium cēpit et ostendit sē nōn esse insānum. Ita et Achilles et Ulixes Trōiam petīvērunt.

Achilles, Achillis, m. – Achilles
agnoscō, ere, agnōvī, agnitum – to recognize
arātrum, ī, n. – plow
arō, āre, āvī, ātum – to plow
callidus, a, um – smart, cunning
fingō, ere, fīnxī, fictum – to pretend
fēminīnus, a, um – feminine
harēna, ae, f. – sand

insānus, a, um – mad, insane
ipse – himself
mente callidā – because of his clever mind. (The ablative expresses in what respect *Ulixes* was *celeberrimus*.)
Ulixes, Ulixis, m. – Odysseus
studiōsus, a, um + genitive – eager for
Trōia, ae, f. – Troy

CONNECTING WITH THE POST-ANCIENT WORLD

UNIVERSITIES IN THE MIDDLE AGES

Both the favor displayed by Charlemagne for scholars, and his promotion of Latin learning at his court, set an important example for Western Europe as a whole. From his reign onward, despite the political chaos following his death, schools were founded in many of the settlements in which there was a cathedral church, or the seat of a bishop. These "cathedral schools" were the first significant educational establishments outside monasteries in Western Europe since the collapse of the ancient Roman Empire in the west. The importance and the number of cathedral schools increased greatly after 1050, owing to the growth of towns.

A relief in the Museo Civico in Bologna, Italy glimpses into the everyday academic life of the medieval university. The professor seated in the *cathedra*, the official professorial chair, lectures to his class of students whose attention is rendered by the unknown sculptor. The size of medieval universities made for excellent student/professor ratios.

By about 1200 a few of these towns witnessed the development of special institutions, devoted to higher learning, known as universities. Educational institutions restricted to more advanced students were by no means new. They had existed in the ancient Greek and Roman world even since the founding of Plato's Academy in the fourth century BCE, and were also known in Islamic society. Nevertheless, the universities that arose in medieval Europe were unlike anything that had preceded them in several ways. The word *ūniversitās* itself denoted a legal society or guild. In this instance the guild was academic, and followed one of two models. The University of Bologna, perhaps the oldest university, with origins dating from the late eleventh century, was a guild of advanced law students, who hired professors to provide them with advanced legal training. It became the prototype of the student-run university, which was imitated in several places, particularly in southern Europe. This form of academic organization, however, gradually faded away. The University of Paris, founded in ca. 1160, and the University of Oxford, founded ca. 1200, represented another prototype, that of the masters' university. In this form of organization, the *Ūniversitās* was a guild of masters, and students associated with them as apprentices.

A university was not only a corporation or a guild but also an institution of higher learning. To qualify as a legitimate university, it had to offer a degree in at least one of the three highest academic disciplines in the Middle

Window from the Spanish College founded in 1367 for Spanish students studying at the University of Bologna, Italy. It was the largest of the colleges at the university in the fourteenth century having thirty students: eight in theology, eighteen in canon law, and four in medicine.

All Souls College was founded by King Henry VI and Henry Chichele, Archbishop of Canterbury, in 1438. Its stated purpose was the "service of Church and State" to learning and society. Today, All Souls College is primarily a research institution devoted to the humanities. This bird's eye view shows the typical Oxford college with its grassy quadrangle.

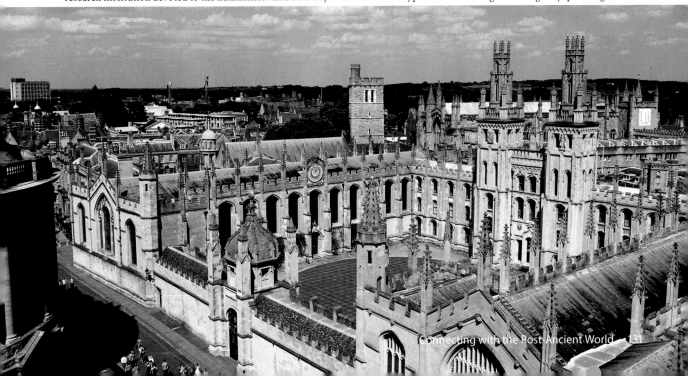

Ages, and preferably all three: law (both Roman civil law and the canon law of the church), theology (which also included what we today would call philosophy), and medicine. All entering students, males typically in their middle teens, would have already acquired some elementary education, especially in Latin. They were required to study the seven subjects comprising the liberal arts: a group of three, known as the *trivium*, consisting of grammar, rhetoric, and dialectic (or logic); and a group of four, known as the *quadrivium*, consisting of arithmetic, geometry, astronomy, and music. One could earn two degrees for studying the arts: the *baccālaureātus, ūs,* m. or "Bachelor of Arts," and the *magisterium, ī,* n. or "Master of Arts." The degree of *doctorātus, ūs,* m. was only awarded in the three highest disciplines. Those who received this degree had—at least in theory if not in practice—the *iūs ubīque docendī,* or "right to teach everywhere." Much of our present-day academic terminology derives from words in medieval Latin, which served as the universal language of academia throughout Europe: not merely the names of the degrees conferred today, but also the words used for various academic positions such as "Dean" (*decānus*), "Rector" (*rector*) and "Regent," and "Faculty" (*facultās*). The mortarboard hat and gown worn by modern students and professors at commencement ceremonies was the official daily garb of medieval university lecturers.

Medieval professors not only lectured, but also held public disputations with other professors on the finer points of their academic disciplines. They published their ideas and arguments in three different types of treatises, *summae* ("overviews"), *quaestiōnēs disputātae* ("debated issues"), or sometimes a *quodlibet* (a "whatever one pleases"), as well as in commentaries of various

The academic gowns seen at formal college functions like convocation and commencement are based on the academic garb of the medieval university. Sunday chapel and dinner at Oxford University requires students to wear their academic gowns while faculty don their doctoral gowns and male guests their tuxedos.

types. Universities, particularly the University of Paris, could possess great cultural prestige, and the views of university professors would weigh heavily in major political and religious events. The theologians at the University of Paris, for example, had a serious impact on settling the Great Schism of the Papacy, which had bitterly divided Europe in the late fourteenth and early fifteenth centuries.

Latin was the exclusive language of all lectures, disputations, official university functions, and publications. The situation only began to change in the late seventeenth century CE, partly in response to the growth of increasingly powerful monarchies, which closely associated their national language with their identity as political states; rulers of these countries favored the use of their own national language in universities located within their borders.

EXPLORING THE MUSLIM INFLUENCE IN SPAIN

AL-ANDALUS AND THE MUDEJAR WAY OF LIFE

Conflicts over religious beliefs have been a regular feature of history. The Romans, however, readily accommodated the gods and religious customs of those they conquered. Their polytheistic religion absorbed new cults and often identified others' gods as related to one in the Roman pantheon. Monotheistic religions like Judaism and Christianity, however, by their very nature precluded such a ready assimilation into Roman religious practice. Indeed, they posed a problem for the Romans. Christians refused to participate in state religious ceremonies and some citing religious grounds refused to undertake military service. Pliny the Younger, while governor of Bithynia, complained that the Christians refused to purchase the meat that had been used in temple sacrifices. Christians were regularly persecuted during the Roman empire until Constantine issued the Edict of Milan in 311 CE which allowed Christians to practice their religion. Soon, Christianity became the state religion of the Roman empire. Friction in Judea led to an outright Jewish revolt in the first century CE against the Romans. As victors, the Romans destroyed the sacred temple in Jerusalem and set in motion the great diaspora whereby the Jews were forced

The panorama of Jerusalem depicts the mount in Jerusalem sacred to all three monotheistic religions—Judaism, Christianity, and Islam. Here, Jews come to the Wailing Wall, the surviving remnant of the Second Temple destroyed by the Romans.

into exile and were scattered. Thus, Jews had settled throughout the Roman empire and on the Iberian peninsula. During the first centuries Christianity especially flourished in North Africa until the seventh century CE when the Prophet Muhammed arose and Islam quickly spread and became the dominant faith. Thus, Jerusalem and the Holy Lands had fallen under the control of the Muslims. To wrest control of those lands from the Muslims, the crusades were born. At that time, the population of Jews in Jerusalem was quite small. Accustomed to living with their Muslim neighbors, the Jews joined their overlords in defending the city against the crusaders.

The Muslim rule over the Iberian peninsula, however, marks a special time in history when, with some periods of exception, people of the three monotheistic religions lived side by side in relative harmony. Indeed, scholars from the three religious communities gathered and discussed great ideas in the courts, libraries, and "universities" of the Muslims. While the crusades pitted warring Christians against Muslims, let us see how the Christians in their reconquest of territories from the Muslims adapted a culture of religious tolerance and scholarly collaboration.

An integral part of the Roman imperium for roughly six centuries, Spain was destined in the fifth century CE to fall into the hands of the Germanic people we know as the Visigoths. Whether as outright invaders or Roman "allies" (*foederātī*) these "West Goths" had filtered into the empire's western provinces and succeeded down to 507 in maintaining a great kingdom extending

Alfonso X made his court an intellectual center which welcomed Christian, Jewish, and Muslim scholars. Under his patronage the translators at Toledo compiled a set of scientific treatises including a revision of the earlier astronomical Tables of Toledo. The image from Alfonso's treatise on chess, a game the crusaders learned from the Muslims, depicts a crusader (left) and a Saracen (right) playing chess.

all the way from the Straits of Gibraltar up to the Loire Valley in Gaul. And while, after that, they were forced to cede their Gaulish territory to victorious Frankish neighbors, their hegemony in the Hispanic peninsula was destined to endure for another two centuries. Only in 711, with the shattering invasion from North Africa of victorious Muslim armies, was Visigothic power finally destroyed and the bulk of the peninsula drawn into the orbit of an Islamic empire.

As a result, it was only in marginal territories clinging in the north to the foothills of the Pyrenees that Christian rulership initially survived. As late as the beginning of the eleventh century, indeed, a full two-thirds of Spain—the territory known as al-Andalus—remained firmly in Muslim hands. Only after 1034, with the disintegration of the caliphate of Córdoba into an array of petty Muslim kingdoms, did the process of Christian reconquest really get under way. That process was to shape much of subsequent Spanish history from the mid-eleventh to the mid-thirteenth centuries, and it was in the arena of that epic struggle for national identity that the great Spanish national hero—the Cid (Arabic sīd, sayyid; lord), Rodrigo Díaz de Vivar (ca. 1043–99)—did his mighty deeds.

Of military aggression, then, there was of course plenty. But it is important to realize that it was only part, and by no means the most intriguing part, of the whole story. That the Cid himself, during his not infrequent quarrels with his lord, Alfonso VI of Castile, chose to fight valiantly

The equestrian statue of Spain's national hero, El Cid, Rodrigo (Ruy) Díaz de Vivar, known as the Campeador, stands in Burgos, the capital of the kingdom of Castile. "Campeador" is a later Latin corruption of the Latin *campī doctor or doctus,* meaning "master of the military arts." El Cid's hometown Vivar is six miles from Burgos.

in the service of Muslim princes says something very important about the nature and intimacy of the relationships that had come to prevail between Muslim and Christian and the degree of acculturation that had come to characterize them. During these initial centuries, at least, Christian reconquest involved not persecution, but a largely tolerant pattern of accommodation that reflected earlier Muslim practice. With the conquest of Toledo in 1085, Alfonso VI adopted the Muslim pattern of preserving conquered communities as "Mudejars," distinctive and in many ways independent enclaves which were allowed to retain more or less intact their traditional religious, legal, and administrative arrangements.

Panoramic view of modern Toledo shows the medieval boundaries of the Visigothic capital. The Alcázar (from the Arabic *al qasr*) is readily recognized rising to the right. The fortified palace built over a Roman barracks has Visigothic, Muslim, and Spanish additions. The present building was restored after major destruction during the civil war in 1936.

It was the constitution of this Mudejar way of life that was to make possible and to promote the complex and creative interpenetration across time of the two cultures, Muslim and Christian. Architecturally speaking, this was to be brilliantly reflected in the intricate interweaving of Muslim and Christian motifs in so many Spanish buildings, not least among them the Alcázar in Seville, the work in part of Mudejars from Toledo.

The Emir of Cordoba Abd el-Rahman III built the Alcázar in Seville over a Roman barracks in 913 CE. Successive caliphs added rooms and gardens as well as magnificent decorations which inspired centuries of Spanish architecture. The Christian kings made it their home. The Islamic palace gardens provided a natural air-cooling system.

It is evident also in the debt that the Provençal court poets (troubadours) of the twelfth and thirteenth centuries clearly owed to the Arabic love-poetry of North Africa and Spain, and not only for the structural form and stylistic traits of their lyrics. That debt appears to have extended also to some of the most striking aspects of the romantic or "courtly" love that formed the central theme of much of troubadour writing and was destined to leave an enduring imprint on the European literary imagination right down to the present. It is evident again, and perhaps most crucially, in the close collaboration of Muslims, Jews, and Christians in the extensive effort at translation that made Spain during the era of reconquest the first route along which the great works of ancient Greek and early-medieval Arabic science and philosophy found their historic way into the intellectual bloodstream of Latin Christendom. Centuries earlier, the Muslim world had assimilated the Greek philosophical and scientific heritage via a complex process of transition involving translation from the original Greek into Hebrew or Syriac and thence into Arabic. Now, during the era of Christian reconquest, and via an array of Spanish centers of translation most notably that at Toledo, the process was reversed and the Greek legacy, often extended and creatively elaborated by Muslim intellectuals, made its way, sometimes circuitously via Hebrew and Spanish translations, into the scholastic Latin that was the international *lingua franca* of the Western Christian intelligentsia.

It was via that route that the great scholastic philosophers and theologians of Paris and Oxford first became acquainted with the full corpus of Aristotle's writings and with the commentaries of such great Muslim philosophers as Ibn Sina and Ibn Rushd. For the Latin scholastics, Aristotle's overriding importance was such that in their own works they referred to him simply as "the Philosopher." And among the admired interpreters of Aristotle Ibn Rushd's stature was such that Christian intellectuals Latinized his name as "Averroës" and fell into the habit of referring to him simply as "the Commentator." New and more accurate Latin translations of Aristotle came later to be made directly from the Greek originals. But it was al-Andalus and the Mudejar way of life that opened up the first gateway through which the world of Latin Christendom was able to reconnect with the full richness of the Greek philosophical legacy. For the unfolding fabric of the European intellectual tradition that historic encounter in Spain was to prove to be nothing less than transformative.

This culture of tolerance was short-lived. As the Christian Spaniards regained more of their territory, they abandoned the practice of tolerance. Indeed, in the fifteenth century, Ferdinand and Isabella, who became known as the Catholic monarchs, used religion both to unify Spain and to diminish Rome's influence in their kingdom. Thus, with the conquest of Granada, they expelled the Muslims from Spain and similarly expelled the Jews who chose not to convert. It should be noted that the Ottoman sultan sent ships to bring the Jews to Muslim territory where they reestablished themselves. Anti-semitism has regularly flared in the modern era—pogroms in parts of Europe and Russia, the rise of the anti-semitic Ku Klux Klan in the United States—reaching its nadir with the Holocaust conducted by the Nazis. The post World War II era has witnessed the erosion of a monolithic European Christianity with the influx of Muslims from former colonies and as guest-workers.

Al-Andalus enjoyed highly developed economic, intellectual, and technological systems. The Islamic rulers took full advantage and improved upon what the Romans had left behind. They made widespread use of the water wheel to irrigate their fields as well as the gardens and fountains of their palaces. The one depicted is on Cordoba's River Guadalquivir.

This tidal wave of change has required the nations of Europe to ponder questions as to what constitutes their national identity. To blur the religious divisions, the French government banned students from wearing dress or accessories that connoted a religious identity. The news of the twenty-first century is filled with stories of religious mistrust, tension, and conflict that continue to pit Christians, Jews, and Muslims against one another. At the same time, political and religious leaders have established and supported programs to encourage mutual understanding and tolerance. Interreligious dialogues, summer camps for children of different faiths, historic overtures like the Roman Catholic Pope's visit with the Chief Rabbi of Rome and visit to an historic mosque in Syria, are all efforts towards reconciliation and tolerance. The example of al-Andalus and the Mudejars offer a special historic lesson.

FRANCIS C. OAKLEY
Edward Dorr Griffin Professor
of the History of Ideas and
President Emeritus,
Williams College
Williamstown, Massachusetts

MĪRĀBILE AUDĪTŪ

MOTTOES, PHRASES, AND TERMS RELEVANT TO CHRISTIAN RELIGION IN MEDIEVAL TIMES AND NOW

MOTTOES

- Ad maiōrem Deī glōriam (A.M.D.G.). "For the greater glory of God." A motto of the Jesuit order, also known as the Company of Jesus or the *Societās Iēsū*, founded by Ignatius of Loyola in 1540. The phrase encapsulates the order's mission.

- Ōrā et labōrā! "Pray and work!" The motto of the Benedictine monastic order. The Rule of St. Benedict was established in the sixth century CE by Benedict, the son of a Roman noble.

PHRASES AND TERMS

- Avē Marīa. "Hail, Mary!" The beginning of the famous prayer to the mother of Jesus which takes its origin from the Gospel according to Luke, 1.28, when the angel foretells to Mary the birth of baby Jesus.

- Ecce homo! "Behold the man!" In the Gospel according to John, 19.5, Pilate with this phrase presents Jesus who was crowned with thorns to the crowd. This is also the title of nineteenth century German philosopher Friedrich Nietzsche's autobiography.

- Meā culpā. "By my own fault." Expression of the inherent failing of human nature used in Christian prayers.

Ignatius of Loyola is regularly depicted with an open book on which the abbreviation A.M.D.G. or the full motto is written. The Jesuits, the popular name for the religious order of men he founded, are known for their educational institutions. In the United States, the Jesuits run twenty-six colleges or universities and some fifty high schools.

Medieval and Renaissance European art abounds with images of the Annunciation when tradition says the archangel Gabriel announced to Mary that she would give birth to the child Jesus. This little relief celebrates that event with its *"Avē Marīa."*

- Mementō morī. "Remember that you <will> die." This expression was used in ancient Rome to remind the triumphing generals that their glory was not perpetual. In Christianity, it became a reminder of the shortness of the terrestrial life. In iconography, it was symbolized by the image of a skull.

- Habēmus pāpam. "We have a pope." With this simple phrase, the election of a new pope is announced from the central balcony of St. Peter's Basilica in the Vatican.

- Sīc trānsit glōria mundī. "Thus goes (across) the glory of the world." The phrase reflects the belief that worldly things are fleeting, they pass quickly. It is a reminder not to trust that present achievement or success will be eternal just as human life is not immortal.

CHAPTER 7

The Irregular Verbs *Volō*, *Nōlō*, and *Mālō*; Use of *volō*, *nōlō*, and *mālō*; Negative Commands

DOMINVS FRANCISCHVS PETRARCHA

Andrea del Castagno (ca. 1419–1457) painted a mural to honor the famous humanist Petrarch.

MEMORĀBILE DICTŪ

Nōlēns volēns.

Literally, "unwillingly or willingly," the English "willy-nilly" tries to capture the effect of the Latin.

READING

The "Renaissance" is the French name for an intellectual movement—fueled by a deep admiration for the culture of ancient Rome and a strong desire to imitate it—that began in the city-states of Italy during the fourteenth century. This enthusiasm for revisiting and perpetuating ancient Roman cultural achievements inspired Italians of that era to immense creativity in many fields. The first major humanist (the term we use for those who championed the cause of the Renaissance) was Petrarch (1304–1374), an Italian who traveled often to other regions of Europe in part because he held a clerical office that required him to remain for several years in Avignon, then the seat of the papacy. But he also traveled alone, for pleasure—a rare practice in the fourteenth century.

Today Petrarch is recognized as a major literary figure in Latin: some of his Latin works, including the meditative *Sēcrētum* (*Secret Writing*) and his many letters, are treasured as classics of humanist Latin.

Petrarch, like other humanists, viewed himself as continuing the Latin literary tradition begun by the classical Romans and felt so close to the long-dead Roman authors that he wrote letters to them. Petrarch ran across some of Cicero's private correspondence that revealed a worried, hesitant man. The contrast between Cicero's personality in his public writings and in his personal letters prompted Petrarch to write to Cicero, who left the world 1300 years before it welcomed Petrarch.

FRANCISCUS CICERŌNĪ SUŌ SALŪTEM DĪCIT

1   Epistulās tuās diū multumque quaesītās atque, cum nōn exspectābam,
     inventās, avidissimē lēgī. Vix crēdēbam, Mārce Tullī, quam multa
     dīcerēs, quantās lacrimās funderēs, quam saepe animum tuum mūtārēs.
     Iam sciēbam quālis magister aliīs fuissēs; nunc tandem intellegō
5   quis tū tibi fueris. Ubicumque es, audiās hoc nōn iam cōnsilium, sed
     lāmentum, quod ūnus posterōrum tuī nōminis studiōsissimus nōn
     sine lacrimīs fundit. Ō, senex semper inquiēte atque anxie, cūr tot
     contentiōnibus et simultātibus haud ūtilibus, interesse voluistī? Ubi
     ōtium quod et aetātī et professiōnī et fortūnae conveniēbat relīquistī?
10   Quī tē falsus glōriae splendor senem adulēscentium bellīs implicuit et
     ad indignam philosophō mortem rapuit? Cūr hoc est factum? Quī furor tē in tot hostēs
     Heu, prō aliīs lūmen tenēbās et viam ostendēbās ut rēctē ambulārent,
     ipse tamen cecidistī. Cūr hoc est factum? Quī furor tē in tot hostēs
     impēgit? Amor, crēdō, reī pūblicae. At sī tantum fidē et lībertāte

15 movēbāris, quid tē ad potentiōrēs trahēbat? Cūr dē virtūtibus verba
semper ōrnātissima dīcēbās, sī tēmetipsum audīre nōlēbās? Utinam
potuissēs in tranquillō locō rūsticō tamquam vērus philosophus
senēscere, utinam nē dē honōribus tam multum cōgitāvissēs, utinam nē
Catilīnās in animō tuō habuissēs!

20 In aeternum valē, mī Cicero!

READING VOCABULARY

*aetās, aetātis, f. – age

anxius, a, um – anxious

avidē (adv.) – eagerly, greedily

Catilīna, ae, m. – Catiline‡

contentiō, contentiōnis, f. – contest, fight

conveniō, īre, convēnī, conventum + dative – to be
becoming to, be appropriate for, meet

falsus, a, um – false

*fidēs, fideī, f. – faith

Franciscus (ī, m.) Petrarca (ae, m.) – Francis Petrarch‡

*fundō, ere, fūdī, fūsum – to pour (out)

furor, furōris, m. – madness, fury

*glōria, ae, f. – glory

haud (adv.) – not

heu (interj.) – alas!

impingō, ere, impēgī, impāctum – to push, drive into

implicō, āre, implicuī, implicitum/āvī, ātum + dative
– to involve

in aeternum – forever

indignus, a, um + dative – unworthy of

inquiētus, a, um – restless, unquiet

intersum, interesse, interfuī, — + dative – to get involved in, participate into

ipse (tū) – yourself

lāmentum, ī, n. – lament, complaint

*lībertās, lībertātis, f. – freedom

*lūmen, lūminis, n. – light

*nōlēbās – you did not want

ō! – oh!

*ōrnātus, a, um – adorned

*ōtium, ī, n. – leisure, free time (usually engaged in
literary activity)

philosophus, ī, m. – philosopher

*potēns, potentis – powerful

posterī, ōrum, m. pl. – descendants, coming generations

professiō, professiōnis, f. – profession

*pūblicus, a, um – common
rēs pūblica – state, republic

*quālis, quāle – what sort of

rapiō, ere, rapuī, raptum – to snatch

rēctē (adv.) – correctly

senēscō, ere, senuī, — – to get old, grow old

simultās, simultātis, f. – rivalry

splendor, splendōris, m. – splendor, glamor

*studiōsus, a, um + genitive – fond of

*tamquam – as

tēmetipsum – yourself

*tot (adv.) – so many

*trahō, ere, trāxī, trāctum – to drag, draw

tranquillus, a, um – quiet, calm

*ubi? – where?

ubicumque (conj.) – wherever

*ūnus, ūna, ūnum –one

*ūtilis, ūtile – useful

*vix (adv.) – hardly

*voluistī – you wanted

*Words marked with an asterisk will need to be memo-
rized later in the chapter.

‡Additional information about the words marked with
the double dagger will be in the **Take Note** section
that follows the Reading Vocabulary.

TAKE NOTE

Catilīna Catiline was a bankrupt revolutionary whose plot to overthrow the republic was exposed by Cicero. More information on Cicero and Catiline can be found in Chapter 9 of Level 1.

Franciscus Petrarca Francis Petrarch's name in Italian is Francesco Petrarca.

tēmetipsum The suffix *–met* added to *tē* (or *mē* or *sē*), with the pronoun *ipse* (in the appropriate case, gender, and number) sometimes added, creates an extra-emphatic form of the personal pronoun "yourself."

COMPREHENSION QUESTIONS

1. What prompts Petrarch to write to Cicero?

2. What kind of objections does Petrarch have against Cicero?

3. What life would Petrarch like for Cicero?

4. What time span divides Petrarch from Cicero?

Petrarch spent some time serving in a clerical position with the papal court which was in Avignon for most of the fourteenth century. The Papal Palace stands as one of the largest and best examples of secular Gothic architecture in Europe. Built onto a natural outcropping of rock, the palace overlooks the Rhône River.

LANGUAGE FACT I

THE IRREGULAR VERBS *VOLŌ*, *NŌLŌ*, AND *MĀLŌ*

In the chapter reading passage, you read the following sentence.

> *Cūr tot contentiōnibus et simultātibus haud ūtilibus, interesse* **voluistī**?
> "Why did you want to participate in so many fights and not useful rivalries?"

The form *voluistī* is a perfect tense form from the irregular verb *volō, velle, voluī, —*, "to want."

In the same passage, there is another sentence.

> *Cūr dē virtūtibus verba semper ōrnātissima dīcēbās, sī tēmetipsum audīre* **nōlēbās**?
> "Why were you always speaking very ornate words about virtues, if you did not want to listen to yourself?"

The form *nōlēbās* is an imperfect tense form from the irregular verb *nōlō, nōlle, nōluī, —*, "not to want, be unwilling."

There is one more irregular verb closely related to *volō*. It is the verb *mālō, mālle, māluī, —*, "to prefer."

These three verbs do not belong to any conjugation, much in the same way the irregular verbs *sum* and *possum* do not belong to any conjugation. Also, like *sum* and *possum*, they have only an active voice.

The Irregular Verbs volō, nōlō, and mālō

volō, velle, voluī, —	to want
nōlō, nōlle, nōluī, —	not to want, be unwilling
mālō, mālle, māluī, —	to prefer

BY THE WAY

The verb *nōlō* is derived from the negative particle *nē–* and the verb *volō*. *Nōlō* is an antonym of *volō*. The verb *mālō* is derived from the adverb *magis* ("more," "rather") and the verb *volō*.

Present Active Indicative of volō, nōlō, and mālō

	Singular			Plural		
First person	volō	nōlō	mālō	volumus	nōlumus	mālumus
Second person	vīs	nōn vīs	māvīs	vultis	nōn vultis	māvultis
Third person	vult	nōn vult	māvult	volunt	nōlunt	mālunt

STUDY TIP

Do not confuse *vīs*, the second person singular of the present indicative that means "you wish," and *vīs*, the noun that means "strength." Context will help you differentiate between the two.

Present Active Subjunctive of volō, nōlō, and mālō

	Singular			Plural		
First person	velim	nōlim	mālim	velīmus	nōlīmus	mālīmus
Second person	velīs	nōlīs	mālīs	velītis	nōlītis	mālītis
Third person	velit	nōlit	mālit	velint	nōlint	mālint

Present Active Infinitive of volō, nōlō, and mālō

velle	nōlle	mālle

Present Imperative of nōlō

Singular	—	nōlī	—
Plural	—	nōlīte	—

STUDY TIP

Note that the endings of the present subjunctive of *volō*, *nōlō*, and *mālō* resemble the endings of the present subjunctive of *sum* and *possum*.

Imperfect Active Indicative of volō, nōlō, and mālō

	Singular			Plural		
First person	volēbam	nōlēbam	mālēbam	volēbāmus	nōlēbāmus	mālēbāmus
Second person	volēbās	nōlēbās	mālēbās	volēbātis	nōlēbātis	mālēbātis
Third person	volēbat	nōlēbat	mālēbat	volēbant	nōlēbant	mālēbant

Imperfect Active Subjunctive of volō, nōlō, and mālō

	Singular			Plural		
First person	vellem	nōllem	māllem	vellēmus	nōllēmus	māllēmus
Second person	vellēs	nōllēs	māllēs	vellētis	nōllētis	māllētis
Third person	vellet	nōllet	māllet	vellent	nōllent	māllent

Future Active Indicative of volō, nōlō, and mālō

	Singular			Plural		
First person	volam	nōlam	mālam	volēmus	nōlēmus	mālēmus
Second person	volēs	nōlēs	mālēs	volētis	nōlētis	mālētis
Third person	volet	nōlet	mālet	volent	nōlent	malent

STUDY TIP

In the imperfect and the future, *volō*, *nōlō*, and *mālō* behave exactly as if they were verbs of the third conjugation. In the imperfect subjunctive these three verbs behave like other verbs also—they feature the personal ending attached directly to the present active infinitive.

In the tenses formed from the perfect stem (perfect, pluperfect, future perfect), the irregular verbs *volō*, *nōlō*, and *mālō* conjugate as any other verb does. You just add to the perfect stem the endings you already know for these tenses.

Perfect Active Indicative of volō, nōlō, and mālō

	Singular			Plural		
First person	voluī	nōluī	māluī	voluimus	nōluimus	māluimus
Second person	voluistī	nōluistī	māluistī	voluistis	nōluistis	māluistis
Third person	voluit	nōluit	māluit	voluērunt	nōluērunt	māluērunt

Perfect Active Subjunctive of volō, nōlō, and mālō

	Singular			Plural		
First person	voluerim	nōluerim	māluerim	voluerimus	nōluerimus	māluerimus
Second person	volueris	nōlueris	mālueris	volueritis	nōlueritis	mālueritis
Third person	voluerit	nōluerit	māluerit	voluerint	nōluerint	māluerint

Perfect Active Infinitive of volō, nōlō, and mālō

voluisse	nōluisse	māluisse

Pluperfect Active Indicative of volō, nōlō, and mālō

	Singular			Plural		
First person	volueram	nōlueram	mālueram	voluerāmus	nōluerāmus	māluerāmus
Second person	voluerās	nōluerās	māluerās	voluerātis	nōluerātis	māluerātis
Third person	voluerat	nōluerat	māluerat	voluerant	nōluerant	māluerant

Pluperfect Active Subjunctive of volō, nōlō, and mālō

	Singular			Plural		
First person	voluissem	nōluissem	māluissem	voluissēmus	nōluissēmus	māluissēmus
Second person	voluissēs	nōluissēs	māluissēs	voluissētis	nōluissētis	māluissētis
Third person	voluisset	nōluisset	māluisset	voluissent	nōluissent	māluissent

Future Perfect Active Indicative of volō, nōlō, and mālō

	Singular			Plural		
First person	voluerō	nōluerō	māluerō	voluerimus	nōluerimus	māluerimus
Second person	volueris	nōlueris	mālueris	volueritis	nōlueritis	mālueritis
Third person	voluerit	nōluerit	māluerit	voluerint	nōluerint	māluerint

▶ EXERCISE 1

Translate into Latin.

1. you do not want
2. to prefer
3. s/he wanted
4. they had not wanted
5. we will have preferred
6. s/he wants
7. s/he prefers
8. I will want

9. you (plural) will not want
10. they were preferring
11. they are unwilling
12. you will have preferred
13. you (plural) had preferred
14. you (plural) want
15. s/he, it will be unwilling

VOCABULARY TO LEARN

NOUNS

aetās, aetātis, f. – age
fidēs, fideī, f. – faith
glōria, ae, f. – glory
lībertās, lībertātis, f. – freedom
lūmen, lūminis, n. – light
ōtium, ī, n. – leisure, free time

ADJECTIVES

ōrnātus, a, um – adorned, ornate, elaborate
potēns, potentis – powerful
pūblicus, a, um – common
quālis, quāle – what sort of
studiōsus, a, um + genitive – fond of
ūtilis, ūtile – useful

NUMERAL

ūnus, ūna, ūnum – one

VERBS

fundō, ere, fūdī, fūsum – to pour
mālō, mālle, māluī, — – to prefer
nōlō, nōlle, nōluī, — – not to want, be unwilling
trahō, ere, trāxī, trāctum – to drag, draw
volō, velle, voluī, — – to want

ADVERBS

tamquam – as
tot – so many
ubi? – where?
vix – hardly

PHRASE

rēs pūblica – state

▶ EXERCISE 2

Find the English derivatives in the following sentences based on the Vocabulary to Learn of this chapter. Write the corresponding Latin word.

1. The changes must be approved by both sides; any unilateral changes are unacceptable.

2. There is considerable traction between the wheels of the car and the road.

3. How much do you pay for utilities every month?

4. In our country, we have opted for a republican form of government.

5. All the products pass through quality control.

6. I signed the affidavit in front of a notary.

7. Anyone who considers war to be glorious is blind to tragedy.

8. I have taken the liberty to write a letter and explain everything on my own initiative.

9. If you are away from the lights of the city in the desert or out in the ocean, the moon can be so luminous on a cloudless night, that you can even read a book by its silver light.

10. The decorations were adorned with gold.

11. This young man demonstrates tremendous potential.

LANGUAGE FACT II

USE OF *VOLŌ*, *NŌLŌ*, AND *MĀLŌ*; NEGATIVE COMMANDS

You have already learned that the present imperative of *nōlō*, i.e., *nōlī*, *nōlīte* with an infinitive, is used for the negative command of any verb.

> *Nōlī fugere!* "Do not run away!"   *Nōlīte fugere!* "Do not run (pl.) away!"

Another way to make a negative command is to use the negative particle **nē** and the perfect subjunctive.

> *Nē fugeris!* "Do not run away!"   *Nē fugeritis!* "Do not run (pl.) away!"

The verbs *volō*, *nōlō* and *mālō* are used with the accusative and infinitive. But it should be noted that if the subject of the infinitive is the same as the subject of the main verb, the subject is normally not expressed by another word but is understood in the ending of the main verb. Notice the contrast between the paired sentences below.

> *Volō ad tē venīre.* "I want to come to you."
> *Volō tē ad mē venīre.* "I want you to come to me."

> *Nōn vīs ad mē venīre.* "You do not want to come to me."
> *Nōn vīs mē ad tē venīre.* "You do not want me to come to you."

> *Mālumus ad vōs venīre.* "We prefer to come to you."
> *Mālumus vōs ad nōs venīre.* "We prefer that you come to us."

▶ EXERCISE 3

Change the *nōlī, nōlīte* and infinitive commands into *nē* and the perfect subjunctive constructions and vice versa. Translate the commands.

Example: Nōlī mē relinquere!
Nē mē relīqueris!   Do not leave me!

1. Nōlī lacrimās fundere!
2. Nōlīte in exercitum trahī!
3. Nē hās discipulās dēcēperis!
4. Nōlīte hērēdem tam saepe laudāre!
5. Nē aurum meum perdideris!
6. Nē dē victōribus tam multum scrīpseritis!

The Ponte Vecchio, Italian for "Old Bridge," in Florence; its present form dates from 1345 when it was rebuilt after floods destroyed the twelfth century bridge twelve years prior. It is believed to be located where the Roman Via Cassia crossed the Arno River. Petrarch may well have shopped here as the bridge has always housed merchants.

▶ EXERCISE 4

Translate into Latin. The Reading Vocabulary may be consulted.

1. Petrarch wants to find Cicero's letters.

2. Petrarch badly (strongly) wants Cicero to be a strong man.

3. Petrarch prefers to read Cicero's speeches.

4. We did not want Petrarch to say that Cicero was not a distinguished man.

5. I will not want to produce poems only about freedom.

A bird's eye view of the Palazzo Vecchio's tower and rooftop which continue to dominate the Florentine skyline just as they did in Petrarch's day. Built in the late thirteenth century to house Florence's city government, the building overlooks the Piazza della Signoria, one of the major public gathering places in Florence through the ages.

▶ EXERCISE 5

Fill in the blanks with the correct degree of the adjective or adverb in parentheses. Translate the sentences. The Reading Vocabulary may be consulted.

1. Petrarca lēgit epistulās Cicerōnis _____ quam aliōs librōs. (avidē)

2. Putāsne Cicerōnem esse omnium Rōmānōrum _____? (celeber)

3. Petrarca vidētur verba _____ scrībere quam Cicero. (ōrnātus)

4. Cicero dīcit nēminem rem pūblicam Rōmānam sē _____ amāre. (vehementer)

5. Ōrātiōnēs Cicerōnis sunt _____ omnium, quās umquam lēgī. (longus)

Petrarch's love for Laura was a classic example of love at first sight as well as unrequited love. The portrait captures the essence of Petrarch's description of the lovely, fair haired, and dignified woman who declined his interest as she was already married. His passion, unleashed in some 366 poems, consumed him even after Laura's death.

▶ EXERCISE 6

Translate into English. You will learn more about Petrarch's life from this passage.

Pater Petrarcae volēbat fīlium iūrisprūdentiam colere. Petrarca tamen dīcēbat nātūram hominum nōn semper esse bonam eamque inīquitātēs saepius amāre quam rēs iūstās. Petrarca igitur iūrisprūdentiae nōn erat studiōsus, sed mālēbat litterīs studēre. Itaque librōs vetustōs quaerere coepit, ut dē rēbus vetustīs disceret. Petrarca quoque multa scrīpsit. Scīmus eum amāvisse fēminam, cui nōmen erat Laura, dē quā carmina scrīpsit, sed numquam eam uxōrem dūxisse. Sōlus cum librīs suīs vīvēbat. Incolae urbis Rōmānae putābant eum esse poētam omnium celeberrimum, et corōnam lauream eī dedērunt.

corōna, ae, f. – crown
iūrisprūdentia, ae, f. – the science of law, jurisprudence
Laura, ae, f. – Laura
laureus, a, um – made of laurel

nātūra, ae, f. – nature
Petrarca, ae, m. – Petrarch
sōlus, a, um – alone

TALKING ABOUT A READING

WHAT IS THE BEST WAY OF LIFE? AND UNADAPTED LATIN: ATTICUS LEAVES ATHENS

QUAE VĪTAE RATIŌ SIT OPTIMA?

Mārcus: Petrarca dīcit Cicerōnem dēbuisse vītam rūsticam agere nec in urbe dē rē pūblicā semper pugnāre. At sī homō vītam rūsticam tantum agit, māgnam fāmam habēre vix potest. Ego volō esse āthlēta praeclārus, cūius fāma erit ingēns.

Christīna: Hominēs, quōrum fāma nōn est māgna, videntur mihi esse fēlīciōrēs. Sī homō bonam familiam habet, sī facit id quod vult, sī aliīs auxilium dare potest, hic homō est fēlīx. Fāma enim nōn sōlum rēs bonās, sed etiam rēs malās sēcum habet. Nam difficile est ab omnibus laudārī et homō quī ab omnibus laudārī vult, esse fēlīx nōn potest. Quid tū putās, Helena?

Helena: Ego volō esse artifex (*artist*) et nōmina artificum multī scīre dēbent.

Marīa: Vōs igitur duo, Mārce et Helena, fāmam petātis! Mihi autem satis est pecūniam habēre. Tunc omnia quae volō facere poterō. Erō fēlīx.

Christīna: Legāmus dē Atticō. Nam volō scīre quid sit factum, postquam Atticus nōluit cum Sullā Athēnīs discēdere et Rōmam petere. Putō Atticum fuisse virum fēlīcem, quia (*because*) aliīs auxilium semper dabat et multōs amīcōs ubīque habēbat.

Helena: Nōlī igitur exspectāre, sed ōrō ut legās.

ATTICUS LEAVES ATHENS

CORNĒLIĪ NEPŌTIS ATTICUS, 4.3–5

Atticus kept in contact with his friends and associates in Rome. He gave financial help to Cicero, when Cicero had to go into exile. Eventually civil disturbances died down in Rome. At that point, Atticus finally decided to leave Athens and move back to his fatherland.

1   3. Hīc complūrēs annōs morātus, cum et reī familiārī tantum operae
     daret, quantum nōn indīligēns dēbēret pater familiās, et omnia reliqua
     tempora aut litterīs aut Athēniēnsium reī pūblicae tribueret, nihilōminus
     amīcīs urbāna officia praestitit. 4. Nam et ad comitia eōrum ventitāvit,
5   et sī quae rēs māior ācta est, nōn dēfuit. Sīcut Cicerōnī in omnibus ēius
     perīculīs singulārem fidem praebuit; cui ex patriā fugientī HS ducenta
     et quīnquāgintā mīlia dōnāvit. 5. Tranquillātīs autem rēbus Rōmānīs
     remigrāvit Rōmam, ut opīnor, L. Cottā et L. Torquātō cōnsulibus.
     Quem discēdentem sīc ūniversa cīvitās Athēniēnsium prōsecūta est, ut
10   lacrimīs dēsīderiī futūrī dolōrem indicāret.

VOCABULARY

1   hīc (adv.) – here
     complūrēs, complūrium – not a few, several
     tantum . . . quantum . . . – so much . . . as . . .
     rēs familiāris – family estate
     operam dō + dative – give care to

2   indīligēns, indīligentis – careless, negligent
     reliquus, a, um – remaining
     familiās – archaic genitive singular of *familia*

3   aut . . . aut . . . – either . . . or . . .
     tribuō, ere, tribuī, tribūtum – to assign, give
     nihilōminus – nevertheless

4   officium, ī, n. – favor, duty
     praestō, āre, praestitī, — – fulfill, perform
     ventitō, āre, āvī, ātum – to go often

5   sī quae – if any
     māior (m./f.) – greater
     dēsum, dēesse, dēfuī, — – to be absent, fail
     sīcut – just as, just in the same way

6   singulāris, singulāre – special, unparalleled
     praebeō, ēre, praebuī, praebitum – to offer, give
     sesterius, ī, m. – sesterce, Roman silver coin
     ducenta et quīnquāgintā mīlia – 250,000
     HS – an abbreviation for *sestertiōrum*

7   dōnō, āre, āvī, ātum – to give, bestow
     tranquillō, āre, āvī, ātum – to make peaceful

8   remigrō, āre, āvī, ātum – to go back, return
     ut + indicative – as, when

9   quem = et eum
     discēdēns, discēdentis – leaving
     ūniversus, a, um – all together
     cīvitās, cīvitātis, f. – state, community of citizens

10   dēsīderium, ī, n. – grief for something absent
     futūrī – future (the future active participle of *sum*)
     indicō, āre, āvī, ātum – to show, indicate

READING NOTES

1   *Hīc complūrēs annōs morātus* The perfect participle *morātus* from the deponent verb *moror* (see Chapter 8) means "having stayed." The accusative of duration of time *complūrēs annōs* means "for several years."

1–2   *cum et . . . tantum operae daret* "although he gave so much care." The partitive genitive *operae* with *tantum* literally meaning "so much of care," translates more fluidly as "so much care."

2   *quantum nōn indīligēns dēbēret pater familiās* "as much as a head (father) of a family who was not careless ought to <give>."

3   *Athēniēnsium reī pūblicae* Often meaning "state, republic," here the singular collective phrase *rēs pūblica* means "the public affairs of the Athenians"

4   *amicīs* "for <his> friends."
     urbāna The noun *urbs* sometimes means "the city," namely "Rome." Likewise the adjective *urbānus, a, um* can mean "relating to Rome."
     comitia The *comitia* (*ōrum*, n. pl.) was the Roman assembly where magistrates were elected.

6   *cui ex patriā fugientī* Meaning "to him (i.e., Cicero) fleeing from <his> fatherland," *fugientī* is a present active participle (see Chapter 11).

6–7   *HS ducenta et quīnquāgintā mīlia* 250,000 sesterces, a very substantial sum of money.

7   *Tranquillātīs autem rēbus Rōmānīs* Literally, "<with> Roman affairs having been made peaceful," the ablative absolute (see Chapter 13) translates better as "when Roman affairs were made peaceful."

8   *ut opīnor* "as I suppose." *opīnor* is deponent.
     L. Cottā et L. Torquātō cōnsulibus The more fluid translation of this ablative absolute is "during the consulship of Lucius Cotta and Lucius Torquatus."

9   *Quem discēdentem . . . prōsecūta est* The phrase *quem discēdentem* means "him (i.e., Atticus) leaving." The deponent verb *prōsecūta est* means "accompanied."

9–10   *ut . . . indicāret* The result clause (see Chapter 14) means "so that . . . it was showing."

QUESTIONS ABOUT THE TEXT

Answer in complete Latin sentences.

1. Quās rēs cūrābat Atticus, dum erat Athēnīs?

2. Cūrābatne Atticus rēs Rōmānās, dum erat Athēnīs?

3. Cūrābatne amīcōs Rōmānōs eō tempore, quō erat Athēnīs?

4. Quid prō Cicerōne fēcit?

5. Quid factum est, postquam rēs Rōmānae sunt tranquillātae?

6. Quid Athēniēnsēs sentiēbant eō tempore, quō Atticus Athēnīs discēdēbat? Cūr?

QUAE VĪTAE RATIŌ SIT OPTIMA? CONTINUED

Mārcus: Ita, sciēbam Cicerōnem patriam suam relinquere dēbuisse et Graeciam petere. Nesciēbam tamen Atticum Cicerōnī auxilium dare voluisse.

Helena: Hoc est vērum. Atticus et Cicero erant amīcī et multās epistulās scrīpsērunt, quae ad nostrum tempus sunt servātae. Ex eīs possumus multa dē temporibus quibus vīxit Cicero discere. Nam Cicero nōlēbat rēs ab Atticō occultāre et omnia hīs in epistulīs dīcēbat.

Mārcus: Cicero saepe multa dīcit. Hoc quoque Petrarca dīxit in epistulā quam mīsit ad Cicerōnem.

Helena: At illa epistula nōn est vēra. Cum enim Petrarca scrībēbat, Cicero iam nōn erat in vītā.

Mārcus: Hominēs quī litterīs student semper vīvunt. Fortasse hoc putābat Petrarca.

CHAPTER 8

Irregular Comparatives and Superlatives; *Quam* with the Superlative of Adjectives and Adverbs; Deponent Verbs

Artist Paul Joseph Jamin (1853–1903) imagines Brennus, chief of the Gallic Senones gloating over the spoils of victory over the Romans.

MEMORĀBILE DICTŪ

Nōn enim tam praeclārum est scīre Latīnē quam turpe nescīre.

"It is not as praiseworthy to know Latin as it is shameful not to know it." (Cicero, *Brutus*, 37.140)

In this dialogue about oratory, Cicero makes this famous remark, when characterizing the unaffected speech of an orator a generation older than himself, named Marcus Antonius. Cicero observes that although this man gave the impression of speaking in a casual manner, his Latin was pure and correct.

READING

The humanists who championed the Renaissance movement in their support of Latin, however, were not merely motivated by admiration for classical antiquity but also by a more practical concern. In the thirteenth and fourteenth centuries CE a new more technical Latin developed in European universities. There was a serious danger that academic and scientific Latin might develop into a group of hybrid, mutually unintelligible jargons. Hence the humanists made it their mission to restore the international language of the European elite to its classical Roman norms. These efforts at humanistic reform of Latin were astoundingly successful. Latin remained the main language of the well educated and of the scientific community until the mid-eighteenth century. And from the mid-fifteenth century, the norm for nearly all who have written in Latin has been the revived classical Latin championed by the humanists. Even today, the basic Latin grammar taught in modern textbooks is basically that employed by Cicero.

One of the main leaders in the humanistic reform of Latin was Lorenzo Valla (1407–1457), a true "Renaissance man" who made many contributions to different branches of learning. Valla's great work on the Latin language was entitled *Ēlegantiārum linguae Latīnae librī sex* (*Six Books Concerning Proper Uses of the Latin Language*). In the study of rhetoric, the Latin word *ēlegantia* means "carefully chosen and accurate use of words and phrases." Valla's work on this topic was a vast treasure trove of idiomatic phrases and grammatical constructions found in classical Roman authors, all of which Valla's contemporaries could employ when writing and speaking Latin.

The reading below is adapted from the preface to Book I of Valla's *Ēlegantiae*. From the perspective of the European community of the educated elite, Valla demands that Europe's international language be restored to its pure and correct form, a situation which he represents allegorically as Rome, and thereby Latin, captured by the Gauls, who stand for corrupting, non-Latin influences on the language. What is more, Valla, who was not known for his modesty, represents himself as the great general who will expel the Gauls and restore the city. Valla's allegory is based on an incident in earlier, ancient Roman history, memorably narrated by Livy: in 390 BCE, the invading Gauls actually captured Rome, and occupied it for a while, until the Romans regained their city.

This fresco celebrates the Donation of Constantine who is shown presenting his crown to the enthroned Pope Sylvester I. Valla carefully studied the document associated with this event which was designed to legitimize the pope's political power. Valla exposed it as a forgery written in the eighth century CE.

ĒLEGANTIĀRUM LINGUAE LATĪNAE PRAEFĀTIŌ PRĪMA

1   Cum saepe dē nostrōrum māiōrum et aliārum gentium rēbus gestīs
     cōgitō, videntur mihi nostrī māiōrēs nōn sōlum imperiī sed etiam
     linguae prōpāgātiōne aliōs omnēs superāvisse. Cerēs laudābātur, quod
     frūmentum hominibus dederat; Minerva laudābātur, quod oleās

5   hominibus dederat; antīquī hominēs propter beneficia hominibus data
     colēbantur tamquam deī. Eratne minus ūtile linguam Latīnam gentibus
     dedisse, optimam frūgem et vērē dīvīnam, nec corporis sed animī
     cibum? Haec enim lingua gentēs illās omnibus artibus, quae līberālēs
     vocantur, īnstituit. Haec optimās lēgēs docuit. Haec viam ad omnem

10   sapientiam ostendit. Et māiōrēs nostrī aliōs omnēs hortābantur ut et
     Rōmae et in prōvinciīs Latīnē loquerentur.

     At imperium Rōmānum, tamquam onus ingrātum, gentēs
     nātiōnēsque prīdem abiēcērunt. Linguam Latīnam omnī aurō
     meliōrem putāvērunt, et sīcut rem dīvīnam ē caelō missam apud sē

15   servāvērunt! Āmīsimus, Rōmānī, āmīsimus imperium et dominātum:
     tamen per hunc splendidiōrem dominātum in māgnā adhūc parte orbis
     terrārum rēgnāmus. Nostra est Ītalia, nostra Gallia, nostra Hispānia,
     Germānia, Pannonia, Dalmatia, Illyricum multaeque aliae nātiōnēs! Ibi
     enim Rōmānum imperium est, ubicumque Rōmāna lingua dominātur!

20   Quis autem litterārum bonīque pūblicī studiōsus ā lacrimīs
     temperābit, cum vīderit linguam Latīnam eō in statū esse quō ōlim
     Rōma capta ā Gallīs? Quoūsque, Quirītēs—litterārum vocō et linguae
     Latīnae cultōrēs, quī vērī Quirītēs sunt—quoūsque, inquam, urbem
     nostram, parentem litterārum ā Gallīs captam esse patiēminī, id est

25   linguam Latīnam ā barbarīs esse oppressam? Parābō exercitum, quem
     in hostēs dūcam! Animōs vestrōs firmābō. Ībō in aciem! Ībō prīmus!

READING VOCABULARY

abiciō, ere, abiēcī, abiectum – to throw away

aciēs, aciēī, f. – line of battle, sharp edge

*adhūc (adv.) – still, up to this time

*antīquus, a, um – ancient

*ars, artis, f. – science, art, skill

barbarus, ī, m. – barbarian ‡

beneficium, ī, n. – benefit, favor, service

bonum pūblicum, n. – the public good

Cerēs, Cereris, f. – Ceres‡

cultor, cultōris, m. – fosterer, supporter, cultivator

Dalmatia, ae, f. – Dalmatia‡

dominātus, dominātūs, m. – rule, sovereignty

*dominātur – rules

ēlegantia, ae, f. – precision in language, elegance

frūx, frūgis, f. – crop, produce of the earth

frūmentum, ī, n. – grain

Gallia, ae, f. – a region of modern France

Gallī, ōrum, m. pl. – Gauls ‡

Germānia, ae, f. – Germany‡

Hispānia, ae, f. – Spain

*hortābantur ut loquerentur – they were exhorting to speak

ībō – I shall go

id est – namely, that is to say‡

Illyricum, ī, n. – Illyricum‡

ingrātus, a, um – unwelcome, unpleasant

īnstituō, ere, īnstituī, īnstitūtum + accusative + ablative – to train or educate someone in a skill

Ītalia, ae, f. – Italy

*Latīnus, a, um – Latin, pertaining to Latin

*Latīnē (adv.) – in Latin

līberālis, līberāle – befitting a free man, generous; artēs līberālēs – the liberal arts‡

*lingua, ae, f. – language, tongue (as physical part of the mouth)

*māior, māius – bigger, greater; māiōrēs, um, m. pl. - ancestors‡

nostrī – Valla means the ancient Romans

*melior, melius – better

Minerva, ae, f. – Minerva‡

*minus (adv.) – less

nātiō, nātiōnis, f. – a race of people, tribe

olea, ae, f. – olive

ōlim (adv.) – once upon a time

onus, oneris, n. – burden

*optimus, a, um – best

orbis, is, m. – circle, disc, globe
    orbis terrārum – the world

Pannonia, ae, f. – Pannonia‡

*patiēminī – you will tolerate

praefātiō, praefātiōnis, f. – preface

prīdem (adv.) – long ago

prōpāgātiō, prōpāgātiōnis, f. – spreading, propagation

prōvincia, ae, f. – province (territorial), any duty or sphere of activity (not territorial)

Quirītēs, Quirītium, m. pl. – Roman citizens‡

quod (conj.) – because

quoūsque (adv.) – how far, to what extent

rēgnō, āre, āvī, ātum – to reign, rule

rēs (rērum) gestae, ārum, f. pl. – things done, history‡

sapientia, ae, f. – wisdom

sē – here (as very often) the reflexive pronoun of the plural meaning "themselves"

splendidus, a, um – illustrious, distinguished, shining

status, statūs, m. – condition, state, attitude

superō, āre, āvī, ātum – to surpass, conquer

temperō, āre, āvī, ātum āb + ablative – to refrain from

ubicumque (adv.) – wherever

vērē (adv.) – truly

*Words marked with an asterisk will need to be memorized later in the chapter.

‡Additional information about the words marked with the double dagger will be in the **Take Note** section that follows the Reading Vocabulary.

TAKE NOTE

artēs līberālēs The liberal arts typically consisted of grammar, rhetoric, and dialectic (*trivium*); and geometry, arithmetic, music, and astronomy (*quadrivium*).

barbarus, ī, m. Originally this word primarily meant "non-Greek" or "non-Roman;" by Valla's time it meant not only "foreign," but "uneducated."

Cerēs, Cereris f. Ceres was the goddess of grain and agriculture; in Greek she was called Demeter.

Dalmatia The region called Dalmatia was a part of the Roman Empire next to Illyricum on the east coast of the Adriatic Sea. It corresponds in part to the area today called Croatia.

Gallī, ōrum, m. pl. The Gauls were the inhabitants of France: in antiquity they were Celtic, until they mingled with the Romans after the conquest of Gaul by Julius Caesar in the first century BCE.

Germānia The region of Europe called Germany approximately corresponds to modern Germany.

id est This is a common phrase used to make a previous assertion more specific and is sometimes abbreviated i.e.

Illyricum Illyricum is a region situated on the west coast of what is today the Balkan peninsula.

māiorēs, um, m. pl. The idea that one's elders were morally superior and worthy of reverence, especially the ancestors of great families, was very prevalent in Roman society. Hence the use of the word *māiorēs* which essentially means "the greater ones" to be equivalent to "ancestors" is a logical development.

Minerva Minerva is the goddess of wisdom and war; in Greek she is called Athena. She gave the Athenians the gift of the olive tree.

Pannonia This is a region which approximately corresponds to modern Hungary.

Quirītēs, Quirītium, m. pl. Roman citizens called themselves *Quirītēs*. According to legend, the primitive Romans took this name when they combined with the Sabines; originally the *Quirītēs* were inhabitants of a Sabine town.

rēs (rērum) gestae, ārum, f. pl. things done, history: the phrase *Rēs gestae* became a common title for historical or annalistic works in the Roman Empire itself from the time of Augustus onward and especially during the Middle Ages.

COMPREHENSION QUESTIONS

1. Why does Valla consider the Latin language to be a "divine" gift?

2. What is Valla's attitude to the political entity that was the ancient Roman Empire?

3. In what sense does Valla consider that the Roman Empire still exists in his own time?

4. To what historical situation does Valla compare the condition of the Latin language in his day, and why?

5. How did Valla establish philology as an academic discipline?

LANGUAGE FACT I
IRREGULAR COMPARATIVES AND SUPERLATIVES

In the chapter reading passage you noticed three comparative words that are not derived from the positive form of adjectives and adverbs according to the typical pattern you just learned in Chapter 6:

> *māiōr, māiōris*, "greater:" the comparative of *māgnus*;
>
> *minus*, "less:" the comparative adverb (the same form is the neuter singular comparative adjective) of *parvus*;
>
> *melior, meliōris*, "better:" the comparative of *bonus*.

The same passage also contains a superlative that is clearly not derived from the base of the positive adjective:

> *optimus, a, um*, "best:" the superlative of *bonus*.

A whole group of irregular comparatives and superlatives must be learned, since they are all commonly found in works written in Latin.

Common Irregular Comparatives and Superlatives		
Positive degree	**Comparative degree**	**Superlative degree**
bonus, a, um – good	melior, melius – better	optimus, a, um – best
malus, a, um – bad	pēior, pēius – worse	pessimus, a, um – worst
māgnus, a, um – great	māior, māius – greater	maximus, a, um – greatest
parvus, a, um – small	minor, minus – smaller	minimus, a, um – smallest
multus, a, um – much	plūs (neuter noun) – more	plūrimus, a, um – most
multī, ae, a – many	plūrēs, plūra – more	plūrimī, ae, a – most

BY THE WAY

The comparative adverb of *māgnus* is *magis*, which means "more greatly" or "rather."

The comparative and superlative forms above, though not regularly derived from the base of the positive adjective, are declined according to the patterns for comparatives and superlatives you have already learned.

Declension of pēior, pēius

	Singular		Plural	
	Masculine and Feminine	Neuter	Masculine and Feminine	Neuter
Nominative	pēior	pēius	pēiōrēs	pēiōra
Genitive	pēiōris	pēiōris	pēiōrum	pēiōrum
Dative	pēiōrī	pēiōrī	pēiōribus	pēiōribus
Accusative	pēiōrem	pēius	pēiōrēs	pēiōra
Ablative	pēiōre	pēiōre	pēiōribus	pēiōribus
Vocative	pēior	pēius	pēiōrēs	pēiōra

Declension of plūs, plūris

	Singular	Plural	
	Neuter	Masculine and Feminine	Neuter
Nominative	plūs	plūrēs	plūra
Genitive	plūris	plūrium	plūrium
Dative	—	plūribus	plūribus
Accusative	plūs	plūrēs	plūra
Ablative	(plūre)	plūribus	plūribus
Vocative	—	plūrēs	plūra

BY THE WAY

Plūs has only a neuter singular. Both the dative and vocative singular do not occur, and the ablative singular rarely occurs. Also unlike other comparatives, the genitive plural of *plūrēs* ends in –**ium**.

Note that *plūs, plūris* is a neuter noun in the singular, which is typically modified by a genitive, e.g., *plūs aquae* "more (of) water." This is known as a genitive of the whole or partitive genitive. In the plural, however, *plūrēs* is an adjective, e.g., *plūrēs mīlitēs* "more soldiers."

Minerva laudābātur, quod oleās hominibus dederat.

▶ EXERCISE 1

Translate the English into Latin and the Latin into English. The Reading Vocabulary may be consulted. Translate the English word "more" with the correct form of *plūs*.

1. Dē plūribus rēbus cōgitō.

2. Ceres gave more grain to humans.

3. I found more letters written by you, Marcus Tullius.

4. Māiōrēs nostrī linguam Latīnam plūribus gentibus dedērunt.

5. Because of the Latin language we have more wisdom.

6. Ē plūribus ūnum.

7. Propter linguam Latīnam apud ("among") plūrēs nātiōnēs nunc rēgnāmus.

8. Plūs honōris et glōriae habēre voluit.

VOCABULARY TO LEARN

NOUNS

ars, artis, f. – science, art, skill

lingua, ae, f. – language, tongue (as physical part of the mouth)

plūs, plūris, n. – more

ADJECTIVES

antīquus, a, um – ancient

Latīnus, a, um – Latin, pertaining to Latin

māior, māius – greater

maximus, a, um – greatest

melior, melius – better

minimus, a, um – smallest

minor, minus – smaller

optimus, a, um – best

pēior, pēius – worse

pessimus, a, um – worst

plūrimus, a, um – most

plūrēs, plūra – more

VERBS

dominor, dominārī, dominātus sum – to dominate, rule

hortor, hortārī, hortātus sum – to exhort, urge

loquor, loquī, locūtus sum – to speak

partior, partīrī, partītus sum – to divide, distribute

patior, patī, passus sum – to endure, tolerate, suffer

sequor, sequī, secūtus sum – to follow

vereor, verērī, veritus sum – to fear, respect

ADVERBS

adhūc – still, up to this time

Latīnē – in Latin

magis – more

minus – less

STUDY TIP

Remember to distinguish between:

> Timeō – fear, be afraid
>
> Vereor – fear, respect, be in awe of

▶ EXERCISE 2

Find the English derivatives in the following sentences based on the Vocabulary to Learn of this chapter. Write the corresponding Latin word.

1. It is difficult for us now to imagine what conditions of daily life must have been like even for well-off people in ancient times.

2. The word "art" in its most narrow sense is restricted to painting and sculpture. In its wider meaning the word can refer to all the skills by which people give creative expression to their culture.

3. Although my uncle is a very loquacious man, I always listen attentively to whatever he says.

4. A person interested in the welfare of society as a whole knows we must maximize the resources available to the poorest members of society.

5. A patient person will persevere until s/he achieves success.

6. Pessimists, who assume the worst outcome for everything, create unnecessary obstacles for themselves.

7. My uncle achieved the rank of major in the army.

8. Avoid words that have a pejorative meaning.

9. Linguists study the structure and evolution of all languages.

10. In ancient warfare, it was customary before a battle for a general to exhort his troops to put forth their supreme effort.

11. You all know that three plus two equal five.

12. Minors are not allowed to purchase or consume alcoholic beverages.

13. Do not minimize the importance of luck in human life!

14. Although economists think inflation is too high now, we expect an amelioration of economic conditions next year.

15. Optimists, who expect the best, are likely to have a higher success rate in all their endeavors.

16. These episodes follow the first installment sequentially.

17. In a painting of a seascape, of course, the dominant color is likely to be blue.

18. Ten minus five equal five.

▶ EXERCISE 3

Change all the positive adjectives into comparatives, and all the comparative adjectives into superlatives. Translate the changed sentences.

Example: Epistulās multās lēgī.
Epistulās plūrēs lēgī.
I have read more letters.

1. Carmen tuum bonum mihi vidētur.
2. Plūrēs gentēs apud sē linguam Latīnam didicērunt.
3. Multīs magistrīs ōtium numquam prōmittitur.
4. Estne glōria Rōmānōrum parva?
5. Cibum hūius gentis malum esse crēdimus.
6. Gallī plūs artium habēre vidēbantur.

LANGUAGE FACT II

QUAM WITH THE SUPERLATIVE OF ADJECTIVES AND ADVERBS

When *quam* is linked to a superlative adjective or adverb, it means "as . . . as possible."

For example, *quam optimē* means "as well as possible," and *quam fortissimus* means "as brave as possible."

Here are some other examples:

> *quam vehementissimē* – as strongly as possible . . .
>
> *quam pulcherrima* – as beautiful as possible . . .
>
> *quam plūrimī* – as many as possible . . .

You have also learned the use of *quam* with comparatives and about *quam* as an accusative singular relative pronoun. Look at the example of each use of *quam*.

> *Haec ars est ūtilior quam illa.*   (*Quam* + comparative)
> This skill is more useful than that one.
>
> *Rēgēs quam ōrnātissimī vidēbantur esse.*   (*Quam* + superlative)
> The kings seemed to be as adorned as possible.
>
> *Haec est rēgīna quam laudāvī.*   (*Quam* as relative pronoun)
> This is the queen whom I praised.

▶ EXERCISE 4

Translate into Latin.

1. As many students as possible should learn the ancient and useful Latin language.

2. More nations used to learn the Latin language than now.

3. We ought to find the best possible teachers for these students.

4. This is the peace which we were seeking.

5. Our armies want to join us as quickly as possible.

6. The king had three daughters, of which the first was beautiful, the second more beautiful, <and> the third most beautiful.

7. Glory is better than fame.

8. There are many languages among you, but more among us.

9. The glory which we have is better than fame.

Valla's work as a philologist and as a theologian regularly earned him academic enemies. King
Alfonso V of Aragon, a humanist, welcomed Valla to his court in Naples making him his Latin secretary in 1435.
Alfonso celebrated his triumphal entrance into Naples in 1443 by adding a triumphal arch (in white) to the Castello Nuovo.

LANGUAGE FACT III

DEPONENT VERBS

In the chapter reading passage you noticed several sentences with new verbs—and these new verbs are distinctive because they have **passive** forms but **active** meanings.

> *Et māiōrēs nostrī aliōs omnēs **hortābantur** ut et Rōmae et in prōvinciīs Latīnē **loquerentur**.*
> "And our ancestors **urged** all the other peoples to **speak** Latin both at Rome and in the provinces."

> *Ibi enim Rōmānum imperium est, ubicumque Rōmāna lingua **dominātur**!*
> "For wherever the Roman language **is dominant**, there is the Roman empire!"

> *. . . Quōusque, inquam, urbem nostram, parentem litterārum ā Gallīs captam esse **patiēminī** . . . ?*
> "To what extent, I say, will **you put up with** <the fact that> our city, the parent of literature, has been captured by the Gauls?"

Some deponent verbs are very common and thus it will be useful to become familiar with them.

Common Deponent Verbs

arbitror, arbitrārī, arbitrātus sum – to think

dominor, dominārī, dominātus sum – to dominate, rule

hortor, hortārī, hortātus sum – to exhort, urge

loquor, loquī, locūtus sum – to speak

partior, partīrī, partītus sum – to divide, distribute

patior, patī, passus sum – to endure, tolerate, suffer

proficīscor, proficīscī, profectus sum – set out, depart

sequor, sequī, secūtus sum – to follow

vereor, verērī, veritus sum – to fear, respect

BY THE WAY

The word "deponent" comes from the Latin verb *dēpōnere*, "to put aside." So you can think of deponent verbs as having "put aside" their active forms but having kept their active meanings.

You already know the endings of deponent verbs because you have learned the passive forms of verbs in all the tenses and conjugations. As you can see from the list above, there are deponent verbs in all the conjugations.

Conjugation of hortor (First Conjugation)

Present

Indicative		Subjunctive
hortor	I exhort	horter
hortāris	you exhort	hortēris
hortātur	s/he exhorts	hortētur
hortāmur	we exhort	hortēmur
hortāminī	you (pl.) exhort	hortēminī
hortantur	they exhort	hortentur

Imperfect

Indicative		Subjunctive
hortābar	I was exhorting	hortārer
hortābāris	you were exhorting	hortārēris
hortābātur	s/he was exhorting	hortārētur
hortābāmur	we were exhorting	hortārēmur
hortābāminī	you (pl.) were exhorting	hortārēminī
hortābantur	they were exhorting	hortārentur

Future

Indicative	
hortābor	I will exhort
hortāberis	you will exhort
hortābitur	s/he will exhort
hortābimur	we will exhort
hortābiminī	you (pl.) will exhort
hortabuntur	they will exhort

Perfect

Indicative		Subjunctive
hortātus, a, um sum	I (have) exhorted	hortātus, a, um sim
hortātus, a, um es	you (have) exhorted	hortātus, a, um sīs
hortātus, a, um est	s/he (has) exhorted	hortātus, a, um sit
hortātī, ae, a sumus	we (have) exhorted	hortātī, ae, a sīmus
hortātī, ae, a estis	you (pl.) (have) exhorted	hortātī, ae, a sītis
hortātī, ae, a sunt	they (have) exhorted	hortātī, ae, a sint

Pluperfect

Indicative		Subjunctive
hortātus, a, um eram	I had exhorted	hortātus, a, um essem
hortātus, a, um erās	you had exhorted	hortātus, a, um essēs
hortātus, a, um erat	s/he had exhorted	hortātus, a, um esset
hortātī, ae, a erāmus	we had exhorted	hortātī, ae, a essēmus
hortātī, ae, a erātis	you (pl.) had exhorted	hortātī, ae, a essētis
hortātī, ae, a erant	they had exhorted	hortātī, ae, a essent

Future Perfect

Indicative	
hortātus, a, um erō	I will have exhorted
hortātus, a, um eris	you will have exhorted
hortātus, a, um erit	s/he will have exhorted
hortātī, ae, a erimus	we will have exhorted
hortātī, ae, a eritis	you (pl.) will have exhorted
hortātī, ae, a erunt	they will have exhorted

Infinitives

hortārī (present)	to exhort
hortātus, a, um, esse (perfect)	to have exhorted
hortātūrus, a, um, esse (future)	to be about to exhort

Participles

hortātus, a, um (perfect)	having exhorted
hortātūrus, a, um (future)	being about to exhort

Conjugation of vereor (Second Conjugation)
Present

Indicative		Subjunctive
vereor	I fear	verear
verēris	you fear	vereāris
verētur	s/he fears	vereātur
verēmur	we fear	vereāmur
verēminī	you (pl.) fear	vereāminī
verentur	they fear	vereantur

Imperfect

Indicative

verēbar	I was fearing
verēbāris	you were fearing
verēbātur	s/he was fearing
verēbāmur	we were fearing
verēbāminī	you (pl.) were fearing
verēbantur	they were fearing

Subjunctive

verērer
verērēris
verērētur
verērēmur
verērēminī
verērentur

Future

Indicative

verēbor	I will fear
verēberis	you will fear
verēbitur	s/he will fear
verēbimur	we will fear
verēbiminī	you (pl.) will fear
verēbuntur	they will fear

Perfect

Indicative

veritus, a, um sum	I (have) feared
veritus, a, um es	you (have) feared
veritus, a, um est	s/he (has) feared
veritī, ae, a sumus	we (have) feared
veritī, ae, a estis	you (pl.) (have) feared
veritī, ae, a sunt	they (have) feared

Subjunctive

veritus, a, um sim
veritus, a, um sīs
veritus, a, um sit
veritī, ae, a sīmus
veritī, ae, a sītis
veritī, ae, a sint

Pluperfect

Indicative

veritus, a, um eram	I had feared
veritus, a, um erās	you had feared
veritus, a, um erat	s/he had feared
veritī, ae, a erāmus	we had feared
veritī, ae, a erātis	you (pl.) had feared
veritī, ae, a erant	they had feared

Subjunctive

veritus, a, um essem
veritus, a, um essēs
veritus, a, um esset
veritī, ae, a essēmus
veritī, ae, a essētis
veritī, ae, a essent

Future Perfect

Indicative

veritus, a, um erō	I will have feared
veritus, a, um eris	you will have feared
veritus, a, um erit	s/he will have feared
veritī, ae, a erimus	we will have feared
veritī, ae, a eritis	you (pl.) will have feared
veritī, ae, a erunt	they will have feared

Infinitives

verērī (present)	to fear
veritus, a, um, esse (perfect)	to have feared
veritūrus, a, um, esse (future)	to be about to fear

Participles

veritus, a, um (perfect)	having feared
veritūrus, a, um (future)	being about to fear

Conjugation of sequor (Third Conjugation)

Present

Indicative		**Subjunctive**
sequor	I follow	sequar
sequeris	you follow	sequāris
sequitur	s/he follows	sequātur
sequimur	we follow	sequāmur
sequiminī	you (pl.) follow	sequāminī
sequuntur	they follow	sequantur

Imperfect

Indicative		**Subjunctive**
sequēbar	I was following	sequerer
sequēbāris	you were following	sequerēris
sequēbātur	s/he was following	sequerētur
sequēbāmur	we were following	sequerēmur
sequēbāminī	you (pl.) were following	sequerēminī
sequēbantur	they were following	sequerentur

Future

Indicative

sequar	I will follow
sequēris	you will follow
sequētur	s/he will follow
sequēmur	we will follow
sequēminī	you (pl.) will follow
sequentur	they will follow

Perfect

Indicative

secūtus, a, um sum	I (have) followed
secūtus, a, um es	you (have) followed
secūtus, a, um est	s/he (has) followed
secūtī, ae, a sumus	we (have) followed
secūtī, ae, a estis	you (pl.) (have) followed
secūtī, ae, a sunt	they (have) followed

Subjunctive

secūtus, a, um sim
secūtus, a, um sīs
secūtus, a, um sit
secūtī, ae, a sīmus
secūtī, ae, a sītis
secūtī, ae, a sint

Pluperfect

Indicative

secūtus, a, um eram	I had followed
secūtus, a, um erās	you had followed
secūtus, a, um erat	s/he had followed
secūtī, ae, a erāmus	we had followed
secūtī, ae, a erātis	you (pl.) had followed
secūtī, ae, a erant	they had followed

Subjunctive

secūtus, a, um essem
secūtus, a, um essēs
secūtus, a, um esset
secūtī, ae, a essēmus
secūtī, ae, a essētis
secūtī, ae, a essent

Future Perfect

Indicative

secūtus, a, um erō	I will have followed
secūtus, a, um eris	you will have followed
secūtus, a, um erit	s/he will have followed
secūtī, ae, a erimus	we will have followed
secūtī, ae, a eritis	you (pl.) will have followed
secūtī, ae, a erunt	they will have followed

Infinitives

sequī (present)	to follow
secūtus, a, um, esse (perfect)	to have followed
secūtūrus, a, um, esse (future)	to be about to follow

Participles	
secūtus, a, um (perfect)	having followed
secūtūrus, a, um (future)	being about to follow

Conjugation of partior (Fourth Conjugation)

Present

Indicative		Subjunctive
partior	I divide	partiar
partīris	you divide	partiāris
partītur	s/he divides	partiātur
partīmur	we divide	partiāmur
partīminī	you (pl.) divide	partiāminī
partiuntur	they divide	partiantur

Imperfect

Indicative		Subjunctive
partiēbar	I was dividing	partīrer
partiēbāris	you were dividing	partīrēris
partiēbātur	s/he was dividing	partīrētur
partiēbāmur	we were dividing	partīrēmur
partiēbāminī	you (pl.) were dividing	partīrēminī
partiēbantur	they were dividing	partīrentur

Future

Indicative	
partiar	I will divide
partiēris	you will divide
partiētur	s/he will divide
partiēmur	we will divide
partiēminī	you (pl.) will divide
partientur	they will divide

Perfect

Indicative		Subjunctive
partītus, a, um sum	I (have) divided	partītus, a, um sim
partītus, a, um es	you (have) divided	partītus, a, um sīs
partītus, a, um est	s/he (has) divided	partītus, a, um sit
partītī, ae, a sumus	we (have) divided	partītī, ae, a sīmus
partītī, ae, a estis	you (pl.) (have) divided	partītī, ae, a sītis
partītī, ae, a sunt	they (have) divided	partītī, ae, a sint

Pluperfect

Indicative   **Subjunctive**

partītus, a, um eram	I had divided	partītus, a, um essem
partītus, a, um erās	you had divided	partītus, a, um essēs
partītus, a, um erat	s/he had divided	partītus, a, um esset
partītī, ae, a erāmus	we had divided	partītī, ae, a essēmus
partītī, ae, a erātis	you (pl.) had divided	partītī, ae, a essētis
partītī, ae, a erant	they had divided	partītī, ae, a essent

Future Perfect

Indicative

partītus, a, um erō	I will have divided
partītus, a, um eris	you will have divided
partītus, a, um erit	s/he will have divided
partītī, ae, a erimus	we will have divided
partītī, ae, a eritis	you (pl.) will have divided
partītī, ae, a erunt	they will have divided

Infinitives

partīrī (present)	to divide
partītus, a, um, esse (perfect)	to have divided
partītūrus, a, um, esse (future)	to be about to divide

Participles

| partītus, a, um (perfect) | having divided |
| partītūrus, a, um (future) | being about to divide |

Conjugation of patior (Third Conjugation –iō Verbs)

Present

Indicative   **Subjunctive**

patior	I endure	patiar
pateris	you endure	patiāris
patitur	s/he endures	patiātur
patimur	we endure	patiāmur
patiminī	you (pl.) endure	patiāminī
patiuntur	they endure	patiantur

Imperfect

Indicative		Subjunctive
patiēbar	I was enduring	paterer
patiēbāris	you were enduring	paterēris
patiēbātur	s/he was enduring	paterētur
patiēbāmur	we were enduring	paterēmur
patiēbāminī	you (pl.) were enduring	paterēminī
patiēbantur	they were enduring	paterentur

Future

Indicative	
patiar	I will endure
patiēris	you will endure
patiētur	s/he will endure
patiēmur	we will endure
patiēminī	you (pl.) will endure
patientur	they will endure

Perfect

Indicative		Subjunctive
passus, a, um sum	I (have) endured	passus, a, um sim
passus, a, um es	you (have) endured	passus, a, um sīs
passus, a, um est	s/he (has) endured	passus, a, um sit
passī, ae, a sumus	we (have) endured	passī, ae, a sīmus
passī, ae, a estis	you (pl.) (have) endured	passī, ae, a sītis
passī, ae, a sunt	they (have) endured	passī, ae, a sint

Pluperfect

Indicative		Subjunctive
passus, a, um eram	I had endured	passus, a, um essem
passus, a, um erās	you had endured	passus, a, um essēs
passus, a, um erat	s/he had endured	passus, a, um esset
passī, ae, a erāmus	we had endured	passī, ae, a essēmus
passī, ae, a erātis	you (pl.) had endured	passī, ae, a essētis
passī, ae, a erant	they had endured	passī, ae, a essent

Future Perfect

Indicative

passus, a, um erō	I will have endured
passus, a, um eris	you will have endured
passus, a, um erit	s/he will have endured
passī, ae, a erimus	we will have endured
passī, ae, a eritis	you (pl.) will have endured
passī, ae, a erunt	they will have endured

Infinitives

patī (present)	to endure
passus, a, um, esse (perfect)	to have endured
passūrus, a, um, esse (future)	to be about to endure

Participles

passus, a, um (perfect)	having endured
passūrus, a, um (future)	being about to endure

BY THE WAY

With each deponent verb, you will learn the first person singular of the present passive indicative and the present passive infinitive. These two forms will give you an indication of the conjugation of the verb and identify it as a deponent.

hortor, hortārī – first conjugation (vowel **ā** in the infinitive)

vereor, verērī – second conjugation (vowel **ē** in the infinitive)

sequor, sequī – third conjugation (infinitive formed only with **ī**)

partior, partīrī – fourth conjugation (vowel **ī** in the infinitive)

patior, patī – third conjugation –*iō* verbs (infinitive formed only with **ī**; first person singular of the present passive indicative looks like fourth conjugation)

▶ EXERCISE 5

Identify the conjugation of each of the following forms.

Example: partīrī   fourth conjugation

1. hortātī estis
2. patiēbāris
3. dominārī
4. loqueris

5. sequimur
6. partiar
7. verētur

STUDY TIP

There are a few exceptions to the rule that deponents have passive forms with active meanings.

1. The present and future participles are active forms with active meanings.

2. The future infinitive is an active form with an active meaning.

BY THE WAY

The perfect participle is a perfect passive form with an **active** meaning. So *secūtus* means "having followed," while *amātus* means "having been loved." Thus you might reasonably ask "How do I say "having loved" in Latin?" You can do this by using one of a variety of other constructions: for example, you could say *postquam amāvit*, which means literally "after s/he loved."

▶ EXERCISE 6

Translate into Latin.

1. We have followed.

2. Let us talk (use *loquī*).

3. They were dominating.

4. You (sg.) will share.

5. Do not put up (pl.) with injustice.

6. I shall not fear the enemies (use *verērī*).

7. We had exhorted the consul.

8. <People> being about to divide the food.

9. I believe the soldiers are going to follow me.

10. Having exhorted the soldiers, I shall follow you.

Valla served at the University of Pavia as a professor of eloquence. One of the oldest universities of Europe, it was established in 1361 by the Visconti family. A school of higher learning, however, had served Pavia since 825. A series of inner courtyards and balconies in the older buildings keeps students protected.

▶ EXERCISE 7

Fill in the blanks with the correct form of the verb in parentheses. Translate each sentence. The Reading Vocabulary may be consulted.

Example: Volō _____. (loquor)

Volō loquī.

I want to speak.

1. Valla nōs _____ ut linguam Latīnam parentem litterārum discāmus. (hortor)

2. Nōs viam ad omnem sapientiam semper _____, sī linguam Latīnam bene didicerimus. (sequor)

3. Illā aetāte, quā vīvēbat Valla, quamquam gentēs Eurōpaeae imperium Rōmānum iam abiēcerant, lingua tamen Latīna multīs in terrīs etiam tum _____. (dominor)

   quamquam (conj.) – although   Eurōpaeus, a, um – European

4. Valla librum dē linguā Latīnā scrīpsit, nē hominēs sapientiam perdī _____. (patior)

5. Sī ducem fortissimum _____, lībertātem habēbimus. (sequor)

6. Sī urbem nostram iterum habēre potuerimus, Gallōs numquam _____. (vereor)

   iterum (adv.) – again

▶ EXERCISE 8

The following passage is adapted from the Roman historian Livy's narrative of the looting of Rome by the Gauls in 390 BCE. It comes from *Ab urbe conditā* (5.41). While young Romans of military age retreated to high ground to defend the citadel and women with children fled from the city, many of the old men of noble status decided to remain in their homes and face the invaders with dignity.

Translate into English.

Seniōrēs domōs regressī adventum hostium firmātō ad mortem animō exspectābant. Vestīmentīs ōrnātissimīs indūtī iānuās aperuērunt et maximā cum dignitāte sedēbant. Gallī urbem intrāvērunt templaque deōrum cōnspiciēbant. Custōdēs posuērunt nē Rōmānī impetum in sē facerent. Tunc aliī aliās viās in urbe secūtī sunt ut praedam peterent. Quīdam ē Gallīs domōs prīncipum apertās vidēbant. Prīmō magis aedificia nōbilium aperta quam casās pauperum clausās verēbantur. Nam prīncipēs vidēre poterant augustōs, quī in ātriīs sedēbant gravissimī māiestāteque deōrum similēs vidēbantur. Cum autem quīdam Gallus Rōmānī sedentis barbam tangere temptāvisset, senex Rōmānus eum scīpiōne percussit. Tunc īrā mōtī Gallī vehementissimā Rōmānōs occīdērunt et urbem vastāre coepērunt.

adventus, adventūs, m. – arrival	nōbilēs, nōbilium, m. pl. – nobles
aedificium, ī, n. – building	percutiō, ere, percussī, percussum – to strike
alius . . . alius . . . – one . . . another . . .	pōnere custōdēs – to station guards
ātrium, ī, n. – the entry hall of a Roman house	praeda, ae, f. – booty, prey
augustus, a, um – venerable, august, majestic	prīnceps, prīncipis, m. – leading citizen
clausus, a, um – closed	quīdam, quaedam, quoddam – a certain
cum temptāvisset = postquam temptāvit	regredior, regredī, regressus sum – to go back
dignitās, dignitātis, f. – dignity (this is an ablative of manner)	scīpiō, scīpiōnis, m. – staff
iānua, ae, f. – door	sē – them(selves)
indūtus, a, um + ablative – clad, dressed in	sedēns, sedentis – sitting
Gallī, ōrum, m. pl. – Gauls	senior, seniōris, m./f. – elder, older (comparative of *senex*)
māiestās, māiestātis, f. – majesty (the ablative here expresses the respect in which they were like gods)	vastō, āre, āvī, ātum – lay waste, ravage

TALKING ABOUT A READING

ABOUT LATIN AND ABOUT OTHER LANGUAGES AND UNADAPTED LATIN: ATTICUS AND HIS UNCLE

DĒ LINGUĀ LATĪNĀ DĒQUE ALIĪS LINGUĪS

Christīna: Laurentius Valla bene loquitur dē linguā Latīnā. Nam lingua Latīna est optima atque pulcherrima.

Marīa: Ego autem putō linguam Hispānam (*Spanish*) esse ūtiliōrem. Nam plūrēs hominēs linguā Hispānā loquuntur.

Helena: At nōnne (*don't you*) intellegis, Marīa, linguam Hispānam esse linguae Latīnae fīliam et linguam Latīnam esse mātrem nōn sōlum linguae Hispānae, sed etiam linguae Ītalicae (*Italian*), linguae Gallicae (*French*), linguae Lūsitānicae (*Portuguese*) et aliārum linguārum? Sī linguam Latīnam bene scīs, facilius est aliās linguās discere.

Mārcus: Putō multōs hominēs linguā Sinēnsī (*Chinese*) nunc loquī. Fortasse etiam linguam Sinēnsem discere dēbēmus.

Christīna: Hoc est vērum. Sī autem linguam Latīnam discimus, discimus quoque dē cultū cīvīlī (*culture*) Eurōpaeō (*European*) et antīquō et recentiōre (*of more recent times*). Cultus cīvīlis Americānus (*American*) ex cultū cīvīlī Eurōpaeō tandem (*ultimately*) vēnit. Sī igitur dē linguā Latīnā discimus, plūra dē nōbīs discere possumus.

Helena: Discāmus dē linguā Latīnā: dē Atticō nunc legāmus!

Mārcus: Quōmodo (*how*) tantam pecūniam (*money*) accēpit Atticus?

Marīa: Avunculum dīvitem habuit, quī eum hērēdem fēcit.

Mārcus: Itaque cāsū (*by chance*), nōn virtūte dīvitiās accēpit.

Marīa: Nōn. Virtūte. Audiās verba Nepōtis.

ATTICUS AND HIS UNCLE

CORNĒLIĪ NEPŌTIS ATTICUS, 5, 1–2

Atticus befriended his maternal uncle, which was no easy task, since this man had a very difficult personality. As it happened, this uncle was a wealthy man, and when he died, Atticus was the heir to three-quarters of the old man's estate.

1   1. Habēbat avunculum Q. Caecilium, equitem Rōmānum, familiārem L. Lūcullī, dīvitem, difficillimā nātūrā. Cūius sīc asperitātem veritus est, ut, quem nēmō ferre posset, hūius sine offēnsiōne ad summam senectūtem retinuerit benevolentiam. Quō factō tulit pietātis frūctum.

5   2. Caecilius enim moriēns testāmentō adoptāvit eum hērēdemque fēcit ex dōdrante; ex quā hērēditāte accēpit circiter centiēs sēstertium.

VOCABULARY

1 Q. – the abbreviation for the praenomen Quīntus

Q. Caecilius (ī, m.) – Quīntus Caecilius

familiāris, familiāris, m./f. – a family member or relation

2 L. – the abbreviation for the praenomen Lucius

L. Lūcullus, ī, m. – a powerful Roman general and politician in the last century BCE

nātūra, ae, f. – nature, character

sīc (adv.) – in such a way

asperitās, asperitātis, f. – harshness

3 ferre – to endure

offēnsiō, offēnsiōnis, f. – offense, cause for offense

summus, a, um – extreme, highest

4 retineō, ēre, retinuī, retentum – to keep, retain

benevolentia, ae, f. – good will

factum, ī, n. – fact, action

tulit – he gained, he got

pietās, pietātis, f. – sense of duty, dutifulness to family and society

frūctus, frūctūs, m. – profit, gain, fruit

5 moriēns, morientis – dying

testāmentum, ī, n. – will

adoptō, āre, āvī, ātum – to adopt

6 ex dōdrante – from a portion of three-quarters, i.e., Atticus was made heir to ¾ of Caecilius' estate

hērēditās, hērēditātis, f. – inheritance

circiter (adv.) – approximately

centiēs sēstertium – ten million sesterces (in Roman currency), a significant sum

READING NOTES

1–2 *Habēbat avunculum . . . difficillimā nātūrā* "He had an uncle . . . <a man of> difficult nature." The ablative of quality, usually consisting of a noun and an adjective, is often used to indicate the quality of a person, as in the phrase *difficillimā nātūrā*.

2 *Cūius . . . asperitātem* The relative pronoun can be used at the beginning of a sentence to refer to something specific or even to a general idea in the previous sentence. In such cases as here it almost has the meaning of a demonstrative and thus *Cūius asperitātem* means "< And> . . . <this man's> harsh nature."

3–4 *ut, quem nēmō ferre posset, hūius sine offēnsiōne ad summam senectūtem retinuerit benevolentiam* Again *ut* introduces a result clause (see Chapter 14) "that he retained the good will of this man, whom no one could endure, without offense right up to his <the uncle's> extreme old age."

4 *Quō factō tulit pietātis frūctum* "By this action he got the gain of his dutifulness." Compare the use of the relative *quō* here with that of *cūius*, explained in the note above.

5 *Caecilius enim moriēns testāmentō adoptāvit eum* The present participle *moriēns* means "while/when dying" (see Chapter 11). The pronoun *eum* or "him" refers to Atticus.

During Atticus' time, the *sestertius* was cast in silver but under Augustus' monetary reforms it was made of brass. On the left a god figure sits between the abbreviation for *Senātūs cōnsultō*, "by decree of the Senate," and on the right a profile of emperor Augustus with the engraving *Augustus pater*, "Augustus father."

QUESTIONS ABOUT THE TEXT

Answer in complete Latin sentences.

1. Cūius hominis erat Q. Caecilius familiāris?

2. Quālis erat Caecilius?

3. Quis Caecilium ferre poterat?

4. Quōmodo Atticus Caeciliī benevolentiam sine offēnsiōne ūsque ad summam senectūtem retinuit?

5. Quālem pietātis frūctum tulit Atticus?

DĒ LINGUĀ LATĪNĀ DĒQUE ALIĪS LINGUĪS CONTINUED

Mārcus: Itaque quia (*because*) Atticus mōrēs bonōs habuit, nōn sōlum doctrīnam (*learning*), sed etiam dīvitiās accēpit.

Marīa: Cāsū (*by chance*) hominēs dīvitiās invenīre et accipere possunt, sed nōn doctrīnam.

CHAPTER 9

The Irregular Verbs *Ferō* and *Fīō*; Imperatives *dīc*, *dūc*, *fac*, and *fer*;
Superlatives ending in *-limus*

Quentin Matsys' (ca. 1466–1530) portrait of Erasmus in his study lined with books.

MEMORĀBILE DICTŪ

Dulce bellum inexpertīs.

"War is sweet for those who have not experienced it." (Erasmus, *Proverbs*)

The celebrated humanist Erasmus, who was a committed pacifist, included this proverb in his collection, thereby indicating his own views of war.

READING

Desiderius Erasmus of Rotterdam (1466–1536) was the leading intellectual of the northern European Renaissance. Although Rotterdam, where he was born, is in the Netherlands, Erasmus considered himself "Latin," a citizen of the republic of literature, *rēs pūblica litterārum*. He belongs to a tradition of Latin writers from outside of Italy that dates back to Roman antiquity itself, and has for centuries since then extended over the wider world. For in ancient Roman times, authors such as the younger Seneca, who came from Spain, and Augustine, who came from North Africa, nonetheless identified themselves, and were viewed, as "Latin." Like these men, Erasmus was thoroughly steeped in Latin learning and left posterity a monumental collection of works in Latin: in his case on theology, religion, education and philosophy. While Erasmus was steadfastly devoted to the Roman church throughout his life, he criticized many of its beliefs and practices, in this way anticipating the developments of the Protestant Reformation. After the early death of his parents, Erasmus was brought up in a monastery, but later obtained a special license to live independently. He spent most of his life traveling in Europe, staying with friends who were also intellectuals. His enemies jokingly turned his name into *mūs errāns*, "wandering mouse." And, because of his sharp tongue, Erasmus did not lack enemies. A superb Latin writer, he did not limit himself to imitations of Cicero as did many of his contemporaries, against whom he wrote a satirical dialogue called *Cicerōniānus*, "The Ciceronian." Rather, he availed himself of all the riches the Latin language had to offer, emulating later Roman authors such as Seneca and the early Christian Fathers as well. Erasmus ranks among the most significant Latin writers, and could easily be judged an equal to Cicero. The adapted letter below provides a glimpse into Erasmus' more personal side. He wrote it to an English friend after a traveling adventure on the European continent.

GUILHELMŌ MONTŌIŌ COMITĪ ANGLŌ ERASMUS ROTERODAMUS S.D.

1   Guilhelmō Montōiō Comitī Anglō Erasmus Roterodamus S.D.

    Post iter difficillimum tandem pervēnimus. Quī Ulixes nunc mē māior esse vidēbitur? Deī ventīs, frīgore acerrimō, pluviā, nive, grandine, contrā nōs pugnābant. Prīmā nocte diū pluerat; deinde pluvia

5   in nivem est mūtāta; vīs nivium erat ingēns; posteā grandō est addita; tum subitō iterum pluere coepit. Simul ac pluvia terram vel arborēs tangēbat, glaciēs ibi fīēbat. Ubīque in terrā glaciēs cōnspiciēbātur nec terra erat aequa, sed multīs in locīs altior vidēbātur. Arborēs sunt glaciē vestītae, cūius onere opprimēbantur. Itaque eārum cacūmina terram

10   tangēbant, rāmī scindēbantur, arborēs cadēbant et in terrā iacēbant. Hominēs, quōs in agrīs vīdimus, dīcēbant sē numquam in vītā rem similem vīdisse. Equī per glaciem et nivēs prōgredī cōnābantur.

Fortasse rogābis quid in Erasmī tuī animō illō tempore fuerit.

Sedēbam in equō et quotiēs equus aurēs ērigēbat, animum dēmittēbam;
15 quotiēs ille in genua procumbēbat, mihi pectus saliēbat. Sed audiās hoc.
Putābis tē verba ex fābulā audīre. Dum per montem dēscendēbāmus, ita
ventīs ferrī coepī et lābī ac sī vēlificārer. Hastīlī cursum moderārī sum
cōnātus. Novum nāvigandī genus!

Ita prōgrediēbāmur. Sōlem vix quartō diē aspeximus. At nunc bene
20 valeō. Tū quoque, mī optime Guilhelme, valeās!

READING VOCABULARY

ac sī (conj.) + imperfect subjunctive – as if

*addō, ere, addidī, additum – to add

Anglus, a, um – English

*auris, auris, f. – ear

cacūmen, cacūminis, n. – top

comes, comitis, m. – count‡

*cōnor, cōnārī, cōnātus sum – to try

cursus, cursūs, m. – course, direction, way

*dēmittō, ere, dēmīsī, dēmissum – to send down;
  animum dēmittō – to let my spirit sink, become
  dejected

difficillimus, a, um – superlative of *difficilis*

Erasmus (ī) Roterodamus (ī, m.) – Erasmus of Rotterdam ‡

ērigō, ere, ērēxī, ērēctum – to raise, set up

*ferrī – present passive infinitive of *ferō, ferre, tulī,
  lātum* – to carry, bear

*fīēbat – was being made, became

*frīgus, frīgoris, n. – cold

genū, genūs, n. – knee

*genus, generis, n. – type, kind

*glaciēs, glaciēī, f. – ice

grandō, grandinis, f. – hail

Guilhelmus (ī) Montōius (ī, m.) – William Mountjoy

hastīle, hastīlis, n. – shaft

illō tempore – at that time

*iter, itineris, n. – road, trip

iterum (adv.) – again

*lābor, lābī, lāpsus sum – to slide, slip, glide down

*moderor, moderārī, moderātus sum – to manage,
  direct, guide

nāvigandī genus – a type of sailing‡

*nix, nivis, f. – snow

*onus, oneris, n. – weight, burden

*perveniō, īre, pervēnī, perventum – to arrive

pluit, ere, pluit, —, an impersonal verb (used only in
  3rd person singular) – to rain

pluvia, ae, f. – rain

prīmā nocte – on the first night

prōcumbō, ere, prōcubuī, prōcubitum – to fall forward, prostrate oneself

*prōgredior, prōgredī, prōgressus sum – to go forward,
  proceed

quartō diē – on the fourth day

quartus, a, um – fourth

*quotiēs (conj.) – as often as

rāmus, ī, m. – branch

s.d. = salūtem dīcit

saliō, īre, saluī, saltum – to jump, leap

scindō, ere, scidī, scissum – to tear, cut

*simul ac (conj.) – as soon as

Ulixes, Ulixis, m. – Odysseus or Ulysses‡

vēlificor, vēlificārī, vēlificātus sum – to sail

vestiō, īre, vestīvī, vestītum – to dress

*Words marked with an asterisk will need to be memo-
  rized later in the chapter.

‡Additional information about the words marked with
  the double dagger will be in the **Take Note** section
  that follows the Reading Vocabulary.

TAKE NOTE

comes This word that also means "companion, associate" came to mean "count."

Erasmus The name Erasmus means in Greek "beloved" and *Roterodamus* "from Rotterdam"; the first name of Erasmus was *Dēsīderius*, which in Latin means "longing."

nāvigandī This word is a gerund (see Chapter 15).

Ulixes Ulysses was one of the heroes of the Trojan war and was famous for his ten-year journey home described by Homer in the *Odyssey*.

Erasmus' letter details the kind of winter storms and dramatic weather that began in the fourteenth century. Letters, diaries, and other personal writings have helped scholars document the Little Ice Age which hit full swing in 1650 beginning with glacial expansion around 1550. The discussion of global warming in the twenty-first century has spurred study of earlier climate change.

COMPREHENSION QUESTIONS

1. In what respect does Erasmus compare himself with Ulysses?

2. What was the main problem in Erasmus' journey?

3. What is the most arresting thing in the landscape that Erasmus describes?

4. What event during the journey does Erasmus describe as a fairytale?

5. What was Erasmus' state of mind during the journey?

LANGUAGE FACT I
THE IRREGULAR VERB *FERŌ*

In the chapter reading passage you read:

> *... ventīs ferrī coepī ...*   "... I began to be carried by the winds ..."

Ferrī is the present passive infinitive of the irregular verb *ferō, ferre, tulī, lātum,* "to carry, bear."

Like a few other irregular verbs, e.g., *sum, possum, volō, nōlō, mālō,* the verb *ferō* does not belong to any conjugation, but follows its own patterns.

The verb *ferō* is transitive and has both an active and a passive voice.

Present Indicative: ferō

	Singular		Plural	
	Active	**Passive**	**Active**	**Passive**
First person	ferō	feror	ferimus	ferimur
Second person	fers	ferris	fertis	feriminī
Third person	fert	fertur	ferunt	feruntur

Present Subjunctive: ferō

	Singular		Plural	
	Active	**Passive**	**Active**	**Passive**
First person	feram	ferar	ferāmus	ferāmur
Second person	ferās	ferāris	ferātis	ferāminī
Third person	ferat	ferātur	ferant	ferantur

Present Active Imperative: ferō

Second person singular	Second person plural
fer	ferte

Present Infinitive: ferō

Active	Passive
ferre	ferrī

In the imperfect and in the future, *ferō* conjugates like a regular verb of the third conjugation.

Imperfect Indicative: ferō

	Singular		Plural	
	Active	**Passive**	**Active**	**Passive**
First person	ferēbam	ferēbar	ferēbāmus	ferēbāmur
Second person	ferēbās	ferēbāris	ferēbātis	ferēbāminī
Third person	ferēbat	ferēbātur	ferēbant	ferēbantur

Imperfect Subjunctive: ferō

	Singular		Plural	
	Active	**Passive**	**Active**	**Passive**
First person	ferrem	ferrer	ferrēmus	ferrēmur
Second person	ferrēs	ferrēris	ferrētis	ferrēminī
Third person	ferret	ferrētur	ferrent	ferrentur

Future Indicative: ferō

	Singular		Plural	
	Active	**Passive**	**Active**	**Passive**
First person	feram	ferar	ferēmus	ferēmur
Second person	ferēs	ferēris	ferētis	ferēminī
Third person	feret	ferētur	ferent	ferentur

Future Active Participle

lātūrus, lātūra, lātūrum

Future Active Infinitive

lātūrus, lātūra, lātūrum esse

In the perfect, pluperfect, and future perfect the verb *ferō* behaves like a regular verb. Once you know the third and fourth principal part of this verb, you see that these tenses are formed in the usual way.

Perfect Indicative: ferō

	Singular		Plural	
	Active	**Passive**	**Active**	**Passive**
First person	tulī	lātus, a, um sum	tulimus	lātī, ae, a sumus
Second person	tulistī	lātus, a, um es	tulistis	lātī, ae, a estis
Third person	tulit	lātus, a, um est	tulērunt	lātī, ae, a sunt

Perfect Passive Participle

lātus, a, um

Perfect Infinitive

Active	**Passive**
tulisse	lātus, lāta, lātum esse

Perfect Subjunctive: ferō

	Singular		Plural	
	Active	**Passive**	**Active**	**Passive**
First person	tulerim	lātus, a, um sim	tulerimus	lātī, ae, a sīmus
Second person	tuleris	lātus, a, um sīs	tuleritis	lātī, ae, a sītis
Third person	tulerit	lātus, a, um sit	tulerint	lātī, ae, a sint

Pluperfect Indicative: ferō

	Singular		Plural	
	Active	**Passive**	**Active**	**Passive**
First person	tuleram	lātus, a, um eram	tulerāmus	lātī, ae, a erāmus
Second person	tulerās	lātus, a, um erās	tulerātis	lātī, ae, a erātis
Third person	tulerat	lātus, a, um erat	tulerant	lātī, ae, a erant

Pluperfect Subjunctive: ferō

	Singular		Plural	
	Active	**Passive**	**Active**	**Passive**
First person	tulissem	lātus, a, um essem	tulissēmus	lātī, ae, a essēmus
Second person	tulissēs	lātus, a, um essēs	tulissētis	lātī, ae, a essētis
Third person	tulisset	lātus, a, um esset	tulissent	lātī, ae, a essent

Future Perfect Indicative: ferō

	Singular		Plural	
	Active	**Passive**	**Active**	**Passive**
First person	tulerō	lātus, a, um erō	tulerimus	lātī, ae, a erimus
Second person	tuleris	lātus, a, um eris	tuleritis	lātī, ae, a eritis
Third person	tulerit	lātus, a, um erit	tulerint	lātī, ae, a erunt

▶ EXERCISE 1

Change the verbs from active to passive voice and vice versa. Translate the changed forms.

1. fers
2. tulī
3. ferrī
4. ferēbāmus
5. feruntur
6. ferēs
7. tulistis
8. lātus erās
9. fertur
10. fertis
11. ferimur
12. feror

VOCABULARY TO LEARN

NOUNS

auris, auris, f. – ear

frīgus, frīgoris, n. – cold

genus, generis, n. – type, kind

glaciēs, glaciēī, f. – ice

iter, itineris, n. – road, trip

nix, nivis, f. – snow

onus, oneris, n. –weight, burden

ADJECTIVES

dissimilis, dissimile – dissimilar

facilis, facile – easy

humilis, humile – low, humble

gracilis, gracile – slender

VERBS

addō, ere, addidī, additum – to add

cōnor, cōnārī, cōnātus sum – to try

dēmittō, ere, dēmīsī, dēmissum – to send down

ferō, ferre, tulī, lātum – to carry, bear

fīō, fierī, factus sum – to be made, become; (impersonally) to happen

lābor, lābī, lāpsus sum – to slide, slip, glide down

moderor, moderārī, moderātus sum – to manage, direct, guide

perveniō, īre, pervēnī, perventum – to arrive

prōgredior, prōgredī, prōgressus sum – to go forward, proceed

CONJUNCTIONS

quotiēs – as often as

simul ac – as soon as

PHRASE

animum dēmittō – to let my spirit sink, become dejected

▶ EXERCISE 2

Find the English derivatives in the following sentences based on the Vocabulary to Learn of this chapter. Some sentences have more than one derivative. Write the corresponding Latin word(s).

1. Here is the latest addition to my collection.

2. Put the groceries in the fridge, please!

3. Human progress has its limitations.

4. This is the itinerary for your trip.

5. Quite a few people learn better if they use both visual and aural faculties.

6. High up in the mountains, we saw spectacular glaciers.

7. Gender studies are a part of many university programs.

8. As a moderator of this conference I have to decide how it will be organized.

9. I am sorry for this lapse of which I was unaware.

10. Let us look at the facts!

11. The ablative originally indicated separation.

LANGUAGE FACT II

THE IMPERATIVES *DĪC, DŪC, FAC,* AND *FER*

In the first language fact of this chapter, you learned that the present active imperative, second person singular of *ferō* is *fer*. Three other verbs (*dīcō, dūcō,* and *faciō*) have irregular present active imperatives in the second person singular. Their imperatives in the singular end in a consonant.

The verb *dīcō* has the present active imperative, second person singular *dīc*.

The verb *dūcō* has the present active imperative, second person singular *dūc*.

The verb *faciō* has the present active imperative, second person singular *fac*.

All these verbs have regular present active imperatives in second person plural.

STUDY TIP

Dīc, dūc, fac, and *fer.*

Don't look for the –*e*,

'cause it isn't there.

Present Active Imperatives of dīcō, dūcō, faciō, and ferō					
		Singular		**Plural**	
Dīcō	Second person	dīc!	"say!"	dīcite!	"say (pl.)!"
Dūcō	Second person	dūc!	"lead!"	dūcite!	"lead (pl.)!"
Faciō	Second person	fac!	"do!"	facite	"do (pl.)!"
Ferō	Second person	fer!	"carry!"	ferte!	"carry (pl.)!"

▶ EXERCISE 3

Complete each sentence with the imperative of *dīcō, dūcō, faciō,* or *ferō* according to the sense of each sentence. Translate the sentence.

1. _____, dux, exercitum tuum per nivem glaciemque!

2. _____ nōs, victōrēs clārissimī!

3. _____, magister, iocōs quōs in animō habēs!

4. _____ mē, frāter! Nam vetus sum et ambulāre nōn possum.

5. Incolae, _____ onera vestra et prōgrediminī!

6. _____ nunc, discipulae, iocōs quōs Latīnē scītis!

7. _____, magistrī, semper rēs meliōrēs, numquam peiōrēs!

8. _____, optime amīce, id quod prōmīsistī!

LANGUAGE FACT III
THE IRREGULAR VERB *FĪŌ*

In the chapter reading passage, you read:

> . . . *glaciēs ibi fīēbat,*
> ". . . ice was created/being made there."

The form *fīēbat* is an imperfect verb form from the irregular verb *fīō, fierī, factus sum.*

You have already learned the verb *faciō, ere, fēcī, factum,* "to do, make." In the present system, i.e., in the present, imperfect and future tenses, this verb has no passive. The passive forms of the present system of this verb are supplied by the irregular verb *fīō,* which means "to be made, become," and impersonally, in the third person singular "to happen."

Present Tense: fīō

	Indicative		Subjunctive	
	Singular	**Plural**	**Singular**	**Plural**
First person	fīō	fīmus	fīam	fīāmus
Second person	fīs	fītis	fīās	fīātis
Third person	fit	fīunt	fīat	fīant

Present Infinitive

fierī

Imperfect Tense: fīō

	Indicative		Subjunctive	
	Singular	**Plural**	**Singular**	**Plural**
First person	fīēbam	fīēbāmus	fierem	fierēmus
Second person	fīēbās	fīēbātis	fierēs	fierētis
Third person	fīēbat	fīēbant	fieret	fierent

Future Tense: fīō

	Indicative	
	Singular	**Plural**
First person	fīam	fīēmus
Second person	fīēs	fīētis
Third person	fīet	fīent

STUDY TIP

In many of its forms, the verb *fīō* very much resembles the fourth conjugation.

BY THE WAY

The verb *fīō* has a very rare present imperative but you will not need to learn it at this time.

In the perfect system, i.e., in the perfect, pluperfect and future perfect tenses, the forms of the verb *fīō* are the same as the passive forms of *faciō*: in the perfect system *fīō* has passive forms.

Perfect Tense: fīō

	Indicative		Subjunctive	
	Singular	**Plural**	**Singular**	**Plural**
First person	factus, a, um sum	factī, ae, a sumus	factus, a, um sim	factī, ae, a sīmus
Second person	factus, a, um es	factī, ae, a estis	factus, a, um sīs	factī, ae, a sītis
Third person	factus, a, um est	factī, ae, a sunt	factus, a, um sit	factī, ae, a sint

Perfect Passive Participle
factus, facta, factum

Perfect Passive Infinitive
factus, facta, factum esse

Pluperfect Tense: fīō

	Indicative		Subjunctive	
	Singular	**Plural**	**Singular**	**Plural**
First person	factus, a, um eram	factī, ae, a erāmus	factus, a, um essem	factī, ae, a essēmus
Second person	factus, a, um erās	factī, ae, a erātis	factus, a, um essēs	factī, ae, a essētis
Third person	factus, a, um erat	factī, ae, a erant	factus, a, um esset	factī, ae, a essent

Future Perfect Tense: fīō

	Indicative	
	Singular	**Plural**
First person	factus, a, um ero	factī, ae, a erimus
Second person	factus, a, um eris	factī, ae, a eritis
Third person	factus, a, um erit	factī, ae, a erunt

BY THE WAY

Since *fīō* is the passive of *faciō* in the present, imperfect, and future, it has only one voice, passive. Note, however, that the endings of *fīō* are not the passive ones. That is because the verb itself does not have a truly passive meaning, but rather an **intransitive** one—i.e., it takes no direct object, but only links a subject and a predicate (the verb "to be" functions in the same way).

> *Volō fierī melior discipula.*
> I want to become a better student.

▶ EXERCISE 4

Translate into Latin.

1. What is happening in the world today?

2. The northern roads become more difficult.

3. Why have the northern roads become more difficult?

4. From the heavy rain and the cold much ice was being made.

5. What will happen to (i.e., 'about') us in the morning?

6. Learn good habits so that things may become better for you!

7. I am trying to ask what happened to (i.e., 'about') Erasmus at first.

   Erasmus, ī, m. – Erasmus

8. Erasmus begged God that things become better.

LANGUAGE FACT IV

SUPERLATIVES ENDING IN *–LIMUS*

Erasmus refers to his trip as *iter difficillimum*, "a very difficult trip."

Six third declension adjectives that end in *–lis* in the masculine/feminine nominative singular form their superlative by dropping the *–is* of the genitive singular ending and adding to the stem the ending *–limus*, *lima*, *limum*. Here are these adjectives.

The nineteenth-century bronze statue of Martin Luther stands outside the Lutheran Frauenkirche, "Church of Our Lady," in Dresden, Germany. The Protestant reformer Martin Luther and Erasmus cultivated a strong friendship on both the personal and intellectual levels. However, when Erasmus proclaimed his belief in free will, the friendship ceased.

MARTIN LUTHER

Positive degree	Superlative degree
facilis, facile – easy	facillimus, a, um – easiest
difficilis, difficile – difficult	difficillimus, a, um – most difficult
similis, simile – similar	simillimus, a, um – most similar
dissimilis, dissimile – dissimilar	dissimillimus, a, um – most dissimilar
gracilis, gracile – slender	gracillimus, a, um – most slender
humilis, humile – low, lowly	humillimus, a, um – lowest, lowliest

▶ EXERCISE 5

Fill in the blanks with the correct degree of the adjectives in parentheses. Translate the sentences.

1. "Hoc iter," dīxit Erasmus, "mihi fuit omnium _____." (difficilis)

2. Omnium itinerum quae in terrā fīunt iter illud fuit _____ nāvigātiōnī. (similis)
   nāvigātiō, nāvigātiōnis, f. – sailing

3. Equus erat _____ equōrum quōs umquam vīdī et vix prōgrediēbātur. (gracilis)

4. Hominēs dīvitēs et clārī in equīs sedēbant, _____ autem ambulābant et onera ferēbant. (humilis)

5. Erasmus multās rēs scrīpsit, nōn sōlum inter sē dissimilēs, sed interdum etiam _____. (dissimilis)

King's College Chapel, Cambridge, England was begun in 1446 by King Henry VI and completed in 1547. Erasmus would have witnessed its construction while he was in Cambridge working on his translation of the New Testament. Erasmus introduced ancient Greek into the Cambridge curriculum and is credited with sowing the seeds of Renaissance thought at the university.

▶ EXERCISE 6

Translate into Latin. The Reading Vocabulary may be consulted.

1. The trip was becoming more difficult and we were being carried by the winds.

2. Ice was being made everywhere; for it had rained and there was cold.

3. I am asking what weight carried the trees' branches toward the ground.

4. People were saying that this thing was most similar to death.

5. I entreat you, Erasmus, to tell me what attitude (i.e., 'mind' or 'spirit') you had on that trip.

6. Erasmus had been carried on the horse as if on a ship. When this happened, he thought that he was sailing.

Rotterdam's favorite son Erasmus is honored by the Erasmusbrug, "Erasmus Bridge," designed by Ben van Berkel and completed in 1996. The cable-stay bridge links the northern and southern halves of Rotterdam with a 2,600-foot span over the Nieuwe Maas River. The bridge, nicknamed "The Swan" for its 456-foot pylon, is featured in the city's logo.

TALKING ABOUT A READING

ABOUT AN ICE STORM AND UNADAPTED LATIN: THE FRIENDSHIP OF CICERO AND ATTICUS

DĒ PROCELLĀ GLACIĀLĪ

Marīa: Hīc Vasintōniae (*in Washington, D.C.*) similem procellam habuimus procellae dē quā nārrat Erasmus.

Mārcus: Quandō (*when*) hoc factum est?

Marīa: Annō praeteritō (*last*). Illō tempore in Californiā fortasse erās.

Helena: Ita. Hanc procellam memoriā teneō. Nūllam vim ēlectricam (*electricity*) per duōs vel trēs diēs habēbāmus. Domī in tenebrīs et frīgore sedēbāmus nec nōbīs coquere licēbat.

Marīa: Mihi tamen placēbat in popīnīs (*restaurants*) comedere!

Christīna: Ego memoriā teneō arborēs glaciē esse opertās (*covered*) tamquam in fābulā. Quam pulchra omnia erant!

At multae arborēs sunt onere glaciēī oppressae eārumque rāmī fractī.

Helena: At multae arborēs sunt onere glaciēī oppressae eārumque rāmī (*branches*) fractī (*broken*).

Christīna: Hoc est vērum. Et viae erant valdē lūbricae (*slippery*) et perīculōrum plēnae.

Marīa: Nōs domī sedēbāmus prope focum (*fireplace*).

Mārcus: In Californiā erat semper sōl nec ūllae procellae fīēbant. Utinam nē hīc sint plūrēs procellae glaciālēs! . . . Ferte nunc librum Nepōtis dē Atticō scrīptum! Nam plūra dē eō discere volō.

Helena: Liber iam est allātus.

Marīa et Christīna intrant.

Marīa et Christīna: Quid fit?

Helena: Locum librī dē Atticō scrīptī legēmus.

Marīa: Hic liber nōn facillimus lēctū (*to read*) . . .

Helena: Shh . . . Legāmus!

THE FRIENDSHIP OF ATTICUS AND CICERO

CORNĒLIĪ NEPŌTIS ATTICUS, 5.3–4

Cicero's brother was married to Atticus' sister, but Atticus had been a good friend of Cicero since his school days, a time well before the relationship through family marriage had come about. Atticus' friendship with Cicero existed because of common interests and similar outlook, not because of family ties. Atticus was also a close friend of another great orator of the day named Quintus Hortensius.

1　　3. Erat nūpta soror Atticī Q. Tulliō Cicerōnī, eāsque nūptiās M. Cicero conciliārat, cum quō ā condiscipulātū vīvēbat coniūnctissimē, multō etiam familiārius quam cum Quīntō, ut iūdicārī possit plūs in amīcitiā valēre similitūdinem mōrum quam affīnitātem. 4. Ūtēbātur autem
5　　intimē Q. Hortēnsiō, quī hīs temporibus prīncipātum ēloquentiae tenēbat, ut intellegī nōn posset, uter eum plūs dīligeret, Cicero an Hortēnsius, et, id quod erat difficillimum, efficiēbat, ut, inter quōs tantae laudis esset aemulātiō, nūlla intercēderet obtrectātiō essetque tālium virōrum cōpula.

VOCABULARY

1   nūbō, ere, nūpsī, nūptum + dative – to marry
     (used for a woman marrying a man)

     Q. = Quīntus

     Quīntus (ī) Tullius (ī) Cicero (Cicerōnis, m.) –
     Quintus Tullius Cicero

     nūptiae, ārum, f. pl. – wedding, marriage

     M. = Mārcus

     Mārcus (ī) Cicero (Cicerōnis, m.) – Marcus (Tul-
     lius) Cicero

2   conciliō, āre, āvī, ātum – to bring together

     condiscipulātus, condiscipulātūs, m. – compan-
     ionship at school

     coniūnctissimē (adv.) – in a very friendly manner

     multō (adv.) – by much

3   familiārius (adv.) – comparative degree of
     familiāriter, "as family, on friendly terms"

     plūs (adv.) – more

     amīcitia, ae, f. – friendship

4   valeō – to be of value

     similitūdō, similitūdinis, f. – similarity

     affīnitās, affīnitātis, f. – relationship by marriage

     ūtor, ūtī, ūsus sum + abl. – to use somebody or
     something, to enjoy the friendship of

     autem – on the other hand

5   intimē (adv.) – as a close friend, on intimate terms

     Quīntus Hortēnsius – a famous orator

     prīncipātus, prīncipātūs, m. – first place

     ēloquentia, ae, f. – eloquence

6   uter, utra, utrum – who, which (of two)

     an – or (in a disjunctive question)

7   efficiō, ere, effēcī, effectum – to bring to effect,
     accomplish

     inter quōs = inter eōs, inter quōs

8   laus, laudis, f. – praise

     aemulātiō, aemulātiōnis, f. – emulation, envy

     nūllus, a, um – none

     intercēdō, ere, intercessī, intercessum – to go
     between, intervene

     obtrectātiō, obtrectātiōnis, f. – an envious de-
     tracting, disparaging

9   tālis, tāle – such

     cōpula, ae, f. – bond, connection

READING NOTES

1   *Q. Tulliō Cicerōnī* Quintus Tullius Cicero was the
     brother of the famous orator, Mārcus Tullius
     Cicero.

2   *conciliārat = conciliāverat*

     cum quō ā condiscipulātū vīvēbat coniūnctissimē
     The subject of *vīvēbat* is Atticus; "with whom
     (i.e., with Cicero) he <Atticus> lived from the
     time of <their> school companionship in a very
     friendly manner."

3–4   *ut iūdicārī possit plūs in amīcitiā valēre
     similitūdinem mōrum quam affīnitātem* This
     phrase means "so that it may be judged that in
     friendship similarity of habits has more value
     than relationship by marriage." This is a result
     clause (see Chapter 14).

5   *hīs temporibus* This ablative of time when means
     "at this time" but literally translates "at these
     times."

6   *ut intellegī nōn posset, uter eum plūs dīligeret,* The
     result clause *ut intellegī nōn posset* "so that it
     could not be understood which of the two men
     esteemed him (i.e., Atticus) more . . ."

7–8   *id quod erat difficillimum, efficiēbat ut . . . nūlla
     intercederet obtrectātiō . . . essetque* This entire
     parenthetical clause refers to the action implicit
     in *efficiēbat*. The sense is: "and, a thing that was
     very difficult, he (i.e., Atticus) brought it about
     that . . . no disparaging would intervene . . . and
     there would exist."

9   *tālium virōrum* Translate this genitive phrase
     "between such men."

QUESTIONS ABOUT THE TEXT

Answer in complete Latin sentences.

1. Eratne affīnitās inter Atticum et Mārcum Tullium Cicerōnem?

2. Quis erat Quīntus Cicero?

3. Utrum Atticus plūs dīligēbat Quīntum an Mārcum? Cūr?

4. Quem alium amīcum habēbat Atticus?

5. Quid erat inter Cicerōnem et Hortēnsium?

6. Quid Atticus effēcit ut inter Cicerōnem et Hortēnsium fieret?

DĒ PROCELLĀ GLACIĀLĪ CONTINUED

Marīa: Numquam dē Hortēnsiō audīvī. Quis erat ille?

Helena: Ōrātiōnēs scrīpsit, ut Cicero, quae autem ad nōs nōn pervēnērunt. Nōmen igitur Cicerōnis clārissimum mānsit, sed nōn Hortēnsiī.

Marīa: Sī Cicero hoc audīre potuerit, māgnō gaudiō ferētur. Nam nōmen suum valdē amāre vidētur.

REVIEW 3: CHAPTERS 7–9

VOCABULARY TO KNOW

NOUNS

aetās, aetātis, f. – age

ars, artis, f. – science, art, skill

auris, auris, f. – ear

fidēs, fideī, f. – faith

frīgus, frīgoris, n. – cold

genus, generis, n. – type, kind

glaciēs, glaciēī, f. – ice

glōria, ae, f. – glory

iter, itineris, n. – road, trip

lībertās, lībertātis, f. – freedom

lingua, ae, f. – language, tongue (the physical part of the mouth)

lūmen, lūminis, n. – light

nix, nivis, f. – snow

onus, oneris, n. –weight, burden

ōtium, ī, n. – leisure, free time

plūs, plūris, n. – more

ADJECTIVES

antīquus, a, um – ancient

dissimilis, dissimile – dissimilar

facilis, facile – easy

gracilis, gracile – slender

humilis, humile – low

Latīnus, a, um – Latin, pertaining to Latin

māior, māius – greater

maximus, a, um – greatest

melior, melius – better

minimus, a, um – smallest

minor, minus – smaller

optimus, a, um – best

ōrnātus, a, um – adorned

pēior, pēius – worse

pessimus, a, um – worst

plūrēs, plūra – more

plūrimus, a, um – most

potēns, potentis – powerful

pūblicus, a, um – common

quālis, quāle – what sort of

studiōsus, a, um + genitive – fond of

ūtilis, ūtile – useful

NUMERAL

ūnus, ūna, ūnum – one

VERBS

addō, ere, addidī, additum – to add

cōnor, cōnārī, cōnātus sum – to try

dēmittō, ere, dēmīsī, dēmissum – to send down

dominor, dominārī, dominātus sum – to dominate, rule

ferō, ferre, tulī, lātum – to carry, bear

fīō, fierī, factus sum – to be made, become; (impersonally) to happen

fundō, ere, fūdī, fūsum – to pour

hortor, hortārī, hortātus sum – to exhort, to urge

lābor, lābī, lāpsus sum – to slide, slip, glide down

loquor, loquī, locūtus sum – to speak

mālō, mālle, māluī, — – to prefer

moderor, moderārī, moderātus sum – to manage, direct, guide

nōlō, nōlle, nōluī, — – not to want, be unwilling

partior, partīrī, partītus sum – to divide, distribute

patior, patī, passus sum – to endure, tolerate, suffer

perveniō, īre, vēnī, ventum – to arrive

prōgredior, prōgredī, prōgressus sum – to go forward, proceed

sequor, sequī, secūtus sum – to follow

trahō, ere, trāxī, tractum – to drag

vereor, verērī, veritus sum – to fear, respect

volō, velle, voluī, — – to want

ADVERBS

adhūc – still, up to this time

Latīnē – in Latin

magis – more

minus - less

tamquam – as

tot – so many

ubi? – where?

vix – hardly

CONJUNCTIONS

quotiēs – as often as

simul ac – as soon as

PHRASES

rēs pūblica – state

animum dēmittō – to let my spirit sink, become
   dejected

▶ EXERCISE 1

Give the requested forms of the verbs *volō*, *nōlō*, *mālō*, *ferō*, and *fīō*.

1. imperfect active indicative, second person singular

2. present active subjunctive, third person plural

3. present active infinitive

4. future active indicative, third person singular

5. imperfect active subjunctive, first person plural

6. present active indicative, second person plural

▶ EXERCISE 2

Change the positive commands into negative commands (both constructions) and vice versa.
Translate the changed form.

Example: fuge!   Nōlī fugere!   Nē fūgeris!   Do not flee!

1. nōlī dūcere!
2. adde!
3. nē tuleris!
4. dēmitte!

5. nōlīte facere!
6. nē dīxeris!
7. funde!
8. trahite!

▶ EXERCISE 3

Translate into Latin.

1. we will become
2. Let us become!
3. it has been made
4. they become
5. it had been made
6. they will have become
7. you were becoming
8. it will be done
9. you (pl.) were becoming
10. you (pl.) have become

▶ EXERCISE 4

Translate into Latin.

1. Up to this time we were trying.
2. The powerful (ones) had dominated.
3. to distribute the burden
4. I will endure the trip.
5. Let us proceed at the same time!
6. Do not exhort the guards!
7. You will follow the marching column.
8. I had spoken lightly.
9. He will have managed easily.
10. You (pl.) will slide on the ice.

▶ EXERCISE 5

Translate into Latin.

1. We will try seriously to learn the best arts from our teachers.

2. The Latin language is not the most difficult language.

3. The leader was seeking the greatest glory by better rule.

4. I am very slender and cannot carry the least burden.

5. Most horsemen praise the sun more than the ice.

▶ EXERCISE 6

Translate into English.

1. Petrarca Cicerōnem rogat ut rēs difficiliōrēs animō māiōre patiātur.

2. Cicero est maximus vir omnium virōrum antīquōrum quī Latīnē scrīpsērunt.

3. Valla putābat linguam Latīnam magis in terrīs dominārī quam aliās linguās.

4. Valla omnēs quī linguam Latīnam amant vocat ut prō eā vehementissimē pugnent eamque servent.

5. Erasmus propter fortissimōs ventōs in glāciē facillimē lābēbātur.

6. Simul ac equus Erasmī tamquam nāvis ferrī coepit, Erasmī animus quam maximō timōre est correptus.

CONSIDERING THE HEROES OF CLASSICAL MYTHOLOGY

In Chapter 9 you read how Erasmus compared himself to Odysseus because of travel woes. Now you will learn in more detail about the travels of Odysseus.

THE ODYSSEY

Ancient Greek and Roman sources relate that after the Greek hero Odysseus fought at Troy for ten years, it took him ten more years to sail home to his kingdom of Ithaca. In narrating its hero's travels, the *Odyssey*—Homer's epic poem about Odysseus' travels in different parts of the Mediterranean—portrays many of his adventures as fraught with danger, and all of them as learning experiences.

Among the first stops made by Odysseus and his crew is the land inhabited by the **Lotus-eaters**. They make his men ingest a narcotic plant called the lotus that causes them to forget everything, including the reason for their travels. But Odysseus forces his comrades to continue the journey, refusing to accept the easier option of oblivion. Instead, he insists that they endure difficulties and overcome their fear of the unknown.

They next stop at the island of the **Cyclops Polyphemus**, a gigantic shepherd with only one, huge eye. While Polyphemus is out, tending his flocks, Odysseus and his men enter the Cyclops' cave and eat some of his cheese. Upon returning, the angry Polyphemus devours several of the crew members, violating the Greek laws of hospitality. Odysseus saves himself and the remainder of his crew by getting the Cyclops drunk. Then, when the inebriated Polyphemus asks Odysseus his name, Odysseus identifies himself as "No-man"; this cautious response may also suggest a desire to be an ordinary, nameless individual rather than a well-known warrior. Later Odysseus blinds the sleeping Cyclops by thrusting a fiery plank of wood into his eye. The Cyclops starts to scream to his neighbors, seeking their help. However, they interpret his cries that "No-man" is attacking him as evidence

Odysseus holds an offering of wine, his guest-friendship gift, to the Cyclops Polyphemus. The uncivilized Cyclops drinks to excess and while he's sleeping, Odysseus and his men plot their escape. As his gift, Polyphemus promises to eat Odysseus last. This Roman copy of a Hellenistic original is in the Vatican Museum.

that he is not in danger, and fail to aid him. Finally, Odysseus manages to escape by having his comrades attach themselves to the undersides of the Cyclops' sheep when Polyphemus leads his flock out of the cave to go grazing. Nevertheless, Odysseus makes matters more difficult for himself by shouting to Polyphemus, boastfully, as they sail away, that it was Odysseus of Ithaca who blinded him. The Cyclops then calls upon his divine father Poseidon, god of the sea, to impede Odysseus' homeward journey. Fortunately for Odysseus, he can rely on the support of another deity, Athena, goddess of wisdom.

On his journey Odysseus also receives help from **Aeolus**, god of the winds, who ties up all the storm winds in a bag and hands the bag over to Odysseus. Although he and his men consequently enjoy smooth sailing on their trip homeward, as they approach their destination his comrades open the bag, suspecting that Odysseus has hidden a treasure in it. The storm winds that they release proceed to take them far from home, prolonging and complicating their journey.

Odysseus stays for an entire year on the island of a sorceress named **Circe**, who becomes his lover. She eventually advises him to travel to the underworld in order to obtain instructions about the rest of his journey from a famous blind prophet named Tiresias. Following Tiresias' orders, he and his men sail near the place occupied by the **Sirens**. With their lovely voices these mythic female creatures enchant, and then destroy, passing sailors— who jump into the sea and drown in their efforts to hear the Sirens' song at closer range. To immunize his crew from these fatally attractive sounds, Odysseus puts wax in their ears; ever-curious, he listens in safety to their melodies by having them tie him to the mast.

Odysseus' men plunge the massive plank into Polyphemus' single eye. Homer's simile likens the hissing and sizzling of the burned eye to the sound of a hot axe thrust by the blacksmith into cold water. The early Attic, seventh century BCE, black-figured amphora captures this moment as Odysseus (in white) strikes the seated giant.

Odysseus subsequently passes through the Greek mythic equivalent of our "a rock and a hard place," **Scylla and Charybdis**, a voracious monster and a raging whirlpool. Odysseus is only able to get through this danger only by sacrificing some of his friends. In the end, Odysseus alone of his entire crew survives. Another irresistible woman, the nymph **Calypso**, then detains him on her island for seven years. She would like to keep him as her lover permanently, and even offers him immortality—which so many Greek heroes would gladly have accepted. But he, surprisingly, declines, preferring to return to his wife Penelope and son Telemachus on Ithaca, and grow old at home.

Penelope proves herself a resourceful woman as well as a loyal wife. While awaiting her husband's return for twenty years, she not only takes care of their household but also fends off the advances of many suitors seeking her hand in marriage. Odysseus' equal in shrewdness and cunning, she devises a strategem to prolong the time for deciding among them. After promising to marry one of the suitors only when she has completed weaving a shroud for Odysseus' father Laertes, she works all day at her weaving but each night unravels what she has woven that day. Once Odysseus returns, she also devises several tests to make him establish his identity beyond any doubt, since she is not entirely certain that he is her husband. Thus, in his presence, she asks her household staff to move their conjugal bed: only Odysseus could know that the bed was immovable, built into an olive tree trunk, around which he had constructed their house. Finally Odysseus defeats all of the suitors in a bow-stringing competition, re-establishing himself with his family and in his kingdom.

The goddess Athena serves as Odysseus' protector throughout the *Odyssey*. She plays a similar role for Odysseus' son Telemachus who after searching is reunited with his father in Ithaca where together they avenge the suitors. At Peterhof, Tsar Peter the Great built a grand neoclassical estate which abounds in works like the Athena.

READ THE FOLLOWING PASSAGE

Achilles et Ulixes sunt virī Graecī celeberrimī, sed inter sē dissimillimī. Vīs maxima Achillis erat in ēius corpore; Ulixes autem mente dominābātur. Achilles volēbat nōmen suum servāre et putābat per glōriam sē posse fierī immortālem. Itaque māluit bellum gerere et occīdī, dum erat iuvenis et fortissimus. Ulixes autem pugnāre nōlēbat, sed domī manēre ut cum familiā suā esset. Tandem necesse eī erat bellum gerere, sed post bellum domum petīvit. Dea eum immortālem facere cupīvit: Ulixes tamen fierī nōluit immortālis. Māluit enim semper esse homō solitus. Haec quoque fuit causa cūr, ā Cyclōpe rogātus quod nōmen habēret, respondēret sē esse Nēminem. Uter, Achilles an Ulixes, viam meliōrem est secūtus?

Achilles, Achillis, m. – Achilles

an – or (introducing the second part of a disjunctive question)

Cyclōps, Cyclōpis, m. – Cyclops

immortālis, immortāle – immortal

solitus, a, um – simple, common

Ulixes, Ulixis, m. – Ulysses

uter, utra, utrum – who (of two)

CONNECTING WITH THE POST-ANCIENT WORLD

THE RENAISSANCE

The English word "Renaissance," which—as already noted—is a French term meaning "rebirth," was first applied to the history of European civilization between the mid-fourteenth and seventeenth centuries by historians writing in the nineteenth century CE. These scholars employed the word "Renaissance" to describe a cultural movement that began in the Italian city states and eventually spread to the whole of Europe, which they characterized not only as a rebirth of interest in Greek and Roman antiquity, but also a rebirth in general of the arts, sciences, and creativity after the "darkness" of the Middle Ages. Although the word "Renaissance" was not used to describe this cultural development prior to the nineteenth century, the idea that it represented may have been inspired by the writings of the Renaissance humanists themselves, who often expressed the view that they lived in an age of revived learning, and spoke scornfully of the medieval period preceding their own era.

Modern historians see the situation differently. They regard the so-called "high" Middle Ages from ca. 1050–1300 as a period of immense creativity and cultural energy, anything but "dark." Nevertheless, the era we conventionally call the Renaissance actually witnessed a major cultural change and this change indeed began in Italian cities. This change was closely connected with esteem for the values and literature of ancient Rome, and for the Latin language itself.

The city-state of Florence emerged as one of the key centers of the Renaissance. Under the Medici rulers, scholars and artists met and discussed the works of Greece and Rome. While thinkers like Leonardo Bruni sought insight from ancient texts, artists like Filippo Brunelleschi studied Roman art and architecture. After twenty years of such study in Rome, inspired by the Pantheon, Brunelleschi conceived the dome for Florence's Cathedral. The cathedral, the Duomo, continues to dominate the skyline.

240

In one sense no "rebirth" occurred at this time because, as we have seen, Latin had remained the universal language of communication by intellectuals throughout the Middle Ages, and many works by classical Latin authors such as Vergil, Cicero, and Ovid had never ceased to be read by the educated. Yet the culture of late medieval Italy was distinctly different from that which existed in most other parts of Europe. For one thing, it was an urban culture, with the city-state as a common form of political organization. For another, in these city-republics the aristocracies often owed their status to the money they made and the political offices they occupied, rather than to feudal landholding. Thus those living in late medieval Italy could more easily relate to the cultural practices of ancient Rome, especially those of the Roman republic, than could other Europeans. A Florentine politician, writer, and humanist such as Leonardo Bruni could easily admire and identify with Cicero, inasmuch as Cicero too desired the political glory that accrued from holding public office and combined a career in law and politics with a life of writing and learning.

Therefore the Italian humanists emulated Petrarch (see Chapter 7) in reading well-known ancient Roman texts with closer attention, and in seeking out other works by Latin authors that had dropped out of circulation during the Middle Ages. The humanists began to notice that the Latin of these ancient Roman writings differed in some respects from the rather technical academic jargon which had come into vogue at the universities of the late Middle Ages, particularly in the fields of dialectic, law, and theology. They accorded particular scrutiny to how these Roman authors used rhetoric—a science which had special appeal in a culture where holding office and engaging in public life was so important. Following the lead of Lorenzo Valla (see Chapter 8) and others, the humanists launched an educational and cultural revolution which made the ancient Roman classics, along with some humanist texts, the basis of formal learning, and which sought to reform the use of Latin itself so that it would conform more closely to the norms of ancient classical writing. This revolution proved immensely successful. Humanist culture and classical literature gradually became the basis of education not only in Italy, but also, eventually, in Northern Europe and Spain. Latin continued to be the language of learning and the sciences for another three centuries after ca. 1400, but humanist or neoclassical Latin became the norm of Latin literary usage after around 1500.

Two events of the mid-fifteenth century CE greatly spurred this development. The first was the invention of the printing press, which allowed books to be distributed in large numbers at previously unimagined rates. Many successful humanists, such as Erasmus (see Chapter 9), associated themselves with presses.

The second was the capture of Constantinople, the center of the Eastern Roman Empire, by the Turks in 1453, which occasioned the migration of many Byzantine

This German stamp celebrates the 500th anniversary of Johannes Gutenberg (ca. 1398–1468) printing the Bible ca. 1454. He is credited with the invention of moveable type which made it possible to stamp multiple copies of a text in a short time. Written material became available to a much wider range of people, significantly impacting the world of ideas.

This map shows how Constantinople with parts on both Europe and Asia sits at the crossroads of trade and cultures. The fall of Constantinople in 1453 CE also meant that the Turks controlled significant trade routes—goods from the Baltic arrived via rivers to Constantinople while other items, especially spices and silk, came from China, Japan, and India via the Silk Road.

intellectuals to Italy and Western Europe. They brought with them their knowledge of the Greek language, and of Greek manuscripts. The increased awareness that Roman culture had deep Greek roots deepened the roots of Renaissance humanist culture itself.

Finally, not only humanist Latin but also a humanist curriculum penetrated the universities. The importance of rhetoric increased in the *trivium,* and the fields of history and moral philosophy were added to the three traditional disciplines of higher education in medieval times: law, theology and medicine.

EXPLORING CICERO'S ENDURING INFLUENCE

CICERO, THE HUMANISTS, AND THE AMERICAN FOUNDING FATHERS

"I think if I could have known Cicero, and been his friend, and talked with him in his retirement at Tusculum (beau-ti-ful Tusculum!), I could have died contented." Mrs. Blimber, a character of Charles Dickens' 1848 novel *Dombey and Son*, speaks these words with a simple admiration. Her daughter in the story remarks that she often resorts to this empty comment at evening parties to cover the fact that she had no education, formal or otherwise. But for our purposes her comment illustrates a firm assumption held by many people since the time of the Renaissance: A passion for Cicero reflects a mind well-grounded in mankind's highest intellectual achievements.

Of all the Romans whose writings were emerging during the Renaissance, Cicero proved to be the most appealing because of his breadth and depth. As a master of rhetoric, that is, the persuasive use of language, he could deliver a well-crafted, rhythmic speech that would sway a jury or move his fellow citizens to a course of action. He wrote essays in beautiful style on such topics as friendship and old age. He composed handbooks to educate the youth. And when political circumstances forced him into retirement, he turned to adapting Greek philosophy, in which he had fully immersed himself, to Roman tastes. He left behind more than 900 letters, correspondence with friends and family members that touch on current events and the human condition, and he even had a reputation in his day as a poet, though very little of his poetry has survived.

M· TVLLIO CICER·

The variety and beautiful style of his writings, coupled with his staunch and often heroic defense of liberty in the face of dictatorship, put him at the center of the humanistic movement. To both understand the human condition and give expression to it, the belief went, one must start with Cicero. In fact, Cicero seemed a model of virtue itself. Imagine the surprise of Petrarch when first he stumbled on letters of Cicero such as the one that appears in Chapter 5, Level 1 of *Latin for the New Millennium*! Writing there to his wife Terentia, Cicero appears inconsolable. He reads her letter with tears as he wallows in

Federico da Montefeltro for his service as a papal officer was made the Duke of Urbino. To embellish his Renaissance palace, he enlisted a Flemish painter believed to be Joos van Ghent (fl. 1460–1480) as court painter. In that capacity, Joos van Ghent painted portraits of twenty-eight famous men like Cicero for the duke's library.

the misery of his exile. His mind grieves (*animus dolet*). The evil machinations of his enemies overwhelm him. "Where is all the emotional fortitude and self-control offered by the philosophy that you espoused?" Petrarch wonders as he writes to Cicero in the fictitious letters you have read. "Why such spiritual weakness?"

In the end, Petrarch opted to separate the *man* Cicero from the *writer* Cicero. No one could deny that in his writings Cicero left behind a roadmap to ethical and cultural living. He also provided the standard for the artistic use of language. He even demonstrated—though Petrarch criticizes him for this as well—that the man of culture must also be a man of action. It is not sufficient to bury oneself in the abstract study of philosophy, Cicero often argued. One must be ready to enter the fray of politics in devotion to one's country. This latter aspect of Cicero's character was what most attracted the founders of America, as we shall see momentarily.

Where Cicero most made his mark in the Renaissance, however, is in the area of rhetoric and style. The man credited for establishing Cicero as the primary model for elegant Latin was Gasparino Barzizza, who lectured throughout Italy in the 1430s and attained an almost perfect imitation of the master. A whole generation followed his lead. In fact, many, such as the humanists Gianfrancesco Pico (1469–1533) and Pietro Bembo (1470–1547), became so slavish to the style of Cicero that they formed a society in which they swore not to use any words or phrases that were not one of his. One famous humanist, Erasmus of Rotterdam (see Chapter 9), ridiculed these Ciceronians for losing sight of the spirit and cultural contributions of Cicero in favor of words and mechanics. He welcomed any reputable Latin, whether it was from Seneca or Tacitus or some other later writer, and rejected Cicero as the only "standard." After all, Erasmus pointed out, how can anyone write about Christian themes using only the pagan words of Cicero? Will Jesus Christ be called Jupiter Optimus Maximus and the apostles Conscript Fathers? One of Erasmus' disciples, Peter Ramus, who became noted for his ideas on logic, introduced further objections to the aping of Cicero's writings. Cicero himself, he said, loved books, study, debate, and listening to orators. He borrowed from them as was appropriate, coined new words when needed, and constantly refined

his own style. He also developed the idea that the character of the orator affects what he speaks or writes. And so to be "Ciceronian" truly, Ramus concluded, one must imitate the habits and ideals of Cicero, not copy his words.

By the late sixteenth century, the ideas of Erasmus and Ramus had won out. Cicero could be admired for his traits, particularly his love of virtue and speaking well, but students would learn good usage from a number of sources and adapt

A product of Trinity College Dublin where he studied Latin, Edmund Burke (1729–1797) addresses the English House of Commons. Burke was considered the most eloquent speaker of his day. A political philosopher, Burke spoke in support of the American colonists seeking to repeal the tea tax and encouraged his colleagues to see the colonists as fellow Englishmen.

their writing to contemporary issues. What is remarkable, however, is that even with the defeat of the old Ciceronian movement, Cicero's many and varied works still played an important role in the educational curriculum in the West. In England, in particular, the study of Cicero was seen as a necessary grounding for legal careers, proper oratory in the House of Commons, and social activity. Thus we have Mrs. Blimber pretending to know something about Cicero while at a dinner party. In France Cicero was the darling of generations who appreciated his accessible and practical philosophy and who found in his eloquence an inspiration for liberty and revolution.

Nowhere do we see the influence of Ciceronian ideas and language more clearly than in the writings of America's founding fathers. In fact, throughout the seventeenth and eighteenth centuries, a thorough grounding in the study of the Classics was required for entry into university studies. Most prominent among the authors to be studied was Cicero. By the time one had graduated from the grammar schools, one would have read his more popular orations, letters, and philosophical treatises. The leaders of the American Revolution found Cicero's resistance to Caesar's and Mark Antony's rise to total power to be especially attractive. In a pamphlet written against the British government, the Boston lawyer Josiah Quincy revered Cicero as the "best of men and first of patriots" for warning his fellow citizens against Caesar's attempts to become king.

A detail from the two dollar bill shows principal contributors like John Adams and Thomas Jefferson presenting the draft of the *Declaration of Independence* to Congress. The image is adapted from painter John Trumbull's Declaration of Independence, a 12- by 18-foot canvas in the United States Capitol Rotunda. The Founding Fathers were steeped in Cicero and the Roman republican tradition.

In recent years, the kind of skill in speaking that dominated in the Revolutionary period has all but disappeared in American politics. The stunning rise of Barack Obama, however, has often been attributed to his gift for oratory which more than once has been called "Ciceronian." Obama, as a lawyer, shared something in common with one of the most famous lawyers in history, who himself rose to the heights of political power even though he was not born into the aristocracy. For example, the constant emotional repetition of the refrain, "Yes we can!" in Obama's speeches is an old tool that Cicero used to similar effect. Compare the passage from Cicero's speech *On the agrarian law*: "Who proposed the law? Rullus. Who stopped the majority of the population from voting? Rullus. Who led the assem-

bly . . . ? Rullus as well." Such similarities in no way prove that Obama borrowed rhetorical tricks from Cicero directly, but it does show that Cicero's influence survives in enough places in American culture that it is possible still to sound like him, even when one is not trying.

KIRK SUMMERS
Associate Professor of Classics
The University of Alabama
Tuscaloosa, Alabama

MĪRĀBILE AUDĪTŪ

PHRASES AND TERMS RELEVANT TO EXPRESSIONS USED IN WRITING AND SPEAKING TODAY

PHRASES AND TERMS

- Ad hoc. "For this." Indicates something designed for a specific purpose.

- Ad rem. "To the matter." I.e., without digressions, directly to the point of the discussion.

- Addendum. "A thing to be added," a supplement.

- Agenda. "Things to be done," a to-do-list.

- Aliās. "Otherwise." This expression is used to denote the same as "pseudonym."

- Circā (abbreviated *ca*). "Approximately, around." Used in indicating dates.

- Curriculum vītae. "Course of life." Another expression for a "résumé." More commonly used in academic circles.

- Dīxī. "I have said/spoken." A frequent way to end a speech.

- Ex cathedrā. "From the chair." The phrase is used to indicate that something is said or done with authority, sometimes connoting dogmatic authority.

- Fac simile. "Make a similar thing." Used for an identical image of a thing. Thence comes the word "fax."

- Īdem. "The same." Used for quoting the same author in a bibliography.

- Ibīdem. "In the same place." Used for quoting the same source in a bibliography.

- In sitū. "In the place." About examination of material performed in the original, real condition, often referring to archaeological finds.

- Interim. "Temporary," literally "in the meantime." It is used to indicate an office held only temporarily, e.g., "interim principal."

- Per annum. "Through a year," i.e., "for a year." Usually used for an income.

- Per diem. "Through a day," i.e., "for a day." Usually used for travel expenses.

- Scīlicet (abbreviated sc.). "Of course," literally *scīre licet*, "it is permitted to know."
- Sīc. "Thus." Used to indicate that the citation of a certain source is exact, although there may be a grammatical or another mistake in it. Often seen as an editor's addition to letters to the editor.
- Viā. "By road of, by way of." Could be used as means of travel ("I flew to Paris via Chicago") or of communication ("I will contact you via e-mail.")
- Vidēlicet (abbreviated viz.). "Namely," literally *vidēre licet*, "it is permitted to see."

CHAPTER 10

T he Irregular Verb *Ēo*; Reflexive Pronoun and Reflexive Possessive Adjective;
The Postposition of the Preposition *cum* in Such Phrases as *sēcum*, *quōcum*, etc.

Holbein the Younger (ca. 1497–1543) who served as court painter
for King Henry VIII painted this portrait of Erasmus in
1523 probably as a gift for Thomas More.

MEMORĀBILE DICTŪ

Ūnī nāvī nōlī omnia committere!

"Do not entrust all <your> things to one ship!" (Anonymous)

This proverb, apparently composed at some point during the Middle Ages, urges merchants and investors to be cautious. Its meaning is equivalent to that of our modern English "Do not put all of your eggs in one basket." In this chapter's reading passage, however, we read of an occasion when having one's possessions in more than one ship proved a bad idea.

READING

Erasmus visited England several times. His friendships with leading English men of letters greatly helped to popularize humanistic literature and the humanistic style of Latin among the British. Erasmus also aided the effort to establish the study of Greek language and literature in England in institutions of learning, and was in fact a professor of Greek at Cambridge University for a time. Despite his academic successes in England, Erasmus' memories of the English were not entirely favorable, as we learn from this letter, in which he narrates his experiences on a sea trip from England to France.

ERASMUS ANDREAE AMMŌNIŌ RĒGIS ANGLŌRUM Ā SĒCRĒTĪS SALŪTEM DICIT

1   Ad aedēs tuās nōn semel īvī, ut optimō amīcōrum meōrum valēdīcerem
    et ut tēcum paulisper loquerer, quōcum numquam nōn iūcundissimē
    manēre soleō. Necesse autem mihi fuit nāvem māne petere. Mare erat
    placidum, caelum serēnum, omnia prospera vidēbantur. Ventīs

5   secundīs ībāmus, sed anxius eram. Nautae illī, quī potius vocārī dēbent
    maritimī fūrēs quam nautae, manticam meam librīs plēnam in aliā nāve
    posuerant. Nam duōbus modīs lūcrum faciunt ex sarcinīs vectōrum,
    quās cōnsultō in aliīs nāvibus pōnunt. Aut rēs in sarcinīs inveniunt,
    quās fūrārī dēcernunt, aut praemia ē vectōribus pōscunt, ut sarcinae

10 vectōribus reddantur. Vectōrēs igitur sciunt sē dēbēre pecūniam suam
    illīs dare ut rēs suās recipiant. Mē meōs librōs perdidisse crēdēbam.
    Putābam mē nōn sōlum librōs sed etiam labōrēs multōrum annōrum
    perdidisse. Nam in quibusdam librīs multās rēs scrīpseram. Nūllus
    parēns dē līberīs āmissīs magis dolet quam ego dē librīs āmissīs

15 dolēbam. Cūr rēgēs Anglōrum fūrēs tam scelestōs ferunt? Fāma
    omnium Anglōrum propter hōs scelestōs valdē laeditur, sī hominēs
    externī aliōs Anglōs esse similēs crēdunt!

READING VOCABULARY

ā sēcrētīs – private secretary‡

*aedēs, aedis, f. – temple; pl. dwelling, house

Andreās (ae) Ammōnius (ī, m.) – Andrew Ammo-
nius‡

Anglī, ōrum, m. pl. – the English

anxius, a, um – anxious, worried

aut . . . aut . . . – either . . . or . . .

cōnsultō (adv.) – on purpose

Erasmus, ī, m. – Erasmus

ferunt – ferō‡

*fūror, fūrārī, fūrātus sum – to steal

*ībāmus – we were going

*iūcundissimē – superlative adverb from iūcundus, a,
um which means "pleasant, nice"

īvī – I went

*labor, labōris, m. – labor, toil

*laedō, ere, laesī, laesum – to harm

*līber, lībera, līberum – free‡

līberī, ōrum, m. pl. – children‡

*lūcrum, ī, n. – profit, gain

mantica, manticae, f. – briefcase, travel bag

*maritimus, a, um – maritime

*modus, ī, m. – way, method, manner

nūllus, a, um – none, no one, no thing

*paulisper (adv.) – for a little while

*pecūnia, ae, f. – money

*placidus, a, um – peaceful, calm

pōscō, ere, popōscī, —— – to demand

*potius (adv.) – rather

*prosper, prospera, prosperum – fortunate, prosperous

quibusdam – ablative plural, meaning "some, certain,
a certain" ‡

quōcum – with whom

recipiant – the verb recipiō, as in this passage, often
means "to take back"

*reddō, ere, reddidī, redditum – to give back

*sarcina, ae, f. – burden, baggage (most commonly
used in the plural)

*scelestus, a, um – wicked

secundus, a, um – favorable (you already know the
meaning "second")

*semel (adv.) – once

*serēnus, a, um – calm, clear

suus, a, um – "his, her, its, their own" (referring back
to the subject)

valēdīcō, ere, valēdīxī, valēdictum – to say goodbye

vector, vectōris, m. – passenger

*Words marked with an asterisk will need to be
memorized later in the chapter.

‡Additional information about the words marked with
the double dagger will be in the **Take Note** section
that follows the Reading Vocabulary.

TAKE NOTE

ā sēcrētīs This entire prepositional phrase, which literally means "from the private affairs," functions like a title or a noun in apposition and comes to mean "private secretary." During the Roman Empire many official titles were formed this way; so, for
example, *ā libellīs* is a "secretary in charge of documents," and *ā ratiōnibus* is an "official in charge of accounting." Kings, nobles, towns, universities, and even some professional associations in the period of Erasmus had secretaries to take care of their
Latin correspondence.

Andreās (ae) Ammōnius (ī, m.) Andrew Ammonius, Italian in origin, secretary to the
British King Henry VIII, and friend of Erasmus.

ferunt The verb *ferō* is the equivalent of the English "to bear" not only in the sense of
"to carry," but also "to endure."

līber, lībera, līberum This adjective means "free." In the plural, however, *līberī, ōrum*, m. pl. means "children;" the word usually only has this meaning when parents are also mentioned or understood in the same sentence. Do not confuse either of these words with the noun *liber, librī* which means "book."

quīdam, quaedam, quoddam This indefinite adjective/pronoun means "some certain, a certain." Note that the declension of *quīdam, quaedam, quoddam* follows the pattern of *quī, quae, quod.*

Portrait of King Henry VIII as a young man by an unknown artist. His bejeweled garments signify his wealth. Henry VIII encouraged humanistic thought in England, inviting scholars and artists like Holbein to participate in his court. He also served as a generous patron to both Cambridge and Oxford Universities.

COMPREHENSION QUESTIONS

1. Why was Erasmus unable to say goodbye to his friend Andrew?

2. How was the weather on the day of Erasmus' voyage?

3. Why were the sailors who put Erasmus' travelbag in the other ship certain to make some money—no matter what happened?

4. When expressing how he felt about his lost books, to what does Erasmus compare his feelings?

LANGUAGE FACT I

THE IRREGULAR VERB *EŌ*

In the chapter reading passage, you noticed two sentences containing forms of a verb that has not yet been included in the Vocabulary to Learn.

> *Ad aedēs tuās nōn semel **īvī** . . .*
> "I went to your house not just once . . ."

> *Ventīs secundīs **ībāmus**.*
> "We were going (i.e., sailing) with favorable winds."

In these sentences *īvī* and *ībāmus* are forms of the irregular verb *eō, īre, īvī, itum*, which means "to go." Learn the forms of this verb thoroughly because *eō* and its many compound verbs are very common.

While Erasmus' journey to France enjoyed favorable winds and a calm, clear sky, crossing the English Channel was often a less than smooth journey. Today's ships are better equipped to protect passengers from the vagaries of weather unlike the type of ship Erasmus would have sailed on.

The Irregular Verb eō

Present Indicative

	Singular	Plural
First person	eō	īmus
Second person	īs	ītis
Third person	it	eunt

Present Subjunctive

	Singular	Plural
First person	eam	eāmus
Second person	eās	eātis
Third person	eat	eant

Present Infinitive

īre

Present Imperative

Second person singular	ī
Second person plural	īte

Imperfect Indicative

	Singular	Plural
First person	ībam	ībāmus
Second person	ībās	ībātis
Third person	ībat	ībant

Imperfect Subjunctive

	Singular	Plural
First person	īrem	īrēmus
Second person	īrēs	īrētis
Third person	īret	īrent

Future Indicative

	Singular	Plural
First person	ībō	ībimus
Second person	ībis	ībitis
Third person	ībit	ībunt

Future Active Participle

itūrus, a, um

Future Infinitive

itūrum esse

The perfect system of *eō* is formed according to the rules you have already learned—once you know the third principal part *īvī*.

Perfect Indicative

	Singular	Plural
First person	īvī	īvimus
Second person	īvistī	īvistis
Third person	īvit	īvērunt

Perfect Infinitive

īvisse

Perfect Subjunctive

	Singular	Plural
First person	īverim	īverimus
Second person	īveris	īveritis
Third person	īverit	īverint

Pluperfect Indicative

	Singular	Plural
First person	īveram	īverāmus
Second person	īverās	īverātis
Third person	īverat	īverant

Pluperfect Subjunctive

	Singular	Plural
First person	īvissem	īvissēmus
Second person	īvissēs	īvissētis
Third person	īvisset	īvissent

Future Perfect Indicative

	Singular	Plural
First person	īverō	īverimus
Second person	īveris	īveritis
Third person	īverit	īverint

BY THE WAY

A fairly common alternate form of the third principal part of *eō* is *iī* instead of *īvī*. The conjugation of *iī* in the various perfect tenses and moods is the same as that of the longer form *īvī*, except the stem is not *īv*– but rather the simple short *i*– prefixed to all the perfect endings. In this book only the forms of *īvī* (and not *iī*) are used.

STUDY TIP

The verb *eō* is intransitive—it never has a direct object in the accusative. This also means that *eō* is not used with a personal subject in the passive. Occasionally, however, the impersonal use of the third person singular passive is used to indicate a general action. For example, the sentence *ībātur/itum est ad portam* would mean "There was a going to the gate," or, in other words, "There was a movement in the direction of the gate." This is the same as saying "People went/were going to the gate."

▶ EXERCISE 1

Translate into Latin using a form of *eō* in each sentence. The Reading Vocabulary may be consulted.

1. If you go to the dwelling, you will get profit. (use the future perfect in the subordinate clause)

2. We went to the dwelling through snow, ice, and cold in order to give back the money.

3. We did not steal the money, so that we might not harm the people.

4. You (pl.) will go to the maritime city in order to receive the baggage.

5. Go (pl.) to the maritime city in order to give back the money!

6. Erasmus was accustomed to go to the dwelling of <his> friend.

7. Erasmus was going to the dwelling of his friend.

8. Erasmus will go to the dwelling of his friend.

9. Erasmus had gone to the dwelling of his friend.

BY THE WAY

The present singular imperative of *eō* constitutes the shortest sentence in the Latin language: *Ī!* "Go!"

VOCABULARY TO LEARN

NOUNS

aedēs, aedis, f. – temple; pl. dwelling, house

labor, labōris, m. – labor, toil

lūcrum, ī, n. – profit, gain

modus, ī, m. – way, method, manner

pecūnia, ae, f. – money‡

sarcina, ae, f. – burden, baggage‡

PRONOUNS

suī, sibi, sē, sē – reflexive pronoun of the third person

ADJECTIVES

iūcundus, a, um – pleasant, nice

līber, lībera, līberum – free

maritimus, a, um – maritime

placidus, a, um – peaceful, calm

prosper, prospera, prosperum – fortunate, prosperous

scelestus, a, um – wicked

serēnus, a, um – calm, clear

suus, a, um – his, her, its, their own (referring back to the subject)

VERBS

fūror, fūrārī, fūrātus sum – to steal

eō, īre, īvī (iī), itum – to go

laedō, ere, laesī, laesum – to harm

reddō, ere, reddidī, redditum – to give back

ADVERBS

paulisper – for a little while

potius – rather

semel – once

‡Additional information about the words marked with the double dagger will be in the **Take Note** section that follows the Reading Vocabulary.

TAKE NOTE

pecūnia, ae, f. This word that means "money" comes from the word *pecus, oris,* n. which means a "herd of cattle." The derivation is hardly surprising, since wealth in the earliest times consisted of the number of cattle a farmer owned. Compare the use of "buck" for "dollar" in English.

sarcinae, ārum, f. In the plural, the word *impedīmenta, ōrum,* n. pl. denotes the baggage of an army, including the beasts of burden and their drivers, while *sarcinae, ārum,* f. pl., also in the plural, refers more specifically to the packs and luggage of the soldiers.

▶ EXERCISE 2

In the sentences below, find the words derived from the Vocabulary to Learn in this chapter. Write the corresponding Latin word.

1. Children who catch chicken pox suffer from a high fever for days and the disease causes lesions on the surface of the skin.

2. Her mode of teaching is very effective.

3. My father was able to accumulate a certain amount of wealth, so our family did not often have to worry about pecuniary matters.

4. When I learned that my application to the program had been successful, my mind was liberated from a great anxiety.

5. My dog never gets perturbed about anything as he has a very placid disposition.

6. My friend is very interested in ships, maritime culture, and history.

7. My parents were well-off because my father's business was a lucrative one.

8. I wish that you may prosper in every way!

9. Suicide is not accepted by many religions.

10. Quite a bit of labor goes into acquiring a skill.

LANGUAGE FACT II

REFLEXIVE PRONOUN AND REFLEXIVE POSSESSIVE ADJECTIVE

In the chapter reading passage you read:

> *Vectōrēs igitur sciunt **sē** dēbēre pecūniam **suam** illīs dare ut rēs **suās** recipiant.*
> "The passengers therefore know they must give their money to them in order to get their things back."

The words *sē, suam, suās* are all reflexive because they refer back to the subject (the passengers). You have already learned the accusative form *sē*.

These words all pertain to the third person. Contrast these words to the pronoun *illīs*, which is also third person, but refers to a third person entity that is **not** the subject (in this case, the sailors).

Here are all the cases of the reflexive pronoun of the third person, which has the same forms for both singular and plural. Its meaning may be "her(self)," "him(self)," "it(self)," "them(selves)," depending on what the subject of the verb is to which the reflexive pronoun refers. Note its similarity to the singular of the pronouns of the first and second person.

Third Person Singular and Plural Reflexive Pronoun	
Nominative	—
Genitive	suī
Dative	sibi
Accusative	sē
Ablative	sē

Sē videt means "S/he sees him/her self."

Eum videt means "S/he sees him (someone else)."

You have already learned that in indirect speech with the accusative and infinitive construction the accusative *sē* is the subject of the infinitive if the subject of the infinitive is the same as the subject of the main verb. If the subject of the infinitive is **not** the same as that of the main verb, it is expressed by the accusative of some other non-reflexive pronoun of the third person, e.g., *eam, eum, eōs, eās, hās, illās*, etc.

*Erasmus dīxit **sē** velle iter facere.*
"Erasmus said that he wanted to travel."

*Erasmus nautae dīxit **eum** nōn dēbēre fūrārī.*
"Erasmus said to the sailor that he should not steal."

France's northern coast facing England offers beautiful views. Erasmus would have enjoyed such landscapes en route to the French harbor towns which continue to host travelers from England.

Note that just as happens in the pronouns of the first and second person, the genitive *suī* is not used to indicate **possession**. To express this meaning you should use the **reflexive possessive adjective** of the third person *suus, sua, suum,* which always agrees in number, gender, and case with the thing possessed.

> *Erasmus librōs suōs āmīsit.*
> "Erasmus lost his (own) books."

As happens in the pronouns of the first and second person, the **genitive of the reflexive pronoun** is used with a **partitive** or **objective** sense.

> *Erasmus putābat librōs esse partem suī.* (partitive sense)
> "Erasmus thought that the books were a part of himself."

> *Erasmī amor suī est satis māgnus.* (objective)
> "Erasmus' love (appreciation) of himself is great enough."

STUDY TIP

Note that *suī, sibi, sē, sē* has no nominative because it is **never** the subject. Since the reflexive often refers back to the subject, it cannot be the subject.

▶ EXERCISE 3

Translate into Latin. The Reading Vocabulary may be consulted.

1. For a little while they think about their (i.e., own) toil.

2. For a little while they think about their (i.e., of other people) toil.

3. They say that they think for a little while about their (i.e., own) toil.

4. They say that they think for a little while about their (i.e., of other people) fame.

5. The kings of the English do not put up with (use *ferō*) wicked thieves in their (i.e., own) lands.

6. The kings of the English do not put up with (use *ferō*) wicked thieves in their (i.e., other people's) lands.

7. The kings of the English say that they do not put up with (use *ferō*) wicked thieves in their (i.e., own) lands.

8. The poet was grieving about his (i.e., own) lost books.

9. The poet was grieving about his (i.e., another person's) lost books.

10. The sailor realized that he ought to give the money back to him (i.e., another person) once.

11. The sailor realized that he (i.e., another person) ought to give the money back to him (i.e., the sailor himself) once.

▶ EXERCISE 4

Translate into English. Then rewrite each Latin sentence changing the reflexive pronoun *suī, sibi, sē, sē* to the third person demonstrative *is, ea, id* and vice versa. The genitives *ēius, eōrum, eārum* should be changed to the correct form of the possessive adjective *suus, a, um*. Translate the changed Latin sentences into English. The Reading Vocabulary may be consulted.

Example: Pecūniam sibi darī crēdidit.
S/he believed the money was being given to her/him (self).
Pecūniam eī darī crēdidit.
S/he believed the money was being given to her/him (the other person).

1. Erasmus necesse sibi esse nāvem petere sciēbat.

2. Vidēbant caelum esse serēnum et eōs ventīs secundīs ferrī.

3. Nautae eōrum sarcinās tenēbant.

4. Crēdēbant librōs esse suōs.

5. Eōs sibi manticam reddidisse crēdēbat.

6. Nautae putābant manticam eīs datam esse.

Following his trip from England to France, Erasmus visited the Swiss city of Basle for the first time. Subsequently, he settled in Basle for a time where he served as an editor, taught at the university, and had his Greek New Testament published. The panoramic view of Basle shows the Rhine river and the cathedral.

BY THE WAY

In English the third person pronouns "he," "they," etc. can often refer either to someone other than the subject or to the subject without the addition of "self/selves." Therefore in English we rely on the context to understand whether the second "he" in a sentence like "He said that he was happy" refers to the subject or some other person. This distinction in Latin is always indicated by the use of different pronouns—reflexive or non-reflexive.

LANGUAGE FACT III

THE POSTPOSITION OF THE PREPOSITION *CUM* IN SUCH PHRASES AS *SĒCUM, QUŌCUM*, ETC.

Look again at this sentence which you have already read in the chapter reading passage.

> *Ad aedēs tuās nōn semel īvī, ut optimō amīcōrum meōrum valēdīcerem et ut **tēcum** paulisper loquerer, **quōcum** numquam nōn iūcundissimē manēre soleō.*

> "I went to your house not <just> once, in order to say goodbye to the best of my friends and to talk with you for a little while, <you> with whom I am never accustomed to spend time in a way that is not extremely pleasant."

When the preposition *cum* refers to the first or second person pronoun in the ablative (*mē, tē, nōbīs, vōbīs*) or the third person reflexive (*sē*) or the ablative of the relative pronoun (*quō, quā, quibus*) it does not **precede** the word, but is **added** on to the end of it like a suffix.

Phrases with Postponed cum	
mēcum	with me
tēcum	with you
nōbīscum	with us
vōbīscum	with you (pl.)
sēcum	with himself/herself/itself/themselves
quōcum	with whom (masculine or neuter)
quācum	with whom (feminine)
quibuscum	with whom (plural)

Occasionally but not very often, Latin shows *cum* before the pronoun as in "*cum quō*" (p. 202, line 2).

▶ EXERCISE 5

Fill in the blanks as required. Translate into English. The Reading Vocabulary may be consulted.

Example: Cīvēs rēgīnae, _____ ad portam vēnerāmus, multa dōna dedērunt. (with whom)
Cīvēs rēgīnae, quācum ad portam vēnerāmus, multa dōna dedērunt.
The citizens gave many gifts to the queen with whom we had come to the gate.

1. Hī fūrēs scelestī sarcinās meās _____ ferunt. (with them)

2. Hic est vir gracilis _____ loquī dēbēbis. (with whom)

3. Sunt ibi multī mīlitēs, _____ pugnāre nōlunt hominēs tam paucī frīgoreque laesī. (with whom)

4. Quī sunt hī vectōrēs, quī _____ nāvigant? (with you)

5. Sciō eōs esse amīcōs tuōs. _____ sunt amīcī meī (with them), _____ iter faciunt. (with whom)

6. Librōs tibi ostendam quōs _____ habeō. (with me)

▶ EXERCISE 6

Erasmus composed the *Colloquia familiāria* as models for conversational Latin on a wide variety of subjects. They were intended to teach good Latin and good morals. Erasmus revised them many times during his life. The earliest versions of the *Colloquia familiāria* are little more than formulaic phrases appropriate for different situations. As Erasmus expanded them, they developed into witty little plays that often portrayed human failings in a satiric light. The subject of this dialogue is *ars nōtōria*, a mysterious, quasi-magical lore believed to enable those who use it to learn all the sciences without effort and in a very short time.

Translate into English. The dialogue is adapted from one of Erasmus' *Colloquia familiāria*.

Ars nōtōria

Magister: Spērō tē hīs diēbus fēlīciter litterīs studēre.

Discipulus: Mūsae mihi auxilium nōn dant. Fēlīcius litterīs studēbō, sī tū mihi auxilium dederis.

Magister: Nihil nōn faciam, ut auxilium vērum habeās. Quid ē mē accipere vīs?

Discipulus: Omnēs tē artēs didicisse crēdō.

Magister: Utinam haec verba essent vēra!

Discipulus: Audiō artem esse quandam nōtōriam. Auxiliō hūius artis hominēs dīcuntur litterās et omnēs artēs līberālēs paene sine labōre discere posse.

Magister: Quid audiō!? Vīdistīne librum in quō haec ars dēscrībitur?

Discipulus: Ita! In illō librō multās rēs novās vīdī: imāginēs animālium, fōrmās litterārum arcānās, signa magica.

Magister: Quam celeriter hominēs dīcuntur auxiliō hūius artis artēs aliās discere posse?

Discipulus: Intrā paucōs diēs—et sine labōre.

Magister: Suntne tibi nōtī hominēs, quī per hanc artem artēs aliās didicērunt?

Discipulus: Nōn sunt. Sed hanc artem discere volō. Volō hanc artem esse vēram.

Magister: Ita dē hāc arte sentīs, quia maximī labōrēs tibi nōn videntur esse iūcundī.

Discipulus: Ita vērō! Nōn sunt iūcundī.

Magister: Dīvitiās illās vulgārēs: aurum, vīllās pulchrās, pecūniam, imperium etiam indignī hominēs sine labōre interdum accipiunt. Artēs et doctrīna vēra nōn aliō modō parantur et accipiuntur nisi studiō et labōre. Labōrāre nōbīs necesse est ut rēs optimās habeāmus. Sī homō diū discit, et plūra discere semper cōnātur, labor discendī tandem fit iūcundus.

Discipulus: Memoria mea nōn vult tot rēs tenēre.

Magister: Volō tē cottidiē pauca verba ex optimīs auctōribus sēlēcta discere. Post multōs diēs haec pauca verba fīent multa. Dēbēbis etiam tēcum habēre hominēs quī bene Latīnē loquuntur. Litterās discēs amōre, cūrā, assiduitāte. Nōn alia mihi nōta est ars nōtōria!

arcānus, a, um – secret, hidden, mysterious

assiduitās, assiduitātis, f. – diligence, assiduity, application

auctor, auctōris, m. – author, originator

cottidiē (adv.) – daily

cūra, ae, f. – effort, labor

dēscrībō, ere, dēscrīpsī, dēscrīptum – to describe, copy

discendī (genitive case) – of learning

doctrīna, ae, f. – science, erudition, teaching

fēlīciter (adv.) – with good success

imāgō, imāginis, f. – image

indignus, a, um – unworthy

intrā + accusative – within

labōrō, āre, āvī, ātum – to labor, toil at

līberālis, līberāle – pertaining to a free man; *artēs līberālēs* – the liberal arts‡

magicus, a, um – magic

Mūsae, ārum, f. pl. – the Muses, the nine ancient Greek goddesses of the arts of expression

nisi – unless, except

nōtus, a, um – known

nōtōrius, a, um – that makes something known: *ars nōtōria* would be a science or technique that helps people learn other things, "the science that imparts learning power"

quīdam, quaedam, quoddam – a certain‡

sēlēctus, a, um – chosen

signum, ī, n. – sign, marker, standard

spērō, āre, āvī, ātum – to hope

studium, ī, n. – study, zeal

vērō (following *ita*) – yes indeed

vulgāris, vulgāre – ordinary, common, belonging to the many

TAKE NOTE

artēs līberālēs The liberal arts, typically grammar, rhetoric, and dialectic.

quīdam, quaedam, quoddam The accusative forms *quendam* and *quandam*, and the genitive plural forms, *quōrundam* and *quārundam,* all have the letter "n" before the suffix *–dam.*

TALKING ABOUT A READING

ABOUT AN AIRPLANE TRIP AND UNADAPTED LATIN: ATTICUS TRIES TO AVOID POLITICAL TURMOIL

DĒ ITINERE ĀEREŌ

Christīna: Dum legimus dē rēbus difficiliōribus quās Erasmus in itinere est passus, cōgitō dē itinere āereō quod cum parentibus in Americam merīdiānam (*South America*) fēcī. Dēbēbāmus diū exspectāre ut sēcūritātis probātiō (*security check*) fieret.

Marīa: At putō temporibus Erasmī sēcūritātis probātiōnēs nōn fuisse. Itinera igitur nōn erant tam similia.

Christīna: Audiās tamen hoc. Nōs pervēnimus sed sarcinae nostrae nōbīscum nōn pervēnērunt. In sarcinā meā habēbam vestīmenta pulchra quae gerere cupiēbam, sed sarcinam nōn accēpī. Per duōs diēs exspectāvimus nec vestīmenta mūtāre poterāmus.

Cōgitō dē itinere āereō quod cum parentibus in Americam merīdiānam fēcī. Dēbēbāmus diū exspectāre ut sēcūritātis probātiō fieret.

Marīa: Erasmus librōs suōs cūrābat, tū autem tantum vestīmenta.

Christīna: Sciō tē, Marīa, dē vestīmentīs nōn cōgitāre. Ego et dē vestīmentīs et dē librīs cōgitō . . . Quid dē Atticō herī (*yesterday*) lēgimus?

Helena: Atticus viam mediam (*middle*) vidētur semper secūtus esse. Potuitne hōc modō efficere (*bring it about*) ut rēs essent meliōrēs? Cicero contrā hominēs scelestōs pugnāre cōnātus est.

Christīna: Ita. Cicero autem saepe errāvit et tandem occīsus est. Atticus eum cōnārī rem pūblicam iuvāre (*help*) sciēbat sed crēdēbat sē aliō modō Rōmānōs iuvāre (*help*) posse. Nam Atticus ūsque (*all the way*) ad senectūtem vīxit multīsque hominibus auxilium dare potuit.

ATTICUS TRIES TO AVOID POLITICAL TURMOIL

CORNĒLIĪ NEPŌTIS ATTICUS, 6.1–3

Although Atticus was sympathetic to the senatorial party, he wanted to avoid the political turmoils so prevalent in that period. Hence he avoided holding political office, because he thought nobody could do so without yielding to corrupt political tactics such as bribery which had become so universal in the Roman republic. He also stayed away from prosecutions and court cases.

1   1. In rē pūblicā ita est versātus, ut semper optimārum partium et esset et existimārētur, neque tamen sē cīvīlibus fluctibus committeret . . .

2. Honōrēs nōn petīvit, cum eī patērent propter vel grātiam vel dignitātem, quod nec petī mōre māiōrum nec capī possent cōnservātīs lēgibus in tam effūsī ambitūs largītiōnibus, nec gerī ē rē pūblicā sine perīculō corrūptīs cīvitātis mōribus . . . 3 . . . Nēminem nec suō nōmine nec subscrībēns accūsāvit; in iūs dē suā rē numquam īvit: iūdicium nūllum habuit.

VOCABULARY

1   versor, versārī, versātus sum – to be occupied in, be involved in

optimārum partium – this phrase means "of the aristocratic/senatorial party" in Roman politics

2   existimō, āre, āvī, ātum – to deem, think, suppose

cīvīlis, cīvīle – pertaining to the state, civil

fluctus, fluctūs, m. – wave, breaker

committō, ere, commīsī, commissum – to entrust

3   pateō, ēre, patuī, — – to lie open, be available

vel . . . vel . . . – either . . . or . . .

grātia, ae, f. – influence

4   dignitās, dignitātis, f. – status

quod (conj.) – because

mōre māiōrum – in accord with the custom of <our> ancestors

cōnservō, āre, āvī, ātum – to preserve

5   effūsus, a, um – lavish, unrestrained

ambitus, ambitūs, m. – bribery to obtain office

largītiō, largītiōnis, f. – prodigality, lavish expenditure, corruption

gerō, ere, gessī, gestum – this verb (already learned) means "to administer" in civil politics

ē rē pūblicā – this phrase means "in accord with the public good"

6   corrumpō, ere, corrūpī, corrūptum – to corrupt

cīvitās, cīvitātis, f. – state

suō nōmine – in his own name

7   iūs, iūris, n. – law, right; the phrase in iūs īre means "to go to court" or "take legal action"

iūdicium, ī, n. – court, court case: the phrase iūdicium . . . habēre means "be involved in a court case"

8   nūllus, a, um – none

READING NOTES

1–2   *In rē pūblicā ita est versātus, ut semper . . . esset et existimārētur, neque . . . sē . . . committeret* Here *ut* introduces a result clause (see Chapter 14). The meaning is: "He was involved in the state in such a way that he was always of the senatorial party and thought <to be of this party>, but he would not entrust himself to . . ."

2   *cīvīlibus fluctibus* Note the metaphor here. It means "to the storms of public affairs." The literal translation "to the public waves" would not make sense in English.

3   *cum eī patērent* In this sentence *cum* is a subordinating conjunction with a subjunctive verb and it means "although."

4–5   *quod . . . cōnservātīs lēgibus* Here *quod* is a causal conjunction and it means "because." Note also the ablative absolute *cōnservātīs lēgibus* (see Chapter 13). The phrase means "with the laws having been preserved," or simply "in accord with the laws."

5   *in tam effūsī ambitūs largītiōnibus* "in the corruptions of such lavish bribery."

nec gerī Understand *possent* with this phrase also.

6   *corrūptīs cīvitātis mōribus* This ablative absolute means "with the morals of the state having been corrupted," or "because the morals of the state had been corrupted."

6–7   *Nēminem . . . subscrībēns accūsāvit* Note that *subscrībēns* is a present active participle (see Chapter 11) of *subscrībere* ("to sign, to subscribe"). Here *subscrībēns* means "being a signatory to an accusation."

QUESTIONS ABOUT THE TEXT

Answer in complete Latin sentences.

1. Quārum partium semper erat Atticus?

2. Quibus rēbus sē numquam commīsit Atticus?

3. Propter quās rēs honōrēs Atticō patēbant?

4. Nōluitne Atticus honōrēs petere, quod (*because*) honōrēs nōn amābat, an (*or*) quod honōrēs mōre māiōrum nōn iam petī posse crēdēbat?

5. Quem Atticus accūsāvit?

6. Quandō (*when*) in iūs dē suā rē īvit Atticus?

7. Quandō iūdicium habuit Atticus?

DĒ ITINERE ĀEREŌ CONTINUED

Marīa: Atticus sē hōc modō sapienter (*wisely*) fortasse gerēbat. Nam manifēstum est (*it is obvious*) eum hominibus aliīs auxilium multīs modīs dare potuisse.

Helena: Via media (*middle*), quam Atticus saepe secūtus est, vidētur mihi fuisse optima.

CHAPTER 11

Present Active Participle; Use of Participles; Adjectives with Genitive Singular in –*īus* and Dative Singular in –*ī*

1518 edition of *Utopia* with Ambrosius Holbein's woodcut of 1518 showing the island of Utopia and the facing page of type.

MEMORĀBILE DICTŪ

Potius mendācium dīcam, quam mentiar.

"I would rather speak a lie, than lie." (Thomas More, *Utopia*, Preface)

These words epitomize the message of More's *Utopia*. He tells many stories that seem unbelievable but his message to the reader is truthful and important.

READING

Thomas More (1478–1535) was chancellor of England under King Henry VIII, but he was ultimately executed by royal order when he refused to acknowledge the king's supremacy over the church. More was renowned not only as a statesman but also as a literary giant in neo-Latin, owing to his celebrated novel *Ūtopia*. His title *Ūtopia* is a Greek word, coined by More himself, meaning "No Place." The second book of the novel relates the narrative of Raphael Hythlodaeus, whose name means "dispenser of nonsense." A sailor and explorer, he describes the customs and way of life among the Utopians, a perfectly organized and just (although altogether imaginary) society on a remote island. While *Ūtopia* is to some extent a work of satire, More also seems to portray the Utopians in various respects as offering a better alternative to European societies.

In the passage below we learn what occurred when foreign ambassadors arrived in Utopia, unaware of the great differences between their own customs and those of the Utopians.

DĒ LEGĀTĪS ANEMŌLIŌRUM

1   Multī legātī illō tempore in Ūtopiam convēnērunt, inter quōs erant
Anemōliī quī vītam mōrēsque Ūtopiēnsium minimē intellegēbant.
Nescientēs autem aurum et argentum ab Ūtopiēnsibus māgnī nōn
habērī sed signa esse servitūtis, vestīmenta ōrnātissima nōn amārī,

5   et puerōs gemmīs lūdere, audīvērunt hīs omnibus rēbus Ūtopiēnsēs
nōn ūtī. Putantēs igitur Ūtopiēnsēs nōn habēre id quō nōn ūtēbantur,
dēcrēvērunt ēlegantiā suā deōs quōsdam repraesentāre et miserōrum
Ūtopiēnsium oculōs splendōre suō praestringere. Itaque Anemōliī in
urbem ingressī sunt vestīmenta pulcherrima gerentēs, anulīs aureīs,

10 monīlibus ex pilleīs pendentibus, margarītīs fulgentibus ōrnātī. Operae
pretium erat vidēre quōmodo cristās ērēxerint, cum ōrnātum suum
cum Ūtopiēnsium ōrnātū contulērunt—nam omnis populus erat
in viīs ut spectāret; nec minus operae pretium erat vidēre quōmodo
Ūtopiēnsēs Anemōliōrum servōs reverenter salūtantēs legātōs sine

15 ūllō honōre praetermitterent. Eīs enim tōtus ille splendor turpis
vidēbātur. Poterās quoque vidēre puerōs, quī iam gemmās et
margarītās abiēcerant, postquam Anemōliōs gemmīs et margarītīs
ōrnātōs vīdērunt, vocāre mātrem latusque fodere atque dīcere: "Ēn

māter! Ille nebulō adhūc margarītīs et gemmīs ūtitur tamquam parvus
20   puer." Māter autem sēriō respondit: "Tacē, fīlī! Putō esse mōriōnem
legātōrum." Aliī putantēs monīlia esse vincula et legātōs esse servōs,
illa vincula reprehendēbant. Dīcēbant enim servōs illīs vinculīs nōn
tenērī, sed facile fugere posse.

READING VOCABULARY

abiciō, ere, abiēcī, abiectum – to throw away

Anemōliī, ōrum, m. pl. – the Anemolians (the name of
    a population)‡

anulus, ī, m. – ring

aureus, a, um – golden

cōnferō, cōnferre, contulī, collātum – to compare,
    bring together

crista, ae, f. – a tuft on the head of animals

cristās ērigō, ere, ērēxī, ērēctum – to carry the head
    high, be conceited

ēlegantia, ae, f. – elegance

ēn! (interjection!) – see there!

fodiō, ere, fōdī, fossum – to dig
    latus fodere – to jab someone's side with an elbow

fulgentibus – shining

fulgeō, ēre, fulsī, —— – to shine

*gemma, ae, f. – gem, precious stone

gerentēs – wearing

ingredior, ingredī, ingressus sum – to enter

latus, lateris, n. – side, flank

*legātus, ī, m. – ambassador

*māgnī habeō – esteem a lot

margarīta, ae, f. – pearl

*minimē (adv.) – least, very little

monīle, monīlis, n. – necklace

mōriō, mōriōnis, m. – fool, clown

nebulō, nebulōnis, m. – a worthless fellow

nescientēs – not knowing

*nesciō, īre, nescīvī, nescītum – not to know

*operae pretium est – it is worthwhile

ōrnātus, ōrnātūs, m. – apparel, attire

pendentibus – hanging

pendeō, ēre, pependī, —— – to hang (intransitive)

pilleus, ī, m. – hat

*populus, ī, m. – people

praestringō, ere, praestrīnxī, praestrictum – to bind
    fast, to strike
    oculōs praestringere – to blind

praetermittō, ere, praetermīsī, praetermissum – to
    allow to go, let pass

putantēs – thinking

*quōmodo (adv.) – how

quōsdam (masc. pl.) – some, certain

repraesentō, āre, āvī, ātum – to represent

reverenter (adv.) – respectfully

salūtantēs – greeting

*salūtō, āre, āvī, ātum – to greet

sēriō (adv.) – seriously

servitūs, servitūtis, f. – slavery

*servus, ī, m. – slave, servant

signum, ī, n. – sign

*spectō, āre, āvī, ātum – to watch

splendor, splendōris, m. – brilliance, splendor

*taceō, ēre, tacuī, tacitum – to be silent, keep quiet

*tōtus, a, um – whole, entire

*turpis, turpe – shameful, disgraceful

Ūtopia, ae, f. – Utopia (in Greek "No Place")

Ūtopiēnsis, Ūtopiēnsis, m. – Utopian

*ūtor, ūtī, ūsus sum + ablative – to use

*Words marked with an asterisk will need to be
    memorized later in the chapter.

‡Additional information about the words marked with
    the double dagger will be in the **Take Note** section
    that follows the Reading Vocabulary.

TAKE NOTE

Anemōliī, ōrum, m. pl. The name of these people is derived from Greek and means "wind-men."

COMPREHENSION QUESTIONS

1. Who were the Anemolians?

2. How did they dress when they came to Utopia, and why?

3. What did the Utopians do when they saw the Anemolians, and why?

4. Why was the exchange between the little Utopian boy and his mother funny?

LANGUAGE FACT I

PRESENT ACTIVE PARTICIPLE

In the chapter reading passage, you saw the form *putantēs* twice. The verb *putō* is already known to you but the form is a new one—the present active participle.

The present active participle is formed from the present stem.

For the verbs of the **first, second** and **third** conjugation, find the present stem of the verb and add the ending *–ns* for the nominative singular and the ending *–ntis* for the genitive singular (these endings are for masculine, feminine, and neuter). Thus formed, the participle declines just like an adjective of the third declension.

For the verbs of the **fourth** conjugation, find the present stem of the verb and add the ending *–ēns* for the nominative singular and the ending *–entis* for the genitive singular (these endings are for the masculine, feminine, and neuter genders). Thus formed, the participle also declines in the same way as an adjective of the third declension. The present participle of the *–iō* **verbs of the third conjugation** looks exactly like the present participle of the fourth conjugation verbs.

BY THE WAY

We may think of all participles as "verbal adjectives." They are not only derived from verbal stems, but they also actually work both like verbs and adjectives. Like verbs they can take an object (if they are active); like adjectives they agree with nouns, expressed or implied.

STUDY TIP

The prese**NT** active participle is readily recognized by the presence of **NT** in the participle's base which comes from its genitive singular form, e.g., *paraNTis*. Similarly, the fut**UR**e active participle is readily recognized by the presence of **UR** in all of its forms, e.g., *parātŪRus*.

Present Active Participle	
First Conjugation	parāns, parantis
Second Conjugation	tenēns, tenentis
Third Conjugation	colēns, colentis
Fourth Conjugation	audiēns, audientis
Third Conjugation –iō Verbs	capiēns, capientis

Note that the third conjugation has a long –*ē*– in the nominative.

Present Active Participle: Declension of parāns

	Singular			Plural		
	Masculine	Feminine	Neuter	Masculine	Feminine	Neuter
Nominative	parāns	parāns	parāns	parantēs	parantēs	parantia
Genitive	parantis	parantis	parantis	parantium	parantium	parantium
Dative	parantī	parantī	parantī	parantibus	parantibus	parantibus
Accusative	parantem	parantem	parāns	parantēs	parantēs	parantia
Ablative	parantī	parantī	parantī	parantibus	parantibus	parantibus
Vocative	parāns	parāns	parāns	parantēs	parantēs	parantia

You usually translate the present active participle with the suffix -*ing*: *parāns*, "preparing," or sometimes with a relative clause "who prepares."

You have already learned that **deponent verbs** are mostly passive with an active meaning. So you might at first be surprised to learn that they have a present **active** participle.

> ūtor – ūtēns, ūtentis "using," "who uses"

BY THE WAY

There is no present passive participle in Latin.

Present Active Participles: Irregular Verbs

eō	iēns, euntis
ferō	ferēns, ferentis
nōlō	nōlēns, nōlentis
possum	potēns, potentis
volō	volēns, volentis

BY THE WAY

In classical Latin, the verbs *sum, fīō,* and *mālō* do not have a present active participle.

▶ EXERCISE 1

Find five more present participles in the chapter reading.

VOCABULARY TO LEARN

NOUNS

gemma, ae, f. – gem, precious stone

legātus, ī, m. – ambassador

populus, ī, m. – a people, populace

servus, ī, m. – slave, servant

ADJECTIVES

alter, altera, alterum – the other (of two)

neuter, neutra, neutrum – neither, none (of two)

nūllus, a, um – none

sōlus, a, um – alone, only

tōtus, a, um – whole, entire

turpis, turpe – shameful, disgraceful

uter, utra, utrum – who, which (of two)?

VERBS

nesciō, īre, nescīvī, nescītum – not to know

salūtō, āre, āvī, ātum – to greet

spectō, āre, āvī, ātum – to watch

taceō, ēre, tacuī, tacitum – to be silent, keep quiet

ūtor, ūtī, ūsus sum + ablative – to use

ADVERBS

minimē – least, very little

quōmodo – how

PHRASE

māgnī habeō – esteem a lot

operae pretium est – it is worthwhile

▶ EXERCISE 2

In the sentences below, find the words derived from the Vocabulary to Learn in this chapter. Write the corresponding Latin word.

1. For Valentine's day I received a ring with a beautiful gem on it.

2. We all need to keep in mind the legacy of the Founding Fathers.

3. What is the total amount due?

4. This view is not very popular in our region.

5. The old man died in solitude.

6. This country remained neutral during the war.

7. This man's servile manner toward the more powerful was repulsive.

8. An army man needs to salute his superiors.

9. He is helping the other student for altruistic reasons.

10. This contract is null and void.

11. The view from the top of the mountain was spectacular.

12. How much do you pay for utilities every month?

13. She does not speak a lot; in fact, her nature is rather taciturn.

▶ EXERCISE 3

Write the present active participles (both nominative and genitive singular) of the following verbs. Translate the participles.

Example: amō   amāns, amantis loving/who loves

1. spectō
2. taceō
3. ūtor
4. nesciō
5. addō

6. sequor
7. salūtō
8. trahō
9. dēleō
10. aspiciō

LANGUAGE FACT II

USE OF PARTICIPLES

You have learned the present active participle (*parāns*), the perfect passive participle (*parātus*), and the future active participle (*parātūrus*).

The participles very often have a **temporal** meaning.

- The perfect passive participle indicates an action that happened **before** the action of the main verb. It can often be translated into English by "having been."

> *Puerī Anemōliōs gemmīs et margarītīs ōrnātōs vīdērunt.*
> "The boys saw the Anemolians (having been) adorned with gems and pearls."

The time sequence in this sentence is clear—the Anemolians were first adorned and then seen by the boys.

- The present active participle indicates an action that happens **at the same time** as the action of the main verb. It is usually translated with -*ing* in English (or with a relative clause "who is doing . . .").

> *Anemōliī in urbem ingressī sunt vestīmenta pulcherrima gerentēs.*
> "The Anemolians entered the city wearing most beautiful garments."

Here again, note the time sequence—the Anemolians are entering the city and wearing the beautiful garments at the same time.

- The future active participle indicates an action that is intended to happen **after** the the action of the main verb.

> *Anemōliī intrāvērunt Ūtopiēnsibus ostentūrī quam essent dīvitēs.*
> "The Anemolians entered about to/intending to show the Utopians how rich they were."

The Anemolians first enter the city with the future action (and sometimes the intention) of showing how rich they are.

Look at the following sentence:

> *Ad labōrem parātus poēta verba parāns domī manēbat carmen parātūrus.*
> "The poet having been prepared for the effort (labor) stayed at home preparing words, about to prepare a poem."

The same sentence can be diagrammed in the following way to show the time sequence of the participles.

Time Before Main Verb	*ad labōrem* **parātus**		
Same Time as Main Verb		*poēta verba* **parāns** *domī manēbat*	
Time After Main Verb			*carmen* **parātūrus**

Sometimes participles have nuances that go beyond the temporal meaning.

Here is an example of a **causal** ("because") meaning of the participle.

> *Aliī putantēs monīlia esse vincula et legātōs esse servōs, illa vincula reprehendēbant.*
> "Other people, thinking that the necklaces were chains and the ambassadors were slaves, criticized those chains."

The idea here is that some people reproached the necklaces **because** they thought that the necklaces were chains.

STUDY TIP

Remember that the present and the future participles have an active meaning (*parāns*, "preparing"; *parātūrus*, "going to prepare") and that the perfect participle has a passive meaning (*parātus*, "prepared"). Deponent verbs have a present active participle and a future active participle with an active meaning (*ūtēns*, "using," *ūsūrus*, "going to use") and a perfect passive participle with an active meaning also (*ūsus*, "having used").

BY THE WAY

The temporal meaning of the participles occurs more often the causal meaning. The future participle is encountered less frequently than the present and the perfect ones.

At Erasmus' recommendation, Thomas More engaged Holbein's services. In this portrait, Thomas More is richly dressed and wears the necklace signifying his position as Lord Chancellor. Thomas More has been called "a man for all seasons," a nickname reflecting his multi-talented life as an author, humanist, statesman, and man of moral principle.

▶ EXERCISE 4

In the chapter reading passage, find the three sentences with participles not discussed in Language Fact II. Translate into English. Identify the form of each participle and explain its use.

Example:

Nescientēs aurum et argentum ab Ūtopiēnsibus māgnī nōn habērī, sed signa esse servitūtis, vestīmenta ōrnātissima nōn amārī, et puerōs gemmīs lūdere, audīvērunt hīs omnibus rēbus Ūtopiēnsēs nōn ūtī.

Not knowing that gold and silver was not esteemed a lot by the Utopians, but that they were signs of slavery, that very adorned garments were not loved <by them>, that <only> children played with gems, they heard that the Utopians did not use all these things.

Nescientēs – present active participle, causal meaning

The entrance to King's Hall founded by Edward II in 1317 and refounded by his son Edward III in 1337 bears tribute to the latter. As part of his reforms, Henry VIII combined King's Hall and Michaelhouse to form Trinity College, Cambridge which he founded in 1546 to produce leaders for the Church of England. Henry prized learning and received an excellent education from his tutors. As an adult he was an accomplished musician, author, and poet who presided over an intellectually lively court.

▶ EXERCISE 5

Translate into English. Identify the form of each participle and explain its use. The Reading Vocabulary may be consulted.

Example: Puerum fugientem vīdī.

I saw a boy who was running away/fleeing.

fugientem – present active participle, temporal meaning

1. Anemōliōs ōrnātissimōs spectantēs Ūtopiēnsēs oculīs suīs crēdere nōn poterant.

2. Puer mātrem tacentem aspexit, legātum digitō ostendit et exclāmāvit: "Spectā, māter, nebulōnem illum!"

3. Māter filium exclāmantem rogāvit ut tacēret.

4. Nōn putāns legātum gracilem posse vestīmenta tam pulchra et tot monīlia gerere, māter dīxit eum esse mōriōnem legātōrum.

5. Ūtopiēnsēs igitur Anemōliōs tam bene cūrātōs atque parātōs sine honōribus accēpērunt.

6. Nescientēs mōrēs Ūtopiēnsium esse tam dissimilēs mōrum suōrum, Anemōliī nōn potuērunt facere id quod volēbant.

LANGUAGE FACT III

ADJECTIVES WITH THE GENITIVE SINGULAR IN –ĪUS AND THE DATIVE SINGULAR IN –Ī

The following sentence is taken from the chapter reading passage.

> *Tōtus ille splendor turpis vidēbātur.*
> "All that splendor seemed disgraceful."

The adjective *tōtus, a, um,* "whole, entire," looks like an adjective of the first and second declension (type *bonus, a, um*), but it has some peculiarities in its declension. Its genitive singular, in all genders, ends in *–īus,* and its dative singular, in all genders, ends in *–ī*.

There are nine adjectives which follow this peculiar declension. You already know the adjectives *alius, alia, aliud,* "another, other," *ūnus, a, um,* "one," and *ūllus, a, um,* "any." The last one also occurs in the chapter reading: *sine ūllō honōre,* "without any honor"; it is used in negative phrases and sentences.

The other five adjectives are:

> *alter, altera, alterum* – the other (of two)
>
> *neuter, neutra, neutrum* – neither, none (of two)
>
> *nūllus, a, um* – none; the difference between *nēmō* and *nūllus* is that *nēmō* is used as a noun and *nūllus* as an adjective

sōlus, sōla, sōlum – alone, only

uter, utra, utrum – who, which (of two?)

BY THE WAY

The word *uter* is used instead of *quis* when asking about the choice between two people; for example *uter cōnsulum?* "which of the (two) consuls?" or *uter coniugum?* "which of the (two) spouses?"

Adjectives with a genitive in –*īus* and dative in –*ī*

1. alius, alia, aliud – another, other
2. alter, altera, alterum – the other (of two)
3. neuter, neutra, neutrum – neither, none (of two)
4. nūllus, nūlla, nūllum – none
5. sōlus, sōla, sōlum – alone, only
6. tōtus, tōta, tōtum – whole, entire
7. ūllus, ūlla, ūllum – any
8. ūnus, ūna, ūnum – one
9. uter, utra, utrum – who, which (of two)

STUDY TIP

The "naughty nine" can be remembered by keeping in mind the phrase UNUS NAUTA, which is made up of the first letters of each of these words: *Ūnus, Neuter, Uter, Sōlus, Nūllus, Alter, Ūllus, Tōtus, Alius.*

Ūnus
Neuter
Uter
Sōlus
Nūllus
Alter
Ūllus
Tōtus
Alius

The declension of all these adjectives, except for the genitive and dative singular and some slight variants in the nominative singular (and, in the case of *alius*, the neuter accusative singular), follows the pattern of *iūstus, iūsta, iūstum; pulcher, pulchra, pulchrum;* or *miser, misera, miserum.* To illustrate this, let us look at the declensions of *sōlus, alter,* and *neuter.*

Declension of *sōlus*: type *iūstus* (only the forms in bold are new)

	Singular			Plural		
	Masculine	**Feminine**	**Neuter**	**Masculine**	**Feminine**	**Neuter**
Nominative	sōlus	sōla	sōlum	sōlī	sōlae	sōla
Genitive	**sōlīus**	**sōlīus**	**sōlīus**	sōlōrum	sōlārum	sōlōrum
Dative	**sōlī**	**sōlī**	**sōlī**	sōlīs	sōlīs	sōlīs
Accusative	sōlum	sōlam	sōlum	sōlōs	sōlās	sōla
Ablative	sōlō	sōlā	sōlō	sōlīs	sōlīs	sōlīs
Vocative	sōle	sōla	sōlum	sōlī	sōlae	sōla
	(masculine vocative rarely seen)					

Alius, ūnus, tōtus, nūllus, and *ūllus* decline like *sōlus*.

Declension of *alter*: type *miser* (only the forms in bold are new)

	Singular			Plural		
	Masculine	**Feminine**	**Neuter**	**Masculine**	**Feminine**	**Neuter**
Nominative	alter	altera	alterum	alterī	alterae	altera
Genitive	**alterīus**	**alterīus**	**alterīus**	alterōrum	alterārum	alterōrum
Dative	**alterī**	**alterī**	**alterī**	alterīs	alterīs	alterīs
Accusative	alterum	alteram	alterum	alterōs	alterās	altera
Ablative	alterō	alterā	alterō	alterīs	alterīs	alterīs
Vocative	alter	altera	alterum	alterī	alterae	altera

BY THE WAY

Note also that the genitive singular *alīus* and the dative *aliī* are very rarely used. Instead, for its genitive and dative singular, *alius* borrows the genitive and dative of *alter*, namely *alterīus* and *alterī*.

Declension of *neuter*: type *pulcher* (only the forms in bold are new)

	Singular			Plural		
	Masculine	**Feminine**	**Neuter**	**Masculine**	**Feminine**	**Neuter**
Nominative	neuter	neutra	neutrum	neutrī	neutrae	neutra
Genitive	**neutrīus**	**neutrīus**	**neutrīus**	neutrōrum	neutrārum	neutrōrum
Dative	**neutrī**	**neutrī**	**neutrī**	neutrīs	neutrīs	neutrīs
Accusative	neutrum	neutram	neutrum	neutrōs	neutrās	neutra
Ablative	neutrō	neutrā	neutrō	neutrīs	neutrīs	neutrīs
Vocative	neuter	neutra	neutrum	neutrī	neutrae	neutra

Uter declines like *neuter*.

STUDY TIP

The genitive singular ending *–īus* and the dative singular ending *–ī* can also be seen in the declension of some pronouns: *hūius, cūius, illīus, ēius; cui, illī, eī.*

BY THE WAY

The ending *–īus* is distinctive for its long vowel before another vowel (usually a vowel before another vowel is short).

Antoine Caron (1521–1599) served as court painter to Catherine de' Medici and Henry II, the Catholic monarchs of France, who would have approved the subject matter of this painting. "The Arrest and Supplication of Thomas More" shows a long-bearded More being arrested in the foreground with the execution scene in the background.

▶ EXERCISE 6

Translate into Latin.

1. The entire populace was watching the ambassadors.

2. No ambassador understood the customs of the people.

3. In that city people never used any gems.

4. Two brothers watching the ambassadors were not silent. One believed they were slaves, the other shouted: "Mother, watch that man!"

5. Which of the brothers did not know they were slaves?

6. Neither of the slaves esteemed jewels a lot.

7. Other people thought it was worthwhile to have jewels.

8. Being about to write about that thing, I was keeping silent.

9. Only to me these customs seemed disgraceful.

▶ EXERCISE 7

Rewrite the sentences changing the relative clauses into present active participle phrases. Translate the sentences. The Reading Vocabulary may be consulted.

Example: Vīdī discipulam, quae legēbat.
Vīdī discipulam legentem.
I saw a student who was reading.

1. Anemōliī, quī ad iter sē parābant, vestīmenta ōrnātissima habēre volēbant.

2. Anemōliī cupiēbant Ūtopiēnsium, quī in viīs stābant, oculōs splendōre suō praestringere.

3. Ūtopiēnsēs tamen putāvērunt legātōs, quī vestīmenta pulcherrima gerēbant, esse servōs.

4. Māter dīxit puerō, quī exclāmābat, eum tacēre dēbēre.

5. Nam puer, quī putābat legātum tamquam puerum sē gerere, mātrī hoc dīcere voluerat.

Erected by William the Conqueror in the 1080s, the Tower of London looms over the River Thames. Thomas More spent a week here prior to his execution. Today's tourists enjoy seeing the Crown Jewels kept in a high security part of the palace, the iconic Beefeater Guards, and the ravens whose presence, according to legend, is necessary lest the monarchy and the kingdom fall.

TALKING ABOUT A READING

ABOUT OUR STATE AND UNADAPTED LATIN: ATTICUS AVOIDS HOLDING OFFICES IN THE PROVINCES

DĒ NOSTRĀ RĒ PŪBLICĀ

Mārcus: Thomas Morus in librō suō rem pūblicam fictam (*invented*) dēscrīpsit (*described*), in quā nōn sunt hominēs dīvitēs nec hominēs pauperēs, sed omnēs sunt aequī. Nōn est in illā rē pūblicā inīquitās, sed rēs sunt omnibus iūstae.

Christīna: Interdum tamen lībertās in illā rē pūblicā nōn plēna vidētur. Fortasse tōtus liber, quem scrīpsit Morus, est iocus.

Mārcus: Nesciō . . . Utinam nostra rēs pūblica esset tam iūsta quam est Ūtopia!

Utinam nostra rēs pūblica esset tam iūsta quam est Ūtopia!

Christīna: At apud nōs sunt rēs iūstae. Nam omnēs hominēs suffrāgia ferre (*to vote*) possunt et ēligere (*to elect*) regimen (*government*) quod volunt: licet ēligere magistrātūs (*officials*) in comitātū (*county*), urbis praefectum (*mayor*), vicāriōs (*congressmen*), senātōrēs (*senators*), reī pūblicae praesidem (*president*). Omnēs possunt līberē dē omnibus rēbus loquī atque dīcere quid sentiant: et quī novitātis fautōribus (*liberals – Democrats*) favent et quī rērum cōnservātōribus (*conservatives – Republicans*) favent. Nōn omnibus in cīvitātibus licet cīvibus dīcere quid sentiant.

Mārcus: Hoc est vērum. Sed sunt quoque hominēs quī multō (*by much*) maiōrēs dīvitiās habent quam aliī et sunt multō potentiōrēs.

Christīna: Sed tālēs (*such*) sunt rēs hūmānae. Nōn omnia possunt esse perfecta (*perfect*). Plūrēs hominēs pecūniam petere solent.

Mārcus: Legēns dē Atticō intellēxī eum honōrēs et dīvitiās nōn māgnī habuisse.

Helena: Tūne, Mārce, honōrēs dīvitiāsque māgnī habēs?

Mārcus: Neutram rem tantī habeō quantī multī hominēs tālēs rēs habent. Discēns dē Atticō illās rēs fortasse etiam minus amābō . . .

ATTICUS AVOIDS HOLDING OFFICE IN THE PROVINCES

CORNĒLIĪ NEPŌTIS ATTICUS, 6.4–5

Consuls and praetors offered Atticus positions in provincial adminstrations, but Atticus avoided duties of this nature. After he had refused the praetorship itself, he did not want to be on the staff of a praetor. He also wanted to avoid the suspicion of illegitimate behavior (and in fact extortion, bribery, plundering were all too prevalent in Roman provincial administration during the late Republic).

1   4. Multōrum cōnsulum praetōrumque praefectūrās dēlātās sīc accēpit, ut nēminem in prōvinciam sit secūtus, honōre fuerit contentus, reī familiāris dēspexerit frūctum; quī nē cum Q. quidem Cicerōne voluerit īre in Āsiam, cum apud eum lēgātī locum obtinēre posset. Nōn enim
5   decēre sē arbitrābātur, cum praetūram gerere nōluisset, asseclam esse praetōris. 5. Quā in rē nōn sōlum dignitātī serviēbat, sed etiam tranquillitātī, cum suspiciōnēs quoque vītāret crīminum. Quō fīēbat, ut ēius observantia omnibus esset cārior, cum eam officiō, nōn timōrī neque speī tribuī vidērent.

VOCABULARY

1 praetor, praetōris, m. – praetor

   praefectūra, ae, f. – an office in governing a province

   dēlātās – perfect passive participle from *dēferō, dēferre, dētulī, dēlātum* – to bring to, confer upon

2 prōvincia, ae, f. – province

   sīc (adv.) – in such a way

   contentus, a, um + abl. – contented with

2–3 rēs familiāris – personal property, estate

3 dēspiciō, ere, dēspexī, dēspectum – to despise

   frūctus, frūctūs, m. – fruit, gain, revenue

   nē . . . quidem . . . – not even

   Q. = Quīntus

4 īre – to go

   Āsia, ae, f. – Asia

   obtineō, ēre, obtinuī, obtentum – to hold onto

5 decet, decēre (impersonal verb) – it is becoming

   arbitror, arbitrārī, arbitrātus sum – to be of the opinion

   praetūra, ae, f. – praetorship

   assecla, ae, m. – follower, attendant

6 dignitās, dignitātis, f. – dignity

   serviō, īre, īvī, ītum – to be of service, comply with

7 tranquillitās, tranquillitātis, f. – calmness, quiet way of life

   suspiciō, suspiciōnis, f. – suspicion

   vītō, āre, āvī, ātum – to avoid

   crīmen, crīminis, n. – crime, illegal action

   quō fīēbat – thus it happened…

8 observantia, ae, f. – regard

   cārus, a, um – dear

   cum . . . vidērent – because people saw

   officium, ī, n. – service, kindness, duty

9 spēs, speī, f. – hope

   tribuō, ere, tribuī, tribūtum – to attribute

READING NOTES

1 *praetor, praetōris,* m. A praetor was a magistrate charged with the administration of justice or was a governor of a province.

1–2 *Multōrum cōnsulum praetōrumque praefectūrās dēlātās sīc accēpit, ut nēminem in prōvinciam sit secūtus* The word *ut* introduces a result clause (see Chapter 14). This phrase means "He accepted the office of many consuls and praetors conferred upon <him> in such a way that he did not follow anyone to a province." In other words, he accepted the honor of appointment but did not physically undertake the office offered.

2–4 *honōre fuerit contentus, reī familiāris dēspexerit frūctum; quī nē cum Q. quidem Cicerōne voluerit īre in Āsiam* All the subjunctive verbs are continuations of the idea of result introduced by *ut* (see the previous note): "<and that> he was content with the honor, <and that> he despised gain of family property/wealth; and he did not even want to go to Asia with Quintus Cicero." Note how the relative *quī* is sometimes used at the beginning of a sentence or a coordinate clause with a meaning closer to that of a demonstrative (e.g., *ille*) than a relative. Note also that *nē . . . quidem* encloses the words to which the idea of "not . . . even" refers.

4 *in Āsiam* The Roman province of Asia contained an area also known as Phrygia which today is Turkey. Asia Minor is also used to refer to the area in ancient times.

   cum apud eum lēgātī locum obtinēre posset Here *cum* with a verb in the subjunctive has the meaning "although" (see Chapter 12) and *apud eum* means "with him."

5 *cum praetūram gerere nōluisset* Here *cum* means "when" or "after." In this context *gerere* means "to hold."

   Quā in rē The meaning is "And in this matter."

7 *cum suspiciōnēs quoque vītāret crīminum* Here *cum* is causal and means "because he was avoiding suspicions of illegal actions."

7–8 *Quō fīēbat, ut ēius observantia omnibus esset cārior* Here again the word *ut* introduces a result clause. "Thus it happened that his regard was dearer to everybody . . ."

8 *cum eam officiō . . . vidērent* The word *cum* again has the causal meaning "because" and *eam* "it," refers to *observantia*.

QUESTIONS ABOUT THE TEXT

Answer in complete Latin sentences.

1. Cūr Atticus praefectūrās in prōvinciīs accipere nōlēbat?

2. Cūr nōluit cum Quīntō Cicerōne Āsiam petere?

3. Quid fīēbat, cum hominēs intellegēbant eum nōlle praefectūrās habēre? Cūr?

DĒ NOSTRĀ RĒ PŪBLICĀ CONTINUED

Mārcus: Melius est nihil ab aliīs petere et amīcōs amāre propter ipsōs, nōn propter dīvitiās et honōrēs.

Helena: Haec audiēns intellegō Atticum fuisse optimum hominem atque fēlīcem.

CHAPTER 12

Temporal, Causal, Concessive Clauses; Conditional Clauses

Nicolò Barabino (1832–1891) presents Columbus on board ship with maps and charts displayed as he explains the journey.

MEMORĀBILE DICTŪ

Nāvigāre necesse est; vīvere nōn est necesse.

It is necessary to sail, it is not necessary to live.

This is the Latin version of a phrase attributed to the first century BCE Roman general Pompey by the Greek author Plutarch, who lived in the late first and early second centuries CE. Though Plutarch wrote in Greek, Pompey presumably said these words in Latin to his soldiers, when exhorting them to complete a mission of supplying grain in very dangerous conditions.

READING

The Spanish priest Juan Ginés de Sepúlveda (1494 CE–1573 CE) came from a well-to-do family and decided on a career as a scholar while still a young man. Like several prominent intellectuals of his time, he traveled to Italy for his training in literature and philosophy, and it was there that he seems to have perfected his excellent Latin style. At the University of Bologna, which he entered in 1515, he began the challenging project of producing more accurate Latin translations of Aristotle's works; his efforts in this field were held in such high regard that in 1526 he was named the official translator of Aristotle for the Papacy. Upon his return to Spain he served as advisor to Charles V, King of Spain and Holy Roman Emperor, who in 1550 convened a council of jurists, theologians, and prominent churchmen at Valladolid to consider the legal basis for the Spanish to subjugate the indigenous peoples in America. At this congress, Sepúlveda upheld the right of the Spanish empire not only to subdue and subjugate the natives of the New World, but also to convert them to Christianity. He applied the concept of "natural slavery" as expounded by Aristotle in his *Politics*. Claiming that these peoples were by nature incapable of rational government and best suited for physical labor, he argued that it was better for them to be ruled by humans naturally adapted to ruling, namely the Europeans. Bartolomé de las Casas, a Dominican friar, opposed Sepúlveda's arguments and upheld the rights of the indigenous peoples, maintaining that they should be free individuals subject to Spanish government, like those who resided in Spain itself. Sepúlveda elaborated his argument for Spanish enslavement of native Americans in a dialogue entitled *Dēmocratēs alter, sive dē iustīs bellī causīs apud Indōs* (*The Second Democrates or On the Just Reasons for War in the Case of the Indians*).

In the passage below, adapted from Book 1 of his historical work *Dē orbe novō* (*On the New World*), Sepúlveda tells how close the expedition of Columbus, sponsored by the Spanish King and Queen, almost came to being abandoned. Columbus is called by the Latinized name *Colōnus*.

DĒ ORBE NOVŌ

1   Ex īnsulīs Fortūnātīs nautae Hispānī discesserant cursumque inter
    merīdiem et occidentem dīrēxerant. Iam tricēsimō diē nāvis per vastum
    ōceanum ferēbātur necdum ūlla terra est vīsa. Nautae iam spērāre
    nōlēbant. Nōn sōlum dē sorte suā dēspērābant, sed etiam Colōnum
5   temeritātis palam accūsābant. Perīcula illīus nāvigātiōnis sibi vidērī esse
    nimis māgna dīcēbant; mare esse vacuum; sē nūllam terram cōnspicere
    posse. "Nisi nōs in Hispāniam statim redūxeris," inquiunt, "moriēris."

    Cum haec omnia audīvisset, nautās quidem timēre coepit Colōnus,
    quamquam dē nāvigātiōne ipsā numquam dēspērāvit. "Vidēminī,"
10 inquit, "ō nautae, omnem glōriae spem perdere dē vītā vestrā tantum
    cōgitantēs. Vīta quoque mea mihi est cāra, quia omnēs hominēs vītam

suam esse cāram putant. Sed haec nāvigātiō est ā rēge probāta. Sī ab officiō vestrō discesseritis, quid dē vōbīs in Hispāniā dīcētur? Virīne fortēs vocābiminī? Itaque rogō ut hanc meam sententiam audiātis. Per

15 trēs aliōs diēs exspectāre dēbēbimus. Sī post trēs diēs terram nūllam cōnspexerimus, cursum mūtābimus et ad Hispāniam nāvigābimus."

His verbīs mōtī nautae tacuērunt et per trēs aliōs diēs exspectāvērunt. Per duōs diēs nāvigābant, nec ūllam terram vīdērunt. Eā autem nocte lūmen procul ā nāvibus positum vīdit nauta. Postquam hoc est factum,

20 Colōnus et nautae canere coepērunt: "Tē Deum laudāmus!"

READING VOCABULARY

canō, ere, cecinī, cantum – to sing

*cārus, a, um – dear

Colōnus, ī, m. – (Christophorus) Columbus

*cum + pluperfect subjunctive – after

cursus, cursūs, m. – course, going

dēspērō, āre, āvī, ātum – to despair

dīrigō, ere, dīrēxī, dīrēctum – to guide, direct, aim, send

Hispānia, ae, f. – Spain

Hispānus, a, um – Spanish

*inquiunt (plural of *inquit*) – they say (only introducing direct speech)

Īnsulae Fortūnātae, –ārum, f. pl. – Canary Islands‡

*morior, morī, mortuus sum – to die

nāvigātiō, nāvigātiōnis, f. – sea voyage

necdum (adv.) – and not yet

*nimis (adv.) – too much

*nisi (conj.) – if not, unless

ō! (interjection) – oh!

occidēns, occidentis, m. – west

ōceanus, ī, m. – ocean

*officium, ī, n. – duty

*orbis, orbis, m. – circle

   orbis terrārum – the earth, the world

palam (adv.) – openly

*probō, āre, āvī, ātum – to approve

*quamquam (conj.) – although

*quia (conj.) – because

*quidem (adv.) – indeed

redūcō, ere, redūxī, reductum – to lead back

*sententia, ae, f. – opinion, point of view

*sors, sortis, f. – lot, fate‡

*spērō, āre, āvī, ātum – to hope

*spēs, speī, f. – hope

temeritās, temeritātis, f. – rashness, recklessness

tricēsimus, a, um – thirtieth

vastus, a, um – empty, vast

*Words marked with an asterisk will need to be memorized later in the chapter.

‡Additional information about the words marked with the double dagger will be in the **Take Note** section that follows the Reading Vocabulary.

TAKE NOTE

Īnsulae Fortūnātae Literally "Islands Blessed by Fortune," this phrase refers to the Canary Islands.

sors, sortis, f. In the literal sense, this word means a lot that one draws but in a metaphorical sense it refers to fate as in one's condition in life.

COMPREHENSION QUESTIONS

1. What was the reason for the frustration of Columbus' crew?

2. What did Columbus's crew request?

3. What was Columbus' response and the reason for it?

4. What happened before the third day?

Orazio Marinali (1643–1720), a late baroque sculptor from Venice, sculpted some 150 statues for the Villa Lampertico in Vicenza, Italy. Marinali captures Aristotle as an older man with furrowed brow and wrinkled cheeks. In a characteristic baroque flourish, the robes are a swirl of folds.

LANGUAGE FACT I

TEMPORAL CLAUSES

In the chapter reading passage, you encountered the following sentence:

> *Cum haec omnia audīvisset, nautās quidem timēre coepit Colōnus.*
> "After he had heard all these things, Columbus began to fear the sailors indeed."

You already know the conjunction *cum*, which means "**when**" and is used with the indicative. The same conjunction, however, may also be used with the subjunctive, and sometimes means "**after**."

The conjunction *cum* is used with the **indicative** when it indicates a **general unspecified circumstance** which could occur any time. This *cum* with the **indicative** occurs most often when the tense of the main verb is present and it means "**when**."

> ***Cum*** *nimis* **dolēmus***, lacrimās fundimus.*
> "When we feel too much pain, we shed tears."

The conjunction *cum* with the **imperfect subjunctive** refers to a concrete or specific circumstance in the past during which the action in the main clause occurred. It is translated with "**when**."

Sometimes a causal meaning of conjunction *cum* is stronger than the temporal one. Then *cum* means "**since**."

> ***Cum*** *tam diū* **nāvigārent***, nautae cupere coepērunt domum petere.*
> "Since they were sailing for such a long time, the sailors began to desire to go home."

The conjunction *cum* with the **pluperfect subjunctive** refers to a concrete or specific circumstance in the past, which occurred before the action in the main clause. In this case *cum* means "**after**."

> ***Cum*** *lūmen* **cōnspexissent***, nautae intellēxērunt sē novam terram invēnisse.*
> "After they had observed a light, the sailors understood that they had found a new land."

Look at this list of all the temporal conjunctions you have learned so far. There are quite a few more uses of most of the above-mentioned conjunctions, as well as other temporal conjunctions, which you will learn as you become more experienced in Latin.

Temporal Conjunctions			
Conjunction	Mood/Tense	Meaning	Example
Cum	indicative	when	**Cum legimus**, discimus. "When we read, we learn."
Cum	imperfect subjunctive	when	**Cum** nimis diū **legerem**, oculī dolēre coepērunt. "When I was reading for a too long time, my eyes began to hurt."
Cum	pluperfect subjunctive	after	**Cum** librum **lēgissem**, alium petīvī. "After I had read the book, I looked for another one."
Dum	indicative	while	**Dum est** spēs, spērāre dēbēmus. "While there is hope, we must hope."
Postquam	indicative	after	**Postquam** mē **vocāvistī**, ad tē vēnī. "After you called me, I came to you."
Quotiēs	indicative	as often as	**Quotiēs** tē **videō**, gaudium mē capit. "As often as I see you, joy seizes me."
Simul ac	indicative	as soon as	**Simul ac** verba illa **audīvī**, timēre coepī. "As soon as I heard those words, I began to fear."

BY THE WAY

When *postquam* occurs in a sentence that talks about an action in the past, it very often introduces a subordinate clause whose verb is in the perfect indicative. Although a pluperfect indicative might be expected since the action of the subordinate clause is necessarily prior to the action of the main clause, Latin uses a perfect indicative in this situation.

Example:

> *Postquam mē vocāvistī, ad tē vēnī.* "After you called me, I came to you."

Lorado Taft's monument stands in front of Union Station in Washington, D.C. Columbus faces the US Capitol standing at the prow of a ship whose winged figure represents democracy. He is flanked by images of the Old World, a patriarchal figure, and the New World, a Native American.

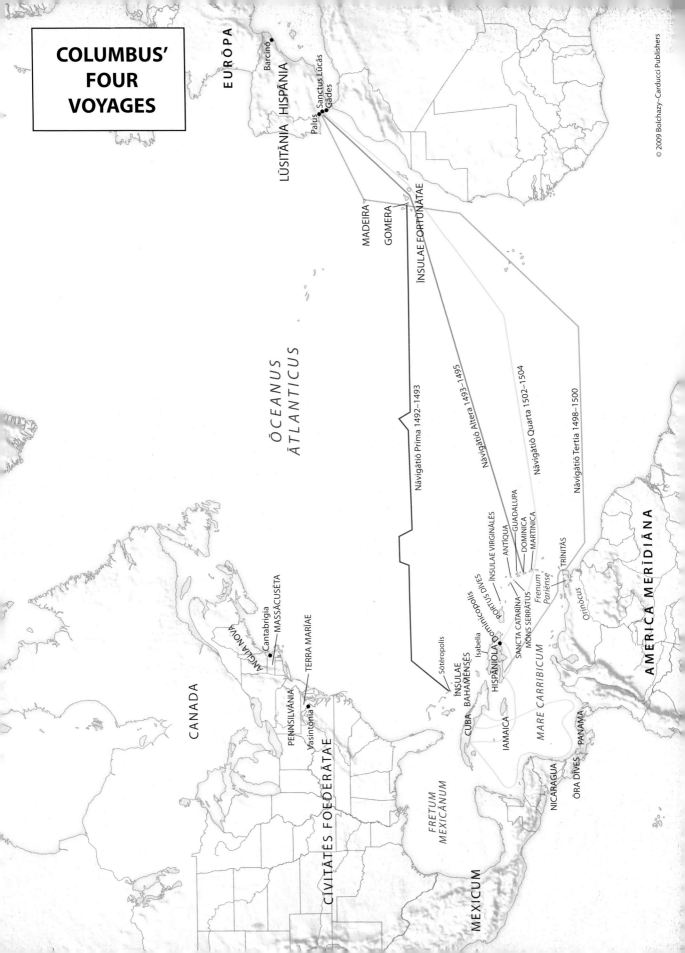

COLUMBUS' FOUR VOYAGES

© 2009 Bolchazy–Carducci Publishers

EURŌPA

Barcinō

LŪSITĀNIA   HISPĀNIA

Sanctus Lūcās
Gādes
Palus

MADEIRA

GOMERA

ĪNSULAE FORTŪNĀTAE

ŌCEANUS ĀTLANTICUS

Nāvigātiō Prīma 1492–1493

Nāvigātiō Altera 1493–1495

Nāvigātiō Quarta 1502–1504

Nāvigātiō Tertia 1498–1500

CANADA

Cantabrigia
MASSĀCUSETA
ANGLIA NOVA

TERRA MARĪAE

Sōtēropolis

PENNSILVĀNIA
Vasintōnia

CĪVITĀTĒS FOEDERĀTAE

ĪNSULAE BAHAMĒNSĒS

INSULAE VIRGINĀLĒS

ANTĪQUA
GUADALUPA
DOMINICA
MARTINĪCA

TRĪNITĀS

Frenum Pariēnse

Orīnōcus

AMERICA MERĪDIĀNA

ĪNSULAE DĪVES

PORTUS DĪVES

Isabella
Dominicopolis
HISPĀNIOLA

SANCTA CATARINA
MŌNS SERRĀTUS

CUBA

IAMAICA

MARE CARRIBICUM

NICARAGUA
ŌRA DĪVES
PANAMA

FRETUM MEXICĀNUM

MEXICUM

▶ EXERCISE 1

Translate into Latin. In some cases, more than one construction will work.

1. As soon as Columbus' opinion was approved, he prepared the ship.

    Colōnus, ī, m. – Columbus

2. As often as the sailors thought of their lot, they lost hope.

3. After they did not see anything for a long time, the sailors said, "We shall not die in this ship. Columbus hopes too much."

4. The sailors were not silent; when they were speaking, their anger became greater.

5. "While we are on the ship," said Columbus, "it is not worthwhile to abandon our duty."

6. When people have a strong spirit, they fear least.

VOCABULARY TO LEARN

NOUNS

officium, ī, n. – duty

orbis, orbis, m. – circle

sententia, ae, f. – opinion, point of view

sors, sortis, f. – lot

spēs, speī, f. – hope

ADJECTIVES

cārus, a, um – dear

VERBS

inquiunt (plural of *inquit*) – they say (only introducing direct speech)

morior, morī, mortuus sum – to die

probō, āre, āvī, ātum – to approve

spērō, āre, āvī, ātum – to hope

ADVERBS

nimis – too much

quidem – indeed

tamen – however, nevertheless

CONJUNCTIONS

cum + pluperfect subjunctive – after

nisi – if not, unless

quamquam – although

quamvīs – although

quia – because

quod – because

PHRASE

orbis terrārum – the earth, the world

▶ EXERCISE 2

In the sentences below, find the words derived from the Vocabulary to Learn in this chapter. Write the corresponding Latin word.

1. After his last offense, he is on probation.

2. The office will be closed today.

3. After the last catastrophic events, I am desperate.

4. You should always write complete sentences.

5. We need to sort things out.

6. The Earth's orbit around the sun is elliptical.

7. The governor issued an official statement earlier today.

LANGUAGE FACT II

CAUSAL CLAUSES

In the chapter reading passage, you met the following sentence:

> *Vīta quoque mea mihi est cāra, quia omnēs hominēs vītam suam esse cāram putant.*
> "My life is also dear to me, because all humans think their lives are dear."

The subordinate clause beginning with *quia* is causal. It explains why Columbus' life was dear to him.

The two most used causal conjunctions in Latin are **quia** and **quod.** If a causal clause presents the cause as a statement, its verb is in the indicative.

> *Discimus **quia** plūra scīre **necesse est**.*
> "We learn because it is necessary to know more."

If a causal clause presents the cause as the thought of a person in the narrative, but **not** necessarily that of the author, its verb is often in the subjunctive.

> *Ille nōn vēnit **quod** tempus nōn **habēret**.*
> "He did not come because <according to what he said/thought> he did not have (the) time."

The conjunction *cum* with the subjunctive may also be employed to introduce a causal clause. The causal meaning (rather than temporal or concessive) is typically clear from the context.

> *Cum mare esset vacuum, nautae spērāre nōlēbant.*
> "Since the sea was empty, the sailors were unwilling to hope."

LANGUAGE FACT III

CONCESSIVE CLAUSES

In the chapter reading passage, Sepúlveda makes this statement:

> *Nautās quidem timēre coepit Colōnus, quamquam dē nāvigātiōne ipsā numquam dēspērāvit.*
> "Columbus began to fear the sailors indeed, although he never lost hope about the voyage itself."

The subordinate clause beginning with *quamquam* is **concessive**. We call it this, because it states a fact **despite which** the action in the main clause happens or is true. Columbus begins to fear the sailors **despite the fact** that he still does not despair about the voyage.

The two most used concessive conjunctions in Latin are **quamquam**, which is used with the indicative and presents the concession as a fact, and **quamvīs,** which is used with the subjunctive and presents the concession as the thought of a person in the narrative, but not necessarily that of the author.

> **Quamquam** *iter* **est** *longum, īre dēbēbimus.*
> "Although the trip is long, we will need to go."

The Columbus Foundation reconstructed Columbus' favorite ship the Niña to celebrate the quincentary anniversary of the famous voyage of 1492. The Niña, a classic caravel with lateen (triangular) sails for maneuverability was launched in 1991. The ship travels as a museum and here sails in Morro Bay, California.

> ***Quamvīs*** *mēcum venīre nōlīs, hoc tamen facere dēbēs.*
> "Although you do not want to come with me, nevertheless you have to do this."

The conjunction *cum* may also be used with a concessive meaning. When *cum* has this meaning, the verb in the subordinate clause it introduces is in the subjunctive, and in the main clause the adverb *tamen* is usually present, so that it is obvious that the meaning of *cum* is not temporal or causal. Here are some examples:

> ***Cum*** *mēcum venīre nōlīs, hoc tamen facere dēbēs.*
> "Although you do not want to come with me, nevertheless you have to do this."

Note that in this sentence *cum* has the same meaning as *quamvīs* (in the example shown earlier). We can put the same sentence in the past, and the construction will be the same, with only a change in the tenses of the verbs.

> ***Cum*** *mēcum venīre nōllēs, hoc tamen facere dēbēbās.*
> "Although you did not want to come with me, nevertheless you were obliged to do this."

BY THE WAY

The presence of the word *tamen* in the main clause often functions as a clue to the reader that a concessive clause may be present.

▶ EXERCISE 3

Fill in the blanks with the appropriate causal or concessive conjunction. Translate the sentences.

Example: Māter fīlium cūrat _____ eum amat.
Māter fīlium cūrat quia eum amat.
The mother takes care of \<her\> son because she loves him.

1. Colōnus nāvigābat _____ novam terram quaerēbat.
    Colōnus, ī, m. – Columbus

2. Nautae īrā sunt captī _____ iam diū nihil cōnspiciēbātur.

3. Nautae Colōnum occīdere volēbant _____ ille in perīcula eōs dūceret.

4. Colōnus ā nautīs tandem nōn occīsus est _____ nautae dīxerant eum moritūrum esse.

5. _____ nautae exspectāre nōlēbant, tamen dēcrēvērunt per trēs diēs exspectāre.

6. _____ trēs diēs essent tempus longum, operae pretium fuit exspectāre.

7. Omnēs tandem maximō gaudiō sunt captī _____ lūmen cōnspicere potuērunt.

LANGUAGE FACT IV
CONDITIONAL CLAUSES

In the chapter reading passage, you saw the following conditional statements.

The sailors threaten Columbus:

> *Nisi nōs in Hispāniam statim redūxeris, moriēris.*
> "Unless you lead us back to Spain at once, you will die!"

Then Columbus tries to dissuade the sailors from doing what they desire.

> *Sī ab officiō vestrō discesseritis, quid dē vōbīs in Hispāniā dīcētur?*
> "If you abandon your duty, what will be said about you in Spain?"

At last Columbus proposes a deal to the sailors.

> *Sī post trēs diēs terram nūllam cōnspexerimus, cursum mūtābimus et ad Hispāniam nāvigābimus.*
> If we see no land after three days, we will change course and will sail to Spain."

In these three examples, there is a **condition that could be fulfilled in the future**. Something will happen (or not), if something else happens (or not) before it. There is a **future perfect indicative in the subordinate clause** and a **future indicative in the main clause**. In many grammar books, this is called a **future more vivid condition**.

Sometimes the simple future indicative can take the place of the future perfect in the subordinate clause, if both parts of the future more vivid condition refer to events that will happen at the same time in the future.

A seven-meter-tall Christopher Columbus stands atop a forty-meter-high column designed by Rafael Atché (1854–1923) for the Exposición Universal de Barcelona held in 1888. The massive monument overlooks the sea and the medieval shipyards. Upon his return to Spain, Columbus reported to Ferdinand and Isabella at Barcelona.

Other times, however, we want to express what would happen if a certain condition was present which actually is not present. An **unfulfilled condition in the present** is indicated with an **imperfect subjunctive** both **in the main clause** and **in the subordinate clause**. Such conditions are often called **present contrary-to-fact conditions.**

Before spotting the light, the sailors might have said to Columbus:

> *Sī terram nunc **vidērēmus**, **nōn cuperēmus** domum petere.*
> "If we were seeing land now, we would not want to go home." (but they do not see land and therefore want to go home).

Sometimes we want to express what would have happened, if a certain condition had been present which in fact never existed. An **unfulfilled condition in the past** is indicated with a **pluperfect subjunctive** both **in the main clause** and **in the subordinate clause.** This is a **past contrary-to-fact condition.**

Columbus might have recalled the commitment of the sailors to the king in the following way:

> *Sī rēx nōs **nōn mīsisset**, in terrā **mānsissēmus**.*
> "If the king had not sent us, we would have remained on land." (but he did send us, and therefore we did not remain on land—and are now at sea).

We have seen above that conditions are called future more vivid when the condition refers to something that **could** be fulfilled in the future. A conditional sentence, however, can also make a much more hesitant statement about the future. In English these are called "should-would" conditions, or **future less vivid conditions**. These are constructed in Latin with the present subjunctive in both clauses. The perfect subjunctive is used in the "if-clause," and the present subjunctive in the conclusion, if the action in the "if-clause" must definitely happen before that described in the conclusion. We can rewrite the **future more vivid condition** quoted above to make it a **future less vivid** condition—i.e., a less definite statement about future action.

> *Sī post trēs diēs terram nūllam cōnspexerimus, cursum mūtēmus et ad Hispāniam nāvigēmus.*
> If we should see no land after three days, we would change course and sail to Spain."

Finally, a conditional statement that makes a general remark about the present or past is called a **present or past general condition**. In these conditions, as you would expect, the appropriate tense of the indicative (i.e., present, imperfect, perfect, or pluperfect) appears in each clause.

Here is a present general condition.

> *Sī terram nūllam cōnspicimus, timēmus.*
> "If we see no land, we are afraid."

And we can easily turn this into a past general condition:

> *Sī terram nūllam cōnspiciēbāmus, timēbāmus.*
> "If we were seeing no land, we were afraid."

Type of Conditional Sentence	Subordinate Clause	Main Clause
Future More Vivid	Future Perfect Indicative (or Future Indicative)	Future Indicative
	Sī pecūniam **habuerō**,	*dōnum pulcherrimum tibi* **parābō**.
	"If I have money,	I will prepare for you a very beautiful gift."

Type of Conditional Sentence	Subordinate Clause	Main Clause
Future Less Vivid	Perfect Subjunctive (or Present Subjunctive)	Present Subjunctive
	Sī pecūniam **habuerim**,	*dōnum pulcherrimum tibi* **parem**.
	"If I should have money,	I would prepare for you a very beautiful gift."

Type of Conditional Sentence	Subordinate Clause	Main Clause
Present Contrary-to-Fact	Imperfect Subjunctive	Imperfect Subjunctive
	Sī pecuniam **habērem**,	*dōnum pulcherrimum tibi* **parārem**.
	"If I were to possess money,	I would prepare for you a very beautiful gift." (but I don't have money and I am not preparing you any gift)

Type of Conditional Sentence	Subordinate Clause	Main Clause
Past Contrary-to-Fact	Pluperfect Subjunctive	Pluperfect Subjunctive
	Sī pecūniam **habuissem**,	*dōnum pulcherrimum tibi* **parāvissem**.
	"If I had possessed money,	I would have prepared for you a very beautiful gift." (but I did not have money and I did not prepare you any gift)

Type of Conditional Sentence	Subordinate Clause	Main Clause
Present General	Present Indicative	Present Indicative
	Sī pecūniam **habeō**	*dōnum pulcherrimum tibi* **parō**.
	"If I have money (i.e., if the condition of my having money exists),	I prepare for you a very beautiful gift."

Type of Conditional Sentence	Subordinate Clause	Main Clause
Past General Condition	Past Indicative	Past Indicative
	Sī pecūniam **habēbam**,	*dōnum pulcherrimum tibi* **parābam**.
	"If I had money (i.e., if the condition of my having money was present),	I used to prepare for you a very beautiful gift."

The negative of *sī* is *sī nōn* or *nisi*.

▶ EXERCISE 4

Identify the type of condition in each sentence. Translate the sentence into Latin.

1. If the sailors had watched the island, they would have hoped indeed.

2. If you (pl.) were thinking about your duty, your point of view would now be different.

3. If this trip had not been approved by the king, we would not have received the ships.

4. If you do not do this, you will die.

5. If we had hope, we would be going to the end of the world.

6. If my lot were better, I would now be with my dear friends.

▶ EXERCISE 5

Fill in the blanks, using the appropriate conjunctions (choose from *cum, dum, postquam, quamquam, quamvīs, quia, quod, quotiēs, nisi, sī, simul ac*). Translate the sentences.

1. _____ dē sorte suā miserrimā cōgitārent, Colōnum esse hominem turpem dīcēbant.

2. Nautae dē vītā suā timēbant _____ vidēbant sē esse in māgnō perīculō.

3. "_____ nōs servāveris," dīxērunt nautae, "tē occidēmus."

4. "_____ plūra intellegerētis," respondit Colōnus, "ita nōn loquerēminī."

5. _____ Colōnus turpis nautīs vidērētur, tamen exspectāre dēcrēvērunt.

6. _____ per duōs diēs nihil cōnspexērunt, tandem lūmen est vīsum.

7. _____ lūmen cōnspexērunt, omnēs intellēxērunt sē novam terram invēnisse.

An official decree of the government of Guatemala called for a newly designed one centavo coin to celebrate the life of "Fray" Bartolomé de las Casas. The Dominican friar is much respected for his defense of the rights of the indigenous peoples of the Americas.

▶ EXERCISE 6

Translate the following text adapted from the beginning of Book 1 of Sepúlveda's *Dē orbe novō*.

Eō annō Colōnus nautam Lūsitānum aegrōtum apud sē accēpit ut ille cūrārētur. Cum nauta Lūsitānus iam prope mortem esset, viam Colōnō aperuit, quā ad terrās novās nāvigāre licēbat, quia novae illae terrae ā Lūsitānō iam vīsae erant. Colōnus statim intellēxit sē rem maximam audīvisse et illās terrās invenīre cupīvit. Omnēs dīcēbant Colōnum auxilium et pecūniam petere dēbēre. "Sī rēx," inquiunt, "hoc cōnsilium probāverit et accēperit, imperium māgnum māgnumque lūcrum in illīs terrīs novīs habēre poterit."

Colōnus prīmō Lūsitānōrum rēgem petīvit, quod Lūsitānī itinera maritima longa ante aliōs fēcissent. Cōnsilium autem Colōnī ā Lūsitānōrum rēge neglēctum est. Hoc quoque fēcit rēx Britannōrum, quem etiam petīverat Colōnus.

Tandem Colōnus ad Ferdinandum et Isabellam, Hispānōrum rēgem et rēgīnam, venīre dēcrēvit. Rem ā nautā Lūsitānō nārrātam eōs docuit. Quamquam eō tempore rēgēs Hispānōrum bellum māgnum gerēbant et pecūniā egēbant, tamen dēcrēvērunt trēs nāvēs et paucōs mīlitēs et nautās Colōnō dare. Propter hoc cōnsilium Hispānī imperium novum et māgnum habēre poterant.

aegrōtus, a, um – sick	Ferdinandus, ī, m. – Ferdinand
Britannus, a, um – British	Hispānus, a, um – Spanish
Colōnus, ī, m. – Columbus	Isabella, ae, f. – Isabella
eō annō – that year	Lūsitānus, a, um – Portuguese
eō tempore – at that time	

TALKING ABOUT A READING

ABOUT THE FIRST AMERICANS AND UNADAPTED LATIN: ATTICUS AND THE CIVIL WAR

DĒ AMERICĀNĪS PRĪMĪS

Marīa: Placet mihi Latīnē discere quae fuerint reī pūblicae nostrae initia. Sī Colōnus timuisset, fortasse nōs hodiē hāc in terrā nōn habitārēmus.

Mārcus: Multī, quī hanc terram novam post Colōnum petīvērunt, perīcula nōn timēbant. Hī vītam meliōrem et prosperam quaerēbant. Aliī fortēs quidem sed invītī (*unwilling*) ductī sunt, ut essent servī (*slaves*).

Helena: Aliī (*some*) vītam bonam, aliī (*others*) vītam malam in terrā novā invēnērunt. Sed omnēs sē ad novās rēs accommodāre (*adapt*) dēbēbant. Multīs aliīs in terrīs hominēs in rēbus vetustīs manēre solent nec rēs facile mūtant. Difficilius enim est rēs quās facere solēmus relinquere et novās petere. At tantum fortiōribus praemia māgna dantur.

Christīna: Bene dīcis. Antīquī quoque hoc dīcēbant: **fortēs fortūna adiuvat** (*helps*).

Helena: Sī homō labōrēs nōn timet, tandem habēre poterit id quod habēre vult. Nōs quoque labōrēs timēre nōn dēbēmus. Interdum lingua Latīna difficilis potest vidērī, sed sī tandem eam bene didicerimus, per tōtam vītam nostram auxiliō nōbīs esse poterit.

Mārcus: Sī igitur nunc volueritis, poterimus plūra dē Atticō legere.

Helena: Legāmus! Nam ex eō librō plūrima ūtilia discere licet.

Marīa: Ita. Quamquam liber est difficilis, mihi tamen placet.

ATTICUS AND THE CIVIL WAR

CORNĒLIĪ NEPŌTIS ATTICUS, 7

When Atticus was about sixty years old, the Roman state was torn by civil war between the partisans of Julius Caesar and the senatorial party commanded by Pompey. Because of his age, Atticus was exempt from military service. He remained at Rome, and freely gave supplies from his estates to some of his friends who were setting out to war in the service of Pompey, with whom Atticus remained on good terms. But Atticus accepted no rewards or distinctions from Pompey. Atticus' refusal to take an active part in the conflict was very gratifying to Caesar, so that Caesar not only refrained from demanding money from Atticus (which he did demand from other private parties) but he also pardoned his sister's son and Quintus Cicero, who had been followers of Pompey.

1   1. Incidit Caesariānum cīvīle bellum, cum habēret annōs circiter
     sexāgintā. Ūsus est aetātis vacātiōne neque sē quōquam mōvit ex urbe.
     Quae amīcīs suīs opus fuerant ad Pompēium proficīscentibus, omnia ex
     suā rē familiārī dedit. Ipsum Pompēium coniūnctum nōn offendit. 2.
5   Nūllum ab eō habēbat ōrnāmentum, ut cēterī, quī per eum aut honōrēs
     aut dīvitiās cēperant; quōrum partim invītissimī castra sunt secūtī,
     partim summā cum ēius offēnsiōne domī remānsērunt. 3. Atticī autem
     quiēs tantopere Caesarī fuit grāta, ut victor, cum prīvātīs pecūniās per
     epistulās imperāret, huic nōn sōlum molestus nōn fuerit, sed etiam
10   sorōris fīlium et Q. Cicerōnem ex Pompēiī castrīs concesserit. Sīc
     vetere īnstitūtō vītae effūgit nova perīcula.

VOCABULARY

1   incidō, ere, incidī, — –to fall upon, happen
    Caesariānus, a, um – of Caesar
    cīvīlis, cīvīle – civil
    circiter (adv.) – around

2   sexāgintā (numeral) – sixty
    vacātiō, vacātiōnis, f. – freedom, exemption from
        military service
    neque (conj.) = nec
    quōquam (adv.) – to any place

3   opus est – is necessary
    Pompēius, ī, m. – Pompey
    proficīscor, proficīscī, profectus sum – to set out,
        depart

4   rēs familiāris – estate
    ipsum – himself
    coniungō, ere, coniūnxī, coniūnctum – to con-
        nect
    offendō, ere, offendī, offēnsum – to offend

5   ōrnāmentum, ī, n. – ornament, distinction
    cēterī, ae, a – the rest

5–6 aut . . . aut . . . – either . . . or . . .

6   invītus, a, um – unwilling

7   summus, a, um – highest, utmost
    offēnsiō, offēnsiōnis, f. – offense
    rēmaneō, ēre, rēmānsī, rēmānsum – to remain

8   quiēs, quiētis, f. – rest, quiet
    tantopere (adv.) – so greatly
    Caesar, Caesaris, m. – Caesar
    grātus, a, um – gratifying
    prīvātus, ī, m. – private citizen

9   molestus, a, um – troublesome

10 Q. Cicero (Cicerōnis, m.) = Quīntus Cicero
    concēdō, ere, concessī, concessum – to allow,
        pardon
    sīc (adv.) – in this way

11 īnstitūtum, ī, n. – way, manner
    effugiō, ere, effūgī, — – to escape

READING NOTES

1   *Incidit Caesariānum cīvīle bellum* The verb *incidit*
    means "happened" and the subject is *bellum*.

2   *Ūsus est aetātis vacātiōne* "He used the exemption
    of his age." A man of sixty years was exempt
    from military service.

3   *Quae amīcīs suīs opus fuerant* The meaning is
    "Those things which his friends had need of."
    When a neuter adjective or pronoun is a subject
    of the verb *esse* and the noun *opus*, *opus* means
    "needed" or "necessary." The dative case is used
    for the person or people for whom there is need.

4   *Ipsum Pompēium coniūnctum* The phrase means
    "Pompey himself, who was connected <with
    him by friendship>." Pompey was a Roman
    political and military leader, first an ally, then a
    rival of Caesar.

5   *ut cēterī* The phrase *ut cēterī* means "as did the
    others."

6–7 *quōrum partim . . . partim . . .* Here *partim . . .
    partim . . .* means almost the same as "some . . .
    others . . ." Adverbs like *partim* can sometimes
    be used so that their meaning approaches that
    of nouns or pronouns. Here, *quōrum* is a parti-
    tive genitive and means "of these."

7   *ēius* Translate this genitive pronoun "to him."

7–10 *Atticī autem quiēs tantopere Caesarī fuit grāta, ut
    victor . . . nōn sōlum molestus nōn fuerit, sed etiam
    sorōris fīlium et Q. Cicerōnem . . . concesserit* The
    word *ut* introduces a result clause. (See Chapter
    14.) *quiēs* ordinarily means "rest, quiet" but here
    means "quiet life." "The quiet life of Atticus, on
    the other hand, was so greatly gratifying to Cae-
    sar that as a winner . . . not only was he (Caesar)
    not troublesome to <Atticus>, he also pardoned
    the son of <his> sister and Quintus Cicero."
    Quintus Cicero, the husband of Atticus' sister.

8–9 *cum prīvātīs pecūniās per epistulās imperāret* Note
    that *imperāret* means "requisition" or "make
    demand for." With this meaning, the thing
    demanded is in the accusative and the person
    from whom the thing is demanded is in the da-
    tive. "when through letters he was demanding
    money from private people . . . "

QUESTIONS ABOUT THE TEXT

Answer in complete Latin sentences.

1. Quid fēcit Atticus, cum bellum Caesariānum incidisset? Cūr?

2. Quid fēcit Atticus prō amīcīs quī ad Pompēium proficīscēbantur?

3. Accēperatne Atticus ōrnāmentum ā Pompēiō?

4. Quid fēcērunt hominēs quī ā Pompēiō ōrnāmenta accēperant?

5. Quid Caesar dē Atticō sēnsit?

6. Quid Caesar prō Atticī familiā fēcit?

DĒ AMERICĀNĪS PRĪMĪS CONTINUED

Marīa Atticus erat fēlīx quia nec Caesar nec Pompēius eī erant hostēs.

Mārcus At sī Atticus iūnior (*younger*) fuisset, ad bellum īvisset nec potuisset habēre et Caesarem et Pompēium amīcōs.

REVIEW 4: CHAPTERS 10–12

VOCABULARY TO KNOW

NOUNS

aedēs, is, f. – (sing.) a temple; (pl.) a dwelling or house

gemma, ae, f. – gem, precious stone

labor, labōris, m. – labor, toil

legātus, ī, m. – ambassador

lūcrum, ī, n. – profit, gain

modus, ī, m. – way, method, manner

officium, ī, n. – duty

orbis, orbis, m. – circle

pecūnia, ae, f. – money

populus, ī, m. – people

sarcina, ae, f. – burden, baggage (this word is most commonly used in the plural)

sententia, ae, f. – opinion, point of view

servus, ī, m. – slave, servant

sors, sortis, f. – lot, fate

spēs, speī, f. – hope

PRONOUNS

suī, sibi, sē, sē – reflexive pronoun of the third person

ADJECTIVES

alter, altera, alterum – the other (of two)

cārus, a, um – dear

iūcundus, a, um – pleasant, nice

līber, lībera, līberum – free

maritimus, a, um – maritime

neuter, neutra, neutrum – neither, none (of two)

nūllus, a, um – none

placidus, a, um – peaceful, calm

prosper, prospera, prosperum – fortunate, prosperous

scelestus, a, um – wicked

serēnus, a, um – calm, clear

sōlus, sōla, sōlum – alone

suus, a, um – his, her, its, their own (referring back to the subject)

tōtus, a, um – whole, entire

turpis, turpe – shameful, disgraceful

uter, utra, utrum – who, which (of two)?

VERBS

eō, īre, īvī (iī), itum – to go

fūror, fūrārī, fūrātus sum – to steal

inquiunt (plural of *inquit*) – they say (only introducing direct speech)

laedō, ere, laesī, laesum – to harm

morior, morī, mortuus sum – to die

nesciō, īre, nescīvī, nescītum – not to know

probō, āre, āvī, ātum – to approve

reddō, ere, reddidī, redditum – to give back

salūtō, āre, āvī, ātum – to greet

spectō, āre, āvī, ātum – to watch

spērō, āre, āvī, ātum – to hope

taceō, ēre, tacuī, tacitum – to be silent, keep quiet

ūtor, ūtī, ūsus sum + ablative – to use

ADVERBS

paulisper – for a little while

potius – rather

semel – once

minimē – least, very little

nimis – too much

quōmodo – how

quidem – indeed

tamen – however, nevertheless

CONJUNCTIONS

cum + pluperfect subjunctive – after

nisi – if not, unless

quamquam – although

quamvīs – although

quia – because

quod – because

PHRASES

māgnī habeō – esteem a lot

operae pretium est – it is worthwhile

orbis terrārum – the earth, the world

▶ EXERCISE 1

Translate into Latin.

1. Go!

2. You were going.

3. Going (i.e., while going) we were watching everything.

4. They went.

5. Will you go?

6. I hope that I will go.

7. You (pl.) had gone.

8. S/he will have gone.

▶ EXERCISE 2

Change the relative clauses into phrases using present participles. Translate the changed sentences.

1. Erasmus, quī iter faciēbat, librōs suōs servāre cupiēbat.

2. Nautae rēs ex hominibus, quī iter faciēbant, fūrārī solēbant.

3. Mōrēs hominum, quī in Ūtopiā vīvēbant, sunt valdē dissimilēs mōrum aliōrum hominum.

4. Legātō, quī in urbem intrābat, omnēs pauperēs sunt vīsī.

5. Colōnus rogāvit nautās, quī patriam petere volēbant, ut exspectārent.

6. Nautae, quī lūmen vidēbant, maximō gaudiō capiēbantur.

▶ EXERCISE 3

Translate into Latin.

1. another lot

2. which of the two opinions?

3. the whole island

4. the other (of the two) ambassador

5. in no way

6. to any servant

7. one hope

8. the duty of neither consul

9. (we) alone

▶ EXERCISE 4

Fill in the blanks using either the present active or the perfect passive participle of the verbs in parentheses. Translate the sentences.

1. In sarcinā Erasmī erant librī ab eō _____. (scrībō)

2. Dē librō _____ Erasmus tam dolēbit quam dē fīliō. (āmittō)

3. Populus _____ legātōs spectābat et nesciēbat cūr vestīmenta tam pulchra illī habērent. (maneō)

4. Inter hominēs _____ erat puer quī mala verba dē legātīs exclāmāvit. (taceō)

5. Colōnus nautīs iam nōn _____ haec dīxit. (spērō)

6. Lūmen _____ nautārum sententiam mūtāvit. (videō)

▶ EXERCISE 5

Fill in the blanks with the correct form of the reflexive pronoun, reflexive possessive adjective, or the demonstrative pronoun *is, ea, id.* Translate the sentences.

1. Erasmus putābat nautās librōs _____ esse fūrātōs.

2. Erasmus librōs _____ cārissimōs _____ cum ferēbat.

3. Legātī dē Ūtopiēnsibus nōn multa audīverant _____ que mōrēs nōn intellegēbant.

4. Legātī cōgitābant Ūtopiēnsēs numquam vīdisse vestīmenta _____ pulchriōra.

5. Nautae putābant Colōnum _____ sortemque _____ nōn māgnī habēre.

6. Colōnus nautīs dīxit _____ vītam _____ et vītās eōrum esse cārās.

▶ EXERCISE 6

Translate into Latin.

1. If the wicked sailors had stolen Erasmus' bag, Erasmus would have grieved a lot.
    Erasmus, ī, m.

2. Although the sea was peaceful and the sky was calm, the trip was not the easiest.

3. The boy thought that the ambassador was playing with the gems (use ablative of means) because in Utopia only boys and girls had gems.
    Ūtopia, ae, f.

4. If people did not love gold and silver too much, they would be happier.

5. If Columbus discovers a new land, this will give prosperous power to the king.

6. Although the trip was full of dangers, the queen gave money so that it could happen.

CONSIDERING THE HEROES OF CLASSICAL MYTHOLOGY

THE HOUSE OF ATREUS

Atreus, father of Agamemnon, offended by his brother Thyestes, had killed, cooked and served to Thyestes his own sons. Owing to his perpetration of this horrendous crime, a heavy family curse hung upon the house of Atreus. When Atreus' son Agamemnon, the Greek commander-in-chief at Troy, came home after the Trojan War, his wife Clytemnestra slaughtered him. His female captive, the Trojan princess and prophetess Cassandra, had warned him what fate awaited them both, but in vain; though she had been endowed by Apollo with the gift of true prophecy, Cassandra's gift was limited by the condition that no one would believe her words. While Agamemnon was away at Troy, the strong-minded Clytemnestra had taken Thyestes' sole surviving son, Agamemnon's cousin Aegisthus, as her lover. Thus both Agamemnon and Cassandra ended their lives in a bath of blood.

The tholos or beehive tomb constructed between 1350 and 1250 BCE is located near the citadel at Mycenae. The tomb's size, the largest known, and the careful construction led to its being named the "Treasury of Atreus" for such a magnificent tomb had to enshrine someone of great importance like Atreus.

Yet Clytemnestra's vengeful act was followed by revenge against her. For Agamemnon's son Orestes, who had been sent away by his mother in her despotic scheming, returned home, and, with the aid of his sister Electra, killed Clytemnestra to avenge his father's murder. Apollo himself had advised him to do so. However, as soon as he had murdered his mother, the Furies began to persecute him. Three female monsters with snakes instead of hair, and torches and whips in their hands, the Furies customarily tortured those who had shed the blood of family members. After wandering around the world in pain and torment, Orestes finally asked Apollo for help. At last, Athena arranged that a court of law be organized in Athens to judge Orestes. The Furies were the prosecutors, Apollo the chief witness for the defense, and Athena the judge. An assembly of Athenian citizens comprised the jury; Orestes was acquitted owing to extenuating circumstances. According to Greek legend, his trial was the first time when a lawful procedure was used to settle a crime, instead of bloody vengeance.

Amateur archaeologist Heinrich Schliemann, whose reading of Homer's poems as a youth inspired him to find Troy and Mycenae, with great enthusiasm declared this gold death mask "Agamemnon's." Found in shaft grave 5 within the citadel of Mycenae, the sixteenth century BCE mask predates Agamemnon. Presumably he was buried with something comparable.

THE HOUSE OF LABDACUS

Another cursed Greek family is the house of Labdacus, a grandson of the man who founded the city of Thebes. Labdacus' son Laius and his wife Jocasta, king and queen of Thebes, were warned not to have any children. They were told that if they were to have a son, he would kill his father and marry his mother. It happened nonetheless that Jocasta bore a child. Fearing the prophecy, the parents exposed the baby on the hills near Thebes, piercing his ankles and tying them with leather thongs. Hence he was called Oedipus, which means "swollen feet." A shepherd, however, found the child and gave him to a foster family in another town. When Oedipus grew up, he was himself told that he would kill his father and marry his mother. To avoid that terrible prophecy, he left his foster parents, believing them to be his true

Adapted from its male Egyptian predecessor, the Greek version represents the sphinx as a monster with a head and breasts of a woman, the body of a lion, the wings of an eagle, and a serpent-headed tail. This Rococo version guards the gardens of the royal summer palace of Queluz outside Lisbon, Portugal.

father and mother. On the way he happened to encounter his actual father Laius. After a quarrel arose between the two travelers, Oedipus, in his anger, unknowingly killed his father. He then arrived in the city of Thebes. It was at that time troubled by a monster called the Sphinx.

The monster had agreed to free the city if someone could guess the answer to a riddle: "What walks on four legs in the morning, two at noon, and three at twilight?" Oedipus correctly guessed that this described a human being: a baby, an adult, and an old person with a walking stick. Thus he was welcomed as a liberator in the city, and the queen wed him as a token of her gratitude. In this way the prophecy was fulfilled, once more showing that no one could escape his fate. After Oedipus and Jocasta realized that they were son and mother, Jocasta killed herself, and Oedipus gouged out his own eyes. Blinded, he became much wiser, and could "see" better than when endowed with full sight.

READ THE FOLLOWING PASSAGE

Oedipodī et Iocastae erant duo fīliī, Eteōclēs et Polynīcēs, et duae fīliae, Antigona et Ismēna. Cum omnēs intellēxissent Oedipodem patrem suum occīdisse et mātrem suam in mātrimōnium dūxisse, Eteōclēs et Polynīcēs patrem vehementissimē reprehendērunt et rogāvērunt ut patriam relinqueret. Tunc Oedipūs fīliīs suīs maledīxit. Postquam Oedipūs in exsilium īvit, Eteōclēs et Polynīcēs alternīs annīs Thēbīs rēgnābant. Semel Eteōclēs imperium frātrī reddere nōluit et Polynīcēs ad aliōs populōs īvit ut auxilium quaereret. Tandem Thēbās cum septem exercitibus redīvit, in urbem impetum fēcit et cum Eteōcle rēge pugnāvit. In turpī illā pugnā alter frāter alterum occīdit. Rēx Thēbārum tunc est factus Creōn, Iocastae frāter. Ille sīvit Eteōclem sepelīrī, sed iussit corpus Polynīcis relinquī, ut ā canibus vulturibusque comederētur, quia Polynīcēs ex aliīs populīs auxilium contrā Thēbās petīverat. Hoc quoque dīxit: "Sī quis Polynīcem sepelīverit, eum morte pūniam." Antigona tamen Polynīcis soror, cui animus erat fortissimus, frātrem sepelīvit, quod hoc esset iūstum. Cum hoc didicisset, īrae plēnus Creōn Antigonam vīvam sepelīvit. At ēius fīlius, quī Antigonam amābat, hoc audiēns sē occīdit. Tandem Creōn intellēxit sē nōn bene fēcisse.

alterum . . . alterum . . . – each other
alternīs annīs – alternate years
Antigona, ae, f. – Antigone
canis, canis, m. – dog
Creōn, Creōntis, m. – Creon
Eteōclēs, Eteōclis, m. – Eteocles
exsilium, ī, n. – exile
Iocasta, ae, f. – Jocasta
Ismēna, ae, f. – Ismene
maledīcō, ere, maledīxī, maledictum + dative – to curse someone

Oedipūs, Oedipodis, m. – Oedipus
Polynīcēs, Polynīcis, m. – Polyneices
redeō, redīre, redīvī, reditum – to return
rēgnō, āre, āvī, ātum – to rule as a king
sepeliō, īre, sepelīvī, sepultum – to bury
septem (numeral) – seven
sī quis – if anyone
Thēbae, ārum, pl. – Thebes
vultur, vulturis, m. – vulture

CONNECTING WITH THE POST-ANCIENT WORLD

THE NEW WORLD

While it has not been customary in our time to think of the discovery and opening up of the Americas as closely related to the history of Latin, Latin and the New World are very much connected with each other. The name "America" itself comes from a Renaissance Latin text entitled *Quattuor Americī Vespucciī nāvigātiōnēs* (*The Four Voyages of Amerigo Vespucci*), printed in 1505 CE. This volume narrates the voyages to America made by an Italian merchant and explorer named Amerigo Vespucci; "America" is adapted from *Americus*, the Latinized version of his first name.

From the early sixteenth century onwards, many Latin accounts of voyages by Columbus and others, as well of the Spanish conquests of Mexico and South America were published. Some were originally written in Latin; others first written in vernacular languages, especially Spanish, but translated into Latin in order to be read by an international audience, since Latin was the international language of Europe's educated elite. To reach an international audience Latin was also the language employed in the explanations, and for place names, on maps made in the Renaissance, including those of the New World.

The pride of a nation's navy is the building, upkeep, and sailing of a "tall ship," a traditionally rigged sailing vessel. The Italian navy maintains a tall ship named for Amerigo Vespucci (1454–1512) whose golden figure graces the ship's prow.

Latin was widely used in early America itself. The first universities in South America, Mexico, and the British colonies in North America produced writings in Latin. To this day, many college and university diplomas in the Western hemisphere continue to be written in Latin. The commencement ceremonies at Harvard and Princeton Universities each year feature an address in Latin by a graduating student. Several explorers also employed Latin when recording their travels and discoveries. They include William Morrell, who wrote the *Nova Anglia*, a hexameter poem about an expedition to Massachusetts printed in London in 1625; the Jesuit Andrew White, who wrote the *Relātiō itineris in Marylandiam*, first published in 1634, and Thomas Makin, whose *Dēscriptiō Pennsylvāniae* was published in 1729.

Latin remained, however, primarily a language of the European elite, although the Spanish Jesuits tried to provide education in Latin to the children of the inhabitants in regions that they occupied. America also figured prominently in Latin writings produced in Europe. Not surprisingly, several Latin epic poems written in hexameters feature Columbus as their hero: among them *Dē nāvigātiōne Christophorī Columbī* by Laurentius Gambara, published in 1581 CE; the *Columbēis* of Julius Caesar Stella in 1585; and the *Columbus* by the Jesuit Hubertinus Carrara in 1715. We should also not forget that the voyages of discovery, opening up of new lands, and the encounters with cultures previously unknown had an immense impact on the European imagination, and in this way influenced literary works such as More's *Ūtopia*. Indeed, *Ūtopia* emerges from a process of synthesis that characterizes much of Renaissance Latin: ideas inspired by new global discoveries creatively combined with classical learning.

Amerigo Vespucci's work for Florentine banks took him to Spain where he heard the call of the sea. In his letters from his second New World voyage in 1501 Vespucci is the first to speak of the new lands as being separate from Asia. This statue joins other Florentine heroes along the Uffizi Museum colonnade.

EXPLORING NEW WORLDS

SEARCHING THE GLOBE AND THE UNIVERSE

The adventures of Columbus and his crews form just one chapter in a long story of exploration, spreading back to ancient times and forward into the twenty-first century, a story full of risks of disaster and death in the face of the unknown. Courage, curiosity, and the search for profit or power are recurrent elements in the tale. Columbus' expedition would have been impossible without the financial backing of Spain's monarchs Ferdinand and Isabella, who expected a financial return.

This was not the first time that exploration sprang from commercial motives. Ancient stories told of voyages for gain. No one doubts that there were bold seafarers among the ancient Greeks; early on, they spread outward from the Greek homeland and the Aegean Sea, eastward into present-day Asiatic Turkey, and westward to southern Italy, Sicily, and ports in the western Mediterranean. Questions abound, though, over how reliable the details are of the stories they passed down to us about early voyages.

The tale of Jason and the voyage of the Argo is an example of how the Greeks may have employed myth as a means of remembering their early eastward seagoing expansion. No one knows the real age of the story. The Argonauts sailed from the Aegean Sea, along the Black Sea's south coast, to the distant land of Colchis, the site of the modern state of Georgia, in quest of the Golden Fleece. By the time of Homer's *Odyssey* (8th century BCE), the story was already well known. Does the myth conceal a historical reality? People debate about this. By retracing the Argo's outward voyage in a ship modeled after those of the thirteenth century BCE, modern seaman Tim Severin proved that the voyage was not impossible in the Bronze Age. Ancient Greeks themselves, including Strabo the geographer, believed the journey had actually happened, if not exactly as recounted. Greek commercial activity along the south shore of the Black Sea had a long history. But whether or not there was a Jason or an Argo, there certainly were early mariners pushing out beyond the safety of familiar coasts, searching out new lands on the edges of the world they knew.

The story of Pytheas is similarly one of mixed doubt and possibility. Ancient writers including Pliny the Elder and Strabo report that a fourth century BCE Greek cartographer and astronomer, Pytheas of Massilia (now Marseilles in France), voyaged to the northwestern edge of the known world. He reputedly travelled to a land called "Thule" (possibly Norway, Iceland, or the Shetlands), where he encountered what could have been fog-bound drift ice, and observed nights that were only two or three hours long. While details such as these indicate that he really did explore the far north, just where he landed on the way is not so clear. It is possible that he arrived in Cornwall, the southwestern tip of Britain, home of a busy tin mining and processing industry, which he is reputed to have examined. If this surmise is accurate, Pytheas would have preceded Julius Caesar into Britain by over two and a half centuries. From records like the tale of the Argo and the better attested stories of Pytheas, we do know that ancient exploration was carried on, even if we cannot always retrieve exact details.

Fast forward to the early 1400s CE, when commercial motives again took a hand. Trade in silks, spices, and precious stones between Europe and the Far East had to run through the lands east of the Mediterranean Sea. But the traffic was hampered by Muslim domination in those lands. If a southern route around the then unknown coast of Africa could be found, voyagers could by-pass the barriers of overland travel. The Portuguese, beginning with Prince Henry the Navigator, started the search. Portugal fronts the Atlantic Ocean; hence there were Portuguese familiar with the Atlantic coast, who did not share the terror of the waters out beyond the Straits of Gibraltar that affected others. After Prince Henry built the seagoing infrastructure, Portuguese mariners probed further and further down the African coast in stages. In 1488 Bartholomew Diaz reached the Cape of Good Hope, Africa's southern tip. Now the Portuguese had an idea of the continent's length. Finally, in 1497–98, Vasco da Gama captained a perilous two year voyage that took the lives of a third of his seamen. He rounded the Cape and pushed on to Calcutta, known as Kolkata today, in India. The way was open. The Portuguese empire in Southeast Asia resulted.

The competition for alternate routes to the East Asian islands, called the Indies by the Europeans, was not at an end. The conviction that the earth was round had been well established. That meant that one could reach the east by sailing west. This was Columbus' idea, but no one would

To commemorate the 500th anniversary in 1960 of the death of Prince Henry the Navigator, the Portuguese dictator António Salazar erected the "Monument to the Discoveries" in Lisbon. Designed as a caravel like the one in Prince Henry's hands, the monument is lined with statues of the key participants in Portugal's explorations.

pay to have him try it out just to satisfy curiosity. Columbus had to make the argument that any backers of his expedition could become rich. Ferdinand and Isabella, joint rulers of Spain, had two reasons for buying into the project. Not only were they interested in profit; as committed Catholics, they saw value in the spread of Catholicism to any new lands that might be reached. Columbus arrived at the Spanish court just when the centuries-long Christian campaign to drive Muslim rulers out of Iberia came to an end, with the fall of the Muslim kingdom of Granada in 1492. In embracing Columbus' Atlantic voyage, the Spanish monarchs followed one Christianizing enterprise with another, as well as investing in a moneymaking proposition. And in reaching the islands of the Caribbean Sea, Columbus thought he had indeed arrived at the Asian "Indies," an idea that was only gradually dispelled. Thus the islands off the southeast coast of the U.S. are to this day called the West Indies.

The aftermath of Columbus' voyages, of course, includes modern American history itself. Spanish, English, and French explorers and colonizers changed the face of North, Central, and South America. The year 1492 was but the beginning of further adventures mapping and subduing the newfound lands. Hernán Cortés reached and overthrew the Aztec Empire in Mexico (1519–21); Vasco Nuñez de Balboa led the first Europeans to see the Pacific Ocean in 1513 at the Isthmus of Panama; Francisco Pizarro destroyed the Inca Empire of Peru in the 1530s.

To mark the quincentennial of Columbus' first journey, the Bank of Spain issued a commemorative series of banknotes in the 1990s. The thousand peseta note featured the portrait of Francisco Pizarro as seen in this photograph and on the obverse of the banknote that of conquistador Hernán Cortés.

In North America, after the creation of the United States and Canada, the search to discover a northwest sea passage through the sub-Arctic from Atlantic to Pacific, north of Canada, entailed death-defying voyages through uncharted ice-bound waters. Failure was frequent. Sir John Franklin set out from England in 1845 with two ships, good equipment, and plenty of optimism. The expedition never returned. Rescue missions came to the north and pieced together Franklin's fate. When ice fields held his ships frozen in immobility, the desperate crews abandoned the vessels and struck out across land by sled in a vain attempt to survive. All were dead by 1848. Later explorers were not deterred.

The Passage was finally negotiated in 1906, and activity has continued. Today, commercial use of the Northwest Passage is still being developed, against a background of disputes over whether Canada has sovereignty over the waterways. Meanwhile, climate change has led to large-scale melting of Arctic ice and easier navigation through the region.

In 1803 President Thomas Jefferson brokered the purchase of the vast Louisiana Territory from France, adding over 800,000 square miles of mostly unexplored territory to the United States. A survey in search of opportunities for trade and settlement was needed. Also, people were hoping to find an easy overland route from the Mississippi to the Pacific coast. The result was the expedition led by Meriwether Lewis and William Clark up the Missouri River from Saint Louis, over

Pompeys Pillar is one of the most famous sandstone buttes in America and appears much as it did two centuries ago. It bears the only remaining physical evidence of the Lewis and Clark Expedition. On the face of the 150-foot butte, Captain William Clark carved his name on July 25, 1806, during his return to the United States through the beautiful Yellowstone Valley.

the Rockies, and down to the already inhabited Oregon coast, in 1804–06. It has been noted that astronauts landing on the moon knew more clearly what was in store for them than did the hardy Lewis and Clark explorers. They had a narrow escape from a potentially disastrous winter, thanks to timely contact with friendly Native Americans enabled by Sacagawea, a Native American woman who accompanied the expedition. The hoped-for easy transcontinental river route was never found, but the region was now accessible for settlement and commercial exploitation.

Sacagawea on the dollar coin carrying her son Jean Baptiste Charbonneau in a papoose. Captain Clark nicknamed the boy "Pomp" whom he honored when the butte was named "Pompeys Pillar." Jean Baptiste more than likely studied Latin when he was a student at the high school division of St. Louis University.

Now that satellites have disclosed every square mile of the earth's surface, space is the new frontier for exploration. Human adventures beyond earth began in 1957 with the Soviets' unmanned Sputnik satellite, followed by cosmonaut Yuri Gagarin's pioneering ride into space in 1961. The context was the Cold War, the name given to the decades of competition between the United States and the Soviet Union for political, economic, and military domination of the globe. The US embarked on a project aimed at human lunar travel. It culminated with the Apollo 11 vehicle that landed astronauts

Headline celebrates American astronaut Neil Armstrong becoming the first man to walk on the moon. After their spaceship landed safely on the moon, Armstrong announced, "Houston, Tranquility Base here. The Eagle has landed." Then, as he put his left foot down first he declared, "That's one small step for man, one giant leap for mankind."

Lunar module pilot James Irwin works at the Lunar Roving Vehicle during the first Apollo 15 lunar surface extravehicular activity, July 1971, at the Hadley-Apennine landing site. The shadow of the Lunar Module "Falcon" is in the foreground. This photograph looking northeast, with Mount Hadley in the background, was taken by mission commander David Scott.

Neil Armstrong and "Buzz" Aldrin on the moon in 1969, followed by six more Apollo missions. (You will note how fitting it was to name these missions after the Greek god of the sun.) As with fifteenth-century mariners, space pioneers still needed the courage to face the risks and dangers of the unknown.

However, since no immediately exploitable commercial potential was generated by the lunar landings, no humans have gone to the moon since 1972. Now, a variety of unmanned probes throughout and beyond the solar system, aided by extraterrestrial devices like the Hubble Telescope, continue to throw floods of light on the nature and origins of the universe. Human space travel is confined to projects like the International Space Station, dedicated to research. And the role of international competition, which played so important a part in Columbus' day, has changed somewhat. Conflict between countries has not yet led to the militarization of space. There are two further striking indications that nations now see advantages in certain types of cooperation rather than competition in exploration. First, exploration in Antarctica takes place under a 1961 international treaty that bans military activity on the continent.

Scientists from around the world conduct a variety of research projects in Antarctica studying such subjects as geology, global warming, and meteorology. Thanks to international agreements, such studies are not impeded by national boundaries. The photograph depicts a telecommunications unit of an Antarctic research center.

Secondly, the International Space Station is a joint venture of the USA, Russia, Japan, Canada, and eleven European countries; it thus embraces nations with a past history as Cold War foes. Emerging powers such as China and India, with their own space programs, have widened the circle of nations involved in space exploration.

Exploration in space has built upon exploration of the earth. Mankind continues to seek commercial rewards, now perhaps more evenly balanced by the pursuit of knowledge for its own sake. Technological successes have diminished, but not eliminated, the risks; nothing has diminished the human appetite for unveiling the unknown.

PROFESSOR EDWARD V. GEORGE
Professor of Classics Emeritus
Texas Tech University
Lubbock, Texas

MĪRĀBILE AUDĪTŪ

ANCIENT LATIN PHRASES AND PROVERBS REVIVED IN HUMANIST LATIN AND RELEVANT TO THE TWENTY-FIRST CENTURY

- Ad Kalendās Graecās. "To the Greek Kalends," i.e., never, because the Greeks did not use the Kalends for calculating the days of the month. Compare the expression "when pigs fly." Suetonius, in *Dē vītā duodecim Caesarum* (*Lives of the Twelve Caesars*), 87, quotes this as a favorite proverb of Augustus. Augustus applied it when he wanted to say that someone would never pay his debts.

- Alter ego. "Another I," i.e., "another self." Cicero, *Laelius vel Dē amīcitiā* (*Laelius or About Friendship*), 80, uses a similar expression to describe what a true friend is.

- Ars longa, vīta brevis. "Art is long, life is short." Latin translation of the aphorism of the Greek medical doctor Hippocrates.

- Cum grānō salis. "With a grain of salt," i.e., not completely seriously. Pliny the Elder, *Historia nātūrālis* (*Natural History*), 23.8, uses this expression as part of a recipe for a poison antidote. The expression, however, is mainly used in a figurative way.

- Damnātiō memoriae. "Damnation of memory." Erasing the name of disgraced Roman emperors in the pretence that they never existed.

Known as the "Father of Medicine," Hippocrates (ca. 460–370 BCE) is credited for establishing medicine as a distinct field of study. He probably began his training at the Asklepieion on the island of Kos depicted here.

- Deus ex māchinā. "A god from a machine." A way to resolve a complicated drama plot in an ancient Greek tragedy: with mechanical help, often a crane, a god appears from the sky. Applied to any artificial solution of a problem.

- Ēiusdem farīnae. "From the same flour," i.e., from the same nature. Compare the expression "cut from the same cloth."

- Festīnā lentē! "Hurry slowly!" This oxymoron is attributed to Augustus by Suetonius, *Dē vītā duodecim Caesarum* (*Lives of the Twelve Caesars*), 25. The phrase came from Greek.

- Homō hominī lupus est. "A man to man is a wolf." Plautus, *Asināria* (*The Ass-Dealer*), 495. Used by the English philosopher Thomas Hobbes (1588–1679) in his description of human nature. In the beginning of his fundamental work *Leviathan* Hobbes states "Man to Man is an Arrant Wolfe."

- In vīnō vēritās. "In wine there is the truth," that is, wine loosens one's tongue. This well-known Latin phrase came from Greek and is first quoted by Pliny the Elder, *Historia nātūrālis* (*Natural History*), 14.28.

- Mēns sāna in corpore sānō. "A sound mind in a sound body." Juvenal, *Saturae* (*Satires*) 10.356. A caveat concerning the dangers of over-exercising, although usually applied in the opposite sense.

Founded in 1909, Hargrave Military Academy in Chatham, Virginia provides a college preparatory military school education to young men. Hargrave states that the motto is the basic tenet of the development of the whole person and that Hargrave helps a cadet grow academically, athletically, and spiritually—mind, body, and soul.

A blative Absolute; *Īdem, ipse, iste*

Based on Theodore de Bry's (1528–1598) illustration which blends Columbus erecting a cross on the island of Guanahari and receiving presents from the Caciques of Hispaniola.

MEMORĀBILE DICTŪ

Nūlla terra exsilium est sed altera patria.

"No land is a place of exile, but merely another native land." (Seneca, *About Remedies for Unexpected Grievances*)

This thought is expressed in the *Dē remediīs fortuitōrum*, which is sometimes attributed to the first century CE Stoic philosopher Seneca. It articulates the characteristically Stoic idea that wise people who achieve harmony with themselves and with nature are at home anywhere. The sailors who accompanied Columbus to the New World, however, were unlikely to have been motivated by Stoic philosophy.

READING

Here is another passage from Book I of Sepúlveda's *Dē orbe novō* (1.8). The island first sighted by Columbus' men was probably in the Bahamas. Afterward Columbus explored the coasts of Cuba and Hispaniola. On Hispaniola, Columbus' flagship, the *Santa María*, ran aground. Here he realized that he needed more people if a permanent settlement were to be established.

RIXA INTER COLŌNUM ĒIUSQUE DUCĒS EST SŌPĪTA

1   Colōnus sē in Hispāniam redīre dēbēre intellēxit, ut aliōs mīlitēs cum
maiōre classe ad īnsulās ā sē inventās dūceret. Sed Colōnus omnēs
in Hispāniam redīre posse negāvit, et paucōs Hispānōs in illā īnsulā
relinquere voluit. Colōnus igitur turrim ligneam aedificārī iussit, ut
5   hominēs ibi relictī castra habērent. Tālia iubentī Colōnō vehementer
restitit Martīnus Alfōnsus Pinzon, quī inter Hispānōrum ducēs
numerābātur. "Cōnsilium istud," inquit Martīnus, "nōn probō. Absente
maiōre Hispānōrum parte, hī paucī in tantā barbarōrum multitūdine
relictī in perīculō maximō versābuntur." Animus Colōnī hīs Martīnī
10   verbīs est offēnsus. Martīnus quoque īrātus est et cum nōnnūllīs sociīs
in aliam īnsulae partem discessit.

Hominēs, quī cum Colōnō manēbant, eum hortābantur, ut Martīnō
veniam daret. Colōnus, litterīs hūmānissimē scrīptīs, suam in
Martīnum benevolentiam dēclārāvit. Epistulam Colōnī et epistulās,
15   quās frātrēs Martīnī ad eum scrīpserant, ut ēius animum plācārent et
firmārent, barbarī tulērunt. Eīdem barbarī, cum epistulās Martīnō
dedissent, vīdērunt Martīnum, epistulīs lēctīs, Colōnī absentis verba et
animum et voluntātem ipsam intellegere, velut sī Colōnus ipse adesset.
Hanc rem vehementer mīrābantur: nam dē litterārum vī nihil omnīnō
20   sciēbant. Vim igitur dīvīnam in epistulīs esse putantēs et nefās esse
rem sacram manibus tenēre, litterās ā Martīnō scrīptās fissā virgā ad
Colōnum rettulērunt.

READING VOCABULARY

*absēns, absentis – away, absent: this adjective is also a present participle from *absum, abesse, āfuī*, which means "be away"

absente . . . parte – with a part . . . being absent

adesset – imperfect subjunctive of *adsum, adesse, adfuī*, which means "to be present"

barbarus, ī, m. – barbarian, native‡

*benevolentia, ae, f. – good will

Colōnus, ī, m. – Columbus

*dēclārō, āre, āvī, ātum – to demonstrate, show

eīdem (nom. pl. masc.) – the same

epistulīs . . . lēctīs –when the letters had been read

fissā – perfect passive participle from *findō, ere, fidī, fissum*, which means "split"

Hispānia, ae, f. – Spain

Hispānus, a, um – Spaniard

hūmānissimē (superlative adverb from *hūmānus, a, um*) – very kindly

*īdem, eadem, idem – the same

in Martīnum – towards Martín‡

*ipse, ipsa, ipsum – self ‡

*īrāscor, īrāscī, īrātus sum – to be angry

*iste, ista, istud – that (of yours)

litterīs . . . scrīptīs – a letter having been written <by him> with great kindness . . .

Martīnus (ī) Alfōnsus (ī) Pinzon (the word 'Pinzon' is indeclinable), m. – Martín Alonso Pinzón

*mīror, mīrārī, mīrātus sum – to marvel, be surprised at

*multitūdō, multitūdinis, f. – crowd, throng

nefās (indeclinable), n. – crime, sacrilege

*negō, āre, āvī, ātum – to deny

nōnnūllī, ae, a – a good number, quite a few, some

*numerō, āre, āvī, ātum – to number, count among

*offendō, ere, offendī, offēnsum – to offend, happen upon

omnīnō (adv.) – wholly, entirely

plācō, āre, āvī, ātum – to placate, soothe

*redeō, redīre, redīvī, reditum – to go back, return

*rettulērunt – perfect tense of *referō, referre, rettulī, relātum* which means "to carry back," and sometimes "to report"

rixa, ae, f. – quarrel

sacer, sacra, sacrum – sacred

*socius, ī, m. – associate, partner, ally

sōpiō, īre, īvī, ītum – to lull to sleep, settle

*tālis, tāle – such a

*turrim – accusative singular of *turris, is*, f., which means "tower"

velut sī – just as if‡

*venia, ae, f. – pardon, indulgence, forgiveness

*versor, versārī, versātus sum – to be situated in, be occupied in

*virga, ae, f. – twig, stick

*voluntās, voluntātis, f. – will

*Words marked with an asterisk will need to be memorized later in the chapter.

‡Additional information about the words marked with the double dagger will be in the **Take Note** section that follows the Reading Vocabulary.

TAKE NOTE

barbarus, ī, m. This word, with its meaning of "barbarian," which had been used by both Greeks and Romans to indicate non-Greeks and non-Romans, whose languages sounded to Greco-Roman ears like "bar . . . bar . . . bar," was reused by Latin authors of Sepúlveda's time to denote native Americans, and sometime other non-Europeans. The unfortunate prejudice inherent in this word continues to have very negative effects.

in Martīnum The preposition *in* with the accusative can mean, as here, "towards," when referring to feelings or attitude to someone.

ipse, ipsa, ipsum This word which means "self" is used not in the reflexive sense, but the intensive one, as in the phrase "here is the man himself."

velut sī Note that this phrase which means "just as if" is normally joined with a verb in the subjunctive.

COMPREHENSION QUESTIONS

1. Why did Columbus want to go back to Spain?

2. Why did Martín Pinzón oppose Columbus' plan?

3. After the dispute had arisen between Pinzón and Columbus, what did Pinzón do?

4. Why did Columbus write a letter to Pinzón?

5. How was Columbus' letter delivered to Martín?

6. Why did the inhabitants/natives of the island think letters were sacred?

A
CRISTOFORO COLOMBO
LA PATRIA

LANGUAGE FACT I

ABLATIVE ABSOLUTE

Look at this sentence from the chapter reading passage.

> *Absente māiōre Hispanōrum parte, hī paucī in tantā barbarōrum multitūdine relictī in perīculō maximō versābuntur.*
> "With the larger part of the Spaniards being absent, these few left among such a great multitude of barbarians will be situated in very great danger."

Note the long ablative phrase at the beginning of the sentence before the subject. This construction expresses circumstances logically linked to what is going on in the main clause (in this case—the fact that the few left on the island will be in danger) but makes no grammatical ties between the main and subordinate clauses (note that there are no subordinating conjunctions like *cum, postquam, quamquam,* etc.). The ablative absolute is made up of a **noun or pronoun in the ablative agreeing with a participle**, along with other words depending on them or modifying them. Sometimes an adjective or another noun can take the place of the participle, e. g., *Caesare duce* ("with Caesar as general").

Dedicated in 1862, the citizens of Genoa honor their native son. In the tradition of Roman monuments, though in Italian, the inscription states "To Christopher Columbus, the Fatherland <erects this.>" On the back of the forty-square-foot base is inscribed "Having divined a world, he found it for the perennial benefit of the old one."

This construction is called the **ablative absolute**. The name comes from the Latin verb *absolvō, ere, absolvī, absolūtum*, which has the basic meaning "to loosen." The ablative absolute, therefore, is a phrase logically linked to the main sentence but grammatically "loosened" from it. It functions like one large adverb made up of many words. Hence it is not surprising that the case of the subject and its modifiers is ablative—since this is the case in Latin that expresses adverbial relations.

The subject of the ablative absolute is, with only very rare exceptions, different from the subject of the main clause.

The perfect participle in an ablative absolute refers to a time before the time of the verb in the main clause while a present participle refers to the same time as that of the verb in the main clause.

When the perfect participle is necessary in the ablative absolute, the action indicated in the ablative absolute has to be said passively, even if the same action could be expressed actively using a different type of construction. For example:

with an ablative absolute

Epistulīs lēctīs, Martīnus Colōnī absentis verba et animum et voluntātem ipsam intellēxit.

"When the letter had been read, Martín understood the words and the mind and the will itself of the absent Columbus."

with a temporal clause

Cum epistulās lēgisset, Martīnus Colōnī absentis verba et animum et voluntātem ipsam intellēxit.

"When he had read the letters, Martín understood the words, and the mind and the will itself of the absent Columbus."

BY THE WAY

Since only deponent verbs in Latin can have a perfect participle with an active meaning, an exception occurs to perfect participles being phrased in the passive in ablative absolutes. The use of a deponent perfect participle in an ablative absolute is not common and is limited (in classical Latin) to deponent verbs without an object. For example:

Caesare mortuō, multī cīvēs bellum timēre coepērunt.
"After Caesar had died, many citizens began to fear war."

▶ EXERCISE 1

Translate into English. The Reading Vocabulary may be consulted.

1. Turrī ligneā aedificātā, hominēs ibi relictī castra tandem habēbant.

2. Verbīs Colōnī audītīs, Martīnus īrātus est et cum nōnnūllīs sociīs in aliam īnsulae partem discessit.

3. Cōnsiliō Colōnī ā Martīnō nōn probātō, multī tamen Hispānī in īnsulā cum duce manēre dēcrēvērunt.

4. Hortantibus nōnnūllīs Colōnum ut Martīnō veniam daret, multī tamen nautae nūllam pācem inter ducēs fierī posse crēdēbant.

5. Litterīs Martīnī ad Colōnum relātīs, pāx inter ducēs tandem est facta.

6. Lūmine procul ā nāvibus vīsō, nautae Colōnī sententiam esse bonam nōn negābant.

VOCABULARY TO LEARN

NOUNS

benevolentia, ae, f. – good will

multitūdō, multitūdinis, f. – crowd, throng

socius, ī, m. – associate, partner, ally

turris, turris, f. – tower

venia, ae, f. – pardon, indulgence, forgiveness

virga, ae, f. – twig, stick

voluntās, voluntātis, f. – will

ADJECTIVES

absēns, absentis – away, absent

tālis, tāle – such a

VERBS

absum, abesse, āfuī, — – be away

dēclārō, āre, āvī, ātum – to demonstrate, show, make known, reveal

īrāscor, īrāscī, īrātus sum + dative – to be angry at

mīror, mīrārī, mīrātus sum – to marvel, be surprised at

negō, āre, āvī, ātum – to deny

numerō, āre, āvī, ātum – to number, count among

offendō, ere, offendī, offēnsum – to happen upon, offend

redeō, redīre, redīvī, reditum – to go back, return

referō, referre, rettulī, relātum – to carry back, report

versor, versārī, versātus sum – to be situated in, be occupied in (from the passive of *versō, āre*)

PRONOUNS

īdem, eadem, idem – the same

ipse, ipsa, ipsum – self

iste, ista, istud – that (of yours)

CONJUNCTIONS

atque – as (when linked with some form of *īdem*)

▶ EXERCISE 2

In the sentences below, find the words derived from the Vocabulary to Learn in this chapter. Write the corresponding Latin word.

1. A good historian always makes reference to his sources.

2. People who act without thinking about other people's feelings are often offensive.

3. He received a large gift from a benevolent uncle.

4. His resignation was completely voluntary; that was what he wanted, and no one forced him to do it.

5. A person who is absent from class without a legitimate excuse cannot make up the test.

6. So large was the multitude of pilgrims that no traffic could move in the street outside the shrine.

7. My associate must sign all the documents signed by me.

8. The history of the United States is considered by some historians to begin with the signing of the Declaration of Independence.

9. An irate person may do things which later evoke great self-regret.

10. Thirsty people in the desert who think they see water are often seeing only a mirage.

11. If we hope to maximize our chances of success, we should try hard to avoid negative thoughts.

LANGUAGE FACT II

MORE ON THE ABLATIVE ABSOLUTE

As you probably noticed in the chapter reading passage and in the sentences in Exercise 1, the ablative absolute can fulfill the same functions as temporal, causal, conditional, and concessive clauses. The temporal, causal, conditional, or concessive meaning is inferred from the context. Sometimes the presence of the word *tamen* in the main clause is an indication that the meaning is concessive. Study the following examples.

> **Temporal Meaning**
> *Caesare duce dictō, mīlitēs sē ad iter parāre coepērunt.*
> "When Caesar had been named leader, the soldiers prepared themselves for the road."
>
> **Causal Meaning**
> *Hostibus appropinquantibus, cōnsul exercitum parāvit.*
> "Because the enemy was approaching, the consul prepared an/the army."
>
> **Concessive Meaning**
> *Hostibus appropinquantibus, cōnsul tamen exercitum nōn parāvit.*
> "Although the enemy was approaching, nevertheless the consul did not prepare an/the army."

The ablative absolute sometimes allows the writer to express shades of more than one meaning in the subordinate clause. For example:

> *Absente māiōre Hispanōrum parte, hī paucī in tantā barbarōrum multitūdine relictī in perīculō maximō versābuntur.*
> "**If** (and/or) **when** the larger part of the Spaniards is absent, these few left among such a great multitude of barbarians will be situated in very great danger."

> *Colōnus, litterīs hūmānissimē scrīptīs, suam in Martīnum benevolentiam dēclārāvit.*
> "Columbus, **because** (and/or) **when** he had written a letter in a very kind way, made clear his good will towards Martín."

Queen Isabella "the Catholic" at the Royal Palace in Madrid which continues to serve as the official residence for the Kings of Spain. Though a Castilian royal possession since the Moorish outpost fell to Alfonso VI in 1065, it was Philip II who made it and Madrid the center of the kingdom in 1561. The current palace was built in 1734 by Philip V after a fire had devastated the original building.

BY THE WAY

When a present participle is in an ablative absolute, it usually ends in –*e*, not in –*ī*.

STUDY TIP

Note that many of the functions of the ablative absolute are equivalents for expressions with *cum*: either temporal, or concessive, or causal. Here is just one example:

> *Absente māiōre Hispanōrum parte, hī paucī in tantā barbarōrum multitūdine relictī in perīculō maximō versābuntur.*

or

> *Cum māior Hispanōrum pars aberit/afutūra erit, hī paucī in tantā barbarōrum multitūdine relictī in perīculō maximō versābuntur.*

> "**If** (and/or) **when** the larger part of the Spaniards is absent, these few left among such a great multitude of barbarians will be situated in very great danger."

▶ EXERCISE 3

Translate the sentences into English treating the ablative absolute as indicating either **time, cause, concession, or condition.** Consider the ablative absolutes as equivalents to sentences in Latin that begin with the conjunctions *cum, postquam, quia/quod, quamquam,* or *sī*. Sometimes more than one meaning—or combination of meanings—is possible. Give at least one plausible translation.

Examples:

Lūmine cōnspectō, nautae intellēxērunt sē novam terram invēnisse.
"When (or "because") the light had been observed, the sailors understood that they had found a new land."

Benevolentiā Hispānōrum cōnspectā, incolae tamen eōs esse amīcōs negāvērunt.
"Although the good will of the Spaniards had been made clear, the inhabitants nevertheless denied they were friends."

1. Verbīs Colōnī audītīs, nautae per trēs aliōs diēs exspectāre dēcrēvērunt.

2. Nūllā terrā multōs per diēs vīsā, nautae iam spērāre nōlēbant.

3. Martīnō epistulam Colōnī legente, incolae exspectābant.

4. Omnibus nautīs in Hispāniam redīre cupientibus, Colōnus tamen paucōs Hispānōs in illā īnsulā manēre dēbēre putābat.

5. "Multīs mīlitibus et nautīs absentibus," inquit Martīnus, "paucī Hispānī in tantā incolārum multitūdine relictī in perīculō maximō versābuntur."

▶ EXERCISE 4

Translate the following sentences into Latin using ablative absolutes for the subordinate clauses. The Reading Vocabulary may be consulted.

Example:

When the letter had been read, Martín understood the words of the absent Columbus.
Epistulīs lēctīs, Martīnus Colōnī absentis verba intellēxit.

1. When/since their good will has been revealed, we are not easily angry.

2. When/since the letter has been carried back on a slender stick, we are not surprised that pardon has been given to your associate.

3. If the island has been sighted/seen, we will not deny that Columbus' plan is good.

4. While the Spaniards were building a tower, Martin made known his good will.

5. Although the Spaniards do not approve of Columbus' opinion, no one however will deny that he (himself) ought to think about his own duty.

6. When many islands had been found by Columbus, a multitude of Spaniards afterwards was living there.

LANGUAGE FACT III

THE DEMONSTRATIVE PRONOUN *ĪDEM, EADEM, IDEM*

In the chapter reading passage, you encountered the following sentence:

> *Eīdem barbarī, cum epistulās Martīnō dedissent, vīdērunt Martīnum, epistulīs lēctīs, Colōnī absentis verba et animum et voluntātem ipsam intellegere.*

> "The same inhabitants/natives, when they had given the letters to Martín, saw that, when the letters had been read, Martín understood the words and the mind and the will itself of the absent Columbus."

The demonstrative prounoun/adjective *īdem, eadem, idem* means "the same." It is composed of *is, ea, id* plus the suffix *–dem*. Certain modifications take place before *–dem*.

- The *s* of the nominative masculine singular and the *d* of the neuter nominative singular drop out before *–dem*.

- The *i* of the nominative masculine singular becomes long.

- The letter *m* becomes *n* before *–dem*.

Pronoun/Adjective: *īdem, eadem, idem*						
	Singular			**Plural**		
	Masculine	**Feminine**	**Neuter**	**Masculine**	**Feminine**	**Neuter**
Nominative	īdem	eadem	idem	eīdem	eaedem	eadem
Genitive	ēiusdem	ēiusdem	ēiusdem	eōrundem	eārundem	eōrundem
Dative	eīdem	eīdem	eīdem	eīsdem	eīsdem	eīsdem
Accusative	eundem	eandem	idem	eōsdem	eāsdem	eadem
Ablative	eōdem	eādem	eōdem	eīsdem	eīsdem	eīsdem

The Latin equivalent of the English phrase "**the same as**" is

īdem quī, with, of course, the pronoun and the relative taking the case, number, and gender appropriate for their contexts

or

īdem atque. Note carefully that when *atque* is used in this way with some form of *īdem*, the conjunction *atque* does not have its usual meaning "and;" in this context it means "as." Some examples:

> *Eaedem sunt puellae, quās anteā vīdimus.*
> "They are the same girls as/whom we saw earlier."

> *Eīsdem āthlētīs praemia dedimus, quī ab omnibus laudātī erant.*
> "We gave rewards to the same athletes as/who had been praised by everybody."

> *Īdem cibus mihi placet atque tibi.*
> "The same food pleases me as <pleases> you."

> *Eadem dōna accēpī atque tū.*
> "I received the same gifts as you <received>."

▶ EXERCISE 5

Translate into English. The Reading Vocabulary may be consulted.

1. Colōnus eōsdem sociōs sēcum manēre volēbat.

2. Incolae eāsdem epistulās, quae Martīnō datae erant, manibus tangere nōlēbant.

3. Colōnus eōdem modō īrātus est Martīnō, quō Martīnus Colōnō īrāscēbātur.

4. Ad eandem īnsulam nāvigāre volumus atque tū.

5. Incolae eandem vim dīvīnam in epistulīs esse putābant atque in rēbus sacrīs.

LANGUAGE FACT IV

THE INTENSIVE PRONOUN *IPSE, IPSA, IPSUM*

Have another look at the same sentence taken from the chapter reading passage.

> *Eīdem barbarī, cum epistulās Martīnō dedissent, vīdērunt Martīnum, epistulīs lēctīs, Colōnī absentis verba et animum et voluntātem ipsam intellegere, velut sī Colōnus ipse adesset.*
>
> "The same inhabitants/natives, when they had given the letters to Martín, saw that, when the letters had been read, Martín understood the words and the mind and the will itself of the absent Columbus, just as if Columbus himself were present."

The intensive pronoun/adjective *ipse, ipsa, ipsum* means "self" and should be carefully distinguished from the reflexive pronoun *suī, sibi, sē, sē*, which we also translate as "self." While English uses one word to express these two distinct notions, Latin has separate words for each. The intensive pronoun/adjective **agrees** with what it refers to and has a nominative, whereas the reflexive pronoun refers to something else in the sentence with which it does **not** agree grammatically and has no nominative. The difference is illustrated in these sentences.

> *Nauta ipse haec dīxit.*   **intensive pronoun/adjective**
> "The sailor himself said these things."
>
> *Nauta haec sibi dīxit.*   **reflexive pronoun**
> "The sailor said these things to himself."
>
> *Nauta ipse amat.*   **intensive pronoun/adjective**
> "The sailor himself loves/is in love."
>
> *Nauta sē amat.*   **reflexive pronoun**
> "The sailor loves himself."

Intensive Pronoun/Adjective: *ipse, ipsa, ipsum*

	Singular			Plural		
	Masculine	Feminine	Neuter	Masculine	Feminine	Neuter
Nominative	ipse	ipsa	ipsum	ipsī	ipsae	ipsa
Genitive	ipsīus	ipsīus	ipsīus	ipsōrum	ipsārum	ipsōrum
Dative	ipsī	ipsī	ipsī	ipsīs	ipsīs	ipsīs
Accusative	ipsum	ipsam	ipsum	ipsōs	ipsās	ipsa
Ablative	ipsō	ipsā	ipsō	ipsīs	ipsīs	ipsīs

The marriage of Queen Isabella of Castile and Aragón and King Ferdinand of León and Navarre in 1469 joined the two largest kingdoms of Spain. The two monarchs ruled independently and Isabella sponsored Columbus' expedition. On the coat of arms are: clockwise, León, Navarre, Aragón, and Castile. The fleurs-de-lis at the center stand for the Bourbons.

▶ EXERCISE 6

Translate into Latin.

Colōnus, ī, m. – Columbus   Martīnus, ī, m. – Martín

1. Columbus said all these things to himself.

2. Columbus himself said all these things.

3. Columbus heard all the words of the sailors themselves.

4. Martín himself led quite a few associates into another part of the island.

5. Columbus himself said that he was angry.

6. The inhabitants saw that Martín, when the letters had been read, understood the words themselves of the absent Columbus.

7. I do not praise myself but glory itself.

8. Columbus did not praise himself but the sailors themselves.

LANGUAGE FACT V

DEMONSTRATIVE PRONOUN *ISTE, ISTA, ISTUD*

In yet another sentence in the chapter reading passage you can see a new demonstrative pronoun/adjective.

> *"Cōnsilium istud," inquit Martīnus, "nōn probō".*
> "I do not approve of that plan of yours," said Martín."

The demonstrative *iste, ista, istud* means "that <of yours>." The notion "of yours" may be literally true or it may simply refer figuratively to a connection between the thing indicated by the pronoun and something else. In some cases—but certainly not always—the use of this pronoun can have a derogatory or dismissive connotation.

Demonstrative Pronoun/Adjective: *iste, ista, istud*

	Singular			Plural		
	Masculine	**Feminine**	**Neuter**	**Masculine**	**Feminine**	**Neuter**
Nominative	iste	ista	istud	istī	istae	ista
Genitive	istīus	istīus	istīus	istōrum	istārum	istōrum
Dative	istī	istī	istī	istīs	istīs	istīs
Accusative	istum	istam	istud	istōs	istās	ista
Ablative	istō	istā	istō	istīs	istīs	istīs

STUDY TIP

Notice the genitive and dative singular of the demonstratives *īdem, ipse,* and *iste*. These forms closely resemble the genitive and dative singular of *ille* or of the naughty nine adjectives like *ūnus* and *sōlus*.

▶ EXERCISE 7

Translate into English.

1. "Dē istīs officiīs," inquiunt nautae, "semper cōgitāre vidēris."

2. "Iste," inquit Martīnus, "dē castrīs ipsīs nec autem hominum relictōrum perīculō loquitur."

3. Istōs tē mīlitēs in illam urbem ductūrum esse dīcis. In labōre ibi semper versābuntur nec redībunt.

4. Istī armīs suīs ūtuntur; nōs virtūte nostrā et benevolentiā dēfendimur.

5. Istī lēgātī epistulās ad Martīnum tulērunt. Ille voluntātem Colōnī intellēxit.

6. Istīs litterīs benevolentiam tuam in Martīnum dēclārāvistī.

▶ EXERCISE 8

The following text is adapted from another history entitled *Dē orbe novō*, which narrates the explorations of Columbus. Peter or Petrus Martyr (1457–1526) was born in Italy and migrated to Spain as an adult. He wrote a great deal about the explorations of Central and South America, including the history *Dē orbe novō*. In this passage Peter describes the first encounter between the Spaniards and the Native Americans upon Columbus' arrival in the West Indies. The happy end of this encounter was, sadly, all too rare on future occasions.

Translate this passage into English. The Reading Vocabulary may be consulted. Some other new words are explained below the passage.

Ibi prīmum ad terram ēgressī incolās nōn paucōs vīdērunt. Incolae, cum gentem inaudītam cōnspexissent, in silvam māgnam, agmine factō, fūgērunt. Nostrī incolās secūtī mulierem tandem capiunt. Hanc cum ad nāvēs dūxissent, nostrīs cibīs et vīnō bene saturātam atque ōrnātam vestibus līberāvērunt et in terrā relīquērunt. Cum ad suōs mulier vēnisset—sciēbat enim illa quō aliī incolae fūgissent—ostendissetque mīram esse nostrōrum hominum līberālitātem, omnēs ad lītora certātim currunt. Hanc gentem novam esse missam ē caelō dīcēbant. Ē nāvibus dēscendunt nostrī et ā rēge et aliīs incolīs honōrificē accipiuntur.

capiunt – although this verb is in the present tense, it refers of course to an action in the past; this historical present is used in narration to make action seem more vivid and present.

certātim (adv.) – eagerly

currunt – another example of the historical present

ēgressī – nominative plural of the perfect participle of *ēgredior, ēgredī, ēgressus sum*, which means "to set forth" or "to go out"

honōrificē (adv.) – with honor and respect

inaudītus, a, um – unheard of

līberālitās, līberālitātis, f. – generosity

mīrus, a, um – marvelous, amazing

prīmum (adv.) – for the first time

quō – to where, whither

saturātus, a, um – filled up

The Cathedral of Seville incorporating a mosque is the world's largest church in terms of volume. La Giralda tower, formerly a minaret, in its present form, is echoed in buildings like Chicago's Wrigley Building. Columbus set sail from Seville's port of San Lucar and an elaborate tomb in the cathedral is said to hold his remains.

TALKING ABOUT A READING
ABOUT ALL PEOPLE BEING EQUAL AND UNADAPTED LATIN: THE ASSASSINATION OF JULIUS CAESAR

DĒ HOMINIBUS INTER SĒ AEQUĀLIBUS

Marīa: Populī quōs Colōnus in terrā novā invēnit nōn erant doctī. Nesciēbant enim scrībere et legere nec sciēbant quālēs essent litterae. Dēbuērunt igitur ab Eurōpaeīs (*Europeans*) vincī.

Helena: Litterārum quidem vīs est ingēns. At male agis, Marīa, sī putās hominēs indigenōs (*native*) fuisse propter hanc causam īnferiōrēs (*inferior*). Nam hominēs indigenī aliās rēs sciēbant, quās Eurōpaeī nōn sciēbant.

Mārcus: Putō Helenam bene dīcere. Omnēs hominēs nōn sunt eīdem. Vīs ūnīuscūiusque (*each one*) hominis est in suīs rēbus posita. Cōgitāte dē omnibus gentibus ex quibus fit nunc populus Americānus: sunt Hibernī (*Irish*), Afrī (*African-Americans*), Ītalī (*Italians*), Sinēnsēs (*Chinese*), multī aliī. Omnēs rēs suās bonās sēcum ferunt et ita populum Americānum meliōrem atque fortiōrem faciunt. Nūllus populus est aliīs īnferior.

Marīa: Nunc intellegō, Mārce, tē et Helenam bene dīcere. Multa bella in orbe terrārum sunt gesta, quia quīdam (*some*) hominēs putābant sē esse aliīs superiōrēs (*superior*).

Helena: Sed signum (*statue*) Lībertātis omnēs eōdem modō salūtat omnibusque eandem lībertātem prōmittit ...

Nunc cōgitēmus dē Atticō. Mārcō enim vītam Atticī legente, mē Nepōtem loquentem paene audīre crēdō.

Mārcus: Ista verba mihi placent. Putāsne mē bene legere?

Helena: Bene legis. Tē recitante (*recitō, āre* "to recite, read aloud"), verba Nepōtis facile intelleguntur.

Marīa: Satis dē hāc rē locūtī estis. Vōs, Mārce et Helena, nimis inter vōs laudāre solētis. Recitā, Mārce, locum, quī sequitur. Mentibus nostrīs fingēmus (*fingō, ere* "to create, pretend") ipsum Nepōtem recitāre!

Sed signum (statue) *Lībertātis omnēs eōdem modō salūtat omnibusque eandem lībertātem prōmittit ...*

Julius Caesar stands guard in the Tuileries Gardens in Paris. Originally a royal retreat near the Louvre, the royal palace and the gardens were begun by Catherine de' Medici. Today they are a much beloved public park where families stroll.

THE ASSASSINATION OF JULIUS CAESAR

CORNĒLIĪ NEPŌTIS ATTICUS, 8.1–3

After Julius Caesar had been assassinated, the conspirators against Caesar seemed to be in control of the state. Atticus remained on good terms with Marcus Brutus, who, together with Cassius, had been at the head of the conspirators. Members of the anti-Caesarian party wanted the Roman equestrians to establish a private fund for the assassins of Caesar. Atticus was asked to be in charge of this project.

1   1. Secūtum est illud tempus, occīsō Caesare, cum rēs pūblica penes
Brūtōs vidērētur esse et Cassium ac tōta cīvitās sē ad eōs convertisse
vidērētur. 2. Sīc M. Brūtō ūsus est, ut nūllō ille adulēscēns aequālī
familiārius quam hōc sene <ūterētur>, neque sōlum eum prīncipem
5   cōnsiliī habēret, sed etiam in convictū. 3. Excōgitātum est ā
quibusdam, ut prīvātum aerārium Caesaris interfectōribus ab equitibus
Rōmānīs cōnstituerētur. Id facile efficī posse arbitrātī sunt, sī prīncipēs
ēius ōrdinis pecūniās contulissent. Itaque appellātus est ā C. Flāviō,
Brūtī familiārī, Atticus, ut ēius reī prīnceps esse vellet.

VOCABULARY

1 penes + accusative – in the possession of

2 Brūtōs – the conspirators Marcus Brutus and
Decimus Brutus

cīvitās, cīvitātis, f. – the state, political entity

convertō, ere, convertī, conversum – to turn

3 aequālis, aequāle – equal, compory in age

4 familiārius – comparative degree of the adverb
familiāriter, which means "familiarly," or "inti-
mately"

4–5 neque sōlum . . . sed etiam . . . – the same meaning
as *nōn sōlum . . . sed etiam*, but *neque* means the
same as *et nōn*

4 prīnceps, prīncipis, m. – leader, chief

5 convictus, convictūs, m. – social relationships, a
living together

excōgitō, āre, āvī, ātum – to think up, devise

5–6 ā quibusdam – by some

6 prīvātus, a, um – private, apart from the public
sphere

aerārium, ī, n. – treasury, fund, account

interfector, interfectōris, m. – slayer, assassin

equitēs, m. pl. – the order of knights

7 cōnstituō, ere, cōnstituī, cōnstitūtum – to establish, institute, decide

efficiō, ere, effēcī, effectum – to bring about, effect

arbitror, arbitrārī, arbitrātus sum – to suppose,
judge

8 ōrdō, ōrdinis, m. – order, class (in society)

cōnferō, cōnferre, contulī, collātum – to contribute, confer, bring together.

appellō, āre, āvī, ātum – to call upon, name,
address

C. Flāvius = Gāius Flāvius

9 familiāris, familiāre – belonging to the same
family

READING NOTES

1–3 *rēs pūblica penes Brūtōs vidērētur esse et Cassium
ac tōta cīvitās sē ad eōs convertisse vidērētur* The
preposition *penes* literally meaning "in the
possession" of the two Bruti and Cassius, here
means they seemed to be in charge and in control. Marcus Brutus headed the conspirators
(including Decimus Brutus, who had formerly
been a soldier under Caesar) who assassinated
Julius Caesar.

3–5 *Sīc M. Brūtō ūsus est, ut nūllō ille adulēscēns
aequālī familiārius quam hōc sene <ūterētur>,
neque sōlum eum prīncipem cōnsiliī habēret, sed
etiam in convictū* Again *ut* introduces a result
clause. (See Chapter 14.) When it refers to the
interactions of people, *ūsus est* can mean "to
treat someone" in a particular way. In apposition to another noun, *prīnceps* means "first of its
kind or class." The sentence means "He treated
Marcus Brutus in such a way that the young
man (Brutus) treated no one of his own age in
a more familiar manner than he did this older
man (i.e., Atticus) and he not only had him (i.e.,
Atticus) as chief in counsel, but also <had him
as a best friend> in social relationships."

5–7 *Excōgitātum est ā quibusdam, ut prīvātum
aerārium . . . cōnstituerētur* The verb *excōgitātum
est* is an impersonal passive linked to an *ut*
clause with the verb *cōnstituerētur* in the
subjunctive because the construction after the
phrase "it was devised that . . ." is like a purpose
clause or an indirect command: "it was devised
. . . that . . . an account should be set up . . ."

7–8 *Id facile efficī posse arbitrātī sunt, sī prīncipēs ēius
ōrdinis pecūniās contulissent* The demonstrative
id refers back to the *aerārium*. And *ēius ōrdinis* is
the equestrian order.

QUESTIONS ABOUT THE TEXT

Answer in complete Latin sentences.

1. Penes quōs, occīsō Caesare, rēs pūblica vidēbātur esse?

2. Quō homine aequālī Mārcus Brūtus adulēscēns familiārius ūtēbātur quam Atticō sene?

3. Quod auxilium Caesaris interfectōribus ab equitibus Rōmānīs cōnstituī volēbant quīdam hominēs?

4. Quōs hominēs pecūniās in prīvātum aerārium cōnferre volēbant illī, quī hortābantur ut hoc auxilium Caesaris interfectōribus cōnstituerētur?

5. Cūius reī ut prīnceps esse vellet, appellātus est Atticus?

DĒ HOMINIBUS INTER SĒ AEQUĀLIBUS CONTINUED

Marīa: Eadem verba dīcō, quae Helena dīxit—Mārcum bene legere!

Mārcus: Grātiās tibi agō.

14

Result Clauses; More Ways to Express Purpose: Supine in *-m*; Formation of Adverbs

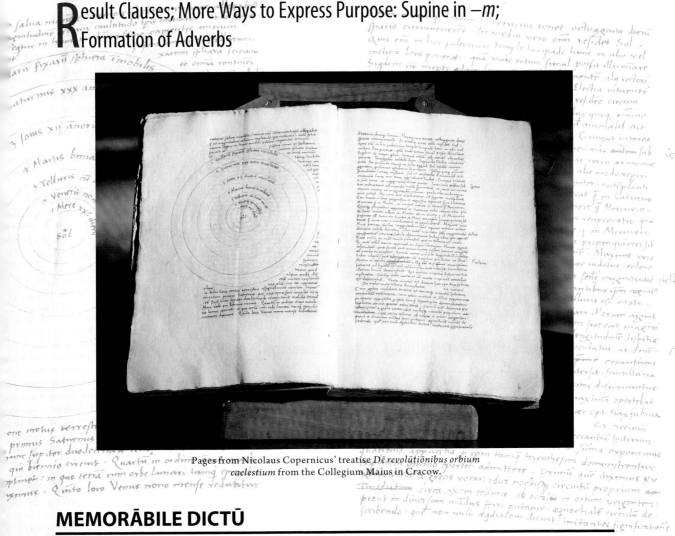

Pages from Nicolaus Copernicus' treatise *Dē revolūtiōnibus orbium caelestium* from the Collegium Maius in Cracow.

MEMORĀBILE DICTŪ

Hypothesēs nōn fingō.

"I make no guesses." (Isaac Newton, *Mathematical Principles of Natural Philosophy*)

Words of Isaac Newton, who in 1687 published *Philosophiae nātūrālis prīncipia mathēmatica*, a discussion of gravity and the laws of motion that is often referred to simply as the *Prīncipia* and is generally considered the most important scientific work ever written. The Latin phrase above comes from a supplement to the *Prīncipia*. Newton's research brought the scientific work of Copernicus, Galileo, and the German astronomer Kepler to its crowning glory. With the exception of Galileo, who wrote in both Italian and Latin, all of these illustrious and influential physical scientists wrote primarily in Latin. Latin remained the official language of scientific communication for centuries.

READING

Nicolaus Copernicus (1473–1543), born in Prussian territory today located in Poland, was the first scholar to formulate scientifically the heliocentric concept of the universe and to prove that the earth was not at its center. The idea that the universe centered on the earth had been propagated in the west by the writings of the ancient astronomer Ptolemy, who lived in the second century CE and the theories of Aristotle. This earth-centered view remained dominant for centuries, even though ancient Greek scholars had advanced the hypothesis that the earth was part of a heliocentric solar system with the sun at the center of the universe. Copernicus propounded his scientific theories in a seminal book written in Latin, *Dē revolūtiōnibus orbium caelestium* (*About the Revolutions of the Celestial Bodies*), which laid the foundations of modern astronomy. Copernicus wrote about mathematics and geometry as well as astronomy. In the early seventeenth century the Italian mathematician and astronomer Galileo Galilei suffered persecution at the hands of an Inquisition for promoting the Copernican theory and arguing that the earth moved around the sun. In front of the Inquisition while he recanted his controversial views he also uttered his famous "And yet it moves…" The excerpt below is adapted from *Dē revolūtiōnibus orbium caelestium*.

CŪR ANTĪQUĪ PUTĀVERINT TERRAM ESSE IN MEDIŌ MUNDĪ TAMQUAM CENTRUM ET CŪR HOC NŌN SIT VĒRUM <NUNC DĪCAM>

1 Antīquī cōnātī sunt affirmāre terram esse sitam in mediō mundī, quod propter gravitātem putābant, quia elementum, ex quō terra est facta, maximē est ponderōsum. Omnia enim undique pondere suō tracta in terram cadunt. Hoc quoque cōgitābant: sī terra volverētur, nōn esset

5 tam stabilis quam nunc est; sī hoc fieret, tam vehementer terra volvī dēbēret ut nūllus homō, nūllum animal in eā stāre posset atque ipsa dissipārētur.

Perperam tamen antīquī putābant terram dissipārī posse. Nam mōtūs quī per nātūram fiunt aliī sunt quam mōtūs quī per artem hūmānam

10 fiunt nec rēs dissipāre solent. Deinde ipsum caelum, quod est immēnsum, maximō impetū atque vēlōcitāte volvī dēbēret, ut terram circumīret. At caelum est tam māgnum et paene īnfīnītum; rēs īnfīnītae nōn moventur; ergō necessāriō stābit. Dē terrā autem scīmus eam fīnēs habēre. Cūr nōlumus sinere eam movērī? Idem Aenēās dīcere potest:

15   "maria, lītora, terrae moventur; ipse stō." Nam nāvigantī omnia alia movērī videntur, dum sē stāre putat. Absurdum est quoque ascrībere mōtum eī reī quae continet; movētur enim potius rēs quae continētur, i.e., terra. Mōbilitās igitur terrae, praesertim in cottīdiānā revolūtiōne, multō probābilior est quam ēius quiēs.

READING VOCABULARY

absurdus, a, um – absurd, irrational

Aenēās, Aenēae, m. – Aeneas

*affirmō, āre, āvī, ātum – to assert, maintain

ascrībō, ere, ascrīpsī, ascrīptum – to impute, ascribe, attribute

centrum, ī, n. – center

*circumeō, circumīre, circumīvī, circumitum – to go around

*contineō, ēre, continuī, contentum – to hold, keep together, contain

*cottīdiānus, a, um – of every day, daily

dissipō, āre, āvī, ātum – to scatter, disperse

elementum, ī, n. – element

*ergō (conj.) – therefore

*gravitās, gravitātis, f. – weight, gravity

i.e. = id est – i.e., that is

*immēnsus, a, um – immeasurable, immense, endless

*īnfīnītus, a, um – boundless, unlimited

*maximē (adv.) – most

*medius, a, um – middle

medium, ī, n. – the middle, midst

mōbilitās, mōbilitātis, f. – mobility

*mōtus, mōtūs, m. – motion, movement

moveō, movēre, movī, mōtum – move‡

*multō (adv.) – by much

*nātūra, ae, f. – nature

*necessāriō (adv.) – necessarily

*perperam (adv.) – wrongly, incorrectly

ponderōsus, a, um – heavy

*pondus, ponderis, n. – weight

*praesertim (adv.) – especially

probābilis, probābile – probable

*quiēs, quiētis, f. – rest, repose

revolūtiō, revolūtiōnis, f. – revolving

stabilis, stabile – steady, stable

*tam vehementer . . . ut . . . – so vehemently . . . that . . .

*undique (adv.) – from all parts, from everywhere

vēlōcitās, vēlōcitātis, f. – speed, velocity

*volvō, ere, volvī, volūtum – to turn round

*Words marked with an asterisk will need to be memorized later in the chapter.

‡Additional information about the words marked with the double dagger will be in the **Take Note** section that follows the Reading Vocabulary.

TAKE NOTE

movētur, moventur, movērī The active form *movēre* in Latin means "to move something." The verb is transitive. So while someone speaking English says something "moves," Latin has a different idiom. If we want to say the same thing in Latin, we must say *movētur* (i.e., "the thing is moved").

BY THE WAY

The passage below is only one small part of the arguments, which Copernicus used to construct a new model of the Solar System. This brief excerpt that helps to explicate the arguments of the chapter reading passages is about the turning of earth itself. Here Copernicus rejects the ancient idea that earth is immobile (which was part of the theory that placed earth in the center of the universe). Copernicus' insightful arguments proceed as follows:

The ancient notion of the earth's position was based on these assumptions:

1. The ancients thought the earth must be at the center of the universe (or "solar system" as we call it), because the earth is very heavy and all heavy things tend downwards—i.e., to the center of the system.

2. The ancients did not think that the earth was always turning because it seems to be steady and we have no sense of its motion, and the earth, if spun violently, would be scattered or dissipated. Therefore they thought the whole heavenly system, including the planets and the sun, traveled in orbits around the earth, and not vice versa.

Copernicus uses these arguments to refute the ancient notion:

1. We can see that many movements of bodies in nature result in no dislocation or "scattering" of the parts of the thing—as we see in the movements of the sky itself.

2. The heavens are infinite in size. It is much less likely that something infinite in size would be turning at an immense velocity (needed to go all the way around the earth in a limited time).

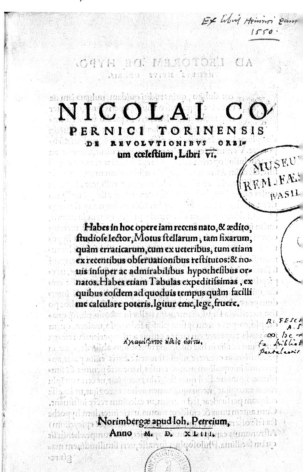

3. We know that the earth is limited in *size* (by comparison to the universe). Hence it is more logical to assume that the earth's rotation causes the apparent revolution of the heavens that we see with our eyes.

4. We on earth are compared to Aeneas sailing on a ship. The shore seems to Aeneas to be moving past him, when in actual fact, the shore is not moving, but rather Aeneas is moving on the ship past the shore.

5. It is more probable that something contained is moving rather than the thing that contains it.

The title page of Copernicus' treatise *Dē revolūtiōnibus orbium caelestium* which was published in Nuremberg, Germany in 1543. Note that the third part of the author's name *Torinēnsis* refers to Torum, his birthplace in what is today Poland. The note, in Greek, *Ageometretos oudeis eisito* warns "Let no one untutored in geometry enter here."

COMPREHENSION QUESTIONS

1. What was the concept that ancient people held about the earth and why?

2. How does Copernicus answer the argument that the earth would be dispersed if it turned around?

3. For what two reasons, according to Copernicus, was it more likely that the earth moved than that the skies moved?

4. For what purpose does Copernicus introduce the comparison with Aeneas?

LANGUAGE FACT I

RESULT CLAUSES

In the chapter reading passage, Copernicus exposes the following argument advanced by the ancients to defend that the earth was immobile in the center of the universe:

> *Sī terra volverētur, nōn esset tam stabilis quam nunc est; sī hoc fieret, **tam** vehementer terra volvī dēbēret **ut nūllus homō, nūllum animal in eā stāre posset atque ipsa dissipārētur.***
>
> "If the earth were turned around, it would not be so steady as it is now; if this happened, the earth would need to be turned around so vehemently that no person, no animal could stay on it and it would be scattered itself."

The subordinate clauses *ut nūllus homō, nūllum animal stāre posset* and *<ut> ipsa dissipārētur* are result clauses. They show what would happen as a result of the action in the main clause: if the earth was turning around, thought the ancients, the result of this turning would be that no man or no animal could stand on it and the earth itself would fall apart.

STUDY TIP

When trying to recognize a result clause in Latin, look for a **TIP OFF** word in the main clause. These tip offs like *tam*, "so," *ita*, "in such a way," *tantus*, "so great," *tālis*, "such," *tot* "so many," etc., often contain the letter "**t.**"

Look at some more examples of result clauses.

> *Terra est tam ingēns ut ā nōbīs tōta cōnspicī nōn possit.*
> "The earth is so huge that it cannot be observed by us whole."

> *Antīquōrum ars nōn erat ita māgna ut illī omnia dē terrā intellegerent.*
> "The science of the ancients was not so large that they understood everything about the earth."

> *Copernicus tam multa dē terrā et dē sōle invēnit ut librum celeberrimum scrīpserit.*
> "Copernicus discovered so many things about the earth and the sun that he wrote a very famous book."

A result clause is introduced by *ut* ("<so> that") or *ut nōn* ("<so> that not"), and always has a **subjunctive** verb. The tense of the subjunctive does not depend on the tense of the main clause, but on the actual time when the result occurred. The present subjunctive is used for a result in the present (even coming out of a past action), imperfect subjunctive for a prolonged result in the past, perfect subjunctive for completed result in the past. Look at the above examples again, paying attention to what tense is used in each result clause.

STUDY TIP

Result and purpose clauses have similar components but they are two different types of propositions. Consider the sentence: "I fell so badly that I broke my leg." The subordinate clause here expresses result but no purpose. Also, the negative for the purpose clause is *nē*, while the negative for the result clause is *ut nōn*.

Reconstruction of the triquetrum, an astronomical instrument, first described by Ptolemy (second century CE) and also discussed by Copernicus in Book IV of *Dē revolūtiōnibus orbium caelestium*. Two intersecting arms hinged to a vertical post enable one to calculate the angular elevation of a heavenly body observed through a sight mounted on the upper arm.

Finally, purpose clauses have present or imperfect subjunctives according to the tense of the main clause, while the result clauses have present, imperfect, or perfect subjunctives according to the time when the result occurred.

If you are still not sure about recognizing result clauses, remember that result clauses answer the question "What happened?," while purpose clauses answer the question "Why?"

The 1973 stamp with a portrait and images of space stations commemorates the 500th anniversary of Copernicus' birth. The African nation of Liberia was founded by freed slaves from the United States who established a Republic in 1847. Following a brutal civil war, Ellen Johnsonn Sirleaf was democratically elected president in 2005.

▶ EXERCISE 1

Translate the Latin into English and the English into Latin.

1. Copernicus is so renowned that all people know about him.

2. Hic liber tam difficilis mihi est vīsus ut eum legere nōn possem.

3. If you want me to read Copernicus, find such an easy part that I can understand it!

4. Rēs quās Copernicus scrīpsit tam māgnī habentur ut etiam hodiē ea legāmus.

5. Multī hominēs tam vehementer affirmābant terram nōn movērī ut Copernicus et aliī contrā hās sententiās diū pugnāre dēbērent.

6. Good will was so absent (i.e., away) that many people, asserting that the earth was being moved, were punished.

VOCABULARY TO LEARN

NOUNS

elementum, ī, n. – element

gravitās, gravitātis, f. – weight, gravity

mōtus, mōtūs, m. – motion, movement

nātūra, ae, f. – nature

pondus, ponderis, n. – weight

quiēs, quiētis, f. – rest, repose

ADJECTIVES

cottīdiānus, a, um – of every day, daily

immēnsus, a, um – immeasurable, immense, endless

īnfīnītus, a, um – boundless, unlimited

medius, a, um – middle; medium, ī, n. – the middle, midst

VERBS

affirmō, āre, āvī, ātum – to assert, maintain

circumeō, circumīre, circumīvī, circumitum – to go around

contineō, ēre, continuī, contentum – to hold, keep together, contain

volvō, ere, volvī, volūtum – to turn round

ADVERBS

maximē – most

multō – by much

necessāriō – necessarily

perperam – wrongly, incorrectly

praesertim – especially

undique – from all parts, from everywhere

CONJUNCTIONS

ergō – therefore

ut – that (sense of result)

▶ EXERCISE 2

In the sentences below, find the words derived from the Vocabulary to Learn in this chapter. One sentence contains more than one derivative. Write the corresponding Latin word.

1. Let me ponder the situation carefully and decide how to act.

2. Please keep quiet in the museum!

3. The answer is affirmative.

4. After the hurricane we all understood how powerful the elemental forces of nature are.

5. I do not want to get involved in this affair.

6. We all are fascinated to learn about the infinity of the cosmos.

7. If I had enough money, I would buy myself a Volvo.

8. This is the highest mountain on our continent.

▶ EXERCISE 3

Fill in the blanks using the sentence in parentheses. The sentence in parentheses should make either a purpose or a result clause, according to context. Change the tense and mood accordingly. Translate the sentence and indicate whether it contains a purpose or a result clause.

Example: Copernicus exemplum dē Aenēā scrīpsit _____. (sententiam suam ostendit)
Copernicus exemplum dē Aenēā scrīpsit <u>ut sententiam suam ostenderet</u>.
Copernicus wrote an example about Aeneas in order to show his opinion. purpose

1. Copernicus tam bonum exemplum dē Aenēa scrīpsit _____. (omnēs, quī nunc legunt, statim intellegunt quid dīcere velit)

2. Copernicus omnia ita mūtāvit _____. (sōl, nōn terra in mediō mundī esse iam putābātur)

3. Multī Copernicō resistere volēbant _____. (sententia vetus servābātur)

The original nineteenth-century tribute to Copernicus with astrolabe in hand is in Warsaw. During the Nazi occupation, a plaque in German covered the original Latin inscription. A Polish Boy Scout removed the plaque and in retaliation the statue itself was removed. Following the war, it was restored to its rightful place.

LANGUAGE FACT II

MORE WAYS TO EXPRESS PURPOSE: SUPINE IN -*M*

Most often purpose is expressed by an *ut*-clause. However, there are some more ways to express purpose which you will learn in this chapter and the next.

You have already seen the fourth principal part of verbs: *parātum, tentum, cultum, audītum, captum*. From this part of the verb the perfect passive participle is formed. This part of the verb itself, with the –*um* ending, is called the "first supine." The supine ending in –*m* has its own special meaning. It is used after verbs of movement to indicate purpose.

> *Eō dormītum.*
> "I go to sleep."

> *Veniō petītum pācem.*
> "I come to ask for peace."

STUDY TIP

While commenting on the motives of the Roman women for visiting the theatre, the poet Ovid in his *Ars Amātōria* gives two good examples expressing purpose, using both the supine in *–m* and the purpose *ut*-clause in the same sentence (*Art of Loving*, 1.99).

> *Spectātum veniunt, veniunt spectentur ut ipsae.*
> "They come to watch, they come to be watched themselves.' (i.e., so that they themselves may be/are watched.)

BY THE WAY

The supine in *–m* is thought of as an accusative singular of a fourth declension noun.

▶ EXERCISE 4

Translate into Latin. When possible, translate in two ways: with an *ut*-clause and with the supine in *–m*.

1. I go around the house to look for a thing I have lost.

2. He was walking in order to observe the nature of the elements.

3. The learned man asserted this especially in order to show the movement, not the rest, of the earth.

4. I returned home in order to find rest.

The United Nations declared 2009 "The International Year of Astronomy" to celebrate the 400th anniversary of Galileo's use of the first complete astronomical telescope to gather evidence that the Earth moved around the sun. Galileo had transformed the spyglass into the astronomical telescope.

▶ EXERCISE 5

Below you will find an adapted excerpt from *Nūntius sīdereus* (*Starry Messenger*), by Galileo Galilei (1564–1642), the first scientific work based on observations with a telescope. It relates observations that the moon did not have a smooth body, as well as the discovery of four planets around Jupiter, and casts serious doubts on Aristotle's assertions about the structure of the universe. The work of Galileo supported Copernicanism. Galileo is called by some "the father of modern physics and astronomy."

Translate the text.

Saepissimē pars altera lūnae clārior, pars obscūrior ā nōbīs cōnspicitur. Perspicillō autem armātī tam bene lūnam observāvimus ut invenīre potuerimus ēius superficiem nōn esse aequam nec lūnam esse sphaeram exāctissimam, ut plūrimī doctī affirmāverant, sed asperam, montium atque cavitātum plēnam. Linea enim quā pars clārior ā parte obscūriōre sēparātur, nōn est ōvālis, ut in vērā sphaerā esse dēbet, sed valdē aspera. Similēs sunt rēs in terrā, quia sōl lūmine suō prīmō montēs tangit, deinde plānitiēs, tandem vallēs. In lūnā ergō sunt cavitātēs et montēs et ita fit ut eōdem tempore quō montēs lūmen accipiunt, cavitātēs adhūc sint in tenebrīs. Itaque linea inter partem clāriōrem et obscūriōrem est aspera.

alter . . . alter . . . – one (of the two) . . . the other (of the two) . . .	obscūrus, a, um – dark, obscure
asper, aspera, asperum – rough, uneven	ōvālis, ōvāle – oval
cavitās, cavitātis, f. – crater	perspicillum, ī, n. – telescope (something we look through: *per* + *-spiciō*, as in *cōnspiciō*)
exāctus, a, um – accurate, precise	plānitiēs, plānitiēī, f. – plain
linea, ae, f. – line	sphaera, ae, f. – sphere
lūna, ae, f. – moon	superficiēs, superficiēī, f. – surface
observō, āre, āvī, ātum – to observe	vallis, vallis, f. – valley

▶ EXERCISE 6

Translate into Latin. The vocabulary supplied in Exercise 5 may be consulted.

1. We use the telescope in order to observe the moon.

2. The telescope can show so many things that it is necessary for us to use it if we are interested in the sky.

3. Come with me to observe the moon! (Translate in two ways.)

4. The ancients thought that the surface of the moon was so even that it seemed a true sphere.

5. Galileo (*Galilaeus*), however, used the telescope so well that he understood that on the moon there were mountains and craters.

6. The sun does not touch the mountains and the craters at the same time in such a way that on the surface of the moon could be seen the clearer and the more obscure parts.

The New Deal's Public Works of Art Project (PWAP) set six sculptors to work in 1934 on an astronomers' monument for the soon to be opened Griffiths Observatory in Los Angeles. This image shows Kepler flanked to the left by Copernicus and to the right by Galileo. Not shown are Hipparchus, Newton, and Herschel.

LANGUAGE FACT III
FORMATION OF ADVERBS

By now you have seen many adverbs, and you have noticed that, although each adverb has just one ending, these endings can vary. In general, adverbs can be divided into words that appear only as adverbs, such as *undique*, meaning "from all sides," and those derived directly from adjectives, like *fēlīciter* ("happily"), which is the adverbial form of the adjective *fēlīx, fēlīcis* ("happy"). There are some general rules about how adverbs may be formed from adjectives, though these rules have very many exceptions. The rules, nonetheless, are helpful, since they account for quite a number of words, and the exceptions can be learned as you meet them.

Adjectives (First and Second Declensions)	**Adverbs** are often formed by adding –*ē* to the base of the adjective.
studiōsus, a, um	*studiōsē*
pulcher, pulchra, pulchrum	*pulchrē*

Adjectives (Third Declension)	**Adverbs** are often formed by adding –*iter* to the base of the adjective.
fortis, e	*fortiter*

Comparative Adjectives	**Comparative Adverbs** often are the same as the neuter nominative/accusative comparative adjective.
studiōsior, studiōsius	*studiōsius*
fortior, fortius	*fortius*

Superlative Adjectives	**Superlative Adverbs** are typically formed by adding –*ē* to the base of the superlative adjective.
studiōsissimus, a, um	*studiōsissimē*
fortissimus, a, um	*fortissimē*
pulcherrimus, a, um	*pulcherrimē*

This chart shows how the comparative and superlative adverbs have the same endings regard-less of the declension of the adjective.

Comparison of Adverbs			
Positive Adjective	Positive Adverb	Comparative Adverb	Superlative Adverb
studiōsus, a, um	studiōsē	studiōsius	studiōsissimē
pulcher, pulchra, pulchrum	pulchrē	pulchrius	pulcherrimē
fortis, forte	fortiter	fortius	fortissimē

A few very common adjectives which you have learned in this book have adverbs related to them which are not formed in accordance with the rules outlined above.

Adjective	Adverb
bonus, a, um	bene
māgnus, a, um	māgnopere
multus, a, um	multō/multum
malus	male
parvus	parum
facilis, facile	facile
tristis, triste	triste
tūtus, a, um	tūtō is more common than tūtē

▶ EXERCISE 7

Change the adjectives into adverbs, keeping the adverbs in the same degree as the adjective. Translate the adverbs into English.

Example: vērissimus, a, um   vērissimē   most/very truly

1. dulcis, dulce
2. sevērus, a, um
3. levis, leve
4. longior, longius
5. praeclārissimus, a, um
6. scelestus, a, um
7. facillimus, a, um
8. ācer, ācris, ācre

TALKING ABOUT A READING

ABOUT TECHNOLOGY AND UNADAPTED LATIN: IN THE MIDDLE OF CIVIL STRIFE

DĒ TECHNOLOGIĀ

Mārcus: Copernicus et Galilaeus fundāmenta (*fundamentals*) scientiae (*knowledge*) et technologiae hodiernae (*modern*) iēcērunt (*established* with *fundāmenta*). Cōgitāte quantum sint hominēs ab illōrum tempore prōgressī! Nunc possumus cum amīcīs telephōnō gestābilī (*cell phone*) omnī locō loquī. Possumus per Rēte ūniversāle (*internet*) imāginēs (*pictures*) et modōs mūsicōs (*music*) statim mittere. Possumus quoque āēroplanīs (*airplanes*) loca longē ā nōbīs sita citō (*quickly*) petere. Medicī vītam hūmānam extendere (*prolong*) semper cōnantur. Quam fēlīcēs sunt nunc hominēs!

Christīna: Technologiam hominēs fēlīcēs facere nōn putō. Prō certō technologia hominibus hodiernīs māgnō est auxiliō. At nōn propter technologiam fit ut sīmus fēlīcēs.

Mārcus: Nōn intellegō cūr hoc dīcās.

Christīna: Hoc exemplum dīcam: hominēs possunt citō aliōs per telephōnum gestābile vel per rēte ūniversāle petere, sed hominēs nōn sunt minus sōlī quam temporibus quibus nec telephōna gestābilia nec rēte ūniversāle habēbant. Necesse est hominibus plūra habēre quam rēs technologiā datās. Promētheus (*Prometheus*), quī hominibus flammās et ipsam technologiam dōnō dedit, aliud quoque dōnum addidit.

Mārcus: Quod erat illud dōnum?

Christīna: Spem caecam (*blind*). Etiam sine technologiā hominēs spērāre possunt. Nōn sōlum technologia, sed etiam amor et amīcī nōs faciunt fēlīcēs.

Mārcus *looking at Helen*: Hoc sciō.

Marīa: Satis dē technologiā, sed satis quoque dē Atticō. Tot rēs dē Atticō dictās iam lēgimus ut illum librum relinquere mālim.

Helena: Nōlī hoc dīcere, Marīa, sed venī audītum. Ipsa enim legam.

IN THE MIDDLE OF CIVIL STRIFE

CORNĒLIĪ NEPŌTIS ATTICUS, 8.4–6

Atticus preferred to help friends without taking political sides, and so he refrained from being
involved in the fund for the assassins of Caesar. He thought that Brutus could use his funds, as
far as these funds would suffice, but he, Atticus, would not enter into any arrangements about
this matter. Without Atticus, this agreement came to nothing. Mark Antony began to be more
powerful in Rome, and he forced Brutus and Cassius into exile. Although Atticus had not wanted
to make a compact with the anti-Caesarian party when it was prospering, he now sent financial
aid to Brutus, when he (Brutus) was cast down and exiled. Atticus neither excessively fawned on
Antony nor abandoned those who were desperate.

1   4. At ille, quī officia amīcīs praestanda sine factiōne existimāret
semperque ā tālibus sē cōnsiliīs remōvisset, respondit: sī quid Brūtus
dē suīs facultātibus ūtī voluisset, ūsūrum, quantum hae paterentur: sē
neque cum quōquam dē eā rē collocūtūrum neque coitūrum. Sīc ille
5   cōnsēnsiōnis globus hūius ūnīus dissēnsiōne disiectus est. 5. Neque
multō post superior esse coepit Antōnius, ita ut Brūtus et Cassius . . .
dēspērātīs rēbus in exsilium proficīscerentur. 6. Atticus, quī pecūniam
simul cum cēterīs cōnferre nōluerat flōrentī illī partī, abiectō Brūtō
Ītaliāque cēdentī HS centum mīlia mūnerī mīsit, eīdem in Ēpīrō absēns
10   trecenta iussit darī, neque eō magis potentī adūlātus est Antōniō neque
dēspērātōs relīquit.

VOCABULARY

1 officium, ī, n. – favor, duty

   praestō, āre, praestitī, praestitum – to perform, offer

   factiō, factiōnis, f. – political preference, party

   existimō, āre, āvī, ātum – to think, consider

2 removeō, ēre, remōvī, remōtum – to move back, remove

   sī quid – if something

3 sī voluisset (indirect discourse) = sī voluerit (direct discourse)

   facultās, facultātis, f. – ability, pl. resources, riches

   quantum – as much as

   pateō, ēre, patuī, — – be open, be available

4 neque = nec; neque . . . neque . . . = nec . . . nec . . .

   quōquam (abl. singular masculine) – anybody (in a negative sentence)

   colloquor, colloquī, collocūtus sum – to converse

   coeō, coīre, coīvī, coitum – to come together, meet

   sīc (adv.) – in such a way

5 cōnsēnsiō, cōnsēnsiōnis, f. – agreement

   globus, ī, m. – mass, association of men, band

   dissēnsiō, dissēnsiōnis, f. – disagreement

   disiciō, ere, disiēcī, disiectum – to break up and scatter

6 post = posteā

   superior, superiōris – more powerful

7 dēspērātus, a, um – desperate

   exsilium, ī, n. – exile

   proficīscor, proficīscī, profectus sum – to set out, depart

8 cēterus, a, um – other, remaining

   cōnferō, cōnferre, contulī, collātum – to bring together, collect

   flōreō, ēre, flōruī, — – to bloom, flourish

   abiciō, ere, abiēcī, abiectum – to cast down

9 cēdō, ere, cessī, cessum – to move, go away from

   mūnus, mūneris, n. – gift

10 trecenta (HS trecenta mīlia) – 300,000 sesterces

   eō (adv.) – for that reason

   adūlor, adūlārī, adūlātus sum – to fawn upon, flatter

READING NOTES

1 *At ille, quī officia amīcīs praestanda sine factiōne existimāret* Note the form *praestanda* that means "to be offered/performed." (See Chapter 15.) "But he (Atticus), because he thought that favors were to be performed for friends without political preference" The word *quī* in the relative clause with a causal sense means "because."

3 *usurum* "That he (i.e., Brutus) would use them (i.e., Atticus' resources).

   quantum hae paterentur The demonstrative *hae* refers to *facultātibus*. The clause means "in so far as these <resources> would allow (i.e., last)."

3–4 *se neque cum quōquam dē eā rē collocūtūrum neque coitūrum* Understand the subject of this indirect statement to be *sē* (i.e., Atticus).

5–6 *Neque multō post superior esse coepit Antōnius* Here *post* is an adverb (not a preposition) that means "afterwards." Antony was an important political figure, a triumvir, and a mortal enemy of Cicero.

7 *dēspērātīs rēbus* Referring to the affairs of Brutus and Cassius, the ablative absolute means "<their> situation being desperate."

7–8 *pecūniam simul cum cēterīs cōnferre . . . flōrentī illī partī* Here *simul cum ceterīs* means "together with the other <anti-Caesarians>." The dative phrase *flōrentī illī partī*, "to that party flourishing" is an indirect object with *pecūniam* and *cōnferre*. The party refers to the anti-Caesarian conspirators.

8–9 *abiectō Brūtō Ītaliāque cēdentī HS centum mīlia mūnerī mīsit* "<He> sent 100,000 sesterces as a gift to Brutus, who, having been cast down, was retreating from Italy." The dative of purpose *mūnerī* and the dative of the person affected *Brūtō* go together.

9 *eīdem in Ēpīrō* The dative singular demonstrative *eīdem* refers to Brutus. Epirus was a province in Greece.

QUESTIONS ABOUT THE TEXT

Answer in complete Latin sentences.

1. Deditne Atticus pecūniam factiōnī Brūtī atque Cassiī? Cūr?

2. Volēbatne Atticus cum factiōne Brūtī atque Cassiī colloquī et coīre?

3. Quid factum est dē factiōne Brūtī atque Cassiī?

4. Quid nōn multō posteā est factum?

5. Quid tunc dē Brūtō et dē Cassiō est factum?

6. Quid fēcit Atticus eō tempore quō Brūtus in exsilium proficīscēbātur?

7. Quid fēcit Atticus postquam Brūtus est in exsilium profectus?

8. Estne Atticus Antōniō adūlātus?

9. Cūr Atticus Brūtō et Cassiō auxilium dedit?

DĒ TECHNOLOGIĀ CONTINUED

Helena: Vidēsne, Marīa? Atticus fuit tam fortis ut potentēs nōn timēret et hominibus, quī iam nōn erant potentēs, auxilium daret. Bonum est dē tālī homine legere. Et tū volēbās discēdere lūsum!

Marīa: Atticus erat māgnus homō. At nunc, postquam dē eō lēgimus, possumus discēdere lūsum . . .

CHAPTER 15

Gerund and Gerundive; Passive Periphrastic; Dative of Agent

Nicolaus Klim asks his friends to lower him by rope into
the cave and thus begins his fantastic adventure.

MEMORĀBILE DICTŪ

Splendidē mendāx.

"Brilliantly deceitful." (Horace, *Odes*, 3.11.35)

Some first editions of Jonathan Swift's *Gulliver's Travels* (1726)—a fantastic account of a trip to foreign lands which satirizes human nature—feature this Latin phrase on their title pages. Swift's book has much in common with Thomas More's *Ūtopia*: Horace's phrase could just as easily apply to More's work, or to any other work of fiction describing impossible journeys and imaginary societies.

READING

Ludvig Holberg (1684–1754), called Ludovīcus Holbergius in Latin, was a Norwegian and Danish writer who is considered to be the father of Danish literature. In 1741, however, he published *Nicolāī Klimī iter subterrāneum* (*The Underground Journey of Nicolaus Klim*), in Latin, one of the masterpieces of world literature. In this novel, the title character Nicolaus—also referred to as Niels by speakers of Scandinavian languages and as Nicholas by English speakers—is an impoverished native of Bergen in Norway who has recently received a degree in philosophy from the University of Copenhagen. Nicolaus' amazing underground journey takes him to the land of Potu, whose population includes highly intelligent and civilized walking trees. His satire of European society owes much to an earlier Latin work, More's *Ūtopia* (indeed, the name "Potu" is the first four letters of "Utopia" spelled backwards) as well as to an English work, *Gulliver's Travels* by Jonathan Swift, published only fifteen years before Holberg's Latin novel. In 1864 the celebrated French science fiction writer, Jules Verne, depicted a similar subterranean itinerary in his *Journey to the Center of the Earth*.

LUDVIG HOLBERG

Having been at different times a professor of metaphysics, of rhetoric, and of history at the University of Copenhagen where his works on law were the standard texts for two hundred years, Holberg was a prolific writer. His thirty-one comedies earned him this permanent seat in front of the Royal Theatre in Copenhagen. Theobald Stein's sculpture of Holberg was placed here in 1898.

DĒ ITINERE SUBTERRĀNEŌ

1   Prope oppidum nostrum erat spēlunca quam ego, discendī studiōsus, iam diū investigāre volēbam. Quōdam diē ūnā cum amīcīs ad eam īvī et cum nēmō alius vellet in spēluncam dēscendere, mē ipsum fūne ligāvī amīcōsque rogāvī ut mē dēmitterent dum mē clāmantem audīrent.

5   Dēmittēbar dextrā tēlum tenēns, sed vix multum dēscenderam, cum rumpitur fūnis. Tunc ingentī celeritāte coepī in profundum ferrī. Ferēbar, circā mē spectābam et cum sīdera in caelō cernerem, fingēbam mē iam esse mortuum et ad sēdem beātōrum vehī. Eōdem tamen tempore rīdēbam, quia cōnspiciēbam mē tēlum manū tenēre et

10   parte fūnis esse adhūc ligātum. Tandem animadvertī mē ad planētam quendam vehī et mōtum iam nōn esse perpendiculārem, sed circulārem. Tunc comae mihi stetērunt; nam timēbam nē illīus planētae satelles fierem. At, rē perpēnsā, dēcrēvī esse corpus caeleste nihil ex dignitāte meā dētrahere posse. Per aliquot igitur diēs sīc ferēbar, cum quoddam

15   mōnstrum ad mē appropinquāvit; ad quod repellendum māgnō impetū tēlum in id impēgī. Mōnstrum, cūius strīdor aurēs percussit, est vulnerātum et mox mortuum. Tum animadvertī mōtum meum esse iterum perpendiculārem et mē in planētam circā quem vehēbar iam cadere. Cum cecidissem, statim vīdī animal ferōx ad mē appropinquāre

20   et, ut id fugerem, cōnātus sum in arborem proximam ascendere. At arbor vōcem tenuem, quālēs mulierēs habēre solent, ēdidit et rāmō suō colaphum vehementem mihi īnflīxit, ita ut in terram timōre percussus ceciderim. Cum oculōs aperuissem, vīdī multās arborēs ad mē undique appropinquantēs. Posteā intellēxī arborēs illās esse animālia animō

25   menteque praedita, quae quoque ambulāre poterant. Arbor enim quae mihi colaphum īnflīxit erat ipsa uxor virī potentissimī, quae cōgitāverat mē sibi malum īnflīgere velle. Arborum iussū causa erat mihi dīcenda ante iūdicem, sed cum arborēs intellēxissent mē nihil malī in mente habuisse, tamquam amīcae mē accēpērunt.

READING VOCABULARY

ad quod repellendum – in order to drive it (*quod*) away

aliquot (adj.) – some, a few

amīca, ae, f. – friend

*animadvertō, ere, animadvertī, animadversum – to notice

*appropinquō, āre, āvī, ātum (usually with *ad* or + dative) – to approach

ascendō, ere, ascendī, ascēnsum – to climb

beātus, a, um – blessed

caelestis, caeleste – caelestial

causa erat mihi dīcenda – I had to plead my case

celeritās, celeritātis, f. – speed

*cernō, ere, crēvī, crētum – to see, distinguish with the eyes

*circā + accusative – around

circulāris, circulāre – circular

*clāmō, āre, āvī, ātum – to scream

colaphus, ī, m. – slap, blow with a fist

coma, ae, f. – hair

cum + imperfect subjunctive – since

dētrahō, ere, dētrāxī, dētrāctum – to take off, take away, detract from

dignitās, dignitātis, f. – dignity

discendī – of learning

dum + subjunctive – until

eōdem tempore – at the same time

esse corpus caeleste – accusative and infinitive used as a subject

*fingō, ere, fīnxī, fictum – to imagine, form in the mind

fūnis, fūnis, m. – rope

*impingō, ere, impēgī, impāctum – to push, strike, drive into

*īnflīgō, ere, īnflīxī, īnflīctum – to strike on or against, inflict

investīgō, āre, āvī, ātum – to investigate, search into

*iterum (adv.) – again

ligō, āre, āvī, ātum – to tie

mihi erat eundum – I had to go

mōnstrum, ī, n. – monster

*oppidum, ī, n. – town

*percutiō, ere, percussī, percussum – to strike through

perpendiculāris, perpendiculāre – perpendicular

perpendō, ere, perpendī, perpēnsum – to ponder, weigh carefully

planēta, ae, m. – planet

*praeditus, a, um + ablative – endowed with, possessed of

profundus, a, um – deep, profound, bottomless

quālis, quāle – of which sort

quendam (masculine sing. acc.) – some, a certain

quōdam diē – on a certain day, one day

quoddam (neuter singular) – some, a certain

rāmus, ī, m. – branch

*repellō, ere, reppulī, repulsum – to push back, thrust back

*rīdeō, ēre, rīsī, rīsum – to laugh

*rumpō, ere rūpī, ruptum – to break, tear

satelles, satellitis, m. – satellite

*sēdēs, sēdis, f. – seat, abode

*sīc (adv.) – in such a way

*sīdus, sīderis, n. – constellation

strīdor, strīdōris, m. – harsh, shrill, or hissing sound

subterrāneus, a, um – underground

*tēlum, ī, n. – spear, javelin

tenuis, tenue – thin

*vehō, ere, vēxī, vectum – to drive, carry

*Words marked with an asterisk will need to be memorized later in the chapter.

COMPREHENSION QUESTIONS

1. How did it happen that Nicholas (the main hero) fell into a cave?

2. Where did Nicholas inadvertently find himself, and what did he think was happening to him?

3. What happened when Nicholas approached a planet?

4. How did Nicholas fare on the planet?

. . . cōnātus sum in arborem proximam ascendere. At arbor vōcem tenuem, quālēs mulierēs habēre solent, ēdidit et rāmō suō colaphum vehementem mihi īnflīxit . . .

LANGUAGE FACT I

FORMATION OF THE GERUND

In the chapter reading passage, the author says he was *discendī studiōsus,* "fond of learning."

The form *discendī* is the genitive of the gerund.

The gerund in Latin is a second declension neuter singular noun. **The gerund is a noun made from a verb** but does **not** have a nominative form with a nominative ending. **The present active infinitive of the verb functions instead as the nominative of the gerund.** The gerund is a partly verbal, partly noun form, **often called a verbal noun.**

Consider the infinitive *discere*. It means "to learn," but it can also have a noun-like meaning, for example "learning" or "the fact of learning." In this meaning, the infinitive may function as a subject.

> *Discere est ūtile.*
> "Learning is useful" or "To learn is useful/is a useful thing."

However, if we need to put *discere* in any case other than the nominative, a gerund is used.

How is the gerund formed? In order to form the genitive singular of the gerund, add the ending *–ndī* to the stem of verbs of the first, second, and third conjugation, and *–endī* to the stem of verbs of the fourth conjugation. The gerund of the *–iō* verbs of the third conjugation looks just like the gerund of the verbs of the fourth conjugation because, in forming the gerund of verbs of this type, the ending *–endī* is added to the *–i* that is left if we subtract the *–ō* of the first principal part.

Formation of the Gerund

First person singular, infinitive	Gerund (genitive singular)
parō, parāre	parandī
teneō, tenēre	tenendī
colō, colere	colendī
audiō, audīre	audiendī
capiō, capere	capiendī

Gerunds of Irregular Verbs

First person singular, infinitive	Gerund (genitive singular)
eō, īre	eundī
ferō, ferre	ferendī

BY THE WAY

The verbs *sum, possum, volō, nōlō, mālō,* and *fīō* do not have a gerund.

Once formed, the gerund declines like a neuter noun of the second declension. It does not have any plural.

Declension of the Gerund (parō)

Genitive	parandī
Dative	parandō
Accusative	(ad) parandum
Ablative	parandō

BY THE WAY

Just as the gerund does not have a nominative (the present active infinitive is considered its nominative), it does not have a vocative either. The accusative of the gerund is normally used only with a preposition, which is usually *ad*.

STUDY TIP

The gerund in Latin can often be translated with a gerund in English. Gerunds in English end in *–ing*.

▶ EXERCISE 1

Form the gerund of the following verbs.

1. animadvertō, ere
2. appropinquō, āre
3. cernō, ere
4. clāmō, āre
5. fingō, ere
6. impingō, ere
7. īnflīgō, ere
8. percutiō, ere
9. repellō, ere
10. rīdeō, ēre
11. vehō, ere

VOCABULARY TO LEARN

NOUNS

oppidum, ī, n. – town
sēdēs, sēdis, f. – seat, abode
sīdus, sīderis, n. – constellation
tēlum, ī, n. – spear, javelin

ADJECTIVES

praeditus, a, um + ablative – endowed with, possessed of

VERBS

animadvertō, ere, animadvertī, animadversum – to notice
appropinquō, āre, āvī, ātum (usually with *ad* + acc. or + dative) – to approach
cernō, ere, crēvī, crētum – to see, distinguish with the eyes
clāmō, āre, āvī, ātum – to shout, scream

fingō, ere, fīnxī, fictum – to imagine, form in the mind
impingō, ere, impēgī, impāctum – to push, strike, drive into
īnflīgō, ere, īnflīxī, īnflīctum – to strike on or against, inflict
percutiō, ere, percussī, percussum – to strike through
repellō, ere, reppulī, repulsum – to push back, thrust back
rīdeō, ēre, rīsī, rīsum – to laugh
rumpō, ere, rūpī, ruptum – to break, tear
vehō, ere, vēxī, vectum – to drive, carry

ADVERBS

iterum – again
sīc – in such a way

PREPOSITIONS

circā + accusative – around

▶ EXERCISE 2

In the sentences below, find the words derived from the Vocabulary to Learn in this chapter. Write the corresponding Latin word.

1. The astronauts were enchanted by their sidereal journey.

2. Have you filed a claim with the insurance company?

3. I would like to buy a more gas-efficient vehicle.

4. The dam was ruptured near the middle and tons of water poured through the gap into the surrounding fields.

5. What is the impact of the war on the common people?

6. This is nothing more than a work of fiction.

7. Do you realize that your actions will have serious repercussions?

8. Everybody should try to avoid a sedentary life.

9. If you had more judgment, you would be able to discern between these two facts.

10. This is truly ridiculous!

11. We need to buy an insect repellent for our trip to the tropics.

12. We want to reiterate our readiness to negotiate.

LANGUAGE FACT II

USE OF THE GERUND

The gerund has a specific use in each of its four cases.

- **Genitive**

    The gerund is used with nouns or adjectives that take the genitive.

    > *Eram discendī studiōsus.*
    > "I was fond of/eager for learning."

    > *Mihi erat spēs fugiendī.*
    > "I had a hope of fleeing."

- **Dative**

    The dative is sometimes used to indicate the purpose of the action.

    > *Quaerō locum aedificandō.*
    > "I am looking for a place for building (i.e., to build)."

- **Accusative**

    The accusative, usually accompanied by the preposition *ad,* indicates the purpose of the action. This is a very frequent use.

    > *Parātus sum ad pugnandum.*
    > "I am ready to fight/I am ready for fighting."

- **Ablative.**

> The ablative indicates means or instrument.
>
> > *Discimus legendō.*
> > "We learn through/by reading."

▶ EXERCISE 3

Translate into English.

1. Cōnsilium cēpī appropinquāndī ad oppidum.

2. Postquam diū circumīvī, tandem invēnī locum dēscendendō.

3. Multī amīcī vēnerant ad spectandum.

4. Spectandō intellēxī mē esse in caelō cum sīderibus.

5. Percutiendō occīdī animal, quod ad mē iterum appropinquāverat.

6. Dum per immēnsum caelum cadēbam, lībertās mihi fuit cōgitandī.

7. Arborēs undique convēnērunt ad loquendum.

Arborum iussū causa erat mihi dīcenda ante iūdicem, sed cum arborēs
intellēxissent mē nihil malī in mente habuisse, tamquam amīcae mē accēpērunt.

LANGUAGE FACT III

GERUNDIVE

In Latin, there is not only a gerund (which is a verbal noun) but also a gerundive (which is a verbal adjective). The gerundive has the same appearance as the gerund, but the gerundive has all the forms of the three genders and all the cases, both singular and plural. (Remember that the gerund exists in only four cases of the neuter singular: look again at the declension of the gerund *parō* above). **This is because the gerund is a verbal NOUN and the gerundive is a verbal ADJECTIVE.**

STUDY TIP

It is easy to remember that the gerund*ive* is a verbal adject*ive*.

The gerundive is formed by adding the endings *–ndus, a, um* to the stem of verbs of the first, second, and third conjugation, and *–endus* for the verbs of the fourth conjugation. The *–iō* verbs of the third conjugation have a gerundive that looks like the gerundive of the fourth conjugation verbs.

Gerundives	
First conjugation	parandus, paranda, parandum
Second conjugation	tenendus, tenenda, tenendum
Third conjugation	colendus, colenda, colendum
Fourth conjugation	audiendus, audienda, audiendum
Third conjugation –iō verbs	capiendus, capienda, capiendum

Note also that while the basic meaning of the gerund is ACTIVE, the basic meaning of the gerundive is PASSIVE. Compare the following phrases:

Laudandī studiōsus . . .   **gerund**
"Eager for praising . . ."

Puella laudanda . . .   **gerundive**
"A girl to be praised . . ."

Legendō discimus . . .   **gerund**
"We learn by reading . . ."

Liber legendus . . .   **gerundive**
"A book to be read . . ."

Amandō amīcōs parāmus . . .   **gerund**
"By loving we make friends . . ."

Puella amanda . . .   **gerundive**
"A girl to be loved . . ."

The gerund is normally used only if it has no direct object. In cases where the gerund could take a direct object, the gerund usually turns into what is called a gerundive construction. Consider the following examples.

> *Eram studiōsus **videndī**.*
> "I was fond of seeing."

If, however, a direct object is to be added to the gerund, observe the transformation.

> *Eram studiōsus **videndae spēluncae**.*
> "I was eager to see the cave (literally "the cave to be seen")."

The gerund changes into a gerundive, taking the **gender** and **number** of the direct object. But the former direct object now agrees with the **case** of the gerund. This construction made up of a noun with the gerundive agreeing with it as an adjective is normally used INSTEAD OF a gerund with an object.

Here are some more examples for the different cases.

Gerund	Gerundive Transformation When a Direct Object Is Added
*Quaerō locum **aedificandō**.* "I am looking for a place to build."	*Quaerō locum **aedificandae domuī**.* "I am looking for a place to build a house (literally "for a house to be built")."
*Habēbam tēlum **ad repellendum**.* "I had a spear for repelling."	*Habēbam tēlum **ad repellenda animālia**.* "I had a spear to repel animals (literally "for animals to be repelled")."
*Discimus **legendō**.* "We learn through/by reading."	*Discimus **legendīs librīs**.* We learn through/by reading books (literally "by books to be read").

▶ EXERCISE 4

Find a gerundive construction in the chapter reading passage. Translate the sentence.

▶ EXERCISE 5

Change the gerund in each sentence into a gerundive construction adding the noun in parentheses as a direct object. Translate the sentences. The Reading Vocabulary may be consulted.

Example: Studiōsus sum scrībendī. (liber)
Studiōsus sum librī scrībendī.
I am fond of writing a book.

1. Multī sunt studiōsī spectandī. (caelum)

2. Nicolāus erat studiōsus investīgandī. (spēlunca)

3. Cernendō ille intellēxit sē esse in caelō. (sīdera)

4. Ad repellendum Nicolāus ūsus est tēlō. (mōnstrum)

5. Cum Nicolāus arborem ascendere esset cōnātus, ad pūniendum arbor rāmō suō colaphum īnflīxit. (ille)

6. Audiendō Nicolāus intellēxit sē esse in terrā animālium animō menteque praeditōrum. (arborēs)

LANGUAGE FACT IV

PASSIVE PERIPHRASTIC AND DATIVE OF AGENT

The gerundive is used not only in substitution for the gerund when it has a direct object; it is often used on its own. Look at this example that you encountered in the chapter reading passage.

> *Arborum iussū causa erat mihi dīcenda ante iūdicem.*
> "By order of the trees <my> case had to be pleaded by me before a judge."

Erat . . . dīcenda is a passive periphrastic formed by the gerundive and the verb *sum*.

The gerundive itself is an adjective with a meaning denoting necessity:

> parandus, a, um – who has to be prepared
>
> tenendus, a, um – who has to be held
>
> colendus, a, um – who has to be worshipped
>
> audiendus, a, um – who has to be heard
>
> capiendus, a, um – who has to be taken

Very often, the gerundive is linked to the verb *sum* (the tense and the mood is used according to the needs of the sentence) in order to indicate necessity.

Librī sunt legendī.	**present passive periphrastic**
"Books must be read."	
Librī erunt legendī.	**future passive periphrastic**
"Books will have to be read."	

> *Librī erant legendī.*
> "Books had to be read."

past passive periphrastic

In order to indicate who is the agent of the action, the **dative of agent** is used (not the ablative of agent, which is usually used with the passive voice).

> *Librī mihi sunt legendī.*
> "Books have to be read by me (or its active equivalent)/I have to read books."

Sometimes, the passive periphrastic conjugation is used impersonally, i.e., no person is specified with association to the necessary action. In this case, of course, the gerundive is neuter—since the subject is impersonal.

> *Legendum est.*
> "There must be reading./People have to read./One has to read./One must read."

BY THE WAY

Note again that the gerund has an active, while the gerundive has a passive meaning.

> studiōsus legendī – fond of reading (*legendī* is active voice)
>
> liber legendus – a book to be read (*legendus* is passive voice)

Bergen is famous for its port and harborside warehouses in Norway. A member of the medieval Hanseatic League, Bergen was founded in 1070 and served as capital of Norway from 1110 until 1299. In Holberg's day, Norway was part of the Danish-Norwegian Kingdom. Holberg was a native of Bergen as was Nicholas Klim.

▶ EXERCISE 6

Change the following sentences so that the duty expressed by *dēbeō* becomes obligation expressed by the passive periphrastic. Translate the sentences. The Reading Vocabulary may be consulted.

Example: Patriam servāre dēbeō.
Patria est mihi servanda.
I have to save the fatherland.

1. Nicolāus in spēluncam dēscendere dēbēbat.

2. Amīcī fūnem bene tenēre dēbēbant.

3. Fūnis rumpī nōn dēbēbat.

4. Nicolāus mōnstrum repellere dēbēbat.

5. Deinde is illum planētam fingere dēbuit.

6. Cum in planētā iam erat, is dēbēbat ā mōnstrō fugere.

7. Nicolāus nōn dēbēbat in arborem ascendere.

8. Arborēs dē Nicolāō iūdicāre dēbēbant.

Like the hero of his science fiction novel, Ludvig Holberg attended the University of Copenhagen whose main administrative building is depicted. The University of Copenhagen is the oldest and largest research and education institution in Denmark dating back to 1479 and with more than 35,000 students and 7,000 employees.

▶ EXERCISE 7

Add the noun in parentheses to the sentences as an ablative of agent or dative of agent as required. Translate the sentences. The Reading Vocabulary may be consulted.

Examples: Fābula est nārranda. (ego)
Fābula mihi est nārranda.
I have to tell a story.

Fābula est nārrāta. (ego)
Fābula est ā mē nārrāta.
The story was told by me.

1. Colaphus vehemēns est Nicolāō sīc īnflīctus. (arbor)

2. Respondendum erat cūr in arborem ascendere voluisset. (homō)

3. Ille tunc est vocātus ut ad sēdem iūdicis īret. (potentiōres)

4. Diū erat cōgitandum ut intellegeret quid esset factum. (iūdex)

5. Tandem haec verba sunt dicta: "Ille homō nihil malī facere voluit." (iūdex)

6. In oppidō arborum cum arboribus erat vīvendum. (homō)

De itineribus in intermundiīs faciendīs. The nearby dwarf galaxy NGC 1569 is a hotbed of vigorous star birth activity which blows huge bubbles. The galaxy's "star productions" also manufacture brilliant blue star clusters. This galaxy experienced an onset of star birth some 25 million years ago which subsided just as the very earliest human ancestors appeared on earth.

TALKING ABOUT A READING

ABOUT SPACE TRAVEL AND UNADAPTED LATIN: MARK ANTONY IN EXILE WHILE ENEMIES PREPARE TO ATTACK HIS FAMILY

DĒ ITINERIBUS IN INTERMUNDIĪS FACIENDĪS

Helena: Mīror hominēs abhinc saecula aliquot (*some centuries ago*) dē itineribus in intermundiīs (*space*) faciendīs iam cōgitāvisse eaque dēscrīpsisse (*described*). Nam et Keplerius iter ad lūnam (*moon*) dēscrīpsit, et Holbergius iter in intermundiīs nārrāvit. Putābantne haec fierī posse vēra?

Christīna: Fortasse ita putābant. Et tandem hoc est factum. Nōnne (*an interrogative particle which expects a positive response*), Mārce, pater tuus est astrōnauta (*astronaut*)?

Mārcus: Ita vērō. Eō tempore (*at that time*) quō in Californiā habitābāmus, pater mūnus (*job*) astrōnautae habēbat. Nunc Vasintōniae in regīmine pūblicō (*government*) est.

Helena: Utrum mūnus eī magis placet? Putō melius esse in intermundiīs itinera facere.

Mārcus: At pater semper sē parābat, sed numquam in intermundiīs fuit.

Helena: Hoc quoque est māgnī momentī (*important*). Cum clādēs facta esset in nāve intermundiālī (*spaceship*) cui nōmen Apollō Tertius Decimus, astrōnautae quī erant in terrā māgnum auxilium astrōnautīs quī erant in ipsā nāve intermundiālī dedērunt, sine quō auxiliō illī tandem nōn essent servātī.

Christīna: Temporibus autem futūrīs omnēs hominēs poterunt itinera in intermundiīs facere, nōn sōlum astrōnautae.

Marīa intrat: Ad legendum "Atticum" conveniāmus, amīcī!

Helena: Optimē. Nam studiōsa sum sciendī quid aliud fēcerit ille māgnus vir.

MARK ANTONY IN EXILE WHILE ENEMIES PREPARE TO ATTACK HIS FAMILY

CORNĒLIĪ NEPŌTIS ATTICUS, 9.1–2

Nepos does not merely assert that Atticus behaved prudently during the conflict at Mutina, he is even prepared to describe Atticus' qualities as "divine." Mark Antony had been driven from Italy and there was no hope of his return. So Antony's political enemies, as well as others, who decided to side with his enemies in order to make the most of the situation, began to persecute Antony's family.

1. Secūtum est bellum gestum apud Mutinam. In quō sī tantum eum prūdentem dīcam, minus quam dēbeam, praedicem, cum ille potius dīvīnus fuerit, sī dīvīnātiō appellanda est perpetua nātūrālis bonitās, quae nūllīs cāsibus agitur neque minuitur. 2. Hostis Antōnius iūdicātus
5 Ītaliā cesserat; spēs restituendī nūlla erat. Nōn sōlum inimīcī, quī tum erant potentissimī et plūrimī, sed etiam, quī adversāriīs ēius sē dabant et in eō laedendō aliquam cōnsecūtūrōs spērābant commoditātem, Antōniī familiārēs īnsequēbantur: uxōrem Fulviam omnibus rēbus spoliāre cupiēbant, līberōs etiam exstinguere parābant.

VOCABULARY

1   Mutina, ae, f. – Mutina

     tantum – only (*adv.*)

2   prūdēns, prūdentis – prudent

     dēbeam – would have to (a potential sense of the subjunctive)

     praedicō, āre, āvī, ātum – to proclaim

3   dīvīnātiō, dīvīnātiōnis, f. – divination, foreseeing, predicting the future (here the meaning seems to be "divine quality")

     perpetuus, a, um – continuous, permanent

     nātūrālis, nātūrāle – natural

     bonitās, bonitātis, f. – moral excellence, goodness

4   cāsus, cāsūs, m. – accident, chance occurrence

     minuō, ere, minuī, minūtum – to diminish

5   cēdō, ere, cessī, cessum – to go away, withdraw

     inimīcus, ī, m. – enemy

6   adversārius, ī, m. – opponent

7   aliquam (accusative singular feminine) - some

     cōnsequor, cōnsequī, cōnsecūtus sum – to acquire, gain

     commoditās, commoditātis, f. – advantage, convenience

8   familiāris, familiāris, m. – family member

     īnsequor, īnsequī, īnsecūtus sum – to pursue (in a hostile manner)

9   spoliō, āre, āvī, ātum + ablative –to strip of

     līberī, ōrum, m. pl. – children

READING NOTES

1–2   *Secūtum est bellum gestum apud Mutinam. In quō sī tantum eum prūdentem dīcam* The relative pronoun, used at the beginning of a sentence to refer to something specific in the previous sentence or even to the general idea in the previous sentence, almost has the meaning of a demonstrative. Thus *In quō* means "In this war." Mutina is a town in Cisalpine Gaul, where Brutus was besieged by Mark Antony; Mutina, located in northern Italy, is today called Modena.

2   *dicam* This present subjunctive verb is in a future less vivid condition and translates "I should call." The conclusion to this condition is *praedicem*, "I would proclaim."

2–3   *cum ille potius dīvīnus fuerit* Here *cum* has a causal meaning.

5   *spēs restituendī nūlla erat* With *restituendī,* understand *Antōniī.* The meaning is "there was no hope of restoring Antony."

6   *quī adversāriīs ēius sē dabant* This relative clause refers to those who had not been opposed to Antony earlier, but who, after his exile, joined themselves with his consistent adversaries. The phrase *sē dabant* in this context means "went over to."

QUESTIONS ABOUT THE TEXT

Answer in complete Latin sentences.

1. Quōmodo sē gessit Atticus in bellō apud Mutinam gestum?

2. Propter quam causam Nepos Atticum dīvīnum vocat?

3. Quid factum erat Antōniō?

4. Quōmodo hominēs ergā (*toward*) Antōnium sē gerēbant?

5. Quid malī hominēs Antōniō facere volēbant?

6. Quī rēs malās contrā Antōnium facere volēbant?

DĒ ITINERIBUS IN INTERMUNDIĪS FACIENDĪS CONTINUED

Helena: Quam malī possunt esse hominēs! Sī vident alium esse oppressum, eōdem homine magis laedendō cōnantur commoditātēs cōnsequī!

Marīa: Dē hīs rēbus dolendum est. Sed hominēs nōn semper tālī modō sē gerunt. Caesar hostibus victīs aliquandō (*sometimes*) parcēbat.

REVIEW 5: CHAPTERS 13–15

VOCABULARY TO KNOW

NOUNS

benevolentia, ae, f. – good will

elementum, ī, n. – element

gravitās, gravitātis, f. – weight, gravity

mōtus, mōtūs, m. – motion, movement

multitūdō, multitūdinis, f. – crowd, throng

nātūra, ae, f. – nature

oppidum, ī, n. – town

pondus, ponderis, n. – weight

quiēs, quiētis, f. – rest, repose

sēdēs, sēdis, f. – seat, abode

sīdus, sīderis, n. – constellation

socius, ī, m. – associate, partner, ally

tēlum, ī, n. – spear, javelin

turris, turris, f. – tower

venia, ae, f. – pardon, indulgence, forgiveness

virga, ae, f. – twig, stick

voluntās, voluntātis, f. – will

PRONOUNS

īdem, eadem, idem – the same

ipse, ipsa, ipsum – self

iste, ista, istud – that (of yours)

ADJECTIVES

absēns, absentis – away, absent

cottīdiānus, a, um – daily, of every day

immēnsus, a, um – immeasurable, immense, endless

īnfīnītus, a, um – boundless, unlimited

medius, a, um – middle; medium, ī, n. – the middle, midst

praeditus, a, um + ablative – endowed with, possessed of

tālis, tāle – such a

VERBS

absum, abesse, āfuī, — – be away

affirmō, āre, āvī, ātum – to assert, maintain

animadvertō, ere, animadvertī, animadversum – to notice

appropinquō, āre, āvī, ātum – to approach

cernō, ere, crēvī, crētum – to see, distinguish with the eyes

circumeō, circumīre, circumīvī, circumitum – to go around

clāmō, āre, āvī, ātum – to shout, scream

contineō, ēre, continuī, contentum – to hold, keep together, contain

dēclārō, āre, āvī, ātum – to demonstrate, show

fingō, ere, fīnxī, fictum – to imagine, form in the mind

impingō, ere, impēgī, impāctum – to push, strike, drive into

īnflīgō, ere, īnflīxī, īnflīctum – to strike on or against, inflict

īrāscor, īrāscī, īrātus sum – to be angry

mīror, mīrārī, mīrātus sum – to marvel, be surprised at

negō, āre, āvi, ātum – to deny

numerō, āre, āvī, ātum – to number, count among

offendō, ere, offendī, offēnsum – to happen upon, offend

percutiō, ere, percussī, percussum – to strike through

redeō, redīre, redīvī, reditum – to go back, return

referō, referre, rettulī, relātum – to carry back, report

repellō, ere, reppulī, repulsum – to push back, thrust back

rīdeō, ēre, rīsī, rīsum – to laugh

rumpō, ere, rūpī, ruptum – to break, tear

vehō, ere, vexī, vectum – to drive, carry

versor, versārī, versātus sum – to be situated in, be occupied in

volvō, ere, volvī, volūtum – to turn round

ADVERBS

iterum – again

maximē – most

multō – by much

necessāriō – necessarily

perperam – wrongly, incorrectly

praesertim – especially

sīc – in such a way

undique – from all parts, from everywhere

CONJUNCTIONS

atque – as (when linked with a form of *īdem*)

ergō – therefore

ut – that (sense of result)

PREPOSITIONS

circā + accusative – around

▶ EXERCISE 1

Identify which construction (a purpose clause, a supine in *–m*, or a result clause) is needed to complete the sentence correctly using the phrase in parentheses. Add a conjunction as appropriate and use the correct mood and tense of the verb. In some instances either a purpose clause or a supine could be appropriate. Translate the sentences.

Example: Ad tē veniam _____ (tēcum loquī).
Purpose clause
Ad tē veniam ut tēcum loquar.
I will come to you in order to talk with you.

1. Necesse erat Colōnō in Hispāniam redīre _____. (plūrēs mīlitēs in novam terram dūcere)

2. Martīnus Alfōnsus Pinzon propter hoc cōnsilium tam est Colōnō irātus _____. (cum sociīs in aliam īnsulae partem discēdere)

3. Sociī autem Colōnī īnsulam circumīvērunt _____. (Martīnum Alfōnsum quaerere)

4. Colōnus ipse epistulam Martīnō Alfōnsō scrīpsit _____. (benevolentiam suam dēclārāre)

5. Tantā benevolentiā scrīpserat Colōnus _____. (Martīnus Alfōnsus epistulā lēctā veniam eī dare)

6. Incolae quī epistulam tulerant et quī dē litterārum vī nihil sciēbant tam sunt mīrātī Martīnum Alfōnsum animum hominis absentis intellegere _____. (putāre esse in epistulā vim dīvīnam)

▶ EXERCISE 2

Fill in the blanks with a gerund or gerundive construction to complete the sentences correctly. Translate the sentences. Specify whether you have used the gerund or gerundive construction.

Example: _____ semper plūra scīmus.
Legendō semper plūra scīmus. (legere)
By/Through reading we always know more. gerund

1. Copernicus erat studiōsus _____ cūr terra nōn esset in mediō mundī. (dēclārāre)

2. _____ hominibus plūra dē caelō, dē terrā, dē sōle discere licuit. (sīdera spectāre)

3. Ut sīdera bene spectārī possint, necessāriō bonus locus _____ invenīrī dēbet. (spectāre)

4. _____ Copernicus ostendit exemplum Aenēae quī iter facit et putat sē stāre, maria autem et lītora movērī. (mōtum terrae dēclārāre)

5. _____ necesse est perspicillum (*telescope*) habēre. (sīdera cernere)

6. _____ terram nōn movērī antīquī in multīs rēbus errāvērunt. (perperam putāre)

▶ EXERCISE 3

Change the clauses introduced by *cum* and *postquam* into ablatives absolutes. Translate the sentences.

Example: Postquam librum lēgī, cōgitāre coepī.
Librō lēctō, cōgitāre coepī.
After I read the book, I started thinking.

1. Postquam Nicolāus in spēluncam est dēmissus, amīcī vōcem audīre exspectābant.

2. Postquam fūnis (*fūnis, fūnis,* m., rope) est ruptus, Nicolāus coepit in caelō vehī.

3. Cum Nicolāus dēscendēbat, multa sīdera ibi volvēbantur.

4. Cum animal ferōx appropinquat, Nicolāus tēlum suum parat.

5. Postquam aliud animal ferōx vīdit, Nicolāus in arborem ascendere est cōnātus.

6. Postquam Nicolāus est ductus ad iūdicem, arborēs intellēxērunt sē contrā hostem nōn pugnāre.

▶ EXERCISE 4

Translate into Latin using the passive periphrastic.

1. Copernicus had to write about the movement of the earth around the sun.
   Copernicus, ī, m.

2. Nobody has to think that because of gravity the earth is in the center of the universe.

3. Nicholas had to leave the repose of his town and look for new lands.
   Nicolāus, ī, m.

4. Nicholas had to imagine with his mind why those (of yours) trees were approaching from everywhere.

5. Columbus had to write a letter to Martin Alfonso himself in order to seek forgiveness.
   Colōnus, ī, m.   Martīnus (ī) Alfōnsus, ī, m.

6. Those (of yours) people who carried the letter thought that it was not to be touched and carried it on a stick.

A characteristic Chinese blue and white teapot and cup surrounded by black tea leaves. Europe imported not only tea from China but also such dishware and the term "china" as well. Imports of "china" became so popular that the potters of Delft, Netherlands made their own blue and white version which remains in production and is highly popular.

▶ EXERCISE 5

Accounts of missionary works written in Latin take us to lands and continents far beyond the ancient Roman empire. Petrus Maffeius (1536–1603) was a Jesuit who wrote, in pure classical Latin, *Historiae Indicae*, a work on the Jesuit missions in America, India, and Japan. He lived in Lisbon, Portugal, from where many of the sea voyages started and where original sources about them were available. The "Histories" of Maffeius were received with enormous interest throughout Europe where many were curious to know more about remote exotic lands and their customs.

Translate the excerpt below which is adapted from Maffeius' description of China. It contains the first, or one of the first, references to what is now one of the world's most popular beverages.

Sinēnsēs ūvīs nōn ūtuntur ad vīnum parandum, sed ad condīmentum faciendum. Bibunt autem liquōrem calidum ex herbā expressum nōmine *Chiā*, quī tam salūtāris vidētur ut illī saepe sine morbīs vītam longissimam agant. Īdem liquor apud Iapōnēs quoque bibitur. Hunc liquōrem Sinēnsēs tam māgnī habent ut tantum in vāsīs fictilibus māgnae nōbilitātis eum bibant. Comedentēs cibum manibus tangere nōlunt, sed bracteātīs paxillīs eum in ōs ferunt. Bibunt autem haustū tam parvō ut saepe bibere dēbeant. Dum bibunt, māgnō cum honōre mutuō sibi propīnant.

bracteātus, a, um – covered with gold

calidus, a, um – warm

Chia – the Chinese name for tea, according to Maffeius

condīmentum, ī, n. – condiment

exprimō, ere, expressī, expressum – to express

fictilis, fictile – made of clay

haustus, haustūs, m. – sipping

Iapon, Iapōnis, m. – Japanese

liquor, liquōris, m. – liquid, beverage

māgnī habēre – to esteem a lot

morbus, ī, m . – illness, sickness

mūtuō (adv.) – mutually (**not** an adjective to be joined with *honōre*)

nōbilitās, nōbilitātis, f. – nobility, distinction

paxillus, ī, m. – small stake/stick

propīnō, āre, āvī, ātum – to make toast to one's health

salūtāris, salūtāre – wholesome

Sinēnsis, Sinēnsis, m. – Chinese

tantum – only (an adverb here)

ūva, ae, f. – grape

vās, vāsis, n.; pl. vāsa, ōrum – vessel, dish; vāsa fictilia – earthenware, china (in fact, the name "china" comes from the name of the region)

The accoutrements are laid out in preparation for a traditional tea service. The tea service remains an important feature of a Chinese wedding celebration. Note the Chinese love of poetry indicated by the two wall hangings that flank the painting.

▶ EXERCISE 6

Antōnius dē Leeuwenhoek (1632–1723) from Holland was one of the earliest investigators to make extensive use of the microscope and is considered the father of microbiology. Unlike the professional scientists of his day, Leeuwenhoek was a simple tradesman. He had no higher education, and knew no Latin—which was the standard language of scientific discourse in the seventeenth century. So Leeuwenhoek wrote letters in his native Dutch to the Royal Society of London to describe his discoveries. Robert Hooke, a fellow of the Royal Society and himself a pioneer in research about microbes, who had taught himself Dutch, translated Leeuwenhoek's more significant letters into Latin for the benefit of the scientific community.

Translate the adapted excerpt from one of Leeuwenhoek's Latinized letters discussing the bacteria he had observed with a microscope.

Dentēs meōs labōre cottidiānō sale fricāre soleō et deinde aquā colluere ita ut albī semper maneant. At animadvertī etiam dentibus bene frictīs inter eōs māteriem quandam albam manēre. Hūius māteriēī partem acū capere potuī, aquae pluviātilī vel salīvae meae miscēre et deinde in mīcroscopiō spectāre. Cernēbantur mīlle animālcula, quōrum alia celerrimē movēbantur, alia circā sē ipsa volvēbantur. Cēpī quoque māteriem ex dentibus duārum mulierum, quās sciō ōra bene colluere et cum eārum salīvā miscuī. Ibi eandem multitūdinem animālculōrum cernere potuī. Fēminārum animī hāc rē sunt percussī. Quid sī hominēs scīverint in suīs ōribus plūs esse animālculōrum quam cīvēs in rē pūblicā!

acus, acūs, f. – needle, pin
alius . . . alius . . . – one . . . another . . .
animālculum, ī, n. – small animal
colluō, ere, colluī, collūtum – to wash thoroughly, rinse
dēns, dentis, m. – tooth
fricō, āre, fricuī, frictum – to rub
māteriēs, māteriēī, f. – material
mīlle – thousand (in the singular an indeclinable adjective)
misceō, ēre, miscuī, mixtum + dative – to mix to/with
mīcroscopium, ī, n. – microscope
plūs + genitive – more of
pluviātilis, pluviātile – of rain
quandam (accusative singular feminine) – some
sāl, salis, m. – salt
salīva, ae, f. – saliva

Leeuwenhoek's legacy to the world of science and medicine is immeasurable. Using a microscope which he himself had constructed led to his discovery of bacteria. In his home in Delft, he assembled microscopes which enabled others to study microbes. Leeuwenhoek's letters which detailed his work are a paradigm for the scientific method.

CONSIDERING THE HEROES OF CLASSICAL MYTHOLOGY

THE BEGINNINGS OF ROME

AENEAS

Rome is said to have begun in the city of Troy, after its defeat by the Greeks. According to Vergil's epic *Aeneid*, Aeneas—one of the last surviving Trojans, son of the mortal shepherd Anchises and Venus, goddess of love—left the city in search of a new fatherland on the night that Troy fell (much like Columbus, many centuries later, set out in quest of new lands and a passage to the Indies). Carrying his father on his back, he led his little son Ascanius through the flames and destruction.

Aeneas' wife, the Trojan princess Creusa, was lost in the confusion. When he returned to search for her, she had already died, but her ghost encouraged him to pursue his quest. You have already encountered the travels of Aeneas in Level 1, where you learned that his guiding principle was devotion to gods, family, and fatherland. Vergil portrays Aeneas as a stable, determined hero who places the call of duty before all else, and is rarely torn by conflicting emotions.

After Aeneas' father Anchises died during their travels on the island of Sicily, Aeneas and his companions were not far from Italy, the western land they were seeking as their new fatherland. But a sudden storm shipwrecked them on the shores of North Africa, in the kingdom of the Carthaginian queen Dido. You will recall that Dido fell passionately in love with Aeneas,

Gian Lorenzo Bernini (1598–1680), the virtuoso architect and sculptor of the baroque age, presents the incarnation of Roman *pietās* in his statue of Aeneas bearing his elderly father while his young son Ascanius tugs on his leg. As they depart the defeated Troy, Anchises carries in his hands the household gods of Troy.

and that during a rainstorm they found refuge in the same cave, where they became lovers. Jupiter then sent Mercury to reproach Aeneas for his "enslavement to a woman," and to remind him of his duty to settle in Italy and become the progenitor of the Roman people. By telling Dido that he had made no commitment to her, and furtively leaving Carthage, Aeneas drove the desperately unhappy queen to suicide. Once he was on Italian soil, Aeneas needed to consult a prophetess of the god Apollo, the Sibyl, at Cumae about his future, and to descend to the underworld in order to confer with his deceased father Anchises.

You remember Anchises' encouragement to his son, and his prediction of Rome's future greatness. In relating these details, the first six books of Vergil's *Aeneid* recall Homer's *Odyssey*, an earlier Greek epic poem narrating Odysseus' journey home after the Trojan War. The final six books of the *Aeneid* evoke Homer's *Iliad*, because their focus is on war and battle scenes. Once he reaches Italy, Aeneas fights battles and forges alliances until he finally defeats and kills his enemy, the Italic king Turnus. Aeneas also wins the hand of Lavinia, whose father King Latinus had promised her to Turnus, and founds the town of Lavinia, while his son Ascanius founds the city of Alba Longa. Both settlements are said to be ancestors of Rome, which was not founded until several centuries later, in 753 BCE. Vergil ends his epic poem with the death of Turnus.

ROMULUS AND REMUS

The information that follows about the early history of Rome derives from the work of Vergil's contemporary Titus Livius, known as Livy. In the first chapter of Level 1 you read about Amulius' overthrowing of his brother Numitor, the king of Alba Longa, after which he forced

An Italian postage stamp bears the likeness of the Cumaean Sibyl whose advice and instructions are key to Aeneas establishing the future Rome. The image is taken from Michelangelo's masterpiece, the ceiling of the Sistine Chapel on which the sibyls of the ancient Greeks and Romans are juxtaposed with the prophets of the Hebrew scriptures.

While tradition holds that Siena was founded by Senius, son of Remus, who fled his "wicked" uncle, archaeological evidence found in 2003 verify a Roman "refounding" of Siena which had Etruscan origins. The city has long honored its Roman heritage as this column showcasing the she-wolf and twins attests.

Numitor's daughter Rhea Silvia to become a Vestal Virgin. There you read, too, how she was impregnated by the god Mars, gave birth to the twins, Romulus and Remus, and exposed them on the banks of the Tiber River. But they were suckled by a she-wolf, and found by a shepherd named Faustulus, who raised them.

According to Livy, when Romulus and Remus grew up, they formed a gang of bandits with other young men, and were eventually brought to justice at the royal court. Their grandfather Numitor recognized them, and they helped him engineer his return to the throne of Alba Longa. Later the twins decided to found a city on their own, the city which would become Rome. But an unfortunate quarrel arose between the two brothers as to who would rule over the new city and where it would be located. They decided to resolve the issue through bird omens. When Romulus' site received a more favorable omen, however, Remus challenged him, and Romulus killed him. Hence Romulus became the first king of Rome, but his hands were stained with the blood of fratricide.

HORATII AND CURIATII

The new city of Rome grew and gradually absorbed the settlements nearby. A long war between Rome and Alba Longa was settled in a memorable and curious way. To limit the amount of blood shed on both sides, two sets of triplets were sent from Rome and Alba Longa, named the Horatii and Curiatii respectively. Which of the two cities was to rule over the other was decided by a combat between these brothers alone. At the start of the battle, two Horatii were killed and three Curiatii wounded. One of the Horatii, therefore, had to fight against three of the Curiatii. He pretended to flee, but then turned and killed all three of them, one at a time. He, and Rome, were victorious. Yet upon his triumphant return to Rome, he saw that his sister was weeping: she had been betrothed to one of the Curiatii whom he had slain. Without a moment of reflection, Horatius killed her on the spot, claiming that no one should be allowed to mourn an enemy. He was taken to court, but acquitted owing to the testimony of his own father, who condemned his daughter's act of betrayal.

MUCIUS SCAEVOLA, CLOELIA, AND HORATIUS COCLES

Later Rome had to fight with the Etruscans. You have read about Mucius Scaevola, who did not shrink from thrusting his right hand into a blazing fire to show the Etruscan king what Roman courage was; you have also read about Cloelia, who rescued her fellow female hostages from Etruscan captivity, and was honored by an equestrian statue. Roman legend also records the heroism of a third individual, Horatius Cocles. He was on duty at a bridge when the Etruscans approached in large numbers. At the sight of the Etruscans, the Romans began to flee towards the city. Horatius, after warning them about the dangers of abandoning the bridge to the enemy, asked his fellow Romans to destroy the bridge while he and two other companions fought alone against the Etruscan troops. Upon hearing that the bridge had collapsed, he swam across the Tiber and joined the other Romans.

Legends such as these emphasize the Roman patriotic belief that their city was destined to grow and expand.

Since the third century BCE construction of a Temple to Aesculapius, the god of medicine, the Tiber Island has housed a medical facility, today called Fatebenefratelli Hospital. The bridge to the left was built by Lucius Fabricius in 62 BCE as its inscription evidences while the Pōns Cestius to the right was built sometime in the same century.

READ THE FOLLOWING PASSAGE

Adapted from the history of Titus Livius, this passage tells why and how the kings were expelled in 509 BCE and the Roman republic was then established. The story involves Sextus Tarquinius, the son of the last king, Tarquinius Superbus ("The Proud/Haughty").

Lucrētia erat uxor mīlitis Collātīnī, quī ūnā cum Sextō Tarquiniō, fīliō rēgis, erat in castrīs et bibēbat. Multō vīnō cōnsūmptō omnēs coepērunt uxōrēs suās laudāre. Tunc Collātīnus dīxit illīs licēre domum suam petere vīsum quālis esset Lucrētia. Cum ad aedēs Collātīnī pervēnissent, Lucrētiam invēnērunt cum ancillīs lānam facientem. Omnēs Lucrētiae virtūtem sunt mīrātī, et praesertim Sextus Tarquinius. Postrīdiē Sextus Tarquinius ad aedēs Collātīnī iterum sōlus vēnit.

Bene ab Lucrētiā acceptus, cēnāvit et in conclāve est ductus, in quō dormīre dēbēbat. At noctū gladiō strictō ad Lucrētiam violandam īvit. Prīmō cōnātus est precibus et minīs virtūtem ēius vincere, sed nōn potuit. Tandem dīxit sē eam occīsūrum et nūdum servum quoque occīsum prope ēius corpus positūrum ut omnēs putārent eam cum servō peccāvisse. Tunc Lucrētia est victa et Sextus Tarquinius habuit id quod voluit. Postquam discessit, Lucrētia mīsit hominēs ad marītum vocandum. Cum Collatīnus vēnisset, Lucrētia omnia eī narrāvit et deinde sē occīdit. Nam dīxit sē nōlle ūllam mulierem Rōmānam putāre veniam darī eīs quae peccāvissent. Collatīnus et amīcī sunt tam īrātī ut hominēs collēgerint et rēgem cum ēius familiā Rōmā expulerint.

ancilla, ae, f. – maid, woman servant

colligō, ere, collēgī, collectum – to gather

conclāve, conclāvis, n. – room

expellō, ere, expulī, expulsum – to expel

lāna, ae, f. – wool

minae, ārum, f. pl. – threats

nūdus, a, um – naked

peccāvissent – (who) had committed sin

postrīdiē (adv.) – the following day, the next day

prex, precis, f. – prayer

stringō, ere, strinxī, strictum – to pull off, draw from the sheath, unsheathe

violō, āre, āvī, ātum – to violate

CONNECTING WITH THE POST-ANCIENT WORLD

THE SCIENTIFIC REVOLUTION

We have already noted that Latin was the language employed in the medieval European university for lecturing, publishing, and other official communications, and remained so until the late seventeenth-century CE (see Review 2), when the national languages began to be used for lecturing and teaching. Even then Latin remained the language of scientific and mathematical writing by professors and researchers for quite a while longer. We owe our entire system of classifying plants to the great eighteenth century Swedish botanist Carl Linnaeus (1707 CE–1778 CE), whose beautifully illustrated botanical books written in Latin are a pleasure to view. Until

the early 1800s CE leading scientists regularly published their findings in simple, accurate, humanist Latin. Two figures stand out in this company: Leonard Euler (1707 CE–1783 CE), a pioneer in the sciences of ballistics

Botanical gardens throughout the world have honored Carl Linnaeus by erecting statues and monuments to him. A beloved professor at Sweden's prestigious University of Uppsala, Linnaeus trained a generation of botanists, including the naturalists on Captain James Cook's expeditions, who traveled the world collecting specimens.

Mathematician Euler's number 2.718281828 . . . found by taking the limit as x approaches infinity of this equation:$(1 + 1/x)^x$.

and hydrodynamics, and the German mathematician Carl Gauss (1777 CE–1855 CE). It has been claimed that the "logical" grammatical constructions and the verbal precision of classical Latin made it especially attractive to mathematicians; they were the most reluctant of all scholars to give up the use of Latin as the language best suited to express their ideas. Calculus students among you may find the affinity between the mathematicians who laid the groundwork in their field and the Latin language particularly inspirational, and take special pleasure in the "classical" beauty of equations for that reason.

The field of medicine owes a huge debt to the Latin language as well. In the Middle Ages and Renaissance, Latin was the language in which medicine—like all other sciences and learned disciplines—was taught, studied, and disseminated. Medical books written in Latin were printed with copious diagrams and annotated illustrations. Perhaps the most spectacular were the books on anatomy by the sixteenth-century scholar Vesalius, which were illustrated with magnificent but at times gruesome woodcuts of scenes set in the midst of classical architecture. Vesalius is said to have used bodies of executed criminals as the basis of his meticulous descriptions and drawing of muscles and bones. To this very day, because of Latin's dominant linguistic role in medicine, our medical terminology—like our botanical and zoological words—is for the most part Latin.

You have seen that Latin was also the language of astronomers, and that the conceptual revolution resulting from the assumption that the sun and not the earth was at the center of the solar system came from works published in Latin. Astronomers today still employ Latin terminology; until very recently they nearly always used the names of figures from Greek mythology for new stars or other celestial bodies, such as Callisto, the moon of Jupiter, which takes its name from a nymph in the entourage of Diana, or the galaxy Andromeda, named after the Ethiopian princess rescued by Perseus.

Andreas Vesalius (1514–1564) wrote, illustrated, and supervised the drawing, engraving, and printing of anatomy's first comprehensive illustrated textbook, *Dē hūmānī corporis fabricā* (1543). By setting his figures in classical landscapes and giving them a classical pose, people more readily accepted what was otherwise a revolutionary work whose accuracy was based on human dissection. Vesalius' original manuscript is one of the treasures of the University of Padua library.

EXPLORING THE DEVELOPMENT OF THE SCIENCES

AUTODIDACTS, POLYMATHS, AND THEIR THEORIES

Humankind has always sought to understand the natural world and unravel its mysteries. From the beginnings of recorded literature, scientists (people of knowledge, from the Latin verb *scio*, "I know") have asked of what is the world made, how are things related to each other, what is the relative size of the earth to celestial bodies, what is the arrangement of the cosmos (universe), and how does humankind fit into the cosmos. The Greek poet Hesiod (around 700 BCE) tried to explain earthquakes as resulting from the anger of the Greek god of the sea, Poseidon, who thrust his trident into the earth when angry. Thales (around 600 BCE) was the first Greek who tried to explain the world on the basis of the properties of natural substances. Thales believed that everything derived from water and that the properties of water explained why things happened. For example, Thales suggested that the earth was a flat disc floating on a cosmic sea. Consequently, ripples in the sea jolted the earth, resulting in earthquakes. Early Greek scientists believed that every event could be explained rationally on the basis of scientific causes.

Greek and Roman thinkers were often autodidacts (self-taught, from the Greek pronoun *autos*, "self, oneself," and the verb *didasko*, "I teach") and invariably polymaths (people who know many things, from the Greek adjective *polus*, "much" and verb *manthano*, "I learn, know") with broad interests and knowledge. Aristotle (384–322 BCE), the famous tutor of Alexander the Great, wrote books in Greek on almost every topic of human knowledge except mathematics. Aristotle studied and lectured on astronomy, biology, physics, literary criticism, ethics, politics, and rhetoric. In gratitude for his education, Alexander, himself a polymath, sent biological specimens from his campaigns back to his mentor in Greece. Archimedes (287–212 BCE) made important discoveries in many scientific fields, including theoretical mathematics (especially in

Greece's ten drachma coin minted in 1990 celebrates the famous philosopher Aristotle. With its membership in the European Union, Greece, like the other member nations, began to mint Euro coins in 2002. Such coins bear images of significance to the country circulating them.

Around 250 BCE, Archimedes calculated the ratio of a circle's circumference to its diameter. An earlier Egyptian document dated to 1650 BCE gives a value of 3.1605. Archimedes' value, however, was not only more accurate, it was the first theoretical, rather than measured, calculation of pi.

measuring the surface area and volume of curved objects like spirals and in calculating extremely large numbers such as the number of grains of sand required to fill up the universe), mechanics (properties of simple machines such as levers), optics (the apparent size of the sun), and hydrostatics (the nature of liquids). The story about Archimedes running naked through the streets and shouting *Eureka* (Greek for "I have discovered it!") after discovering the theory of specific density (the ratio between an object's mass and its volume) is probably just an urban myth.

Ancient Greek scientists would consider our own modern approach of narrow specializations and the strict divisions of scientific fields artificial and unhelpful. Strabo (63/62 BCE –24 CE), a Greek historian who wrote an extensive geography of the *oikoumene* (from the Greek verb *oikeō*, "I dwell, inhabit;" compare the Greek noun, *oikos* "home," and verb, *oikonomeō* "I manage a household"

from which the English word "economy" derives), says "wide learning, which alone makes it possible to undertake a work on geography, is possessed solely by the man who has investigated things both human and divine—knowledge of which, they say, constitutes philosophy. And so, too, the utility of geography—and its utility is manifold, not only as regards the activities of statesmen and commanders but also as regards knowledge both of the heavens and of things on land and sea, animals, plants, fruits, and everything else to be seen in various regions—the utility of geography, I say, presup-

The Roman architect Vitruvius relates the legend of Archimedes whom King Hieron II of Syracuse had asked to ascertain without inflicting damage whether his crown was actually made from pure gold. As Archimedes watched the water spill from the tub as he stepped in, he realized how he could answer the king's query.

poses in the geographer the same philosopher, the man who busies himself with the investigation of the art of life, that is, of happiness" (Strabo, *Geography* 1.1.1). In other words, all knowledge is interconnected, and a true understanding of one discipline (geography) cannot be attained in ignorance of others (philosophy or zoology).

Although Greek science continued to advance steadily from Thales to Aristotle, a real scientific boom occurred after Alexander the Great.

Alexander the Great astride Bucephalus leads his troops with their characteristic Greek helmets against an eastern army identified by their dress and their "orientalized" eyes. The profile of the youthful Alexander is an image replicated on ancient coins. Alexander was a lifelong student who learned from the lands and peoples he conquered.

Alexander himself helped to advance Greek science through gathering all sorts of information on his campaigns and by establishing contacts with different cultures of diverse approaches to science. But the golden age of Greek science occurred a little later at Alexandria in Egypt, where the son of one of Alexander's generals founded the famous *Mūsēum*, a center of learning. The *Mūsēum* served as a central meeting place for people of knowledge to discuss and exchange their ideas. At the *Mūsēum*, Archimedes advanced the science of hydrostatics; Aristarchus (around 280 BCE) proposed a theory of heliocentrism; Herophilus (330–260 BCE) pioneered the study of human anatomy by performing human dissection; and Hipparchus (190–120 BCE) discovered the precession of the equinoxes (as if at the edges of a very slowly spinning toy top, the stars appear to shift over the centuries as they rise in the night sky at particular times of the year). The Library attached to the school quickly housed the largest collection of manuscripts, including classic works of Greek literature, science, bibliographic surveys, commentaries (especially on the *Iliad* and *Odyssey*), and Greek translations of important works in other languages including the Jewish *Septuagint* (*Old Testament*). Customs officials at the port of Alexandria were under strict orders to confiscate any manuscripts brought into the city by travelers. The originals were usually deposited in the Library, and copies were then delivered only to the luckiest book owners.

Eratosthenes served as the director of the *Mūsēum* for forty years (around 245–205 BCE). A polymath who lived in a time of intellectual giants (e.g., Archimedes), he earned the rather unkind nicknames "Beta" ("second best," from the second letter of the Greek alphabet, *beta*), and "Pentathlos" (an all around athlete, good enough to win only at three out of five set competitions at the Olympics: from the Greek adjective *pente*, "five" and noun *athlos*, "contest"); that is to say, Eratosthenes was a "jack-of-all-trades." Born in Cyrene (modern-day Libya), Eratosthenes studied philosophy and mathematics in Athens, a city whose reputation as an academic center remained strong throughout antiquity. Eratosthenes came to Alexandria to direct the *Mūsēum* and to tutor the king's son, Ptolemy Philopater (born around 245 BCE). As head librarian of the *Mūsēum*, Eratosthenes, who was deeply interested in all aspects of human knowledge, wrote on chronology, mythology, grammar, literary criticism, astronomy, harmonics, and geography. He also wrote poetry.

Eratosthenes is most famous for estimating the circumference of the earth. To estimate the earth's circumference, Eratosthenes used astral data together with a simple and elegant ratio, based on the geometry of the sphere. He made three simple assumptions: that the earth was a perfect sphere; that the sun was sufficiently far enough away from the earth that its rays were parallel when striking the earth; and that two Egyptian cities from which he made his calculations, Syene (Aswan) and Alexandria, lay on the same meridian (Alexandria is actually 3° west of Syene). Eratosthenes compared readings from these two cities on the same day, the summer solstice, at high noon. At Syene no shadows were cast at midday because the sun was precisely at its zenith, but a slight shadow was cast at Alexandria, because of the curvature of the earth and the fact that Alexandria is north of Syene. He then measured the angle of the shadow cast at Alexandria as one-fiftieth of a circle, and he knew that the distance between Syene and Alexandria was approximately 5,000 *stadia* (a *stadion* is the Greek unit of distance, equal to 600 Greek feet, but varies from place

In the lower right quadrant of this photograph of the stadium at Olympia one can see the white starting blocks that run across the field. The stone wall by the edge of the grassy knoll is the entrance through which the athletes entered the running field. Spectators sat on the banks along the running area.

to place: the *stadion* at Olympia was 632.5 feet, the length of the stadium there; the Athenian *stadion* measured 606.9 feet, the Egyptian *stadion* was 516.7 feet). Eratosthenes multiplied 5,000 *stadia* (the length of the arc between Syene and Alexandria) by 50 (the number of units in his circle) to find the earth's circumference: 250,000 *stadia* (24,412.5 miles; we assume that Eratosthenes employed the Egyptian *stadion*). This value is remarkably close to our own estimate of 24,901 miles. Eratosthenes later adjusted his estimate to 252,000 (24,608 miles), a number divisible by 60, and even closer to modern calculations. Unfortunately, many of his successors rejected the estimate because Eratosthenes was not recognized as an important mathematician. Instead, the "orthodox" estimate of the earth's circumference was calculated by the mathematician Poseidonius (around 100 BCE) as 180,000 *stadia* (between 17,615 and 21,564 miles, depending on which *stadion* Poseidonius used). Poseidonius' value, considerably smaller than that of Eratosthenes, was accepted by the Greek astronomer and mathematician Ptolemy (second century CE), whose geocentric arrangement of the cosmos was accepted without question until the ninth century when a Muslim astronomer, Ibn al-Haytham, noticed numerous errors and scathingly attacked Ptolemy's astronomical system as "utterly impossible." Columbus, incidentally, bowing to the authority of Ptolemy, also accepted the smaller value and, hence, assumed that he made landfall in China, when he actually fell short by some 7,000 miles, landing instead somewhere in the Bahamas.

Most science in antiquity was written in Greek. A shift occured in the Middle Ages when Latin became the common language of communication, the *lingua franca* of philosophers and the universities. Although Copernicus wrote in Latin, his approach to science had more similarities than differences from his Greco-Roman predecessors. Like Greek and Roman scientists before, Nicolaus Copernicus (1473–1543) was a man of great genius and deep intellectual curiosity. At the University of Cracow, Poland, while training for the priesthood, Copernicus also took classes

The Jagiellonian University in Cracow was established in 1364. The *Collegium Māius* is a fine example of fifteenth-century Gothic architecture: its inner courtyard is surrounded by arcades and features a staircase leading from the ground floor with its lecture rooms to the first floor halls for official ceremonies.

in mathematics, astronomy, and astrology, which at the time was considered a rigorous branch of mathematical astronomy. Before earning a degree from the University of Cracow, he moved to Bologna in northern Italy to study Canon Law of the Roman Catholic Church. At Bologna, Copernicus continued to study mathematics and astronomy, and there he learned Greek, a language which was not commonly taught at universities in the fifteenth century. Knowing Greek was important to a budding astronomer since the works of Ptolemy and other great astronomers from antiquity were written in Greek and had not been translated into Latin. Copernicus was able to analyze directly the ancient Greek astronomical observations which were at best poorly understood by his colleagues. Like Eratosthenes at the *Mūsēum*, Copernicus was lucky enough to have access to resources that helped him develop his own theories: knowledge of Greek and friendship with Bologna astronomy professor Domenico Maria Novara, one of the few who dared to question the authority of Ptolemy. Furthermore, Copernicus consulted Arabic scholars including the Muslim mathematician and astronomer al-Battani (around 858–929) whose *Dē mōtū stellārum* (*Kitab al-Zij*) was translated into Latin in 1116, and Greek scientific treatises which were translated into Arabic and then into Latin, before the original Greek texts were lost. Copernicus also studied medicine at Padua where the medical curriculum included an emphasis on astrology in medical diagnosis and treatment; this branch of astrology, called iatro-astrology (from the Greek noun

iatreia, "healing"), dated back to antiquity when it was believed that the stars and other heavenly bodies could have a real effect on the lives of people on earth. Copernicus finally earned a doctorate in Canon Law from the University of Ferrara, also in northern Italy, in 1503.

Through his official career as a Church administrator, Copernicus helped to stabilize eastern European currency, offered political advice in wartime, and was a consulting physician for Prussian nobles (southeast Baltic coast). Nonetheless, fascinated by astronomy, he made astronomical observations when he could: as a Church official, his responsibilities were pressing, and the frequent fog at Frombork in northern Poland, where Copernicus lived his adult life and where he had a roofless tower to observe the heavens, was not conducive to astronomical observation.

Founded in 1222, the University of Padua boasted one of the finest medical schools on the continent. Copernicus studied medicine at Padua in 1501. One can visit the anatomy theater where he attended classes as did Andreas Vesalius. One can also see the podium from which lectures were given.

Copernicus is most famous for the theory of heliocentrism, first suggested by Aristarchus, but rejected in antiquity because of the lack of visible stellar parallax (the apparent displacement of stationary objects resulting when the observer moves). Copernicus described his system first in *Dē hypothesibus mōtuum caelestium ā sē cōnstitūtīs commentāriolus* (*Commentāriolus*) and later published a more developed explanation in *Dē revolūtiōnibus orbium caelestium*.

Copernicus analyzed astronomical observations at Cracow and Frombork (which he assumed was on the same meridian with Cracow, but is actually ¼° west) using the same type of data, records of lunar and solar eclipses, that Eratosthenes and other Greeks had used to calculate the latitudes of different places. Copernicus suggested that the earth was not the center of the universe, but rather that the earth (and the other planets) revolved around the sun. He argued that the earth only seemed not to move, and that the apparent daily rotation of the heavens, in fact, results from the real daily rotation of the earth on its axis (diurnal axial rotation had first been proposed by the Greek astronomer, Heracleides, born 387 BCE). Furthermore, the apparent journey of the sun through the constellation of the zodiac results from the earth's real annual revolution around the sun, and the apparent retrograde motion of the planets (occurring when planets, usually moving from west to east in the night sky, seem to move westward for a short time and then to resume their eastward trajectory) results from the fact that the planets, including the earth, revolve around the sun at different rates. Although, for example, both Mars and Earth revolve around the sun in the same direction, Earth, which is closer to the sun, takes less time to make a complete circuit. When Earth is "behind" Mars, Mars seems to travel eastward; but when Earth "overtakes" Mars, Mars seems to move "backwards" or westward.

This image of Copernicus is from a statue at the castle of Olsztyn, Poland. While living in the castle, Copernicus made observations of the movement of the planets and included these findings in his life's work *Dē revolūtiōnibus orbium caelestium*. He wrote the first chapter of that work while at the castle.

Copernicus countered the ancient arguments against Aristarchus' theory of heliocentrism by suggesting that the universe was so large and the stars were so far away that any stellar parallax would be undetectable to the naked eye. Copernicus was also able to reconcile heliocentrism with Aristotle's definition of natural motion and doctrine of natural place: celestial bodies move in perpetual circles; terrestrial bodies move in straight lines, stopping when they reach their natural places, "sinking of their own weight." Any other motion, according to Aristotle, is "violent." Copernicus recategorized the earth as a celestial body (hence it could move circularly), but conceded that displaced parts of the earth (rocks, tree branches, etc.) are subjected to "violent motion." Centuries earlier, Ptolemy had objected to the idea of the earth's axial rotation. He argued that terrestrial axial rotation, a violent motion, would result in the earth bursting apart and dropping out of the sky, in the shaking up of loose objects on the ground, and in clouds constantly floating away westward. Copernicus answered, "Ptolemy has no cause to fear that the earth and everything earthly will be disrupted by a rotation" because such an earth, constantly threatened by violent motion, would simply not last long and the system "brought into existence by nature is well ordered and well preserved in its best state" (Copernicus, *Dē revolūtiōnibus* 1.8). Furthermore, Copernicus argued, the air and water on the earth "conform to the same nature (i.e., same rules of physics) as the earth" because of their proximity to the earth, and so clouds and lakes rotate eternally with the earth. Copernicus accepted the ancient theory that the earth was tilted on its axis to explain the varying length of days and the precession of the equinoxes.

Heliocentrism seemed to contradict the Bible, and Copernicus proceeded cautiously. He published *Commentāriolus* anonymously and agreed to publish *Dē revolūtiōnibus* only after his friend Georg Joachim Rheticus, a mathematician, astronomer, and Lutheran minister, published *Nārrātiō prīma* (1540), a sort of book review of *Dē revolūtiōnibus*. *Nārrātiō prīma* did not attract a great deal of controversy, so Copernicus wrote a dedication to the reigning pope, Paul III (*regnat* 1534–1549), and added a preface in which he declared *mathēmata mathēmaticīs scrībuntur* (Greek astronomers called themselves *mathēmaticī*), which is to say that Copernicus believed in a separation of church and science. The publisher, Andrew Osiander (1498–1552), however, disagreed with the book's potentially controversial content. Osiander anonymously appended another preface asserting that *Dē revolūtiōnibus* was not a true account of the universe but more of a thought experiment. Rheticus and others protested Osiander's contradictory disclaimer, and Rheticus even crossed out the preface in his own copy.

Nonetheless, probably because of Osiander's preface, the book did not attract as much controversy as it could have. Although most clergy and even some astronomers (including the brilliant Tycho Brahe: 1546–1601) rejected Copernicus' system, the Polish astronomer was highly admired, and his theory was selectively accepted. Nor did the Church render an official stand on Copernicus' system, much less declare it a heresy. Eventually, Copernicus' theory was accepted as sound. In fact, Copernicus' estimates for the distances of the planets from the sun are remarkably close to modern values. Galileo Galilei (1564–1642) promoted Copernicus' theory, leading to official Church condemnation of Copernicus' *Dē revolūtiōnibus* and charges of heresy against Galileo. In the Protestant Netherlands, Johannes Kepler (1571–1630), who also improved the design for the newly developed refracting telescope, advanced Copernicus' work to develop an even more accurate description of the solar system.

Kepler who had moved frequently in the course of his career, sometimes because his religious beliefs conflicted with those of his patrons, spent the last years of his life in Regensburg, Germany, the cultural capital of southern Germany. Regensburg paid tribute to this famous resident with the Kepler Memorial.

Although modern professional scientists tend to specialize in very narrow fields, they continue to explore broad interests. For example, Albert Einstein (1879–1955), best known for the theories of general and special relativity, was also an outspoken critic of Nazi Germany, wrote philosophical books about Zionism and pacifism, was interested in cosmology (how the universe came into existence, a guiding question of early Greek astronomy), and played the violin.

Richard Feynman (1911–1988), a quantum physicist who contributed to the atomic bomb theory and worked on the "Manhattan Project" (the joint venture between the United States, United Kingdom, and Canada to develop nuclear weapons during World War II), was also an expert safe cracker, a noted practical joker, and he deciphered Mayan hieroglyphics. Isaac Asimov (1920–1992), best known as a writer of science fiction, studied and taught biochemistry but wrote widely on everything from commentaries on the Bible and Shakespeare to treatises on theoretical physics. Astronomer and cosmologist Carl Sagan (1934–1996) was a political activist, successful popularizer of theoretical astronomy (*Cosmos* was filmed for PBS), and a novelist. The paleontologist and evolutionary biologist Stephen Jay Gould (1941–2002) also wrote broadly on the history of science as it connects to all branches of human knowledge, and he even played himself on *The Simpsons*.

Like his fellow modern scientists and like his Greek and Renaissance predecessors, Stephen Hawking (1942–) pursues broad scientific interests in mathematics, thermodynamics, relativity, quantum mechanics, astronomy, and cosmology. His works of popular science are lucid and full of humor (he claims to have sold more books on physics than Madonna has on sex). Not taking his own genius too seriously, he has even played himself on *Red Dwarf*, *Star Trek: the Next Generation*, and several episodes of the *Simpsons* and *Futurama*.

In the late twentieth and early twenty-first centuries, we come full circle, back to the foundations of Greek scientific inquiry. Hawking is asking the very same questions that the earliest Greek scientists had asked: what is the world (the universe) made of; what are its parts; how do these parts fit and work together; how did the universe come to be; and what factors will determine the universe's passing away. Although the past millennia have seen countless changes in scientific approaches, philosophy, tools, and even the sheer scope of human imagination, the human quest for knowledge remains eternal and perpetual, like Aristotelian celestial motion. Just as Thales had proposed a unified theory of physics based on the properties of water, Hawking seeks to develop a unified theory of physics that will describe everything that occurs in the universe. Together with other scientists, Hawking is working to combine Einstein's general theory of relativity with the uncertainty principle, a random element of quantum theory espoused by Niels Bohr (1885–1962) and with Feynman's notion that the universe has multiple histories, each with its own probability rating. For example, Einstein's general theory of relativity suggests that the universe has a beginning and that the universe began with a "Big Bang." But Einstein's theory fails to account for all events especially those further back in time, closer to the moment of the "Big Bang," perhaps because he had not taken into account the uncertainty principle. Einstein famously declared that "God does not play dice." Hawking, however, suggests that "God is quite

This lifelike statue of Einstein depicts him as one might find him in a park when he lived in Princeton, New Jersey. The sculpture in the Science Park of Granada, Spain invites one to sit and join the genius on the bench. The open air museum offers a variety of hands-on science-related activities.

a gambler," and he compares the universe to a casino with dice being rolled on every occasion. In our large and expanding universe, the number of rolls of the dice is very high and the results average out to something mathematically predictable. But when the universe is small (since the universe is expanding, it must have once been tiny), the number of rolls of the dice is few, the results are less predictable, and the uncertainty principle becomes important.

Like Eratosthenes who not only estimated the earth's circumference but also mapped the *oik-oumene*, Hawking seeks to explain the relationship between events (if not places) in the universe. Like Copernicus who remapped the solar system in developing a unified theory of astronomy that explained all the events that we can see in the night sky, Hawking attempts to understand various deep space phenomena, such as the conversion of matter into energy in black holes (regions in space-time with gravity so strong nothing can escape) and the radiation of energy from black holes, the existence of wormholes (thin tubes of space-time connecting distant regions of space) and their ramifications for travel in space and time. Although time has uncovered flaws in every scientific idea from the Greeks onward, and although Hawking admits that his own questions may be unanswerable (at least during this century), he speaks for all scientists from Thales to himself when he says, "We must try to understand the beginning of the universe on the basis of science. It may be a task beyond our powers, but we should at least make the attempt" (Stephen Hawking, *The Universe in a Nutshell* [2001] 79).

GEORGIA IRBY-MASSIE
Assistant Professor of Classics
The College of William and Mary
Williamsburg, Virginia

MĪRĀBILE AUDĪTŪ

EARLY MODERN AND MEDIEVAL LATIN PHRASES AND TERMS RELEVANT TO THE TWENTY-FIRST CENTURY

PHRASES AND TERMS FROM THE EARLY MODERN PERIOD

- Ab incūnābulīs. "From the cradle," i.e., "from childhood, from the beginning." The word *incūnābula* is often used to describe the first printed books around 1500. These books were in the "infancy" of the art of printing.

- Ad ūsum Delphīnī. "For the use of the Dauphin." The French king Louis XIV (1638 CE–1715 CE) expurgated the editions of classical works in order to render them appropriate for reading by his heir, the Dauphin. The phrase is used generally for a work with indecent or improper passages deleted.

- Cōgitō, ergō sum. "I think; therefore I am/exist." A rationalistic argument by the French philosopher René Descartes (1596 CE–1650 CE).

- Ēditiō prīnceps. "First edition." First printed edition of a certain work.

- Mūtātīs mūtandīs. "After having changed what needs to be changed," i.e., with the necessary changes.

- Prōsit! "To your good health!" Literally, "Let it be useful." A toast in German (and thence used in other languages) that came from Latin.

A French stamp honors the "Father of Modern Philosophy," René Descartes.

- Tabula rāsa. "Scraped table," i.e., blank slate. The origin of this phrase is in the wax tablets that the Romans used for writing, on which anything written could be erased by the back of the stylus. The English philosopher John Locke (1632 CE–1704 CE) used this phrase to describe the human state of mind at birth.

PHRASES AND TERMS FROM THE UNIVERSITIES IN THE MIDDLE AGES

- Ēmeritus/ēmerita. "Retired." Normally used for retired academic professors.

- Doctor honōris causā. "Doctor for the sake of honor." An honorary university title given for other than academic merits.

- Summā cum laude/māgnā cum laude/cum laude. "With highest praise/with great praise/with praise." These designations are based upon a student's cumulative academic grades at the time of graduation.

1. THE PEOPLE OVER FORTUNE

Atticus is friend to the people, not to fortune.

CORNĒLIĪ NEPŌTIS ATTICUS, 9.3–6

In the previous section you read that Antony was sent into exile, and that his wife Fulvia and his children were threatened by persecution. Marcus Antonius, or Mark Antony, a fascinating and contradictory political figure (since tradition has presented him either as a villain or as a powerful and enchanting leader destroyed by his own weakness), was losing ground at that time. Everybody seemed to be against him, backed by the authority of the senate and fueled by Cicero's eloquence, who delivered his famous orations called *The Philippics*. These were named after the speeches of the Greek orator Demosthenes and were delivered against the Macedonian king Philip. The word "Philippic" remained proverbial for any fiery accusation. Atticus, literary adviser, publisher and banker, as well as an intimate friend of Cicero, found himself in a delicate situation with regard to his relationship with Antony.

1   9. 3. Atticus cum Cicerōnis intimā familiāritāte ūterētur, amīcissimus

        esset Brūtō, nōn modo nihil hīs indulsit ad Antōnium violandum, sed

        ē contrāriō familiārēs ēius ex urbe profugientēs, quantum potuit, tēxit,

        quibus rēbus indiguērunt, adiūvit. 4. . . . Ipsī Fulviae, cum lītibus

5   distinērētur māgnīsque terrōribus vexārētur, tantā dīligentiā officium

        suum praestitit, ut nūllum illa stiterit vadimōnium sine Atticō; spōnsor

        omnium rērum fuerit.

VOCABULARY

1 cum + subjunctive – although
   *intimus, a, um – most intimate, closest
   *familiāritās, familiāritātis, f. – familiarity
   ūtor + ablative – to avail oneself of, use, enjoy
   *amīcus, a, um – friendly

2 modo (adv.) – only
   indulgeō, ēre, indulsī, indultum + dative – to be
      indulgent, grant as a favor to
   violō, āre, āvī, ātum – to violate, harm

3 ē contrāriō – on the contrary
   *familiāris, familiāris, m./f. – family member
   profugiō, ere, profūgī, —— – to run away, flee
   *tegō, ere, tēxī, tēctum – to cover, protect

4 indigeō, ēre, indiguī, —— + ablative – to lack, need
   *adiuvō, āre, adiūvī, adiūtum – to help

5 distineō, ēre, distinuī, distentum – to hold apart,
      distract
   terror, terrōris, m. – terror
   vexō, āre, āvī, ātum – to trouble, harass
   *dīligentia, ae, f. – carefulness, attentiveness
   officium, ī, n. – favor, duty

6 *praestō, āre, praestitī, praestitum – to make
      available, supply
   vadimōnium, ī, n. – guarantee that the defendant
      will appear before the judge: vadimōnium
      sistere (sistō, sistere, stitī) – to show up in court
      to answer bail
   spōnsor, spōnsōris, m. – guarantor, one who
      formally guarantees the good faith of another

READING NOTES

1–2 *Atticus cum . . . nōn modo nihil . . . sed* Note that
      cum in this sentence has a meaning similar to
      "although," and the thought contrasting with
      cum is marked by *nōn modo nihil . . . sed . . . .*

3 *familiārēs ēius* "His family members" refers to Ant-
      ony's relatives.

6 *illa* "she" refers to Fulvia.

5. Quīn etiam, cum illa fundum secundā fortūnā ēmisset in diem neque post calamitātem versūram facere potuisset, ille sē interposuit pecūniamque sine faenore sineque ūllā stipulātiōne crēdidit, maximum existimāns quaestum memorem grātumque cognōscī simulque aperiēns sē nōn fortūnae, sed hominibus solēre esse amīcum. 6. Quae cum faciēbat, nēmō eum temporis causā facere poterat existimāre. Nēminī enim in opīniōnem veniēbat Antōnium rērum potītūrum . . .

10

VOCABULARY

7   quīn etiam – and furthermore

     fundus, ī, m. – country estate, farm

     secundus – following, favorable, second

8   *emō, ere, ēmī, emptum – to buy

     in diem – for a future day

     *calamitās, calamitātis, f. – disaster, misfortune, calamity

     versūra, ae, f. – exchanging one creditor for another

9   interpōno, ere, interposuī, intepositum – to put between; sē interpōnere – to intervene, interfere

     faenus, faenoris, n. – interest, profit

     stipulātiō, stipulātiōnis, f. – demanding of a guarantee from a prospective debtor

10 crēdō – to lend money, believe

     *existimō, āre, āvī, ātum – to value, esteem, think

     quaestus, quaestūs, m. – profit

     *memor, memoris – remembering, mindful (of one's obligations)

     *grātus, a, um – thankful, appreciative

11 *cōgnōscō, ere, cōgnōvī, cōgnitum – to get to know, find to be

12 quae = et haec

     temporis causā – to suit the occasion

13 *opīniō, opīniōnis, f. – opinion, mind

14 potior, potīrī, potītus sum + genitive – to make oneself master of, take possession of

     *Words marked with an asterisk will need to be memorized later in the chapter.

READING NOTES

7–8 *cum illa fundum secundā fortūnā ēmisset* The phrase *secundā fortūnā* means "in favorable circumstances." Originally meaning "following," or "blowing in the direction of one's course," here *secundus* means "favorable." You have already learned that *secundus* can mean "second."

in diem This expression which means "by a future day" indicates that the farm she bought was to be paid for by a future, agreed-upon day.

9 *versūram facere* The phrase *versūram facere* means "to refinance a loan with a new creditor."

10–11 *maximus existimāns quaestum memorem grātumque cognōscī* "Thinking that the greatest profit was to be found mindful of his obligations and thankful . . ."

12 *aperiēns* The verb *aperiō, -īre, aperuī, apertum* can mean not only "to open," but also "to reveal."

eum This accusative subject of an indirect statement refers to Atticus.

14 *Nēminī . . . in opīniōnem veniēbat* The phrase *in opīniōnem venīre* (with the dative indicating the person involved) means "to occur to" someone.

Antōnium rērum potītūrum The word *rēs* in the plural often means simply "affairs" or "circumstances."

COMPREHENSION QUESTIONS

Answer the following questions in Latin using the text on pp. 378 and 380. The Reading Vocabulary may be consulted.

1. Eratne Atticus Cicerōnis amīcus?

2. Eratne Atticus Brūtī amīcus?

3. Erantne Cicero et Brūtus Antōniī amīcī?

4. Quōcum stābat Atticus, cum Cicerōne et Brūtō, an (or) cum Antōniō?

5. Quid fēcit Atticus, cum Antōniī familiārēs Rōmā fugerent?

6. Quid fīēbat illō tempore Fulviae, Antōniī uxōrī?

7. Quibus duōbus modīs Atticus Fulviam adiūvit?

8. Quid Atticus maximum quaestum existimābat?

9. Putābantne hominēs ab Atticō Fulviam temporis causā adiuvārī? Cūr?

VOCABULARY TO LEARN

NOUNS

calamitās, calamitātis, f. – disaster, misfortune, calamity

familiāritās, familiāritātis, f. – familiarity

dīligentia, ae, f. – carefulness, attentiveness, diligence

opīniō, opīniōnis, f. – opinion, mind

ADJECTIVES

amīcus, a, um – friendly

familiāris, familiāris, m./f. – family member, close friend

grātus, a, um – thankful, appreciative

intimus, a, um – most intimate, closest

memor, memoris + genitive – remembering, mindful of (usually of one's obligations)

VERBS

adiuvō, āre, adiūvī, adiūtum – to help

cōgnōscō, ere, cōgnōvī, cōgnitum – to get to know, find to be

emō, ere, ēmī, emptum – to buy

existimō, āre, āvī, ātum – to value, esteem, think

praestō, āre, praestitī, praestitum – to make available, supply

tegō, ere, tēxī, tēctum – to cover, protect

▶ EXERCISE 1

The following conversation might have taken place between Atticus and Fulvia during the period in which she was in trouble. Fulvia, married to Mark Antony (this was her third marriage), was a very active person in the politics of the late republic, and in some ways a prototype of the future empresses.

Fill in the blanks using the correct form of the verbs and phrases in parentheses. Then translate the dialogue into English. The Reading Vocabulary may be consulted.

Atticus: Salvē, Fulvia! Quōmodo hodiē valēs?

Fulvia: Tot lītibus distineor et tantīs terrōribus vexor ut _____ (mihi vīrēs iam nōn sunt). Quis mē miserrimam adiuvābit?

Atticus: Ipse ad tē vēnī ut _____ (auxilium tibi ferō). Parātus sum omnia prō tē facere. Quid est mihi faciendum?

Fulvia: Ad iūdicem mihi est eundum. Licetne mihi tē rogāre ut _____ (spōnsor meus fīēs)?

Atticus: Nūllum vadimōnium sistere dēbēbis sine mē. Semper veniam ut tē _____ (adiuvō). Tēcum semper ambulābō.

Fulvia: Grāta sum, Attice, vir optime, prō benevolentiā tuā, et semper hūius reī memor erō. Sī marītus meus Rōmam redīre _____ (potest), multa officia tibi praestābit.

Atticus: Tē adiuvāre volō, quia nōn mihi placet amīcōs in calamitātibus relinquere. Nūlla alia est causa.

Fulvia: At mihi est quoque alia calamitās.

Atticus: Dīcās mihi _____ (quid est)!

Fulvia: Fundum in diem ēmī, sed nunc versūram facere nōn possum, quamquam cōnor.

Atticus: Pecūniam tibi crēdam sine faenore et sine stipulātiōne.

Fulvia: At pecūniā sine faenore mihi crēditā, nūllus quaestus erit tibi.

Atticus: Existimō _____ (maximus quaestus est grātum memoremque cognōscī). Valē nunc, Fulvia! Posteā veniam ut _____ (pecūniam tibi dō) et ut _____ (ad iūdicem īmus).

Fulvia: Valē, vir amīcissime!

2. THE SHIP OF STATE

Atticus is compared to a captain who brings his ship to a safe harbor after a storm.

CORNĒLIĪ NEPŌTIS ATTICUS, 10

As Cornelius Nepos himself would observe, fortune changed easily in the turbulent times of the first century BCE. In November 43 BCE, Antony, together with his allies Lepidus and Octavian, were appointed triumvirs for the restoration of the state for the period of five years. What followed, of course, was the proscription of their enemies. The proscribed people were declared outlaws and executed, and all their property was confiscated. Atticus' close friend Cicero met his death in Antony's proscription.

1   10. 1. Conversa subitō fortūna est. Ut Antōnius rediit in Ītaliam,
      nēmō nōn māgnō in perīculō Atticum putārat propter intimam
      familiāritātem Cicerōnis et Brūtī. 2. Itaque ad adventum imperātōrum
      dē forō dēcesserat, timēns prōscrīptiōnem . . . tanta varietās hīs
5   temporibus fuit fortūnae, ut modo hī, modo illī in summō essent aut
      fastīgiō aut perīculō . . .

VOCABULARY

1   convertō, ere, convertī, conversum – to rotate, invert

    *ut + perfect indicative – as soon as, when

    rediit – an alternative form of *redīvit* from *redeō, redīre, redīvī, reditum* ("to go back, return")

    *Ītalia, ae, f. – Italy

2   nēmō nōn – everybody (two negatives make a positive)

3   *adventus, adventūs, m. – arrival

    ad adventum – by (the time of) the arrival

    *imperātor – general, commanding officer, emperor

4   *forum, ī, n. – Forum Rōmānum, the main square in Rome

    dēcēdō, ere, dēcessī, dēcessum – to go away, withdraw

    prōscrīptiō, prōscrīptiōnis, f. – proscription, publishing the names of citizens declared to be outlaws

    varietās, varietātis, f. – variety, diversity, changeable nature

5   *modo . . . modo . . . – at one time . . . at another . . . , now . . . now . . .

    *summus, a, um – highest, upmost

    *aut – or; aut . . . aut . . . – either . . . or . . .

6   fastīgium, ī, n. – highest part, roof, top, peak

READING NOTES

1   *Ut . . . rediit* When an *ut* clause has a perfect indicative verb, it translates "as soon as" or "when."

2   *nēmō nōn* Double negatives like this amount to a strong affirmation. The meaning is "virtually everyone."

    putārat This is a shortened/contracted form of *putāverat*. The *–ve–* or *–vi–* in the perfect or pluperfect can sometimes be lost: for example, *amāsset=amāvisset, amārunt=amāvērunt.*

3   *Cicerōnis et Brūtī* Translate these two genitives as "with Cicero and Brutus."

4–5   *tanta varietās hīs temporibus fuit fortūnae* The phrase means there was "so much shifting of fortune." The phrase *hīs temporibus* is an ablative of time meaning "in/at these times."

4. Antōnius autem etsī tantō odiō ferēbātur
in Cicerōnem, ut nōn sōlum eī, sed etiam omnibus ēius amīcīs esset
inimīcus eōsque vellet prōscrībere, multīs hortantibus tamen Atticī
memor fuit officiī et eī, cum requīsisset ubinam esset, suā manū scrīpsit,
10   nē timēret statimque ad sē venīret: sē eum . . . dē prōscrīptōrum
numerō exēmisse. Ac nē quod perīculum incideret, quod noctū fīēbat,
praesidium eī mīsit . . . 5–6. Quod sī gubernātor praecipuā laude fertur,
quī nāvem ex hieme marīque scopulōsō servat, cūr nōn singulāris ēius
existimētur prūdentia, quī ex tot tamque gravibus procellīs cīvīlibus ad
15   incolumitātem pervēnit?

VOCABULARY

6 *etsī (conj.) – although

8 *inimīcus, ī, m. – enemy, opponent
   prōscrībō, ere, prōscrīpsī, prōscrīptum – to proscribe, publish someone's name in a list of outlaws

9 *officium – favor, duty
   requīrō, ere, requīsīvī, requīsītum – to try to find, inquire about
   requīsisset = requīsīvisset
   ubinam? – where in the world?

11 *numerus, ī, m. – number
   eximō, ere, exēmī, exēmptum – to take out, remove
   nē quod – quis and quī after nē mean "somebody," "any," "something," "some"
   incidō, ere, incidī, incāsum – to fall into

12 *praesidium, ī, n. – military escort, garrison
   gubernātor, gubernātōris, m. – helmsman, pilot
   praecipuus, a, um – peculiar, special, exceptional
   laus, laudis, f. – praise

13 *hiems, hiemis, f. – winter, storm
   scopulōsus, a, um – full of shoals, rocky
   singulāris, singulāre – unique, exceptional

14 *prūdentia, ae, f. – practical intelligence, wisdom
   procella, ae, f. – violent storm, gale
   cīvīlis, cīvīle – civil

15 incolumitās, incolumitātis, f. – freedom from harm, safety

   *Words marked with an asterisk will need to be memorized later in the chapter.

READING NOTES

6 *ferēbātur* In this context the verb means "was carried away with."

6–7 *odiō ferēbātur in Cicerōnem* The preposition *in* with the accusative can mean "against."

7 *ut nōn sōlum eī* The dative singular pronoun *eī*, "to him," refers to Cicero.

7–8 *ēius . . . eōsque* The word *ēius*, meaning "his," refers to Cicero and *eōsque*, meaning "and them," refers to Cicero's friends.

8 *multīs hortantibus* This phrase is an ablative absolute.

9 *eī . . . scrīpsit* "He <i.e., Antony> wrote to him <i.e., Atticus>."

11 *Ac nē quod* The indefinite adjective *quī, qua, quod* is a form of *aliquī, aliqua, aliquod*, which means "some" or "any." The forms of *quī* are used instead of forms of *aliquī* after the words *sī, nisi, nē, num, quō,* and *quantō* because the "ali-s" drop away! So the phrase here means "and lest any . . ." or "so that no . . ."

12 *Quod sī* The word *quod* at the beginning of a sentence, especially before *sī*, is very often a particle of transition (which has nothing to do with the relative and causal meanings of *quod* which you have learned in other contexts). The phrase *quod sī* means "but if."

   praecipuā laude fertur The passive of *ferre* with an ablative of words indicating praise means "be exalted" or "be celebrated."

14 *existimētur* The subjunctive here adds a note of suggestion and deliberation. Translate with this English helping verb "should."

   procellīs cīvīlibus This metaphorical phrase means "political storms" which shake the state. This is an extension of the famous "ship of state" metaphor common in Greek and Latin literature.

COMPREHENSION QUESTIONS

Answer the following questions in Latin using the text on pp. 384 and 386. The Reading Vocabulary may be consulted.

1. Poteratne fortūna facile mūtārī illīs temporibus?
2. Quid fierī poterat hominibus quī erant in summō fastīgiō?
3. Quid factum est Antōniō?
4. Quid factum est Antōniī inimīcīs?
5. Quid Atticus timēbat? Quid propter timōrem fēcit?
6. Quid fēcit Antōnius, cum vīdisset Atticum nōn esse in forō?
7. Quid Antōnius Atticō dēclārāvit?
8. Quid rogāvit Antōnius ut Atticus faceret?
9. Cūr est Atticus laudandus tamquam bonus gubernātor?

Nepos' reference to a ship's helmsman draws on a metaphor used by the Greek poet Alcaeus and by Plato in *The Republic*. The first-century BCE poet Horace expounds on the image in *Ode* 1.14. The reconstruction of the Greek trireme honors its significant contribution to Athenian naval power which defeated the Persians.

VOCABULARY TO LEARN

NOUNS

adventus, adventūs, m. – arrival

forum, ī, n. – Forum Rōmānum

hiems, hiemis, f. – winter, storm

imperātor, imperatoris, m. – general, commanding officer, emperor

inimīcus, ī, m. – enemy, opponent‡

Ītalia, ae, f. – Italy

numerus, ī, m. – number

officium, ī, n. – favor, duty

praesidium, ī, n. – military escort, garrison

prūdentia, ae, f. – practical intelligence, wisdom

ADJECTIVES

summus, a, um – highest, the top of

CONJUNCTIONS

aut – or; aut . . . aut . . . – either . . . or . . .

etsī – although

modo . . . modo . . . – at one time . . . at another . . . , now . . . now . . .

ut + perfect indicative – as soon as, when

‡Additional information about the words marked with the double dagger will be in the **Take Note** section that follows the Vocabulary to Learn.

TAKE NOTE

inimīcus The word *inimīcus* tends to refer more to a personal enemy while *hostis* is more typically a public enemy—but the distinction is not rigidly observed.

▶ EXERCISE 1

Below is a letter that Antony might have written to Atticus. Translate it into Latin.

Antony greets Atticus

I returned to Rome from external (foreign) lands, and after my arrival I searched for you in the forum. As soon as I did not see you there, I thought that you, fearing, had left. You should fear nothing, Atticus (*use the passive periphrastic*). Do you think that I am not mindful of your favor and not thankful? I know well that you have helped my family members and especially my wife. Your help was so great that you have saved her. Although you are a friend of my utmost enemy Cicero, however, I will not count you yourself in the number of my enemies. I am sending to you a military escort so that you can come immediately to me and we may speak. Your prudence is to be praised, Atticus.

Be well!

The center of Roman political life, the Roman Forum, witnessed the turbulence of the first century BCE. After the assassination of Julius Caesar, the Senate declared him a god to whom a temple was erected in the forum. The triumvirs published the proscription list in the forum.

3. SKILLFUL NAVIGATION

Because of his prudence and astuteness, Atticus shaped his own fate.

CORNĒLIĪ NEPŌTIS ATTICUS, 11

Here you will read more about Atticus' behavior during the proscriptions of Antony. The author, Atticus' friend Cornelius Nepos, tries to explain how this man, coming from the class of Roman knights (who were not the highest Roman nobility), and even during a time of terrible political turmoil, managed to lead such an extraordinary existence of cultured leisure, to be incredibly successful in business, and to emerge from the most difficult circumstances unscathed and with friendships intact.

1   11.1. Quibus ex malīs ut sē ēmersit, nihil aliud ēgit, quam ut quam plūrimīs, quibus rēbus posset, esset auxiliō . . . 3. Difficile est omnia persequī et nōn necessārium. Illud ūnum intellegī volumus, illīus līberālitātem neque temporāriam neque callidam fuisse. 4. Id ex ipsīs

5   rēbus ac temporibus iudicārī potest, quod nōn flōrentibus sē vēnditāvit, sed afflīctīs semper succurrit; quī quidem Servīliam, Brūtī mātrem, nōn minus post mortem ēius quam flōrentem coluerit. 5. Sīc līberālitāte ūtēns nūllās inimīcitiās gessit, quod neque laedēbat quemquam neque, sī quam iniūriam accēperat, nōn mālēbat oblīvīscī quam ulcīscī. Īdem

10   immortālī memoriā percepta retinēbat beneficia; quae autem ipse tribuerat, tamdiū meminerat, quoad ille grātus erat, quī accēperat. 6. Itaque hic fēcit, ut vērē dictum videātur.

   Suī cuique mōrēs fingunt fortūnam hominibus . . .

VOCABULARY

1   quibus = et hīs

     ēmergō, ere, ēmersī, ēmersum – to come out of the water, emerge

     *quam + superlative degree – as . . . as possible

2   auxiliō – a source of help

3   persequor, persequī, persecūtus sum – to follow persistently, to go over (cf. "persecution")

     *necessārius, a, um – necessary

4   *līberālitās, līberālitātis, f. – generosity

     *neque = nec; neque . . . neque . . . – neither . . . nor . . .

     temporārius, a, um – suited for the occasion, temporary

     callidus, a, um – clever, cunning

5   tempus – circumstance, time

     *flōreō, ēre, flōruī, — – to blossom, flourish

     vēnditō, āre, āvī, ātum – to try to sell, advertise

6   *afflīgō, ere, afflīxī, afflīctum – to strike, distress, afflict

     succurrō, ere, succurrī, succursum – to hasten to help

8   inimīcitia, ae, f. – hostility

     quemquam (accusative singular masculine) – anybody

9   *iniūria, ae, f. – unjust treatment, injury

     *oblīvīscor, oblīvīscī, oblītus sum – to forget

     ulcīscor, ulcīscī, ultus sum – to take revenge

10   *immortālis, immortāle – undying, immortal

     *percipiō, ere, percēpī, perceptum – to take, earn, acquire

     retineō, ēre, retinuī, retentum – to retain

     *beneficium, ī, n. – service, kindness, favor

11   *tribuō, ere, tribuī, tribūtum – to grant, bestow

     tamdiū . . . quoad . . . – as long . . . as . . .

     *meminī, meminisse – to remember

12   vērē (adv.) – correctly

     *Words marked with an asterisk will need to be memorized later in the chapter.

READING NOTES

1   *nihil aliud ēgit quam ut* The phrase *id agere* joined with *ut* and a purpose clause means "to aim at." With *nihil aliud . . . quam ut*, the expression has the meaning "to aim at nothing other than . . ."

1–2   *quam plūrimīs . . . auxiliō esset* Understand *hominibus* with *plūrimīs*. The case of *plūrimīs* is dative of the person affected by the dative of purpose *auxiliō*. The phrase means "to be of help to as many people as possible."

2   *quibus rēbus posset* Meaning "with what things (resources) he could," here *rēs* refers to financial resources. The verb *posset* is subjunctive because it is considered part of the purpose clause that begins with *ut*.

3   *illīus* Meaning "his," this word refers to Atticus.

5   *nōn flōrentibus sē vēnditāvit* With *flōrentibus*, understand *hominibus*, i.e., "flourishing people."

6–7   *quī quidem Servīliam, Brūtī mātrem, nōn minus post mortem ēius quam flōrentem coluerit* The accusative case participle *flōrentem* refers to *Servīliam* with whom Atticus maintained his friendship no less after her son's death than when she was "flourishing," (i.e., when her son was alive). The verb *colō, ere, coluī, cultum*, when it refers to interactions between people, has the special meaning "cultivate" or "look after."

8   *nūllās inimīcitiās gessit* The verb *gerere*, when it takes the accusative of a noun of enmity or friendship, means "foster" or "nurture."

8–9   *neque laedēbat quemquam neque . . . nōn mālēbat oblīvīscī quam ulcīscī* Note the strongly positive force of the double negative: "he did not harm anyone, nor did he not prefer (i.e., he **always** preferred) to forget than to avenge."

9   *sī quam* Remember that *quis* and *quī* after *sī* have the meaning "somebody," "any."

10   *quae* "the favors which . . ."

12   *itaque hic fēcit* "And he so behaved . . ."

13   *suī cuique* Keep in mind that *suī* goes with *mōrēs*, and *cuique* is a dative singular of an indefinite pronoun. When the possessive and reflexive adjective of the third person is combined with an indefinite pronoun in another case (as here), the meaning is "one's own."

COMPREHENSION QUESTIONS

Answer the following questions in Latin using the text on p. 390. The Reading Vocabulary may be consulted.

1. Quid fēcit Atticus, postquam ab Antōniō est servātus?

2. Cūr Nepōs nōn vult numerāre omnēs hominēs quōs adiūvit Atticus?

3. Quālis fuit līberālitās Atticī?

4. Quālēs hominēs adiuvābat Atticus?

5. Quid fēcit Atticus Servīliae, Brūtī mātrī?

6. Gerēbatne Atticus inimīcitiās? Cūr?

7. Cūr Nepōs dīcit Atticum fēcisse ut vērē dictum vidērētur "Suī cuique mōrēs fingunt fortūnam hominibus"?

VOCABULARY TO LEARN

NOUNS

beneficium, ī, n. – service, kindness, favor

iniūria, ae, f. – unjust treatment, injury

līberālitās, līberālitātis, f. – generosity

ADJECTIVES

immortālis, immortāle – undying, immortal

necessārius, a, um – necessary

VERBS

afflīgō, ere, afflīxī, afflīctum – to strike, distress, afflict

flōreō, ēre, flōruī, — – to flourish, blossom

meminī, meminisse – to remember‡

oblīvīscor, oblīvīscī, oblītus sum + genitive – to forget

percipiō, ere, percēpī, perceptum – to take, earn, acquire

tribuō, ere, tribuī, tribūtum – to grant, bestow

ADVERBS

quam + superlative degree – as . . . as possible

CONJUNCTIONS

neque = nec; neque . . . neque . . . – neither . . . nor . . .

‡Additional information about the words marked with the double dagger will be in the **Take Note** section that follows the Vocabulary to Learn.

TAKE NOTE

meminī This verb is defective, i.e., it has only perfect, pluperfect, and future perfect tenses which are used with the meanings of the present, imperfect, and future tenses.

The familiar image of the television journalist, microphone ever ready for the interviewee's responses.

▶ EXERCISE 1

Imagine that Atticus was interviewed (in Latin!) by a modern journalist about the principles of his life. Fill in the blanks using the correct form of the verbs and phrases written in parentheses. Sometimes the mood and person of verbs will have to be changed. Sometimes verbs will need to be changed into participles. Add conjunctions as needed. Then translate the dialogue into English.

Diurnārius (*journalist*): Salvē, Attice, vir celeberrime. Omnēs dīcunt tē esse fēlīcem et bonam fortūnam tē semper esse secūtam. Quōmodo hoc facere potuistī?

Atticus: Sī quis (*if anybody*) mē rōgābat _____ (sē adiuvāre), semper hoc facere sum cōnātus.

Diurnārius: Dum adiuvābās, faciēbāsne ita _____ (prō auxiliō praemium accipere)?

Atticus: Beneficia mea nōn _____ (flōreō) tribuēbam, sed _____ (afflīgō). Ex illīs vix ūllum praemium _____ (spērō; *use the passive periphrastic*), quamquam interdum fortūna celeriter mūtābātur.

Diurnārius: Sī hominēs beneficiī ā tē factī iam nōn erant memorēs, quid fīēbat?

Atticus: Tunc ipse quoque tōtīus reī oblīvīscī mālēbam.

Diurnārius: Sī tū ab aliīs es adiūtus, erāsne hūius reī memor?

Atticus: Omnium beneficiōrum tam memor sum ut _____ (ea semper grātō animō in memoriā tenēre).

Diurnārius: Quid fēcistī illīs hominibus quī tē laesērunt? Dīcās ōrō.

Atticus: Exīstimāvī _____ (ego potius oblīvīscī quam ulcīscī; *use the passive periphrastic construction and an indirect statement*).

Diurnārius: Prūdentia tua, Attice, _____ (laudō; *use the passive periphrastic*). Grātiās tibi agō (*thank you*).

Atticus: Libenter (*my pleasure*).

The print media journalist commits the interviewee's responses to his notes and often to a tape recorder as well.

4. ATTICUS AND THE EMPEROR'S BEST FRIEND

Atticus not only befriends Agrippa, right-hand man to Augustus, but he also becomes Agrippa's father-in-law.

CORNĒLIĪ NEPŌTIS ATTICUS, 12

Marcus Vipsanius Agrippa, a simple and modest man, was a lifelong friend of the first Roman emperor Augustus. It is said that in a critical moment Augustus even entrusted Agrippa with his own signet ring, thus unofficially allowing Agrippa to exercise the emperor's power. Agrippa became a close friend of Atticus, and this friendship resulted in the marriage of Atticus' daughter to Agrippa. This girl was the first of Agrippa's three wives (the third one was the daughter of Augustus himself).

1   12. 1. Hīs igitur rēbus effēcit, ut M. Vipsānius Agrippa, intimā familiāritāte coniūnctus adulēscentī Caesarī, cum propter suam grātiam et Caesaris potentiam nūllīus condiciōnis nōn habēret potestātem, potissimum ēius dēligeret affīnitātem praeoptāretque

5   equitis Rōmānī fīliam generōsārum nūptiīs. 2. Atque hārum nūptiārum conciliātor fuit—nōn est enim cēlandum—M. Antōnius, triumvir reī pūblicae cōnstituendae. Cūius grātiā cum augēre possessiōnēs posset suās, tantum āfuit ā cupiditāte pecūniae, ut nūllā in rē ūsus sit eā nisi in dēprecandīs amīcōrum aut perīculīs aut incommodīs.

READING VOCABULARY

1 *efficiō, ere, effēcī, effectum (often + *ut*) – to cause to happen, bring about

2 *coniungō, ere, coniūnxī, coniūnctum – to connect, join together

   *Caesar, Caesaris, m. – emperor, Caesar

3 *grātia, ae, f. – agreeableness, favor, influence, prestige

   *potentia, ae, f. – power

   *condiciō, condiciōnis, f. – condition

4 *potestās, potestātis, f. – command, control, power

   potissimum (adv.) – especially, above all

   dēligō, ere, dēlēgī, dēlēctum – to choose

   affīnitās, affīnitātis, f. – relationship by marriage, marriage connection

   praeoptō, āre, praeoptāvī, praeoptātum + accusative + dative – to prefer something to something

5 *eques – knight, member of the equestrian order

   generōsus, a, um – high-born, of noble birth

   *nūptiae, ārum, f. pl. – wedding, marriage

6 conciliātor, conciliātōris, m. – mediator

   cēlō, āre, āvī, ātum – to hide

   triumvir, triumvirī, m. – member of a committee of three men

7 *cōnstituō, ere, cōnstituī, cōnstitūtum – to set up, establish

   cūius = et hūius

   *cum + imperfect subjunctive – although

   *augeō, ēre, auxī, auctum – to increase

   possessiō, possessiōnis, f. – possession

8 *tantum (adv.) – so much, only

   cupiditās, cupiditātis, f. – greed, immoderate desire

9 dēprecor, dēprecārī, dēprecātus sum – to try to avert (by prayer)

   *incommodum, ī, n. – disadvantage, harm

   *Words marked with an asterisk will need to be memorized later in the chapter.

READING NOTES

1 *hīs igitur rēbus* The word *rēbus* refers to Atticus' prudent and moral actions described in Section 3 and the phrase is an ablative of means.

2 *adulēscentī Caesarī* The word *Caesarī* here refers to Augustus.

2–4 *Cum . . . habēret potestātem* Here *cum* is concessive and means "although" or "despite the fact that."

3–4 *nūllīus condiciōnis nōn habēret potestātem* The double negative **nūllīus** condiciōnis **nōn** habēret . . . amounts to a strong affirmative: "he could have power over <**absolutely**> **every** condition . . ."

4–5 *praeoptāretque equitis Rōmānī fīliam generōsārum nuptiīs* The word *generōsārum* means "of women of noble birth."

6–7 *M. Antōnius, triumvir reī pūblicae cōnstituendae* The three powerful men who emerged after the civil strife between Julius Caesar and the senatorial party (which had been led by Pompey) were Antony, Lepidus, and Octavian. In 43 BCE, amid a great political crisis, they were appointed as a commision of three for restoring the state: *triumvirī reī pūblicae cōnstituendae*. In this title, note the gerundive construction in a dative of purpose.

7–8 *Cūius grātiā cum augēre possessiōnēs posset suās* The connecting relative refers to something or someone mentioned in the previous sentence and translates as a demonstrative or personal pronoun. Here, therefore, *cūius* means the equivalent of "his," which refers to Antony.

8 *nūllā in rē ūsus sit eā* The pronoun *eā* refers back to *grātiā*.

8–9 *in dēprecandīs perīculīs aut incommodīs* Note here the gerundive construction. The phrase means "in trying to avert the dangers and disadvantages . . ."

COMPREHENSION QUESTIONS

Answer the following questions in Latin using the text on p. 394. The Reading Vocabulary may be consulted.

1. Quis fuit Mārcus Vipsānius Agrippa?

2. Quid factum est inter Agrippam et Atticum?

3. Potuitne Agrippa aliam uxōrem habēre? Cūr?

4. Quis adiūvit Atticum et Agrippam ad nūptiās parandās?

5. Voluitne Atticus possessiōnēs suās augēre ūtēns grātiā Antōniī?

6. Ad quam rem faciendam Atticus Antōniō est ūsus?

The Pantheon, Rome's most famous temple, bears witness to Augustus' right-hand man and Atticus' personal friend, Marcus Agrippa. Restored by Hadrian in the second century CE, the Pantheon retains the dedicatory inscription—M • AGRIPPA • L • F • COS • TERTIUM • FECIT—from the original built in 27 BCE.

VOCABULARY TO LEARN

NOUNS

Caesar, Caesaris, m. – emperor‡

condiciō, condiciōnis, f. – condition

eques, equitis, m. – knight, member of the equestrian order‡

grātia, ae, f. – agreeableness, favor

incommodum, ī, n. – disadvantage, harm

nūptiae, ārum, f. pl. – wedding, marriage

potentia, ae, f. – power

potestās, potestātis, f. – command, control, power

VERBS

augeō, ēre, auxī, auctum – to increase

coniungō, ere, coniūnxī, coniūnctum – to connect, join together

cōnstituō, ere, cōnstituī, cōnstitūtum – to set up, establish

efficiō, ere, effēcī, effectum (often + ut) – to cause to happen, bring about

ADVERBS

tantum (adv.) – so much, only

CONJUNCTIONS

cum + imperfect subjunctive – although

‡Additional information about the words marked with the double dagger will be in the **Take Note** section that follows the Vocabulary to Learn.

TAKE NOTE

Caesar This was initially the name of Julius Caesar. Octavian, having been adopted by Caesar in his will, according to Roman convention took the name Caesar. So did the others who succeeded Augustus. By the latter part of the first century CE, Caesar had simply become one of the official titles for the emperor.

eques Literally a "horseman" because an *eques* came to battle equipped with a horse, an *eques* was a knight or a member of the equestrian order, to which both Cicero and Atticus belonged. The knights were rather high in social standing, although they had less political responsibility than the highest order, the patricians. Both orders were closer together than the third lowest order, the plebeians: that made Cicero propose the concept of *concordia ōrdinum*, "agreement of orders," including in it, however, only patricians and knights.

▶ EXERCISE 1

The following exercise is an imaginary dialogue between Agrippa and Atticus, when the bethrothal of Agrippa and Atticus' daughter Caecilia Attica was arranged in Atticus' home with the mediation of Mark Antony. Translate the English parts into Latin and the Latin parts into English.

ānulus, ī, m. – ring   dōs, dōtis, f. – dowry

Agrippa: Salvē, Attice! Esne domī? Veniō enim petītum ut fīliam tuam uxōrem mihi dēs.

Atticus: Come in, Agrippa! I am expecting you, so that we may speak.

Agrippa: Volō coniungī cum familiā optimī virī. Itaque, quamquam mihi licet aliās fēminās dīvitēs petere, dēcrēvī mē mālle fīliam tuam habēre.

Atticus: You ought to learn, Agrippa, that my daughter is not poor. I have such great riches that I am able to give her a huge dowry.

Agrippa: At ipse cupiō fīliam tuam nōn sōlum propter dōtem, sed etiam propter virtūtēs. Nam dēbet esse patrī suō similis.

Atticus: My daughter is endowed indeed with the very best morals. You also seem a good man. If you were not a good man, I would not give you my daughter. Did you bring a ring with you?

Agrippa: Ita, ānulum mēcum tulī ut illum fīliae tuae darem.

Atticus: I will call my daughter. After the ring is given, we will all eat together. Now is the time for (i.e., "of") drinking (*use a gerund*).

5. BE IT EVER SO HUMBLE, THERE IS NO PLACE LIKE HOME

Despite his social prominence, Atticus preferred a simple and serene lifestyle at home.

CORNĒLIĪ NEPŌTIS ATTICUS, 13

Now you will read how Atticus used to live at home with his family. The word *familia* in Latin, when referring to the noble class, often means the whole household, slaves included. The head of the family was called by the archaic word *paterfamiliās*, i.e., *pater familiae*. Atticus' grumpy uncle, about whom you read in Chapter 8, is mentioned here again. Despite the sternness of his uncle, Atticus was persistently kind to him, and was rewarded for his kindness—the uncle left his nice home to Atticus!

1   13. 1. Neque vērō ille vir minus bonus pater familiās habitus est quam cīvis. Nam cum esset pecūniōsus, nēmō illō minus fuit emāx, minus aedificātor. Neque tamen nōn in prīmīs bene habitāvit omnibusque optimīs rēbus ūsus est. 2. Nam domum habuit in colle

5   Quirīnālī Tamphiliānam, ab avunculō hērēditāte relictam; cūius amoenitās nōn aedificiō, sed silvā cōnstābat. Ipsum enim tēctum antīquitus cōnstitūtum plūs salis quam sūmptūs habēbat; in quō nihil commūtāvit, nisi sī quid vetustāte coāctus est.

VOCABULARY

1   vērō (adv.) – in fact, truly

2   pecūniōsus, a, um – moneyed, provided with
     money

     emāx, emācis – fond of buying

3   aedificātor, aedificatōris, m. – builder; devoted to
     building (functioning as an adjective)

     in prīmīs (imprīmīs) – especially, above all

4   *collis, collis, m. – hill; collis Quirīnālis – the
     Quirinal is one of the seven hills of Rome

5   Tamphiliāna (domus) – made by the architect
     Tamphilus

     *hērēditās, hērēditātis, f. – inheritance

6   amoenitās, amoenitātis, f. – pleasantness (of a
     place)

     *aedificium, ī, n. – building

     *cōnstō, āre, cōnstitī, — + ablative – to consist in

     *tēctum, ī, n. – roof, house

7   antīquitus (adv.) – from old times

     plūs + partitive genitive – more (of)

     *sāl, salis, m. – salt, a quality that gives taste, wit

     *sūmptus, sūmptūs, m. – expense

8   commūtō, āre, āvī, ātum – to change (completely)

     vetustās, vetustātis, f. – old age

     *cōgō, ere, coēgī, coāctum – to compel, force

READING NOTES

1–2 *Neque vērō ille vir minus bonus pater familiās habi-
     tus est quam cīvis* Here *habitus est* means "was
     considered as." *Ille vir* refers to Atticus.

3   *Neque tamen nōn in prīmīs bene habitāvit* The
     double negative virtually constitutes an
     affirmative—"yet he did live very well."

4   *optimīs rēbus ūsus est* The verb *ūtor* often as here
     has the meaning "enjoy."

5–6 *cūius amoenitās* Translate "its pleasantness" or
     "the pleasantness of this <house>."

6–7 *tēctum . . . plūs salis quam sūmptūs habēbat* In the
     singular *plūs* is a neuter noun that takes the
     genitive, whereas *plūrēs* (the plural form) is an
     adjective that agrees with the case, number,
     and gender of the noun it modifies. *Salis* in this
     context means "taste."

8   *nihil commūtāvit, nisi sī quid vetustāte coāctus
     est* Understand the infinitive *commūtāre* to
     complete the meaning of *coāctus est*, i.e., ". . .
     unless he was forced to change anything." And
     on *sī quid*, remember the rule already quoted in
     a note in Chapter 10, "after *sī, nisi, nē, num, quō,*
     and *quantō* the 'ali-s' drop away."

3. Ūsus est
familiā, sī ūtilitāte iūdicandum est, optimā; sī fōrmā, vix mediocrī.

10 Namque in eā erant puerī litterātissimī, anagnōstae optimī et plūrimī
librāriī, ut nē pedisequus quidem quisquam esset, quī nōn utrumque
hōrum pulchrē facere posset, parī modō artificēs cēterī, quōs cultus
domesticus dēsīderat, apprīmē bonī . . . 5. Ēlegāns, nōn māgnificus;
splendidus, nōn sūmptuōsus: omnisque dīligentia munditiam, nōn

15 affluentiam affectābat.

VOCABULARY

9 ūtilitās, ūtilitātis, f. – usefulness

   ūtilitāte – according to usefullness

   fōrmā – according to appearance

   *mediocris, mediocre – commonplace, mediocre, moderate

10 namque (conj.) – indeed, for, because

   *litterātus, a, um – versed in literature, cultured

   anagnōstēs, ae, m. – slave whose job is to read aloud, reader

11 librārius, ī, m. – a slave trained in copying, copy-ist, secretary

   *nē . . . quidem . . . – not even

   pedisequus, ī, m. – manservant

   uterque, utraque, utrumque – each of the two

12 pulchrē (adv.) – beautifully

   *pār, paris – equal

   *artifex, artificis, m. – craftsman, artisan

   *cēterus, a, um – the rest, remaining

   cultus, cultūs, m. – care, maintenance

13 domesticus, a, um – domestic

   dēsīderō, āre, āvī, ātum – to long for, need, desire

   apprīmē (adv.) – to the highest degree, especially

   *ēlegāns, ēlegantis – careful in choosing, tasteful

   māgnificus, a, um – magnificent

14 splendidus, a, um – splendid

   sūmptuōsus, a, um – involving expenses, sumptu-ous, extravagant

   munditia, ae, f. – neatness, cleanliness

15 affluentia, ae, f. – opulence, extravagance

   affectō, āre, āvī, ātum – to try to achieve, strive after

   *Words marked with an asterisk will need to be memorized later in the chapter.

READING NOTES

9 *sī ūtilitāte iūdicandum est . . . optimā; sī fōrmā, vix mediocrī* Understand *iūdicandum est* again after the word *fōrmā*. Latin writers typically do not repeat words to complete a parallel structure. The words *ūtilitāte* and *fōrmā* are both ablatives of respect and mean "in respect to/according to usefulness" and "in respect to/according to appearance."

11 *nē pedisequus quidem quisquam esset* "there was not even any man-servant . . ."

11–12 *quī nōn utrumque hōrum pulchrē facere posset* Note the verb is in the subjunctive because the nega-tive relative clause illustrates a quality of the antecedent. Such relative clauses are analogous to result clauses.

COMPREHENSION QUESTIONS

Answer the following questions in Latin using the text on pp. 398 and 400. The Reading Vocabulary may be consulted.

1. Fuitne Atticus melior cīvis quam pater familiās?
2. Amābatne Atticus rēs novās emere et rēs novās aedificāre?
3. Eratne Atticō bona domus? Ubi erat et quālis?
4. Quās rēs Atticus domī mūtāre cupiēbat?
5. Quālēs erant Atticī servī?

VOCABULARY TO LEARN

NOUNS

aedificium, ī, n. – building
artifex, artificis, m. – craftsman, artisan
collis, collis, m. – hill
hērēditās, hērēditātis, f. – inheritance
sāl, salis, m. – salt, a quality that gives taste, wit
sūmptus, sūmptūs, m. – expense
tēctum, ī, n. – roof, house

ADJECTIVES

cēterus, a, um – remaining
ēlegāns, ēlegantis – careful in choosing, tasteful

litterātus, a, um – versed in literature, cultured
mediocris, mediocre – commonplace, mediocre, moderate
pār, paris – equal

VERBS

cōgō, ere, coēgī, coāctum – to compel, force
cōnstō, āre, cōnstitī, — + ablative – to consist in

CONJUNCTIONS

nē . . . quidem . . . – not even

Excavations of an upper-class Roman home in Ephesus, Turkey, share the decorative elements of homes back in the capital city—frescos on the walls, mosaic floors, *opus sectile* (cut stone) floors, an inner courtyard as evidenced by the column bases. One can imagine that the home of Atticus' uncle enjoyed similar features.

► EXERCISE 1

Two friends talk about Atticus' household. Each asks the other for repetition of his questions, answers, and requests, thus requiring the other to use indirect statements, indirect questions, and indirect commands when he repeats these things, as asked. Fill in the blanks in the answers with the needed indirect statements, indirect questions, and indirect commands as appropriate. The words to be changed into indirect expressions to fill each blank will be found in the lines of the previous speaker.

Amīcus prīmus Fuistīne, amīce, apud Atticum? Quid tē rogō?

Amīcus secundus Rogās, amīce, _____ .

Ita, fuī apud Atticum. Quid dīxī, amīce?

Amīcus prīmus Dīxistī, amīce, _____ .

Nārrā mihi dē tēctō Atticī. Quid tē ōrāvī, amīce?

Amīcus secundus Ōrāvistī mē, amīce, _____ .

Tēctum Atticī erat antīquum et bonum atque pulchram circā sē habēbat silvam. Quid nārrāvī?

Amīcus prīmus Nārrāvistī, amīce, _____ .

Quis domum Atticō hērēditāte dedit? Quid tē rogāvī?

Amīcus secundus Rogāvistī, amīce, _____ .

Avunculus domum Atticō hērēditāte dedit.

Vīsne mē plūra dē Atticī familiā tibi nārrāre? Quid tē rogō?

Amīcus prīmus Rogās, amīce, _____ . Ita. Ōrō ut plūra dē servīs quōs Atticus habēbat mihi dīcās. Quālibus servīs Atticī familia cōnstābat? Quid rogō?

Amīcus secundus Rogās, amīce, _____ . Atticī servī erant litterātī. Quid dīxī?

Amīcus prīmus Dīxistī, amīce, _____ .

Quālis ipse Atticus fuit? Quid rogāvī?

Amīcus secundus Rogāvistī, amīce, _____ .

Ipse Atticus fuit ēlegāns. Nōlēbat tamen ostendere sē multōs sūmptūs habēre posse.

6. LIKE A TRUE EPICUREAN

Atticus found true wealth and happiness in the quality of life rather than the quantity of possessions. This lifestyle matches the doctrines of the Greek philosopher Epicurus, who had lived several centuries before Atticus, and had asserted that the greatest good was pleasure. But for Epicurus (as for Atticus) the highest pleasure consists in moderation in all habits and the joys of an active, studious mind.

CORNĒLIĪ NEPŌTIS ATTICUS, 14–15

1 14. 1. Nēmō in convīviō ēius aliud acroāma audīvit quam anagnōstēn;
quod nōs quidem iūcundissimum arbitrāmur; neque umquam sine
aliquā lēctiōne apud eum cēnātum est, ut nōn minus animō quam
ventre convīvae dēlectārentur. 2. Namque eōs vocābat,
5 quōrum mōrēs ā suīs nōn abhorrērent. Cum tanta pecūniae facta
esset accessiō, nihil dē cottidiānō cultū mūtāvit, nihil dē vītae
cōnsuētūdine . . . 3. Nūllōs habuit hortōs, nūllam suburbānam aut
maritimam sūmptuōsam vīllam, neque in Italiā, praeter Ārrētīnum et
Nōmentānum, rūsticum praedium . . .

VOCABULARY

1   *convīvium, ī, n. – dinner party, feast

    acroāma, acroāmatis, n. – any form of entertainment

    anagnōstēs, ae, m. – reader

2   *arbitror, arbitrārī, arbitrātus sum –to judge, consider

3   *aliquis, aliqua, aliquid (used as a noun); aliquī, aliqua, aliquod (used as an adjective) – some

    lēctiō, lēctiōnis, f. – reading

    *cēnō, āre, āvī, ātum – to dine

4   venter, ventris, m. – stomach, belly

    convīva, ae, m./f. – dinner companion, guest

    *namque (conj.) – indeed, for, because

5   abhorreō, ēre, abhorruī, — + ablative – to be averse to, be different from

6   accessiō, accessiōnis, f. – addition, increase

    *cultus, cultūs, m. – care, management, way of living

7   *cōnsuētūdō, cōnsuētūdinis, f. – custom, habit

    *hortus, ī, m. – garden

    suburbānus, a, um – situated near Rome

8   maritimus, a, um – belonging to the sea, near the sea, maritime

    sūmptuōsus, a, um – costly, sumptuous

    *praeter + accusative – except, beside

    Ārrētīnus, a, um – connected with, near Arrētium, a town in Etruria

9   Nōmentānus, a, um – belonging to, near Nōmentum, a town in Latium

    praedium, ī, n. – estate, land

READING NOTES

1   *Nēmō in convīviō ēius aliud acroāma audīvit quam anagnōstēn* The Greek word *anagnōstēn* is in the Greek accusative case. The word *ēius*, "his," refers to Atticus.

2   *quod* This relative means "which thing" or "this thing."

2–3   *neque umquam . . . cēnātum est* The verb *cēnātum est* means "dinner took place" or "people dined." This is a common impersonal use of the third person singular passive.

3–4   *nōn minus animō quam ventre* The ablatives *animō* and *ventre* are ablatives of respect or specification. They specify in what respect the statement is true. "not less in <their> spirit than in <their> mind."

4   *eōs vocābat* "He called (invited) them (i.e., his guests)."

5   *quōrum mōrēs ā suīs nōn abhorrērent* The verb *abhorrērent* is subjunctive because it describes a general characteristic of the subject; it is similar to a subjunctive in a result clause.

5–6   *cum tanta . . . accessiō* "After so great an increase . . ."

10   15. 1. Mendācium neque dīcēbat neque patī poterat. Itaque ēius cōmitās nōn sine sevēritāte erat neque gravitās sine facilitāte, ut difficile esset intellēctū, utrum eum amīcī magis verērentur an amārent. Quidquid rogābātur, religiōsē prōmittēbat, quod nōn līberālis, sed levis arbitrābātur pollicērī, quod praestāre nōn posset.

15   2. Īdem in nītendō, quod semel annuisset, tantā erat cūrā, ut nōn mandātam, sed suam rem vidērētur agere . . .

VOCABULARY

10 *mendācium, ī, n. – lie

11 cōmitās, cōmitātis, f. – friendliness, courtesy
    sevēritās, sevēritātis, f. – sternness, severity
    facilitās, facilitātis, f. – easygoing, good nature

12 *utrum . . . an . . . (introducing a disjunctive question) – whether . . . or . . .

13 quisquis, quidquid – whoever, whatever
    religiōsē (adv.) – scrupulously, conscientiously

14 līberālis, līberāle – generous
    *polliceor, pollicērī, pollicitus sum – to promise

15 *nītor, nītī, nīsus/nīxus sum – to strive to achieve
    in nītendō – in striving
    annuō, ere, annuī, annūtum – to nod, grant, approve, assent
    *cūra, ae, f. – care, diligent

16 mandō, āre, āvī, ātum – to assign, order

    *Words marked with an asterisk will need to be memorized later in the chapter.

READING NOTES

10 *Mendācium neque dīcēbat neque patī poterat* Understand *mendācium* again as the object of *patī*.

11–12 *ut difficile esset intellēctū* The expression *difficile intellēctū* means "difficult to understand." The form *intellēctū* is a supine ending in –*u*, which, after certain adjectives, indicates the respect in which the meaning of the adjective is true.

13–14 *nōn līberālis, sed levis arbitrābātur pollicērī* The genitive of certain adjectives indicating the personality or quality of a person with a noun like *hominis* understood is joined with a linking verb to mean "it is the characteristic/mark of" the type of person indicated by the adjective. So in this passage the genitive means "he judged that it was not the mark of a generous person, but of a trivial one, to promise . . ."

15 *in nītendō* The word *nītendō* is a gerund in the ablative with the preposition *in*.
    quod The relative pronoun translates "for that which."
    tantā erat cūrā The phrase *tantā erat cūrā* is an ablative of quality which indicates a quality of the person to whom it refers. The phrase means "was of such great diligence" or "was so diligent."

COMPREHENSION QUESTIONS

Answer the following questions in Latin using the text on pp. 404 and 406. The Reading Vocabulary may be consulted.

1. Quōmodo in Atticī convīviīs convīvae dēlectābantur?
2. Quae alia acroāmata erant in Atticī convīviīs praeter lēctiōnēs?
3. Cum Atticus dīves factus esset, quid in ēius cōnsuētūdine est mūtātum?
4. Habēbatne Atticus vīllās sūmptuōsas atque hortōs?
5. Quid habēbat Atticus?
6. Quid Atticus dē mendāciīs putābat?
7. Fuitne Atticus sevērus an (or) facilis?
8. Amābantne magis Atticum ēius amīcī an (or) verēbantur?
9. Prōmittēbatne Atticus rēs facile?
10. Quid faciēbat Atticus, sī semel rem prōmīsit?

VOCABULARY TO LEARN

NOUNS

cōnsuētūdō, consuētūdinis, f. – custom, habit

convīvium, ī, n. – dinner party, feast

cultus, cultūs, m. – care, management, way of living

cūra, ae, f. – care

hortus, ī, m. – garden

mendācium, ī, n. – lie

PRONOUNS

aliquis, aliquid (used as a noun) – some ‡

aliquī, aliqua (aliquae), aliquod (used as an adjective) – some‡

VERBS

arbitror, arbitrārī, arbitrātus sum – to judge, consider

cēnō, āre, āvī, ātum – to dine

nītor, nītī, nīsus/nīxus sum – to strive, achieve

polliceor, pollicērī, pollicitus sum – to promise

CONJUNCTIONS

namque – indeed, for, because

PREPOSITION

praeter + accusative – except, beside

INTERROGATIVE PARTICLES

utrum . . . an . . . (introducing a disjunctive question) – whether . . . or . . .

‡Additional information about the words marked with the double dagger will be in the **Take Note** section that follows the Vocabulary to Learn.

TAKE NOTE

aliquis, aliquid The second part of this indefinite pronoun, the part after **ali–**, is declined like the interrogative pronoun *quis, quid*.

aliquī, aliqua (aliquae), aliquod Used as an adjective, the second part of this word, the part after **ali–**, is declined like the interrogative adjective *quī, quae, quod*.

▶ EXERCISE 1

Translate into Latin.

1. Atticus prepared dinner parties in order to please the spirits of his friends (*use a gerundive construction*).

2. While (i.e., among) dining (*use a gerund*), servants were reading with the greatest diligence.

3. People used to go to the dinner parties of Atticus not only in order to dine but in order to listen (*use supines in -um*).

4. Atticus was calling/inviting to the dinner parties only people most similar to himself.

5. To us Atticus' dinner parties seemed most delightful of all.

6. Atticus did not consider that gardens were to be bought.

7. Atticus tolerated lies less than the other vices.

8. I ask you to say whether you judge Atticus to have been too severe or too easygoing.

9. Atticus always strove/made effort in order that the promised things happened and never promised that which he could not do.

The British Museum, London, houses this marble bust of the Greek philosopher Epicurus. It is a Roman copy of what was probably a second or third century BCE Greek original. Epicurus influenced western thinking through the ages including the United States Declaration of Independence which notes that the "pursuit of happiness" is an "inalienable right."

7. ATTICUS AND CICERO

Here we learn about the friendship between Cicero and Atticus and their correspondence.

CORNĒLIĪ NEPŌTIS ATTICUS, 16

Some people mentioned by Nepos earlier in the text appear again in this excerpt. You met the dictator and the civil war leader Lucius Cornelius Sulla Felix in Chapters 3 and 6. Atticus emigrated to Athens in order to avoid the civil disturbances and conflicts which rocked the Roman world during the last century BCE. It was his long sojourn in Athens, the main city in the region of Greece called Attica, that gave him the surname "Atticus." Sulla nevertheless strove to have Atticus' friendship. Marcus Brutus, an extremely ambitious political figure and the leader of the conspiracy that led to Caesar's assassination, yet also a great orator and a scholar in philosophy, was mentioned in Chapters 13, 14, and 15 of this book, as well as in sections 1, 2, and 3 on pp. 378–390. Atticus did not abandon Brutus' family, when Brutus, after his final defeat, committed suicide.

The famous orator Quintus Hortensius, Cicero's rival and friend, appeared in Chapter 9. The same chapter also provided some information about Atticus' familiarity with Cicero. Atticus was a friend of Cicero's family from an early stage in his life. Atticus' sister was given in marriage to Cicero's brother Quintus. With Cicero, however, he was bound by special ties. Cicero's letters to Atticus, a major source of information about the late republic, were published in the first century CE. Nepos mentions a collection of eleven books of letters. Actually sixteen books have come down to us and so the collection was probably augmented after Nepos' time. No letters by Atticus to Cicero have survived.

1   16. 1. Hūmānitātis vērō nūllum afferre māius testimōnium possum,
quam quod adulēscēns īdem senī Sullae fuit iūcundissimus, senex
adulēscentī M. Brūtō, cum aequālibus autem suīs, Q. Hortēnsiō et M.
Cicerōne, sīc vīxit, ut iūdicāre difficile sit, cui aetātī fuerit aptissimus.

5   2. Quamquam eum praecipuē dīlēxit Cicero, ut nē frāter quidem eī
Quīntus cārior fuerit aut familiārior. 3. Eī reī sunt indiciō praeter eōs
librōs, in quibus dē eō facit mentiōnem, quī in vulgus sunt ēditī, ūndecim
volūmina epistulārum ab cōnsulātū ēius ūsque ad extrēmum tempus
ad Atticum missārum; quae quī legat, nōn multum dēsīderet historiam

10   contextam eōrum temporum. 4. Sīc enim omnia dē studiīs prīncipum,
vitiīs ducum, mūtātiōnibus reī pūblicae perscrīpta sunt, ut nihil in hīs
nōn appāreat et facile existimārī possit prūdentiam quōdam modō esse
dīvīnātiōnem. Nōn enim Cicero ea sōlum, quae vīvō sē accidērunt,
futūra praedīxit, sed etiam, quae nunc ūsū veniunt, cecinit ut vātēs.

READING VOCABULARY

1   *hūmānitās, hūmānitātis, f. – human character, kindness

    vērō (adv.) – moreover (introducing a further argument)

    afferō, afferre, attulī, allātum – to bring

    *testimōnium, ī, n. – testimony

3   aequālis, aequālis, m./f. – a person of the same age

4   *aptus, a, um – fitted, appropriate

5   *praecipuē (adv.) – particularly, especially

6   indicium, ī, n. – indication

7   mentiō, mentiōnis, f. – mention

    *vulgus, ī, n. – common people, general public

    ūndecim – eleven

8   volūmen, volūminis, n. – book

    cōnsulātus, cōnsulātūs, m. – consulship

    *ūsque (adv.) – right up; ūsque ad – up to

    *extrēmus, a, um – situated or occurring at the end, last

9   quae = et ea

    *dēsīderō, āre, āvī, ātum – to long for, desire, need, require

    historia, ae, f. – history, written account of past events

10   contexō, ere, contexuī, contextum – to join by weaving, compose

    *studium, ī, n. – pursuit, activity to which one is devoted

    *prīnceps, prīncipis, m. – leading citizen

11   mūtātiō, mūtātiōnis, f. – change

    perscrībō, ere, perscrīpsī, perscrīptum – to write a detailed account of

12   *appāreō, ēre, appāruī – to appear, be found

    *quīdam, quaedam, quiddam (used as a noun); quīdam, quaedam, quoddam (used as an adjective) – a certain

13   dīvīnātiō, dīvīnātiōnis, f. – prophecy, foreseeing

    *accidō, ere, accidī, — – to fall upon, happen

    praedīcō, ere, praedīxī, praedictum – to predict

14   *ūsus, ūsūs, m. – use; ūsū venīre – to occur

    *canō, ere, cecinī, cantum – to sing, make a prophetic statement

    vātēs, vatis, m. – prophet

    *Words marked with an asterisk will need to be memorized later in the chapter.

READING NOTES

1–2   *nūllum afferre māius testimōnium possum, quam quod.* The conjunction *quod* does not always have a causal meaning. Sometimes, as here, it introduces a clause with its verb(s) in the indicative, and it means "the fact that."

3–4   *cum aequālibus autem suīs* In this clause *autem* has no adversative meaning, it just continues the argument.

5   *Quamquam eum praecipuē dīlēxit Cicero* Here *quamquam*, with the meaning "however," does **not** introduce a subordinate clause.

6   *eī . . . indiciō* The dative of purpose *indiciō* means "as a sign, as an indication" Translate the dative of reference *eī reī* "of this thing."

7   *quī in vulgus sunt ēditī* The phrase *in vulgus ēdere* means "to publish," or, literally, "to give out into the populace at large."

9   *quae quī legat* Here *quae* is a relative, which refers to *volūmina* and means "these." And *quī* (the subject of *legat*) has the force of *quīcumque*, which means "whoever." The subjunctive verb *legat* has a potential sense.

10–11   *Sīc enim omnia . . . perscrīpta sunt* Understand with *perscrīpta sunt* ("have been written") the additional thought "in these letters," which follows from the preceding context.

11–12   *ut nihil in hīs nōn appāreat* The double negative *nihil . . . nōn* means "everything."

12   *possit* Use the impersonal meaning "it is able" to translate this word.

13   *vīvō sē* This ablative absolute means "while he (i.e., Cicero) was alive."

13–14   *ea . . . futūra* Translate "that those things would happen."

14   *ut vātēs* Translate "as a prophet."

COMPREHENSION QUESTIONS

Answer the following questions in Latin using the text on p. 410. The Reading Vocabulary may be consulted.

1. Cūr Nepōs dīcit Atticum habuisse hūmānitātem?

2. Quis Atticum optimē omnium dīligēbat?

3. Dīligēbatne Cicero magis Atticum an (or) frātrem suum?

4. Ubi discimus Cicerōnem Atticum valdē dīlēxisse?

5. Cūr Nepōs vocat Cicerōnis epistulās historiam illōrum temporum contextam?

6. Cūr Nepōs Cicerōnem vātem vocat?

VOCABULARY TO LEARN

NOUNS

hūmānitās, hūmānitātis, f. – human character, kindness

prīnceps, prīncipis, m. – leading citizen

studium, ī, n. – pursuit, activity to which one is devoted

testimōnium, ī, n. – testimony

ūsus, ūsūs, m. – use; ūsū venīre – to occur

vulgus, ī, n. – common people, general public

PRONOUNS

quīdam, quaedam, quiddam (used as a noun); quīdam, quaedam, quoddam (used as an adjective) – a certain

ADJECTIVES

aptus, a, um – fitted, appropriate

extrēmus, a, um – situated or occurring at the end, last

VERBS

accidō, ere, accidī, — – to fall upon, happen

appāreō, ēre, appāruī – to appear, be found

canō, ere, cecinī, cantum – to sing

dēsīderō, āre, āvī, ātum – to long for, desire, need, require

ADVERBS

praecipuē – particularly, especially

ūsque – right up; ūsque ad – up to

▶ EXERCISE 1

The following excerpt is adapted from Cicero's letter to Atticus (*Ad Atticum*, 2.21). Translate into English.

Cicero Atticō salūtem dīcit.

Dē rē pūblicā nesciō quid sit mihi scrībendum. Tōta perdita est et etiam miserior quam eō tempore quō eam relīquistī. Nam tum dominātiō vidēbātur cīvitātem oppressisse, quae iūcunda esset multitūdinī, bonīs autem molesta, sed sine perniciē. Nunc autem tantō in odiō est omnibus ut terribilia timeāmus. Utinam tempestātis trānsitum hominēs exspectāre potuissent! Sed iam diū tacentēs doluērunt et iam omnēs loquī atque clāmāre coepērunt.

Tē et ego dēsīderō et rēs ipsae iam vocant. Cūrā ut sciam quid agās atque ēgeris.

cīvitās, cīvitātis, f. – community of citizens, city, state

dominātiō, dominātiōnis, f. – rule, regime, dominion, tyranny

molestus, a, um – unpleasant

perniciēs, perniciēī, f. – ruin

transitus, transitūs, m. – transition, passing

The Münster church in Ulm, Germany, founded in 1377, boasts beautiful wooden choir stalls where the sculptor Jörg Syrlin (ca. 1470) carved this bust of Cicero. Cicero joins other ancient "pagans" like Terence and Ptolemy and the sibyls along with the apostles, various Christian saints, and the prophets and heroes of the Jewish scriptures.

8. ATTICUS THE AUTHOR

Nepos describes Atticus' writings.

CORNĒLIĪ NEPŌTIS ATTICUS, 18

Although nothing written by Atticus has come to us, he was not only a literary adviser to Cicero, but a writer in his own right, as we learn from Nepos' narrative.

1 18. 1. Mōris etiam māiōrum summus imitātor fuit antīquitātisque amātor; quam adeō dīligenter habuit cognitam, ut eam tōtam in eō volūmine exposuerit, quō magistrātūs ōrdināvit. 2. Nūlla enim lēx neque pāx neque bellum neque rēs illūstris est populī Rōmānī,

5 quae nōn in eō suō tempore sit notāta, et, quod difficillimum fuit, sīc familiārum orīginem subtexuit, ut ex eō clārōrum virōrum propāginēs possēmus cōgnoscere . . . 5. Attigit quoque poēticēn, crēdimus, nē ēius expers esset suāvitātis. Namque versibus, quī honōre rērumque gestārum amplitūdine cēterōs Rōmānī populī praestitērunt, 6. exposuit

10 ita, ut sub singulōrum imaginibus facta magistrātūsque eōrum nōn amplius quaternīs quīnīsque versibus dēscrīpserit: quod vix crēdendum sit, tantās rēs tam breviter potuisse dēclārārī. Est etiam ūnus liber Graecē cōnfectus, dē cōnsulātū Cicerōnis.

READING VOCABULARY

1   māiōrēs, māiōrum, m. pl. – ancestor

    imitātor, imitātōris, m. – imitator, emulator

    antīquitās, antīquitātis, f. – antiquity

2   amātor, amātōris, m. – lover

    *adeō (adv.) – to such an extent, so

    *dīligenter (adv.) – diligently, carefully

    habuit cognitam = cognōvit

3   *volūmen, volūminis, n. – book, volume

    expōnō, ere, exposuī, expositum – to set forth in words, describe, explain, relate about

    *magistrātus, magistrātūs, m. – office of a magistrate, magistracy

    ordinō, āre, āvī, ātum – to place in order

4   *illūstris, illūstre – distinguished, illustrious

5   notō, āre, āvī, ātum – to indicate, note

6   *orīgō, orīginis, f. – origin

    subtexō, ere, subtexuī, subtextum – to add as a supplement

    propāgō, propāginis, f. – offspring, progeny

7   attingō, ere, attigī, attāctum – to touch, engage in

8   *expers, expertis + genitive – having no share in, devoid of

    *suāvitās, suāvitātis, f. – sweetness, charm

    *versus, versūs, m. – line of writing, line of verse

8–9 *rēs gestae – past actions, deeds, exploits

9   amplitūdō, amplitūdinis, f. – size, importance

    praestō, āre, praestitī, praestitum – to be superior, make available, supply

10 *sub + ablative – under

    *singulī, ae, a – one apiece, one each (a distributive)

    *imāgō, imāginis, f. – image

11 *amplius (adv.) – a greater amount, a greater number, more

    quaternī, ae, a – four each (a distributive)

    quīnī, ae, a – five each (a distributive)

    dēscrībō, ere, dēscrīpsī, dēscrīptum – to describe

12 *breviter (adv.) – shortly, briefly

13 Graecē (adv.) – in Greek

    cōnficiō, ere, cōnfēcī, cōnfectum – to make, compose

    cōnsulātus, cōnsulātūs, m. – consulship

    *Words marked with an asterisk will need to be memorized later in the chapter.

READING NOTES

2   *quam* Translate the relative pronoun as the demonstrative "this," which refers to *antīquitātis*.

2–3 *eam tōtam in eō volūmine exposuerit, quō magistrātūs ordināvit* Apparently Atticus provided some sort of historical chronology in this work. Translate *quō* "in which."

5   *quae nōn in eō suō tempore sit notāta* The meaning is "which has not been indicated in this book (*in eō*) in the order of the time when it happened," or, more literally "at its own time."

6   *familiārum orīginem subtexuit* This seems to be a genealogy of distinguished families.

7   *poēticēn* This word is the accusative in Greek of *poēticē, poēticēs* which means "poetry."

8   *ēius* This pronoun means "its" or "of it" and refers to poetry, *poēticēn*.

    quī . . . praestitērunt Understand *illōs* as an antecedent to *quī* and translate "those who . . . were superior to."

8–9 *rērumque gestārum amplitūdine . . . praestitērunt* The phrase *rēs gestae* often (as here) has the simple meaning of "deeds."

10 *singulōrum* "of each one."

11–12 *quod vix crēdendum sit* The subjunctive here conveys potential sense. Translate *quod* "this thing."

COMPREHENSION QUESTIONS

Answer the following questions in Latin using the text on p. 414. The Reading Vocabulary may be consulted.

1. Cūius reī erat Atticus imitātor atque amātor?

2. Quās rēs scrīpsit Atticus?

3. Scrīpsitne Atticus tantum Latīnē?

4. Potuitne Atticus dē rēbus gestīs populī Rōmānī bene nārrāre?

5. Cūr Atticus carmina quoque scrīpsit?

6. Quid dē familiīs scrīpsit Atticus?

7. Quōmodo virōs illūstrēs dēscrīpsit Atticus?

VOCABULARY TO LEARN

NOUNS

imāgō, imāginis, f. – image, bust, painting

magistrātus, magistrātūs, m. – office of a magistrate, magistracy, magistrate

orīgō, orīginis, f. – origin

rēs gestae – past actions, deeds, exploits

suāvitās, suāvitātis, f. – sweetness, charm

versus, versūs, m. – line of writing, line of verse

volūmen, volūminis, n. – book, volume

ADJECTIVES

expers, expertis + genitive – having no share in, devoid of

illūstris, illūstre – distinguished, illustrious

singulī, ae, a – one apiece, one each (a distributive)

ADVERBS

adeō – to such an extent

amplius – a greater amount, a greater number, more

breviter – shortly, briefly

dīligenter – diligently, carefully

PREPOSITIONS

sub + ablative – under

▶ EXERCISE 1

In the following sentences, change all the relative and temporal clauses into participles or ablative absolute constructions. Remember that the subject of the main clause should always be different from the noun in the ablative absolute. Translate the sentences.

1. Atticus, quī mōribus antīquīs dēlectābātur, rēs gestās antīquōrum nārrāre voluit.

2. Cum omnia bella, lēgēs, pācēs, rēs illūstrēs dīligenter essent dēclārāta, liber Atticī nūllā rē eget.

3. Cum orīginēs clārōrum virōrum ostendere cuperet, Atticus dē māgnīs et antīquīs familiīs quoque scrīpsit.

4. Cum carmina vēram suāvitātem hominibus praestārent, Atticus illīus reī expers esse nōluit.

5. Postquam versūs dē singulīs clārīs virīs sunt scrīptī, Atticus librum carminum plēnum habuit.

6. Atticus, quī ā Cicerōne semper amīcus colēbātur, magistrātum Cicerōnis in volūminibus suīs neglegere nōn potuit.

9. ATTICUS, FRIEND OF THE EMPEROR

Nepos tells us more about Atticus' dealings with Augustus.

CORNĒLIĪ NEPŌTIS ATTICUS, 19–20

Despite his rather humble equestrian origin, Atticus becomes not only a relative, but also a friend to the first Roman emperor Octavian Augustus.

1　　19. 2 . . . Hic contentus ōrdine equestrī, quō erat ortus, in affīnitātem
pervēnit imperātōris, dīvī fīliī; cum iam ante familiāritātem ēius esset
cōnsecūtus nūllā aliā rē quam ēlegantiā vītae . . . 4. Nāta est autem
Atticō neptis ex Agrippā, cui virginem fīliam collocārat. Hanc

5　　Caesar vix anniculam Ti. Claudiō Nerōnī, Drusillā nātō, prīvignō
suō, despondit; quae coniūnctiō necessitūdinem eōrum sānxit,
familiāritātem reddidit frequentiōrem.

VOCABULARY

1   contentus, a, um – content

    *ōrdō, ōrdinis, m. – order, social class

    equester, equestris, equestre – equestrian; ordo equester – the order of knights

    *orior, orīrī, ortus sum + ablative – to be born of, be descended from, originate

    *affīnitās, affīnitātis, f. – relationship by marriage, connection

2   dīvus, ī, m. – god, deified emperor

3   *cōnsequor, cōnsecūtus sum, cōnsequī – to acquire, gain

    ēlegantia, ae, f. – fineness of taste, elegance

    *nāscor, nāscī, nātus sum – to be born

4   neptis, neptis, f. – granddaughter

    *virgō, virginis, f. – virgin, girl of marriageable age

    collocō, āre, āvī, ātum – to set up, give in marriage

5   anniculus, a, um – one year long (old), yearling

    prīvignus, ī, m. – stepson

6   dēspondeō, ēre, dēspondī, dēspōnsum – to promise a woman in marriage, betroth

    coniūnctiō, coniūnctiōnis, f. – connection

    *necessitūdō, necessitūdinis, f. – bond between people, relationship, connection

    *sanciō, īre, sānxī, sānctum – to ratify solemnly, confirm

7   reddō, ere, reddidī, redditum – to render, make, give back

    *frequēns, frequentis – frequent, assiduous

READING NOTES

1–2   *in affīnitātem pervēnit imperātōris, dīvī fīliī* The word *affīnitās* here means a family connection. The phrase *dīvī fīliī* refers to the fact that Augustus was the successor and the adopted son of the deified Julius Caesar.

2   *familiāritātem ēius* Translate "a familiarity with him (i.e., Augustus)"

3   *Nāta est autem Atticō neptis* In this sentence *autem* has virtually no adversative meaning but merely continues the narrative.

4   *collocārat* This is the syncopated/contracted form of *collocāverat.*

    Hanc Translate "this girl."

5   *Ti. Claudiō Nerōnī, Drusillā nātō,* The abbreviation *Ti.* stands for Tiberius and this complete name refers to Tiberius Claudius Nerō, also known as the emperor Tiberius. Livia Drusilla was Tiberius' mother and later a wife of Octavian Augustus.

6   *quae coniūnctiō* Translate this phrase "this connection."

7   *familiāritātem reddidit frequentiōrem.* I.e., the communication between them became more frequent. "It made the familiarity more frequent."

20. 1. Quamvīs ante haec spōnsālia nōn sōlum, cum ab urbe abesset, numquam ad suōrum quemquam litterās mīsit, quīn Atticō mitteret,

10 quid ageret, in prīmīs, quid legeret quibusque in locīs et quamdiū esset morātūrus, 2. sed etiam, cum esset in urbe et propter īnfīnītās suās occupātiōnēs minus saepe quam vellet, Atticō fruerētur, nūllus diēs temerē intercessit, quō nōn ad eum scrīberet, cum modo aliquid dē antīquitāte ab eō requīreret, modo aliquam quaestiōnem poēticam eī

15 prōpōneret, interdum iocāns ēius verbōsiōrēs ēliceret epistulās . . .

VOCABULARY

8   ante (adv.) – before

spōnsālia, ium, n. pl. – the act or the ceremony of betrothal

9   *quisquam, quicquam (quidquam) – any

*quīn (conj.) + subjunctive – without its being the case that

10   in prīmīs – in the first place

*quamdiū (interrogative adverb) – for how long

11   *moror, morārī, morātus sum – to stay for a long or short period, spend time

morātūrus esset – would be going to stay

12   occupātiō, occupātiōnis, f. – preoccupation with business, engagement

*fruor, fruī, fruitus/frūctus sum + ablative – to enjoy, enjoy the society of

13   temerē (adv.) – hardly, heedlessly, without good cause

intercēdō, ere, intercessī, intercessum – to intervene

14   *antīquitās, antīquitātis, f. – antiquity

requīrō, ere, requīsīvī, requīsītum – to ask, inquire about

quaestiō, quaestiōnis, f. – question, dispute

poēticus, a, um – poetic

15   prōpōnō, ere, prōposuī, prōpositum – to propose

iocor, iocārī, iocātus sum – to joke

verbōsus, a, um – containing many words, lengthy

ēliciō, ere, ēlicuī, ēlicitum – to coax, entice, elicit, call forth

*Words marked with an asterisk will need to be memorized later in the chapter.

READING NOTES

8   *cum ab urbe abesset* The subject is Augustus.

9   *ad suōrum quemquam* "To any of his (i.e., Augustus') people."

9–10   *quīn Atticō mitteret, quid ageret* With the phrase *quīn Atticō mitteret* ("without sending a letter to Atticus"), understand "telling him," and this thought governs the indirect question *quid ageret.*

12   *vellet* This imperfect subjunctive here has a contrary-to-fact sense.

13   *scrīberet* The subjunctive depends on the preceding negative clause *nūllus diēs intercessit.*

13–15   *cum modo . . . aliquid dē antīquitāte . . . requīreret, modo aliquam quaestiōnem poēticam . . . prōpōneret* The coordinating adverbs *modo . . . modo . . .* mean "at one time . . . at another time . . ."

COMPREHENSION QUESTIONS

Answer the following questions in Latin using the text on pp. 418 and 420. The Reading Vocabulary may be consulted.

1. Quō ōrdine ortus erat Atticus? Quid dē eō ōrdine sentiēbat?

2. Quōmodo familiāritātem imperātōris cōnsecūtus erat Atticus?

3. Quae erat affīnitās Atticī et imperātōris?

4. Scrībēbatne Augustus ad Atticum, cum ab urbe abesset? Sī scrībēbat, quā dē rē scrībēbat?

5. Cum Augustus Rōmae esset, vidēbatne Atticum tam saepe quam volēbat? Cūr?

6. Scrībēbatne Augustus ad Atticum, cum Rōmae esset? Sī scrībēbat, quā dē rē scrībēbat?

Augustus' forty-five-year reign brought prosperity and relative peace to the Roman Empire. Such a length ensured that his reforms and his transformation of the republic into the principate took deep root. This bronze coin celebrates Augustus.

VOCABULARY TO LEARN

NOUNS

affīnitās, affīnitātis, f. – relationship by marriage, connection

antīquitās, antīquitātis, f. – antiquity

necessitūdō, necessitūdinis, f. – bond

ōrdō, ōrdinis, m. – order, social class

virgō, virginis, f. – virgin, girl of marriageable age

PRONOUNS

quisquam, quicquam (quidquam) – any ‡

ADJECTIVES

frequēns, frequentis – frequent, assiduous

VERBS

cōnsequor, cōnsequī, cōnsecūtus sum – to acquire, gain

fruor, fruī, fruitus / frūctus sum + ablative – to enjoy, enjoy the society of

moror, morārī, morātus sum – to stay for a long or short period, spend time

nāscor, nāscī, nātus sum – to be born

orior, orīrī, ortus sum + ablative – to be born of, be descended from, originate

sanciō, īre, sānxī, sānctum – to ratify solemnly, confirm

ADVERBS

quamdiū (interrogative adverb) – for how long

CONJUNCTION

quīn + subjunctive – but that, without (after negative clauses)

‡Additional information about the words marked with the double dagger will be in the Take Note section that follows the Vocabulary to Learn.

TAKE NOTE

quisquam, quicquam (*quidquam*) Meaning "any," this word is used mainly in negative sentences. The part before *–quam* declines like the interrogative pronoun *quis, quid*.

▶ EXERCISE 1

Translate into Latin.

1. Although he was a knight, Atticus became familiar (i.e., came into familiarity) with the emperor.

2. Relationship by marriage originated between Atticus and the emperor, because Atticus' granddaughter was promised to the son of the emperor.

3. If Atticus' granddaughter had not been promised to the son of the emperor, the bond between (i.e., of) Atticus and the emperor would have nevertheless remained assiduous.

4. "If you give your granddaughter to my son, Atticus," said Augustus, "I will solemnly ratify this marriage."

5. "I would always enjoy your company, Atticus," said Augustus, "if there were not so many things which I had to do (*use the passive periphrastic*)."

The most famous statue of Augustus known as the "Augustus of Prima Porta" because it was found at his wife Livia's villa just outside Rome in Prima Porta. Tradition dates it to 15 CE just after Augustus' death. Probably based on an earlier bronze statue, Tiberius' commission added the conquest of the Parthians to Augustus' breastplate.

This view of the Forum of Augustus emphasizes its central feature, the Temple to Mars Ultor ("The Avenger"), built in thanksgiving for the defeat of the conspirators Brutus and Cassius at the Battle of Philippi in 42 BCE. Statues of famous Romans lined the side porticoes culminating in Aeneas and Romulus, the ancestral founders of the Julio-Claudian line.

10. THE DEATH OF ATTICUS

CORNĒLIĪ NEPŌTIS ATTICUS, 21–22

Atticus lived a very full life. In old age, however, he was beset by a painful illness, for which no cure could be found. So Atticus chose his own death (32 BCE).

1 21. Tālī modō cum VII et LXX annōs complēsset . . . tantāque
prosperitāte ūsus esset valētūdinis, ut annīs XXX medicīnā nōn
indiguisset, 2. nactus est morbum, quem initiō et ipse et medicī
contempsērunt . . . 3. . . . Postquam in diēs dolōrēs accrēscere
5 febrēsque accessisse sēnsit, Agrippam generum ad sē arcessī iūssit
et cum eō duōs amīcōs. 5. Hōs ut vēnisse vīdit, in cubitum innīxus
"Quantam" inquit "cūram dīligentiamque in valētūdine meā tuendā
hōc tempore adhibuerim, cum vōs testēs habeam, nihil necesse est
plūribus verbīs commemorāre. Quibus quoniam, ut spērō, satisfēcī
10 mē nihil reliquī fēcisse, quod ad sānandum mē pertinēret, reliquum
est, ut egomet mihi cōnsulam. 6. Id vōs ignōrāre nōluī.

VOCABULARY

1   cum + subjunctive – since, although

    VII et LXX = septem et septuāgintā – 77

    *compleō, ēre, complēvī, complētum – to fill, complete

2   prosperitās, prosperitātis, f. – fortunate state of things, prosperity

    *valētūdō, valētūdinis, f. – health

    XXX = trīgintā – 30

    medicīna, ae, f. – medicine

3   *indigeō, ēre, indiguī, — + ablative – to need, lack

    nancīscor, nancīscī, nactus (nānctus) sum – to gain possession of, acquire

    *morbus, ī, m. – illness, sickness

    medicus, ī, m. – doctor

4   *contemnō, ere, contempsī, contemptum – to regard with contempt, despise

    in diēs – daily, as the days proceed

    accrēscō, ere, accrēvī, accrētum – to increase in size

5   *febris, febris, f. – fever

    *accēdō, ere, accessī, accessum – to approach, be added

    gener, generī, m. – son-in-law

    arcessō, ere, arcessīvī, arcessītum – to send for, fetch

6   cubitum, cubitī, n. – elbow

    innītor, innītī, innīxus (innīsus) sum – to lean on

7   *tueor, tuērī, tuitus (tūtus) sum – to look at, protect

8   *adhibeō, ēre, adhibuī, adhibitum – to apply

    testis, testis, m. – witness

    nihil (adv.) – in no way, not at all

9   commemorō, āre, āvī, ātum – to recall

    satisfaciō, ere, satisfēcī, satisfactum – to satisfy

10   *reliquus, a, um – the rest of, the remaining

    pertineō, ēre, pertinuī, pertentum – to relate to, pertain to

11   *cōnsulō, ere, cōnsuluī, cōnsultum + dative – to take thought for

    ignōrō, āre, āvī, ātum – to have no knowledge, be ignorant of

READING NOTES

1   *complēsset* This is the syncopated or contracted form of *complēvisset.*

6   *Hōs ut vēnisse vīdit* The indicative with *ut* means "when."

7   *in valētūdine meā tuendā.* A gerundive construction with the preposition *in.*

9–10   *Quibus quoniam, ut spērō, satisfēcī mē nihil reliquī fēcisse* The connecting relative *quibus* refers back to *vōs testēs* and translates as a personal pronoun. It is dative because *satisfacere* takes the dative. The meaning is "Since, as I hope, I have satisfied you that . . ." The common phrase *nihil reliquī facere* contains a partitive genitive and means "leave nothing undone" (or, literally, "to make nothing of a remainder").

10   *quod ad sānandum mē pertinēret* The subjunctive verb *pertinēret* has a potential sense here.

10–11   *reliquum est, ut egomet mihi cōnsulam* While *cōnsulō, cōnsulere* + acc. means "to consult," with the dative, as here, the verb means "take thought for oneself" which is a less direct way of saying "think about ending one's life." The particle *–met* on *egomet* is used to emphasize the pronoun.

Nam mihi stat alere morbum dēsinere. Namque hīs diēbus quidquid cibī sūmpsī, ita prōdūxī vītam, ut auxerim dolōrēs sine spē salūtis. Quārē ā vōbīs petō, prīmum, ut cōnsilium probētis meum, deinde, nē frūstrā dehortandō

15 impedīre cōnēminī."

22. 1. Hāc ōrātiōne habitā tantā cōnstantiā vōcis atque vultūs, ut nōn ex vītā, sed ex domō in domum vidērētur migrāre, 2. cum quidem Agrippa eum flēns atque ōsculāns ōrāret atque obsecrāret, nē id, quod nātūra cōgeret, ipse quoque sibi accelerāret, et, quoniam tum

20 quoque posset temporibus superesse, sē sibi suīsque reservāret, precēs ēius taciturnā suā obstinātiōne dēpressit. 3. Sīc cum bīduum cibō sē abstinuisset, subitō febris dēcessit leviorque morbus esse coepit. Tamen prōpositum nihilō sētius perēgit. Itaque diē quīntō, postquam id cōnsilium inierat . . . dēcessit . . .

VOCABULARY

12   *dēsinō, ere, dēsiī, dēsitum – to stop

      quisquis, quidquid (quicquid) – whoever, what-
ever

      *sūmō, ere, sūmpsī, sūmptum – to take

13   prōdūcō, ere, prōdūxī, prōductum – to bring
forth, lengthen

      *quārē (conj.) – therefore, hence

14   *prīmum (adv.) – first

      *frūstrā (adv.) – in vain, to no avail

      dehortor, dehortārī, dehortātus sum – to discour-
age, dissuade

15   *impediō, īre, impedīvī, impedītum – to impede,
prevent

17   migrō, āre, āvī, ātum – to move from one place to
another

18   *fleō, ēre, flēvī, flētum – to cry

      ōsculor, ōsculārī, ōsculātus sum – to kiss

      obsecrō, āre, āvī, ātum – to beseech, entreat

19   accelerō, āre, āvī, ātum – to quicken, accelerate

20   supersum, superesse, superfuī, —— + dative – to
survive something

      reservō, āre, āvī, ātum – to keep, reserve

      *prex, precis, f. – prayer

21   taciturnus, a, um – silent

      obstinātiō, obstinātiōnis, f. – obstinacy, stub-
bornness

      dēprimō, ere, dēpressī, dēpressum – to repress

      bīduum, ī, n. – a period of two days

22   abstineō, ēre, abstinuī, abstentum – to keep away;
sē abstinet – s/he abstains

      *dēcēdō, ere, dēcessī, dēcessum – to go away, die

23   prōpositum, ī, n. – intention, proposition

      nihilō sētius – none the less, just the same

      peragō, ere, perēgī, perāctum – to carry out, per-
form

      quīntus, a, um – fifth

24   ineō, īre, inīvī (iniī), initum – to go into;
cōnsilium inīre – to form a plan

      *Words marked with an asterisk will need to be
memorized later in the chapter.

READING NOTES

11–12   *Nam mihi stat alere morbum dēsinere* The phrase
mihi stat, or sometimes *sententia stat*, completed by an infinitive, means "I am resolved to" or
"I have made up my mind to"

12   *quidquid cibī* The genitive is partitive.

14–15   *nē frūstrā dehortandō impedīre cōnēminī* Understand the pronoun "me" with both *dehortandō*
and *impedīre*.

16   *Hāc ōrātiōne habitā* The phrase *ōrātiōnem habēre*
means "to make a speech" and here is found in
an ablative absolute.

18–20   *nē id, quod nātūra cōgeret, ipse quoque sibi
accelerāret, et, quoniam tum quoque posset temporibus superesse, sē sibi suīsque reservāret, precēs
ēius* The meaning of *tempora* here is "crisis." It
is dative because it is to be understood with
superesse. Also, understand *ut* after *et*, in a parallel construction with *nē* at the beginning of the
clause. Both *cōgeret* and *posset* are subjunctives
due to the attraction of moods (if a subordinate
clause already has an infinitive or a subjunctive,
any other subordinate clause depending on it
will often have a subjunctive verb also). Translate *sē sibi suīsque reservāret* " to save himself
for himself and for his own people." The phrase
precēs ēius, "his prayers," refers to Agrippa's
prayers.

COMPREHENSION QUESTIONS

Answer the following questions in Latin using the text on pp. 424 and 426. The Reading Vocabulary may be consulted.

1. Quālis fuit valētūdō Atticī per tōtam vītam?
2. Solēbatne Atticus medicīnās capere?
3. Cūr Atticus Agrippam cum duōbus amīcīs arcessīvit?
4. Quod erat Atticī prōpositum?
5. Quid putābat Atticus dē cibō quem sūmpserat?
6. Quam rem nōlēbat Atticus impedīre?
7. Quō animō Atticus dīxit sē velle morī?
8. Quid tum fēcit Agrippa?
9. Fēcitne Atticus id quod Agrippa rogāverat?
10. Quid tandem est factum?

VOCABULARY TO LEARN

NOUNS

febris, febris, f. – fever
morbus, ī, m. – illness, sickness
prex, precis, f. – prayer
valētūdō, valētūdinis, f. – health

ADJECTIVES

reliquus, a, um – the rest of, the remaining

VERBS

accēdō, ere, accessī, accessum – to approach, be added
adhibeō, ēre, adhibuī, adhibitum – to apply
compleō, ēre, complēvī, complētum – to fill, complete
cōnsulō, ere, cōnsuluī, cōnsultum + dative – to look after; + accusative – to consult
contemnō, ere, contempsī, contemptum – to regard with contempt, despise

dēcēdō, ere, decessī, decessum – to go away, die
dēsinō, ere, dēsiī, dēsitum – to stop
fleō, ēre, flēvī, flētum – to cry
impediō, īre, impedīvī, impedītum – to impede, prevent
indigeō, ēre, indiguī, — + ablative – to need, lack
sūmō, ere, sūmpsī, sūmptum – to take
tueor, tuērī, tuitus (tūtus) sum – to look at, protect

ADVERBS

frustrā – in vain, to no avail
prīmum – first

CONJUNCTIONS

quārē – therefore, hence

▶ EXERCISE 1

The following sentences may have been exchanged in the dialogue between Atticus and Agrippa. Translate them into Latin paying special attention to the use of the subjunctive in a main clause.

1. (Please) approach me, friend!

2. Let us stop weeping and let us talk!

3. If only you were not regarding your life with contempt!

4. If only my health had remained prosperous!

5. Do not impede me with your prayers!

6. (Please) take food and protect your health!

7. May the fevers leave!

8. May you complete many years!

9. Let us apply every cure and diligence so that our friend may be healed!

10. You ask in vain. (Please) allow me to die now!

APPENDIX A

HISTORICAL TIMELINE

Authors and Literature		Roman and European History
		Later Roman History*
	379–395	Reign of Theodosius in both halves of the Roman Empire
	ca. 405	The Vulgate Latin translation of the Bible is completed by Jerome
	408–450	Reign of Theodosius II in the Eastern Empire
	ca. 461	St. Patrick dies
	476	Romulus Augustulus abdicates
Early Middle Ages	**ca. 500–ca. 1000**	**Early Middle Ages**
Boethius	ca. 480–524	
	493–526	Theodoric the Ostrogoth, *Rēx Ītaliae*, rules Italy
	507	Frankish king Clovis defeats Visigoth kings in Southern Gaul: they rule in Spain
	511	Clovis dies; kingdom in Gaul is divided among his four sons
	527–565	Justinian rules Eastern Roman Empire, conquers Vandals in North Africa, establishes Exarchate of Ravenna, codifies Roman law
	ca. 540–600	Anglo-Saxon heptarchy rises
	552	Justinian crushes Ostrogoths in Italy, takes part of Spain from Visigoths
	558	Lombards invade northern Italy
Isidore of Seville	ca. 560–636	
	590	Gregory the Great becomes Pope. The first Archbishop of Canterbury named Augustine, baptizes Aethelbert of Kent first Anglo-Saxon Christian king
	623	Pepin I becomes Mayor of the Palace and *dē factō* ruler in Gaul
	ca. 610–632	The Quran, sacred book of Islam, is compiled
	634–41	Muslims conquer Syria and Egypt

*Earlier Roman History can be found on pp. 411–414 of Level 1.
NB: Sometimes historical periods overlap due to geographical differences. For example, while the Renaissance began in Italy in the fifteenth century, northern Europe was still in the midst of the Late Middle Ages.

	655	Penda of Mercia, last pagan king in Anglo-Saxon England, dies
Venerable Bede	ca. 673–735	
	698	Carthage, last Byzantine stronghold in Africa, taken by Muslims
	711	Muslims defeat Visigoths in Spain
	732	Muslims advance into southern Gaul from Spain; stopped by Charles Martel at Poitiers
	756	Donation of Pepin begins the Papal States
	768	Charlemagne becomes King of the Franks
	757–77	Offa II of Mercia gains power over much of Britain
Einhard	775–840	
	787	Viking ships appear on coast of Britain
	800	Charlemagne crowned *Imperātor Rōmānōrum* in Rome
	814	Charlemagne dies, leaves huge kingdom, including France, Germany, the Low Countries and much of Italy, to his surviving son Louis the Pious
	833	Moravian Empire founded
	844–5	Vikings attack Spain, Hamburg, and Paris
	859	University of Al-Karaouine is founded in Fes, Morocco
	862	St. Cyril and St. Methodius sent to Christianize Slavs; Slavonic joins Latin and Greek as a liturgical language
	871	Alfred the Great becomes King of Wessex
	896	Magyars pillage eastern Danube region
	910	William of Aquitaine founds monastery of Cluny
	912	Charles the Simple, Frankish king, cedes Norman land to Rollo the Viking
	924	Aethelstan becomes king of much of Britain
	955	Treaty between Muslims and Christians strengthens Christian kingdoms in Spain
	962	Otto I of Germany crowned Holy Roman Emperor by Pope John XII
	980–1037	Avicenna, renowned Muslim thinker, flourishes in intellectual center Baghdad
	987	Hugh Capet becomes King of Île de France in western Francia
High Middle Ages	**ca. 1000–ca. 1300**	**High Middle Ages**
	1020	Danish king Cnut unites England, Norway, and Denmark—North Sea Empire
	1018	Byzantine Basil II takes Bulgaria
	1034	Caliphate of Cordova disintegrates into petty Muslim fiefdoms

	1037	William becomes Duke of Normandy; Seljuk Turks expand Ghaznavid Empire in Persia
	1043–60	Seljuks gain Iran and Iraq
	1043–99	"El Cid," Rodrigo Díaz de Vivar, national hero of Spain
	1046	German king Henry III calls Synod of Sutri, resolves disputes between three rival popes, is crowned Holy Roman Emperor on Christmas Day by new Pope Clement II
	1060	Normans take parts of Italy and Sicily
	1066	Battle of Hastings: William of Normandy (becomes the "Conqueror") takes Anglo-Saxon England
	1076	Seljuk Turks capture Jerusalem
	1078	Sulayman declared Sultan of Rum, laying claim to former Roman/Byzantine lands in Asia Minor
Peter Abelard	1079–1142	
	1085	Christians capture Toledo, Alfonso VI preserves Mudejar community system
	ca. 1088	University of Bologna founded
	1095	Pope Urban II preaches First Crusade at Council of Clermont
	1098	First Crusader state, Edessa, founded
	1099	Crusaders take Jerusalem
	1100–1145	Geoffrey of Monmouth chronicles Arthurian Legend
	1106	Henry I of England takes Normandy
	1108	Louis VI becomes King of France
	1109	Crusader Raymond of Toulouse takes Tripoli
	ca. 1110	Abul-Qasim Ferdowsi publishes the Persian epic, *Shahnameh* (*Book of Kings*)
	1115	Florence becomes commune ruled by nobles; Bernard of Clairvaux founds Abbey of Cîteaux
	1116	al-Battani's *Kitab al-Zij* is translated into Latin as *Dē motū stellārum*
	1118	Knights Templar founded in Jerusalem
	1124	Crusaders take Tyre from Muslims
	1126–98	Ibn Rushd, "Averroës," great Muslim commentator on Aristotle
William of Tyre	1130–1185	
	1143	Rome and Venice become communes ruled by nobles
	1144	Seljuks overrun Edessa, triggering the Second Crusade
	1147	Alfonso I and Crusaders defeat Muslims in Spain
	ca. 1150	*Carmina Burāna* compiled

	1152	Henry of Anjou marries Eleanor of Aquitaine, founding the Plantagenet dynasty of England and France
	1155	Frederick Barbarossa becomes Holy Roman Emperor
	ca. 1160	University of Paris founded
Archpoet	fl. ca. 1163	
	1169	Saladin becomes ruler of Egypt under Seljuks
	1174–87	Saladin takes most of the Crusader cities
	1176	Seljuks defeat Byzantium
	1180	Philip II Augustus becomes King of France
	1189	Richard the Lionhearted becomes King of England & leader of Third Crusade
	1190	Frederick Barbarossa, one of the leaders of the Third Crusade, drowns in Turkey
	1192	Richard the Lionhearted and Saladin sign a truce that gives Christians access to Jerusalem
	ca. 1200	University of Oxford founded
	1204	Crusaders of Fourth Crusade loot Constantinople
	ca. 1214–1294	Roger Bacon conducts scientific experiments
	1215	King John of England signs *Māgna Carta*
	1220	Frederick II, King of Germany, Italy and Burgundy, becomes Holy Roman Emperor
	ca. 1225–1274	Thomas Aquinas synthesizes Aristotelianism and Christian theology
	1230	Teutonic Knights conquer pagan Prussians
	1236–48	Muslim strongholds in Spain fall to Christians
	1240–1	Mongols invade Poland and Hungary; withdraw on the death of Ogedei Khan
	1259	Louis IX, King of France, launches Seventh Crusade
	ca. 1280	Simon of Keza compiles *Gesta Hungarōrum*
	1284–96	Edward I of England takes Wales and Scotland
Late Middle Ages	**ca. 1300–ca.1500**	**Late Middle Ages**
Petrarch*	1304–74	
	1309–77	Papal Court in Avignon
	1315	Major famine brought on by Little Ice Age
	1326–71	Ottoman Empire expands into Balkans
	1337	Hundred Years War between England and France begins
	1338	Declaration of Rense; Holy Roman Emperor chosen by German electors, not Pope
	1347	Black Death reaches Europe

*Petrarch is considered the first Renaissance humanist.

	1370–1444	Leonardo Bruni, Florentine politician and humanist*
	1377	Papacy returns to Rome
	1378–1417	Western Schism in Roman Catholic Church
	1382	Wycliffe translates Bible into English
Lorenzo Valla**	1407–57	
	ca. 1418	Prince Henry founds a school of navigation
Renaissance	**ca. 1400–ca. 1600**	**Renaissance**
	1451–1506	Christopher Columbus
	1453	Constantinople taken by Ottomans; last battle of Hundred Years War fought
	1454–1512	Amerigo Vespucci
	1455	English Wars of the Roses begin; Gutenberg prints his Bible
Erasmus	1466–1536	
Peter Martyr	1457–1526	
Copernicus	1473–1543	
Thomas More	1478–1535	
	1485	Ferdinand and Isabella begin Spanish Inquisition
	1486–1576	Bartolomé de las Casas, defender of the rights of indigenous peoples of New World
	1488	Dias sails around the Cape of Good Hope
Juan Sepúlveda	1494–1573	
	1492	Columbus crosses the Atlantic
	1492	Ferdinand and Isabella drive the last Moorish ruler from Spain
	1492	Expulsion of Jews from Spain; Ottoman Sultan invites refugees to Salonika, Greece
	1495	Maximilian I shores up Holy Roman Empire
	1497–98	Vasco da Gama sails around Africa to India
	1515	Francis I becomes King of France
	1517	Luther presents his Ninety-Five Theses beginning Protestant Reformation
	1519	Charles V, King of Spain, becomes Holy Roman Emperor
	1521	Cortés takes Aztec capital
	1533	Pizarro takes Inca Empire
	1534	Henry VIII establishes Church of England
	1536–39	Dano-Norwegian Kingdom becomes Lutheran
	1538	University of Santo Domingo begun

* Bruni flourished during the Italian Renaissance.
**Valla flourished during the Italian Renaissance.

Petreus Maffeius	1536–1603	
	1540	Ignatius of Loyola founds Jesuit Order, key group in Catholic Counter Reformation
	1541	John Calvin starts Reformed Church
	1545–1563	Council of Trent formulates Counter Reformation
Galileo Galilei	1564–1642	
Johannes Kepler	1571–1630	
	1571	Don Juan of Austria defeats the Turks
	1577–80	Francis Drake sails around the world
	1580	Spain, Portugal, and their vast empires united
	1584	English colony Virginia founded
	1588	English defeat Spanish Armada
	1592–1670	John Amos Comenius, Czech reformer advocates universal education, compiles Latin picture dictionary
	1594	Henry IV becomes Catholic and king of France
	1596	Ottoman European advance ends in Hungary
	1596–1650	René Descartes
	1616	Thirty Years War between France and Holy Roman Empire Habsburgs begins
	1620	English immigrants arrive in Massachusetts
	1636	Harvard College founded in Cambridge, Massachusetts
Antonius de Leeunwenhoek	1632–1723	
	1642	Civil War in England between king and Parliament
	1643	Louis XIV becomes King of France
	1649	Charles I, King of England, executed
	1660	Charles II regains throne of England
Ludvig Holberg	1684–1754	
	1726	Swift's *Gulliver's Travels* published

APPENDIX B

GRAMMATICAL FORMS AND PARADIGMS

Only forms taught in *Latin for the New Millennium*, Levels 1 and 2, are listed in this appendix.

NOUNS

DECLENSIONS OF NOUNS

First Declension: *lupa**

	Singular	Plural
Nominative	lupa	lupae
Genitive	lupae	lupārum
Dative	lupae	lupīs
Accusative	lupam	lupās
Ablative	lupā	lupīs
Vocative	lupa	lupae

*The nouns *dea* and *filia* have irregular dative and ablative plurals: *deābus* and *filiābus*.

Second Declension: *amīcus*

	Singular	Plural
Nominative	amīcus	amīcī
Genitive	amīcī	amīcōrum
Dative	amīcō	amīcīs
Accusative	amīcum	amīcōs
Ablative	amīcō	amīcīs
Vocative	amīce	amīcī

Second Declension: *puer*

	Singular	Plural
Nominative	puer	puerī
Genitive	puerī	puerōrum
Dative	puerō	puerīs
Accusative	puerum	puerōs
Ablative	puerō	puerīs
Vocative	puer	puerī

Second Declension: *ager*

	Singular	Plural
Nominative	ager	agrī
Genitive	agrī	agrōrum
Dative	agrō	agrīs
Accusative	agrum	agrōs
Ablative	agrō	agrīs
Vocative	ager	agrī

Second Declension: *vir*

	Singular	Plural
Nominative	vir	virī
Genitive	virī	virōrum
Dative	virō	virīs
Accusative	virum	virōs
Ablative	virō	virīs
Vocative	vir	virī

Second Declension: *bellum*

	Singular	Plural
Nominative	bellum	bella
Genitive	bellī	bellōrum
Dative	bellō	bellīs
Accusative	bellum	bella
Ablative	bellō	bellīs
Vocative	bellum	bella

Third Declension: Masculine and Feminine Nouns

	Singular	Plural
Nominative	passer	passerēs
Genitive	passeris	passerum
Dative	passerī	passeribus
Accusative	passerem	passerēs
Ablative	passere	passeribus
Vocative	passer	passerēs

Third Declension: Neuter Nouns

	Singular	Plural
Nominative	tempus	tempora
Genitive	temporis	temporum
Dative	temporī	temporibus
Accusative	tempus	tempora
Ablative	tempore	temporibus
Vocative	tempus	tempora

Third Declension: *I*-stem Nouns
Same Number of Syllables (Masculine and Feminine)

	Singular	Plural
Nominative	cīvis	cīvēs
Genitive	cīvis	cīvium
Dative	cīvī	cīvibus
Accusative	cīvem	cīvēs
Ablative	cīve	cīvibus
Vocative	cīvis	cīvēs

Third Declension: *I*-stem Nouns
Different Number of Syllables (Masculine and Feminine)

	Singular	Plural
Nominative	urbs	urbēs
Genitive	urbis	urbium
Dative	urbī	urbibus
Accusative	urbem	urbēs
Ablative	urbe	urbibus
Vocative	urbs	urbēs

Third Declension: *I*-stem Nouns
(Neuters in -*al*, -*ar*, -*e*)

	Singular	Plural
Nominative	mare	maria
Genitive	maris	marium
Dative	marī	maribus
Accusative	mare	maria
Ablative	marī	maribus
Vocative	mare	maria

Third Declension Irregular Noun: *vīs*

	Singular	Plural
Nominative	vīs	vīrēs
Genitive	—	vīrium
Dative	—	vīribus
Accusative	vim	vīrēs
Ablative	vī	vīribus
Vocative	vīs	vīrēs

Fourth Declension: Masculine and Feminine Nouns

	Singular	Plural
Nominative	tumultus	tumultūs
Genitive	tumultūs	tumultuum
Dative	tumultuī	tumultibus
Accusative	tumultum	tumultūs
Ablative	tumultū	tumultibus
Vocative	tumultus	tumultūs

Fourth Declension: Neuter Nouns

	Singular	Plural
Nominative	cornū	cornua
Genitive	cornūs	cornuum
Dative	cornū	cornibus
Accusative	cornū	cornua
Ablative	cornū	cornibus
Vocative	cornū	cornua

Fourth Declension Irregular Noun: *domus*

	Singular	Plural
Nominative	domus	domūs
Genitive	domūs	domuum (domōrum)
Dative	domuī (domō)	domibus
Accusative	domum	domōs (domūs)
Ablative	domō (domū)	domibus
Vocative	domus	domūs

Fifth Declension: *rēs*

	Singular	Plural
Nominative	rēs	rēs
Genitive	reī	rērum
Dative	reī	rēbus
Accusative	rem	rēs
Ablative	rē	rēbus
Vocative	rēs	rēs

Fifth Declension: *diēs*

	Singular	Plural
Nominative	diēs	diēs
Genitive	diēī	diērum
Dative	diēī	diēbus
Accusative	diem	diēs
Ablative	diē	diēbus
Vocative	diēs	diēs

ADJECTIVES

DECLENSIONS OF POSITIVE ADJECTIVES

Adjectives of the First and Second Declension: *iūstus*

	Singular			Plural		
	Masculine	Feminine	Neuter	Masculine	Feminine	Neuter
Nominative	iūstus	iūsta	iūstum	iūstī	iūstae	iūsta
Genitive	iūstī	iūstae	iūstī	iūstōrum	iūstārum	iūstōrum
Dative	iūstō	iūstae	iūstō	iūstīs	iūstīs	iūstīs
Accusative	iūstum	iūstam	iūstum	iūstōs	iūstās	iūsta
Ablative	iūstō	iūstā	iūstō	iūstīs	iūstīs	iūstīs
Vocative	iūste	iūsta	iūstum	iūstī	iūstae	iūsta

Adjectives of the First and Second Declension: *pulcher*

	Singular			Plural		
	Masculine	Feminine	Neuter	Masculine	Feminine	Neuter
Nominative	pulcher	pulchra	pulchrum	pulchrī	pulchrae	pulchra
Genitive	pulchrī	pulchrae	pulchrī	pulchrōrum	pulchrārum	pulchrōrum
Dative	pulchrō	pulchrae	pulchrō	pulchrīs	pulchrīs	pulchrīs
Accusative	pulchrum	pulchram	pulchrum	pulchrōs	pulchrās	pulchra
Ablative	pulchrō	pulchrā	pulchrō	pulchrīs	pulchrīs	pulchrīs
Vocative	pulcher	pulchra	pulchrum	pulchrī	pulchrae	pulchra

Adjectives of the First and Second Declension: *miser*

	Singular			Plural		
	Masculine	Feminine	Neuter	Masculine	Feminine	Neuter
Nominative	miser	misera	miserum	miserī	miserae	misera
Genitive	miserī	miserae	miserī	miserōrum	miserārum	miserōrum
Dative	miserō	miserae	miserō	miserīs	miserīs	miserīs
Accusative	miserum	miseram	miserum	miserōs	miserās	misera
Ablative	miserō	miserā	miserō	miserīs	miserīs	miserīs
Vocative	miser	misera	miserum	miserī	miserae	misera

Adjectives of the Third Declension: Three Nominative Endings

	Singular			Plural		
	Masculine	Feminine	Neuter	Masculine	Feminine	Neuter
Nominative	ācer	ācris	ācre	ācrēs	ācrēs	ācria
Genitive	ācris	ācris	ācris	ācrium	ācrium	ācrium
Dative	ācrī	ācrī	ācrī	ācribus	ācribus	ācribus
Accusative	ācrem	ācrem	ācre	ācrēs	ācrēs	ācria
Ablative	ācrī	ācrī	ācrī	ācribus	ācribus	ācribus
Vocative	ācer	ācris	ācre	ācrēs	ācrēs	ācria

Adjectives of the Third Declension: Two Nominative Endings

	Singular		Plural	
	Masculine/Feminine	Neuter	Masculine/Feminine	Neuter
Nominative	fortis	forte	fortēs	fortia
Genitive	fortis	fortis	fortium	fortium
Dative	fortī	fortī	fortibus	fortibus
Accusative	fortem	forte	fortēs	fortia
Ablative	fortī	fortī	fortibus	fortibus
Vocative	fortis	forte	fortēs	fortia

Adjectives of the Third Declension: One Nominative Ending

	Singular			Plural		
	Masculine	Feminine	Neuter	Masculine	Feminine	Neuter
Nominitive	fēlīx	fēlīx	fēlīx	fēlīcēs	fēlīcēs	fēlīcia
Genitive	fēlīcis	fēlīcis	fēlīcis	fēlīcium	fēlīcium	fēlīcium
Dative	fēlīcī	fēlīcī	fēlīcī	fēlīcibus	fēlīcibus	fēlīcibus
Accusative	fēlīcem	fēlīcem	fēlīx	fēlīcēs	fēlīcēs	fēlīcia
Ablative	fēlīcī	fēlīcī	fēlīcī	fēlīcibus	fēlīcibus	fēlīcibus
Vocative	fēlīx	fēlīx	fēlīx	fēlīcēs	fēlīcēs	fēlīcia

DECLENSIONS OF COMPARATIVE ADJECTIVES

Declension of Comparative Adjectives

	Singular		Plural	
	Masculine/Feminine	Neuter	Masculine/Feminine	Neuter
Nominative	fortior	fortius	fortiōrēs	fortiōra
Genitive	fortiōris	fortiōris	fortiōrum	fortiōrum
Dative	fortiōrī	fortiōrī	fortiōribus	fortiōribus
Accusative	fortiōrem	fortius	fortiōrēs	fortiōra
Ablative	fortiōre	fortiōre	fortiōribus	fortiōribus
Vocative	fortior	fortius	fortiōrēs	fortiōra

Declension of Comparative Adjectives ending in –er: *pulcher*

	Singular		Plural	
	Masculine/Feminine	Neuter	Masculine/Feminine	Neuter
Nominative	pulchrior	pulchrius	pulchriōrēs	pulchriōra
Genitive	pulchriōris	pulchriōris	pulchriōrum	pulchriōrum
Dative	pulchriōrī	pulchriōrī	pulchriōribus	pulchriōribus
Accusative	pulchriōrem	pulchrius	pulchriōrēs	pulchriōra
Ablative	pulchriōre	pulchriōre	pulchriōribus	pulchriōribus
Vocative	pulchrior	pulchrior	pulchriōrēs	pulchriōra

Declension of Comparative Adjectives ending in –er: *miser*

	Singular		Plural	
	Masculine/Feminine	Neuter	Masculine/Feminine	Neuter
Nominative	miserior	miserius	miseriōrēs	miseriōra
Genitive	miseriōris	miseriōris	miseriōrum	miseriōrum
Dative	miseriōrī	miseriōrī	miseriōribus	miseriōribus
Accusative	miseriōrem	miserius	miseriōrēs	miseriōra
Ablative	miseriōre	miseriōre	miseriōribus	miseriōribus
Vocative	miserior	miserior	miseriōrēs	miseriōra

DECLENSIONS OF SUPERLATIVE ADJECTIVES

Declension of Superlative Adjectives

Singular

	Masculine	Feminine	Neuter
Nominative	fortissimus	fortissima	fortissimum
Genitive	fortissimī	fortissimae	fortissimī
Dative	fortissimō	fortissimae	fortissimō
Accusative	fortissimum	fortissimam	fortissimum
Ablative	fortissimō	fortissimā	fortissimō
Vocative	fortissime	fortissima	fortissimum

Plural

	Masculine	Feminine	Neuter
Nominative	fortissimī	fortissimae	fortissima
Genitive	fortissimōrum	fortissimārum	fortissimōrum
Dative	fortissimīs	fortissimīs	fortissimīs
Accusative	fortissimōs	fortissimās	fortissima
Ablative	fortissimīs	fortissimīs	fortissimīs
Vocative	fortissimī	fortissimae	fortissima

Declension of Superlative Adjectives ending in –er

Singular

	Masculine	Feminine	Neuter
Nominative	pulcherrimus	pulcherrima	pulcherrimum
Genitive	pulcherrimī	pulcherrimae	pulcherrimī
Dative	pulcherrimō	pulcherrimae	pulcherrimō
Accusative	pulcherrimum	pulcherrimam	pulcherrimum
Ablative	pulcherrimō	pulcherrimā	pulcherrimō
Vocative	pulcherrime	pulcherrima	pulcherrimum

Plural

	Masculine	Feminine	Neuter
Nominative	pulcherrimī	pulcherrimae	pulcherrima
Genitive	pulcherrimōrum	pulcherrimārum	pulcherrimōrum
Dative	pulcherrimīs	pulcherrimīs	pulcherrimīs
Accusative	pulcherrimōs	pulcherrimās	pulcherrima
Ablative	pulcherrimīs	pulcherrimīs	pulcherrimīs
Vocative	pulcherrimī	pulcherrimae	pulcherrima

Declension of Superlative Adjectives ending in –*lis**

Singular

	Masculine	Feminine	Neuter
Nominative	facillimus	facillima	facillimum
Genitive	facillimī	facillimae	facillimī
Dative	facillimō	facillimae	facillimō
Accusative	facillimum	facillimam	facillimum
Ablative	facillimō	facillimā	facillimō
Vocative	facillime	facillima	facillimum

Plural

	Masculine	Feminine	Neuter
Nominative	facillimī	facillimae	facillima
Genitive	facillimōrum	facillimārum	facillimōrum
Dative	facillimīs	facillimīs	facillimīs
Accusative	facillimōs	facillimās	facillima
Ablative	facillimīs	facillimīs	facillimīs
Vocative	facillimī	facillimae	facillima

*Only the Latin adjectives *facilis, difficilis, similis, dissimilis, gracilis,* and *humilis* are formed in this way in the superlative.

IRREGULAR COMPARATIVE AND SUPERLATIVE DEGREES OF ADJECTIVES

Common Irregular Comparatives and Superlatives

Positive degree	Comparative degree	Superlative degree
bonus, a, um – good	melior, melius – better	optimus, a, um – best
malus, a, um – bad	pēior, pēius – worse	pessimus, a, um – worst
māgnus, a, um – great	māior, māius – greater	maximus, a, um – greatest
multus, a, um – much	plūs (neuter noun) – more	plūrimus, a, um – most
multī, ae, a – many	plūrēs, plūra – more	plūrimī, ae, a – most
parvus, a, um – small	minor, minus – smaller	minimus, a, um – smallest

Declension of *plūs*, plūris*

	Singular	Plural	
	Neuter	**Masculine and Feminine**	**Neuter**
Nominative	plūs	plūrēs	plūra
Genitive	plūris	plūrium	plūrium
Dative	—	plūribus	plūribus
Accusative	plūs	plūrēs	plūra
Ablative	(plūre)	plūribus	plūribus
Vocative	—	plūrēs	plūra

*The singular of *plūs, plūris* is a neuter noun while in the plural it is an adjective.

Adjectives with a Genitive in –*īus* and Dative in –*ī*

1. alius, alia, aliud – another, other
2. alter, altera, alterum – the other (of two)
3. neuter, neutra, neutrum – neither, none (of two)
4. nūllus, nūlla, nūllum – none
5. sōlus, sōla, sōlum – alone, only
6. tōtus, tōta, tōtum – whole, entire
7. ūllus, ūlla, ūllum – any
8. ūnus, ūna, ūnum – one
9. uter, utra, utrum – who, which (of two)

Declension of *sōlus**

	Singular			Plural		
	Masculine	**Feminine**	**Neuter**	**Masculine**	**Feminine**	**Neuter**
Nominative	sōlus	sōla	sōlum	sōlī	sōlae	sōla
Genitive	sōlīus	sōlīus	sōlīus	sōlōrum	sōlārum	sōlōrum
Dative	sōlī	sōlī	sōlī	sōlīs	sōlīs	sōlīs
Accusative	sōlum	sōlam	sōlum	sōlōs	sōlās	sōla
Ablative	sōlō	sōlā	sōlō	sōlīs	sōlīs	sōlīs
Vocative	sōle	sōla	sōlum	sōlī	sōlae	sōla

(masculine vocative rarely seen)

**Alius, ūnus, tōtus, nūllus*, and *ūllus* decline like *sōlus*.

Declension of *alter*

	Singular			Plural		
	Masculine	**Feminine**	**Neuter**	**Masculine**	**Feminine**	**Neuter**
Nominative	alter	altera	alterum	alterī	alterae	altera
Genitive	alterīus	alterīus	alterīus	alterōrum	alterārum	alterōrum
Dative	alterī	alterī	alterī	alterīs	alterīs	alterīs
Accusative	alterum	alteram	alterum	alterōs	alterās	altera
Ablative	alterō	alterā	alterō	alterīs	alterīs	alterīs
Vocative	alter	altera	alterum	alterī	alterae	altera

Declension of *neuter**

	Singular			Plural		
	Masculine	**Feminine**	**Neuter**	**Masculine**	**Feminine**	**Neuter**
Nominative	neuter	neutra	neutrum	neutrī	neutrae	neutra
Genitive	neutrīus	neutrīus	neutrīus	neutrōrum	neutrārum	neutrōrum
Dative	neutrī	neutrī	neutrī	neutrīs	neutrīs	neutrīs
Accusative	neutrum	neutram	neutrum	neutrōs	neutrās	neutra
Ablative	neutrō	neutrā	neutrō	neutrīs	neutrīs	neutrīs
Vocative	neuter	neutra	neutrum	neutrī	neutrae	neutra

Uter declines like neuter.

DECLENSIONS OF PARTICIPLES

Declension of the Present Active Participle

	Singular			Plural		
	Masculine	**Feminine**	**Neuter**	**Masculine**	**Feminine**	**Neuter**
Nominative	parāns	parāns	parāns	parantēs	parantēs	parantia
Genitive	parantis	parantis	parantis	parantium	parantium	parantium
Dative	parantī	parantī	parantī	parantibus	parantibus	parantibus
Accusative	parantem	parantem	parāns	parantēs	parantēs	parantia
Ablative	parantī	parantī	parantī	parantibus	parantibus	parantibus
Vocative	parāns	parāns	parāns	parantēs	parantēs	parantia

Declension of the Perfect Passive Participle

	Singular			Plural		
	Masculine	Feminine	Neuter	Masculine	Feminine	Neuter
Nominative	parātus	parāta	parātum	parātī	parātae	parāta
Genitive	parātī	parātae	parātī	parātōrum	parātārum	parātōrum
Dative	parātō	parātae	parātō	parātīs	parātīs	parātīs
Accusative	parātum	parātam	parātum	parātōs	parātās	parāta
Ablative	parātō	parātā	parātō	parātīs	parātīs	parātīs
Vocative	parāte	parāta	parātum	parātī	parātae	parāta

Declension of the Future Active Participle

	Singular			Plural		
	Masculine	Feminine	Neuter	Masculine	Feminine	Neuter
Nominative	parātūrus	parātūra	parātūrum	parātūrī	parātūrae	parātūra
Genitive	parātūrī	parātūrae	parātūrī	parātūrōrum	parātūrārum	parātūrōrum
Dative	parātūrō	parātūrae	parātūrō	parātūrīs	parātūrīs	parātūrīs
Accusative	parātūrum	parātūram	parātūrum	parātūrōs	parātūrās	parātūra
Ablative	parātūrō	parātūrō	parātūrō	parātūrīs	parātūrīs	parātūrīs
Vocative	parātūre	parātūra	parātūrum	parātūrī	parātūrae	parātūra

NUMBERS

Declension of Numbers*

	Ūnus			Duo			Trēs	
Nominative	ūnus	ūna	ūnum	duo	duae	duo	trēs	tria
Genitive	ūnīus	ūnīus	ūnīus	duōrum	duārum	duōrum	trium	trium
Dative	ūnī	ūnī	ūnī	duōbus	duābus	duōbus	tribus	tribus
Accusative	ūnum	ūnam	ūnum	duōs	duās	duo	trēs	tria
Ablative	ūnō	ūnā	ūnō	duōbus	duābus	duōbus	tribus	tribus

*Other numbers can be found in Appendix D.

ADVERBS

Comparison of Adverbs

Positive		Comparative		Superlative	
iūstē	justly	iūstius	more/too/rather justly	iūstissimē	most/very justly
pulchrē	beautifully	pulchrius	more/too/rather beautifully	pulcherrimē	most/very beautifully
fortiter	bravely	fortius	more/too/rather bravely	fortissimē	most/very bravely

Irregular Positive Degree of Adverbs

Adjective	Adverb
bonus, a, um	bene
māgnus, a, um	māgnopere
multus, a, um	multō/multum
malus	male
parvus	parum
facilis, facile	facile
trīstis, trīste	trīste
tūtus, a, um	tūtō (tūtē is a rare form)

PRONOUNS

DECLENSIONS OF PERSONAL AND REFLEXIVE PRONOUNS

Personal Pronouns: First and Second Person

	First singular	Second singular	First plural	Second plural
Nominative	ego	tū	nōs	vōs
Genitive	meī	tuī	nostrī/nostrum	vestrī/vestrum
Dative	mihi	tibi	nōbīs	vōbīs
Accusative	mē	tē	nōs	vōs
Ablative	mē	tē	nōbīs	vōbīs

Personal Pronoun: Third Person; Demonstrative Pronoun and Adjective: *is, ea, id*

	Singular			Plural		
	Masculine	Feminine	Neuter	Masculine	Feminine	Neuter
Nominative	is	ea	id	eī (iī)	eae	ea
Genitive	ēius	ēius	ēius	eōrum	eārum	eōrum
Dative	eī	eī	eī	eīs (iīs)	eīs (iīs)	eīs (iīs)
Accusative	eum	eam	id	eōs	eās	ea
Ablative	eō	eā	eō	eīs (iīs)	eīs (iīs)	eīs (iīs)

Third Person Singular and Plural Reflexive Pronoun

Nominative	—
Genitive	suī
Dative	sibi
Accusative	sē
Ablative	sē

Possessive Adjectives

First Person Singular	meus, mea, meum
Second Person Singular	tuus, tua, tuum
Third Person Singular	suus, sua, suum/ēius
First Person Plural	noster, nostra, nostrum
Second Person Plural	vester, vestra, vestrum
Third Person Plural	suus, sua, suum/eōrum, eārum, eōrum

DECLENSIONS OF DEMONSTRATIVE PRONOUNS/ADJECTIVES

Demonstrative Pronoun/Adjective: *hic, haec, hoc*

	Singular			Plural		
	Masculine	Feminine	Neuter	Masculine	Feminine	Neuter
Nominative	hic	haec	hoc	hī	hae	haec
Genitive	hūius	hūius	hūius	hōrum	hārum	hōrum
Dative	huic	huic	huic	hīs	hīs	hīs
Accusative	hunc	hanc	hoc	hōs	hās	haec
Ablative	hōc	hāc	hōc	hīs	hīs	hīs

Demonstrative Pronoun/Adjective: *ille, illa, illud*

	Singular			Plural		
	Masculine	Feminine	Neuter	Masculine	Feminine	Neuter
Nominative	ille	illa	illud	illī	illae	illa
Genitive	illīus	illīus	illīus	illōrum	illārum	illōrum
Dative	illī	illī	illī	illīs	illīs	illīs
Accusative	illum	illam	illud	illōs	illās	illa
Ablative	illō	illā	illō	illīs	illīs	illīs

Demonstrative Pronoun/Adjective: *iste, ista, istud*

	Singular			Plural		
	Masculine	**Feminine**	**Neuter**	**Masculine**	**Feminine**	**Neuter**
Nominative	iste	ista	istud	istī	istae	ista
Genitive	istīus	istīus	istīus	istōrum	istārum	istōrum
Dative	istī	istī	istī	istīs	istīs	istīs
Accusative	istum	istam	istud	istōs	istās	ista
Ablative	istō	istā	istō	istīs	istīs	istīs

Demonstrative Pronoun/Adjective: *īdem, eadem, idem*

	Singular			Plural		
	Masculine	**Feminine**	**Neuter**	**Masculine**	**Feminine**	**Neuter**
Nominative	īdem	eadem	idem	eīdem	eaedem	eadem
Genitive	ēiusdem	ēiusdem	ēiusdem	eōrundem	eārundem	eōrundem
Dative	eīdem	eīdem	eīdem	eīsdem	eīsdem	eīsdem
Accusative	eundem	eandem	idem	eōsdem	eāsdem	eadem
Ablative	eōdem	eādem	eōdem	eīsdem	eīsdem	eīsdem

DECLENSION OF THE INTENSIVE PRONOUN/ADJECTIVE

Intensive Pronoun/Adjective: *ipse, ipsa, ipsum*

	Singular			Plural		
	Masculine	**Feminine**	**Neuter**	**Masculine**	**Feminine**	**Neuter**
Nominative	ipse	ipsa	ipsum	ipsī	ipsae	ipsa
Genitive	ipsīus	ipsīus	ipsīus	ipsōrum	ipsārum	ipsōrum
Dative	ipsī	ipsī	ipsī	ipsīs	ipsīs	ipsīs
Accusative	ipsum	ipsam	ipsum	ipsōs	ipsās	ipsa
Ablative	ipsō	ipsā	ipsō	ipsīs	ipsīs	ipsīs

DECLENSION OF THE RELATIVE PRONOUN

Relative Pronoun: *quī, quae, quod*

	Singular			Plural		
	Masculine	**Feminine**	**Neuter**	**Masculine**	**Feminine**	**Neuter**
Nominative	quī	quae	quod	quī	quae	quae
Genitive	cūius	cūius	cūius	quōrum	quārum	quōrum
Dative	cui	cui	cui	quibus	quibus	quibus
Accusative	quem	quam	quod	quōs	quās	quae
Ablative	quō	quā	quō	quibus	quibus	quibus

DECLENSIONS OF INTERROGATIVE PRONOUNS AND ADJECTIVES

Interrogative Pronoun: *quis, quid?*

| | Singular | | Plural | | |
	Masculine/Feminine	Neuter	Masculine	Feminine	Neuter
Nominative	quis	quid	quī	quae	quae
Genitive	cūius	cūius	quōrum	quārum	quōrum
Dative	cui	cui	quibus	quibus	quibus
Accusative	quem	quid	quōs	quās	quae
Ablative	quō/quā	quō	quibus	quibus	quibus

Interrogative Adjective: *quī, quae, quod?*

| | Singular | | | Plural | | |
	Masculine	Feminine	Neuter	Masculine	Feminine	Neuter
Nominative	quī	quae	quod	quī	quae	quae
Genitive	cūius	cūius	cūius	quōrum	quārum	quōrum
Dative	cui	cui	cui	quibus	quibus	quibus
Accusative	quem	quam	quod	quōs	quās	quae
Ablative	quō	quā	quō	quibus	quibus	quibus

VERBS

CONJUGATIONS OF REGULAR VERBS

Present Active Indicative

	First conjugation	Second conjugation	Third conjugation	Fourth conjugation	Third conjugation -*iō*
First person singular	parō	teneō	petō	audiō	capiō
Second person plural	parās	tenēs	petis	audīs	capis
Third person plural	parat	tenet	petit	audit	capit
First person plural	parāmus	tenēmus	petimus	audīmus	capimus
Second person plural	parātis	tenētis	petitis	audītis	capitis
Third person plural	parant	tenent	petunt	audiunt	capiunt

Present Passive Indicative

	First conjugation	Second conjugation	Third conjugation	Fourth conjugation	Third conjugation -*iō*
First person singular	paror	teneor	petor	audior	capior
Second person singular	parāris	tenēris	peteris	audīris	caperis
Third person singular	parātur	tenētur	petitur	audītur	capitur
First person plural	parāmur	tenēmur	petimur	audīmur	capimur
Second person plural	parāminī	tenēminī	petiminī	audīminī	capiminī
Third person plural	parantur	tenentur	petuntur	audiuntur	capiuntur

Imperfect Active Indicative

	First conjugation	Second conjugation	Third conjugation	Fourth conjugation	Third conjugation -*iō*
First person singular	parābam	tenēbam	petēbam	audiēbam	capiēbam
Second person singular	parābās	tenēbās	petēbās	audiēbās	capiēbās
Third person singular	parābat	tenēbat	petēbat	audiēbat	capiēbat
First person plural	parābāmus	tenēbāmus	petēbāmus	audiēbāmus	capiēbāmus
Second person plural	parābātis	tenēbātis	petēbātis	audiēbātis	capiēbātis
Third person plural	parābant	tenēbant	petēbant	audiēbant	capiēbant

Imperfect Passive Indicative

	First conjugation	Second conjugation	Third conjugation	Fourth conjugation	Third conjugation -*iō*
First person singular	parābar	tenēbar	petēbar	audiēbar	capiēbar
Second person singular	parābāris	tenēbāris	petēbāris	audiēbāris	capiēbāris
Third person singular	parābātur	tenēbātur	petēbātur	audiēbātur	capiēbātur
First person plural	parābāmur	tenēbāmur	petēbāmur	audiēbāmur	capiēbāmur
Second person plural	parābāminī	tenēbāminī	petēbāminī	audiēbāminī	capiēbāminī
Third person plural	parābantur	tenēbantur	petēbantur	audiēbantur	capiēbantur

Future Active Indicative

	First conjugation	Second conjugation	Third conjugation	Fourth conjugation	Third conjugation -*iō*
First person singular	parābō	tenēbō	petam	audiam	capiam
Second person singular	parābis	tenēbis	petēs	audiēs	capiēs
Third person singular	parābit	tenēbit	petet	audiet	capiet
First person plural	parābimus	tenēbimus	petēmus	audiēmus	capiēmus
Second person plural	parābitis	tenēbitis	petētis	audiētis	capiētis
Third person plural	parābunt	tenēbunt	petent	audient	capient

Future Passive Indicative

	First conjugation	Second conjugation	Third conjugation	Fourth conjugation	Third conjugation -iō
First person singular	parābor	tenēbor	petar	audiar	capiar
Second person singular	parāberis	tenēberis	petēris	audiēris	capiēris
Third person singular	parābitur	tenēbitur	petētur	audiētur	capiētur
First person plural	parābimur	tenēbimur	petēmur	audiēmur	capiēmur
Second person plural	parābiminī	tenēbiminī	petēminī	audiēminī	capiēminī
Third person plural	parābuntur	tenēbuntur	petentur	audientur	capientur

	Perfect Active Indicative*	Perfect Passive Indicative*
First person singular	parāvī	parātus, parāta, (parātum) sum
Second person singular	parāvistī	parātus, parāta, (parātum) es
Third person singular	parāvit	parātus, parāta, parātum est
First person plural	parāvimus	parātī, parātae, (parāta) sumus
Second person plural	parāvistis	parātī, parātae, (parāta) estis
Third person plural	parāvērunt	parātī, parātae, parāta sunt

* The third principal part of verbs of all conjugations supplies the perfect active stem from which the perfect active, pluperfect active, and future perfect active tenses are formed. The fourth principal part of verbs of all conjugations supplies the first word of the perfect passive, pluperfect passive, and future perfect passive tenses.

	Pluperfect Active Indicative	Pluperfect Passive Indicative
First person singular	parāveram	parātus, parāta, (parātum) eram
Second person singular	parāverās	parātus, parāta, (parātum) erās
Third person singular	parāverat	parātus, parāta, parātum erat
First person plural	parāverāmus	parātī, parātae, (parāta) erāmus
Second person plural	parāverātis	parātī, parātae, (parāta) erātis
Third person plural	parāverant	parātī, parātae, parāta erant

	Future Perfect Active Indicative	Future Perfect Passive Indicative
First person singular	parāverō	parātus, parāta, (parātum) erō
Second person singular	parāveris	parātus, parāta, (parātum) eris
Third person singular	parāverit	parātus, parāta, parātum erit
First person plural	parāverimus	parātī, parātae, (parāta) erimus
Second person plural	parāveritis	parātī, parātae, (parāta) eritis
Third person plural	parāverint	parātī, parātae, parāta erunt

Present Active Subjunctive

	First conjugation	Second conjugation	Third conjugation	Fourth conjugation	Third conjugation -iō
First person singular	parem	teneam	petam	audiam	capiam
Second person singular	parēs	teneās	petās	audiās	capiās
Third person singular	paret	teneat	petat	audiat	capiat
First person plural	parēmus	teneāmus	petāmus	audiāmus	capiāmus
Second person plural	parētis	teneātis	petātis	audiātis	capiātis
Third Person plural	parent	teneant	petant	audiant	capiant

Present Passive Subjunctive

	First conjugation	Second conjugation	Third conjugation	Fourth conjugation	Third conjugation -iō
First person singular	parer	tenear	petar	audiār	capiar
Second Person singular	parēris	teneāris	petāris	audiāris	capiāris
Third Person singular	parētur	teneātur	petātur	audiātur	capiātur
First Person plural	parēmur	teneāmur	petāmur	audiāmur	capiāmur
Second Person plural	parēminī	teneāminī	petāminī	audiāminī	capiāminī
Third person plural	parentur	teneantur	petantur	audiantur	capiantur

Imperfect Active Subjunctive

	First conjugation	Second conjugation	Third conjugation	Fourth conjugation	Third conjugation -iō
First person singular	parārem	tenērem	peterem	audīrem	caperem
Second person singular	parārēs	tenērēs	peterēs	audīrēs	caperēs
Third person singular	parāret	tenēret	peteret	audīret	caperet
First Person plural	parārēmus	tenērēmus	peterēmus	audīrēmus	caperēmus
Second person plural	parārētis	tenērētis	peterētis	audīrētis	caperētis
Third person plural	parārent	tenērent	peterent	audīrent	caperent

Imperfect Passive Subjunctive

	First conjugation	Second conjugation	Third conjugation	Fourth conjugation	Third conjugation -iō
First person singular	parārer	tenērer	peterer	audīrer	caperer
Second person singular	parārēris	tenērēris	peterēris	audīrēris	caperēris
Third person singular	parārētur	tenērētur	peterētur	audīrētur	caperētur
First person plural	parārēmur	tenērēmur	peterēmur	audīrēmur	caperēmur
Second person plural	parārēminī	tenērēminī	peterēminī	audīrēminī	caperēminī
Third person plural	parārentur	tenērentur	peterentur	audīrentur	caperentur

	Perfect Active Subjunctive*	**Perfect Passive Subjunctive***
First person singular	parāverim	parātus, parāta, (parātum) sim
Second Person singular	parāveris	parātus, parāta, (parātum) sīs
Third person singular	parāverit	parātus, parāta, parātum sit
First person plural	parāverimus	parātī, parātae, (parāta) sīmus
Second Person plural	parāveritis	parātī, parātae, (parāta) sītis
Third person plural	parāverint	parātī, parātae, parāta sint

*The third principal part of verbs of all conjugations supplies the perfect active stem
from which the perfect active and pluperfect active subjuctives are formed.

	Pluperfect Active Subjunctive*	**Pluperfect Passive Subjunctive***
First person singular	parāvissem	parātus, parāta, (parātum) essem
Second person singular	parāvissēs	parātus, parāta, (parātum) essēs
Third person singular	parāvisset	parātus, parāta, parātum esset
First Person plural	parāvissēmus	parātī, parātae, (parāta) essēmus
Second Person plural	parāvissētis	parātī, parātae, (parāta) essētis
Third person plural	parāvissent	parātī, parātae, parāta essent

*The fourth principal part of verbs of all conjugations supplies the first
word of the perfect passive and pluperfect passive subjunctives.

Present Imperatives

	First conjugation	Second conjugation	Third conjugation	Fourth conjugation	Third conjugation -iō
Second person singular positive	parā	tenē	pete*	audī	cape*
Second person plural positive	parāte	tenēte	petite	audīte	capite
Second person singular negative	nōlī parāre	nōlī tenēre	nōlī petere	nōlī audīre	nōlī capere
Second person plural negative	nōlīte parāre	nōlīte tenēre	nōlīte petere	nōlīte audīre	nōlīte capere

*The second person singular positive imperatives of third conjugation verbs dīcō, dūcō
and of the third –io verb faciō are irregular: dīc, dūc, fac.

Participles

	Active	Passive
Present	parāns, parantis	—
Perfect		parātus, parāta, parātum
Future	parātūrus, parātūra, parātūrum	

Infinitives

	Active	Passive
Present	parāre	parārī
Perfect	parāvisse	parātus, parāta, parātum esse
Future	parātūrus, parātūra, parātūrum esse	—

CONJUGATIONS OF DEPONENT VERBS

Present Passive Indicative

	First conjugation	Second conjugation	Third conjugation	Fourth conjugation	Third conjugation -io
First person singular	hortor	vereor	sequor	partior	patior
Second person singular	hortāris	verēris	sequeris	partīris	pateris
Third person singular	hortātur	verētur	sequitur	partītur	patitur
First person plural	hortāmur	verēmur	sequimur	partīmur	patimur
Second person plural	hortāminī	verēminī	sequiminī	partīminī	patiminī
Third person plural	hortantur	verentur	sequuntur	partiuntur	patiuntur

Imperfect Passive Indicative

	First conjugation	Second conjugation	Third conjugation	Fourth conjugation	Third conjugation -io
First person singular	hortābar	verēbar	sequēbar	partiēbar	patiēbar
Second person singular	hortābāris	verēbāris	sequēbāris	partiēbāris	patiēbāris
Third person singular	hortābātur	verēbātur	sequēbātur	partiēbātur	patiēbātur
First person plural	hortābāmur	verēbāmur	sequēbāmur	partiēbāmur	patiēbāmur
Second person plural	hortābāminī	verēbāminī	sequēbāminī	partiēbāminī	patiēbāminī
Third person plural	hortābantur	verēbantur	sequēbantur	partiēbantur	patiēbantur

Future Passive Indicative

	First conjugation	Second conjugation	Third conjugation	Fourth conjugation	Third conjugation -io
First person singular	hortābor	verēbor	sequar	partiar	patiar
Second person singular	hortāberis	verēberis	sequēris	partiēris	patiēris
Third person singular	hortābitur	verēbitur	sequētur	partiētur	patiētur
First person plural	hortābimur	verēbimur	sequēmur	partiēmur	patiēmur
Second person plural	hortābiminī	verēbiminī	sequēminī	partiēminī	patiēminī
Third person plural	hortābuntur	verēbuntur	sequentur	partientur	patientur

Perfect Passive Indicative

	First conjugation	Second conjugation	Third conjugation	Fourth conjugation	Third conjugation -io
First person singular	hortātus, a, um sum	veritus, a, um sum	secūtus, a, um sum	partītus, a, um sum	passus, a, um sum
Second person singular	hortātus, a, um es	veritus, a, um es	secūtus, a, um es	partītus, a, um es	passus, a, um es
Third person singular	hortātus, a, um est	veritus, a, um est	secūtus, a, um est	partītus, a, um est	passus, a, um est
First person plural	hortātī, ae, a sumus	veritī, ae, a sumus	secūtī, ae, a sumus	partītī, ae, a sumus	passī, ae, a sumus
Second person plural	hortātī, ae, a estis	veritī, ae, a estis	secūtī, ae, a estis	partītī, ae, a estis	passī, ae, a estis
Third person plural	hortātī, ae, a sunt	veritī, ae, a sunt	secūtī, ae, a sunt	partītī, ae, a sunt	passī, ae, a sunt

Pluperfect Passive Indicative

	First conjugation	Second conjugation	Third conjugation	Fourth conjugation	Third conjugation -io
First person singular	hortātus, a, um eram	veritus, a, um eram	secūtus, a, um eram	partītus, a, um eram	passus, a, um eram
Second person singular	hortātus, a, um erās	veritus, a, um erās	secūtus, a, um erās	partītus, a, um erās	passus, a, um erās
Third person singular	hortātus, a, um erat	veritus, a, um erat	secūtus, a, um erat	partītus, a, um erat	passus, a, um erat
First person plural	hortātī, ae, a erāmus	veritī, ae, a erāmus	secūtī, ae, a erāmus	partītī, ae, a erāmus	passī, ae, a erāmus
Second person plural	hortātī, ae, a erātis	veritī, ae, a erātis	secūtī, ae, a erātis	partītī, ae, a erātis	passī, ae, a erātis
Third person plural	hortātī, ae, a erant	veritī, ae, a erant	secūtī, ae, a erant	partītī, ae, a erant	passī, ae, a erant

Future Perfect Passive Indicative

	First conjugation	Second conjugation	Third conjugation	Fourth conjugation	Third conjugation -*io*
First person singular	hortātus, a, um erō	veritus, a, um erō	secūtus, a, um erō	partītus, a, um erō	passus, a, um erō
Second person singular	hortātus, a, um eris	veritus, a, um eris	secūtus, a, um eris	partītus, a, um eris	passus, a, um eris
Third person singular	hortātus, a, um erit	veritus, a, um erit	secūtus, a, um erit	partītus, a, um erit	passus, a, um erit
First Person plural	hortātī, ae, a erimus	veritī, ae, a erimus	secūtī, ae, a erimus	partītī, ae, a erimus	passī, ae, a erimus
Second Person plural	hortātī, ae, a eritis	veritī, ae, a eritis	secūtī, ae, a eritis	partītī, ae, a eritis	passī, ae, a eritis
Third person plural	hortātī, ae, a erunt	veritī, ae, a erunt	secūtī, ae, a erunt	partītī, ae, a erunt	passī, ae, a erunt

Present Passive Subjunctive

	First conjugation	Second conjugation	Third conjugation	Fourth conjugation	Third conjugation -*io*
First person singular	horter	verear	sequar	partiar	patiar
Second person singular	hortēris	vereāris	sequāris	partiāris	patiāris
Third person singular	hortētur	vereātur	sequātur	partiātur	patiātur
First person plural	hortēmur	vereāmur	sequāmur	partiāmur	patiāmur
Second person plural	hortēminī	vereāminī	sequāminī	partiāminī	patiāminī
Third person plural	hortentur	vereantur	sequantur	partiantur	patiantur

Imperfect Passive Subjunctive

	First conjugation	Second conjugation	Third conjugation	Fourth conjugation	Third conjugation -*io*
First person singular	hortārer	verērer	sequerer	partīrer	paterer
Second person singular	hortārēris	verērēris	sequerēris	partīrēris	paterēris
Third person singular	hortārētur	verērētur	sequerētur	partīrētur	paterētur
First person plural	hortārēmur	verērēmur	sequerēmur	partīrēmur	paterēmur
Second person plural	hortārēminī	verērēminī	sequerēminī	partīrēminī	paterēminī
Third Person plural	hortārentur	vererentur	sequerentur	partīrentur	paterentur

Perfect Passive Subjunctive

	First conjugation	Second conjugation	Third conjugation	Fourth conjugation	Third conjugation -io
First person singular	hortātus, a, um sim	veritus, a, um sim	secūtus, a, um sim	partītus, a, um sim	passus, a, um sim
Second person singular	hortātus, a, um sīs	veritus, a, um sīs	secūtus, a, um sīs	partītus, a, um sīs	passus, a, um sīs
Third person singular	hortātus, a, um sit	veritus, a, um sit	secūtus, a, um sit	partītus, a, um sit	passus, a, um sit
First person plural	hortātī, ae, a sīmus	veritī, ae, a sīmus	secūtī, ae, a sīmus	partītī, ae, a sīmus	passī, ae, a sīmus
Second person plural	hortātī, ae, a sītis	veritī, ae, a sītis	secūtī, ae, a sītis	partītī, ae, a sītis	passī, ae, a sītis
Third person plural	hortātī, ae, a sint	veritī, ae, a sint	secūtī, ae, a sint	partītī, ae, a sint	passī, ae, a sint

Pluperfect Passive Subjunctive

	First conjugation	Second conjugation	Third conjugation	Fourth conjugation	Third conjugation -io
First person singular	hortātus, a, um essem	veritus, a, um essem	secūtus, a, um essem	partītus, a, um essem	passus, a, um essem
Second person singular	hortātus, a, um essēs	veritus, a, um essēs	secūtus, a, um essēs	partītus, a, um essēs	passus, a, um essēs
Third person singular	hortātus, a, um esset	veritus, a, um esset	secūtus, a, um esset	partītus, a, um esset	passus, a, um esset
First Person plural	hortātī, ae, a essēmus	veritī, ae, a essēmus	secūtī, ae, a essēmus	partītī, ae, a essēmus	passī, ae, a essēmus
Second Person plural	hortātī, ae, a essētis	veritī, ae, a essētis	secūtī, ae, a essētis	partītī, ae, a essētis	passī, ae, a essētis
Third person plural	hortātī, ae, a essent	veritī, ae, a essent	secūtī, ae, a essent	partītī, ae, a essent	passī, ae, a essent

Participles

	Active	Passive
Present	hortāns, horantis	—
Perfect		hortātus, a, um
Future	hortātūrus, a, um	

Infinitives

	Active	Passive
Present	—	hortārī
Perfect	—	hortātus, a, um, esse
Future	hortātūrus, a, um, esse	

CONJUGATIONS OF IRREGULAR VERBS

SUM, ESSE, FUĪ, FUTŪRUM

Indicative

	Present	Imperfect	Future	Perfect	Pluperfect	Future perfect
First person singular	sum	eram	erō	fuī	fueram	fuerō
Second person singular	es	erās	eris	fuistī	fuerās	fueris
Third person singular	est	erat	erit	fuit	fuerat	fuerit
First person plural	sumus	erāmus	erimus	fuimus	fuerāmus	fuerimus
Second person plural	estis	erātis	eritis	fuistis	fuerātis	fueritis
Third person plural	sunt	erant	erunt	fuērunt	fuerant	fuerint

Subjunctive

	Present	Imperfect	Future	Perfect	Pluperfect	Future perfect
First person singular	sim	essem	—	fuerim	fuissem	—
Second person singular	sīs	essēs	—	fueris	fuissēs	—
Third person singular	sit	esset	—	fuerit	fuisset	—
First person plural	sīmus	essēmus	—	fuerimus	fuissēmus	—
Second person plural	sītis	essētis	—	fueritis	fuissētis	—
Third person plural	sint	essent	—	fuerint	fuissent	—

Present Imperatives

Second person singular positive	es
Second person plural positive	este

Infinitives

	Active	Passive
Present	esse	
Perfect	fuisse	
Future	futūrus, a, um esse	

POSSUM, POSSE, POTUĪ, —

Indicative

	Present	Imperfect	Future	Perfect	Pluperfect	Future perfect
First person singular	possum	poteram	poterō	potuī	potueram	potuerō
Second person singular	potes	poterās	poteris	potuistī	potuerās	potueris
Third person singular	potest	poterat	poterit	potuit	potuerat	potuerit
First person singular	possumus	poterāmus	poterimus	potuimus	potuerāmus	potuerimus
Second person plural	potestis	poterātis	poteritis	potuistis	potuerātis	potueritis
Third person plural	possunt	poterant	poterunt	potuērunt	potuerant	potuerint

Subjunctive

	Present	Imperfect	Future	Perfect	Pluperfect	Future perfect
First person singular	possim	possem	—	potuerim	potuissem	—
Second person singular	possīs	possēs	—	potueris	potuissēs	—
Third person singular	possit	posset	—	potuerit	potuisset	—
First person plural	possīmus	possēmus	—	potuerimus	potuissēmus	—
Second person plural	possītis	possētis	—	potueritis	potuissētis	—
Third person plural	possint	possent	—	potuerint	potuissent	—

Participles

Active

Present	potēns, potentis

Infinitives

Active

Present	posse
Perfect	potuisse

EŌ, ĪRE, ĪVĪ, ITUM

Indicative

	Present	Imperfect	Future	Perfect	Pluperfect	Future perfect
First person singular	eō	ībam	ībō	īvī	īveram	īverō
Second person singular	īs	ībās	ībis	īvistī	īverās	īveris
Third person singular	it	ībat	ībit	īvit	īverat	īverit
First person plural	īmus	ībāmus	ībimus	īvimus	īverāmus	īverimus
Second person plural	ītis	ībātis	ībitis	īvistis	īverātis	īveritis
Third person plural	eunt	ībant	ībunt	īvērunt	īverant	īverint

Subjunctive

	Present	Imperfect	Future	Perfect	Pluperfect	Future perfect
First person singular	eam	īrem	—	īverim	īvissem	—
Second person singular	eās	īrēs	—	īveris	īvissēs	—
Third person singular	eat	īret	—	īverit	īvisset	—
First person plural	eāmus	īrēmus	—	īverimus	īvissēmus	—
Second person plural	eātis	īrētis	—	īveritis	īvissētis	—
Third person plural	eant	īrent	—	īverint	īvissent	—

Present Imperatives

Second person singular positive	ī
Second person plural positive	īte
Second person singular negative	nōlī īre
Second person plural negative	nōlīte īre

Participles

	Active	Passive
Present	iēns, euntis	—
Perfect	—	—
Future	itūrus, itūra, itūrum	—

Infinitives

	Active
Present	īre
Perfect	īvisse
Future	itūrus, a, um esse

VOLŌ, VELLE, VOLUĪ

Indicative

	Present	Imperfect	Future	Perfect	Pluperfect	Future perfect
First person singular	volō	volēbam	volam	voluī	volueram	voluerō
Second person singular	vīs	volēbās	volēs	voluistī	voluerās	volueris
Third person singular	vult	volēbat	volet	voluit	voluerat	voluerit
First person plural	volumus	volēbāmus	volēmus	voluimus	voluerāmus	voluerimus
Second person plural	vultis	volēbātis	volētis	voluistis	voluerātis	volueritis
Third person plural	volunt	volēbant	volent	voluērunt	voluerant	voluerint

Subjunctive

	Present	Imperfect	Future	Perfect	Pluperfect	Future perfect
First person singular	velim	vellem	—	voluerim	voluissem	—
Second person singular	velīs	vellēs	—	volueris	voluissēs	—
Third person singular	velit	vellet	—	voluerit	voluisset	—
First person plural	velīmus	vellēmus	—	voluerimus	voluissēmus	—
Second person plural	velītis	vellētis	—	volueritis	voluissētis	—
Third person plural	velint	vellent	—	voluerint	voluissent	—

Participles

Active

Present	volēns, volentis

Infinitives

Active

Present	velle
Perfect	voluisse

NŌLŌ, NŌLLE, NŌLUĪ

Indicative

	Present	Imperfect	Future	Perfect	Pluperfect	Future perfect
First person singular	nōlō	nōlēbam	nōlam	nōluī	nōlueram	nōluerō
Second person singular	nōn vīs	nōlēbās	nōlēs	nōluistī	nōluerās	nōlueris
Third person singular	nōn vult	nōlēbat	nōlet	nōluit	nōluerat	nōluerit
First person plural	nōlumus	nōlēbāmus	nōlēmus	nōluimus	nōluerāmus	nōluerimus
Second Person plural	nōn vultis	nōlēbātis	nōlētis	nōluistis	nōluerātis	nōlueritis
Third person plural	nōlunt	nōlēbant	nōlent	nōluērunt	nōluerant	nōluerint

Subjunctive

	Present	Imperfect	Future	Perfect	Pluperfect	Future perfect
First person singular	nōlim	nōllem	—	nōluerim	nōluissem	—
Second person singular	nōlīs	nōllēs	—	nōlueris	nōluissēs	—
Third person singular	nōlit	nōllet	—	nōluerit	nōluisset	—
First person plural	nōlīmus	nōllēmus	—	nōluerimus	nōluissēmus	—
Second person plural	nōlītis	nōllētis	—	nōlueritis	nōluissētis	—
Third person plural	nōlint	nōllent	—	nōluerint	nōluissent	—

Present Imperatives

Second person singular positive	nōlī
Second person plural positive	nōlīte

Participles

Active

Present	nōlēns, nōlentis

Infinitives

Active

Present	nōlle
Perfect	nōluisse

MĀLŌ, MĀLLE, MĀLUĪ

Indicative

	Present	Imperfect	Future	Perfect	Pluperfect	Future perfect
First person singular	mālō	mālēbam	mālam	māluī	mālueram	māluerō
Second person singular	māvīs	mālēbās	mālēs	māluistī	māluerās	mālueris
Third person singular	māvult	mālēbat	mālet	māluit	māluerat	māluerit
First person plural	mālumus	mālēbāmus	mālēmus	māluimus	māluerāmus	māluerimus
Second Person plural	māvultis	mālēbātis	mālētis	māluistis	māluerātis	mālueritis
Third person plural	mālunt	mālēbant	mālent	māluērunt	māluerant	māluerint

Subjunctive

	Present	Imperfect	Future	Perfect	Pluperfect	Future perfect
First person singular	mālim	māllem	—	māluerim	māluissem	—
Second person singular	mālīs	māllēs	—	mālueris	māluissēs	—
Third person singular	mālit	māllet	—	māluerit	māluisset	—
First person plural	mālīmus	māllēmus	—	māluerimus	māluissēmus	—
Second person plural	mālītis	māllētis	—	mālueritis	māluissētis	—
Third person plural	mālint	māllent	—	māluerint	māluissent	—

Infinitives

Active

Present	mālle
Perfect	māluisse

FERŌ, FERRE, TULĪ, LĀTUM

Indicative Active

	Present	Imperfect	Future	Perfect	Pluperfect	Future perfect
First person singular	ferō	ferēbam	feram	tulī	tuleram	tulerō
Second person singular	fers	ferēbās	ferēs	tulistī	tulerās	tuleris
Third person singular	fert	ferēbat	feret	tulit	tulerat	tulerit
First person plural	ferimus	ferēbāmus	ferēmus	tulimus	tulerāmus	tulerimus
Second Person plural	fertis	ferēbātis	ferētis	tulistis	tulerātis	tuleritis
Third person plural	ferunt	ferēbant	ferent	tulērunt	tulerant	tulerint

Indicative Passive

	Present	Imperfect	Future	Perfect	Pluperfect	Future perfect
First person singular	feror	ferēbar	ferar	lātus, a, um sum	lātus, a, um eram	lātus, a, um erō
Second person singular	ferris	ferēbāris	ferēris	lātus, a, um es	lātus, a, um erās	lātus, a, um eris
Third person singular	fertur	ferēbātur	ferētur	lātus, a, um est	lātus, a, um erat	lātus, a, um erit
First person plural	ferimur	ferēbāmur	ferēmur	lātī, ae, a sumus	lātī, ae, a erāmus	lātī, ae, a erimus
aecond person plural	feriminī	ferēbāminī	ferēminī	lātī, ae, a estis	lātī, ae, a erātis	lātī, ae, a eritis
Third person plural	feruntur	ferēbantur	ferentur	lātī, ae, a sunt	lātī, ae, a erant	lātī, ae, a erunt

Subjunctive Active

	Present	Imperfect	Future	Perfect	Pluperfect	Future perfect
First person singular	feram	ferrem	—	tulerim	tulissem	—
Second person singular	ferās	ferrēs	—	tuleris	tulissēs	—
Third person singular	ferat	ferret	—	tulerit	tulisset	—
First person plural	ferāmus	ferrēmus	—	tulerimus	tulissēmus	—
Second person plural	ferātis	ferrētis	—	tuleritis	tulissētis	—
Third person plural	ferant	ferrent	—	tulerint	tulissent	—

Subjunctive Passive

	Present	Imperfect	Future	Perfect	Pluperfect	Future perfect
First person singular	ferar	ferrer	—	lātus, a, um sim	lātus, a, um essem	—
Second person singular	ferāris	ferrēris	—	lātus, a, um sīs	lātus, a, um essēs	—
Third person singular	ferātur	ferrētur	—	lātus, a, um sit	lātus, a, um esset	—
First Person plural	ferāmur	ferrēmur	—	lātī, ae, a sīmus	lātī, ae, a essēmus	—
Second person plural	ferāminī	ferrēminī	—	lātī, ae, a sītis	lātī, ae, a essētis	—
Third person plural	ferantur	ferrentur	—	lātī, ae, a sint	lātī, ae, a essent	—

Present Imperatives

Second person singular positive	fer
Second person plural positive	ferte
Second person singular negative	nōlī ferre
Second person plural negative	nōlīte ferre

Participles

	Active	Passive
Present	ferēns, ferentis	—
Perfect	—	lātus, lāta, lātum
Future	lātūrus, lātūra, lātūrum	

Infinitives

	Active	Passive
Present	ferre	ferrī
Perfect	tulisse	lātus, lāta, lātum esse
Future	latūrus, a, um, esse	

FĪŌ, FIERĪ, FACTUS SUM

Indicative

	Present	Imperfect	Future	Perfect	Pluperfect	Future perfect
First person singular	fīō	fīēbam	fīam	factus, a, um sum	factus, a, um eram	factus, a, um ero
Second person singular	fīs	fīēbās	fīēs	factus, a, um es	factus, a, um erās	factus, a, um eris
Third person singular	fit	fīēbat	fīet	factus, a, um est	factus, a, um erat	factus, a, um erit
First person plural	fīmus	fīēbāmus	fīēmus	factī, ae, a sumus	factī, ae, a erāmus	factī, ae, a erimus
Second person plural	fītis	fīēbātis	fīētis	factī, ae, a estis	factī, ae, a erātis	factī, ae, a eritis
Third person plural	fīunt	fīēbant	fīent	factī, ae, a sunt	factī, ae, a erant	factī, ae, a erunt

Subjunctive

	Present	Imperfect	Future	Perfect	Pluperfect	Future perfect
First person singular	fīam	fierem	—	factus, a, um sim	factus, a, um essem	—
Second person singular	fīās	fierēs	—	factus, a, um sīs	factus, a, um essēs	—
Third person singular	fīat	fieret	—	factus, a, um sit	factus, a, um esset	—
First person plural	fīāmus	fierēmus	—	factī, ae, a sīmus	factī, ae, a essēmus	—
Second person plural	fīātis	fierētis	—	factī, ae, a sītis	factī, ae, a essētis	—
Third person plural	fīant	fierent	—	factī, ae, a sint	factī, ae, a essent	—

Participles

	Active	Passive
Present		
Perfect		factus, facta, factum

Infinitives

	Active	Passive
Present	fierī	
Perfect		factus, facta, factum esse

GERUNDS AND GERUNDIVES

Formation of the Gerund

Conjugation		Gerund in the Genitive Singular
First	parō, parāre	parandī
Second	teneō, tenēre	tenendī
Third	colō, colere	colendī
Fourth	audiō, audīre	audiendī
Third –io	capiō, capere	capiendī

Gerunds of Irregular Verbs

eō, īre	eundī
ferō, ferre	ferendī

Declension of the Gerund

Genitive	parandī
Dative	parandō
Accusative	(ad) parandum
Ablative	parandō

Formation of Gerundives

Conjugation		Gerundives in the Nominative Singular
First	parō, parāre	parandus, paranda, parandum
Second	teneō, tenēre	tenendus, tenenda, tenendum
Third	colō, colere	colendus, colenda, colendum
Fourth	audiō, audīre	audiendus, audienda, audiendum
Third –io	capiō, capere	capiendus, capienda, capiendum

Declension of the Gerundive

	Singular			Plural		
	Masculine	**Feminine**	**Neuter**	**Masculine**	**Feminine**	**Neuter**
Nominative	parandus	paranda	parandum	parandī	parandae	paranda
Genitive	parandī	parandae	parandī	parandōrum	parandārum	parandōrum
Dative	parandō	parandae	parandō	parandīs	parandīs	parandīs
Accusative	parandum	parandam	parandum	parandōs	parandās	paranda
Ablative	parandō	parandā	parandō	parandīs	parandīs	parandīs

APPENDIX C

LATIN SYNTAX

Only syntax taught in *Latin for the New Millennium*, Levels 1 and 2, is listed in this appendix. For additional syntax not taught in this book, see Appendix D.

NOUNS

BASIC USE OF CASES*

Case	Function
Nominative	Subject. Predicate nominative (noun or adjective).
Genitive	Modifier (often possession). Partitive genitive. Objective genitive.
Dative	Indirect object. Possession. Purpose. Agent (with passive periphrastic).
Accusative	Direct object. Place to which.
Ablative	Agent (with passive voice). Manner. Instrument (means). Separation. Place from which. Place where. Accompaniment. Partitive. Comparison.
Vocative	Address

*For additional case uses, see Appendix D.

PRONOUNS

EXPRESSION OF POSSESSION WITH PERSONAL PRONOUNS, DEMONSTRATIVES, AND POSSESSIVE ADJECTIVES

The genitive of the personal pronouns, *ego, tū, nōs, vōs*, and of the reflexive pronoun of the third person, *suī, sibi, sē, sē*, are **not** used to indicate possession. If you need to express possession with these words, use the possessive adjectives, *meus, tuus, noster, vester, suus*.

Examples:

Librum meum habeō.	"I have my book."
Librum tuum habeō.	"I have your book."
Librum vestrum habeō.	"I have your (pl.) book."
Librum nostrum habētis.	"You (pl.) have our book."
Librum suum habent.	"They have their (own) book."
Librum suum habet.	"S/he has her/his (own) book."

However, the genitive of the third person non-reflexive pronouns **is** used to indicate possession.

Examples:

Librum ēius habet.	"S/he has her/his (someone else's) book."
Librum eōrum habent.	"They have their (other people's) book."

In general, the genitive of other words often shows possession.

Example:

liber puellae	"the book of the girl"

Possession can also be expressed by dative of possession.

Example:

Mihi sunt multī librī.	"I have many books."

USE OF THE RELATIVE PRONOUN

The relative pronoun always refers back to a preceding word, which is usually expressed, but sometimes implied. The preceding word is called an antecedent. The relative pronoun has the gender and number of the antecedent, but its case is determined by its function in its own clause.

Example:

Hī sunt librī, **quōs** *habēmus.*	"These are the books, which we have."

INTENSIVE AND REFLEXIVE PRONOUNS

The intensive pronoun/adjective *ipse, ipsa, ipsum* means "self" and should be carefully distinguished from the reflexive pronoun *suī, sibi, sē, sē*, which we also translate as "self." The intensive pronoun/adjective **agrees** with what it refers to and has a nominative, whereas the reflexive pronoun refers to something else in the sentence with which it does **not** agree grammatically and has no nominative.

Examples:

Nauta ipse haec dīxit.	"The sailor himself said these things."
Nauta haec sibi dīxit.	"The sailor said these things to himself."

DEMONSTRATIVE PRONOUNS/ADJECTIVES

The demonstratives *is, ea, id*; *hic, haec, hoc*; and *ille, illa, illud* may be used as pronouns or adjectives. As pronouns, all three demonstratives are the third person pronouns "he, she, it, they." As with other pronouns, the case of the demonstrative pronoun is determined by its use in the sentence.

As adjectives , the demonstratives agree with the noun they modify in case, number, and gender. The demonstrative *is, ea, id* means "this/these" or "that/those" while *hic, haec, hoc* means "this/these" and *ille, illa, illud* means "that/those."

Examples:

Hic mox respondēbit.	"He (this \<man\>) will reply soon."
Hic vir mox respondēbit.	"This man will reply soon."

The demonstrative *īdem, eadem, idem* means "same."

Example:

Īdem vir mox respondēbit.	"The same man will reply soon."

The demonstrative *iste, ista, istud* means "that \<of yours\>." The notion "of yours" may be literally true or it may simply refer figuratively to a connection between the thing indicated by the demonstrative and something else. In some cases—but certainly not always—the use of this pronoun can have a derogatory or dismissive connotation.

Example:

Cōnsilium istud nōn probō.	"I do not approve of that plan of yours."

ADJECTIVES

NOUN-ADJECTIVE AGREEMENT

The adjective agrees with the noun in number, gender, and case.

Examples:

Ōrātiōnem longam audīvī.	"I heard a long speech."
Librum celebrem legō.	"I am reading a renowned book."

SUBSTANTIVE ADJECTIVES, ESPECIALLY NEUTER PLURAL

Sometimes adjectives, used in the appropriate gender, and when the context makes the frame of reference clear, may be used without an expressed noun to indicate persons or things.

Examples:

Fortēs *fugere nōn solent.*	"Brave people are not accustomed to flee."
Bonī mala *nōn laudant.*	"Good people do not praise bad things."

WAYS OF EXPRESSING A COMPARISON

When two or more things are compared with a comparative adjective or adverb, the word for "than" is the adverb **quam** or the second member of the comparison is put in the ablative case.

This is called the ablative of comparison and is not used unless the first of the two things being compared is in the nominative or accusative, and it is usually avoided when the second member of the comparison has a modifier.

Examples:

Nēmō est miserior quam ego.	"No one is more wretched than I."
Nēmō est miserior mē.	"No one is more wretched than I."

Sometimes comparatives, but especially superlatives, express a part of a whole. The whole then is expressed by a genitive. Sometimes this "part of the whole" or "partitive" relationship can be expressed with the prepositions *ex* or *inter* instead of the genitive.

Examples:

> *Fīliam rēgī omnium praeclārissimō dedit.*
> "He gave <his> daughter to the most distinguished king of all."
>
> *Fīliam rēgī ex omnibus praeclārissimō dedit.*
> "He gave <his> daughter to the most distinguished king of all."

THE USES OF *QUAM*

When *quam* is linked to a superlative adjective or adverb, it means "as . . . as possible."

Examples:

> *quam fortissimus*   "as brave as possible"
> *quam vehementissimē*   "as strongly as possible"
> *quam plūrimī*   "as many as possible"

When *quam* is used with a comparative adjective or adverb, it means "than."

Example:

> *Haec ars est ūtilior quam illa.*   "This skill is more useful than that one."

The accusative singular feminine of the relative pronoun is *quam* and it means "whom, which," or "that."

Example:

> *Haec est rēgīna quam laudāvī.*   "This is the queen whom I praised."

PREPOSITIONS AND PREPOSITIONAL PHRASES

Preposition	Case	Meaning	Grammatical Name
ā, ab	ablative	by, from	Agent, Separation
ad	accusative	towards, to, into	Place to Which
ante	accusative	in front of	Miscellaneous
apud	accusative	at the house of	Miscellaneous
circum	accusative	around	Miscellaneous
contrā	accusative	against	Miscellaneous
cum	ablative	with	Accompaniment, Manner
dē	ablative	about, concerning, down from	Miscellaneous, Place from Which
ē, ex	ablative	from, out of	Place from Which, Partitive
in	ablative	in, on	Place where
in	accusative	into, to	Place to which
inter	accusative	between, among	Miscellaneous
per	accusative	through	Miscellaneous
post	accusative	after	Miscellaneous
prō	ablative	for, on behalf of	Miscellaneous
prope	accusative	near	Miscellaneous
propter	accusative	because of	Miscellaneous
sine	ablative	without	Miscellaneous

PLACE WHERE, PLACE TO WHICH, AND PLACE FROM WHICH WITH NAMES OF TOWNS

Place Where:

To express "place where" Latin uses *in* with the ablative.

Examples:

> *Vīvō in pulchrā terrā.*　　　"I live in a nice land."

However, "place where" with the names of cities, towns, and small islands is expressed with a locative for singular nouns of the first and second declension, and with the ablative for plural nouns of the first and second declension, as well as for the nouns of the third declension in both the singular and the plural. The ending of the locative singular for the first declension is -*ae* and for the second declension is –*ī*.

Examples:

> *Vīvō Rōmae.*　　　　　　　"I live in Rome."
>
> *Carolus vīvit Aquīsgrānī.*　　"Charles lives in Aachen."
>
> *Vīvō Athēnīs.*　　　　　　　"I live in Athens."
>
> *Hannibal vīvēbat Carthāgine.*　"Hannibal lived in Carthage."

Place to Which:

To express "place to which" Latin uses *in* or *ad* with the accusative.

Examples:

    Mīlitēs ad Ītaliam dūcō.   "I lead soldiers to Italy."

However, "place to which" with the names of cities, towns, and small islands is expressed with a simple accusative.

Examples:

    Mīlitēs Rōmam, Aquīsgrānum,   "I lead soldiers to Rome, Aachen,

    Athēnās, Carthāginem dūcō.   Athens, Carthage."

Place from Which:

To express "place from which" Latin uses *ā, ab, dē* or *ē, ex* with the ablative.

Example:

    Ab Germāniā veniō.   "I am coming from Germany."

However, "place from which" with the names of cities, towns, and small islands is expressed with a simple ablative.

Examples:

    Rōmā, Aquīsgrānō,   "I am coming from Rome, Aachen,

    Athēnīs, Carthāgine veniō.   Athens, Carthage."

VERBS

SUBJECT-VERB AGREEMENT

The subject agrees with the verb in number.

Example:

    Puer currit.   "The boy is running."

The predicate nominative agrees with the verb in number. If the predicate nominative is a noun, it agrees with the subject in number and case; if it is an adjective, it agrees with the subject in number, gender, and case.

Example:

    Vīta est gaudium.   "Life is joy."

    Praemium est māgnum.   "The prize is great."

TRANSITIVE AND INTRANSITIVE VERBS

Transitive verbs express the subject acting on something else and can take the accusative.

Example:

Librum teneō.	"I hold a book."

Intransitive verbs express the state or condition of the subject and cannot take an accusative.

Examples:

Liber est meus.	"The book is mine."
In casā meā maneō.	"I am staying in my house."

FUNCTIONS OF THE SUBJUNCTIVE IN THE MAIN CLAUSE

The subjunctive in a main clause usually shows the action as desirable or possible.

1. The volitive subjunctive is a somewhat milder command than the imperative **OR** it indicates an exhortation or strong advice, usually in the first or third person. Its negative is accompanied by *nē*.

   Examples:

Rēs parēs!	"Prepare the things!"
	"You should/must prepare the things!"
Ad īnsulam nāvigēmus!	"Let us sail to the island!"

2. The optative subjunctive indicates a wish and is often, but not always, accompanied by the word *utinam*. Its negative is expressed by *nē*. The present subjunctive is used for a wish about the future, which could still come true. The imperfect subjunctive is used for a wish about the present which has not become true. The pluperfect subjuctive is used for a wish about the past which had not become true.

   Examples:

(Utinam) illam vōcem audiam!	"If only I may hear that voice!"
(Utinam) illam vōcem audīrem!	"If only I were hearing that voice!"
(Utinam) illam vōcem audīvissem!	"If only I had heard that voice!"

FUNCTIONS OF THE SUBJUNCTIVE IN A DEPENDENT CLAUSE

Purpose Clauses:

Purpose clauses are introduced by **ut**, "in order to," "so that," or **nē**, "in order not to," "lest" for a negative purpose. They are constructed with the present subjunctive depending on a primary tense (present, future, future perfect), or with the imperfect subjunctive depending on a secondary tense (imperfect, perfect, pluperfect).

Examples:

> *Epistulam mittō **ut sciās** mē bene valēre.*
> "I am sending a letter so that you may know that I am well."

> *Epistulam mīsī **ut scīrēs** mē bene valēre.*
> "I sent a letter so that you might know that I was well."

Indirect Questions:

Indirect questions are introduced by verbs of asking and, more generally, by verbs of thinking. They begin with an interrogative word, such as the interrogative pronoun or adjective, and have a subjunctive verb according to the sequence of tenses.

Examples:

*Interrogō tē **quid agās**.*	"I am asking you what you are doing."
*Interrogō tē **quid ēgeris**.*	"I am asking you what you were doing."
*Interrogāvī tē **quid agerēs**.*	"I asked you what you are doing."
*Interrogāvī tē **quid ēgissēs**.*	"I asked you what you were doing."

Indirect Commands:

An indirect command is used after verbs that express will, like *ōrō*, "to ask, to entreat" or *rogō*, "to ask." It is introduced with the conjunction *ut*, or with the conjunction *nē*, if the command is negative. The indirect command has the present subjunctive, if the tense in the main clause is primary, and the imperfect subjunctive, if the tense in the main clause is secondary.

Examples:

*Ōrō **ut** ad mē **veniās**.*	"I ask you to come to me."
*Ōrāvī **ut** ad mē **venīrēs**.*	"I asked you to come to me."

Result Clauses:

Result clauses show what would happen as a result of the action in the main clause and are introduced by *ut* or by *nē* if the result is negative. When trying to recognize a result clause in Latin, look for a clue word in the main clause such as ***tam***, "so," ***ita***, "in such a way," ***tantus***, "so great," ***tālis***, "such," ***tot*** "so many," etc.

Examples:

> *Terra est **tam** ingēns **ut** ā nōbīs tōta cōnspicī nōn **possit**.*
> "The earth is so huge that it cannot be observed by us whole."

> *Antīquōrum ars nōn erat **ita** māgna **ut** illī omnia dē terrā **intellegerent**.*
> "The science of the ancients was not so large that they understood everything about the earth."

Cum Clauses:

The conjunction *cum* is used with the **indicative** when it indicates a **general unspecified circumstance** which could occur any time. This *cum* with the **indicative** occurs most often when the tense of the main verb is present and it means "**when**."

Example:

> ***Cum*** *nimis* ***dolēmus****, lacrimās fundimus.*
> "When we feel too much pain, we shed tears."

The conjunction *cum* with the **imperfect subjunctive** refers to a concrete or specific circumstance in the past during which the action in the main clause occurred. It is translated with "**when**."

Example:

> ***Cum*** *nimis diū* ***legerem****, oculī dolēbant.*
> "When I was reading for too long a time, my eyes were hurting."

The conjunction *cum* with the **pluperfect subjunctive** refers to a concrete or specific circumstance in the past, which occurred before the action in the main clause. In this case *cum* means "**after**."

Example:

> ***Cum*** *haec omnia* ***audīvisset****, nautās quidem timēre coepit Colōnus.*
> "After he had heard all these things, Columbus began to fear the sailors indeed."

Sometimes a causal meaning of conjunction *cum* is stronger than the temporal one. Then *cum* means "**since**."

Example:

> ***Cum*** *tam diū* ***nāvigārent****, nautae cupere coepērunt domum petere.*
> "Since they were sailing for such a long time, the sailors began to
> desire to go home."

Temporal Clauses:

In addition to *cum* temporal clauses, two of which have subjunctive verbs and one has an indicative verb, there are a number of other temporal clauses that feature indicative verbs.

Temporal Conjunctions			
Conjunction	**Mood/Tense**	**Meaning**	**Example**
Cum	indicative	when	**Cum legimus**, discimus. "When we read, we learn."
Cum	imperfect subjunctive	when	**Cum** nimis diū **legerem**, oculī dolēre coepērunt. "When I was reading for too long a time, my eyes began to hurt."
Cum	pluperfect subjunctive	after	**Cum** librum **lēgissem**, alium petīvī. "After I had read the book, I looked for another one."
Dum	indicative	while	**Dum est** spēs, spērāre dēbēmus. "While there is hope, we must hope."
Postquam	indicative	after	**Postquam** mē **vocāvistī**, ad tē vēnī. "After you called me, I came to you."
Quotiēs	indicative	as often as	**Quotiēs** tē **videō**, gaudium mē capit. "As often as I see you, joy seizes me."
Simul ac	indicative	as soon as	**Simul ac** verba illa **audīvī**, timēre coepī. "As soon as I heard those words, I began to fear."

Causal Clauses:

The two most used causal conjunctions in Latin are **quia** and **quod.**

If a causal clause presents the cause as a statement, its verb is in the indicative.

Example:

> *Discimus* **quia** *plūra scīre* **necesse est**.
> "We learn because it is necessary to know more."

If a causal clause presents the cause as the thought of a person in the narrative, but **not** necessarily that of the author, its verb is often in the subjunctive.

Example:

> *Ille nōn vēnit* **quod** *tempus nōn* **habēret**.
> "He did not come because <according to what he said/thought>
> he did not have (the) time."

The conjunction *cum* with the subjunctive may also be employed to introduce a causal clause. The causal meaning (rather than temporal or concessive) is typically clear from the context.

Example:

> *Cum mare esset vacuum, nautae spērāre nōlēbant.*
> "Since the sea was empty, the sailors were unwilling to hope."

Concessive Clauses:

A subordinate clause beginning with *quamquam* is **concessive**. It states a fact **despite which** the action in the main clause happens or is true. The two most used concessive conjunctions in Latin are **quamquam**, which is used with the indicative and presents the concession as a fact, and **quamvīs**, which is used with the subjunctive and presents the concession as the thought of a person in the narrative, but not necessarily that of the author.

Examples:

Quamquam iter est longum, īre dēbēbimus.
"Although the trip is long, we will need to go."

Quamvīs mēcum venīre nōlīs, hoc tamen facere dēbēs.
"Although you do not want to come with me, nevertheless you have to do this."

The conjunction *cum* may also be used with a concessive meaning. When *cum* has this meaning, the verb in the subordinate clause it introduces is subjunctive, and in the main clause the adverb *tamen* is usually present, so that it is obvious that the meaning of *cum* is not temporal or causal.

Example:

Cum mēcum venīre nōlīs, hoc tamen facere dēbēs.
"Although you do not want to come with me, nevertheless you have to do this."

Note that in this sentence *cum* has the same meaning as *quamvīs*.

CONDITIONAL SENTENCES

Type of Conditional Sentence	Subordinate Clause	Main Clause
Future More Vivid	Future Perfect Indicative (or Future Indicative)	Future Indicative
	Sī pecūniam habuerō, "If I have money,	*dōnum pulcherrimum tibi parābō.* I will prepare for you a very beautiful gift.
Future Less Vivid	Perfect subjunctive (or present subjunctive)	Present Subjunctive
	Sī pecūniam habuerim, "If I should have money,	*dōnum pulcherrimum tibi parem.* I would prepare for you a very beautiful gift."
Present Contrary-to-Fact	Imperfect Subjunctive	Imperfect Subjunctive
	Sī pecūniam habērem, "If I were to possess money,	*dōnum pulcherrimum tibi parārem.* I would prepare for you a very beautiful gift." (but I don't have money and I am not preparing you any gift)
Past Contrary-to-Fact	Pluperfect Subjunctive	Pluperfect Subjunctive
	Sī pecūniam habuissem, "If I had possessed money,	*dōnum pulcherrimum tibi parāvissem.* I would have prepared for you a very beautiful gift." (but I did not have money and I did not prepare you any gift)

Present General (Present Simple)	Present Indicative	Present Indicative
	*Sī pecūniam **habeō**,* "If I have money,	*dōnum pulcherrimum tibi **parō**.* I prepare for you a very beautiful gift." (i.e., if the condition of my having money exists)
Past General (Past Simple)	Past Indicative	Past Indicative
	*Sī pecūniam **habēbam**,* "If I had money,	*dōnum pulcherrimum tibi **parābam**.* I used to prepare for you a very beautiful gift." (i.e., if the condition of my having money was present)

SEQUENCE OF TENSES

The sequence of tenses is the relationship of the tense of the subordinate subjunctive to that of the main verb. Not all subordinate clauses follow the sequence of tenses.

1. If the main verb is in a **present or future tense**, the **present subjunctive** is used in the subordinate clause if the verb in the subjunctive refers to the **same time** as that of the main verb (or to a time after the main verb); the **perfect subjunctive** is used in the subordinate clause if the verb in the subjunctive refers to a **time before** that of the main verb.

   Examples:

   > *Etiam victōrēs sentīre possunt quam terribilis sit haec clādēs.*
   > "Even the victors can feel how terrible this disaster is."

   > *Etiam victōrēs sentīre possunt quam terribilis fuerit haec clādēs.*
   > "Even the victors can feel how terrible this disaster was."

2. If the main verb is in **any past tense**, the **imperfect subjunctive** is used in the subordinate clause if the verb in the subjunctive refers to the **same time** as that of the main verb (or to a time after the main verb), and the **pluperfect subjunctive** is used in the subordinate clause if the verb in the subjunctive refers to a **time before** that of the main verb.

   Examples:

   > *Tunc hostēs intellēxērunt quanta esset clādēs.*
   > "Then the enemy realized how great the disaster was."

   > *Prīmō nec nostrī nec hostēs sciēbant quid hominēs in aliā urbis parte fēcissent.*
   > "At first, neither our men nor the enemy were aware of what people had done in the other part of the city."

Complete Sequence of Tenses		
IndependentClause (Main Verb)	**Subordinate Clause Same Time, Time After**	**Subordinate Clause Time Before**
Primary Tense Verb/ Primary Sequence: Present, Future, Future Perfect Indicative	Present Subjunctive	Perfect Subjunctive
Secondary Tense Verb/ Secondary Sequence: Imperfect, Perfect Indicative	Imperfect Subjunctive	Pluperfect Subjunctive

USE OF THE FIRST SUPINE OR SUPINE ENDING IN –UM

From the fourth principal part of verbs (e.g., *parātum, tentum, cultum, audītum, captum*) the perfect passive participle is formed. This part of the verb itself, with the *–um* ending, is called the supine ending in *–um*. The first supine has its own special meaning. It is used after verbs of movement to indicate purpose.

Examples:

Eō dormītum.	"I go to sleep."
Veniō petītum pācem.	"I come to ask for peace."

USE OF THE GERUND

The gerund has a specific use in each of its four cases.

Genitive:

The gerund is used with nouns or adjectives that take the genitive.

Examples:

Eram discendī studiōsus.	"I was fond of/eager for learning."
Mihi erat spēs fugiendī.	"I had a hope of fleeing."

Dative:

The dative is sometimes used to indicate the purpose of the action.

Example:

Quaerō locum aedificandō.	"I am looking for a place for building (i.e., to build)."

Accusative:

The accusative, usually accompanied by the preposition *ad,* indicates the purpose of the action.

Example:

> *Parātus sum ad pugnandum.* "I am ready to fight/I am ready for fighting."

Ablative:

The ablative indicates means or instrument.

Example:

> *Discimus legendō.* "We learn through/by reading."

USE OF THE GERUNDIVE

The gerund is normally used only if it has no direct object. In cases where the gerund could take a direct object, the gerund usually turns into what is called a gerundive construction. The gerundive takes the **gender** and **number** of the direct object. But the direct object agrees with the **case** of the gerund. This construction made up of a noun with the gerundive agreeing with it as an adjective is normally used INSTEAD OF a gerund with an object.

	Gerund	**Gerundive**
Genitive:	*Eram studiōsus **videndī**.* "I was fond of seeing."	*Eram studiōsus **videndae spēluncae**.* "I was eager to see the cave." (literally "the cave to be seen")
Dative:	*Quaerō locum **aedificandō**.* "I am looking for a place to build."	*Quaerō locum **aedificandae domuī**.* "I am looking for a place to build a house." (literally "for a house to be built")
Accusative:	*Habēbam tēlum **ad repellendum**.* "I had a spear for repelling."	*Habēbam tēlum **ad repellenda animālia**.* "I had a spear to repel animals." (literally "for animals to be repelled")
Ablative:	*Discimus **legendō**.* "We learn through/by reading."	*Discimus **legendīs librīs**.* "We learn through/by reading books." (literally "by books to be read")

When linked to the verb *sum,* the gerundive indicates necessity. This construction is called the passive periphrastic.

Examples:

> *Librī sunt legendī.* **present passive periphrastic**
> "Books must be/have to be read."
>
> *Librī erunt legendī.* **future passive periphrastic**
> "Books will have to be read."
>
> *Librī erant legendī.* **past passive periphrastic**
> "Books had to be read."

In order to indicate who is the agent of the action, the **dative of agent** is used (not the ablative of agent, which is usually used with the passive voice).

Example:

> *Librī mihi sunt legendī.*
> "Books have to be read by me. (or its active equivalent)/I have to read books."

Sometimes, the passive periphrastic is used impersonally, i.e., no person is specified in association with the necessary action. In this situation, the gerundive is neuter—since the subject is impersonal.

Example:

> *Legendum est.*
> "There must be reading./People have to read./One has to read./One must read."

INFINITIVES

FUNCTIONS OF THE INFINITIVE

1. **Complementary with *dēbeō, possum, soleō:***

    The infinitive completes the meanings of these verbs, each of which has an incomplete meaning by itself. Example: in the sentence *legere dēbeō,* which means "I ought to read," the infinitive completes the meaning of "I ought."

2. **Indirect statement after verbs of saying and thinking:**

    In English a subordinate statement after a verb of saying or thinking begins with the conjunction "that." In classical Latin no such conjunction is used: instead the subordinate statement is expressed in the accusative and infinitive as a kind of object of the verb of saying or thinking. Consider the English sentence "I think that the book is good." In Latin the same sentence is *Putō librum esse bonum.*

3. **Nominative and infinitive:**

In Latin, when a verb of saying or thinking is in the passive, the accusative and infinitive is typically not used. The subject of the indirect statement is the same as the subject of the verb of saying or thinking, and it is in the nominative. The verb in the indirect statement is still an infinitive. In this case, Latin is much closer to English. Consider the English sentence "The book is thought to be good." In Latin the same sentence is *Liber bonus esse putātur*.

4. **Accusative and infinitive with *volō, nōlō* and *mālō*:**

The verbs *volō, nōlō*, and *mālō* are used with the accusative and infinitive. But it should be noted that if the subject of the infinitive is the same as the subject of the main verb, the subject is normally not expressed by another word but is understood in the ending of the main verb.

Examples:

Accusative and Infinitive	No Change in Subject
Volō tē ad mē venīre.	*Volō ad tē venīre.*
"I want you to come to me."	"I want to come to you."
Nōn vīs mē ad tē venīre.	*Nōn vīs ad mē venīre.*
"You do not want me to come to you."	"You do not want to come to me."
Mālumus vōs ad nōs venīre.	*Mālumus ad vōs venīre.*
"We prefer that you come to us."	"We prefer to come to you."

TENSES OF THE INFINITIVE IN INDIRECT STATEMENT

In Latin, when the accusative and infinitive construction of indirect statement is used, the tense of the infinitive is always **relative to the main verb** of saying or thinking. This is not quite the same as the situation in English: for in English the tense of the verb within an indirect statement is not always relative to the verb of saying or thinking.

Indirect Statements		
Infinitive	**Time in relation to main clause**	**Example**
Present Infinitive	SAME	*Putō multōs hominēs librum **legere.*** "I think that many people **are reading** the book." *Putābam multōs hominēs librum **legere.*** "I used to think that many people **were reading** the book."
Perfect Infinitive	BEFORE	*Putō multōs hominēs librum **lēgisse.*** "I think that many people **have read** the book." *Putābam multōs hominēs librum **lēgisse.*** "I used to think that many people **had read** the book."
Future Infinitive	AFTER	*Putō multōs hominēs librum **lēctūrōs esse.*** "I think that many people **will read/are going to read/ are going to be reading** the book." *Putābam multōs hominēs librum **lēctūrōs esse.*** "I used to think that many people **would read/were going to read/ were going to be reading** the book."

PARTICIPLES

USE OF PARTICIPLES

A participle is both an adjective and a verb. Like verbs, participles express an action and can be modified by adverbial constructions. Like adjectives, participles agree with a noun, expressed or implied, in case, number, and gender.

Participles have literal meanings but also temporal and occasionally causal meanings.

The **present active participle** indicates an action that happens *at the same time* as the action of the main verb. It is literally translated with *-ing* in English or with a clause beginning with a relative pronoun (e.g., "who, which, that") or a temporal conjunction such as "while."

Example:

> *Anemōliī in urbem ingressī sunt vestīmenta pulcherrima gerentēs.*
> "The Anemolians entered the city wearing most beautiful garments."

The **perfect passive participle** indicates an action that happened *before* the action of the main verb. It can often be translated literally into English by "having been" or by a clause beginning with a temporal conjunction such as "when" or "after."

Examples:

> *Puerī Anemōliōs gemmīs et margarītīs ōrnātōs vīdērunt.*
> "The boys saw the Anemolians (having been) adorned with gems and pearls."

> *Librum ab amīcō datum lēgī.*
> I read the book after it had been given <to me> by a/my friend.

The **future active participle** indicates an action that is intended to happen *after* the action of the main verb. It can be literally translated into English by "about to," "going to," or "intending to" or by a clause beginning with a relative pronoun or temporal conjunction.

Examples:

> *Anemōliī intrāvērunt Ūtopiēnsibus ostentūrī quam essent dīvitēs.*
> "The Anemolians entered about to/intending to show the Utopians how rich they were."

> *Fortūna semper discessūra nihil dat.*
> "Fortune, which is always about to go away, gives nothing."

Sometimes participles have nuances that go beyond the temporal meaning and may express cause by using a causal conjunction to begin a dependent clause.

> *Aliī putantēs monīlia esse vincula et legātōs esse servōs, illa vincula reprehendēbant.*
> "Other people, because they were thinking that the necklaces were chains and the ambassadors were slaves, criticized those chains."

Deponent verbs have a present participle and a future participle with an active meaning (*ūtēns*, "using," *ūsūrus*, "going to use") and a perfect participle with an active meaning also (*ūsus*, "having used").

THE ABLATIVE ABSOLUTE

The ablative absolute is a dependent clause that expresses circumstances logically linked to what is happening in the main clause of a sentence but which is not tied grammatically to the main clause. The ablative absolute is made up of a **noun or pronoun in the ablative agreeing with a participle**, along with other words depending on them or modifying them. Sometimes an adjective or another noun can take the place of the participle, e.g., *Caesare duce* ("with Caesar as general"). Note that there are no subordinating conjunctions like *cum*, *postquam*, *quamquam*, etc.) in an ablative absolute. The subject of the ablative absolute is, with only very rare exceptions, different from the subject of the main clause.

The perfect participle in an ablative absolute refers to a time ***before*** the time of the verb in the main clause while a present participle refers to the ***same*** time as that of the verb in the main clause. When a present participle is in an ablative absolute, it usually ends in *–e*, not in *–ī*.

When the perfect participle is necessary in the ablative absolute, the action indicated in the ablative absolute has to be said passively, even if the same action could be expressed actively using a different type of construction such as a *cum* clause. Since only deponent verbs in Latin can have a perfect participle with an active meaning, an exception occurs to perfect participles being phrased in the passive in ablative absolutes. The use of a deponent perfect participle in an ablative absolute is not common and is limited (in classical Latin) to deponent verbs without an object.

Example:

> *Caesare mortuō, multī cīvēs bellum timēre coepērunt.*
> "After Caesar had died, many citizens began to fear war."

The ablative absolute can fulfill the same functions as temporal, causal, conditional, and concessive clauses. The temporal, causal, conditional, or concessive meaning is inferred from the context. Sometimes the presence of the word *tamen* in the main clause is an indication that the meaning is concessive.

Examples:

Temporal Meaning
Caesare duce dictō, mīlitēs sē ad iter parāre coepērunt.
"When Caesar had been named leader, the soldiers prepared themselves for the road."

Causal Meaning
Hostibus appropinquantibus, cōnsul exercitum parāvit.
"Because the enemy was approaching, the consul prepared an/the army."

Concessive Meaning
Hostibus appropinquantibus, cōnsul tamen exercitum nōn parāvit.
"Although the enemy was approaching, nevertheless the consul did not prepare an/the army."

CONJUNCTIONS

Latin	English
atque	and
autem	however
cum	when, after
dum	while
enim	for, in fact
et	and
itaque	and so
nam	for, in fact
nec	and not, nor
nōn sōlum . . . sed etiam	not only . . . but also
postquam	after
-que	and
sed	but
sī	if
tamen	however

INTERROGATIVE WORDS

Latin	English
cūr?	why?
-ne?	interrogative particle
nōnne?	interrogative expecting a positive answer
num?	interrogative expecting a negative answer
quandō?	when?
quī? quae? quod?	which? what?
quis? quid?	who? what?
quōmodo?	how?
ubi?	where?

APPENDIX D

SUPPLEMENTARY GRAMMAR, MORPHOLOGY AND SYNTAX

This appendix contains additional information on grammar and syntax, which is NOT covered in either Level 1 or Level 2 of *Latin for the New Millennium*. It is meant for students who have completed the entire course of LNM and are embarking on the reading of Latin authors.

SUPPLEMENTARY INFORMATION ON THE USE OF CASES

GENITIVE
Genitive of Quality:
The genitive may describe a quality of the subject. In this case it is always modified by an adjective.

> **Example:**
>
> *Atticus, vir māgnae līberālitātis, multōs habuit amīcōs.*
> "Atticus, a man of great generosity, had many friends."

Genitive of Price:
The genitive is used to indicate general worth with verbs of estimating and buying. It appears in many different neuter adjectives or the genitive of nouns which indicate worth, such as (and these are merely selected examples) *tantī* ("of so much"), *parvī* ("of small worth"), *māgnī* ("of great worth"), *naucī* ("of a trifle"), *floccī* ("of the value of a lock of wool"). Cf. ablative of price, p. 496.

> **Examples:**
>
> *Floccī nōn faciō hōs hominēs.*
> "I don't care a straw (i.e., the value of a lock of wool) for these people."
>
> *Quantī cōnstat hic ager?*
> "How much (i.e., of how much) does this field cost?"
>
> *Parvī aestimō hunc librum.*
> "I consider this book of little worth."

Subjective Genitive:
The genitive indicates the subject.

> **Example:**
>
> *Patriae beneficia.*　　　　"The benefits of the fatherland."
> 　　　　　　　　　　　　　(i.e., the benefits given by the fatherland)

Genitive with Verbs of Memory

Verbs of reminding, remembering, and forgetting take the genitive (some of these verbs also take the accusative).

Example:

> *Hārum rērum semper meminī.* "I always remember these things."

DATIVE

Dative of Purpose:

A noun in the dative may indicate the purpose or tendency of an act or situation. These dative nouns are not modified by any adjectives other than those of magnitude or extent. This dative is often joined with another dative that indicates the person affected. The verb is usually *esse*, although a few other verbs such as *habēre*, *dūcere*, and *dare* are also used in this construction.

Examples:

> *Cōnsilia tua mihi māgnō auxiliō fuērunt.*
> "Your suggestions were a source of great help to me."
>
> *Verba hūius poētae mihi sunt gaudiō.*
> "The words of this poet are a source of joy to me."

Ethical Dative:

This dative indicates a person interested in the action; its grammatical and logical link with the rest of the sentence is quite loose.

Example:

> *Tālia mihi dicta dēfendis?* "Do you defend such sayings (in my sight)?"

ACCUSATIVE

Adverbial Accusative:

A neuter adjective or pronoun expresses the type or extent of an action.

Examples:

> *Plūs valeō quam tū.* "I have more strength than you."
>
> *In carminibus legendīs* "In reading poetry s/he is the most effective."
> *plūrimum potest.*

Double Accusative:

A group of verbs may take two objects, one expressing the thing done, and the other expressing the personal object of the action. This construction occurs with some very common verbs, including *docēre* ("to teach"), *rogāre* ("to ask"), *pōscō* ("to demand"), and *cēlāre* ("to hide").

Examples:

> *Rogō tē tuam sententiam.* "I ask you your opinion."
>
> *Doceō tē hanc artem.* "I teach you this skill."

Note that many of these verbs, including those in the examples above, may also take alternate constructions, such as the accusative of the person affected with the preposition *dē* and the ablative indicating the thing involved, for example *Tē dē hīs rēbus docēbō.* ("I will teach you about these things.")

Greek Accusative:

This use is sometimes called the "accusative of respect" or "Greek middle voice." In the poets and sometimes in post-classical prose authors the accusative (in analogy with Greek usage) may indicate the body part affected.

Example:

> *Vulnerātus pedem . . .*
> "Wounded in his foot (with respect to his foot) . . ."

NB: A not dissimilar poetic usage of the accusative expresses the garment in which a person is dressed, e.g., *Longam indūtus vestem* ("Having put on a long garment").

Accusative of Extent:

The accusative expresses duration of time or extent of space.

Examples:

> *Trēs diēs iter faciēbant.*
> "They were traveling for three days."

> *Iter fēcērunt tria mīlia passuum.*
> "They journeyed for three miles."

ABLATIVE

Ablative with Certain Verbs:

The ablative is used with certain verbs where English speakers might expect the accusative. The most common of these are certain deponents: *ūtor* ("I use"), *fruor* ("I enjoy"), *fungor, fungī, functus sum* ("I fulfill").

> *Officiō meō fungor.*   "I do my duty."

Ablative of Cause:

The ablative typically expresses the cause when that cause is a property or characteristic of the subject of the main verb. When the cause is external to the subject, the prepositions *propter* or *ob* are preferred.

Example:

> *Fortitūdine tuā dīcēbāris esse fortis.*
> "Because of your courage you were said to be brave."

> *Propter fortitūdinem tuam cōnsulēs tē laudāvērunt.*
> "Because of your courage the consuls praised you."

Ablative of Price:
Specific price is expressed by the ablative with verbs of buying and selling. Cf. genitive of price, p. 493.

Example:

> *Agrum eōrum vigintī talentīs ēmī.*
> "I bought their field for twenty talents."

Ablative of Quality:
A noun in the ablative, always modified by an adjective, may denote the quality of a thing—or describe it.

Example:

> *Hī equitēs sunt animō meliōre.*
> "These horsemen are of better spirit."

The genitive may also be used in the same way, but physical (and potentially less permanent) qualities are more often indicated by the ablative.

Ablative of Time:
The ablative (occasionally with the preposition *in* but more often with no preposition) indicates time when (uses the ordinal numbers) or within which (uses the cardinal numbers).

Examples:

> *Tertiō diē terram cōnspexērunt.*
> "On the third day they observed land."
>
> *Tribus diēbus omnem cibum cōnsūmpsērunt.*
> "Within three days they consumed all the food."

NUMBERS

Numbers may be divided into four categories.

Cardinal numbers:
These answer the question *quot?* ("how many?").

Example:

> *Quīnque sunt nautae.*   "There are five sailors."

Ordinal numbers:

These answer the question *quotus?* ("which in order?").

Example:

> *Hic est nauta quīntus.*   "This is the fifth sailor."

Distributive numbers:

These answer the question *quotēnī?* ("how many each?"), and they are regularly used in Latin when one indicates how many items are to be associated with each person or each set of persons/things. The distributives are also used with nouns that have plural forms with singular meanings, such as *castra* ("a camp") and *litterae* ("a letter").

Examples:

> *Quīnquāgēnī nautae in singulīs nāvibus erant.*
> "In each ship there were fifty sailors."

> *Mīlitēs Caesaris in bīnīs castrīs exspectābant.*
> "Caesar's soldiers were waiting in two camps."

Numerical adverbs:

These answer the question *quotiēs?* ("how often?"), and they indicate how many times something happened.

Example:

> *Quīnquiēns rogāvērunt Colōnum ut in Hispāniam redīrent.*
> "Five times they asked Columbus that they turn back to Spain."

The declension of the cardinal number adjectives *ūnus, a, um* ("one"); *duo, duae, duo* ("two"); and *trēs, tria* ("three") are found in Appendix B on p. 448.

The **other cardinal numbers** from *quattuor* to *centum* are **indeclinable.** The rest of the cardinals up to *mīlle* are adjectives of the first and second declension, as are all the ordinals and distributives.

	CARDINAL	ORDINAL	DISTRIBUTIVE	ADVERBS
I.	ūnus, a, um	prīmus, a, um	singulī, ae, a	semel
II.	duo, duae, duo	secundus, alter	bīnī	bis
III.	trēs, trēs, tria	tertius	ternī/trīnī	ter
IV.	quattuor	quārtus	quaternī	quater
V.	quīnque	quīntus	quīnī	quīnquiēns
VI.	sex	sextus	sēnī	sexiēns
VII.	septem	septimus	septēnī	septiēns
VIII.	octō	octāvus	octōnī	octiēns
IX.	novem	nōnus	novēnī	noviēns
X.	decem	decimus	dēnī	deciēns
XI.	ūndecim	ūndecimus	ūndēnī	ūndeciēns
XII.	duodecim	duodecimus	duodēnī	duodeciēns
XIII.	trēdecim	tertius decimus	ternī dēnī	terdeciēns
XIV.	quattuordecim	quārtus decimus	quaternī dēnī	quaterdeciēns
XV.	quīndecim	quīntus decimus	quīnī dēnī	quīndeciēns
XVI.	sēdecim	sextus decimus	sēnī dēnī	sēdeciēns
XVII.	septendecim	septimus decimus	septēnī dēnī	septiēns deciēns
XVIII.	duodēvīgintī	duodēvīcēsimus	duodēvīcēnī	duodēvīciēns
XIX.	ūndēvīgintī	ūndēvīcēsimus	ūndēvīcēnī	ūndēvīciēns
XX.	vīgintī	vīcēsimus	vīcēnī	vīciēns
XXI.	ūnus et vīgintī	ūnus et vīcēsimus	vīcēnī singulī	semel et vīciēns
XXX.	trīgintā	trīcēsimus	trīcēnī	trīciēns
XL.	quadrāgintā	quadrāgēsimus	quadrāgēnī	quadrāgiēns
L.	quīnquāgintā	quīnquāgēsimus	quīnquāgēnī	quīnquāgiēns
LX.	sexāgintā	sexāgēsimus	sexāgēnī	sexāgiēns
LXX.	septuāgintā	septuāgēsimus	septuāgēnī	septuāgiēns
LXXX.	octōgintā	octōgēsimus	octōgēnī	octōgiēns
XC.	nōnāgintā	nōnāgēsimus	nōnāgēnī	nōnāgiēns
C.	centum	centēsimus	centēnī	centiēns
CC.	ducentī	ducentēsimus	ducēnī	ducentiēns
CCC.	trecentī	trecentēsimus	trecēnī	trecentiēns
CCCC.	quadringentī	quadringentēsimus	quadringēnī	quadringentiēns
D.	quīngentī	quīngentēsimus	quīngēnī	quīngentiēns
DC.	sescentī	sescentēsimus	sescēnī	sescentiēns
DCC.	septingentī	septingentēsimus	septingēnī	septingentiēns
DCCC.	octingentī	octingentēsimus	octingēnī	octingentiēns
DCCCC.	nōngentī	nōngentēsimus	nōngēnī	nōngentiēns
M.	mīlle	mīllēsimus	mīllēnī	mīlliēns
MM.	duo mīlia	bis mīllēsimus	bīna mīlia	bis mīlliēns

Mīlle is an **indeclinable adjective** in the singular. The plural *mīlia* is a third declension noun and is used with a partitive genitive.

Examples:

> *Cum mīlle mīlitibus vēnit.*
> "S/he came with a thousand soldiers."

> *Cum decem mīlibus mīlitum vēnit.*
> "S/he came with ten thousand soldiers."

If a smaller number is included with *mīlia* in the plural, the practice varies, but it is not uncommon for the smaller number to follow the genitive.

> *Cum decem mīlibus mīlitum et ducentīs vēnit.*
> "S/he came with ten thousand two hundred soldiers."

INDEFINITE PRONOUNS, ADJECTIVES, AND RELATIVES

INDEFINITE PRONOUNS/ADJECTIVES

Latin is rich in these words, and many of them have subtle distinctions in meaning.

The indefinite *aliquis, aliquid*:

This pronoun means "someone" in an affirmative statement. Its adjective form is *aliquī, aliqua, aliquod*.

Example:

> *Aliquis hoc dīxit.*
> "Somebody said this (though we don't know who.)"

The pronoun *quis, quid* ("anyone, anything") and its adjective *quī, quae/qua, quod* are used instead of *aliquis/aliquī* after *sī, nisi, num,* and *nē*.

Example:

> *Sī quis illam pecūniam mihi dederit, eum amābō!*
> "If anyone gives me that money, I will like him!"

The indefinite *quisquam, quidquam/quicquam*:

This pronoun means "anyone, anything at all," and its adjective *ūllus, a, um* is used after negative words such as *nec* or *vix*, or verbs of prohibiting, preventing, and denying. They are used in questions and *sī*-clauses where a negative force is implied. Unlike *aliquis*, we find *quisquam* in negative or virtually negative statements.

Examples:

> *Ad urbem noctū vēnī, nec quisquam mē cōnspexit.*
> "I arrived at the city by night, and no one saw/caught sight of me."

> *Estne quisquam, quī hoc dīxerit?*
> "Is there anyone who has said this?" (It is implied that there is no one.)

The indefinite *quispiam, quippiam*:

This pronoun means "some one or other" and is not negative but even vaguer than *aliquis*.

Example:

> *Dīxerit tunc quispiam . . .*   "Then someone or other would say . . . "

The indefinite *nesciō quis, nesciō quid*:

This pronoun means "some one or other" and its adjective *nesciō quī, nesciō quae, nesciō quod* is similar to *quispiam*, except that the sense of *nesciō quis* is typically contemptuous. The "verbal" part, *nesciō,* never changes its form, regardless of the construction of *quis/quid*.

Example:

> *Nesciō quis hoc dīxit.*
> "Someone (of little account, i.e., I don't know who) said this."

The indefinite *quīdam, quaedam, quoddam*:

This pronoun/adjective means "a certain one/thing," and it is sometimes used in much the same way as "one" is used in English. Please note that the Latin *ūnus* is very rarely (in the more polished authors, at least) used as an indefinite.

Examples:

> *Erat in Atticī mōribus grātia, sed etiam quaedam gravitās.*
> "There was agreeableness in Atticus' personality, but also a certain seriousness/weightiness."

> *Tertiō autem diē quīdam ē nautīs lūmen cōnspexit.*
> "But on the third day one of the sailors observed a light."

The indefinite *quīvīs, quaevīs, quodvīs* (for adjectives) and *quidvīs* (for pronouns) and *quīlibet, quaelibet, quodlibet* (for adjectives) and *quidlibet* (for pronouns):

These mean "any one/thing you like" or "any one/thing which you please."

Examples:

> *Mūcius Scaevola quodlibet perīculum prō patriā patī parātus erat.*
> "Mucius Scaevola was prepared to endure any danger whatsoever for the sake of <his> fatherland."

THE INDEFINITE RELATIVE

**The indefinite relative *quīcumque, quaecumque, quodcumque*
and *quisquis, quicquid/quidquid*:**

These indefinite relative pronouns mean "whoever, whatever." In later authors they are sometimes used as non-relative indefinite pronouns, but in classical Latin they are almost always relatives (like *quī, quae, quod*).

Example:

> *Quīcumque Rōmam vēnerit, lūcrum faciet.*
> "Whoever comes to Rome, will make a profit."

SUPPLEMENTAL INFORMATION ON VERB FORMS

FUTURE PASSIVE INFINITIVE IN INDIRECT SPEECH

The equivalent of a future passive infinitive in indirect speech may be formed in two ways: one may use the supine ending in *–um* with *īrī* (the passive infinitive of *īre*), or *fore* (the future active infinitive of *esse* in shortened form) with *ut* and a result clause. The supine form in *–um*, of course, never changes its ending, regardless of its implied "subject."

Examples:

> *Caesar multōs cīvēs servātum īrī pollicitus est.*
> "Caesar promised that many citizens would be saved."

> *Caesar fore ut multī cīvēs servārentur pollicitus est.*
> "Caesar promised that many citizens would be saved."

PRESENT PASSIVE IMPERATIVE

	First conjugation	Second conjugation	Third conjugation	Fourth conjugation	Third conjugation *-iō*
Second person singular positive	amāre (be loved)	monēre (be warned)	petere (be sought)	audīre (be heard)	capere (be captured)
Second person plural positive	amāminī (be loved)	monēminī (be warned)	petiminī (be sought)	audīminī (be heard)	capiminī (be captured)

FUTURE IMPERATIVE

There is also a future imperative of most verbs which indicates a more formal sort of request. Note that there are only singular forms in the passive.

	First conjugation	Second conjugation	Third conjugation	Fourth conjugation	Third conjugation -iō
Active					
Second person singular positive	amātō (you shall love)	monētō (you shall warn)	petitō (you shall seek)	audītō (you shall hear)	capitō (you shall capture)
Second person plural positive	amātōte (you shall love)	monētōte (you shall warn)	petitōte (you shall seek)	audītōte (you shall hear)	capitōte (you shall capture)
Passive					
Second person singular positive	amātor (you shall be loved)	monētor (you shall be warned)	petitor (you shall be sought)	audītor (you shall be heard)	capitor (you shall be captured)

ALTERNATE VERB ENDINGS

Very common in verse are alternate endings in *–re* instead of *–ris* of the second person singular present passive in the present, future, and imperfect tenses of the indicative and subjunctive: for example, *monēbāre = monēbāris*, *petere = peteris*, *audiēre = audiēris*, etc. Similarly, and also typically in poetry, though we find this in some prose too, the *–ērunt* ending of the perfect active indicative can end in *–ēre*: so we can sometimes see *laudāvēre* for **laudāvērunt** or *audīvēre* for **audīvērunt**, etc.

SUPINE IN *–Ū*

The supine of some verbs (found always in the fourth principal part) can end in *–ū* instead of *–um*, and then it functions like an ablative of respect. It is used with the noun phrases *opus* ("there is need of"), *fās* ("it is right"), *nefās* ("it is wrong"), and with adjectives denoting ease, difficulty, or the effect on one's feelings and senses. The number of these supines is relatively restricted in classical Latin, including just the following forms: *audītū, dictū, factū, inventū, memorātū* (*memorō, āre*, to mention), *nātū, vīsū*. The number of these supines increases in later Latin.

NB: In each chapter of LNM, you have seen the use of the supine in *–ū* in the section title— *memorābile dictū*— and in the review section title—*mīrābile audītū*.

Examples:

> *Sī hoc est fās dictū.*
> "If this is legitimate to say."

> *Quaerunt quid optimum factū sit.*
> "They ask what is the best thing to do."

IMPERSONAL VERBS

An impersonal verb is a verb with an abstract or impersonal subject in the third person singular only. In English such a subject is often indicated by the words "one" or "it." There are quite a few types of impersonal verbs in Latin.

Many impersonal verbs, such as *cōnstat* ("it is established"), may be completed with an accusative and infinitive.

Example:

> *Cōnstat līberālitātem Atticī ā multīs laudātam esse.*
> "It is established/generally known that Atticus' generosity was praised by many people."

Several impersonal verbs, such as *licet* ("it is permitted/allowed"), are completed with a dative and infinitive.

Example:

> *Licuit Atticō Athēnīs diū manēre.*
> "Atticus was allowed/it was permitted for Atticus to remain in Athens for a long time."

Some impersonal verbs, such as *paenitet* ("it repents/is a cause of regret"), *pudet* ("it causes shame"), *taedet* ("it bores") and *piget* ("it causes regret"), may be constructed with genitive and infinitive.

Example:

> *Īrae meae mē paenitet.*
> "I regret/am sorry for my anger."

Sometimes intransitive verbs can be used impersonally in the third person singular passive to indicate a general action. If the tense is perfect, the participial part of the verb must be in the neuter nominative singular.

Example:

> *Ad forum itur.*
> "There is a going to the forum/One goes to the forum."

> *Ad urbem ventum est.*
> "There was an arrival at the city/<They> came to the city."

Verbs which take a dative instead of an accusative direct object, such as *parcō* ("to spare"), *persuādeō* ("to persuade"), *noceō* ("to harm"), *īgnōscō* ("to pardon") are only used impersonally in the passive.

Example:

Tibi nōn nocētur.	"You are not being harmed."
Nōbīs ā Cicerōne persuādētur.	"We are persuaded by Cicero."
Nēminī parcēbātur.	"No one was being spared."

HISTORICAL PRESENT

In a narration (especially in histories) of a series of actions that took place in the past, the present tense is sometimes employed to make the action seem more vivid and present. This use of the present may occur in the context of other verbs which retain their past tense.

Example:

> *Caesar Gallōs nōn esse parātōs cōnspexerat: itaque mīlitēs suōs*
> *impetum facere iubet.*
> "Caesar had noticed the Gauls were unprepared: so he orders
> (i.e., ordered) his soldiers to launch an attack."

Similar to this "historical present" is the use of the "literary present." In this use of the present tense an author, who may be long since dead, is conventionally said to speak in the present time.

Example:

> *Nepos dīcit Atticum ab omnibus Athēniēnsibus amātum esse.*
> "Nepos says (as if he were speaking now) that Atticus was loved
> by all the Athenians."

HISTORICAL INFINITIVE

In a narration (especially in histories) that involves a rapid sequence of events, the present infinitive instead of the indicative is sometimes employed. In such cases there are usually several infinitives in succession, and their subjects, if expressed, are nominative (not accusative).

Example:

> *Tunc Catilīna cum mīlitibus prīmīs versārī, laesīs auxilium dare, omnia cūrāre,*
> *ferōciter ipse pugnāre . . .*
> "Then Catiline was occupied with the front rank of soldiers: he was helping
> the wounded, he was taking charge of everything, and he himself was
> fighting fiercely . . ."

EXCLAMATORY SENTENCES

Exclamations can be expressed in Latin in a number of ways, two of which are perhaps the most common.

Exclamations are expressed in the accusative case, and verbs, if expressed, are in the infinitive. Some exclamations are also interrogative.

Examples:

> *Ō, mē miserum!*
> "Oh, wretched me!"

> *Mēne in tālem locum dēscendere!?*
> "What! I go down into a place like that!?"

Exclamatory questions may also be expressed with the subjunctive, with or without *ut*.

Example:

> *Egone tibi pauper, hominī tam dīvitī, pecūniam dare dēbeam!?*
> "I, a poor man, ought to give money to you, so wealthy a man!?"

MORE ON THE SUBJUNCTIVE IN MAIN CLAUSES

In addition to the volitive and optative uses of the subjunctive in a main clause, the subjunctive can appear in the principal clause of a sentence with a meaning that is often described as potential (or one of conditioned futurity). In this usage the speaker/writer makes a statement about something which could potentially happen but which is far from certain.

The present, and very often the perfect subjunctive, is used for a **present potential** statement pertaining to some vague future time

Examples:

> *Mōrēs tālium hominum probem . . .*
> "I would approve of the character of such people . . ."
> (should I perchance meet people of such a kind)
>
> *Vix crēdiderim talia esse vēra . . .*
> "I should scarcely believe such things are true . . ."
> (should such things perchance happen).

The **potential of the past,** with its effect often being valid up to the present, is expressed by the imperfect subjunctive (the pluperfect subjunctive is rarely employed for the past potential).

Example:

> *Crēderēs eōs esse victōs . . .*
> "You would think (and would still think) those people were conquered . . ."
> (if you had seen them).

MORE ON THE SUBJUNCTIVE IN DEPENDENT CLAUSES

Futurity in Indirect Questions

If the verb in an indirect question is active and refers to a time **after** that of the main verb, this future time may be indicated by the use of the future active participle with the subjunctive of *esse*. The tense of the subjunctive of *esse* normally conforms to the rules for sequence of tenses.

Examples:

> Mīles rogat *quid dīxerimus.*
> "The soldier is asking what we said."
>
> Mīles rogat *quid dictūrī sīmus.*
> "The soldier is asking what we are going to say."

Mīles rogāvit *quid dīcerēmus.*
"The soldier asked what we were saying."

Mīles rogāvit *quid dictūrī essēmus.*
"The soldier asked what we were going to say."

Statements Dependent on Verbs of Fearing

The subordinate constructions which depend on verbs expressing fear are quite distinctive.

What we fear **might happen in the future** is expressed by a clause whose verb is subjunctive and which depends on *nē.* In such cases, *nē* has a meaning similar to the English "lest."

Example:

Caesar timēbat nē ab hostibus facile cōnspicerētur.
"Caesar was afraid that he would easily be observed by the enemy."

What we fear might **not** happen is expressed by a clause whose verb is subjunctive and which depends on *ut,* or sometimes *nē nōn.*

Examples:

Caesar timēbat ut ā mīlitibus suīs cōnspicerētur.
"Caesar was afraid that he would not be observed by his (own) soldiers."

Caesar timēbat nē mīlitēs tālibus verbīs nōn firmārentur.
"Caesar was afraid that (his) soldiers would not be strengthened by such words."

Clauses after Verbs of Hindering and Preventing: *nē, quōminus, quīn*

If a verb of hindering or preventing is **positive,** the clause depending on it is in the subjunctive mood introduced by *nē* or *quōminus.*

Example:

Impedior nē/quōminus dē hīs rēbus loquar.
"I am prevented from speaking about these things."

If the verb of hindering or preventing is **negative or interrogative** implying a negative or is joined with the adverbs *vix* or *aegrē* (which mean "hardly," or "scarcely"), the clause depending on it is in the subjunctive mood introduced by *quīn* or (more rarely) *quōminus.*

Example:

Mīlitēs impedīrī nōn poterant quīn arma caperent.
"The soldiers could not be prevented from seizing arms."

More Clauses with *quīn*

The word *quīn* has several distinctive and widely differing functions and meanings.

A clause introduced by *quīn* with its verb in the subjunctive depends on **negative** (and **never** affirmative) phrases of doubting.

Examples:

> *Nōn erat dubium quīn mīlitēs arma capere vellent.*
> "There was no doubt that the soldiers wanted to seize arms."

> *Nōn dubitō quīn Vergilius poēta fuerit optimus.*
> "I do not doubt that Vergil was the best poet."

Very often *quīn* is the equivalent of *ut nōn* in result clauses if the main verb is negative, or interrogative implying a negative, or is joined with the adverbs *vix* or *aegrē* (which mean "hardly," or "scarcely"). In such sentences, *quīn* is the equivalent of a relative with a negative (i.e., *quī, quae, quod* + *nōn*). It is generally used instead of a relative in the nominative case (and occasionally in place of a relative in the accusative).

Example:

> *Nūllus homō est tam doctus quīn aliquid aliud discere possit.*
> "No person is so learned that he cannot learn something else."

Quīn introducing an **interrogative sentence** sometimes means "why not(?)."

Example:

> *Quīn pācem petimus?*
> "Why do we not seek peace?"

Explicative Clauses

An entire clause, which has an explicative or "completing the circumstances" meaning and which is introduced by *ut* with its verb in the subjunctive, is used as the **subject** of certain set phrases, the most common of which are: *accidit ut, contingit ut, ēvenit ut, fit ut* (which all mean "it happens that"), *fierī potest ut* ("it can happen that"), and *mōs est ut* ("it is the custom that").

Example:

> *Fit ut āthētae optimī praemia accipiant.*
> "It happens that the best athletes get prizes."

An entire clause, which has an explicative or "completing the circumstances" meaning and is introduced by *quod* with its verb in the indicative, is used as the **object** of certain set phrases, the most common of which are: *addō* ("I add"), *praetereō* ("I pass over"), *mittō* ("I disregard"). *Quod* in such sentences means "the fact that."

Example:

> *Praetereō quod cīvēs nostrī cibō indigent.*
> "I pass over the fact that our citizens need food."

An entire clause, which has an explicative or "completing the circumstances" meaning and is introduced by *quod* with its verb in the indicative, is used as the **subject** of certain set phrases, such as *bonum/malum/(etc.) est* ("it is good or bad that"), *accēdit* ("<the fact> is added that"), *bene/male/(etc.) accidit, ēvenit, fit* ("it turns out well/badly [etc.] that").

Example:

> *Accēdit quod nē ūnum quidem amīcum inter iūdicēs cōnspiciō.*
> "Added is the fact that I do not observe even one friend among the jurors."

Comparative Clauses

In a comparative sentence which expresses likeness or difference **as a fact**, the **indicative** is used in both clauses. Common correlative words expressing likeness are *sīc/ita . . . ut* ("just/so . . . as"), or *perinde/iuxtā . . . atque* ("just/so . . . as"), and *pariter aequē . . . atque* ("equally . . . as").

Example:

> *Perinde fēcī, atque dēbuī.*
> "As I ought <to have acted>, so I acted."

Common correlative words expressing difference or unlikeness in a comparison of fact are *aliter/secus . . . atque* ("differently . . . from," "otherwise . . . than"), *contrā . . . atque/quam* ("contrarily . . . to").

Examples:

> *Contrā quam putāvī, nēmō vēnit.*
> "Contrary to my supposition, no one came."

> *Aliter dīxit atque fēcit.*
> "His words were different from his action."

In comparative sentences which are **hypothetical**, **conditional**, or **contrary to fact**, the verb of the subordinate clause is **subjunctive**. The most common comparative conjunctions in such sentences are *quam sī* ("than/as . . . if"), *quasi, ut sī, tamquam sī, velut sī* ("as . . . if"). Occasionally we find simply *tamquam* or *velut* with a subjunctive verb.

Example:

> *"Mātris tuae negōtia," inquit Atticus, "cūrāvī, velut sī essent mea."*
> "I managed your mother's business affairs," said Atticus, "as though they were mine."

Relative Clauses with the Subjunctive in a Direct Statement

When the meaning of a relative clause includes something more than a mere descriptive statement about the antecedent, the verb of the relative clause is often in the subjunctive.

A relative clause that describes a **characteristic or quality** of the antecedent is often the equivalent of a result clause. Such relative clauses typically refer to negative or indefinite antecedents, or antecedents modified by *sōlus* or *ūnus*.

Example:

> *Sunt quī crēdant Caesarem esse victum.*
> "There are those (the type of people) who would believe that Caesar was defeated."

A relative clause may also be the equivalent of a **purpose clause.**

Example:

> *Atticus servum ad urbem mīsit, quī litterās Antōniō daret.*
> "Atticus sent his slave to the city so that he (the slave) might give the letter to Antony."

A relative clause with the subjunctive may be the equivalent of a **concessive or causal** clause. The concessive relative clause is sometimes (but not always) accompanied by *tamen* in the main clause. The causal meaning of a relative clause is sometimes (but not always) made clear by *quippe, ut,* or *utpote* placed next to the relative pronoun.

Examples:

> *Atticus, quī esset homō dīves, domum (tamen) māgnam habēre nōlēbat.*
> "Although Atticus was a wealthy man, he did not want to have a large home."

> *Atticus, (quippe) quī esset homō dīves, multōs miserōs iuvāre poterat.*
> "Because Atticus was a wealthy man, he was able to help many unfortunate people."

A relative clause with the subjunctive may sometimes have a **restrictive meaning**, and this meaning is sometimes (but not always) emphasized by *quidem.*

Examples:

> *Omnēs, quī (quidem) hīc maneant, Atticum laudāre volunt.*
> "Everyone, at least <of> those who are staying here, want to praise Atticus."

MORE ON CONDITIONAL SENTENCES

Hypothetical conditions may pertain to the **future,** in which case they are often called "future-less-vivid conditions." In such conditions the verbs in both the main and subordinate clause are in the present subjunctive although the verb in the subordinate clause may be in the perfect subjunctive if the action clearly happened before that of the main clause. See Chapter 12 and/or Appendix C for more information.

Examples:

> *Sī Rōmae habitētis, sītis fēlīcēs.*
> "Should you (pl.) live in Rome, you would be happy."

> *Sī aedēs in urbe positās ēmerim, Rōmae saepius maneam.*
> "If I should buy a house located in the city, I would stay in Rome more often."

Hypothetical conditions of the **past** usually have verbs in the imperfect subjunctive in both the "if-clause" and the main clause. In appearance they resemble unfulfilled or contrary-to-fact conditions of the present. In fact, they are to be distinguished from such conditional sentences because of subtle differences in meaning. These conditions are not actually contrary-to-fact or unfulfilled, but rather present a hypothetical or potential statement about a past time.

Example:

> *Sī Caesar mīlitēs in eōrum terram ad eōs iuvandōs mittere vidērētur, nōn tam bellum gerere quam hostēs repellere putārētur.*
> "Were Caesar to seem to send soldiers into their territory in order to help them, he would be thought not so much to wage war as to repel enemies."

MORE ON INDIRECT DISCOURSE/STATEMENT

Subordinate clauses that are really **part of indirect speech** have their verb(s) in the **subjunctive**, even if this/these verb(s) would have been in the indicative in the direct statement.

Example:

> *Caesar sē quoque ā mīlitibus, quōs ipse vidēre posset, facile cōnspicī posse intellēxit.*
> "Caesar realized that he too could be easily observed by the soldiers whom he himself could see." (The phrase *quōs ipse vidēre posset* is a part of what Caesar realized.)

Subordinate clauses in a passage of indirect discourse that are **not part** of the thought of the subject of the indirect discourse (such as explanatory remarks of the author) have verb(s) in the **indicative**.

Example:

> *Thēseus sē in Crētam, quae est īnsula, cum adulēscentibus Athēniēnsibus nāvigātūrum esse prōmīsit.*
> "Theseus promised that he would sail with the Athenian youths to Crete, which is an island." (The phrase *quae est īnsula* is an explanation given by the author rather than a part of what Theseus promised.)

Pronouns, as well as adverbs of place and time, **fit the point of view of indirect speech** introduced by a third person verb. Therefore, *hic* in direct speech becomes *ille* in the indirect speech, *hīc* becomes *ibi*, *nunc* becomes *tunc* (if the main verb introducing the indirect speech is in a past tense), etc.

Examples:

> (Direct) *Haec praemia sunt optima.* (These are the words of the athletes.)
> "These prizes are the best."

> (Indirect) *Āthlētae illa praemia esse optima crēdēbant.* (Someone else is reporting the words/thoughts of the athletes.)
> "The athletes believed that those prizes were the best."

(Direct) *Hīc templum aedificābō.* (These are the words of the queen.)
"Here I shall build a temple."

(Indirect) *Rēgīna sē templum ibi aedificātūram esse dīxit.* (Someone else is reporting the words of the queen.)
"The queen said that she would build a temple there."

(Direct) *Multās nāvēs vidēre nunc possum!* (These are the words of the sailor.)
"Now I can see many ships."

(Indirect) *Nauta multās sē nāvēs vidēre tunc posse clāmāvit.* (Someone else is reporting the words of the sailor.)
"The sailor shouted that he was then able to see many ships."

Questions and commands, which would have indicative and imperative moods in direct speech, are expressed in indirect discourse with **subjunctive** verbs.

Examples:

(Direct) *Hostēs ferōcissimī ā vōbīs sunt victī. Propter virtūtem vestram Carthāginiēnsēs ab omnibus gentibus timentur. Cūr igitur nunc Alpēs, montēs nōn hominēs, montēs nōn hostēs, timētis? Timōrem exstinguite! Sarcinās parāte! Nōlīte in castrīs manēre!*
"The most ferocious enemies have been defeated by you. Because of your courage the Carthaginians are feared by all peoples. Why do you now fear the Alps, mountains not people, mountains not enemies? Destroy fear! Prepare the baggage! Do not stay in the camp!"

(Indirect) *Hannibal īrātus dīxit hostēs ferōcissimōs ab illīs esse victōs. Propter eōrum virtūtem Carthāginiēnsēs ab omnibus gentibus timērī. Cūr igitur tunc Alpēs, montēs nōn hominēs, montēs nōn hostēs, timērent? Timōrem exstinguerent! Sarcinās parārent! Nē in castrīs manērent!*
"Angered Hannibal said that the most ferocious enemies had been defeated by them (i.e., the soldiers). Because of their courage the Carthaginians were feared by all peoples. Why then were they afraid of the Alps, mountains not people, mountains not enemies? They should destroy fear! They should prepare <their> baggage! They must not stay in the camp!"

Sometimes, however, **rhetorical questions**, i.e., questions that are not real questions but are asked just for effect and expect no answer, are expressed with the accusative and infinitive rather than the subjunctive in indirect speech.

Example:

> (Direct) *Hostēs ferōcissimī ā vōbīs sunt victī. Propter virtūtem vestram Carthāginiēnsēs ab omnibus gentibus timentur. Cūr igitur nunc Alpēs, montēs nōn hominēs, montēs nōn hostēs, timētis?* **Quis umquam rem tam turpem vīdit?!** *Timōrem exstinguite! Sarcinās parāte! Nōlīte in castrīs manēre!*
>
> "The most ferocious enemies have been defeated by you. Because of your courage the Carthaginians are feared by all peoples. Why do you now fear the Alps, mountains not people, mountains not enemies? **Who ever saw a thing so shameful?!** Destroy fear! Prepare the baggage! Do not stay in the camp!"

> (Indirect) *Hannibal īrātus dīxit hostēs ferōcissimōs ab illīs esse victōs. Propter eōrum virtūtem Carthāginiēnsēs ab omnibus gentibus timērī. Cūr igitur tunc Alpēs, montēs nōn hominēs, montēs nōn hostēs, timērent?* **Quem umquam rem tam turpem vīdisse?!** *Timōrem exstinguerent! Sarcinās parārent! Nē in castrīs manērent!*
>
> "Angered Hannibal said that the most ferocious enemies had been defeated by them (i.e., the soldiers). Because of their courage the Carthaginians were feared by all peoples. Why were they then afraid of the Alps, mountains not people, mountains not enemies? **Who had ever seen a thing so shameful?!** They should destroy fear! They should prepare <their> baggage! They must not stay in the camp!"

MORE ON INTERROGATIVE WORDS: *NUM, NŌNNE, NECNE, ANNŌN*

Num introducing a direct question expects a negative answer.

Example:

> *Num mōrēs hōrum hominum malōs probās?*
> "Surely you do not approve of the bad character of these people?"
> (Expected answer: "Of course not.")

Num introducing an indirect question does not have this force. In indirect questions, *num* is a neutral interrogative particle which indicates no expectation about the type of answer.

Example:

> *Amīcum meum rogābō num carmina Vergiliī lēgerit.*
> "I shall ask my friend whether he has read the poems of Vergil."
> (I have no expectation about what his answer might be.)

Nōnne introducing a direct question expects an affirmative answer.

Example:

> *Nōnne hoc aedificium esse pulchrum putās?*
> "Don't you think this building is beautiful?"
> (Expected answer: "Yes indeed, I do.")

Annōn means "or not" and is typically used in direct questions.

Example:

> *Suntne hī hominēs cīvēs, annōn?*
> "Are these people citizens, or not?"

Necne means "or not" and is typically used in indirect questions.

Example:

> *Rogāvimus pecūnia mīlitibus esset data necne.*
> "We asked whether the money had been given to the soldiers or not."

ENGLISH TO LATIN GLOSSARY

This glossary contains the English meanings of all the Latin words in the **Vocabulary to Learn** sections from all the chapters.

LIST OF ABBREVIATIONS:

(1) = first conjugation
abl. = ablative
acc. = accusative
adj. = adjective
adv. = adverb
conj. = conjunction
dat. = dative
f. = feminine

gen. = genitive
inf. = infinitive
m. = masculine
n. = neuter
pl. = plural
prep. = preposition
sg. = singular

NOTE:

The genitive of second declension words ending in *-ius* or *-ium* is indicated with a single *-ī,* which is the genitive ending itself. Note that in the full form of the genitive there is normally a double *i*: *fīlius, -ī* (= *filiī*); *gaudium, -ī* (= *gaudiī*).

A

adorned, ornātus, -a, -um, *adj.*

abandon, relinquō, -ere, relīquī, relictum

able, to be, possum, posse, potuī, —

able, to be (= *to have the power to do*), valeō, -ēre, valuī, —, + *infinitive*

abode, sēdēs, -is, *f.*

abound with, abundō (1), + *abl.*

about, dē, *prep.* + *abl.*

about to be, futūrus, -a, -um, *participle*

absent, absēns, absentis, *adj.*

absent, to be, absum, abesse, āfuī, —

accept, accipiō, -ere, -cēpī, -ceptum

account of, on, propter, *prep.* + *acc.*

account, to hold of no, aestimō ūnīus assis

accuse someone of something, accūsō (1), + *acc.* + *gen.*

accustomed, to be, soleō, -ēre, solitus sum, —, + *inf.*

acknowledge, cōgnoscō, -ere, cōgnōvī, cōgnitum

acquire, cōnsequor, cōnsequī, cōnsecūtus sum; percipiō, -ere, percēpī, perceptum

add, addō, -ere, addidī, additum

added, to be, accēdō, -ere, accessī, accessum

adopt, capiō, -ere, cēpī, captum

advice, cōnsilium, -ī, *n.*

after, cum, *conj.* + *pluperfect subjunctive*

after, post, *prep.* + *acc.*

afterwards, posteā, *adv.*

again, iterum, *adv.*

against, contrā, *prep.* + *acc.*

age, aetās, -ātis, *f.*

agreeable, iūcundus, -a, -um, *adj.*

agreeableness, grātia, -ae, *f.*

all, omnis, -e, *adj.*

allow somebody to do something, sinō, -ere, sīvī, situm, + *acc.* + *inf.*

allowed for someone to do something, it is, licet, + *dat.* + *inf.*

ally, socius, -ī, *m.*

almost, paene, *adv.*

alone, sōlus, -a, -um, *adj.*

already, iam, *adv.*

also, etiam, *adv.*; quoque, *adv.*

although, cum, *conj.,* + *imperfect subjunctive*; etsī, *conj.*; quamquam, *conj.*; quamvīs, *conj.*

always, semper, *adv.*

ambassador, lēgātus, -ī, *m.*

among, inter, *prep.* + *acc.* (also one of the meanings of *apud*, prep. + acc.)

ancient, antīquus, -a, -um, *adj.*

and, et, *conj.*; atque, *conj.*; -que, *conj.*

and not, nec, *conj.*; neque, *conj.*

and so, itaque, *conj.*

anger, īra, -ae, *f.*

angry, to be, īrāscor, īrāscī, īrātus sum

animal, animal, -ālis, *n.*

another, alius, alia, aliud, *adj.*

answer, respondeō, -ēre, -spondī, -spōnsum

antiquity, antīquitās, -ātis, *f.*

any, ūllus, -a, -um, *indefinite adj. (mainly in negative sentences)*

appear, appāreō, -ēre, appāruī, appāritum

appearance, fōrma, -ae, *f.*

apply, adhibeō, -ēre, adhibuī, adhibitum

appreciative, grātus, -a, -um, *adj.*

approach, accēdō, -ere, accessī, accessum; appropinquō (1)

appropriate, aptus, -a, -um, *adj.*

approve, probō (1)

argument, argūmentum, -ī, *n.*

armed, armātus, -a, -um, *adj.*

army, exercitus, -ūs, m.

around, circa, *prep. + acc.*; circum, *prep. + acc.*

arrival, adventus, -ūs, m.

arrive, perveniō, -īre, -vēnī, -ventum

art, ars, artis, *f.*

artisan, artifex, -ficis, *m.*

as, tamquam, *adv.*; ut, *conj. + indicative*

as . . . as possible, quam + *superlative degree*

as often as, quotiēs, *conj.*

as soon as, simul ac, *conj.*; ut *conj. + perfect indicative*

ash, cinis, -eris, *m.*

ask, ōrō (1); rogō (1)

assert, affirmō (1)

assiduous, frequēns, -entis, *adj.*

associate, socius, -ī, *m.*

at first, prīmō, *adv.*

at home, domī

at last, tandem, *adv.*

at one time . . . at another . . . , modo . . . modo . . .

at the house of, apud, *prep. + acc.*

at the same time, simul, *adv.*

athlete, āthlēta, -ae, *m.*

attack, impetus, -ūs, *m.*

attain, reach, (verb), cōnsequor, cōnsequī, cōnsecūtus sum

attentiveness, dīligentia, -ae, *f.*

attire, vestis, -is, *f.*

avail, to no, frūstrā, *adv.*

await, exspectō (1)

awaken, excitō (1)

away, absēns, absentis, *adj.*

axis, axis, -is, *m.*

axle, axis, -is, *m.*

B

bad, improbus, -a, -um, *adj.*; malus, -a, -um, *adj.*

baggage, sarcina, -ae, *f.* (used mostly in pl.)

battle, proelium, -ī, *n.*

be surprised at, mīror, mīrārī, mirātus sum

be unwilling, nōlō, nōlle, nōluī, —

be, sum, esse, fuī, —

bear, ferō, ferre, tulī, lātum

beard, barba, -ae, *f.*

beautiful, pulcher, pulchra, pulchrum, *adj.*

because, namque, *conj.*; quia, *conj.*; quod, *conj.*

because of, propter, *prep. + acc.*

become, fīō, fierī, factus sum

befall, accidō, -ere, accidī, —

before, in front of, ante, *prep. + acc.*

begin to, coepī, coepisse, coeptum, + *inf.*

beginning, initium, -ī, *n.*; ortus, -ūs, *m.*

behalf of, on, prō, *prep. + abl.*

behave, act in a certain way, agō, -ere, ēgī, āctum

believe somebody, crēdō, -ere, crēdidī, crēditum, + *dat.*

best, optimus, -a, -um, *adj.*

bestow, tribuō, -ere, tribuī, tribūtum

better, melior, melius, *adj. comparative*

between, inter, *prep. + acc.*

blame, reprehendō, -ere, -prehendī, -prehēnsum

blood, sanguis, -inis, *m.*

blossom, flōreō, -ēre, flōruī, —

body, corpus, -oris, *n.*

bond, necessitūdō, -ūdinis, *f.*

book, liber, librī, *m.*; volūmen, -ūminis, *n.*

born, to be, nascor, nascī, nātus sum

born of, to be, orior, orīrī, ortus sum + *abl.*

bosom, gremium, -ī, *n.*

both . . . and . . . , et . . . et . . .

boundless, infīnītus, -a, -um, *adj.*

boy, puer, puerī, *m.*

brave, fortis, -e, *adj.*

break, rumpō, -ere, rūpī, ruptum

bridge, pōns, pontis, *m.*

briefly, breviter, *adv.*

bring about, efficiō, -ere, -fēcī, -fectum, often + *ut*

brook, rīvus, -ī, *m.*

brother, frāter, -ātris, *m.*

build, aedificō (1)

building, aedificium, -ī, *n.*

burden, onus, oneris, *n.*; sarcina, -ae, *f.* (used mostly in pl.)

burn, be on fire, ārdeō, -ēre, ārsī, —

burst in, invādō, -ere, invāsī, —

but, at, *conj.*; sed, *conj.*

buy, emō, -ere, ēmī, emptum

by, ā *or* ab, *prep. + abl.*

C

calamity, calamitās, -ātis, *f.*

call, vocō (1)

calm, placidus, -a, -um, *adj.*; serēnus, -a, -um, *adj.*

calmly (*of a person's attitude*), aequō animō

camp, castra, -ōrum, *n. pl.*

can, possum, posse, potuī, —

capture, capiō, -ere, cēpī, captum

care, cultus, -ūs, *m.*; cūra, -ae, *f.*

care for, cūrō (1)

care for, not to, aestimō ūnīus assis

careful in choosing, ēlegāns, -antis, *adj.*

carefully, dīligenter, *adv.*

carefulness, dīligentia, -ae, *f.*

carry back, referō, referre, rettulī, relātum

carry, ferō, ferre, tulī, lātum; gerō, -ere, gessī, gestum; (*of vehicles*) vehō, -ere, vexī, vectum

cause, causa, -ae, *f.*

cause to happen, efficiō, -ere, -fēcī, -fectum, often + *ut*

cave, spēlunca, -ae, *f.*

certain, a, quīdam, quaedam, quiddam, *indefinite pronoun;* quīdam, quaedam, quoddam, *indefinite adjective*

certain, for, prō certō, *adverbial phrase*

chain, vinculum, -ī, *n.*

change, mūtō (1)

charm, suāvitās, -ātis, *f.*

chest, pectus, -oris, *n.*

choose, legō, -ere, lēgī, lēctum

circle, orbis, orbis, *m.*

citizen, cīvis, -is, *m./f.*

city (city of Rome), urbs, urbis, *f.*

clear, clārus, -a, -um, *adj.*; serēnus, -a, -um, *adj.*

clear, to be, appāreō, -ēre, appāruī, —

closest, intimus, -a, -um, *adj.*

clothes, vestīmenta, -ōrum, *n. pl.;* vestis, -is, *f.*

cloud, nūbēs, -is, *f.*

cold, frīgus, -oris, *n.*

column of marching or traveling people, agmen, -minis, *n.*

combat, proelium, -ī, *n.*

come, veniō, -īre, vēnī, ventum

come upon, inveniō, -īre, invēnī, inventum

command, potestās, -ātis, *f.*

commanding officer, imperātor, -ōris, *m.*

common, pūblicus, -a, -um, *adj.*

common people, vulgus, -ī, *n.*

compel, cōgō, -ere, coēgī, coactum

complete, to, compleō, -ēre, -ēvī, -ētum

concerning, dē, *prep.* + *abl.*

condition, condiciō, -ōnis, *f.*

confirm, sanciō, -īre, sānxī, sanctum

conflagration, incendium, -ī, *n.*

confusion, tumultus, -ūs, *m.*

connect, coniungō, -ere, -iūnxī, -iūnctum

connection (*usually by marriage*), affīnitās, -ātis, *f.*

conquer, vincō, -ere, vīcī, victum

consider, arbitror, arbitrārī, arbitrātus sum; putō (1)

consist in, cōnstō, -āre, cōnstitī, —, + *abl.*

constancy, cōnstantia, -ae, *f.*

constellation, sīdus, -eris, *n.*

consul, cōnsul, -ulis, *m.*

consult, cōnsulō, -ere, cōnsuluī, cōnsultum, + *acc.*

consume, cōnsūmō, -ere, -sūmpsī, sūmptum

contain, contineō, -ēre, continuī, contentum

contempt, to regard with, contemnō, -ere, contempsī, contemptum

control, potestās, -ātis, *f.*

cook, coquō, -ere, coxī, coctum

cottage, casa, -ae, *f.*

count among, numerō (1)

country house, vīlla, -ae, *f.*

countryside, rūs, rūris, *n.*

courage, fortitūdō, -inis, *f.*; virtūs, -ūtis, *f.*

cover, tegō, -ere, tēxī, tēctum

craftsman, artifex, -ficis, *m.*

crowd, multitūdō, -ūdinis, *f.*

crowded, celeber, -bris, -bre, *adj.*

cruel, crūdēlis, -e, *adj.*

cry, fleō, -ēre, flēvī, flētum

cultivate, colō, -ere, coluī, cultum

cultured, litterātus, -a, -um, *adj.*

custom, consuētūdō, -ūdinis, *f.*; mōs, mōris, *m.*

D

daily, cottīdiānus, -a, -um, *adj.*

danger, perīculum, -i, *n.*

darkness, tenebrae, -ārum, *f. pl.*

daughter, fīlia, -ae, *f.*

day, diēs, -ēī, *m./f.*

deadly, fūnestus, -a, -um, *adj.*

dear, cārus, -a, -um, *adj.*

death, mors, mortis, *f.*

deceive, dēcipiō, -ere, dēcēpī, dēceptum

deception, dolus, -ī, *m.*

decide, dēcernō, -ere, -crēvī, -crētum, + *inf.*

deeds, rēs gestae

deep, altus, -a, -um, *adj.*

defeat, vincō, -ere, vīcī, victum

defend, dēfendō, -ere, dēfendī, dēfēnsum

dejected, to become, animum dēmittō

delight, dēliciae, -ārum, *f. pl., (noun)*

delight, dēlectō (1)

delightful, iūcundus, -a, -um, *adj.*

demonstrate, dēclārō (1)

descend, dēscendō, -ere, -scendī, -scēnsum

descended from, to be, orior, orīrī, ortus sum + *abl.*

design, parō (1)

desire, cupiō, -ere, -īvī, -ītum; dēsīderō (1)

despise, contemnō, -ere, contempsī, contemptum

destiny, fātum, -ī, *n.*

destroy, dēleō, -ēre, dēlēvī, dēlētum; tollō, -ere, sustulī, sublātum

determine, dēcernō, -ere, -crēvī, -crētum, + *inf.*

devastate, dēvastō (1)

devoid of, expers, -ertis, *adj.,* +*gen.*

die, dēcēdō, -ere, decessī, decessum; morior, morī, mortuus sum

difficult, difficilis, -e, *adj.*

diligence, dīligentia, -ae, *f.*

diligently, dīligenter, *adv.*

dine, cēnō (1)

dinner party, convīvium, -ī, *n.*

direct, moderor, -ārī, -ātus sum

disadvantage, incommodum, -ī, *n.*

disaster, calamitās, -ātis, *f.*; clādēs, -is, *f.*

disgraceful, turpis, -e, *adj.*

dispute, līs, lītis, *f.*

dissimilar, dissimilis, -e, *adj.*

distinguish by the eyes, cernō, -ere, crēvī, crētum

distinguished, clārus, -a, -um, *adj.*; illūstris, -e, *adj.*; praeclārus, -a, -um, *adj.*

distribute, partior, partīrī, partītus sum

divide, partior, partīrī, partītus sum

divine, dīvīnus, -a, -um, *adj.*

do, agō, -ere, ēgī, āctum; faciō, -ere, fēcī, factum

dominate, dominor, dominārī, dominātus sum

down from, dē, *prep.* + *abl.*

drag, trahō, -ere, traxī, tractum

drink, bibō, -ere, bibī, —

drive into, impingō, -ere, impēgī, impāctum

drive, agō, -ere, ēgī, āctum

duty, officium, -ī, *n.*

dwell, habitō (1)

dwelling, aedēs, -ium, *f. pl.*

E

each, omnis, -e, *adj.*

eager for, to be, studeō, -ēre, studuī, —, + *dat.*

ear, auris, -is, *f.*

earth, orbis terrārum

east, ortus sōlis

easy, facilis, -e, *adj.*

eat, comedō, -ere, -ēdī, -ēsum

effect, to (to bring about), efficiō, -ere, -fēcī, -fectum, often + *ut*

either . . . or . . . , aut . . . aut . . .

element, elementum, -ī, *n.*

emperor, Caesar, -aris, *m.* (initially the name of Julius Caesar); imperātor, -ōris, *m.*

empire, imperium, -ī, *n.*

empty of, vacuus, -a, -um, + *abl.*

end, fīnis, -is, *m.*

endless, immēnsus, -a, -um, *adj.*

endowed with, praeditus, -a, -um, + *abl.*

endure, patior, patī, passus sum

enemy, hostis, -is, *m.*; inimīcus, -ī, *m., adj.*

enjoy, fruor, fruī, fruitus/frūctus sum, + *abl.*

enjoy the society of, fruor, fruī, fruitus /frūctus sum, + *abl.*

enough, satis, *adv.*

enter, intrō (1)

entire, tōtus, -a, -um, *adj.*

entreat, ōrō (1)

envy someone, invideō, -ēre, invīdī, invīsum, + *dat.*

equal, pār, paris, *adj.*

eruption, incendium, -ī, *n.*

especially, praecipuē, *adv.*; praesertim, *adv.*

establish, cōnstituō, -ere, cōnstituī, cōnstitūtum

esteem a lot, māgnī habeō

esteem highly, dīligō, -ere, dīlēxī, dīlēctum

estimate, aestimō (1); exīstimō (1)

even, aequus, -a, -um, *adj.*

even, etiam, *adv.*

ever, umquam, *adv.*

every, omnis, -e, *adj.*

everywhere, ubīque, *adv.*

example, exemplar, -āris, *n.*; exemplum, -ī, *n.*

exceedingly, valdē, *adv.*

except, beside, praeter, *prep.* + *acc.*

exclaim, exclāmō (1)

exhort, hortor, hortārī, hortātus sum

expect, exspectō (1)

expense, sumptus, -ūs, *m.*

exploits, rēs gestae

extent, to a small, paulō, *adv.*

extent, to such an, adeō, *adv.*

extent, to what, quantum, *interrogative and relative adv.*

external, externus, -a, -um, *adj.*

extinguish, exstinguō, -ere, -stīnxī, -stīnctum

eye, oculus, -ī, *m.*

F

face, faciēs, -ēī, *f.*; vultus, -ūs, *m.*

faith, fidēs, -eī, *f.*

faithful, fidēlis, -e, *adj.*

fall, cadō, -ere, cecidī, cāsum

fame, fama, -ae, *f.*

familiarity, familiāritās, -ātis, *f.*

family member, familiāris, -āris, *m./f.*

family, familia, -ae, *f.*

famous, praeclārus, -a, -um, *adj.*

far away, procul, *adv.*

far, longē, *adv.*; procul, *adv.*

farmer, agricola, -ae, *m.*

fate, fātum, -ī, *n.* fātum, -ī, *n.*; sors, sortis, *f.* (*in the metaphorical sense of one's condition in life*)

father, pater, patris, *m.*

fatherland, patria, -ae, *f.*

favor, beneficium, -ī, *n.*; grātia, -ae, *f.*; officium, -ī, *n.*

fear, timor, -ōris, *m.*, (*noun*)

fear, timeō, -ēre, timuī, —; vereor, -ērī, veritus sum, (*verb*)

feast, convīvium, -ī, *n.*

feed, alō, -ere, aluī, altum/alitum

feel, sentiō, -īre, sēnsī, sēnsum

ferocious, ferōx, -ōcis, *adj.*

fetter, vinculum, -ī, *n.*

fever, febris, -is, *f.*

few, paucī, -ae, -a, *adj.*

field, ager, agrī, *m.*

fierce, ācer, ācris, ācre, *adj.*; ferōx, -ōcis, *adj.*

fight, pugnō (1)

fill, compleō, -ēre, -ēvī, -ētum

finally, tandem, *adv.*

find to be, cōgnoscō, -ere, cōgnōvī, cōgnitum

find, inveniō, -īre, invēnī, inventum

finger, digitus, -ī, *m.*

fire, ignis, -is, *m.*

first, prīmum, *adv.*; **at first,** prīmō, *adv.*

first, prīmus, -a, -um, *adj.*

fish, piscis, -is, *m.*

fitted, aptus, -a, -um, *adj.*

flame, flamma, -ae, *f.*

flee, fugiō, -ere, fūgī, —

fleet, classis, -is, *f.*

flesh, carō, carnis, *f.*

flourish, flōreō, -ēre, flōruī, —

flow, fluō, -ere, flūxī, fluxum

follow, sequor, sequī, secūtus sum

fond of, studiōsus, -a, -um, + *gen.*

food, cibus, -ī, *m.*

for, enim, *conj.*; nam, *conj.*; namque, *conj.*

for, prō, *prep.* + *abl.*

force, impetus, -ūs, *m.*; vīs, —, *f.*, *pl.* vīrēs, vīrium, (*noun*)

force, cōgō, -ere, coēgī, coactum, (*verb*)

foreign to, aliēnus, -a, -um, *adj.* + *prep.* ā/ab + *abl.*

forest, silva, -ae, *f.*

forget, oblīvīscor, oblīvīscī, oblītus sum, + *gen.*

forgetful of, immemor, -oris, *adj.*, + *gen.*

forgiveness, venia, -ae, *f.*

form in the mind, fingō, -ere, finxī, fictum

form, fōrma, -ae, *f.*

fortunate, fēlīx, -īcis, *adj.*; prosper, prospera, prosperum, *adj.*

fortune, fortūna, -ae, *f.*

Fortune, the goddess, Fortūna, -ae, *f.*

Forum Rōmānum, the main square in Rome, forum, -ī, *n.*

free someone from something, līberō (1), + *acc.* + *abl.*

free time, ōtium, -ī, *n.*

free, līber, lībera, līberum, *adj.*

freedom, lībertās, -ātis, *f.*

frequent, frequēns, -entis, *adj.*

friend, amīcus, -ī, *m.*

friendly, amīcus, a, um, *adj.*

from, ā *or* ab, *prep.* + *abl.*; ē *or* ex, *prep.* + *abl.*

from all sides, undique, *adv.*

fruit, pōmum, -ī, *n.*

full of, plēnus, -a, -um, *adj.* + *gen.* or + *abl.*

G

gain, lūcrum, -ī, *n.*

garden, hortus, -ī, *m.*

garment, vestīmentum, -ī, *n.*

garrison, praesidium, -ī, *n.*

gate, porta, -ae, *f.*

gem, gemma, -ae, *f.*

general, dux, ducis, *m.*; imperātor, -ōris, *m.*

generosity, līberālitās, -ātis, *f.*

get, percipiō, -ere, percēpī, perceptum

get ready, parō (1)

get to know, cōgnōscō, -ere, cōgnōvī, cōgnitum

gift, dōnum, -ī, *n.*

girl, puella, -ae, *f.*

girl of marriageable age, virgō, -inis, *f.*

give back, reddō, -ere, reddidī, redditum

give birth to, pariō, -ere, peperī, partum; gignō, -ere, genuī, genitum

give forth, ēdō, -ere, ēdidī, ēditum

give, dō, dăre, dedī, dătum

glide down, lābor, lābī, lapsus sum

glimpse, aspiciō, -ere, aspexī, aspectum

glory, glōria, -ae, *f.*

go, eō, īre, īvī, itum

go around, circumeō, -īre, -īvī, -itum

go away, dēcēdō, -ere, dēcessī, dēcessum

go back, redeō, -īre, -īvī, -itum

go forward, prōgredior, prōgredī, prōgressus sum

go to, petō, -ere, petīvī, petītum

god, deus, -ī, *m.*

goddess, dea, -ae, *f.*

going to be, futūrus, -a, -um, *participle*

gold, aurum, -ī, *n.*

good, bonus, -a, -um, *adj.*

goodbye!, valē!

goodwill, benevolentia, -ae, *f.*

grant, tribuō, -ere, tribuī, tribūtum

gravity, gravitās, -ātis, *f.*

great, măgnus, -a, -um, *adj.*

greater, māior, māius, *adj. comparative*

greatest, maximus, -a, -um, *adj. superlative*

greet, salūtō (1)

greet, I (*a customary way to begin a letter*), salūtem dīcō, + *dat.*

grief, dolor, -ōris, *m.*

grieve, doleō, -ēre, doluī, —

grow, crēscō, -ere, crēvī, —

guard, custōs, -ōdis, *m.*

guide, moderor, moderārī, moderātus sum

H

habit, consuētūdō, -ūdinis, *f.*; mōs, mōris, *m.*

hand, manus, -ūs, *f.*

hang (*intransitive*), pendeō, -ēre, pependī, —

happen, accidō, -ere, accidī, —

happen (*impersonal*), fīō, fierī, factus sum

happen upon, offendō, -ere, offendī, offēnsum

happy, fēlīx, -īcis, *adj.*

hardly, vix, *adv.*

harm, incommodum, -ī, *n.*, (*noun*)

harm, laedō, -ere, laesī, laesum, (*verb*)

hatred, odium, ī, *n.*

hate someone/something, odiō habēre, + *acc.*

have, habeō, -ēre, habuī, habitum

he, she, it, is, ea, id, *personal and demonstrative pronoun and adj.*

head, caput, -itis, *n.*

head for, petō, -ere, petīvī, petītum

heal, sānō (1)

health, salūs, -ūtis, *f.*; valētūdō, -ūdinis, *f.*

health, to be in good, valeō, -ēre, valuī, —, + *infin.*

hear, audiō, -īre, audīvī, audītum

heart, cor, cordis, *n.*

heaven, caelum, -ī, *n.*

heavy, gravis, -e, *adj.*

heir, hērēs, -ēdis, *m./f.*

help, auxilium, -ī, *n.*, (*noun*)

help, adiuvō, -āre, adiūvī, adiūtum, (*verb*)

helplessness, inopia, -ae, *f.*

her (own), suus, a, um, *possessive adj.*

herself, himself, itself, themselves, suī, sibi, sē, *reflexive pronoun*

hide, skin, pellis, -is, *f.*, (*noun*)

hide, occultō (1), (*verb*)

highest, summus, -a, -um, *adj.*

hill, collis, -is, *m.*

hold, contineō, -ēre, continuī, contentum; teneō, -ēre, tenuī, tentum

home, domus, -ūs, *f.*

honor, honor, -ōris, *m.*

hope, spēs, speī, *f.*, (*noun*)

hope, spērō (1), (*verb*)

horn, cornū, -ūs, *n.*

horse, equus, -ī, *m.*

horseman, eques, -itis, *m.*

house, aedēs, -ium, *f. pl.*; domus, -ūs, *f.*; tēctum, -ī, *n.*

household, familia, -ae, *f.*

how great, quantus, -a, -um, *interrogative and relative adj.*

how long, quamdiū, *interrogative and relative adv.*

how much, quantus, -a, -um, *interrogative and relative adj.*

how, quam, *interrogative adv. and exclamation particle*; quōmodo, *adv.*

however, autem, *conj.*; tamen, *conj.*

huge, ingēns, ingentis, *adj.*

human, hūmānus, -a, -um, *adj.*

human character, hūmānitās, -ātis, *f.*

humanity, hūmānitās, -ātis, *f.*

hurt (*i.e., feel pain - intransitive*), doleō, -ēre, doluī, —

husband, marītus, -ī, *m.*

I

I, ego, *personal pronoun*

ice, glaciēs, -ēī, *f.*

if, sī, *conj.*

if not, nisi, *conj.*

if only (*a particle of wishing*), utinam

illness, morbus, -ī, *m.*

illustrious, illūstris, -e, *adj.*

image, imāgō, -inis, *f.*

imagine, fingō, -ere, finxī, fictum

immeasurable, immēnsus, -a, -um, *adj.*

immediately, statim, *adv.*

immense, immēnsus, -a, -um, *adj.*

immortal, immortālis, -e, *adj.*

impede, impediō, -īre, -īvī, -ītum

impetus, impetus, -ūs, *m.*

important, māgnus, -a, -um, *adj.*

in, in, *prep. + abl.*

in fact, enim, *conj.*; nam, *conj.*

in Latin, Latīnē, *adv.*

in order not to, nē, *conj. + subjunctive*

in order to, ut + *subjunctive*

in vain, frūstrā, *adv.*

inconsistent with, aliēnus, -a, -um, *adj. + prep. ā/ab + abl.*

incorrectly, perperam, *adv.*

increase, augeō, -ēre, auxī, auctum

indeed, namque, *conj.*; quidem, *adv.*

indication, argūmentum, -ī, *n.*

indifferently, aequō animō, *adverbial phrase*

indulgence, venia, -ae, *f.*

inert, to be, iaceō, -ēre, iacuī, —

inflict, īnflīgō, -ere, īnflīxī, īnflīctum

inhabitant, incola, -ae, *m.*

inheritance, hērēditās, -ātis, *f.*

injury, iniūria, -ae, *f.*

injustice, inīquitās, -ātis, *f.*

innermost, intimus, -a, -um, *adj.*

interested in, to be, studeō, -ēre, studuī, —, + *dat.*

into, ad, *prep.* + *acc.*; in, *prep.* + *acc.*

invade, to, invādō, -ere, invāsī, —

island, īnsula, -ae, *f.*

Italy, Ītalia, -ae, *f.*

it, she, he, is, ea, id, *personal and demonstrative pronoun and adj.*

J

javelin, tēlum, -ī, *n.*

join together, coniungō, -ere, -iūnxī, -iūnctum

join, iungō, -ere, iūnxī, iūnctum

joke, iocus, -ī, *m.*

joy, gaudium, -ī, *n.*

judge, iudex, -icis, *m.*, (*noun*)

judge, arbitror, -ārī, -ātus sum; iūdicō (1), (*verb*)

just, iūstus, -a, -um, *adj.*

just as, sīcut, *adv.*

K

keen, ācer, ācris, ācre, *adj.*

keep quiet, keep silent, taceō, -ēre, tacuī, tacitum

keep together, contineō, -ēre, continuī, contentum

kill, occīdō, -ere, occīdī, occīsum

kind, genus, -eris, *n.*

kindness, beneficium, -ī, *n.*; hūmānitās, -ātis, *f.*

king, rēx, rēgis, *m.*

knight, member of the equestrian order, eques, -itis, *m.*

know, sciō, -īre, -īvī, -ītum; to know (a person) *cōgnōvī* (perfect tense of *cōgnoscō*)

know, to not, nesciō, -īre, -īvī, -ītum

L

labor, labor, -ōris, *m.*

lack something, to, egeō, -ēre, eguī, —, + *abl.*; indigeō, -ēre, indiguī, —, + *abl.*

lacking in, expers, -ertis, *adj.*, + *gen.*

land, terra, -ae, *f.*

language, lingua, -ae, *f.*

lap, gremium, -ī, *n.*

large, māgnus, -a, -um, *adj.*

last, extrēmus, -a, -um, *adj.*

Latin, Latīnus, -a, -um, *adj.*; **in Latin,** Latīnē, *adv.*

laugh, rīdeō, -ēre, rīsī, rīsum

law, lēx, lēgis, *f.*

lead, agō, -ere, ēgī, āctum; dūcō, -ere, dūxī, ductum

leader, dux, ducis, *m.*

leading citizen, prīnceps, prīncipis, *m.*

learn, discō, -ere, didicī, —

learned, doctus, -a, -um, *adj.*

least, minimē, *adv. superlative*

leave, discēdō, -ere, -cessī, -cessum

leave behind, relinquō, -ere, relīquī, relictum

leave over, reliquum facere

legitimate, iūstus, -a, -um, *adj.*

leisure, ōtium, -ī, *n.*

less, minus, *adv. comparative*

lest, nē, *conj.* + *subjunctive*

letter (epistle), epistula, -ae, *f.*; litterae, -ārum, *f. pl.*

letter of the alphabet, littera, -ae, *f.*

lie, mendācium, -ī, *n.*

lie down, iaceō, -ēre, iacuī, —

life, vīta, -ae, *f.*

lift up, tollō, -ere, sustulī, sublātum

light, levis, -e, (*adj.*)

light, lūmen, -inis, *n.*, (*noun*)

like, similis, -e, *adj.* + *gen.* or + *dat.*

line of verse, versus, -ūs, m.

line of writing, versus, -ūs, m.

listen, audiō, -īre, audīvī, audītum

literate, litterātus, -a, -um, *adj.*

literature, litterae, -ārum, *f. pl.*

little house, casa, -ae, *f.*

little, somewhat, paulō, *adv.*

live, habitō (1); vīvō, -ere, vīxī, vīctum

located, situs, -a, -um, *adj.*

long, longus, -a, -um, *adj.*

long for, dēsīderō (1)

long time, for a, diū, *adv.*

look after, consulō, -ere, consuluī, consultum, + *dat.*

look at, aspiciō, -ere, aspexī, aspectum; cōnspiciō, -ere, -spexī, -spectum; tueor, -ērī, tuitus/tūtus sum

look for, quaerō, -ere, quaesīvī, quaesītum

look here!, ecce, *interj.*

lord, dominus, -ī, *m.*

lose, āmittō, -ere, -mīsī, -missum; perdo, -ere, perdidī, perditum

lot sors, sortis, *f.* (in the literal sense of a lot one draws), fate (in the metaphorical sense of one's condition in life)

love, amor, -ōris, *m.*, (*noun*)

love, amō (1); dīligō, -ere, dīlēxī, dīlēctum, (*verb*)

low, humilis, -e, *adj.*

loyal, fidēlis, -e, *adj.*

M

made, to be, fīō, fierī, factus sum

magistracy, magistrātus, -ūs, *m.*

maintain, affirmō (1)

make, faciō, -ere, fēcī, factum

man (*i.e., human being*), homō, -inis, *m.*

man, vir, virī, *m.*

manage, moderor, moderārī, moderātus sum

management, cultus, -ūs, *m.*

manner, modus, -ī, *m.*

many, multus, -a, -um, *adj.*

maritime, maritimus, -a, -um, *adj.*

marriage, matrimōnium, -ī, *n.*; nūptiae, -ārum, *f. pl.*

marry (*a woman*), uxōrem dūcō

marvel, mīror, mirārī, mirātus sum

master, dominus, -ī, *m.*

matter, rēs, reī, *f.*

meat, carō, carnis, *f.*

mediocre, mediocris, -e, *adj.*

meet, conveniō, -īre, -vēnī, -ventum

memory, memoria, -ae, *f.*

method, modus, -ī, *m.*

midday, merīdiēs, -ēī, *m.*

middle, medius, -a, -um, *adj.*

middle, the, medium, -ī, *n.*

middling, mediocris, -e, *adj.*

midst, medium, -ī, *n.*

might, with all one's, prō vīribus

military escort, praesidium, -ī, *n.*

mind, animus, -ī, *m.*; mens, mentis, *f.*; ōpīnio, opīniōnis, *f.*

mindful of (*usually of one's obligations*), memor, -oris, *adj.* + *gen.*

misfortune, calamitās, -ātis, *f.*

mistake, to make a, errō (1)

mistress, domina, -ae, *f.*

moderate, mediocris, -e, *adj.*

money, pecūnia, -ae, *f.*

morals, mōrēs, -um, *m. pl.*

more (*in amount*), amplius, *adv.*; magis, *adv.*

more (*in number*), *n.*, plūrēs, plūra, *adj. comparative*

more, plūs, plūris, *adj. comparative*

morning, in the, māne, *adv.*

most, maximē, *adv. superlative*

most, plūrimus, -a, -um, *adj. superlative*

mother, māter, mātris, *f.*

motion, mōtus, -ūs, *m.*

mountain, mōns, montis, *m.*

mouth, ōs, ōris, *n.*

move, moveō, -ēre, mōvī, mōtum

movement, mōtus, -ūs, *m.*

much, multum, *adv.*; **by much,** multō, *adv.*

much, multus, -a, -um, *adj.*

must, dēbeō, -ēre, dēbuī, dēbitum, + *inf.*

my, meus, -a, -um, *possessive adj.*

N

name, nōmen, -inis, *n.*; fama, -ae, *f.*

nature, natūra, -ae, *f.*

near, prope, *prep.* + *acc.*

nearest, proximus, -a, -um, *adj.*

necessarily, necessāriō, *adv.*

necessary, necessārius, -a, -um, *adj.*

necessary for someone to do something, it is, necesse est, + *dat.* + *infinitive*

need, dēsīderō (1); indigeō, -ēre, indiguī, —, + *abl.*

neglect, neglegō, -ere, neglēxī, neglēctum

neither, neuter, neutra, neutrum, *adj.*

neither . . . nor . . . , nec . . . nec . . . ; neque . . . neque . . .

never, numquam, *adv.*

new, novus, -a, -um, *adj.*

nice, pulcher, pulchra, pulchrum, *adj.*

night, nox, noctis, *f.*; **by night, at night,** noctū, *adv.*

no, not at all, minimē, *adv. superlative*

no one, nēmō, *m.*

none, nūllus, -a, -um, *adj.*

nor, nec, *conj.*

northern, septentriōnālis, -e, *adj.*

not, nōn, *negative adv.*

not even, nē . . . quidem . . .

not only . . . , but also . . . , nōn sōlum . . . , sed etiam . . .

not to know, nesciō, -īre, -īvī, -ītum

not to want, nōlō, nōlle, nōluī, —

nothing, nihil, *negative pronoun*

notice, animadvertō, -ere, animadvertī, animadversum

nourish, alō, -ere, aluī, altum/ alitum

now, nunc, *adv.*

now . . . now . . . , modo . . . modo . . .

nowhere, nusquam, *adv.*

number, numerus, -ī, *m.,* (*noun*)

number, numerō (1), (*verb*)

O

observe, cōnspiciō, -ere, -spexī, -spectum

obvious, to be, appāreō, -ēre, appāruī, —

occupy, occupō (1)

occur, ūsū venīre

of every day, cottīdiānus, -a, -um, *adj.*

offend, offendō, -ere, offendī, offēnsum

offer, praestō, -āre, praestitī, praestitum

office of a magistrate, magistrātus, -ūs, *m.*

often, saepe, *adv.*

old, vetus, veteris, *conj.*; vetustus, -a, -um, *adj.*

old age, senectūs, -ūtis, *f.*

old man, senex, -is, *m.*

on, in, *prep.* + *abl.*

on account of, propter, *prep.* + *acc.*

on behalf of, prō, *prep.* + *abl.*

once, semel, *adv.*

one, ūnus, ūna, ūnum, *adj.*

one apiece, singulī, -ae, -a, *adj.*

one each (*a distributive*), singulī, -ae, -a, *adj.*

one time . . . at another . . . , modo . . . modo . . .

only, tantum, *adv.*

open, aperiō, -īre, aperuī, apertum

opinion, opīniō, opīniōnis, *f.*; sententia, -ae, *f.*

opponent, inimīcus, -ī, *m.*

or, aut, *conj.*; vel, *conj.*

oracle, ōrāculum, -ī, *n.*

order, ordō, ordinis, *m.*; iussus, -ūs, *m.* (*usually employed in the ablative singular only*)

order somebody to do something, iubeō, -ēre, iussī, iussum, + *acc.* + *inf.*

ordinary, mediocris, -e, *adj.*

origin, orīgō, orīginis, *f.;* ortus, -ūs, *m.*

originate, orior, orīrī, ortus sum + *abl.*

other, alius, alia, aliud, *adj.*

other (*of two*), alter, altera, alterum, *adj.*

ought, dēbeō, -ēre, dēbuī, dēbitum, + *inf.*

our, noster, nostra, nostrum, *possessive adj.*

out of, ē *or* ex, *prep.* + *abl.*

outside, in the open, forīs, *adv.*

outside of, extrā, *prep.* + *acc.*

outward, externus, -a, -um, *adj.*

overwhelm, opprimō, -ere, oppressī, oppressum

owe, dēbeō, -ēre, dēbuī, dēbitum, + *inf.*

P

pain, dolor, -ōris, *m.*

pain, to feel, doleō, -ēre, doluī, —

pardon, venia, -ae, *f.*

parent, parēns, -rentis, *m./f.*

part, pars, partis, *f.*

particularly, praecipuē, *adv.*

partner, socius, -ī, *m.*

passages of a book, locī, -ōrum, *m. pl.*

past actions, rēs gestae

peace, pāx, pācis, *f.*

peaceful, placidus, -a, -um, *adj.*

people, hominēs, -um, *m. pl.;* populus, -ī, *m.*

perceive (with the eyes), cernō, -ere, crēvī, crētum

perhaps, fortasse, *adv.*

permitted for someone to do something, it is, licet, + *dat.* + *inf.*

pet, dēliciae, -ārum, *f. pl.*

place, locus, -ī, *m.,* (*noun*)

place, pōnō, -ere, posuī, positum, (*verb*)

places (*geographical*), loca, -ōrum, *n. pl.*

plan, cōnsilium, -ī, *n.;* **make plans,** cōnsilia capere

plant, herba, -ae, *f.*

play, lūdō, -ere, lūsī, lūsum

pleasant, iūcundus, -a, -um, *adj.*

please, dēlectō (1); placeō, -ēre, placuī, placitum, + *dat.*

please (*to be agreeable to*), placeō, -ēre, placuī, placitum, + *dat*

poem, carmen, -inis, *n.*

poet, poēta, -ae, *m.*

point of view, sententia, -ae, *f.*

poison, venēnum, -ī, *n.*

poor, pauper, pauperis, *adj.*

population, gēns, gentis, *f.*

possess, possideō, -ēre, possēdī, possessum

possessed of, praeditus, -a, -um, + *abl.*

pour, fundō, -ere, fūdī, fūsum

power, imperium, -ī, *n.;* potentia, -ae, *f.;* potestās, -ātis, *f.*

powerful, potēns, potentis, *adj.*

practical intelligence, prūdentia, -ae, *f.*

praise, laudō, -āre, -āvī, -ātum

prayer, prex, precis, *f.*

precious stone, gemma, -ae, *f.*

prefer, mālō, mālle, māluī, —

prepare, parō (1)

preserve, servō (1)

prevent, impediō, -īre, -īvī, -ītum

proceed, prōgredior, prōgredī, prōgressus sum

produce, ēdō, -ere, ēdidī, ēditum; gignō, -ere, genuī, genitum

profit, lūcrum, -ī, *n.*

promise, polliceor, pollicērī, pollicitus sum; prōmittō, -ere, prōmīsī, prōmissum

proof, argūmentum, -ī, *n.*

prosperous, prosper, prospera, prosperum, *adj.*

protect, tegō, -ere, tēxī, tēctum; tueor, -ērī, tuitus/tūtus sum

provide, praestō, -āre, praestitī, praestitum

provided with, praeditus, -a, -um, + *abl.*

public (*belonging to the state*), pūblicus, -a, -um, *adj.*

public office or distinction, honor, -ōris, *m,*

public, the (*i.e., common people*), vulgus, -ī, *n.*

punish, pūniō, -īre, -īvī, -ītum

pursuit, studium, -ī, *n.*

push, impingō, -ere, impēgī, impāctum

push back, repellō, -ere, reppulī, repulsum

put, pōnō, -ere, posuī, positum

Q

quarrel, līs, lītis, *f.*

queen, rēgīna, -ae, *f.*

R

rage, furō, -ere, furuī, —

raise, tollō, -ere, sustulī, sublātum

raising, ortus, -ūs, *m.*

rather, potius, *adv.*

ratify solemnly, sanciō, -īre, sānxī, sānctum

read, legō, -ere, lēgī, lēctum

reason, causa, -ae, *f.*

rebuke, reprehendō, -ere, -prehendī, -prehēnsum

receive, accipiō, -ere, -cēpī, -ceptum; recipiō, -ere, recēpī, receptum

red, ruber, rubra, rubrum, *adj.*

regard, aestimō (1)

relationship by marriage, affīnitās, -ātis, *f.*

remain, maneō, -ēre, mānsī, mānsum

remaining, cēterus, -a, -um, *adj.*

remember, meminī, meminisse

remembering, memor, -oris, *adj.* + *gen.*

renowned, celeber, -bris, -bre, *adj.*

report, referō, referre, rettulī, relātum

repose, quiēs, -ētis, *f.*

reputation, fama, -ae, *f.*

require, dēsīderō (1)

resist (*somebody or something*), resistō, -ere, restitī, — + *dat.*

respect, vereor, verērī, veritus sum

rest, quiēs, -ētis, *f.*

the rest, the remaining, reliquus, -a, -um, *adj.*

restore, restituō, -ere, restituī, restitūtum

retreat, to, sē recipere

return, redeō, -īre, -īvī, -itum

reward, praemium, -ī, *n.*

rich, dīves, dīvitis, *adj.*

riches, dīvitiae, -ārum, *f. pl.*

right hand, dextra, -ae, *f.*

right up, ūsque, *adv.*

river, flūmen, -minis, *n.*

road, iter, -eris, *n.;* via, -ae, *f.*

rock, saxum, -ī, *n.*

Roman, Rōmānus, -a, -um, *adj.*

Rome, Rōma, -ae, *f.*

roof, tēctum, -ī, *n.*

rouse, excitō (1)

rub, terō, -ere, trīvī, trītum

rule, imperium, -ī, *n.* (*noun*)

rule, dominor, dominārī, dominātus sum, (*verb*)

rumor, fama, -ae, *f.*

run, currō, -ere, cucurrī, cursum

run away, fugiō, -ere, fūgī, —

rural, rūsticus, -a, -um, *adj.*

rush to, petō, -ere, petīvī, petītum

rustic, rūsticus, -a, -um, *adj.*

S

sad, trīstis, -e, *adj.*

safe, tūtus, -a, -um, *adj.*

sail, nāvigō (1)

sailor, nauta, -ae, *m.*

salt, sāl, salis, *m.*

same, īdem, eadem, idem, *demonstrative pronoun and adj.*

save, servō (1)

say, dīcō, -ere, dīxī, dictum; **I say/I said** (*only introducing direct speech*), inquam

say, s/he says or said (*only introducing direct speech*), inquit

say, they say or said (*only introducing direct speech*), inquiunt

science, ars, artis, *f.*

sea, mare, maris, *n.*

search, quaerō, -ere, quaesīvī, quaesītum

seat, sēdēs, -is, *f.*

second, secundus, -a, -um, *adj.*

see, videō, -ēre, vīdī, vīsum; cernō, -ere, crēvī, crētum

seek, petō, -ere, petīvī, petītum

seem, videō, -ēre, vīdī, vīsum (passive)

seize, corripiō, -ere, -ripuī, -reptum

self, ipse, ipsa, ipsum, *demonstrative pronoun and adj.*

send, mittō, -ere, mīsī, missum

send down, dēmittō, -ere, -mīsī, -missum

separate, sēparō (1)

serious, gravis, -e, *adj.;* sevērus, -a, -um, *adj.*

servant, servus, -ī, *m.*

service, beneficium, -ī, *n.*

set up, cōnstituō, -ere, cōnstituī, cōnstitūtum

severe, sevērus, -a, -um, *adj.*

shadows, tenebrae, -ārum, *f. pl.*

shameful, turpis, -e, *adj.*

she, he, it, is, ea, id, *personal and demonstrative pronoun and adj.*

she-wolf, lupa, -ae, *f.*

ship, nāvis, -is, *f.*

shore, lītus, -oris, *n.*

short, brevis, -e, *adj.*

shortly, breviter, *adv.*

should, dēbeō, -ēre, dēbuī, dēbitum, + *inf.*

shout, clāmō (1)

show, dēclārō (1); ostendō, -ere, ostendī, ostentum

sickness, morbus, -ī, *m.*

silent, to be, taceō, -ēre, tacuī, tacitum

silver, argentum, -ī, *n.*

similar, similis, -e, *adj.* + *gen.* or + *dat.*

simultaneously, simul, *adv.*

since, cum, *conj.* + *imperfect subjunctive*

sing, canō, -ere, cecinī, cantum

sister, soror, -ōris, *f.*

sit, sedeō, -ēre, sēdī, sessum

situated or occurring at the end, extrēmus, -a, -um, *adj.*

situated, situs, -a, -um, *adj.*

skill, ars, artis, *f.*

skin, pellis, -is, *f.*

sky, caelum, -ī, *n.*

slave, servus, -ī, *m.*

sleep, somnus, -ī, *m., (noun)*

sleep, dormiō, -īre, -īvī, -ītum, (*verb*)

slender, grācilis, -e, *adj.*

slide, lābor, lābī, lapsus sum

slip, lābor, lābī, lapsus sum

small, parvus, -a, -um, *adj.*

smaller, minor, minus, *adj. comparative*

smallest, minimus, -a, -um, *adv. superlative*

smoke, fūmus, -ī, *m.*

snatch away, ēripiō, -ere, -ripuī, -reptum

snow, nix, nivis, *f.*

so, ita, *adv.;* tam, *adv;* sīc, *adv.*

so . . . as . . . , tam . . . quam . . .

so great, tantus, -a, -um, *adj.*

so many, tot, *adv.*

so much, tantum, *adv.*

so that, ut + *subjunctive*

so that not, nē, *conj.* + *subjunctive*

social class, ordō, ordinis, *m.*

soldier, mīles, -itis, *m.*

some, aliquis, aliqua, aliquid, *indefinite pronoun;* aliquī, aliqua, aliquod, *indefinite adj.*

sometimes, interdum, *adj.*

somewhat, paulō, *adv*

son, fīlius, -ī, *m.*

soon, mox, *adv.*

soul, animus, -ī, *m.*

south, merīdiēs, -ēī, *m.*

spare somebody or something, parcō, -ere, pepercī, —, + *dat.*

sparrow, passer, -eris, *m.*

speak, loquor, loquī, locūtus sum

spear, tēlum, -ī, *n.*

speech, ōrātiō, -ōnis, *f.;* **make a speech,** ōrātiōnem habeō

spend time, moror, morārī, morātus sum

spirit, animus, -ī, *m.;* mens, men-tis, *f.*

spouse, coniūnx, -iugis, *m./f.*

stand, stō, -āre, stetī, statum

state, rēs pūblica

stay for a long or short period, moror, morārī, morātus sum

steal, fūror, -ārī, -ātus sum

stick, virga, -ae, *f.*

still, adhūc, *adv.*

stir up, excitō (1)

stone, saxum, -ī, *n.*

stop, dēsinō, -ere, dēsiī, dēsitum

storm, tempestās, -ātis, *f.;* hiems, hiemis, *f.*

story, fābula, -ae, *f.*

stream, rīvus, -ī, *m.*

strength, vīs, —, *f. pl.* vīrēs, vīrium

strengthen, firmō (1)

strict, sevērus, -a, -um, *adj.*

strike, impingō, -ere, impēgī, impāctum

strike on or against, īnflīgō, -ere, īnflīxī, īnflīctum

strike through, percutiō, -ere, percussī, percussum

strive to achieve, nītor, nītī, nīsus/nīxus sum

strong, fortis, -e, *adj.*

strongly, vehementer, *adv.*

student (*female*), discipula, -ae, *f.*

study, studeō, -ēre, studuī, —, + *dat.*

such a, tālis, tāle, *adj.*

such an extent, to, adeō, *adv.*

suddenly, subitō, *adv.*

suffer, patior, patī, passus sum

sufficiently, satis, *adv.*

sun, sōl, sōlis, *m.*

supply, praestō, -āre, praestitī, praestitum

suppress, opprimō, -ere, oppressī, oppressum

sure, for, prō certō, *adverbial phrase*

sweet, dulcis, -e, *adj.*

sweetness, suāvitās, -ātis, *f.*

swiftly, celeriter, *adv.*

sword, gladius, -ī, *m.*

T

take, capiō, -ere, cēpī, captum; dūcō, -ere, dūxī, ductum; percipiō, -ere, percēpī, per-ceptum; sūmō, -ere, sumpsī, sumptum

tall, altus, -a, -um, *adj.*

taste (*as in fine judgement and ap-preciation*), sāl, salis, *m.*

tasteful, ēlegāns, -antis, *adj.*

teach, doceō, -ēre, docuī, doctum

teacher (*male*), magister, magistrī, *m.*

tear, lacrima, -ae, *f.,* (*noun*)

tear, rumpō, -ere, rūpī, ruptum, (*verb*)

tell, nārrō (1)

temple, aedēs, -is, *f.;* templum, -ī, *n.*

terrifying, terribilis, -e, *adj.*

testimony, testimōnium, -ī, *n.*

than, quam, *used with comparative words*

thankful, grātus, -a, -um, *adj.*

that (*of yours*), iste, iste, istud, *demonstrative pronoun and adj.*

that, ut *conj.* + *subjunctive*

that, ille, illa, illud, *demonstrative pronoun and adj.*

that, quī, quae, quod, *relative pronoun*

that not, nē, *conj.* + *subjunctive*

theft, fūrtum, -ī, *n.*

their, suus, a, um, *possessive adj.*

then, deinde, *adv.;* tum, *adv.;* tunc, *adv.*

there, ibi, *adv.*

therefore, ergo, *conj.;* igitur, *adv.;* quārē, *conj.*

thief, fūr, fūris, *m.*

thing, rēs, reī, *f.*

think, cōgitō (1); exīstimō (1); putō (1)

third, tertius, -a, -um, *adj.*

this, hic, haec, hoc, *demonstrative pronoun and adj.;* is, ea, id, *per-sonal and demonstrative pronoun and adj.*

three, trēs, tria, *numeral*

throng, multitūdō, -ūdinis, *f.*

through, per, *prep.* + *acc.*

throw, iaciō, -ere, iēcī, iactum

thrust back, repellō, -ere, reppulī, repulsum

time, tempus, -oris, *n.*

to, ad, *prep.* + *acc.;* in, *prep.* + *acc.*

today, hodiē, *adv.*

together, ūnā, *adv.*

toil, labor, -ōris, *m.*

tolerate, patior, patī, passus sum

tongue (*as physical part of the mouth*), lingua, ae, *f.*

too much, nimis, *adj.*

top of, summus, -a, -um, *adj.*

touch, tangō, -ere, tetigī, tāctum

towards, ad, *prep. + acc.*

tower, turris, -is, f.

town, oppidum, -ī, *n.*

tree, arbor, -oris, *f.*

tribe, gēns, gentis, *f.*

trickery, dolus, -ī, *m.*

trip, iter, itineris, *n.*

true, vērus, -a, -um, *adj.*

try, cōnor, cōnārī, cōnātus sum; temptō (1)

turn round, volvō, -ere, volvī, volūtum

turn, versō (1)

twig, virga, -ae, *f.*

two, duo, duae, dua, *numeral*

type, genus, -eris, *n.*

U

uncle, avunculus, -ī, *m.*

under, sub, *prep. + abl.*

understand, intellegō, -ere, intellēxī, intellēctum

undying, immortālis, -e, *adj.*

unjust treatment, iniūria, -ae, f.

unless, nisi, *conj.*

unlimited, infīnītus, -a, -um, *adj.*

unwilling, to be, nōlō, nōlle, nōluī, —

up to this time, adhūc, *adv.*

up to, ūsque ad + *acc.*

uproar, tumultus, -ūs, *m.*

urge, hortor, hortārī, hortātus sum

use, ūsus, -ūs, *m., (noun)*

use, ūtor, ūtī, ūsus sum, + *abl., (verb)*

useful, ūtilis, -e, *adj.*

V

vain, in, frūstrā, *adv.*

value, exīstimō (1)

vegetation, herba, -ae, *f.*

vehement, vehemēns, vehementis, *adj.*

vehemently, vehementer, *adv.*

versed in literature, litterātus, -a, -um, *adj.*

very, valdē, *adv.*

very little, minimē, *adv. superlative*

vice, vitium, -ī, *n.*

victor, victor, -ōris, *m.*

villa, vīlla, -ae, *f.*

violent, vehemēns, vehementis, *adj.*

virgin, virgō, -inis, *f.*

virtue, virtūs, -ūtis, *f.*

voice, vōx, vōcis, *f.*

volume, volūmen, -ūminis, *n.*

voyage, nāvigō (1)

W

wage war, bellum gerō

wait for, exspectō (1)

wake up, excitō (1)

walk, ambulō (1)

wall, mūrus, -ī, *m.*

wall-fence, mūrus, -ī, *m.*

wander, errō (1)

want, inopia, -ae, f., *(noun)*

want, cupiō, -ere, -īvī, -ītum.; volō, velle, voluī, — , *(verb)*

want, not to, nōlō, nōlle, nōluī, —

war, bellum, -ī, *n.*

waste, perdō, -ere, perdidī, perditum

watch, spectō (1)

water, aqua, -ae, f.

way, modus, -ī, *m.*

way of living, cultus, -ūs, *m.*

we, nōs, *personal pronoun*

wealth, dīvitiae, -ārum, f. pl.

weapons, arma, -ōrum, *n. pl.*

wear, gerō, -ere, gessī, gestum

wear out, terō, -ere, trīvī, trītum

weather, caelum, -ī, *n.*

wedding, nūptiae, -ārum, *f. pl.*

weight, onus, oneris, *n.*; pondus, -eris, *n.*; gravitās, -ātis, f.

welfare, salūs, -ūtis, f.

well, bene, *adv.*

well, to be, valeō, -ēre, valuī, —

well-known, celeber, -bris, -bre, *adj.*

what sort of, quālis, quāle, *interrogative and relative pronoun*

what?, quī, quae, quod?, *interrogative adjective;* quis, quid?, *interrogative pronoun*

wheel, rota, -ae, f.

when, cum, *conj.,* + *indicative;* ut + *perfect indicative*

where?, ubi?, *interrogative adv.*

wherefore, quārē, *conj.*

which (of two)?, uter, utra, utrum, *interrogative adj.*

which, quī, quae, quod, *relative pronoun*

which?, quī, quae, quod?, *interrogative adjective*

while, dum, *conj.*

while, for a little, paulisper, *adv.*

white, albus, -a, -um, *adj.*

who, quī, quae, quod, *relative pronoun*

who? quis, quid?, *interrogative pronoun*

who (of two?), uter, utra, utrum, *interrogative adj.*

whole, tōtus, -a, -um, *adj.*

why?, cūr, *adv.*

wicked, improbus, -a, -um; scelestus, -a, -um, *adj.*

wife, uxor, -ōris, f.

will, voluntās, -tātis, f.

wind, ventus, -ī, *m.*

wine, vīnum, -ī, *n.*

winter, hiems, hiemis, f.

wisdom, prūdentia, -ae, f.

wit, sāl, salis, *m.*

with all one's might, prō vīribus

with me, mēcum = cum mē

with you, tēcum = cum tē

with, cum, *prep. + abl.*

without it being the case that
(*after negative clauses*), quīn, *conj. + subjunctive*

without, sine, *prep. + abl.*

woman, mulier, -ieris, *f.*; woman, fēmina, -ae, *f.*,

wooden, ligneus, -a, -um, *adj.*

word, verbum, -ī, *n.*

world, mundus, -ī, *m.*; orbis terrārum

worse, pēior, pēius, *adj. comparative*

worship, colō, -ere, coluī, cultum

worst, pessimus, a, um, *adj. superlative*

worthwhile, it is, operae pretium est

wound, vulnus, -eris, *n.*, (*noun*)

wound, vulnerō (1), (*verb*)

wretched, miser, -a, -um, *adj.*

write, scrībō, -ere, scrīpsī, scrīptum

wrongly, perperam, *adv.*

Y

year, annus, ī, *m.*

yes, ita, *adv.*

you (pl.), vōs, *personal pronoun*

you (sg.), tū, *personal pronoun*

young man, young lady,
adulēscēns, -entis, *m./f.*

your (pl.), vester, vestra, vestrum, *possessive adj.*

your (sg.), tuus, -a, -um, *possessive adj.*

yours (pl.), vester, vestra, vestrum, *possessive adj.*

yours (sg.), tuus, -a, -um, *possessive adj.*

youth, iuventūs, - ūtis, *f.*

LATIN TO ENGLISH GLOSSARY

This glossary contains the **Vocabulary to Learn*** as well as the **Reading Vocabulary** from all the chapters and the Atticus passages.

*All words from the **Vocabulary to Learn** are starred. Those from Level 2 are additionally coded: e.g., C12 means the word first appeared as **Vocabulary to Learn** in Chapter 12 while A3 means the word first appeared in the third Atticus selection (those following Chapters 1–15) at the back of the text. In a very few instances, an additional meaning for the word is given in a later part of the text. Such additional meanings appear in the Glossary.

Words marked with a star and no chapter or Atticus selection reference are from the **Vocabulary to Learn** of Level 1.

LIST OF ABBREVIATIONS:

(1) = first conjugation
abl. = ablative
acc. = accusative
adj. = adjective
adv. = adverb
conj. = conjunction
dat. = dative
f. = feminine

gen. = genitive
inf. = infinitive
m. = masculine
n. = neuter
pl. = plural
prep. = preposition
sg. = singular

NOTE:

The genitive of second declension words ending in *–ius* or *–ium* is indicated with a single *–ī*, which is the genitive ending itself. Note that in the full form of the genitive there is normally a double *–i*: *fīlius, –ī* (*= filiī*); *gaudium, –ī* (*= gaudiī*).

A

ā *or* **ab**, *prep. + abl.*, by, from*

ā sēcrētīs, private secretary

Abaelardus, -ī, *m.*, Abelard

abhorreō, -ēre, abhorruī, —, + *abl.*, to be averse to, be different from

abiciō, -ere, abiēcī, abiectum, to throw away, to cast down

absēns, absentis, *adj.*, away, absent* C13

abstineō, -ēre, abstinuī, abstentum, to keep away; **sē abstinēre,** to abstain

absum, abesse, āfuī, —, to be away*

absurdus, -a, -um, *adj.*, absurd, irrational

abundō (1), + *abl.*, to abound with*

ac, shortened form of atque

ac sī, *conj.* + *imperfect subjunctive*, as if (*something was happening, which, in fact, was not*)

accēdō, -ere, accessī, accessum, to approach, be added* A10

accelerō (1), to quicken, accelerate

accessiō, -ōnis, *f.*, addition, increase

accidō, -ere, accidī, —, to fall upon, happen* A7

accingō, -ere, accīnxī, accīnctum, to gird on, arm

accipiō, -ere, -cēpī, -ceptum, to accept, receive*

accūsō (1), + *acc.* + *gen.*, to accuse someone of something*

ācer, ācris, ācre, *adj.*, keen, fierce*

aciēs, -ēī, *f.*, line of battle, sharp edge

acroāma, acroāmatis, *n.*, any form of entertainment

ad adventum, before the arrival

ad, *prep. + acc.,* towards, to, into*

addō, -ere, addidī, additum, to add* C9

adeō, *adv.,* to such an extent* A8-

adhibeō, -ēre, adhibuī, adhibitum, to apply* A10

adhūc, *adv.,* still, up to this time* C8

adiungō, -ere, adiūnxī, adiūnctum, + *dative*

adiuvō, -āre, adiūvī, adiūtum, to help* A1

admittō, -ere, admīsī, admissum, to admit, let in

adoptō (1), to adopt

adsum, adesse, adfuī, —, to be present

adulēscēns, -entis, *m./f.,* young man, young lady*

adulēscentulus, -ī, *m.,* young man

adūlor, adūlārī, adūlātus sum, to fawn upon, flatter

adventus, -ūs, m., arrival* A2

adversārius, -ī, *m.,* opponent

adversum, *prep + acc.,* against

aedēs, -is, *f., (in the singular)* a temple; *(in the plural)* a dwelling or house* C10

aedificātor, -ōris, *m.,* builder; *adj.,* devoted to building

aedificium, -ī, *n.,* building* A5

aedificō (1), to build*

aemulātiō, aemulātiōnis, *f.,* emulation, envy

Aenēās, Aenēae, *m.,* Aeneas

aequālis, aequāle, *adj.,* equal, contemporary in age

aequālis, -is, *m./f.,* a person of the same age

aequus, -a, -um, *adj.,* even, fair; **aequō animō,** indifferently*

aerārium, -ī, *n.,* treasury, fund, account

aes, aeris, *n.,* bronze

aestās, -ātis, *f.,* summer; **aestāte,** in the summer

aestimō (1), to regard, esteem; **aestimō ūnīus assis,** I do not care a bit*

aestuō (1), to be in violent commotion, burn

aetās, -ātis, *f.,* age* C7

affectō (1), to try to achieve, strive after

afferō, afferre, attulī, allātum, to bring

affīnitās, -ātis, *f.,* relationship by marriage, connection* A9

affirmō (1), to assert, maintain* C14

afflīgō, -ere, -flīxī, -flīctum, to strike, distress, afflict* A3

affluentia, -ae, *f.,* opulence, extravagance

ager, agrī, *m.,* field*

agmen, -minis, *n.,* marching column* C4

agō, -ere, ēgī, āctum, to drive, lead, do, behave*

agricola, -ae, *m.,* farmer*

albus, -a, -um, *adj.,* white*

aliēnus, -a, -um, *adj. + prep. ā/ab + abl.,* foreign to, inconsistent with*

aliī . . . aliī . . ., some . . .others . . .

aliquis, aliqua, aliquid, *indefinite pronoun;* **aliquī, aliqua, aliquod,** *indefinite adj.,* some* A6

aliquot, *indeclinable indefinite pronoun and adj.,* some, a few

alius, alia, aliud, *adj.,* another, other*

alō, -ere, aluī, altum/alitum, to feed, nourish*

alter, altera, alterum, *adj.,* the other (of two)*

alteruter, alterutra, alterutrum, *adj.,* either of two

altus, -a, -um, *adj.,* tall, deep* C2

amāritūdō, amāritūdinis, *f.,* bitterness

amātor, -ōris, *m.,* lover

ambitus, -ūs, *m.,* bribery to obtain office

ambulō (1), to walk*

amīcitia, ae, *f.,* friendship

amīcus, -a, -um, *adj.,* friendly* A1

amīcus, -ī, *m.,* friend*

āmittō, -ere, -mīsī, -missum, to lose*

amō (1), to love*

amoenitās, -ātis, *f.,* pleasantness (*of a place*)

amor, -ōris, *m.,* love*

amplitūdō, amplitūdinis, *f.,* size, importance

amplius, *adv.,* a greater amount, a greater number, more* A8

an, or (*in a disjunctive question*)

anagnōstēs, -ae, *m.,* reader, slave whose job is to read aloud

ancilla, -ae, *f.,* female servant, maidservant

Andrēas (-ae) Ammōnius, -ī, *m.,* Andrew Ammonius, Italian in origin, secretary to the British King Henry VIII, and friend of Erasmus

Anemōliī, -ōrum, *m. pl.,* the Anemolians, the name of a fictional population

Anglī, -ōrum, *m. pl.,* the English

Anglus, -a, -um, *adj.,* English

animadvertō, -ere, animadvertī, animadversum, to notice* C15

animal, -ālis, *n.,* animal*

animus, -ī, *m.,* spirit, soul, mind*

anniculus, -a, -um, *adj.,* one year long, yearling

annuō, -ere, annuī, annūtum, to nod, grant, approve

annus, -ī, *m.,* year* C2

ante, *adv.,* before

ante, *prep. + acc.,* in front of*

antīquitās, -ātis, *f.,* antiquity, ancient tradition* A9

antīquitus, *adv.,* from old times

antīquus, -a, -um, *adj.,* ancient* C8

ānulus, -ī, *m.,* ring

anxius, -a, -um, *adj.,* anxious, worried

aperiō, -īre, aperuī, apertum, to open* C4

appāreō, -ēre, appāruī, to appear, be found* A7

appāret, -ēre, it is clear, obvious

appellō (1), to call upon, name, address

apprīmē, *adv.,* to the highest degree, especially

appropinquō (1), to approach* C15

aptus, -a, -um, *adj.,* fitted, appropriate* A7

apud, *prep. + acc.,* at the house of*

aqua, -ae, *f.,* water*

Aquīsgrānum, -ī, *n.,* Aachen (Aix-la-Chapelle), a town in western Germany, with mineral waters (as the name indicates), a seat of the Holy Roman Empire

arbitror, ārbitrārī, arbitrātus sum, to judge, consider, be of the opinion, suppose* A6

arbor, -oris, *f.,* tree*

arcessō, -ere, arcessīvī, arcessītum, to send for, fetch

ārdeō, -ēre, ārsī, —, to burn, be on fire*

argentum, -ī, *n.,* silver* C2

argūmentum, -ī, *n.,* proof, indication, argument*

arma, -ōrum, *n. pl.,* weapons*

armātus, -a, -um, *adj.,* armed*

Arrētīnus, -a, -um, *adj.,* connected with Arrētium, a town in Etruria

ars, artis, *f.,* science, art, skill* C8

artifex, -ficis, *m.,* craftsman, artisan* A5

arx, arcis, *f.,* citadel

ascendō, -ere, ascendī, ascēnsum, to climb

ascīscō, -ere, ascīvī, ascītum, to receive, adopt, summon from elsewhere

ascrībō, -ere, ascrīpsī, ascrīptum, to impute, ascribe, attribute

Āsia, -ae, *f.,* Asia

asperitās, asperitātis, *f.,* harshness

aspiciō, -ere, aspexī, aspectum, to look at, catch a glimpse of* C1

assecla, -ae, *m.,* follower, attendant

assiduus, -a, -um, *adj.,* diligent, dedicated

assus, -a, -um, *adj.,* roasted

at, *conj.,* but* C3

Athēnae, -ārum, *f. pl.,* Athens

Athēniēnsēs, Athēniēnsium, *m. pl.,* the Athenians

āthlēta, -ae, *m.,* athlete*

atque, *conj.,* and*

attingō, -ere, attigī, attāctum, to touch, engage in

audiō, -īre, audīvī, audītum, to hear, listen*

augeō, -ēre, auxī, auctum, to increase* A4

Augustīnus, -ī, *m.,* Augustine

aureus, -a, -um, *adj.,* golden

auris, -is, *f.,* ear* C9

aurum, -ī, *n.,* gold* C2

aut, *conj.,* or; **aut . . . aut . . . ,** either . . . or . . .* A2

autem, *conj.,* however, on the other hand

auxilium, -ī, *n.,* help*

avidē, *adv.,* eagerly, greedily

avis, -is, *f.,* bird

avunculus, -ī, *m.,* uncle*

axis, -is, *m.,* axle, axis*

B

bālaena, -ae, *f.,* whale

barba, -ae, *f.,* beard*

barbarus, -ī, *m.,* barbarian; foreign, uneducated

beātus, -a, -um, *adj.,* blessed

bellum, -ī, *n.,* war*

bene, *adv.,* well*

beneficium, -ī, *n.,* service, kindness, favor, benefit* A3

benevolentia, -ae, *f.,* good will* C13

bibō, -ere, bibī, —, to drink* C5

bīduum, -ī, *n.,* a period of two days; **bīduum,** for two days

bonitās, bonitātis, *f.,* moral excellence, goodness

bonum pūblicum, -ī, *n.,* the public good

bonus, -a, -um, *adj.,* good*

Britō, Britōnis, *m.,* a Briton

brevis, -e, *adj.,* short* C2

breviter, *adv.,* shortly, briefly* A8

Brūtī, the conspirators Marcus Brutus and Decimus Brutus

C

C. = Gāius, Roman first name

cacūmen, -ūminis, *n.,* top

cadō, -ere, cecidī, cāsum, to fall*

caelestis, -e, *adj.,* celestial

caelum, -ī, *n.,* sky, heaven, weather*

Caesar, -aris, *m.,* emperor (initially the name of Julius Caesar), Caesar* A4

Caesariānus, -a, -um, *adj.,* of Caesar

calamitās, -ātis, *f.,* disaster, misfortune, calamity* A1

calēns, calentis, *adj.,* hot; **aquae natūrāliter calentēs,** hot water springs

callidus, -a, -um, *adj.,* clever, cunning

canō, -ere, cecinī, cantum, to sing* A7

cānus, -a, -um, *adj.,* grey (for hair)

capillus, -ī, *m.,* hair

capiō, -ere, cēpī, captum, to take, adopt, capture; **cōnsilia capere,** to make plans*

capulus, -ī, *m.,* handle, hilt

caput, -itis, *n.,* head*

carmen, -inis, *n.,* poem, song* C5

carō, carnis, *f.,* meat, flesh*

Carolus, -ī, *m.,* Charles

cārus, -a, -um, *adj.,* dear* C12

casa, -ae, *f.,* little house, cottage*

castra, -ōrum, *n. pl.,* camp*

cāsus, -ūs, m., accident, chance occurrence

Catilīna, -ae, *m.,* Catiline, a bankrupt revolutionary whose plot to overthrow the republic was exposed by Cicero

causa, -ae, *f.,* cause, reason, case*

cēdō, -ere, cessī, cessum, to go away (from), withdraw, move

celeber, -bris, -bre, *adj.,* renowned, well-known, crowded*

celeritās, -ātis, *f.,* speed

celeriter, *adv.,* swiftly*

cēlō (1), to hide

cēnō (1), to dine* A6

centiēs sēstertium, ten million sesterces (in Roman currency)

centrum, -ī, *n.,* center

centum, *numeral and indeclinable adj.,* one hundred

Cerēs, Cereris, *f.,* goddess of grain and agriculture (in Greek, Demeter)

cernō, -ere, crēvī, crētum, to see, distinguish by the eyes* C15

cervīx, cervīcis, *f.,* neck

cēterus, -a, -um, *adj.,* other, remaining; *in pl.,* the rest * A5

cibus, -ī, *m.,* food* C5

cinis, -eris, *m.,* ash*

Cinnānus, -a, -um, *adj.,* related to

Cinna, -ae, *m.* Cinna, leader in Roman civil wars of first century CE

circā, *prep. + acc.,* around* C15

circiter, *adv.,* approximately, around

circulāris, -e, *adj.,* circular

circum, *prep. + acc.,* around*

circumeō, -īre, -īvī, -itum, to go around* C14

cīvīlis, -e, *adj.,* civil, pertaining to the state

cīvis, -is, *m./f.,* citizen*

cīvitās, cīvitātis, *f.,* city, community of citizens, state, political entity

clādēs, -is, *f.,* disaster*

clam, *adv.,* secretly

clāmō (1), to scream* C15

clārus, -a, -um, *adj.,* clear, distinguished* C2

classis, -is, *f.,* fleet*

clāvis, -is, *f.,* key

coeō, coīre, coīvī, coitum, to come together, meet

coepī, coepisse, coeptum, + inf., to begin to* C4

cōgitō (1), to think*

cōgnōscō, -ere, cōgnōvī, cōgnitum, to come to know, find to be* A1

cōgō, -ere, coēgī, coactum, to compel, force* A5

colaphus, -ī, *m.,* slap, blow with a fist

collaudō, -āre, -āvī, -ātum, to praise warmly entry needs to be bolded

collis, -is, *m.,* hill* A5

collocō (1), to set up, give in marriage

colloquor, colloquī, collocūtus sum, to converse

colō, -ere, coluī, cultum, to worship, cultivate*

Colōnus, -ī, *m.,* Columbus

coma, -ae, *f.,* hair

comedō, -ere, -ēdī, -ēsum, to eat*

Comes Flandrēnsium, Robert II, Count of Flanders (a region of Belgium today), one of the principal generals in the First Crusade

Comes Tolosānus, Raymond IV, count of Toulouse (in southern France), one of the leaders of the First Crusade

comes, comitis, *m.,* count; companion, associate

cōmitās, -ātis, *f.,* friendliness, courtesy

commemorō (1), to recall

committō, -ere, commīsī, commissum, to entrust

commoditās, commoditātis, *f.,* advantage, convenience

commūtō (1), to change (completely)

compleō, -ēre, -ēvī, -ētum, to fill, complete* A10

complūrēs, complūrium, *adj.,* not a few, several

concēdō, -ere, concessī, concessum, to allow, pardon

conciliātor, -ōris, *m.,* mediator

conciliō (1), to bring together

condiciō, -ōnis, *f.,* condition, terms of a loan or agreement* A4

condiscipulātus, -ūs, *m.,* companionship at school

condiscipulus, -ī, *m.,* classmate

cōnferō, cōnferre, contulī, collātum, to compare, bring together, collect, contribute

cōnfessiō, -ōnis, *f.,* confession

cōnficiō, -ere, cōnfēcī, cōnfectum, to make, compose

coniūnctiō, -ōnis, *f.,* connection

coninūctissimē, *adv.,* in a very friendly manner

coniungō, -ere, -iūnxī, -iūnctum, to connect, join together* A4

coniūnx, -iugis, *m./f.,* spouse* C3

cōnor, cōnārī, cōnātus sum, to try* C9

cōnsēnsiō, cōnsēnsiōnis, *f.,* agreement

cōnsequor, cōnsequī, cōnsecūtus sum, to acquire, gain* A9

cōnservō (1), to preserve

cōnsilium, -ī, *n.,* plan, advice* C1

consōbrīna, -ae, *f.,* cousin

cōnspiciō, -ere, -spexī, -spectum, to look at, observe*

cōnstantia, -ae, *f.,* constancy*

cōnstituō, -ere, cōnstituī, cōnstitūtum, to establish, set up, institute, decide*A4

cōnstō, -āre, cōnstitī, —, + *abl.,* to consist in* A5

consuētūdō, -ūdinis, *f.,* custom, habit, companionship* A6

cōnsul, -ulis, *m.,* consul*

cōnsulātus, -ūs, *m.,* consulship

cōnsulō, -ere, cōnsuluī, cōnsultum, + *dat.,* to look after; **+** *acc.,* to consult* A10

cōnsultō, *adv.,* on purpose

cōnsūmō, -ere, -sūmpsī, sūmptum, to consume*

contemnō, -ere, contempsī, contemptum, to regard with contempt, despise* A10

cōntentiō, -ōnis, *f.,* contest, fight

contentus, a, um, *adj., +* *abl.,* contented with, content

contexō, -ere, contexuī, contextum, to join by weaving, compose

contineō, -ēre, continuī, contentum, to hold, keep together, contain* C14

contrā, *prep. +* *acc.,* against*

conveniō, -īre, convēnī, conventum, to meet; **+** *dat.,* to be becoming to, be appropriate for*

convertō, -ere, convertī, conversum, to rotate, invert, turn

convictus, -ūs, *m.,* social relationships, a living together

convīva, -ae, *m./f.,* dinner companion, guest

convīvium, -ī, *n.,* dinner party, feast* A6

cōpula, -ae, *f.,* bond, connection

coquō, -ere, coxī, coctum, to cook*

cor, cordis, *n.,* heart*

cornū, -ūs, *n.,* horn*

corpus, -oris, *n.,* body*

corripiō, -ere, -ripuī, -reptum, to seize*

corrumpō, -ere, corrūpī, corrūptum, to corrupt

cottīdiānus, -a, -um, *adj.,* daily, of every day* C14

crēdō, -ere, crēdidī, crēditum, + *dat.,* to believe somebody, lend money*

crēscō, -ere, crēvī, —, to grow*

crīmen, crīminis, *n.,* crime, illegal action

crista, -ae, *f.,* a tuft on the head of animals; **cristās ērigere,** to carry the head high, be conceited

crūdēlis, -e, *adj.,* cruel*

cubitum, -ī, *n.,* elbow

cultor, -ōris, *m.,* fosterer, supporter, cultivator

cultus, -ūs, *m.,* care, management, maintenance, way of living* A6

cum, *conj., +* *indicative,* when; **+** *imperfect subjunctive,* although, since; **+** *pluperfect subjunctive,* after* C12

cum, *prep. +* *abl.,* with*

cupiditās, -ātis, *f.,* greed, immoderate desire

cupiō, -ere, -īvī, -ītum, to desire, want*

cūr, *adv.,* why?*

cūra, -ae, *f.,* care* A6

cūrō (1), to care for, take care of*

currō, -ere, cucurrī, cursum, to run*

cursus, -ūs, *m.,* course, direction, way, going

custōs, -ōdis, *m.,* guard* C2

D

Dalmatia, -ae, *f.,* region of the Roman Empire next to Illyricum on the east coast of the Adriatic sea. It corresponds in part to the area today called Croatia.

dē, *prep. +* *abl.,* about, concerning; down from, from*

dea, -ae, *f.,* goddess*

dēbeō, -ēre, dēbuī, dēbitum, + *inf.,* ought, must, should; to owe*

dēcēdō, -ere, dēcessī, dēcessum, to go away, die, withdraw*

dēcernō, -ere, -crēvī, -crētum, + *inf.,* to decide, determine*

decet, decēre (*impersonal verb*), it is becoming

dēcipiō, -ere, dēcēpī, dēceptum, to deceive* C6

dēclārō (1), to demonstrate, indicate, show* C13

dēdūcō, -ere, dēdūxī, dēductum, to lead away

dēfendō, -ere, dēfendī, dēfēnsum, to defend* C4

deinde, *adv.,* then*

dēlectō (1), to delight, please*

dēleō, -ēre, dēlēvī, dēlētum, to destroy*

dēliciae, -ārum, *f. pl.,* delight, pet*

dēligō, -ere, dēlēgī, dēlectum, to choose

delphīn, delphīnis, *m.,* dolphin

dēmittō, -ere, -mīsī, -missum, to send down; **animum dēmittō,** to let my spirit sink, become dejected* C9

dēprecor, dēprecārī, dēprecātus sum, to try to avert (by prayer)

dēprimō, -ere, dēpressī, dēpressum, to repress

dēscendō, -ere, -scendī, -scēnsum, to descend*

dēscrībō, -ere, dēscrīpsī, dēscrīptum, to describe

dēsīderium, -ī, *n.,* grief for something absent

dēsīderō (1), to long for, desire, need, require* A7

dēsinō, -ere, dēsiī, dēsitum, to stop*

dēspērātus, -a , -um, *adj.,* desperate

dēspērō (1), to despair

dēspiciō, -ere, dēspexī, dēspectum, to despise

despondeō, -ēre, despondī, despōnsum, to promise a woman in marriage, betroth

dēsum, dēesse, dēfuī, —, to be absent, fail

dētrahō, -ere, dētrāxī, dētrāctum, to take off, take away, detract from

dētrīmentum, -ī, *n.,* damage, detriment

deus, -ī, *m.,* god*

dēvastō (1), to devastate*

dēvinciō, -īre, dēvīnxī, dēvīnctum, to tie up, oblige, attach

dextra, -ae, *f.,* right hand*

dīcō, -ere, dīxī, dictum, to say*

diēs, -ēī, *m./f.,* day*

difficilis, -e, *adj.,* difficult*

digitus, -ī, *m.,* finger*

dignitās, dignitātis, *f.,* dignity, status, social position

dīligēns, dīligentis, *adj.,* diligent

dīligenter, *adv.,* diligently, carefully* A8

dīligentia, -ae, *f.,* carefulness, attentiveness, diligence* A1

dīligō, -ere, dīlēxī, dīlēctum, to esteem highly, love* C6

dīmittō, -ere, dīmīsī, dīmissum, to send away

dīrigō, -ere, dīrexī, dīrectum, to guide, direct, aim, send

discēdēns, discēdentis, *participle,* leaving

discēdō, -ere, -cessī, -cessum, to leave*

discipula, -ae, *f.,* student (female)* C3

discō, -ere, didicī, —, to learn* C3

disiciō, -ere, disiēcī, disiectum, to break up and scatter

dissēnsiō, dissēnsiōnis, *f.,* disagreement

dissimilis, -e, *adj.,* dissimilar*

dissipō (1), to scatter, disperse

distineō, -ēre, distinuī, distentum, to hold apart, distract

dītī = dīvite

diū, *adv.,* for a long time*

dīves, dīvitis, *adj.,* rich*

dīvīnātiō, dīvīnātiōnis, *f.,* prophecy, divination, foreseeing, predicting the future

dīvīnus, -a, -um, *adj.,* divine*

dīvitiae, -ārum, *f. pl.,* wealth, riches*

dīvus, -ī, *m.,* god, deified emperor

dō, dăre, dedī, dătum, to give*

doceō, -ēre, docuī, doctum, to teach*

docilitās, docilitātis, *f.,* aptness for being taught, docility

doctrīna, -ae, *f.,* learning, erudition

doctus, -a, -um, *adj.,* learned*

doleō, -ēre, doluī, —, to feel pain, hurt*

dolor, -ōris, *m.,* grief, pain*

dolus, -ī, *m.,* trickery, deception*

domesticus, -a, -um, *adj.,* domestic

domī, at home*

domicilium, -ī, *n.,* dwelling, abode

domina, -ae, *f.,* mistress*

dominātus, -ūs, *m.,* rule, sovereignty

dominor, dominārī, dominātus sum, to dominate, rule* C8

dominus, -ī, *m.,* master, lord* C3

domus, -ūs, *f.,* house, home*

dōnō (1), to give, bestow; + *acc.* + *abl.,* to present someone with something

dōnum, -ī, *n.,* gift*

dormiō, -īre, -īvī, -ītum, to sleep*

Drusilla, -ae, *f.,* Livia Drusilla, a powerful Roman matron, mother of the emperor Tiberius; later a wife of Octavian Augustus

dūcō, -ere, dūxī, ductum, to lead, take*

dulcis, -e, *adj.,* sweet* C5

dum, *conj.,* while; + *subjunctive,* until*

duo, duae, dua, *numeral,* two* C6

dux, ducis, *m.,* leader, general (in medieval Latin often means "duke")*

E

ē contrāriō, on the contrary

ē *or* **ex,** *prep.* + *abl.,* from, out of*

ē rē pūblicā, in accord with the public good

ēbrius, -a, -um, *adj.,* drunk

ecce, *interj.,* look here!*

ēdō, -ere, ēdidī, ēditum, to produce, give forth* C4

efficiō, -ere, -fēcī, -fectum, *often* + *ut,* to cause to happen, bring about, effect, to bring to effect, to accomplish* A4

effugiō, -ere, effūgī, —, to escape

effūsus, -a, -um, *adj.,* lavish, unrestrained

egeō, -ēre, eguī, —, + *abl.,* to lack something*

ego, *personal pronoun,* I*

egomet, *pronoun,* I myself

ēlegāns, -antis, *adj.,* careful in choosing, tasteful* A5

ēlegantia, -ae, *f.,* fineness of taste, elegance

elementum, -ī, *n.,* element*

ēliciō, -ere, ēlicuī, ēlicitum, to coax, entice, elicit, call forth

ēlixus, -a, -um, *adj.,* boiled

ēloquentia, -ae, *f.,* eloquence

emāx, emācis, *adj.,* fond of buying

ēmergō, -ere, ēmersī, ēmersum, to come out of the water, emerge

emō, -ere, ēmī, ēmptum, to buy* A1

ēn, *interj.,* see there!

enim, *conj.,* for, in fact*

eō, *adv.,* for that reason

eō, īre, īvī, itum, to go* C10

eōdem, *adv.,* to the same place

epistula, -ae, *f.,* letter*

eques, -itis, *m.,* horseman, knight, member of the equestrian order* C2 A4

equester, -tris, -tre, *adj.,* equestrian, related to the social class of knights; **ōrdō equester,** the order of the knights (the social class between patricians and plebeians)

equitēs, -itum, *m.,* the order of knights (middle rank in Roman society)

equus, -ī, *m.,* horse*

Erasmus (-ī) Roterodamus, -ī, *m.,* Erasmus of Rotterdam

ergō, *conj.,* therefore* C14

ērigō, -ere, ērēxī, ērēctum, to raise, set up

ēripiō, -ere, -ripuī, -reptum, to snatch away*

errō (1), to wander, make a mistake*

ērudiō, -īre, ērudīvī, ērudītum, to educate, instruct

et, *conj.,* and; **et . . . et . . . ,** both . . .and . . . * C1

etiam, *adv.,* even, also*

etsī, *conj.,* although* A2

Eurōpa, -ae, *f.,* Europe

ex dōdrante, from a portion of three-quarters

excellenter, *adv.,* in an excellent way

excitō (1), to awaken, wake up, rouse, stir up*

exclāmō (1), to exclaim*

excōgitō (1), to think up, devise

exemplar, -āris, *n.,* example*

exemplum, -ī, *n.,* example*

exercitus, -ūs, *m.,* army* C6

eximō, -ere, exēmī, exēmptum, to take out, remove

exīstimō (1), to value, esteem, think, deem, suppose, consider* A1

expers, -ertis, *adj.,* + *gen.,* having no share in, devoid of, free from* A8

explendēscō, -ere, exsplenduī, —, to shine forth, be famous

expōnō, -ere, exposuī, expositum, to set forth in words, describe, explain, relate about

exsilium, -ī, *n.,* exile

exspectō (1), to wait for, await, expect*

exstinguō, -ere, -stīnxī, -stīnctum, to extinguish*

externus, -a, -um, *adj.,* outward, external*

extrā, *prep.* + *acc.,* outside of* C4

extrēmus, -a, -um, *adj.,* situated or occurring at the end, last* A7

F

fābula, -ae, *f.,* story*

faciēs, -ēī, *f.,* face*

facile, *adv.,* easily*

facilis, -e, *adj.,* easy*

facilitās, -ātis, *f.,* an easy, good nature

faciō, -ere, fēcī, factum, to do, make*

factiō, factiōnis, *f.,* political preference, party

factum, -ī, *n.,* fact, action

facultās, facultātis, *f.,* ability; *f. pl.,* resources, riches

faenus, -oris, *n.,* interest, profit

falsus, -a, -um, *adj.,* false

fama, -ae, *f.,* fame, name* C3

familia, -ae, *f.,* family, household*

familiāris, -āris, *m./f.,* family member, a family member or relation* A1

familiāris, familiāre, *adj,* belonging to the same family, intimate person or thing

familiāritās, -ātis, *f.,* familiarity* A1

familiās, *archaic gen. sing. of familia,* of the family

fastīgium, -ī, *n.,* highest part, roof, top

fātum, -ī, *n.,* fate, destiny*

faveō, ēre, fāvī, fautum + *dat.,* to favor

febris, -is, *f.,* fever* A10

fēlīx, -īcis, *adj.,* fortunate, happy*

fēmina, -ae, *f.,* woman*

ferō, ferre, tulī, lātum, to carry, bear, endure* C9

ferōx, -ōcis, *adj.,* fierce, ferocious*

ferrum, -ī, *n.,* iron

fidēlis, -e, *adj.,* fathful, loyal*

fidēs, -eī, *f.,* faith* C7

fīlia, -ae, *f.,* daughter*

fīlius, -ī, *m.,* son*

findō, -ere, fidī, fissum, to split

fingō, -ere, fīnxī, fictum, to imagine, form in the mind* C15

fīnis, -is, *m.,* end* C2

fīō, fierī, factus sum, to be made, become; (*impersonally*) to happen* C9

firmō (1), to strengthen*

flamma, -ae, *f.,* flame*

fleō, -ēre, flēvī, flētum, to cry*

flō (1), to blow

flōreō, -ēre, flōruī, —, to blossom, flourish* A3

fluctus, -ūs, *m.,* wave, breaker

flūmen, -minis, *n.,* river* C5

fluō, -ere, flūxī, fluxum, to flow*

fodiō, -ere, fōdī, fossum, to dig; **latus fodere,** to stab someone's side with an elbow

folium, -ī, *n.,* leaf

forīs, *adv.,* outside, in the open*

fōrma, -ae, *f.,* form, appearance*

fortasse, *adv.,* perhaps*

fortis, -e, *adj.,* brave, strong*

fortitūdō, -inis, *f.,* courage*

fortūna, -ae, *f.,* fortune, the goddess Fortune; *f. pl.,* financial resources

forum, -ī, *n.,* Forum Rōmānum, the main square in Rome* A2

Franciscus (-ī) Petrarca, -ae, *m.,* Francis Petrarch (His name in Italian is Francesco Petrarca.)

Francus, -ī, *m.,* a Frank

frāter, -ātris, *m.,* brother* C3

frequēns, -entis, *adj.,* frequent, assiduous* A9

frīgus, -oris, *n.,* cold* C9

frūctus, -ūs, *m.,* fruit, gain, profit, revenue

frūmentum, -ī, *n.,* grain

fruor, fruī, fruitus/frūctus sum, + *abl.,* to enjoy, enjoy the society of* C10 A9

frūstrā, *adv.,* in vain, to no avail*

frūx, frūgis, *f.,* crop, produce of the earth

fuga, -ae, *f.,* flight

fugiō, -ere, fūgī, —, to flee, run away*

fulgeō, -ēre, fulsī, —, to shine

fūmus, -ī, *m.,* smoke*

fundō, -ere, fūdī, fūsum, to pour* C7

fundus, -ī, *m.,* country estate, farm

fūnestus, -a, -um, *adj.,* deadly*

fūnis, -is, *m.,* rope

fūr, fūris, *m.,* thief*

furō, -ere, furuī, —, to rage, be insane* C4

fūror, fūrārī, fūrātus sum, to steal*

furor, -ōris, *m.,* madness, fury

fūrtum, -ī, *n.,* theft*

futūrus, -a, -um, *participle,* about to be*

G

Galilaeus, -ī, *m.,* Galileo

Gallī, -ōrum, *m. pl.,* the Gauls, the inhabitants of France

Gallia Belgica, -ae, *f.,* Belgium

Gallia, -ae, *f.,* Gaul, a region of modern France

gaudium, -ī, *n.,* joy*

gemma, -ae, *f.,* gem, precious stone* C11

gener, generī, *m.,* son-in-law

generō (1), to give birth, procreate; *pass.,* to descend from

generōsus, -a, -um, *adj.,* highborn, of noble birth

gēns, gentis, *f.,* tribe, population* C1

genu, genūs, *n.,* knee

genus, -eris, *n.,* type, kind* C9

Germānia, -ae, *f.,* the region of Europe approximately corresponding to modern Germany

gerō, -ere, gessī, gestum, to carry, wear; "to administer" in civil politics; **sē gerit,** s/he behaves; **bellum gerō,** to wage war* C2

gesta, -ōrum, *n. pl.,* deeds

gignō, -ere, genuī, genitum, to produce, give birth* C1

glaciēs, -ēī, *f.,* ice* C9

gladius, -ī, *m.,* sword*

globus, -ī, *m.,* mass, association of men, band

glōria, -ae, *f.,* glory* C7

Godefrīdus, -ī, *m.,* Godfrey of Bouillon

Golia, -ae, *m.,* name of a wandering scholar

grācilis, -e, *adj.,* slender*

gradior, gradī, gressus sum, walk

Graecē, *adv.,* in Greek

grandō, grandinis, *f.,* hail

grātia, -ae, *f.,* agreeableness, favor, grace; winning character, influence* A4

grātus, -a, -um, *adj.,* thankful, appreciative, gratifying* A1

gravis, -e, *adj.,* heavy, serious* C2

gravitās, -ātis, *f.,* weight, gravity* C14

gremium, -ī, *n.,* bosom, lap*

gubernātor, -ōris, *m.,* helmsman, pilot

Guilhelmus (-ī) Montoius, -ī, *m.,* William Mountjoy

H

habeō, -ēre, habuī, habitum, to have*

habitō (1), to live, dwell*

habuit cognitam = cognōvit

hastīle, hastīlis, *n.,* shaft

haud, *adv.,* not

Heloīsa, -ae, *f.,* Heloise

herba, -ae, *f.,* plant, vegetation*

hērēditās, -ātis, *f.,* inheritance* A5

hērēs, -ēdis, *m./f.,* heir* C6

heu, *interj.,* alas!

Hibernia, -ae, *f.,* Ireland

hīc, *adv.,* here

hic, haec, hoc, *demonstrative pronoun and adj.,* this*

hiems, hiemis, *f.,* winter, storm* A2

Hierosolyma, -ōrum, *n. pl.,* Jerusalem

Hispānia, -ae, *f.,* Spain

Hispānus, -a, -um, *adj.,* Spaniard

historia, -ae, *f.,* history, written account of past events

historicus, -ī, *m.,* historian

hodiē, *adv.,* today* C1

homō, -inis, *m.,* man (*i.e., human being*); *pl.* people*

honor, -ōris, *m.,* honor, public office or distinction*

hortor, hortārī, hortātus sum, to exhort, urge* C8

hortus, -ī, *m.,* garden* A6

hostis, -is, *m.,* enemy*

HS, an abbreviation for *sestertiōrum,* sesterces

hūc, *adv.,* to this place, hither

hūmānitās, -ātis, *f.,* human character, kindness; culture, humanity, refinement befitting a man* A7

hūmānus, -a, -um, *adj.,* human*

humilis, -e, *adj.,* low*

I

i.e. = id est

iaceō, -ēre, iacuī, —, to lie down, be inert*

iaciō, -ere, iēcī, iactum, to throw*

iam, *adv.,* already; anymore*

ibi, *adv.,* there*

id est, namely, that is to say (*a common phrase used to make a previous assertion more specific*)

īdem, eadem, idem, *demonstrative pronoun and adj.,* the same* C13

igitur, *adv.,* therefore*

ignis, -is, *m.,* fire*

ignōrō (1), to have no knowledge, be ignorant of

ille, illa, illud, *demonstrative pronoun and adj.,* that*

illūstris, -e, *adj.,* distinguished, illustrious* A8

Illyricum, -ī, *n.,* a region situated on the west coast of what is today the Balkan peninsula

imāgō, -inis, *f.,* image* A8

imitātor, -ōris, *m.,* imitator, emulator

immemor, -oris, *adj.,* + *gen.,* forgetful of* C5

immēnsus, -a, -um, *adj.,* immeasurable, immense, endless* C14

immō, *conj.,* on the contrary, nay rather

immortālis, -e, *adj.,* undying, immortal* A3

impediō, -īre, -īvī, -ītum, to impede, prevent*

imperātor, -ōris, *m.,* emperor, general, commanding officer* A2

imperium, -ī, *n.,* rule, power, empire, dominion, command* C6

impertiō, -īre, impertīvī, impertītum, to share, provide (to give a *pars*)

impetus, -ūs, *m.,* impetus, force, attack*

impingō, -ere, impēgī, impāctum, to push, strike, drive into* C15

implicō, -āre, implicuī, implicitum/implicātum, + *dative,* to involve into, implicate

improbus, -a, -um, *adj.,* bad, wicked* C3

in aeternum, forever

in diem, for a future day

in diēs, daily, as the days proceed

in prīmīs (imprīmīs), especially, above all, first of all

in, *prep.* + *abl.,* in, on*

in, *prep.* + *acc.,* in, into, towards (*when referring to feelings or attitude to someone*)*

incendium, -ī, *n.,* conflagration, eruption*

incendō, -ere, incendī, incēnsum, to set fire, irritate

incidō, -ere, incidī, incāsum, to fall into

incitō (1), to stimulate, instigate

incola, -ae, *m.,* inhabitant* C1

incolumitās, -ātis, *f.,* freedom from harm, safety

incommodum, -ī, *n.,* disadvantage, harm* A4

indicium, -ī, *n.,* indication

indicō (1), to show, indicate

indigeō, -ēre, indiguī, —, + *abl.,* to need, lack* A10

indignus, -a, -um, *adj.,* + *dat.,* unworthy of

indīligēns, indīligentis, *adj.,* careless, negligent

indulgeō, -ēre, indulsī, indultum, + *dat.,* to be indulgent, grant as a favor to

induō, -ere, induī, indūtum, to put on (a piece of clothing)

ineō, -īre, inīvī/iniī, initum, to go into; **cōnsilium inīre,** to form a plan

īnfimus, -a, -um, *adj.,* lowest

īnfīnītus, -a, -um, *adj.,* boundless, unlimited, infinite, immense* C14

īnflīgō, -ere, īnflīxī, īnflīctum, to strike on or against, inflict* C15

ingēns, ingentis, *adj.,* huge* C4

ingrātus, -a, -um, *adj.,* unwelcome, unpleasant

ingredior, ingredī, ingressus sum, to enter

inimīcitia, -ae, *f.,* hostility

inimīcus, -ī, *m.,* enemy, opponent* A2

inīquitās, -ātis, *f.,* injustice*

initium, -ī, *n.,* beginning*

iniūria, -ae, *f.,* unjust treatment, injury* A3

innītor, innītī, innīxus/innīsus sum, to lean on

inopia, -ae, *f.,* want, helplessness, scarcity, poverty* C6

inquam, I say/I said (*only introducing direct speech*)*

inquiētus, -a, -um, *adj.,* restless, unquiet

inquit, s/he says or said (*only introducing direct speech*)* C12

inquiunt (plural of *inquit*), they say (*only introducing direct speech*)* C12

īnsequor, īnsequī, īnsecūtus sum, to pursue (in a hostile manner)

īnstituō, -ere, īnstituī, īnstitūtum, + *acc.* + *abl.,* to train or educate someone in some skill

īnstitūtum, -ī, *n.,* way, manner

īnsula, -ae, *f.,* island* C12

Īnsulae Fortūnātae, -ārum, *f. pl.,* Canary Islands

intellegō, -ere, intellēxī, intellēctum, to understand*

inter, *prep.* + *acc.,* between, among*

intercēdō, -ere, intercessī, intercessum, to go between, intervene

interdum, *adj.,* sometimes* C2

interfector, interfectōris, *m.,* slayer, assassin

interficiō, -ere, interfēcī, interfectum, to kill

interpōnō, -ere, interposuī, interpositum, to put between; **sē interpōnere,** to interfere, intervene

intersum, interesse, interfuī, —, + *dat.,* to get involved in, participate in

intimē, *adv.,* as a close friend, on intimate terms

intimus, -a, -um, *adj.,* most intimate, closest* A1

intrīnsecus, *adv.,* on the inside

intrō (1), to enter*

invādō, -ere, invāsī, —, to burst in* C4

inveniō, -īre, invēnī, inventum, to come upon, find* C1

investīgō (1), to investigate, search into

invideō, -ēre, invīdī, invīsum, + *dat.,* to envy someone*

invītō (1), to invite

invītus, -a, -um, *adj.,* unwilling

iocor, iocārī, iocātus sum, to joke

iocus, -ī, *m.,* joke* C5

ipse, ipsa, ipsum, *demonstrative pronoun and adj.,* -self* C13

īra, -ae, *f.,* anger*

īrāscor, īrāscī, īrātus sum, to be angry* C13

is, ea, id, *personal and demonstrative pronoun and adj.,* s/he, it, this*

iste, iste, istud, *demonstrative pronoun and adj.,* that (of yours)* C13

ita, *adv.,* so, in such a way; yes*

Ītalia, -ae, *f.,* Italy* A2

itaque, *conj.,* and so*

item, ad*v.,* likewise

iter, itineris, *n.,* road, trip* C9

iterum, *adv.,* again* C15

iubeō, -ēre, iussī, iussum, + *acc.* + *inf.,* to order somebody to do something*

iūcundus, -a, -um, *adj.,* pleasant, agreeable, delightful* C10

iūdex, -icis, *m.,* judge*

iūdicium, ī, *n.,* court, court case; **iūdicium . . . habēre,** to be involved in a court case

iūdicō (1), to judge*

iungō, -ere, iūnxī, iūnctum, to join* C3

iūs, iūris, *n.,* law, right; **in iūs īre,** to go to court, take legal action

iussus, -ūs, *m.,* order (usually employed in the ablative singular only)*

iūstus, -a, -um, *adj.,* legitimate, just*

iuventūs, -ūtis, *f.,* youth* C5

iūvō, āre, iūvī, iūtum, to help

L

L., the abbreviation for the praenomen Lūcius

L. Lūcullus, ī, *m.,* a powerful Roman general and politician in the first century BCE

lābor, lābī, lāpsus sum, to slide, slip, glide down* C9

labor, -ōris, *m.,* labor, toil* C10

lacrima, -ae, *f.,* tear*

laedō, -ere, laesī, laesum, to harm* C10

lāmentum, -ī, *n.,* lament, complaint

largītiō, largītiōnis, *f.,* prodigality, lavish expenditure, corruption

Latīnē, *adv.,* in Latin* C8

Latīnus, -a, -um, *adj.,* Latin, pertaining to Latin* C8

lātus, -a, -um, *adj.,* broad, wide

latus, lateris, *n.,* side, flank; **latus fodere,** to stab someone's side with an elbow

laudō (1), to praise* C6

laus, laudis, *f.,* praise

lēctiō, -ōnis, *f.,* reading

legātus, -ī, *m.,* ambassador* C11

legō, -ere, lēgī, lēctum, to read, choose*

lepor, lepōris, *m.,* charm, agreeableness

levis, -e, *adj.,* light, trivial* C5

levō (1), lighten, relieve

lēx, lēgis, *f.,* law*

līber, lībera, līberum, *adj.,* free* C10

liber, librī, *m.,* book*

līberālis, -e, *adj.,* befitting a free man, generous; **artēs līberālēs,** the liberal arts (typically grammar, rhetoric, and dialectic)

līberālitās, -ātis, *f.,* generosity* A3

līberī, -ōrum, *m. pl.,* children

līberō (1), + *acc.* + *abl.,* to free someone from something*

lībertās, -ātis, *f.,* freedom* C7

librārius, -ī, *m.,* a slave trained in copying, copyist, secretary

licet, + *dat.* + *inf.,* it is allowed, it is permitted for someone to do something*

ligneus, -a, -um, *adj.,* made of wood* C4

ligō (1), to tie

lingua, -ae, *f.,* language, tongue (*as physical part of the mouth*)* C8

līs, lītis, *f.,* dispute, quarrel* C2

littera, -ae, *f.,* letter of the alphabet; **litterae, -ārum,** *f. pl.,* literature, letter (epistle)*

litterātus, -a, -um, *adj.,* versed in literature, cultured* A5

lītus, -oris, *n.,* shore*

locus, -ī, *m.,* place; **locī, -ōrum,** *m. pl.,* passages of a book; **loca, -ōrum,** *n. pl.,* geographical places*

longē, *adv.,* far*

longus, -a, -um, *adj.,*long*

loquor, loquī, locūtus sum, to speak* C8

lūcidus, -a, -um, *adj.,* bright

lūcrum, -ī, *n.,* profit, gain* C10

lūdō, -ere, lūsī, lūsum, to play*

lūmen, -inis, *n.,* light* C7

lupa, -ae, *f.,* she-wolf*

M

M. = Mārcus, Roman first name

M. Brūtus, -ī, *m.,* Marcus Brutus

magis, *adv.,* more*

magister, magistrī, *m.,* teacher (male)* C3

magistrātus, -ūs, *m.,* office of a magistrate, magistracy* A8

māgnī habeō, esteem a lot* C11

māgnificus, -a, -um, *adj.,* magnificent

māgnus, -a, -um, *adj.,* large, great, important*

māior, māius, *adj. comparative,* greater* C8

māiōrēs, māiōrum, *m. pl.,* ancestors

mālō, mālle, māluī, —, to prefer*

malus, -a, -um, *adj.,* bad*

mandō (1), to assign, order

māne, *adv.,* in the morning* C2

maneō, -ēre, mānsī, mānsum, to remain*

mantica, -ae, *f.,* briefcase, travel bag

manus, -ūs, *f.,* hand*

Mārcus Tullius Cicerō, -ōnis, *m.,* Marcus Tullius Cicero

mare, maris, *n.,* sea*

margarīta, -ae, *f.,* pearl

maritimus, -a, -um, maritime, belonging to the sea, near the sea* C10

marītus, -ī, *m.,* husband*

Marius, -ī, *m.,* civil war leader against Sulla

Martīnus (-ī) Alfōnsus (-ī) Pinzon (indeclinable), *m.,* Martín Alonso Pinzón

māter, mātris, *f.,* mother*

māteria, -ae, *f.,* material

mātrimōnium, -ī, *n.,* marriage* C3

matūrē, *adv.,* early

maximē, *adv. superlative,* most* C14

maximus, -a, -um, *adj. superlative,* greatest*

mēcum = cum mē, with me*

medicīna, -ae, *f.,* medicine

medicus, -ī, *m.,* doctor

mediocris, -e, *adj.,* commonplace, mediocre, moderate* A5

medium, -ī, *n.,* the middle, midst*

medius, -a, -um, *adj.,* middle* C14

melior, melius, *adj. comparative,* better* C8

meminī, meminisse, to remember* A3

memor, -oris, *adj. + gen.,* remembering, mindful of (*usually of one's obligations*)* A1

memoria, -ae, *f.,* memory*

mendācium, -ī, *n.,* lie* A6

mēns, mentis, *f.,* mind, spirit* C5

mentiō, -ōnis, *f.,* mention

mereor, merērī, meritus sum, to deserve

merīdiānus, -a, -um, *adj.,* southern

merīdiēs, -ēī, *m.,* midday, south* C1

meritō, *adv.,* deservedly

metallum, -ī, *n.,* metal

meus, -a, -um, *possessive adj.,* my*

migrō (1), to move from one place to another

mīles, -itis, *m.,* soldier*

Minerva, -ae, *f.,* goddess of wisdom and war (in Greek her name is Athena)

minimē, *adv. superlative,* least, very little; no* C11

minimus, -a, -um, *adj. superlative,* smallest, least*

minor, minus, *adj. comparative,* smaller*

minuō, -ere, minuī, minūtum, to diminish

minus, *adv. comparative,* less* C8 C11

mīror, -ārī, -ātus sum, to marvel, be surprised at* C13

miser, misera, miserum, *adj.,* wretched*

mittō, -ere, mīsī, missum, to send*

mōbilitās, -ātis, *f.,* mobility

moderor, moderārī, moderātus sum, to manage, direct, guide* C9

modo ... modo ..., at one time ... at another ..., now ... now ...* A2

modo, *adv.,* only

modus, -ī, *m.,* way, method, manner* C10

molestus, -a, -um, *adj.,* troublesome

monasterium, -ī, *n.,* monastery

monīle, monīlis, *n.,* necklace

mōns, montis, *m.,* mountain*

monstrum, -ī, *n.,* monster

morbus, -ī, *m.,* illness, sickness* A10

mōre māiōrum, in accord with the custom of <our> ancestors

moriēns, morientis, *adj.,* dying

mōriō, -ōnis, *m.,* fool, clown

morior, morī, mortuus sum, to die* C12

moror, morārī, morātus sum, to stay for a long or short period, spend time* A9

mors, mortis, *f.,* death*

mōs, mōris, *m.,* custom, habit; *pl.,* morals* C1

mōtus, -ūs, *m.,* motion, movement* C14

moveō, -ēre, mōvī, mōtum, to move*

mox, *adv.,* soon*

mulier, -ieris, *f.,* woman*

multitūdō, -ūdinis, *f.,* crown, throng* C13

multō, *adv.,* by much* C14

multum, *adv.,* much*

multus, -a, -um, *adj.,* much, many; **multum** + *partitive gen.,* a lot of

munditia, -ae, *f.,* neatness, cleanliness

mundus, -ī, *m.,* world* C1

mūnus, mūneris, *n.,* gift

mūrus, -ī, *m.,* wall, wall-fence*

mūtātiō, -ōnis, *f.,* change

Mutina, ae, *f.,* Mutina, city in northern Italy, called Modena today

mūtō (1), to change*

N

nam, *conj.,* for, in fact*

namque, *conj.,* indeed, for, because* A6

nancīscor, nancīscī, nactus/ nanctus sum, to gain possession of, acquire

nārrō (1), to tell*

nāscor, nāscī, nātus sum, to be born* A9

Nāsō, -ōnis, *m.,* Ovid

nātiō, -ōnis, *f.,* a race of people, tribe

nātīvus, -a, -um, *adj.,* inborn, native

natō (1), to swim

nātū maxima/minima, oldest/ youngest

nātūra, -ae, *f.,* nature, character* C14

nātūrālis, nātūrāle, *adj.,* natural

nātūrāliter, *adv.,* naturally

nātus, -a, -um, *adj.,* born

nauta, -ae, *m.,* sailor*

nāvigātiō, -ōnis, *f.,* sea voyage

nāvigō (1), to sail, voyage*

nāvis, -is, *f.,* ship*

nē ... quidem ... , not even* A5

-ne, a particle added to the first word of an interrogative sentence*

nē, *conj.* + *subjunctive,* in order not to, lest, that not, not to* C1

nebulō, -ōnis, *m.,* a worthless fellow

nec, *conj.,* and not, nor; **nec ... nec... ,** neither ... nor ... * C4

necdum, *adv., conj.,* and not yet

necessāriō, *adv.,* necessarily* C14

necessārius, -a, -um, *adj.* necessary* A3

necesse est, it is necessary; + *dat.* + *infinitive,* it is necessary for someone to do something* C6

necessitūdō, -ūdinis, *f.,* bond* A9

nefās (indeclinable), *n.,* a crime, a sacrilege

neglegō, -ere, neglēxī, neglēctum, to neglect*

negō (1), to deny* C13

nēmō nōn, everybody

nēmō, *m.,* no one* C6

neptis, -is, *f.,* granddaughter

neque = nec, and not; **neque ... neque ... ,** neither ... nor ... * A3

neque eō sētius, nevertheless

neque sōlum ... sed etiam ... , not only ... but also ...

neque, *conj.* = nec; **neque ... neque ... ** = nec ... nec ...

nesciō, -īre, -īvī, -ītum, not to know* C11

neuter, neutra, neutrum, *adj.,* neither, none of two*

nihil, *adv.,* in no way, not at all

nihil, *negative pronoun,* nothing*

nihilō sētius, nonetheless, just the same

nihilōminus, *conj.,* nevertheless

nimis, *adj.,* too much* C12

nisi, *conj.,* if not, unless* C12

nītor, nītī, nīsus/nīxus sum, to strive to achieve* A6

nix, nivis, *f.,* snow* C9

nōbilis, nōbile, *adj.,* noble, distinguished

noctū, *adv.,* during the night*

nōlō, nōlle, nōluī, —, not to want, be unwilling* C7

nōmen, -inis, *n.,* name*

Nōmentānus, -a, -um, *adj.,* belonging to Nomentum, a town in Latium

nōn sōlum ... , sed etiam ... , not only ... , but also ... *

nōn, *negative adv.,* not*

nōnnūllī, -ae, -a, *adj.,* a good number, quite a few, some

nōs, *personal pronoun,* we*

noster, nostra, nostrum, *possessive adj.,* our*

notō (1), to indicate, note

novus, -a, -um, *adj.,* new*

nox, noctis, *f.,* night*

nūbēs, -is, *f.,* cloud*

nūbō, -ere, nūpsī, nūptum + *dat.,* to marry (*used for a woman marrying a man*)

nūllus, -a, -um, *adj.,* none*

numerō (1), to number, count among* C13

numerus, -ī, *m.,* number* A2

numquam, *adv.,* never*

nunc, *adv.,* now*

nūptiae, -ārum, *f. pl.,* wedding, marriage* A4

nusquam, *adv.,* nowhere* C3

O

ō, *interj.,* oh!

oblīvīscor, oblīvīscī, oblītus sum, + *gen.,* to forget* A3

obsecrō (1), to beseech, entreat

observantia, -ae, *f.,* regard

obstinātiō, -ōnis, *f.,* obstinacy, stubbornness

obtineō, -ēre, obtinuī, obtentum, to hold, hold onto

obtrectātiō, obtrectātiōnis, *f.,* an envious detracting, disparaging

occidēns, occidentis, *m.,* west

occīdō, -ere, occīdī, occīsum, to kill*

occultō (1), to hide*

occupātiō, -ōnis, *f.,* preoccupation with business, engagement

occupō (1), to occupy* C1

ōceanus, -ī, *m.,* ocean

oculus, -ī, *m.,* eye*

odium, ī, *n.,* hatred; **odiō habeō,** + *acc.,* I hate somebody* C2

offendō, -ere, offendī, offēnsum, to happen upon, offend* C13

offēnsiō, offēnsiōnis, *f.,* offense, cause for offense

officium, -ī, *n.,* favor, duty, sense of duty, service, kindness* C12

olea, -ae, *f.,* olive

ōlim, *adv.,* once upon a time

omnīnō, *adv.,* wholly, entirely

omnis, -e, *adj.,* each, every, all*

onus, oneris, *n.,* weight, burden* C9

operae pretium est, it is worthwhile* C11

operam dō + *dat.,* to give care to

opīniō, opīniōnis, *f.,* opinion, mind* A1

oppidum, -ī, *n.,* town* C15

opprimō, -ere, oppressī, oppressum, to overwhelm, suppress*

ops, opis, *f.,* aid, wealth; **opēs, opium,** *f. pl.,* resources, money

optimus, -a, -um, *adj.,* best* C8

opus est, is necessary

ōrāculum, -ī, *n.,* oracle*

ōrātiō, -ōnis, *f.,* speech; **ōrātiōnem habeō,** make a speech*

orbis, orbis, *m.,* circle, disc, globe; **orbis terrārum,** the earth, the world* C12

ōrdinō (1), to place in order

ōrdō, ōrdinis, *m.,* order, social class, class (in society)* A9

orīgō, orīginis, *f.,* origin* A8

orior, orīrī, ortus sum + *abl.,* to be born of, be descended from, originate* A9

ōrnāmentum, -ī, *n.,* ornament, distinction

ōrnātus, -a, -um, *adj.,* adorned* C7

ornātus, -ūs, *m.,* apparel, attire

ōrō (1), to ask, entreat* C5

ortus, -ūs, *m.,* raising, beginning, origin; **ortus sōlis,** east* C1

ōs, ōris, *n.,* mouth*

osculor, osculārī, osculātus sum, to kiss

ostendō, -ere, ostendī, ostentum, to show*

ostrea, -ae, *f.,* oyster

ōtium, -ī, *n.,* leisure, free time* C7

P

P. = Pūblius

paene, *adv.,* almost*

palam, *adv.,* openly

Pannonia, -ae, *f.,* a region which approximately corresponds to modern Hungary

pār, paris, *adj.,* equal*A5

parcō, -ere, pepercī, —, + *dat.,* to spare somebody or something* C4

parēns, -rentis, *m./f.,* parent*

pariō, -ere, peperī, partum, to give birth to* C3

parō (1), to prepare, get ready, design*

pars, partis, *f.,* part*

partior, partīrī, parītus sum, to divide, distribute*

parvus, -a, -um, *adj.,* small*

passer, -eris, *m.,* sparrow*

pateō, -ēre, patuī, —, to be open, be available

pater, patris, *m.,* father*

patior, patī, passus sum, to endure, tolerate, suffer, allow

patria, -ae, *f.,* fatherland*

paucī, -ae, -a, *adj.,* few*

paulisper, *adv.,* for a little while* C10

paulō, *adv.,* a little bit, to a small extent* C6

pauper, pauperis, *adj.,* poor*

pāx, pācis, *f.,* peace*

pectus, -oris, *n.,* chest*

pecūnia, -ae, *f.,* money* C10

pecūniōsus, -a, -um, *adj.,* moneyed, provided with money

pedisequus, -ī, *m.,* manservant

pēior, pēius, *adj. comparative,* worse*

pellis, -is, *f.,* skin, hide*

pendeō, -ēre, pependī, —, to hang (intransitive)*

penes, *prep.* + *acc.,* in the possession of

per, *prep.* + *acc.,* through*

peragō, -ere, perēgī, perāctum, to carry out, perform

percipiō, -ere, percēpī, perceptum, to take, earn, acquire* A3

percutiō, -ere, percussī, percussum, to strike through* C15

perdō, -ere, perdidī, perditum, to lose, waste* C3

peregrīnātiō, peregrīnātiōnis, *f.,* journeying

perīculum, -ī, *n.,* danger*

perpendiculāris, -e, *adj.,* perpendicular

perpendō, -ere, perpendī, perpēnsum, to ponder, weigh carefully

perperam, *adv.,* wrongly, incorrectly* C14

perpetuō, *adv.,* without interruption

perpetuus, a, um, *adj.,* continuous, permanent

perscrībō, -ere, perscrīpsī, perscrīptum, to write a detailed account of

persequor, persequī, persecūtus sum, to follow persistently, go over

persuādeō, -ēre, persuāsī, persuāsum, to persuade

pertineō, -ēre, pertinuī, pertentum, to relate to, pertain to

perturbō (1), to throw into confusion

perveniō, -īre, -vēnī, -ventum, to arrive* C9

pessimus, -a, -um, *adj. superlative,* worst*

petō, -ere, petīvī, petītum, to seek, head for, go to, rush to*

philosophus, -ī, *m.,* philosopher

Pictus, -ī, *m.,* a Pict

pietās, pietātis, *f.,* sense of duty, dutifulness to family and society

pilleus, -ī, *m.,* hat

piscis, -is, *m.,* fish* C1

placeō, -ēre, placuī, placitum, + *dat.,* to please, be agreeable to somebody* C5

placidus, -a, -um, *adj.,* peaceful, calm* C10

plācō (1), to placate, soothe

planēta, -ae, *m.,* planet

plēnus, -a, -um, *adj.* + *gen.* or + *abl.,* full of*

pluit, -ere, pluit, —, *an impersonal verb (used only in 3rd sg.),* to rain

plumbum, -ī, *n.,* lead

plūrēs, plūra, *adj. comparative,* more*

plūrimus, -a, -um, *adj. superlative,* most*

plūs, *adv.,* more

plūs, plūris, *adj. comparative,* + *partitive gen.,* more*

pluvia, -ae, *f.,* rain

poēma, poēmatis, *n.,* poem

poēta, -ae, *m.,* poet*

poēticē, poēticēs (poēticēn), *f.,* poetry

poēticus, -a, -um, *adj.,* poetic

polliceor, pollicērī, pollicitus sum, to promise* A6

Pompēius, -ī, *m.,* Pompey

Pompōnius, -ī, *m.,* the first name of Atticus

pōmum, -ī, *n.,* fruit*

ponderōsus, -a, -um, *adj.,* heavy

pondus, -eris, *n.,* weight* C14

pōnō, -ere, posuī, positum, to put, place*

pōns, pontis, *m.,* bridge* C4

populus, -ī, *m.,* people* C11

porta, -ae, *f.,* gate* C4

pōscō, -ere, popōscī, —, to demand

possessiō, -ōnis, *f.,* possession

possideō, -ēre, possēdī, possessum, to possess*

possum, posse, potuī, —, to be able, can*

post, *prep.* + *acc.,* after*

posteā, *adv.,* afterwards*

posteāquam = postquam

posterī, -ōrum, *m. pl.,* descendants, coming generations

postquam, *conj.,* after*

potēns, potentis, *adj.,* powerful* C7

potentia, -ae, *f.,* power* A4

potestās, -ātis, *f.,* command, control, power* A4

potior, potīrī, potītus sum, + *gen.,* to make oneself master of, take possession of

potissimum, *adv.,* especially, above all

potius, *adv.,* rather* C10

praebeō, -ēre, praebuī, praebitum, to offer, give

praecipuē, *adv.,* particularly, especially* A7

praecipuus, -a, -um, *adj.,* peculiar, special, exceptional

praeclārus, -a, -um, *adj.,* famous, distinguished, excellent, renowned*

praedicō (1), to proclaim

praedīcō, -ere, praedīxī, praedictum, to predict

praeditus, -a, -um, + *abl.,* endowed with, possessed of* C15

praedium, -ī, *n.,* estate, land

praefātiō, -ōnis, *f.,* preface

praefectūra, -ae, *f.,* an office in governing a province

praemium, -ī, *n.,* reward*

praeoptō (1), + *acc.* + *dat.,* to prefer something to something

praesertim, *adv.,* especially* C14

praesidium, -ī, *n.,* military escort, garrison* A2

praestō, -āre, praestitī, praestitum, to make available, supply; fulfill, perform, offer; surpass, exceed, excel* A1

praestringō, -ere, praestrīnxī, praestrictum, to bind fast, to strike; **oculōs praestringere,** to blind

praeter, *prep.* + *acc.,* except, beside, in addition to, beyond * A6

praetermittō, -ere, praetermīsī, praetermissum, to allow to go, let pass

praetor, praetōris, *m.,* praetor

praetūra, ae, *f.,* praetorship

prāvus, -a, -um, *adj.,* crooked, bad

prex, precis, *f.,* prayer*

prīdem, *adv.,* long ago

prīmā nocte, on the first night

prīmō, *adv.,* at first* C4

prīmum, *adv.,* first*

prīmus, -a, -m, *adj.,* first*

prīnceps, prīncipis, *adj.,* distinguished, first

prīnceps, prīncipis, *m.,* leading citizen, leader, chief * A7

prīncipātus, prīncipātūs, *m.,* first place

prīvātus, -a, -um, *adj.,* private, apart from the public sphere

prīvātus, -ī, *m.,* private citizen

prīvignus, -ī, *m.,* stepson

prō certō, *adverbial phrase,* for certain, for sure*

prō, *prep. + abl.,* for, on behalf of*

probābilis, -e, *adj.,* probable

probō (1), to approve* C12

prōcēdō, -ere, prōcessī, prōcessum, to advance, proceed

procella, -ae, *f.,* violent storm, gale

procul, *adv.,* far, far away*

prōcumbō, -ere, prōcubuī, prōcubitum, to fall forward, prostrate oneself

prōdūcō, -ere, prōdūxī, prōductum, to bring forth, lengthen

proelium, -ī, *n.,* battle, combat*

professiō, -ōnis, *f.,* profession

proficīscor, proficīscī, profectus sum, to set out, depart

profugiō, -ere, profūgī, —, to run away, flee

profundus, -a, -um, *adj.,* deep, profound, bottomless

prōgredior, prōgredī, prōgressus sum, to go forward, proceed* C9

prohibeō, -ēre, prohibuī, prohibitum, to prevent

prōiciō, -ere, prōiēcī, prōiectum, to send forth, (*in passive participle*) protruding

prōmittō, -ere, prōmīsī, prōmissum, to promise* C1

prōnūntiō (1), to pronounce, recite, deliver (of a speech)

prōpāgātiō, -ōnis, *f.,* spreading, propagation

propāgō, propāginis, *f.,* offspring, progeny

prope, *prep. + acc.,* near* C1

prōpōnō, -ere, prōposuī, prōpositum, to propose

prōpositum, -ī, *n.,* intention, proposition

propter, *prep. + acc.,* because of, on account of*

prōscrībō, -ere, prōscrīpsī, prōscrīptum, to proscribe, publish someone's name in a list of outlaws

prōscrīptiō, -ōnis, *f.,* proscription, publishing the names of citizens declared to be outlaws

prosper, prospera, prosperum, *adj.,* fortunate, prosperous* C10

prosperitās, -ātis, *f.,* fortunate state of things, prosperity

prout, *conj.,* as

prōvincia, -ae, *f.,* province (territorial), any duty or sphere of activity (not territorial)

proximus, -a, -um, *adj.,* nearest* C5

prūdēns, prūdentis, *adj.,* prudent

prūdentia, -ae, *f.,* practical intelligence, wisdom, prudence, foreseeing* A2

pūblicē, *adv.,* publicly, on behalf of the state

pūblicus, -a, -um, *adj.,* common, public, belonging to the state; **rēs publica,** state* C7

puella, -ae, *f.,* girl*

puer, puerī, *m.,* boy*

puerīlis, puerīle, *adj.,* related to *puer;* **puerīlis aetās,** boyhood

pueritia, -ae, *f.,* childhood

pugnō (1), to fight*

pulcher, pulchra, pulchrum, *adj.,* beautiful, nice*

pulchrē, *adv.,* beautifully

pūniō, -īre, -īvī, -ītum, to punish*

putō (1), to think, consider*

Q

Q. = Quīntus

Q. Caecilius, -ī, *m.,* Quīntus Caecilius

Q. Cicero, Cicerōnis, *m.,* = Quīntus Cicero

Q. Hortēnsius, Quīntus Hortensius

quaerō, -ere, quaesīvī, quaesītum, to look for, search*

quaestiō, -ōnis, *f.,* question, dispute, investigation

quaestus, -ūs, *m.,* profit

quālis, quāle, *interrogative and relative pronoun,* what sort of* C7

quam, + *superlative degree,* as . . . as possible* A3

quam, *interrogative adv. and exclamation particle,* how* C4

quam, *used with comparative words,* than* C6

quamdiū, *adv. and conj.,* as long as

quamdiū, *interrogative adv.,* for how long* A9

quamquam, *conj.,* although* C12

quamvīs, *conj.,* although*

quantum, *interrogative and relative adv.,* as much as, as much; how much, to what extent* C6

quantus, -a, -um, *interrogative and relative adj,* how much, how great* C4

quārē, *conj.,* therefore, hence*

quaternī, -ae, -a, *adj.,* four each (*a distributive*)

-que, *conj.,* and*

quī, quae, quod, *relative pronoun,* which, who, that*

quī, quae, quod?, *interrogative adjective,* which? what?*

quia, *conj.,* because* C12

quīdam, quaedam, quiddam, *indefinite pronoun;* **quīdam, quaedam, quoddam,** *indefinite adjective,* a certain* A7

quidem, *adv.,* indeed* C12

quiēs, -ētis, *f.,* rest, repose* C14

quīn etiam, and furthermore

quīn, *conj. + subjunctive,* without its being the case that (*after negative clauses*)* A9

quīnī, -ae, -a, *adj.,* five each (*a distributive*)

Quīntus (-ī) Tullius (-ī) Cicero (Cicerōnis), *m.,* Quīntus Tullius Cicero

Quīntus Hortēnsius, *m.,* a famous orator

quīntus, -a, -um, *adj.,* fifth

Quirītēs, -ium, *m. pl.,* Roman citizens

quis, quid?, *interrogative pronoun,* who? what?*

quisquam, quicquam (quidquam), *indefinite pronoun* (*mainly in negative sentences*), any* A9

quisquam, quicquam (quidquam), *indefinite pronoun* (*mainly in negative sentences*), anybody

quisquis, quidquid (quicquid), *indefinite pronoun,* whoever, whatever

quōcum = cum quō

quod, *conj.,* because* C12

quod, *conj.,* the fact that, because

quōdam diē, a certain day, one day

quōmodo, *adv.,* how* C11

quōquam, *adv.,* to any place

quoque, *adv.,* also*

quotiēs, *conj.,* as often as* C9

quōusque, *adv.,* how far, to what extent

R

rāmus, -ī, *m.,* branch

rapiō, -ere, rapuī, raptum, to snatch

recipiō, -ere, recēpī, receptum, to receive, take back; **mē recipiō,** I retreat* C4

rēctē, *adv.,* correctly

reddō, -ere, reddidī, redditum, to render, make, give back* C10

redeō, -īre, -īvī, -itum, to go back, return* C13

redūcō, -ere, redūxī, reductum, to lead back

referō, referre, rettulī, relātum, to carry back, report* C13

rēgia, -ae, *f.,* royal palace

rēgīna, -ae, *f.,* queen*

rēgnō (1), to reign, rule

religiōsē, *adv.,* scrupulously, conscientiously

relinquō, -ere, relīquī, relictum, to leave behind, abandon*

reliquus, -a, -um, *adj.,* the rest of, the remaining; **reliquum facere,** to leave over* A10

rēmaneō, -ēre, rēmānsī, rēmānsum, to remain

remigrō (1), to go back, return

removeō, -ēre, remōvī, remōtum, to move back, remove

repellō, -ere, reppulī, repulsum, to push back, thrust back* C15

repraesentō (1), to represent

reprehendō, -ere, -prehendī, -prehēnsum, to blame, rebuke*

requīrō, -ere, requīsīvī, requīsītum, to try to find, inquire about

rēs familiāris (familiāris, familiāre), family resources, wealth, personal property, family estate, estate

rēs (rērum) gestae, -ārum, *f. pl.,* deeds, exploits, things done, history, past actions* A8

rēs, reī, *f.,* thing, matter*

reservō (1), to keep, reserve

resistō, -ere, restitī, — , to resist, oppose; + *dat.,* to resist (*somebody or something*)* C4

respondeō, -ēre, -spondī, -spōnsum, to answer*

restituō, -ere, restituī, restitūtum, to restore* C6

retineō, -ēre, retinuī, retentum, to retain, keep

reverenter, *adv.,* respectfully

revolūtiō, -ōnis, *f.,* revolving

rēx, rēgis, *m.,* king*

rīdeō, -ēre, rīsī, rīsum, to laugh* C15

rīvus, -ī, *m.,* brook, stream*

rixa, -ae, *f.,* quarrel

rogō (1), to ask*

Rōma, -ae, *f.,* Rome*

Rōmānus, -a, -um, *adj.,* Roman*

rota, -ae, *f.,* wheel*

ruber, rubra, rubrum, *adj.,* red*

rumpō, -ere, rūpī, ruptum, to break, tear* C15

rūs, rūris, *n.,* countryside*

rūsticus, -a, -um, *adj.,* rural, rustic*

S

s.d. = salūtem dīcit

sacer, sacra, sacrum, *adj.,* sacred

saepe, *adv.,* often*

sāl, salis, *m.,* salt, a quality that gives taste, wit* A5

saliō, -īre, saluī, saltum, to jump

salūs, -ūtis, *f.,* health, welfare; **salūtem dīcō,** + *dat.,* I greet (a customary way to begin a letter)* C3

salūtō (1), to greet* C11

sanciō, -īre, sānxī, sānctum, to ratify solemnly, confirm* A9

sanguis, -inis, *m.,* blood*

sānō (1), to heal*

sapientia, -ae, *f.,* wisdom

sarcina, -ae, *f.* (*used mostly in pl.*), burden, baggage* C10

satelles, satellitis, *m.,* satellite

satis, *adv.,* enough, sufficiently* C6

satisfaciō, -ere, satisfēcī, satisfactum, to give satisfaction, give all that is required (*often with dat.*)

saxum, -ī, *n.,* stone, rock*

scandō, -ere, —, —, to climb over, mount

scelestus, -a, -um, *adj.,* wicked* C10

scindō, -ere, scindī, scissum, to tear, cut

sciō, -īre, -īvī, -ītum, to know*

scopulōsus, -a, -um, *adj.,* full of shoals, rocky

Scōttus, -ī, *m.,* a Scot

scrībō, -ere, scrīpsī, scrīptum, to write* C3

Scythia, -ae, *f.,* Scythia (a territory in southern Russia today)

sē, *acc. of the reflexive pronoun,* herself, himself, itself, themselves*

sēcum = cum sē

secundus, -a, -um, *adj.,* favorable, second* C6

sed, *conj.,* but*

sedeō, -ēre, sēdī, sessum, to sit*

sēdēs, -is, *f.,* seat, abode* C15

semel, *adv.,* once* C10

semper, *adv.,* always*

senectūs, -ūtis, *f.,* old age*

senēscō, -ere, senuī, —, to get old, grow old

senex, -is, *m.,* old man*

sententia, -ae, *f.,* opinion, point of view* C12

sentiō, -īre, sēnsī, sēnsum, to feel*

sēparō (1), to separate*

septentriōnālis, -e, *adj.,* northern* C1

sequor, sequī, secūtus sum, to follow*

serēnus, -a, -um, *adj.,* calm, clear* C10

sēriō, *adv.,* seriously

sermō, sermōnis, *m.,* conversation, speech

serviō, -īre, servīvī, servītum, to be of service, comply with

servitūs, -ūtis, *f.,* slavery

servō (1), to save, preserve*

servus, -ī, *m.,* slave, servant* C11

sesterius, -ī, *m.,* sesterce, Roman silver coin

sevēritās, -ātis, *f.,* sternness, severity

sevērus, -a, -um, *adj.,* serious, strict, severe*

sexāgintā, *numeral,* sixty

sī, *conj.,* if*

sibi, *dat. of the reflexive pronoun,* to himself/herself/itself/themselves*

sīc, *adv.,* in such a way, in this way, so* C15

sīcut, *adv.,* just as, just in the same way*

sīdus, -eris, *n.,* constellation* C15

signum, -ī, *n.,* sign

silva, -ae, *f.,* forest*

similis, -e, *adj.* + *gen.* or + *dat.,* like, similar*

similitūdō, similitūdinis, *f.,* similarity

simplex, simplicis, *adj.,* simple

simul ac, *conj.,* as soon as* C4 C9

simul, *adv.,* at the same time, simultaneously*

simultās, -ātis, *f.,* rivalry

sine, *prep.* + *abl.,* without*

singulāris, -e, *adj.,* unique, exceptional, special, unparalleled

singulī, -ae, -a, *adj.,* one apiece, one each (*a distributive*)* A8

sinō, -ere, sīvī, situm, + *acc.* + *inf.,* to allow somebody to do something* C2

Siōn, Siōnis, *m./f.,* a hill in Jerusalem

situs, -a, -um, *adj.,* situated, located* C1

socius, -ī, *m.,* associate, partner, ally* C13

sōl, sōlis, *m.,* sun* C1

soleō, -ēre, solitus sum, —, + *inf.,* to be accustomed*

sōlus, -a, -um, *adj.,* alone*

somnus, -ī, *m.,* sleep*

sōpiō, -īre, sōpīvī, sōpītum, to lull to sleep, settle

soror, -ōris, *f.,* sister*

sors, sortis, *f.,* lot (in the literal sense of a lot one draws), fate (in the metaphorical sense of one's condition in life)* C12

specimen, speciminis, *n.,* mark, example, proof

spectō (1), to watch* C11

spēlunca, -ae, *f.,* cave*

spērō (1), to hope* C12

spēs, speī, *f.,* hope* C12

splendidus, -a, -um, *adj.,* illustrious, distinguished, shining

splendor, -ōris, *m.,* brilliance, splendor

spoliō (1), + *abl.,* to strip of

spōnsālia, -ium, *n. pl.,* the act or the ceremony of betrothal

spōnsor, -ōris, *m.,* guarantor, one who formally guarantees the good faith of another

stabilis, -e, *adj.,* steady, stable

statim, *adv.,* immediately*

status, -ūs, *m.,* condition, state, attitude

stipulātiō, -ōnis, *f.,* demanding of a guarantee from a prospective debtor

stirps, stirpis, *f.,* stock, descent, race

stō, -āre, stetī, statum, to stand*

strīdor, -ōris, *m.,* a harsh, shrill, or hissing sound

studeō, -ēre, studuī, —, + *dat.,* to study, be eager for, be interested in*

studiōsus, -a, -um, *adj.,* + *gen.,* fond of, interested in* C7

studium, -ī, *n.,* pursuit, activity to which one is devoted, zeal, eagerness* A7

suāvitās, -ātis, *f.,* sweetness, charm, pleasantness* A8

sub, *prep.* + *abl.,* under* A8

subitō, *adv.,* suddenly*

sublevō (1), to support, to help

subterrāneus, -a, -um, *adj.,* underground

subtexō, -ere, subtexuī, subtextum, to add as a supplement

suburbānus, -a, -um, *adj.,* situated near Rome

succurrō, -ere, succurrī, succursum, to hasten to help

suī, sibi, sē, *reflexive pronoun,* herself, himself, itself, themselves*

Sulla, -ae, *m.,* Sulla

Sullānus, -a, -um, *adj.,* related to Sulla, -ae, *m.*

sum, esse, fuī, —, to be*

summa, -ae, *f.,* high point, sum total; **summa imperiī,** pinnacle of power

summus, -a, -um, *adj.,* extreme, highest, utmost, supreme, at the top of* A2

sūmō, -ere, sūmpsī, sūmptum, to take*

sūmptuōsus, -a, -um, *adj.,* costly, sumptuous

sūmptus, -ūs, *m.,* expense* A5

superior, superiōris, *adj.,* more powerful

superō (1), to surpass, conquer

supersum, superesse, superfuī, —, + *dat.,* to survive something

suprā, *adv.,* beyond, in addition

suspiciō, suspiciōnis, *f.,* suspicion

suus, -a, -um, *possessive adj.,* his, her, its, their*

T

taberna, -ae, *f.,* wineshop

taceō, -ēre, tacuī, tacitum, to be silent, keep quiet* C11

taciturnus, -a, -um, *adj.,* silent

tālis, tāle, *adj.,* such, such a* C13

tam . . . quam . . . , so . . . as . . . * C5

tam, *adv.,* so*

tamdiū . . . quoad . . . , as long . . . as . . .

tamen, *conj.,* however*

tamquam, *adv.,* as* C7

Tancrēdus Normannus, Tancred of Hauteville; along with Bohemond of Taranto, led a powerful contingent of Normans in the First Crusade

tandem, *adv.,* at last*

tangō, -ere, tetigī, tāctum, to touch*

tantopere, *adv.,* so greatly

tantum . . . quantum . . . , as much . . . as . . .

tantum, *adv.,* only, so much* A4

tantus, -a, -um, *adj.,* so great*

tēctum, -ī, *n.,* roof, house* A5

tēcum = cum tē, with you*

tegō, -ere, tēxī, tēctum, to cover, protect* A1

tēlum, -ī, *n.,* spear, javelin* C15

temerē, *adv.,* hardly, heedlessly, without good cause

temeritās, -ātis, *f.,* rashness, recklessness

tēmetipsum, yourself

temperō (1), *ā(b)* + *abl.,* to refrain from

tempestās, -ātis, *f.,* storm*

templum, -ī, *n.,* temple*

temporārius, -a, -um, *adj.,* suited for the occasion, temporary

temporis causā, to suit the occasion

temptō (1), to try*

tempus, -ōris, *n.,* circumstance, time; *pl.,* **tempora,** crisis

tempus, -oris, *n.,* time*

tenebrae, -ārum, *f. pl.,* shadows, darkness*

teneō, -ēre, tenuī, tentum, to hold*

tenuis, -e, *adj.,* thin

tergum, -ī, *n.,* back

terō, -ere, trīvī, trītum, to wear out, rub*

terra, -ae, *f.,* land*

terribilis, -e, *adj.,* terrifying*

territus, -a, -um, *adj.,* terrified

terror, -ōris, *m.,* terror

tertius, -a, -um, *adj.,* third* C6

testāmentum, -ī, *n.,* will

testimōnium, -ī, *n.,* testimony* A7

testis, -is, *m.,* witness

Theodosius, -ī, *m.,* Theodosius

Ti. Claudius Nerō, *m.,* Tiberius Claudius Nero, the emperor Claudius

timeō, -ēre, timuī, —, to fear, be afraid*

timor, -ōris, *m.,* fear*

tolerō (1), to tolerate, bear

tollō, -ere, sustulī, sublātum, to liftup, raise, destroy*

tot, *adv.,* so many* C7

tōtus, -a, -um, *adj.,* whole, entire* C11

trādō, -ere, trādidī, trāditum, to give, to teach

trahō, -ere, trāxī, trāctum, to drag* C7

trāiciō, -ere, trāiēcī, trāiēctum, to transport, transfer

tranquillitās, tranquillitātis, *f.,* calmness, quiet way of life

tranquillō (1), to make peaceful

tranquillus, -a, -um, *adj.,* quiet, calm

trecenta (HS trecenta mīlia), 300,000 sesterces

trēs, tria, *numeral,* three* C6

tribūnus, -ī, *m.* plēbī, tribune of the plebs

tribuō, -ere, tribuī, tribūtum, to grant, bestow, assign, give, attribute* A3

tricēsimus, -a, -um, *adj.,* thirtieth

trīstis, -e, *adj.,* sad* C6

triumvir, triumvirī, *m.,* member of a committee of three men

tū, *personal pronoun,* you (sg.)*

tueor, -ērī, tuitus/tūtus sum, to look at, protect* A10

tum, *adv.,* then*

tumultus, -ūs, *m.,* uproar, confusion*

tunc, *adv.,* then*

turpis, -e, *adj.,* shameful, disgraceful* C11

turris, -is, f., tower* C13

tūtus, -a, -um, *adj.,* safe* C4

tuus, -a, -um, *possessive adj.,* yours, your (sg.)*

U

ubi?, *interrogative adv.,* where?* C7

ubīcumque, *conj.,* wherever; *adv.,* everywhere

ubĭnam, *adv.,* where in the world?

ubīque, *adv.,* everywhere*

ulcīscor, ulcīscī, ultus sum, to take revenge

Ulixēs, -is, *m.,* Odysseus or Ulysses

ūllus, -a, -um, *adj.,* any*

ultimus, -a, -um, *adj.,* last, farthest, most remote

umquam, *adv.,* ever*

ūnā, *adv.,* together*

ūndecim, eleven

undique, *adv.,* from all parts, from everywhere* C14

ūniversus, -a, -um, *adj.,* all together, all, entire

ūnus, ūna, ūnum, *adj.,* one* C7

urbs, urbis, f., city (usually the city of Rome)*

ūsque, *adv.,* right up; **ūsque ad,** up to* A7

ūsūra, -ae, f., interest (of money), interest paid for the use of money

ūsus, -ūs, *m.,* use; **ūsū venīre,** to occur* A7

ut, *conj.,* + *indicative,* as, when, according to; + *perfect indicative,* as soon as, when; + *subjunctive,* in order to, so that, that* C2

uter, utra, utrum, *interrogative adj.,* who?, which (of two)?

uterque, utraque, utrumque, *adj. or pronoun,* each of the two

ūtilis, -e, *adj.,* useful* C7

ūtilitās, -ātis, f., usefulness

utinam, I wish that, if only (a particle of wishing)* C1

Ūtopia, -ae, f., Utopia (in Greek "No Place")

Ūtopiēnsis, Ūtopiēnsis, *m.,* Utopian

ūtor, ūtī, ūsus sum, + *abl.,* to use somebody or something; enjoy the friendship of, avail oneself of* C11

utrum ... an ... (introducing a disjunctive question), whether ... or ...* A6

uxor, -ōris, f., wife; **uxōrem dūcō,** to marry (a woman)* C3

V

vacātiō, vacātiōnis, f., freedom, exemption from military service

vacuus, -a, -um, + *abl.,* empty of* C4

vadimōnium, -ī, *n.,* guarantee that the defendant will appear before the judge

valdē, *adv.,* very, exceedingly*

valē!, goodbye!*

valedīcō, -ere, valedīxī, valedictum, to say goodbye

valeō, -ēre, valuī, —, + *infin.,* to be able; be in good health; be of value* C2

valētūdō, -ūdinis, f., health* A10

vapor, -ōris, *m.,* steam, vapor

varietās, -ātis, f., variety, diversity, changeable nature

vastus, -a, -um, *adj.,* empty, vast

vātēs, vatis, *m.,* prophet

vector, -ōris, *m.,* passenger

vegetus, -a, -um, *adj.,* lively, vigorous

vehemēns, vehementis, *adj.,* violent, vehement* C5

vehementer, *adv.,* vehemently, strongly* C6

vehō, -ere, vexī, vectum, to drive, carry* C15

vel ... vel ..., either ... or ...

vel, *conj.,* or*

vēlificor, -ārī, vēlificātus sum, to sail

vēlōcitās, -ātis, f., speed, velocity

velut sī, just as if (normally joined with a verb in the subjunctive)

vēnātor, -ōris, *m.,* hunter

vēnditō (1), to try to sell, advertise

venēnum, -ī, *n.,* poison*

venia, -ae, f., pardon, indulgence, forgiveness* C13

veniō, -īre, vēnī, ventum, to come*

venter, -tris, *m.,* stomach, belly

ventitō (1), to go often

ventus, -ī, *m.,* wind*

verbōsus, -a, -um, *adj.,* containing many words, lengthy

verbum, -ī, *n.,* word*

vērē, *adv.,* correctly

vereor, verērī, veritus sum, to fear, respect*

vērō, *adv.,* in fact, truly; moreover (introducing a further argument)

versō (1), to turn*

versor, versārī, versātus sum, to be occupied in, be involved in* C13

versūra, -ae, *f.,* exchanging one creditor for another, borrowing, application for a loan

versus, -ūs, m., line of writing, line of verse* A8

vērus, -a, -um, *adj.,* true*

vester, vestra, vestrum, *adj.,* yours (pl.), your*

vestīmentum, -ī, *n.,* garment, (pl.) clothes*

vestiō, -īre, -īvī, -ītum, to dress

vestis, -is, *f.,* clothes, attire* C2

vetus, veteris, *conj.,* old* C5

vetustās, -ātis, *f.,* old age

vetustus, -a, -um, *adj.,* old*

vexō (1), to trouble, harass

via, -ae, *f.,* road*

victor, -ōris, *m.,* victor* C4

videō, -ēre, vīdī, vīsum, to see, (passive) seem*

vīlla, -ae, *f.,* country house, villa*

vincō, -ere, vīcī, victum, to conquer, defeat*

vinculum, -ī, *n.,* chain, fetter*

vīnum, -ī, *n.,* wine* C5

violenter, *adv.,* violently

violō (1), to violate, harm

vir, virī, *m.,* man*

virga, -ae, *f.,* twig, stick* C13

virgō, -inis, *f.,* virgin, girl of marriageable age* A9

virtūs, -ūtis, *f.,* virtue, courage* C5

vīs, —, *f. pl.,* **vīrēs, vīrium,** force, strength; **prō vīribus,** with all one's might*

vīta, -ae, *f.,* life*

vitium, -ī, *n.,* vice* C5

vīvō, -ere, vīxī, victum, to live*

vīvus, -a, -um, *adj.,* alive

vix, *adv.,* hardly* C7

vocō (1), to call*

volō, velle, voluī, —, to want* C7

volūmen, -ūminis, *n.,* book, volume* A8

voluntās, -tātis, *f.,* will* C13

volvō, -ere, volvī, volūtum, to turn round* C14

vōs, *personal pronoun,* you (pl.)*

vōx, vōcis, *f.,* voice* C2

vulgus, -ī, *n.,* common people, general public* A7

vulnerō (1), to wound*

vulnus, -eris, *n.,* wound*

vultus, -ūs, *m.,* face* C2

BIBLIOGRAPHY

LATIN GRAMMAR

Allen, J. H., and J. B. Greenough. *Allen and Greenough's New Latin Grammar.* Edited by Anne Mahoney. Newburyport, MA: Focus Publishing/R. Pullins, 2001.

Gildersleeve, Basil L., and Gonzalez Lodge. *Gildersleeve's Latin Grammar.* 3rd ed. 1895. Reprint, Wauconda, IL: Bolchazy-Carducci Publishers, 2003.

Sidwell, Keith. *Reading Medieval Latin.* Cambridge, UK: Cambridge University Press, 1995.

Tunberg, Terence, "The Latinity of Erasmus and Medieval Latin: Continuities and Discontinuities," *Journal of Medieval Latin* 14 (2004): 145–168.

LATIN COMPOSITION

Minkova, Milena. *Introduction to Latin Prose Composition.* Wauconda, IL: Bolchazy-Carducci Publishers, 2007. First published 2002 by Wimbledon Publishing Co.

Minkova, Milena, and Terence Tunberg. *Readings and Exercises in Latin Prose Composition: From Antiquity to the Renaissance.* Newburyport, MA: Focus Publishing/R. Pullins, 2004.

Mountford, James F., ed. *Bradley's Arnold Latin Prose Composition.* Rev. ed. Wauconda, IL: Bolchazy-Carducci Publishers, 2006.

LATIN DICTIONARIES

Du Cange, C. Du Fresne. *Glossarium mediae et infimae latinitatis.* Seven Volumes. Paris, France: Didot, 1840.

Hoven, René. *Lexique de la prose latine de la Renaissance.* Deuxième édition revue et considérablement augmentée, Leiden: Brill Academic Publishers, 2006.

Lewis, Charlton T., and Charles Short. *A Latin Dictionary.* Oxford: Clarendon Press, 1879.

Niermeyer, Jan Frederik, *Mediae Latinitatis Lexicon Minus*, Leiden: Brill Academic Publishers, 1976.

Oxford Latin Dictionary. Edited by P. G. W. Glare. Oxford: Clarendon Press, 1982.

Smith, William, and Theophilus D. Hall. *Smith's English-Latin Dictionary.* Reprinted from the 1871 American Book Company edition, *A Copious and Critical English-Latin Dictionary*, with a new foreword by Dirk Sacré. Wauconda, IL: Bolchazy-Carducci Publishers, 2000.

Souter, Alexander. *A Glossary of Later Latin to 600 A.D.*, Oxford: Clarendon Press, 1949.

CONVERSATIONAL LATIN

Traupman, John. *Conversational Latin for Oral Proficiency*. 4th ed.: *Audio Conversations*. Performed by Mark Robert Miner et al. Compact discs. Wauconda, IL: Bolchazy-Carducci Publishers, 2006.

LATIN LITERATURE

Albrecht, Michael von. *A History of Roman Literature: From Livius Andronicus to Boethius*. Leiden: Brill Academic Publishers, 1997.

IJsewijn, Jozef. *Companion to Neo-Latin Studies, Part I: History and Diffusion of Neo-Latin Literature*. 2nd ed. Supplementa Humanistica Lovaniensia, 5. Leuven: University Press, 1990.

IJsewijn, Jozef, and Dirk Sacré. *Companion to Neo-Latin Studies, II: Literary, Linguistic, Philological and Editorial Questions*. 2nd. ed. Supplementa Humanistic Lovaniensia, 14. Leuven: Leuven University Press, 1998.

Mantello, Frank, and Arthur G. Rigg. *Medieval Latin. An Introduction and Bibliographical Guide*. Washington, D.C.: The Catholic University of America Press, 1996.

HISTORY OF THE LATIN SPEAKING WORLD

Boatwright, Mary T., Daniel J. Gargola, and Richard J. A. Talbert. *A Brief History of the Romans*. New York: Oxford University Press, 2006.

Holmes, George. *The Oxford History of Medieval Europe*. Oxford: Oxford University Press, 2001.

Thompson, Bard. *Humanists and Reformers: A History of the Renaissance and Reformation*. Grand Rapids and Cambridge: William B. Eerdmans Publishers, 1996.

MYTHOLOGY

Colakis, Marianthe, and Mary Joan Masello. *Classical Mythology and More: A Reader Workbook*. Wauconda, IL: Bolchazy-Carducci Publishers, 2007.

Morford, Mark P. O., and Robert J. Lenardon. *Classical Mythology*. 8th ed. New York: Oxford University Press, 2006.

DAILY LIFE

Brucia, Margaret A., and Gregory Daugherty. *To Be a Roman: Topics in Roman Culture*. Wauconda, IL: Bolchazy-Carducci Publishers, 2007.

Carcopino, Jérôme. *Daily Life in Ancient Rome*. New Haven and London:Yale University Press, 1968.

Newman, Paul B. *Daily Life in the Middle Ages*. Jefferson, NC: McFarland & Company, 2001.

ENGLISH ETYMOLOGY

Oxford Dictionary of English Etymology. Edited by C. T. Onions et al. New York: Oxford University Press, 1966.

PHOTOGRAPHY CREDITS

CHAPTER 1

Female Pict (The Trustees of the British Museum/Art Resource, NY)

Compass Rose (© 2009 Shutterstock Images LLC)

Lindisfarne Priory (© 2009 Shutterstock Images LLC)

Durham Cathedral (© 2009 Shutterstock Images LLC)

Pictish Obelisk (© 2009 Shutterstock Images LLC)

CHAPTER 2

Charlemagne Portrait (Scala/Art Resource, NY)

Tiber and St. Peter's, Rome (© 2009 Shutterstock Images LLC)

City Hall, Mechelen, Belgium (© 2009 Shutterstock Images LLC)

Statue of Charlemagne, Des Invalides, Paris (© 2009 Shutterstock Images LLC)

Aachen Cathedral (© 2009 Shutterstock Images LLC)

Eiffel Tower, Paris (© 2009 Shutterstock Images LLC)

CHAPTER 3

Heloise and Abelard (Erich Lessing/Art Resource, NY)

Astrolabe (© 2009 Jupiter Images Corp.)

Heloise and Letter (© 2009 Jupiter Images Corp.)

Medieval Calligraphy (© 2009 Shutterstock Images LLC)

Thoronet Abbey, France (© 2009 Shutterstock Images LLC)

Heloise and Abelard's Tomb, Paris (DeA Picture Library/Art Resource, NY)

Agora, Athens (© 2009 Shutterstock Images LLC)

REVIEW 1

White Cliffs of Dover (© 2009 Shutterstock Images LLC)

CLASSICAL HEROES 1

Perseus and Medusa's Head (© 2009 Jupiter Images Corp.)

Temple of Hercules, Amman, Jordan (© 2009 Shutterstock Images LLC)

Hercules Mosaic, Volubilis, Morocco (© 2009 Shutterstock Images LLC)

Minotaur Sculpture, Tuileries, Paris (© 2009 Shutterstock Images LLC)

Palace at Knossos, Crete (© 2009 Shutterstock Images LLC)

Argonauts Woodcut (© 2009 Jupiter Images Corp.)

POST-ANCIENT WORLD 1

Bayeaux Tapestry (© 2009 Jupiter Images Corp.)

Battle of Hastings (© 2009 Jupiter Images Corp.)

Reenactment Knight (© 2009 Shutterstock Images LLC)

Carisbrooke Castle, Isle of Wight (© 2009 Shutterstock Images LLC)

Medieval Stained Glass (© 2009 Shutterstock Images LLC)

Carcassone, France (© 2009 Shutterstock Images LLC)

EXPLORATION 1

Sand Sculpture of Plato (© 2009 Shutterstock Images LLC)

Abelard and Heloise (Art Resource, NY)

Dido Mourning Aeneas (Alinari/Art Resource, NY)

Death of Romeo (© 2009 Jupiter Images Corp.)

Titanic Memorial (© 2009 Shutterstock Images LLC)

MĪRĀBILE AUDĪTŪ 1

United States Marine Corps Memorial (© 2009 Shutterstock Images LLC)

Don't Veto (© 2009 Shutterstock Images LLC)

CHAPTER 4

Capture of Jerusalem (Scala/Art Resource, NY)

Statue of Godfrey, Brussels, Belgium (© 2009 Shutterstock Images LLC)

David's Tower, Jerusalem (© 2009 Shutterstock Images LLC)

Second Crusade (© 2009 Jupiter Images Corp.)

Knights Reenactment Group (© 2009 Shutterstock Images LLC)

REVIEW 3
CLASSICAL HEROES 3
Statue of Odysseus (© 2009 Jupiter Images Corp.)

Blinding of Polyphemus (Erich Lessing/Art Resource, NY)

Statue of Athena, Peterhof, Russia (© 2009 Shutterstock Images LLC)

POST-ANCIENT WORLD 3
Duomo, Florence (© 2009 Shutterstock Images LLC)

Gutenberg Stamp (© 2009 Shutterstock Images LLC)

Map with Constantinople (© 2009 Shutterstock Images LLC)

EXPLORATION 3
Cicero Portrait (Alinari/Art Resource, NY)

House of Commons, England (© 2009 Jupiter Images Corp.)

Two Dollar Bill/Drafting Declaration of Independence (© 2009 Shutterstock Images LLC)

Yes We Can (© 2009 Shutterstock Images LLC)

MĪRĀBILE AUDĪTŪ 3
Curriculum Vitae (© 2009 Shutterstock Images LLC)

CHAPTER 10
Holbein's Erasmus (Bildarchiv Preussischer Kulturbesitz/Art Resource, NY)

Henry VIII Portrait (© 2009 Jupiter Images Corp.)

Ship's Mast (© 2009 Shutterstock Images LLC)

France's Northern Coast (© 2009 Shutterstock Images LLC)

Panorama of Basle, Switzerland (© 2009 Shutterstock Images LLC)

Passport Stamps (© 2009 Shutterstock Images LLC)

CHAPTER 11
Utopia Map and Text (The New York Public Library/Art Resource, NY)

Thomas More Portrait (© 2009 Jupiter Images Corp.)

Henry VIII, Trinity College, Cambridge, England (© 2009 Shutterstock Images LLC)

Arrest of Thomas More (© 2009 Jupiter Images Corp.)

Tower of London (© 2009 Shutterstock Images LLC)

Utopia Sign (© 2009 Shutterstock Images LLC)

CHAPTER 12
Columbus Explains His Journey (Scala/Art Resource, NY)

Aristotle Bust (© 2009 Shutterstock Images LLC)

Columbus Monument, Union Station, Washington DC (© 2009 Shutterstock Images LLC)

Niña Reconstruction (Wikimedia)

Columbus Statue Barcelona (© 2009 Shutterstock Images LLC)

Bartolomé de las Casas Coin (© 2009 Jupiter Images Corp.)

REVIEW 4
CLASSICAL HEROES 4
"Treasury of Atreus" (© 2009 Shutterstock Images LLC)

"Mask of Agamemnon" (© 2009 Jupiter Images Corp.)

Sphinx at Queluz Palace, Lisbon (Courtesy of Donald E. Sprague, 2009)

POST-ANCIENT WORLD 4
Amerigo Vespucci Tall Ship (© 2009 Shutterstock Images LLC)

Amerigo Vespucci Statue (© 2009 Shutterstock Images LLC)

EXPLORATION 4
Henry the Navigator Monument, Lisbon, Portugal (Courtesy of Donald E. Sprague, 2009)

Pizarro Banknote (© 2009 Shutterstock Images LLC)

Pompeys Pillar, Montana (© 2009 Shutterstock Images LLC)

Clark's Graffito (© 2009 Shutterstock Images LLC)

Sacagawea Dollar Coin (© 2009 Shutterstock Images LLC)

Man on Moon Headline (© 2009 Shutterstock Images LLC)

Apollo 15 Lunar Exploration (NASA)

Research Station, Antarctica (© 2009 Shutterstock Images LLC)

MĪRĀBILE AUDĪTŪ 4
Hippocrates' Asklepeion, Kos (© 2009 Shutterstock Images LLC)

Hargrave Military Academy School Seal (Permission of Hargrave Military Academy)

CHAPTER 13

Columbus Lands (Bildarchiv Preussischer Kulturbesitz/Art Resource, NY)

Columbus Monument, Genoa, Italy (© 2009 Shutterstock Images LLC)

Queen Isabella Statue (© 2009 Shutterstock Images LLC)

Royal Crest of Spain (© 2009 Jupiter Images Corp.)

La Giralda, Cathedral of Seville, Spain (Courtesy of Donald E. Sprague, 2009)

Statue of Liberty (© 2009 Jupiter Images Corp.)

Julius Caesar Statue, Tuileries, Paris (© 2009 Shutterstock Images LLC)

CHAPTER 14

Copernicus' Treatise (Erich Lessing/Art Resource, NY)

Copernicus Title Page (© 2009 Jupiter Images Corp.)

Triquetrum (© 2009 Jupiter Images Corp.)

Liberian Stamp of Copernicus (© 2009 Jupiter Images Corp.)

Copernicus with Astrolabe (© 2009 Shutterstock Images LLC)

Bust of Galileo (© 2009 Shutterstock Images LLC)

Astronomer's Monument, Los Angeles (© 2009 Shutterstock Images LLC)

CHAPTER 15

Man Rappeling (© 2009 Shutterstock Images LLC)

Statue of Ludwig Holberg (Christian Bickel/Wikimedia)

Tree (© 2009 Shutterstock Images LLC)

Tree (© 2009 Shutterstock Images LLC)

Bergen, Norway (© 2009 Shutterstock Images LLC)

University of Copenhagen (© 2009 Shutterstock Images LLC)

Galaxy (NASA/Hubble)

REVIEW 5

China Tea Cups (© 2009 Shutterstock Images LLC)

Tea Service (© 2009 Shutterstock Images LLC)

Leeuwenhoek's Microscope (Jacopo Werther/Wikimedia)

CLASSICAL HEROES 5

Bernini's Aeneas, Ascanius, Anchises Sculpture (Alinari/Art Resource, NY)

Sibyl Stamp (© 2009 Jupiter Images Corp.)

Siena She-wolf (© 2009 Shutterstock Images LLC)

Tiber River Island (© 2009 Shutterstock Images LLC)

POST-ANCIENT WORLD 5

Carl Linnaeus Statue (© 2009 Jupiter Images Corp.)

Euler's Number (© 2009 Shutterstock Images LLC)

Vesalius Anatomical Drawing (© 2009 Jupiter Images Corp.)

EXPLORATION 5

Aristotle Coin (© 2009 Shutterstock Images LLC)

Archimedes' Pi (© 2009 Shutterstock Images LLC)

Archimedes in Tub (© 2009 Jupiter Images Corp.)

Alexander the Great Relief (© 2009 Shutterstock Images LLC)

Stadium at Olympia (© 2009 Shutterstock Images LLC)

Collegium Maius, Cracow (© 2009 Shutterstock Images LLC)

University of Padua (Erich Lessing/Art Resource, NY)

Copernicus Bust (© 2009 Shutterstock Images LLC)

Kepler Memorial, Regensburg, Germany (© 2009 Shutterstock Images LLC)

Einstein on Bench (© 2009 Shutterstock Images LLC)

MĪRĀBILE AUDĪTŪ 5

Descartes Stamp (© 2009 Shutterstock Images LLC)

ADDITIONAL READINGS FROM NEPOS' *LIFE OF ATTICUS*

Greek Trireme (© 2009 Shutterstock Images LLC)

Roman Forum (© 2009 Shutterstock Images LLC)

Television Journalist (© 2009 Shutterstock Images LLC)

Print Media Journalist (© 2009 Shutterstock Images LLC)

Pantheon, Rome (© 2009 Shutterstock Images LLC)

Roman Home, Ephesus (© 2009 Shutterstock Images LLC)

Bust of Epicurus (© 2009 Jupiter Images Corp.)

Cicero Bust, Ulm, Germany (Joachim Köhler/Wikimedia)

Augustus Coin (© 2009 Shutterstock Images LLC)

Augustus Statue (© 2009 Shutterstock Images LLC)

Forum of Augustus (© 2009 Shutterstock Images LLC)

INDEX

Note: A reference to xxvii or 192 indicates the main text, while xxviip or 192p indicates a picture or its caption.

Bithynia, 134

al-Bittani, *Dē mōtū stellārum (Kitab al-Zij)*, 371

Black holes, 376

Black Sea, 56, 286

Mrs. Blimber, 215, 217

Boccaccio, Giovanni, 106

Bologna, Italy, 130*p*, 131*p*, 371
  University of, 131, 258, 371

Books, 315*p*, 318*p*

Boulanger, Louis, 65*p*

Boy Scouts, 323*p*

Brennus, 159*p*

Briseis, 127

Britain
  Bede's description of, 2–3
  Latin in, 2

British Isles
  map of, 7*p*

British Museum, 409*p*

Bronze Age, 286

Brunelleschi, Filippo, 212*p*

Bruni, Leonardo, 212*p*, 213

Brussels, 72*p*

Brutus, Marcus, 312, 330, 410, 423*p*

Brutus (Cicero), quoted, 159

de Bry, Theodore, 295*p*

Bucephalus, 97*p*, 368*p*

Burgos, 136*p*

Burke, Edmund, 216*p*

Byzantines, 213–214

C

Caesar, Augustus. *See* Augustus Caesar

Caesar, Julius, 2, 128, 217, 274, 286, 311*p*, 389*p*
  assassination of, 312, 330
  invasion of England, 51*p*

Caesar, meanings of, 397

Calcutta, 287

Callisto, 365

Calypso, 210

Cambridge University, 222

Campeador. *See* (El) Cid

Canada, 288–289

Canary Islands, 259

Cape of Good Hope, 287

Capitoline Museum, 62*p*, 85*p*

Carcasonne, 60*p*

Cardinal numbers, 496–498
  declined (1–3), 112–113, 448

Carisbrooke, 59*p*

Carolingian dynasty, 18

Carolus Magnus. *See* Charlemagne

Caron, Antoine, 251*p*

Carrara, Hubertinus, *Columbus*, 285

Carthage, 64, 359–360

Cases
  ablative
    in place constructions, 26–28
  accusative
    in place constructions, 26–28
  basic uses of, 473
  locative, 26–28

Cassandra, 281

Cassiopeia, 54

Cassius, 312, 330, 423*p*

Castello Nuovo, Naples, 170*p*

Castile, 136*p*, 307*p*

cathedra, professorial chair, 130*p*

Cathedral schools, 130

Catherine de' Medici, Queen of France, 251*p*, 311*p*

Catholicism, and conquest, 288

Causal clauses, 265

Causal clauses, with *cum*, 261

Causal use of ablative absolute, 301–303, 490

Causal use of participles, 245–246

Cellini, Benvenuto, 53*p*

Celtic cross, 13*p*

Cerberus, 55

Ceto, 53

Charbonneau, Jean Baptiste, 289*p*

Charlemagne (Carolus Māgnus), 17*p*, 20*p*, 21*p*, 25*p*, 27*p*, 130
  Einhard's biography of, 18–19

Charles, Duke of Orléans, 33*p*, 63*p*

Charles V, King of Spain and Holy Roman Emperor, 258

Charybdis, 210

Chaucer, Geoffrey, 106

Chess, 135*p*

China, 356*p*, 357, 357*p*

Chocolate, 101*p*

Chryseis, 127

Cicero, Marcus Tullius, 14, 213, 215–218, 215*p*, 413*p*
  On the agrarian law, quoted, 218
  Brutus, quoted, 159
  friendship with Atticus, 202
  Letters, 144
    to Atticus, 410
    adapted, 413
    and Mark Antony, 378
  murder of, 384
  Petrarch's letter to, 144–145
  The Philippics, 378

Cicero, Quintus (brother of Marcus), 202–203, 274, 410

El Cid, Rodrigo Díaz de Vivar, 136–137, 136*p*

Circe, 210

Circumference of the Earth, measured, 369–370

Citizenship, Athenian and Roman, 102

Civil War of Caesar and Pompey, 274

Clark, William, 289, 289*p*

Clerics in Medieval society, 58–61

Clermont, Council of, 70

Cloelia, 361

Coins, 422*p*
  Greek, 366*p*
  sestertiī, 185*p*

Late, 213, 434–435

'Middle' (Greek) use of accusative, 495

A Midsummer Night's Dream (Shakespeare), 65

Milky Way, 54

mīlle and *mīlia*, 499

Minerva, 126

Minos, 55, 56*p*

Minotaur, 55, 55*p*, 56, 56*p*

Mississippi River, 289

Mnemonics for Latin grammar, 22, 195, 249

Monotheism, 134

Montefeltro, Federico da, Duke of Urbino, 215*p*

Monument to the Discoveries, Lisbon, 287*p*

Moods. *See also* Imperative, Indicative, Subjunctive
  differences between, 8
  meaning of, 8

Moon, exploration of, 290

Moons, of Jupiter, 325

More, Thomas, 239*p*, 246*p*, 251*p*, 253*p*
  Ūtopia, 285, 333–334
    quoted, 239

Morocco, 55*p*

Morrell, William, *Nova Anglia*, 285

Mosaics, 55*p*

Mottoes and phrases, Latin, 1, 67, 140–141, 143, 221

Movable type, 213*p*

Mudejars, 137–139

Muhammed, 135

Münster, Ulm, 413*p*

Museo Civico, Bologna, 130*p*

Museum, of Alexandria, 368

Muslims, 70
  in Spain, 134–139, 135–139
    expulsion of, 139

Mutina, 350

Mycenae, 281*p*, 282*p*

N

Names, Latinization of, 57*p*

Naples, 170*p*

Napoleon Bonaparte, 25*p*, 43*p*

Nārrātiō prīma (Rheticus), 373

Native Americans, 258, 297

'Natural Slavery,' 258

'Naughty nine' irregular adjectives, 248–250, 446–447

Navarre, 307*p*

Naxos, 56

Nazis, 323*p*

nē
  in clauses of hindering and preventing, 506
  in fear clauses, 506
  in indirect commands, 98
  in purpose clauses, 40–41
  with the volitive and optative subjunctive, 10

necne, 513

Negative
  commands, 151
  of volitive and optative subjunctive, 10

Nemean lion, 55

nēmō, forms of, 108

Neoclassical Latin, 213

Nepos, Cornelius, *Dē virīs illūstribus (About famous men)*, 14
  Atticus, quoted, 15, 30, 46, 86, 102, 120, 156, 184, 202, 236–237, 254, 274, 312, 330, 350, 378–429 (passim)
  Themistocles, 14

Nereids, 54

Netherlands, 356*p*

Neuter
  of comparative adjectives, 109

neuter, 248–250, 447

New Deal, 326*p*

New Testament (Erasmus' edition), 199*p*, 232*p*

New World, 295

Newton, Sir Isaac
  Principia, quoted, 315

Nicolāī Klimī iter subterrāneum (Holberg), 334
  quoted, 336

Nietzsche, Friedrich, 140

Niña (Columbus' ship), 266*p*

nisi, in conditional clauses, 268–270

Nobility in Medieval society, 58–61

nōlō, irregular verb, 147–149, 151, 465
  present participle of, 243

Nominative case, 473

nōnne, 513

Normans, 51*p*, 58*p*, 72

Norman Conquest, 51*p*, 58*p*, 59

Northwest Passage, 288–289

Norway, 346*p*

Nouns, declined, 437–441

Nova Anglia (Morrell), 285

Novara, Domenico Maria, 371

NT, sign of the present active participle, 242

nūllus, 248–250

num, 512

Numbers, 496–499
  cardinal
    with the ablative of time within which, 496
  declined (1–3), 112–113, 448
  ordinal
    with the ablative of time when, 496

Numerical adverbs, 497–498

Numitor, 360–361

Nūntius sīdereus (Galileo), adapted, 325

Nuremberg, 318*p*

O

Obama, Barack, 54*p*, 218

Obelisks, 114*p*

Octavian. *See* Augustus Caesar

Odes (Horace), 388*p*
  quoted, 89, 333

Odysseus, 127–128, 209–211, 209*p*, 210*p*, 211*p*

Odyssey (Homer), 209–211, 211*p*, 360

Oedipus, 282–283

oikoumene, 367, 376

Olsztyn, Poland, 372*p*

Olympia, 369*p*

On the agrarian law (Cicero), quoted, 218

Optative subjunctive
  pluperfect, 77
  present, 9–10

opus sectīle, 402*p*

Ordinal numbers, 497–498

Oregon, 289

Orestes, 282

Osiander, Andrew, 373

Otto I, Holy Roman Emperor, 17

Ovid (Publius Ovidius Naso), 33, 64, 213

Oxford University, 131, 131*p*, 132*p*, 138

P

Pacifism, Erasmus', 187

Padua, 371*p*
  University of, 365*p*, 371*p*

Paintings, 17*p*

Palatine Chapel, Aachen, 27*p*

Palazzo Vecchio, Florence, 153*p*

Panama, Isthmus of, 288

Pantheon, 212*p*, 396*p*

Papal Palace, Avignon, 146*p*

Parchment, 41*p*

Paris (city), 29*p*, 55*p*
  University of, 131, 133, 138

Paris (Trojan), 126–128

Participles
  forms
    of deponent verbs, 460

future active, 448
    of irregular verbs, 461–470
  perfect passive, 448
  present active, 242–243, 447
    ending, in ablative absolute, 303
    of regular verbs, 456
  uses
    causal vs temporal, 245–246

Pascal, Blaise, quoted, 66

Passive periphrastic, 345–346

Past conditions (general and contrary-to-fact), 269–270

paterfamiliās, 398

Patroclus, 127, 127*p*

Paul, *Epistles to Timothy*, quoted, 69

Paul III, Pope, 373

Pavia, University of, 182*p*

Peasants in Medieval society, 58–61

Peleus, 126, 126*p*

Penelope, 210–211

Perfect active infinitive
  and pluperfect subjunctive active, 76

Perfect passive participle, 448

Perfect subjunctive
  active forms of, 73–74

Periphrastic, passive, 345–346

Perseus, 53, 53*p*, 365

Persians, 388*p*

Peru, 288

Peter (Petrus) Martyr, *Dē orbe novō*, adapted, 309

Peter the Great, Tsar, 211*p*

Petrarch, 143*p*, 144, 146*p*, 152*p*, 154*p*, 155, 213, 215–216
  letter to Cicero, quoted, 144–145
  Sēcrētum (Secret Writing), 144

Pevensey, 51*p*

Philip II, King of Macedon, 378

Philippi, Battle of, 423*p*

The Philippics (Cicero), 378

Philosophy, Greek, 215

Phorcys, 53

pi (mathematical constant), 367*p*

Picasso, Pablo, 55*p*

Pico, Gianfrancesco, 216

Picts, 1*p*, 2–4
  monuments, 13*p*

pietās, Roman, 359*p*

Pilate, Pontius, 140

Pippin, 20*p*

Pirates, 116–117

Pizarro, Francisco, 288*p*

Place from which, constructions, 26–28

Place to which, constructions, 26–28

Place where, constructions, 26–28

Plato, 62*p*, 388*p*
  Symposium, 62–63, 65

Plato's Academy, 130

Pliny the Elder, 286

Pliny the Younger, 134

Pluperfect subjunctive
  active forms of, 75–76
    vs future perfect indicative, 76

plūs
  forms of, 166, 446
  use of, 166

Plutarch, 257

Poetry, Chinese, 357*p*

Point of view, and pronouns in indirect speech, 510

Poland, 316

Polymaths, 366

Polynices, 283

Polyphemus, 209–210, 209*p*, 210*p*

Polytheism, 134

Pompey the Great, quoted, 257, 274

Pompeys Pillar, 289*p*

Pons Cestius, 362*p*

Ponte Vecchio, Florence, 152*p*

Poseidon, 54, 210

Poseidonius, 370

LATIN FOR THE NEW MILLENNIUM
ELECTRONIC RESOURCES FOR STUDENTS

VISIT LNM.BOLCHAZY.COM

Latin for the New Millennium provides a variety of online materials that complement your Latin lessons and encourage active use of Latin within fun learning environments. Audio, games, and more await with new content added frequently.

QUIZ YOURSELF ONLINE

REINFORCE YOUR UNDERSTANDING OF LATIN GRAMMAR

Check out *lookingatlatin.com*—with over 5,000 exercises—covering all points of Latin grammar These online exercises build your Latin skills because they are self-correcting. Just ten to thirty-five questions per part of speech or point of grammar make these questions very manageable for students.

Spend some time doing Latin online and watch your understanding of Latin grow!

PRACTICE YOUR LATIN ONLINE AS YOU MEET LATIN STUDENTS FROM AROUND THE WORLD!

Visit Bolchazy-Carducci's Roman villa in Teen Second Life™ where Latin is the *lingua franca*. Students over 18 may visit Bolchazy-Carducci's Latin site in the Main Grid of Second Life™.

Practice writing and speaking Latin as you apply what you are learning through the readings and dialogues presented in each chapter of *Latin for the New Millennium*.

Go solo from home or join your class in the computer lab for speaking Latin aloud.

iPODIUS

For Latin audio, video, vocabulary flashcards, and other software downloads, visit *ipodius.bolchazy.com*, Bolchazy-Carducci's online multimedia store.

eLEARNING

Only Bolchazy-Carducci Publishers offers students and teachers of Latin and Greek an extensive catalogue of digital products and free online resources. New School meets Old School with a 21st century approach to learning ancient languages.

ONLINE

- *eClassics* (eclassics.ning.com). The world's first and largest social network for students and teachers integrating technology into the Classics classroom.
- *iPodius* (ipodius.bolchazy.com). MP3 downloads of the original Oldies (Vergil, Catullus, Cicero, Ovid, Horace, music and more).

SOFTWARE

- *Review Latin Verbs*
- *Roman Town: The Premiere Archaeology Video Game for Kids*
- *Cicero's First Catilinarian: A Digital Tutor*

MULTIMEDIA

- *Latin Aloud* MP3 CD
- *Performing Cicero's Pro Archia* DVD

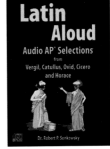

BLENDED LEARNING

- *Aesop's Fables in Latin* (aesopus.ning.com). Video, podcasts, wiki, fable-of-the-day blog, images, more.

See previous page for electronic resources specific to *Latin for the New Millennium*.

TRANSITIONAL LATIN – LEVEL III

TRANSITIONING INTO ANCIENT AUTHORS LEVEL III

The *LEGAMUS Transitional Readers* and *A Little Book of Latin Love Poetry* are innovative texts that form a bridge between the initial study of Latin via *Latin for the New Millennium* and the reading of authentic author texts. Depending on the ability level of a given group of third year Latin students, teachers might choose several titles from the series and cover several authors in a year.

Each LEGAMUS Transitional Reader provides an overview of the life and works of the Latin author, a bibliography, a map of the Roman world with place-names relevant to the author, and a set of illustrations. These readers offer students comprehensive support: both adapted and unadapted Latin passages, facing-page vocabulary and grammatical notes, visual aids that help the students see linguistic patterns, grammar review notes with practice exercises, English derivative exercises, and comprehension and analysis questions. Pre-reading materials and explanations ease students into understanding an author's style. A grammar appendix with examples from the individual author, a customized appendix of figures of speech, and a pull-out vocabulary of words appearing frequently round out each book's innovative features. A discussion on meter is presented for each of the poets.

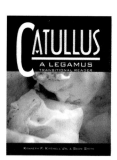

CATULLUS: A LEGAMUS TRANSITIONAL READER

Sean Smith and Kenneth F. Kitchell, Jr.

Student Text: xxx + 162 pp. (2006) Paperback ISBN 978-0-86516-634-9

This reader contains selections (194 lines) from 18 Catullus poems: 1, 5, 7, 8, 11.15–24; 13, 43, 50, 51, 64.1–15; 65.1–24; 70, 72, 83, 85, 86, 87, and 101.

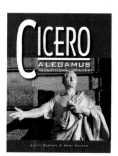

CICERO: A LEGAMUS TRANSITIONAL READER

Mark Haynes and Judith L. Sebesta

Student Text: xxii + 226 pp. (2010) Paperback ISBN 978-0-86516-656-1

The *Cicero LEGAMUS Transitional Reader* contains 103 lines from Cicero's *Pro Archia*: 4.2–4; 5.1–3; 5.4–6; 6.1, 6.2–3; 7.1–3; 12 entire; 13.1; 14.1–3; 18.4–5; 19 entire; 23 entire; 24.1–3; 28 entire; 29 entire; 31 entire; 1 entire; 2 entire; and 3 entire.

 BOLCHAZY-CARDUCCI PUBLISHERS

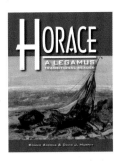

HORACE: A LEGAMUS TRANSITIONAL READER

Ronnie Ancona and David J. Murphy

Student Text: xxiv + 198 pp. (2008) Paperback ISBN 978-086516-676-9

This reader contains 203 lines of Latin selections from Horace (*Satires* 1.4.103–126; 1.6, 70–92; *Odes* 1.5; 1.23; 1.11; 3.9; 2.10; 1.37; 1.9; 3.30).

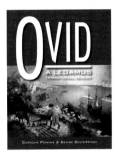

OVID: A LEGAMUS TRANSITIONAL READER

Caroline Perkins and Denise Davis-Henry

Student Text: xxvi + 126 pp. (2008) Paperback ISBN 978-0-86516-604-2

This reader contains selections (202 lines) from Ovid's *Metamorphoses*: Apollo and Daphne, 1.463–473, 490–502, 548–567; Pyramus and Thisbe, 4.65–77, 93–104, 137–153; Daedalus and Icarus, 8.195–208, 220–235; Baucis and Philemon, 8.626–640, 705–720; Pygmalion, 10.243–269, 270–297.

VERGIL: A LEGAMUS TRANSITIONAL READER

Thomas J. Sienkewicz and LeaAnn A. Osburn

Student Text: xxvi + 136 pp. (2004) Paperback ISBN 978-0-86516-578-6

This reader contains selections (227 lines) from Vergil's *Aeneid*, Books 1, 2, and 4, selections included are: *Aeneid* 1.1–11, 195–209, 318–334; *Aeneid* 2.20–222, 526–566; 705–729; 4.65–89, 279–303, 642–666.

CAESAR: A LEGAMUS TRANSITIONAL READER

Hans-Friedrich Mueller and Rose Williams

Student Text: (forthcoming) ISBN 978-0-86516-733-0

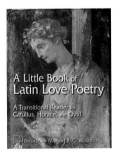

A LITTLE BOOK OF LATIN LOVE POETRY
A TRANSITIONAL READER FOR CATULLUS, HORACE, AND OVID

John Breuker and Mardah Weinfeld

Student Text: x + 124 pp. (2006) Paperback ISBN 978-0-86516-601-1
Teacher's Guide: xii + 156 pp. (2007) Paperback ISBN 978-0-86516-636-3

This reader introduces intermediate Latin students to Catullus, Horace, and Ovid. Selections (156 lines) from 6 poems of Catullus (51, 43, 86, 5, 70, 8), 3 poems of Horace (*Odes* 1.23, 3.9, 3.26), and 2 poems of Ovid (*Amores* 1.5 and 1.9), first modified, then unmodified. It offers a transition to reading these authors by presenting slightly modified versions of poems before the students read the authentic Latin verse as review. Vocabulary, reading helps, grammar reviews with exercises, and discussion questions are included, as well as sections on metrics, poetic devices, and a complete glossary.

WORKBOOKS – LEVEL IV

WORKBOOKS THAT WORK IN LEVEL IV

WRITINGS OF FIVE SIGNIFICANT ANCIENT AUTHORS
CATULLUS • CICERO • HORACE • OVID • VERGIL

LLWS The Latin Literature Workbook Series has been designed to reinforce a set of viable approaches to reading classical authors in the original. An honors level third year class might begin with a Legamus reader and then move to one of these workbooks. These workbooks serve as an excellent resource for all levels of fourth year Latin.

These varying approaches appear as a set of exercises that enables the student to quickly reach a higher degree of comprehension on sight or prepared passages. These approaches include: • Short analysis questions • Translation passages • Short and long essay questions on literary interpretation • Lines for scansion d Short answer questions and multiple choice questions on • The grammatical underpinnings of the passage • Figures of speech and rhetorical devices • Identification of characters, events, places, historical and mythical allusions

By working through passages provided in the books, the student will develop the habit of using these approaches and thereby develop a greater facility in reading and appreciating the ancient authors.

Each workbook was written by a team of authors—one, a university scholar with special expertise in the Latin literary text, and the other, a high school Advanced Placement Latin teacher.

The Latin text in each workbook consists of passages of significant literary and cultural merit. These are representative samplings of the ancient authors' work—small enough perhaps to allow the class to cover several authors in one year, yet comprehensive enough to be significant to the student.

These teacher's manuals provide not only a key or a set of answers! They identify not just one answer but the salient points necessary for complete answers to the short analysis questions. The "chunking" method of evaluating a translation is included for each translation passage. The topics essential to answer the essay question fully and instructions on how to use the six to one grading rubric are given. In addition, selected lines show the scansion marks according to the meter.

> (These) outstanding new titles from Bolchazy-Carducci Publishers in the area of Latin instruction are superbly presented, 'user friendly,' and highly recommended additions to any personal studies, academic library, or school curriculum reference collections.
>
> – *Midwest Book Review*

 BOLCHAZY-CARDUCCI PUBLISHERS

A VERGIL WORKBOOK

Barbara Weiden Boyd and Katherine Bradley

Student Text: x + 262 pp. (2006) 8½" x 11" Paperback ISBN 978-0-86516-614-1
Teacher's Manual: xviii + 320 pp. (2007) Paperback ISBN 978-0-86516-651-6

(1856 lines)

A CATULLUS WORKBOOK

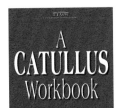

Helena Dettmer and LeaAnn A. Osburn

Glossary by Ronnie Ancona

Student Text: xii + 244 pp. (2006) 8½" x 11" Paperback ISBN 978-0-86516-623-3
Teacher's Manual: xvi + 298 pp. (2007) 6" x 9" Paperback ISBN 978-0-86516-624-0

(771 lines)

A HORACE WORKBOOK

David J. Murphy and Ronnie Ancona

Student Text: xii + 204 pp. (2005) 8½" x 11" Paperback ISBN 978-0-86516-574-8
Teacher's Manual: xvi + 274 pp. (2006) 6" x 9" Paperback ISBN 978-0-86516-649-3

(572 lines)

A CICERO WORKBOOK

Jane Crawford and Judy Hayes

Student Text: x + 238 pp. (2006) 8½" x 11" Paperback ISBN 978-0-86516-643-1
Teacher's Manual: xiv + 250 pp. (2007) 6" x 9" Paperback ISBN 978-0-86516-654-7

(408 lines *Pro Archia Poeta Oratio*; 170 lines *de Amicitia*)

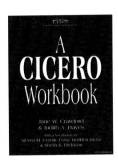

AN OVID WORKBOOK

Charbra Adams Jestin and Phyllis B. Katz

Student Text: x + 166 pp. (2006) 8½" x 11" Paperback ISBN 978-0-86516-635-7
Teacher's Manual: xii +172 pp. (2007) 6" x 9" Paperback ISBN 978-0-86516-626-4

(630 lines)

A CAESAR WORKBOOK

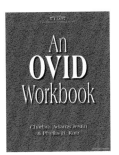

Debra Nousek and Rose Williams

Student Text: (forthcoming) 8½" x 11" Paperback ISBN 978-0-86516-753-7
Teacher's Manual: (forthcoming) 6" x 9" Paperback ISBN 978-0-86516-755-1

RESOURCES AND ENRICHMENT

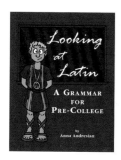

LOOKING AT LATIN
A GRAMMAR FOR PRE-COLLEGE

by Anna Andresian

viii + 280 pp., 288 color illustrations (2006)
8½" x 11" Paperback, ISBN 978-0-86516-615-8

Looking at Latin is a complete illustrated grammar reference book for all levels of pre-college Latin, from middle school through high school.

Lessons are designed to cover single topics—from the subject nominative to the impersonal passive periphrastic—which allows for flexibility in the order in which lessons are covered. Innovative visual elements bring clarity and energy to the presentation of grammatical material, with arrows and colored text emphasizing and connecting important points. Information is delivered via small text boxes that allow students to use a step-by-step approach to learning forms and syntax, and comprehensive example sentences illustrate each topic in detail. Abundant color illustrations add personality and humor, producing a visual appeal unusual to Latin grammars.

Whether the student needs to review declensions and conjugations or would like to learn how to use constructions such as the ablative absolute or purpose clauses, this is the book to use.

Features:

- detailed table of contents makes finding topics easy
- topics are arranged by grammatical category, making the book as useful for later review and reference as for initial learning
- dynamic layout with text boxes, arrows, examples, and color illustrations
- design expressly targets Latin students from middle school through high school
- illustrations represent the diversity of the modern world

A class set of this new grammar, *Looking at Latin,* is a must for every middle and high school Latin classroom. Students continuing in Latin will surely want to purchase personal copies.

- PDF eBook available for purchase with the purchase of a classroom set (10 copies min.)
- On-line quizzes, drills, exercises, and community

Online

BOLCHAZY-CARDUCCI PUBLISHERS

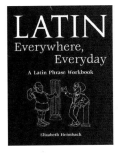

LATIN EVERYWHERE, EVERYDAY
A LATIN PHRASE WORKBOOK

Elizabeth Heimbach

CD in Teacher's Manual by James Chochola

Student Text: viii + 152 pp. (2004) 8½" x 11" Paperback ISBN 978-0-86516-572-4
Teacher's Manual: iv + 164 pp. (2005) 8½" x 11" Paperback ISBN 978-0-86516-589-2

This workbook of Latin phrases and mottoes is filled with exercises, projects, and games designed for students in grades 7–10. There are three parts to the workbook: *sententiae* or Latin phrases, abbreviations, and mottoes. The first section contains 180 Latin phrases, one for each day of the school year. There are five phrases on each page so that students can see a whole week's work at once. A variety of exercises helps students master each group of phrases. The second section of the workbook contains Latin mottoes of states, schools, colleges, and organizations. The third section reviews the 29 Latin abbreviations that were introduced in section one. All three sections are filled with interesting derivatives, engaging information, delightful facts, and ample exercises.

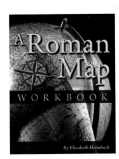

A ROMAN MAP WORKBOOK

Elizabeth Heimbach

Student Text: viii + 144 pp. (2010) 8½" x 11" Paperback ISBN 978-0-86516-726-1
Teacher's Guide: (forthcoming)

A Roman Map Workbook meets the needs of today's students and introduces them to the geography of Rome and the Roman world. Veteran high school and college Latin teacher Elizabeth Heimbach provides students, especially those studying Latin, with a thorough grounding in the geography of the Roman world. The *Workbook* walks students through each map, discussing the importance of each place-name, making connections to Roman history and literature. The carefully chosen maps complement subjects and periods covered in the Latin and ancient history classroom. Every Latin student will find a personal copy or access to a classroom set a valuable learning resource. A Teacher's Guide will be available.

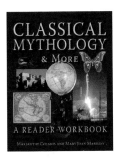

CLASSICAL MYTHOLOGY AND MORE
A READER WORKBOOK

Mary Joan Masello and Marianthe Colakis

Student Text: xii + 460 pp., 559 Illustrations (2007) 8½" x 11" Paperback
    ISBN 978-0-86516-573-1
Teacher's Guide: vi + 158 pp. (2010) 8½" x 11" Paperback ISBN 978-0-86516-747-6

Using Greek and Roman primary sources, this workbook for the twenty-first century offers middle- and high-school aged students in Classics, English and Language Arts classes a fresh retelling of timeless tales from Hesiod, Homer, Ovid and other authors. A wide variety of exercises, illustrations, reflections, and vocabulary enrichment tasks accompany each myth.

Students preparing for the ACL Medusa Myth Exam and the ACL National Mythology Exam will find in this an indispensable tool.

 w w w . B O L C H A Z Y . c o m

ADVANCED LEVELS IV & V
AP* VERGIL

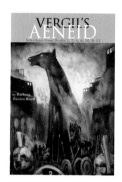

VERGIL'S *AENEID*
SELECTIONS FROM BOOKS 1, 2, 4, 6, 10, AND 12, 2ND EDITION
Barbara Weiden Boyd

Student Text: xxxviii + 410 pp. + pullout (2004, 2nd edition)
Paperback ISBN 978-0-86516-584-7; Hardbound ISBN 978-0-86516-583-0
Teacher's Guide: 176 pp. (2002) Paperback ISBN 978-0-86516-481-9

This edition is designed for high school Advanced Placement and college level courses: a newly updated and revised version of selected passages from *Vergil's Aeneid, Books I–VI*, by Clyde Pharr (whose user-friendly format revolutionized Latin textbooks), plus additional passages from Books 10 and 12, not found in Pharr. Passages included are: 1.1–519; 2.1–56; 199–297, 469–566, 735–804; 4.1–448, 642–705; 6.1–211, 450–476, 847–901; 10.420–509; 12.791–842, 887–952.

Features of the student edition: • all new introduction • introduction to each section • Latin text with selected vocabulary and notes on the same page • 6 new illustrations by Thom Kapheim • ancient illustrations • grammatical appendix, including newly revised sections: "Vergil's Meter" and "Rhetorical Terms, Figures of Speech, and Metrical Devices" • index to grammatical appendix • new, updated selected bibliography • new, full vocabulary at the back of the book • pull-out general word list

Features of the teacher's guide: • introduction • literal translation • questions for discussion and analysis • large-print Latin text (1.1–519; 2.1–56; 199–297, 469–566, 735–804; 4.1–448, 642–705; 6.1–211, 450–476, 847–901; 10.420–509; 12.791–842, 887–952), without macrons or italics, for in-class translation and mock-tests

VERGIL'S *AENEID:* BOOKS I–VI COMPLETE
Clyde Pharr

Student Text: Illus., xvii + 518 pp. + fold-out (1964, Reprint 1998)
Paperback ISBN 978-0-86516-421-5; Hardbound ISBN 978-0-86516-433-8

This is the book that revolutionized Latin textbooks, with its student-friendly format of vocabulary and notes on the same page as the Latin text, and unique pull-out vocabulary of most-often repeated words. Together, these allow for faster reading, unimpeded by the page-turning required to look up vocabulary or consult notes. Pharr's *Aeneid* is the all-time most popular textbook of Vergil's *Aeneid*.

Grammatical notes are supported by a full grammatical appendix; vocabulary memorization is aided by vocabulary drill lists, arranged by frequency of occurrence. The perfect edition for both classroom and home study.

Features of the student edition: • general introduction • full Latin text of Books 1–6 of Vergil's *Aeneid*, with selected vocabulary and notes on the same page • 24 black-and-white illustrations plus map of Aeneas' voyage • grammatical appendix • index to grammatical appendix • word lists for vocabulary drill • updated, extensive selective bibliography • pull-out general word list